ITALIAN

FOR THE

BUSINESS
TRAVELER

Frank G. Rakas

General Manager
Vicenzasped International Agency

BARRON'S

The pronunciation in the Key Industry Terms and Main Dictionary sections
has been provided by Marcel Danesi, University of Toronto

All inquiries should be addressed to:
Barron's Educational Series, Inc.
250 Wireless Boulevard
Hauppauge, NY 11788

Library of Congress Catalog Card No. 93-31810

International Standard Book No. 0-8120-1771-4

Library of Congress Cataloging-in-Publication Data

Rakas, Frank G.
     Italian for the business traveler / by Frank G. Rakas. —2nd ed.
     p. cm. —(Bilingual business guides)
     Rev. ed. of: Talking business in Italian.
     ISBN 0-8120-1771-4
     1. Business—Dictionaries. 2. Commerce—Dictionaries.
     3. Business—Dictionaries—Italian. 4. Commerce—
     Dictionaries–Italian. 5. English language—Dictionaries—Italian. 6.
     Italian language—Dictionaries—English.
     I. Rakas, Frank G. Talking business in Italian. II. Series: Barron's
     bilingual business guides.
HF1001.R35 1994   93-31810
650'.03–dc20   CIP

PRINTED IN THE UNITED STATES OF AMERICA

4567 5500 987654321

CONTENTS

Preface and Acknowledgments   iv

I.   **PRONUNCIATION GUIDE**   v

II.   **INTRODUCTION**   vi
Doing Business in Italian-speaking Countries

Before You Go...   ix

III. **BASIC WORDS AND PHRASES**   1
General words and phrases for getting by, including
amenities, answers to standard questions, and other
essential expressions.

IV. **BUSINESS DICTIONARY**
English to Italian   27
Italian to English   204
Key Words for Key Industries   365

V.   **GENERAL INFORMATION**
Abbreviations   423
Weights and Measures   427
Temperature and Climate   428
Communications Codes   428
Postal Services   430
Time Zones   430
Major Holidays   432
Currency Information   432
Major Periodicals   433
Annual Trade Fairs   434
Travel Times   436
Travel Tips   438
Major Hotels   440
Major Restaurants   444
Useful Addresses   445
Maps   447

PREFACE

It is the nature of business to seek out new markets for its products, to find more efficient ways to bring its goods to more people. In the global marketplace, this often means travel to foreign countries, where language and customs are different. Even when a businessperson knows the language of the host country, the specific and often idiosyncratic terminology of the business world can be an obstacle to successful negotiations in a second language. Pocket phrase books barely scratch the surface of these problems, while standard business dictionaries prove too cumbersome.

Now there is a solution—Barron's *Italian for the Business Traveler*. Here is the essential pocket reference for all international business travelers. Whether your business be manufacturing or finance, communications or sales, this three-part guide will put the right words in your mouth and the best expressions in your correspondence. It is a book you'll carry with you on every trip and take to every meeting. But it is also the reference you'll keep on your desk in the office. This is the business dictionary for people who do business in Italian.

Barron's *Italian for the Business Traveler* offers you the following features:

- a 6,000-entry list of basic business terms, dealing with accounting, advertising and sales, banking, computers, export/import, finance and investment, labor relations, management, manufacturing, marketing, sales, and more.
- a quick guide to basic terms and expressions for getting by in Italian.
- a pronunciation guide for speaking the language.
- a comprehensive list of common business abbreviations.
- reference words for numbers and amounts, days of the week, months and seasons of the year.
- conversion tables for metric and customary measurements.
- lists of major holidays, annual trade fairs, travel times between cities, average temperatures throughout the year.
- information on international currencies, country and city telephone codes, useful addresses in the foreign countries.

Acknowledgments

We would like to thank the following individuals and organizations for their assistance on this project:

John Downes, Business Development Consultant, Office for Economic Development, New York, New York; Gianfranco Paone of Long Island Trust; Luciana Silvers of the Ital Trade USA Corporation; Warren T. Schimmel, Senior Vice-President, Academic Affairs, The Berkeley Schools; the Commercial Office of the Embassy of Italy in the United States for their assistance in preparing the Introduction; and Dolores Maggiore and Viera Morse, for their detailed and careful attention to the manuscript.

Portions of Part I of this book are reprinted with permissions from *Italian at a Glance*, by Mario Costantino, published by Barron's Educational Series, Inc. The information about Switzerland in the Introduction is reprinted with permission from Pierre Weil's Introduction to *Talking Business in French*, also published by Barron's.

I. PRONOUNCIATION GUIDE

This book assumes you are already somewhat familiar with the basic pronunciation rules of Italian, but for those whose knowledge is a little rusty, here are some tips. Many vowels and consonants in Italian are pronounced as they would be in English. There are some exceptions, however, which are given below. Since these sounds don't usually vary, you can follow these guidelines in pronouncing all Italian words. Note: When pronouncing the words in the following examples, stress the vowels that appear in CAPITAL letters.

ITALIAN LETTER(S)	SOUND IN ENGLISH	EXAMPLE
Vowels		
a	ah (y<u>a</u>cht)	casa (kAH-sah), house
è	eh (n<u>e</u>t)	leggere (lEH-jeh-reh), to read
e	ay (h<u>a</u>y)	mela (mAY-lah), apple
i	ee (f<u>ee</u>t)	libri (lEE-bree), books
o	oh (r<u>o</u>pe)	boccone (boh-kOH-neh), mouthful
u	oo (c<u>oo</u>l)	tutto (tOOt-toh), everything
Consonants		
ci	chee (<u>chee</u>se)	cinema (chEE-nay-mah), movies
ce	chay (<u>ch</u>air)	piacere (pee-ah-chAY-reh), pleasure
ca	kah (<u>c</u>ot)	casa (kAH-sah), house
co	koh (<u>c</u>old)	cotto (kOHt-toh), cooked
che	kay (<u>k</u>ent)	perchè (pehr-kAY), because
chi	key (<u>key</u>)	pochi (pOH-key), few
gi	jee (<u>jee</u>p)	giro (jEE-roh), turn
ge	jay (<u>g</u>eneral)	generale (jay-nay-rAH-leh), general
gh	gh (spa<u>gh</u>etti)	spaghetti (spah-ghAY-tee)
gli	ll (mi<u>lli</u>on)	egli (AY-ly-ee), he
		bottiglia (boht-tEE-ly-ee-ah), bottle
gn	ny (can<u>y</u>on)	magnifico (mah-ny-EE-fee-ko), magnificent
qu	koo (<u>qu</u>iet)	aquila (AH-koo-ee-lah), eagle
sce	sh (fi<u>sh</u>)	pesce (pAY-sheh), fish
sci		sciopero (shee-OH-peh-roh), strike
z or zz	ts (ea<u>ts</u>)	pizza (pEE-tsah), pizza
		zero (tsEH-roh), zero

II. INTRODUCTION

DOING BUSINESS IN ITALIAN-SPEAKING COUNTRIES

by Stephanie Siciarz, Cultural Office, Embassy of Italy in the United States

Doing business with another culture and in another language can be a difficult and mystifying experience. Customs and procedures may be quite different from what is perceived as the "normal" way of conducting oneself in a business circumstance.

In this introduction, some important cultural and economic aspects of Italy and Switzerland are outlined. Basic knowledge of these facts will assist you in effectively conducting business in the Italian speaking world.

Usual Hours of Operation

Italy: Monday to Friday 8:30 or 9:00 AM–12:30 and 3:00 PM– 5:30 or 6:00 PM

Switzerland: Monday to Friday 7:30 AM–5:30 PM with 1–2 hours lunch

Business Customs

Italy: Italian business people tend to be quite formal. For instance, when the title of an Italian executive is unknown, he/she should be addressed as *Dottore/Dottoressa*. This title generally denotes one who has earned the equivalent of an American bachelor's degree. Also, at the beginning of a business meeting, casual conversation is appropriate. The aggressive "strictly business" attitude of some American businessmen is not common in the Italian business world, and this American aggressiveness could be mistaken for rudeness or coldness. It is advisable, however, to avoid addressing current political events, as Italians are very politically aware and opinionated; a discussion of politics could lead to heated debate and awkwardness for the American executive.

Switzerland: Discretion is highly valued in all circumstances. Punctuality is important for any occasion, business or social. Refrain from first-name basis also.

General Government Policy and Economic Situation

Italy: The Italian Republic is subdivided into twenty regions, each of which is to a large extent an autonomous entity. Each region is governed by a regional Council within the guidelines set by the Constitution and the laws of the State. Each region is also responsible for its own police, markets, sanitation, tourism, museums and libraries, and education, among others. These legislative functions must not conflict in any way, however, with the national interest or with the interest of other regions.

Although Italy is among the seven most industrialized democracies in the world, agriculture continues to play an important role in the Italian economy. Agricultural production, which has remained extremely stable, engages approximately 10% of Italy's work force. The major crops are wheat, grapes, sugar beets, olives, and fruits. Current improvements in mechanization, fertilization, and irrigation should increase the efficiency of production.

Industry, which accounts for approximately 36% of Italy's labor force, is very diverse, encompassing production of iron and steel, chemicals and fuel oils, electrical machinery, and textiles.

The production of iron and steel is of particular importance, despite the fact that it must rely on the fluctuation of the automobile and building industries. Italy is the fourth world producer of steel and machine tools.

The chemical industry accounts for a major portion of the Italian economy as well. Italy is one of the biggest world producers of such chemical products as fertilizers, dyes, plastics, fuel oils, and pharmaceuticals.

In the field of electrical machinery and appliances, Italy has become the first world producer of electric motors, the second world producer of sewing machines and motorcycles, and the third world producer of household appliances.

The textile industry has a long history and accounts for a generous portion of Italy's foreign trade profit. Italy is the first world producer of leather apparel and ranks third in the world for the production of fabrics after the United States and Japan. Italian clothing and footwear have enjoyed especially strong demand in the foreign market.

The remainder of Italy's work force is divided into the service sector, which accounts for 36% of the labor force and includes such fields as commerce, transportation, and communication; and the field of public administration, which accounts for 18% of those employed.

Italy is largely a free economy, though governmental participation does play an important role particularly in the industrial sector. Through the large holding companies of the State, such as the IRI (Institute for Industrial Reconstruction), the ENI (National Hydrocarbons Agency), and others, the government is able to exercise power in order to further develop this important sector of the economy.

Main imports: Consumer goods, raw materials, fuels, machinery.

Main exports: Automobiles, wines, petroleum derivatives, organic chemical products, textiles, steel and metal products, motors and machinery, industrial equipment, office machinery, furniture, clothing, footwear, jewelry.

Principal trading partners: Countries with which Italy conducts the most business include, the United States, Belgium, Luxembourg, France, Germany, United Kingdom, Austria, Switzerland, Netherlands, Russia, Saudi Arabia, Libya, and Iran. Italy, which conducts a major portion of its trade activity with other European nations, is a member of the European Economic Community (EEC). In 1984, Italy's trade balance showed a deficit of $6 million.

Inflation rate: 10%.

Population: 58 million.

Language: The principal language of Italy is Italian. Accents and dialects vary from region to region, with the purest Italian considered that of the Toscana region (Tuscany). In the Valle d'Aosta region on the French border, French is spoken as well as Italian. Similarly, in the Friuli-Venezia Giulia region bordering Yugoslavia there is a Slovakian language spoken, and in the Alto Adige region bordering Austria and Switzerland one is likely to hear some German. In addition, in the regions of Puglia, Calabria, and Sicily, there are small Greek-speaking and Albanian-speaking communities.

Religion: Roman Catholic (95%).

GDP: $596 billion.

GDP per inhabitant: $10,400.

Unemployment rate: 12%.

Switzerland: The Swiss Confederation is made up of about 3,000 communes that have a great deal of local autonomy. The 26 cantons (or states) each have their own constitution and their own method of choosing representatives to the federal level. The Italian-speaking area of Switzerland is in the canton of Ticino. Bellinzona is its capital and Lugano is its principal city.

Switzerland is a highly industrialized country based on a free market economy.

Major industries: Machinery, machine tools, precision instruments, chemicals, pharmaceuticals, textiles, banking.

Main imports: Foodstuffs, agricultural and forestry products, coal, oil, textiles, clothing, paper, leather goods, construction materials, metal products, motor vehicles, raw materials.

Main exports: Precision instruments, watches, machinery, chemicals, pharmaceuticals, electronics, textiles.

Principal trading partners: Germany, France, the United States, Italy, the United Kingdom.

Inflation rate: 5%.

Population: 6.6 million.

Languages: German 70%, French 20%, Italian 10%.

Religion: Roman Catholic 48%, Protestant 44%, others 8%.

GDP: $96.1 billion.

GDP per inhabitant: $15,000.

Unemployment rate: 1.5%.

In all Italian-speaking countries, during negotiations the pace is usually slower and it would be advisable not to use the hard sell method. As elsewhere, an appointment is preferred and it is recommended to telephone if detained. Courtesy goes a long way to smooth the relationship.

BEFORE YOU GO . . .

Passports

All permanent U.S. residents must carry a valid passport. Application should be made by mail or in person at least eight (and preferably twelve) weeks in advance to either (1) a U.S. Passport Agency office located in twelve major cities and Washington, D.C.; (2) designated U.S. post offices throughout the country; or, (3) State and Federal courthouses. You may also consult your travel agent or international airline office. All of these offices will let you know what documents you need and the proper procedures to follow. Requirements for citizens and non-citizens differ somewhat. No international travel tickets will be issued by an airline or travel agent to persons without valid passports.

Visas

No visas are required for Italy, Malta, or Switzerland for travelers with U.S. passports whose stay does not exceed three months.

Immunizations

There are no immunization requirements for smallpox or other diseases for entry into these countries or upon return to the United States. If you plan to include travel outside Europe to Asia, Africa or the Middle East, consult your doctor or the nearest U.S. Public Health Service office.

Customs and Currency Regulations

In general, travelers with U.S. passports are allowed to bring in fairly generous amounts of duty-free items for their own *personal* use. These items include tobacco, alcohol and perfumes and are typically allowed in the following quantities (despite local variation):

200 cigarettes *or* 50 cigars *or* 250 grams of tobacco (about ½ lb.)

2 liters of wine *or* ¾ liters of liquor

2 ounces of perfume

If you are not well in excess of these amounts, a simple statement of "nothing to declare" will be respected by most customs officials.

For gifts whose final destination is the country you are entering, the rules are a bit stricter. It would be wise to check on the duty-free limits beforehand and to declare whatever is in excess.

For personal valuables like jewelry or furs and foreign-made items like watches, cameras, typewriters, or tape recorders (acquired before your trip) you should have proof of possession or register with U.S. Customs before departure. This will ensure that they are not subject to duty either by the United States upon return or by any country you visit.

Upon returning to the United States, each person has a duty-free allowance of $400, including 100 cigars and 1 carton of cigarettes. Each adult may bring in only 1 liter of wine *or* other liquor duty-free. Gifts worth $50 or less may be sent home subject to certain restrictions. For further up-to-date details, ask your travel agent or airline to provide a copy of U.S. Customs regulations.

There are usually no restrictions on the amounts of *foreign currency* (or checks) which foreign nationals may bring *into* these countries. However, in Italy the equivalent of L 1,000,000 or more must be declared on entry or exit; and in Malta all foreign currency must be declared. If in doubt, consult a travel agent.

Traveler's Checks, Credit Cards, Foreign Exchange

All major international traveler's checks and credit cards are accepted by most hotels, restaurants and shops. However, it is always best to inquire at each establishment beforehand. The checks most recognized are: American Express, Barclays, Visa, CitiBank, and Bank of America. The cards most acceptable are: American Express, MasterCard, Visa, and Diners Club.

However, be advised that the exchange rate on dollar traveler's checks is almost always disadvantageous. If you want, you can buy foreign currency checks and/or actual currency in the United States before leaving at rates equivalent to or better than the bank rate you will get over there. Currency or checks may be purchased from retail foreign currency dealers. The largest of these, Deak-Perera, will send information if you contact them at: 29 Broadway, New York, NY 10006, 212-757-6915.

A warning to credit card users: When charging, make sure that the following information appears on the original and all copies of your bill: the correct date; the type of currency being charged (*francs, marks, kroner,* etc.); the official exchange rate for that currency on that date (if possible); and, the total amount of the bill. Without this information, you may end up paying at an exchange rate less favorable to you and more favorable to your European host, and for a larger bill than you thought!

Driver's License

A valid American (state) license is usually respected. However, if you have time, and want to avoid language problems on the road, it is a good idea to get an international drivers' document through the AAA or a local automobile club.

Electrical Appliances

If you plan to bring along any small electrical appliances for use without batteries, be aware that Europe's system of electric current and voltage differs from ours. If your appliance has no special internal adapters or converters made especially for use in Europe, you will have to supply your own. For most appliances, you will need *plug adapters* (one for continental Europe and one for Great Britain) that provide the proper number and shape prongs for European outlets.

For further information on foreign electricity, contact Franzus Company, 352 Park Avenue South, New York, NY 10010, 212-889-5850.

III. BASIC WORDS AND PHRASES

Fundamental Expressions

Yes.	Sì. (see)
No.	No (noh).
Maybe.	Forse. (fOHr-seh)
Please.	Per piacere. (pEHr pee-ah-chAY-reh)
Thank you very much.	Mille grazie. (mEEI-leh grAH-tsee-eh)
You're welcome.	Prego. (prEH-goh)
Excuse me.	Mi scusi. (mee-skOO-see)
I'm sorry.	Mi dispiace. (mee dee-spee-AH-cheh)
Just a second.	Un momento. (OOn-moh-mEHn-toh)
That's all right/okay.	Va bene. (vah bEH-neh)
It doesn't matter.	Non importa. (nohn eem-pOHr-tah)
Sir	Signore (see-nyOH-reh)
Madame	Signora (see-nyOH-rah)
Miss	Signorina (see-nyoh-rEE-nah)
Good morning/afternoon.	Buon giorno (boo-OHn jee-OHr-noh)
Good evening/night.	Buona sera/notte. (boo-Oh-nah sAY-rah/nOH-teh)
Goodbye.	Arrivederci. (ahr-ree-veh-dAYr-chee)
See you later.	A più tardi. (ah pee-OO tAHr-dee)
So long.	Ciao. (chee-AH-oh)
See you tomorrow.	A domani. (ah doh-mAH-nee).

NOTE: Generally, **buon giorno** is used throughout the day until about 4–6 P.M. The expression **buon pomeriggio** ("good afternoon") is generally not used in conversation. **Buona sera** is used when meeting people in the late afternoon and throughout the evening. **Buena notte** is used when leaving at the end of the evening. The casual expression **ciao** ("hello," "bye," "so long") is used only with friends and family.

Glad to make your acquaintance.	Molto lièto[a]. (mohl-toh lee-AY-toh [ah])
How are you?	Come sta? (kOH-meh stah)
Very well, thank you.	Bene, grazie. (beh-neh grAH-tse-eh)
And you?	E lei? (ay lEH-ee)
Fine.	Bene. (beh-neh)
What is your name?	Come si chiama? (kOH-meh see key-AH-meh)
My name is____.	Mi chiamo____. (mE-Eeh key-AH-moh)
How do you do?	Come sta? (kOH-meh stah)
Glad to meet you.	Lièto[a] di conoscérla. (lee-EH-toh [ah] dee koh-nOH-shehr-lah)
The pleasure is mine.	Il piacere é mio. (eel pee-ah-chAY-reh EH stAH-toh MEE-oh)
Where are you from?	Lei di dov'è? (lEH-ee dee doh-vEH)

How long will you be staying?	Quanto tempo resterà qui? (koo-AHn-toh tEHm-po reh-steh-rAH koo-EE)
What hotel are you staying at?	In quale hotel sta? (een koo-AH-leh oh-tEHl stAH)
Here's my address and my telephone number.	Ecco il mio indirizzo e il mio numero di telefono. (EHk-koh eel mEE-oh een-dee-rEE-tsoh ay eel mEE-OH nOO-meh-roh)
See you tomorrow.	A domani. (ah doh-mAH-nee)
See you later.	A più tardi/ciao. (ah pee-OO tAHr-dee/chee-AH-oh)

Communication

Do you speak English?	Parla inglese? (pAHr-lah een-glAY-seh)
I don't speak Italian.	Lo non parlo italiano. (EE-oh nohn pAHr-loh ee-tah-lee-AH-noh)
I speak a little Italian.	Parlo poco l'italiano. (pAHr-loh pOH-koh lee-tah-lee-AH-noh)
Is there anyone here who speaks English?	C'è qualcuno qui che parla inglese? (chEH koo-ahl-kOO-noh koo-EE key pAHr-lah een-gLAY-seh)
Please speak more slowly.	Parli lentamente, per favore. (pAHr-lee pee-OO pee-AH-noh pehr fah-vOH-reh)
Please repeat.	Ripeta, per favore. (ree-pEH-tah koo-AYs-toh pehr fah-vOH-reh)
How do you say____ in Italian?	Come si dice ____ in italiano? (kOH-meh see dEE-cheh een ee-tah-lee-AH-noh)
What do you call this in Italian?	Come si chiama questo in Italiano? (kOH-meh see key-AH-mah koo-AYS-toh een ee-tah-lee-AH-noh)

Common Questions and Phrases

Where is ____?	Dov'è ____ ? (doh-vEH)
When?	Quando? (koo-AHn-doh)
How?	Come? (kOH-meh)
How much?	Quanto costa? (koo-AHn-toh)
Who?	Chi? (key)
Why?	Perchè? (pehr-kAY)
Which?	Quale? (koo-AH-leh)
Here is ____.	Ecco ____. (EHk-koh)
There is ____.	C'è ____. (chEH)
There are ____.	Ci sono ____. (chee sOH-noh)
That is ____.	Quello[a] è ____. (koo-AYl-loh[ah] EH)
It is ____.	É ____. (EH)

Useful Nouns

address	l'indirizzo (leen-dee-rEE-tsoh)
amount	quantità, il prezzo (koo-AHn-tee-tah, eel prEH-tsoh)

appointment	l'appuntamento (lahp-poon-tah-mEHN-toh)
bill	il conto (eel-kOHn-toh)
business	l'affare (lahf fAH-reh)
car	la macchina, l'auto (lah MAH-key-nah, lAH-oo-toh)
cashier	il cassiere (eel kahs-see-AY-reh)
check	l'assegno (lahs-sAY-ny-oh)
city	la città (lah cheet-tAH)
customs	la dogana (lah doh-gAH-nah)
date	la data (lah dAH-tah)
document	il documento (eel doh-koo-mEHn-toh)
elevator	l'ascensore (lah-shayn-sOH-reh)
flight	il volo (eel vOH-loh)
friend	l'amico[a] (lah-mEE-koh[a])
hanger	l'attaccapanni (laht-tAH-kah-pAHn-nee)
highway	autostrada (lah-oo-toh-strAH-dah)
key	la chiave (lah key-AH-veh)
list	la lista (lah lEEs-tah)
luggage	il bagaglio (eel bah-gAH-ly-e-oh)
maid	la cameriera (lah kah-meh-reeEH-rah)
mail	la posta (lah pOHs-tah)
magazine	la rivista (lah ree-vEEs-tah)
manager	il direttore (eel-dee-reht-tOH-reh)
map	la carta, cartina (lah kAHr-tah, lah-kahr-tEE-nah)
mistake	lo sbaglio (loh-sbAH-ly-ee-oh)
money	il denaro (eel day-nAH-roh)
name	il nome (eel nOH-meh)
newspaper	il giornale (eel jee-ohr-nAH-leh)
office	l'ufficio (loof-fEE-chee-oh)
package	il collo, il pacco, il pacchetto (eel kOH-loh, eel pAH-koh, eel pah-kAY-toh)
paper	la carta (lah kAHr-tah)
passport	il passaporto (eel-pahs-sah-pOHr-toh)
pen	la penna (lah pAYn-nah)
pencil	la matita (lah mah-tEE-tah)
porter	il portabagagli (eel pOHr-tah-bah-gAH-ly-ee)
post office	l'ufficio postale (loof-fEE-chee-oh pohs-tAH-leh)
postage stamp	il francobollo (eel frahn-koh-bOHl-loh)
price	il prezzo (eel prEH-tsoh)
raincoat	l'impermeabile (leem-pehr-mayAH-bee-leh)
reservation	la prenotazione (lah preh-noh-tah-tsee-OH-neh)
rest room	il gabinetto (eel gah-bee-nAYt-toh)
restaurant	il ristorante (eel rEEs-toh-rAHn-teh)
road	la strada (lah strAH-dah)
room	la camera (lah kAH-meh-rah)
shirt	la camicia (lah kah-mEE-chee-ah)

shoes	le scarpe (leh skAHr-peh)
shower	la doccia (lah dOH-chee-ah)
store	il negozio (eel nay-gOH-tsee-oh)
street	la via, la strada (lah vEE-ah, lah strAH-dah)
suit	l'abito (lAH-bee-toh)
suitcase	la valigia (lah vah-lEE-jee-ah)
taxi	il tassì (eel tahs-sEE)
telegram	il telegramma (eel teh-leh-grAHm-mah)
telephone	il telefono (eel teh-lEH-foh-noh)
terminal	il capolinea (eel kah-poh-lEE-neh-ah)
ticket	il biglietto (eel bee-ly-AYt-toh)
time	l'ora, il tempo (lOH-rah, eel tEHm-poh)
tip	la mancia (lah mAHn-chee-ah)
train	il treno (eel trEH-noh)
trip	il viaggio (eel vee-AH-jee-oh)
umbrella	l'ombrello (lohm-brEH-loh)
waiter	il cameriere (eel kah-meh-ree-EH-reh)
watch	l'orologio (loh-roh-lOH-jee-oh)
water	l'acqua (lAH-koo-ah)

Useful Verbs (Infinitive Forms)

accept	accettare (ah-cheht-tAH-reh)
answer	rispondere (rees-pOHn-day-reh)
arrive	arrivare (ahr-ree-vAH-reh)
ask	domandare, chiedere (doh-mahn-dAHr-reh, key-AY-day-reh)
assist	aiutare (ah-ee-oo-tAH-reh)
begin	cominciare (koh-meen-chee-AH-reh)
bring	portare (pohr-tAH-reh)
buy	comprare (kohm-prAH-reh)
call	chiamare (key-ah-mAH-reh)
carry	portare (pohr-tAH-reh)
change	cambiare (kahm-bee-AH-reh)
close	chiudere (key-OO-deh-reh)
come	venire (vay-nEE-reh)
confirm	confermare (kohn-fayr-mAH-reh)
continue	continuare (kohn-tee-noo-AH-reh)
cost	costare (kohs-tAH-reh)
deliver	consegnare (kohn-say-ny-AH-reh)
direct	indicare (een-de-kAH-reh)
do	fare (fAH-reh)
eat	mangiare (mahn-jee-AH-reh)
end	finire (fee-nEE-reh)
enter	entrare (ayn-trAH-reh)
examine	esaminare (ay-sah-mee-nAH-reh)
exchange	scambiare (skahm-bee-AH-reh)
feel	sentire (sayn-tEE-reh)
finish	finire (fee-nEE-reh)
fix	riparare (repair) (ree-pah-rAH-reh)

follow	seguire (say-goo-EE-reh)
forget	non ricordare, dimenticare, scordare (nohn-ree-kohr-dAH-reh, dee-mehn-tee-kAH-reh, skohr-dAH-reh)
forward	spedire (spay-dEE-reh)
get	ottenere (oht-teh-nAY-reh)
give	dare (dAH-reh)
go	andare (ahn-dAH-reh)
hear	sentire (sayn-tEE-reh)
help	aiutare (ah-ee-oo-tAH-reh)
keep	tenere (tay-nAY-reh)
know	sapere (fact) (sah-pAY-reh) conoscere (someone, something) (koh-nOH-shay-reh)
learn	apprendere, imparare (ahp-prAYn-deh-reh, eem-pah-rAH-reh)
leave	partire (go out) (pahr-tEE-reh)
listen	ascoltare (ah-skohl-tAH-reh)
look	guardare (goo-AHr-dAH-reh)
lose	perdere (pEHr-deh-reh)
make	fare (fAH-reh)
mean	significare (see-ny-ee-fee-kAH-reh)
meet	incontrare (een-kohn-trAH-reh)
miss	mancare (mahn-kAH-reh)
need	avere bisogno di (ah-vAY-reh bee-sOH-ny-oh dee)
open	aprire (ah-prEE-reh)
order	ordinare (ohr-dee-nAH-reh)
park	parcheggiare (pahr-kay-jee-AH-reh)
pay	pagare (pah-gAH-reh)
prefer	preferire (preh-fay-rEE-reh)
prepare	preparare (preh-pah-rAH-reh)
present	presentare (preh-sayn-tAH-reh)
prove	provare (pro-vAH-reh)
pull	tirare (tee-rAH-reh)
purchase	comprare (kohm-prAH-reh)
put	mettere (mAYt-tay-reh)
read	leggere (lEH-jeh-reh)
receive	ricevere (ree-chAY-vay-reh)
recommend	raccomandare (rAH-koh-mahn-dAH-reh)
remain	restare (rays-tAH-reh)
repair	riparare (ree-pah-rAH-reh)
repeat	ripetere (ree-pEH-teh-reh)
rest	riposare (ree-poh-sAH-reh)
return	ritornare (ree-tohr-nAH-reh)
run	correre (kOHr-ray-reh)
say	dire (dEE-reh)
see	vedere (vay-dAY-reh)
send	mandare (mahn-dAH-reh)
show	mostrare, indicare (mohst-rAH-reh, een-dee-kAH-reh)

sit	sedersi (say-dAYr-see)
speak	parlare (pahr-lAH-reh)
stand	alzarsi (ahl-tsAr-see)
start	cominciare (koh-meen-chee-AH-reh)
stop	fermare (fayr-mAH-reh)
take	prendere (prayn-dAY-reh)
talk	parlare (pahr-lAH-reh)
tell	dire (dEE-reh)
think	pensare (pehn-sAH-reh)
try	provare (proh-vAH-reh)
turn	girare (jee-rAH-reh)
use	utilizzare, servirsi di, usare (oo-teel-ee-tsAH-reh, sehr-vEEr-see dee, oo-sAH-reh)
visit	visitare (vee-see-tAH-reh)
wait	aspettare (ahs-peht-tAH-reh)
walk	camminare (kahm-mee-nAH-reh)
want	volere, desiderare, (voh-lAY-reh, day-see-day-rAH-reh)
wear	portare (pohr-tAH-reh)
work	lavorare (lah-voh-rAH-reh)
write	scrivere (skrEE-veh-reh)

Useful Adjectives and Adverbs

above/below	sopra/sotto (sOH-prah/sOHt-toh)
best/worst	migliore/peggiore (mee-ly-ee-OH-reh/peh-jee-O-reh)
big/small	grande/piccolo[a] (grAHn-deh/pEE-koh-loh[ah])
early/late	presto/tardi (prEHs-toh/tAHr-dee)
easy/difficult	facile/difficile (fAH-chee-leh/deef-fEE-chee-leh)
few/many	pochi/molti (pOH-kee/mOHl-tee)
first/last	primo[a]/ultimo[a] (prEE-moh[ah]/OOl-tee-moh[ah])
front/back	anteriore/posteriore (ahn-teh-ree-OH-reh/pohs-teh-ree-OH-reh)
full/empty	pieno[a]/vuoto[a] (pee-AY-noh[ah]/voo-OH-toh[ah])
good/bad	buono[a]/cattivo[a] (boo-OH-noh[ah]/kaht-tEE-voh[ah])
hot/cold	caldo[a]/freddo[a] (kAHl-doh[ah]/frAYd-doh[ah])
high/low	alto[a]/basso[a] (AHl-toh[ah]/bAHs-soh[ah])
in front/in back	davanti/dietro (dah-vAHn-tee/dee-EH-troh)
inside/outside	dentro/fuori (dAYn-troh/ fooOH-ree)
large/small	grande/piccolo[a] (grAHn-deh/pEE-koh-loh[ah])
more/less	più/meno (pee-OO/mAY-noh)

near/far	vicino[a], prossimo[a]/lontano[a] (vee-chEE-noh[nah], prOH-see-moh[mah]/lohn-tAH-noh[nah])
old/new	vecchio[a]/nuovo[a] (vEHk-kee-oh/noo-OH-voh)
open/shut	aperto[a]/chiuso[a] ([ah]-pEHr-toh[ah]/key-OO-soh[ah])
right/wrong	giusto[a]/sbagliato[a] (jee-OOs-toh[tah]/sbah-ly-AH-toh[tah])
slow/fast (adj.)	lento[a]/rapido[a] (lEHn-toh[tah]/rAH-pee-doh[dah])
slow/fast (adv.)	piano/presto (pee-AH-noh/prEHs-toh)
thin/thick	magro[a], fine/grosso[a], denso[a] (mAH-groh[grah], fEE-neh/grAH-soh[sah], dEHn-soh[sah])
to be right/wrong	avere ragione/avere torto (ah-vEH-reh rah-jee-OH-neh/ah/vEH-reh tOHr-teh)

Other Useful Words

a, an	un, uno, una (oon, OO-noh, OO-nah)
about	intorno (een-tOHr-noh), circa (chEEhr-kah)
across	attraverso (aht-trah-vEHr-soh)
after	dopo (dOH-poh)
again	un'altra volta, di nuovo (oon-AHl-trah vOHl-tah, dee noo-OH-voh)
all	tutto[a], tutti[e], (tOOt-toh[ah], tOO-tee [teh])
almost	quasi (kwAH-zee)
also	anche (AHn-keh)
always	sempre (sEHm-preh)
among	tra (trAH)
and	e (ay)
any	qualche (koo-AHl-keh)
another	un altro, un'altra (oon-AHl-troh, oon-AHl-trah)
around	intorno (een-tOHr-noh)
at	all', alla, etc. (ahl, ahl-lah)
away	via (vEE-ah)
because	perchè (pehr-kAY)
before	prima di, davanti a (prEE-mah dee, dah-vAHn-tee ah)
behind	dietro a (dee-AY-troh)
between	fra (frAH)
both	tutti e due (toot-tee ay dOO-eh)
but	ma (mah)
down	giù (jee-OO)
each	ogni (OH-ny-ee)
enough	basta (bAHs-tah)
even if	anche se (AHn-keh seh)
every	ogni (OH-ny-ee)

except	eccetto (ay-chEH-toh)
few	pochi[e] (pOH-kee[keh])
for	per (pehr)
from	da, dall', dalla, etc. (dah, dahl, dahl-lah)
however	però (peh-rOH)
if	se (seh)
in	in, nel', nello, nella, etc. (een, nehl, nEHl-loh, nEHl-lah)
instead	invece (een-vAY-cheh)
maybe	forse (fOHr-seh)
more	più (pee-OO)
much	molto (mOHl-toh)
next to	vicino[a] (vee-chEE-noh[nah])
not	no, non (noh, nohn)
now	adesso/ora (ad-dEHs-soh/OH rah)
of	di, del, dell', dello, della, etc. (dee, dehl, dEHl-loh dEHl-lah)
often	spesso (spAYs-soh)
only	solo/solamente (soh-loh/soh-lah-mEHn-teh)
or	o (oh)
other	altro[a] (AHl-troh[ah])
perhaps	forse (fOHr-seh)
same	stesso[a] (stAY-soh[ah])
since	poichè (poh-ee-kEH)
some	qualche (koo-AHl-keh)
still	ancora (ahn-kOH-rah)
that	che (kay)
these	questi[e] (koo-AYs-tee[ay])
this	questo[a] (koo-AYs-toh[ah])
to	a, al, alla, etc. (ah, ahl, AHl-lah)
unless	a meno chè (ah mAY-noh keh)
until	fino a (fEE-noh ah)
very	molto (mohl-toh)
with	con (kohn)

Directions

North	il nord (eel nord)
South	il sud (eel sud)
East	l'est (lehst)
West	l'ovest (lOH-vehst)
Straight ahead	tutto diritto (tOO-toh dee-rEE-toh)
Left	sinistra (see-nEEs-trah)
Right	destra (dEHs-trah)
In the middle	in mezzo (een mEH-tsoh)

Days of the Week

Sunday	domenica (doh-mAY-nee-kah)
Monday	lunedì (loo-neh-dEE)

Tuesday	martedì (mahr-teh-dEE)
Wednesday	mercoledì (mehr-kok-leh-dEE)
Thursday	giovedì (jee-oh-veh-dEE)
Friday	venerdì (veh-nehr-dEE)
Saturday	sabato (sAH-bah-toh)
Today	oggi (OH-jee)
Yesterday	ieri (ee-EH-ree)
Tomorrow	domani (doh-mAH-nee)
Tonight	questa notte/stanotte (koo-AY-stah-nOHt-teh/stah-nOHt-teh)
Next week	la settimana prossima (lah seht-tee-mAH-nah prOH-see-mah)
Last week	la settimana passata (lah seht-tee-mAH-nah pahs-sAH-tah)
Next month	il mese prossimo (eel mAY-seh prOH-see-moh)
The day after tomorrow	dopodomani (dOH-poh-doh-mAH-nee)
This weekend	questa fine di settimana (koo-AYs-tah fEE-neh dee-sayt-tee-mAH-nah)
What day is it today?	Che giorno é oggi? (kAY jee-OHr-noh EH OH-jee)
Today is _____ .	Oggi é _____. (OH-jee EH)

Months of the Year

January	gennaio (jehn-nAH-ee-oh)
February	febbraio (fehb-brAH-ee-oh)
March	marzo (mAHr-tsoh)
April	aprile (ah-prEE-leh)
May	maggio (mAH-jee-oh)
June	giugno (jee-OO-ny-ee-oh)
July	luglio (lOO-ly-ee-oh)
August	agosto (ah-gOH-stoh)
September	settembre (seht-tEHm-breh)
October	ottobre (oht-tOH-breh)
November	novembre (noh-vEHm-breh)
December	dicembre (dee-chEHm-breh)
What's today's date?	Che data é oggi? (kay dAH-ta EH OH-jee)

The first of the month is *il primo* (an ordinal number). All other dates are expressed with *cardinal* numbers.

Today is August first.	Oggi é il primo di agosto. (OH-jee EH eel prEE-moh dee ah-gOH-stoh)
• fourth	• il quattro (eel koo-AHt-troh)
• 25th	• il venticinque (eel vayn-tee chEEn-koo-eh)
This month	questo mese (koo-AY-stoh mAY-seh)
Last month	il mese scorso (eel mAY-seh skOHr-soh)
Next month	il mese prossimo (eel mAY-seh prOHs-see-moh)

Last year	l'anno scorso (lAHn-noh skOHr-soh)
Next year	l'anno prossimo (lAHn-noh prOHs-see-moh)
May 1, 1876	il primo maggio, mille- otto- cento- settanta-sei (EEl prEE-moh mAH-jee-oh mEEl-leh oht-toh-chEHn-toh seht-tAHn-tah-sEH-ee)
July 4, 1984	il quattro luglio, mille- nove- cento- ottanta-quattro (eel koo-AHt-troh 1OO-ly-ee-oh mEEl-leh noh-veh-chEHn toh oht-tAHn-tah koo-AHt-troh)

The Four Seasons

Spring	la primavera (lah pree-mah-vEH-rah)
Summer	l'estate (leh-stAH-teh)
Fall	l'autunno (lah-oo-tOOn-noh)
Winter	l'inverno (leen-vEHr-noh)
How is the weather today?	Che tempo fa oggi? (kay tEHm-poh fAH OH-jee)
It's good (bad) weather.	Fa bel/cattivo tempo. (fah behl/kaht-tEE-voh tEHm-poh)
It's hot.	Fa caldo. (fah kAHl-doh)
• cold	• freddo (frAYd-doh)
• cool	• fresco (frAY-skoh)
It's windy.	Tira vento. (tEE-rah vEEn-toh)
It's sunny.	C'è il sole. (chEH eel sOH-leh)
It's raining.	Piove. (pee-OH-veh)
It's snowing.	Nevica. (nAY-vee-kah)
It's drizziling.	Pioviggina. (pee-oh-vEE-jee-nah)

Time

What time is it?	Che ora é? (kay OH-rah EH)

When telling time in Italian, *it is* is expressed by è for 1:00, noon, and midnight, **sono** is used for all other numbers.

It's 1:00 .	É l'una. (eh 1OO-nah)
It's 12 o'clock (noon).	É mezzogiorno. (eh meh-tsoh-jee-OHr-noh)
It's midnight.	É mezzanotte. (eh meh-tsah-nOHt-teh)
It's early/late.	É presto/tardi. (eh prEH-stoh/tAHr-dee)
It's 2:00.	Sono le due. (sOH-noh leh dOO-eh)
It's 3:00, etc.	Sono le tre. (sOH-noh leh trAY)

The number of minutes after the hour is expressed by adding **e** ("and"), followed by the number of minutes.

It's 4:10.	Sono le quattro e dieci. (sOH-noh leh koo-AHt-roh ay dee-EH-chee)

Fifteen minutes after the hour and half past the hour are expressed by placing *e un quarto* and *e mezzo* after the hour.

It's 5:20.	Sono le cinque e venti. (sOH-noh leh chEEn-koo-eh ay vAYn-tee)
It's 6:15.	Sono le sei e un quarto. (sOH-noh leh sEH-ee ay oon koo-AHr-toh)
It's 7:30.	Sono le sette e mezzo. (sOH-noh leh sEHt-teh ay mEH-tsoh)

After passing the half-hour point on the clock, time is expressed in Italian by *subtracting* the number of minutes to the *next* hour.

It's 7:40.	Sono le otto meno venti (sOH-noh leh OHt-toh mEH-noh vAYn-tee)
It's 8:50.	Sono le nove meno dieci. (sOH-noh leh nOH-veh mAY-noh dee-EH-chee)
At what time?	A che ora? (ah kay OH-rah)
At 1:00.	All'una (ahl-lOO-nah)
At 2:00/3:00, etc.	Alle due/tre (AHl-leh dOO-eh/trAY)
A.M. (in the morning)	del mattino (dAYl-maht-tEE-noh)
P.M. (in the afternoon)	del pomeriggio (dAYl poh-meh-rEE-jee-oh)
At night.	Di notte. (dee nOHt-teh)

Official time is based on the 24-hour clock. You will find train schedules and other such times expressed in terms of a point within a 24-hour sequence.

The train leaves at 15.30.	Il treno parte alle quindici e trenta. (eel trEH-noh pAHr-teh ahl-leh koo-EEn-dee-chee ay trEHn-tah)

Arrival/Hotel

Ny name is _____.	Mi chiamo _____. (mEE-eh keyAH-moh)
I'm American/British, Australian/Canadian.	Sono americano[a] /inglese /australiano[a] /canadese. (sOH-noh ah-mehr-ree-KAh-noh[ah]/een-glAY-seh/ah-oo-strah-lee-AN-noh[ah]/kan-nah-dAY-seh)
I'm staying at _____ .	Sto abitando a _____. (stOH ah-bee-tAHn-doh ah)
Here is my _____.	Ecco il mio _____. (EHk-oh eel-mEE-oh)
• passport	• passaporto (pahs-sah-pOHr-toh)
• business card	• la mia carta (la mEE-ah kAHr-tah), biglietto da visita (beeh-lyEht-toh dah vEEh-zeeh-tah)
I'm on a business trip.	Sono in viaggio d'affari. (sOH-no een vee-AH-jee-oh dahf-fAH-ree)
I'm just passing through.	Sono di passaggio. (sOH-noh dee pahs-sAH-jee-oh)
I'll be staying here for _____ .	Saro li per _____ . (SAH-rah lee pehr)
• a few days	• qualche giorno (koo-AHl-keh jee-OHr-neeoh)
• a week	• una settimana (oo-nah seht-tee-mAH-neh)
• a few weeks	• qualche settimana (koo-AHl-keh seht-tee-mAH-nah)
• a month	• un mese (oon mAY-seh)

I am traveling to _____ .	vado a (vAh-doh ah)
I have nothing to declare.	Non ho niente da dichiarare. (nohn oh neeEHn-tay dah dee-key-ah-rAH-reh)
I'd like to go to the _____ Hotel.	Vorrei andare all'albergo _____. (vohr-rEH-ee ahn-dAH-reh ahl ahl-bEHr-goh)
Where can I get a taxi?	Dov'è si trova un tassì? (dOH-veh see trOH-va oon tahs-sEE)
I have a reservation.	Ho una prenotazione. (OH OO-nah preh-noh-tah-tsee-OH-neh)
I need a room for one night.	Ho bisogno di una camera per una notte. (OH bee-sOH-ny-oh dee OO-nah kAH-meh-rah pehr OO-nah nOHt-teh)
I want a double room with a bath.	Vorrei una camera doppia con bagno. (vohr-rEH-ee OO-nah kAH-meh-rah dOH-pee-eh kohn-bAH-ny-oh)
What is the rate per night?	Quant'é la camera? (koo-AHnt-ay lah kAH-meh-rah)
Does that include breakfast?	É compresa la colazione? (ay kohm-prEH-sah lah Koh-lah-tsee-OH-neh)
Where is the elevator?	Dov'è l'ascensore? (doh-vEH lah-shehn-sOH-reh)
Please send up some mineral water.	Mi mandi una bottiglia d'acqua minerale, per favore. (mee mAHn-dee OO-nah boht-tEE-ly-ee-ah dAH-koo-ah mee-neh-rAHl-leh pehr fah-vOH-reh)
Please wake me tomorrow at _____ .	Per favore, mi svegli alle _____ domani. (pehr fah-vOH-reh mee svay-ly-ee AH-leh doh-mAH-nee)
Are there any messages for me?	Ci sono messaggi per me? (chee sOH-no mehs-sAH-jee pehr may)
I'd like to leave this in your safe.	Vorrei lasciare questo nella sua cassaforte. (vohr-rEH-ee lah-shee-AH-reh koo-AYs-toh nEH-lah soo-ah kAH-sa-fOHR-teh)
Please make this call for me.	Mi faccia questa telefonata, per favore. (mee fAH-chee-ah koo-AYs-tah teh-leh-fOH-nah-tah pehr fah-vOH-reh)
Would you please send someone up for my bags?	Mi faccia scendere il bagaglio, per favore? (mee fAH-chee-ah shAYn-day-reh eel bah-gAH-ly-ee-oh pehr fah-vOH-reh)
I'd like to check out.	Vorrei pagare il conto e partire. (vohr-rEH-ee pah-gAH-reh eel kOHn-to ay pahr-tEE-reh)

Transportation

bus	autobus (ah-oo-toh-bOOs)
train	treno (trEH-noh)
metro	metropolitana (meh-troh-poh-lee-tAH-nah)
ticket	biglietto (bee-ly-ee-AY-toh)
station	stazione (stah-tsee-OH-neh)
map	cartina (kahr-tEE-nah)

stop	fermata (fehr-mAH-tah)
taxi	tassì (tahs-sEE)
Where can I rent a car?	Dove posso noleggiare un macchina? (dOH-veh POHs-soh noh-leh-jee-AH-reh OO-nah mAHk-kee-nah)
I want/I'd like _____ .	Voglio/Vorrei _____ . (vOH-lyee-oh/vohr-rEH-ee)
• a small car	• una macchina piccola (OO-nah mAHk-kee-nah pEE-koh-lah)
• a large car	• una macchina grande (OO-nah mAHk-kee-nah grAHn-deh)
• a sport car	• una macchina sportiva (OO-nah mAHk-kee-nah spohr-tEE-vah)
I prefer automatic transmission.	Preferisco il cambio automatico. (preh-feh-rEE-skoh eel kAHm-bee-oh ah-oo-toh-mAH-tee-koh)
How much does it cost ___ ?	Quanto costa ____? (koo-AHn-toh kOH-stah)
• per day	• al giorno (ahl jee-OHr-noh)
• per week	• alla settimana (AHl-lah seht-tee-mAH-nah)
• per kilometer	• per chilometro (pehr key-lOH-meh-troh)
• for unlimited mileage	• a chilometraggio illimitato (ah key-loh-meh-trAH-jee-oh eel-lee-mee-tAH-toh)
How much is the complete insurance?	Quant'é l'assicurazione completa? (koo-ahn-tEH las-see-koo-rah-tsee-OH-neh kohm-plEH-tah)
Is gas included?	É inclusa la benzina? (EH een-kloo-sah lah behn-tsEE-nah)
Do you accept credit cards?	Accetta carte di credito? (ah-chEHt-tah kAHr-teh dee krEH-dee-toh)
Here's my (international) driver's license.	Ecco la mia patente (internazionale). (EHk-koh lah mEE-ah-pah-tEHn-teh (een-tehr-nah-tsee-oh-nAH-leh)
Do I have to leave a deposit?	Devo lasciare un acconto/un deposito? (dAY-voh lah-shee-AH-reh oon ahk-kOHn-toh/oon day-pOH-see-toh)
Is there a drop-off charge?	C'é un supplemento per la consegna dell'auto? (chEH oon soo-pleh-mEHn-toh pehr lah kohn-seh-ny-ee-ah dayl-lAH-oo-toh)
I want to rent the car here and leave it in Turin.	Desidero noleggiare l'auto qui e consegnarla a Torino. (day-sEE-deh-roh noh-lay-jee-AH-reh lAH-oo-toh koo-EE ay kohn-say-ny-ee-AHr-lah ah toh-rEE-noh)
What kind of fuel does it take?	Che tipo di carburante usa? (kay tEE-poh dee kahr-boo-rAHn-teh OO-sah)
Fill'er up with _____ .	Faccia il pieno di _____. (fAH-chee-ah eel pee-AY-noh dee)
• diesel	• diesel (dEE-eh-sehl) /gasolio (gAHsolioh)
• regular (standard)	• normale (nohr-mAH-leh)

- super (premium) • super (sOO-pehr)

Please check _____ . Per favore mi controlli _____ . (pehr fah-vOH-reh mee kohn-trOHl-leh)

- the battery • la batteria (lah baht-teh-rEE-ah)
- the carburetor • il carburatore (eel kahr-boo-rah-tOH-reh)
- the oil • l'olio (lOH-lee-oh)
- the spark plugs • le candele (leh kahn-dAY-leh)
- the tires • i pneumatici/le gomme (ee pnay-oo-mAH-tee-chee/leh gOHm-meh)
- the tire pressure • la pressione delle gomme (lah prehs-see-OH-neh dAYl-leh gOHm-meh)
- the water • l'acqua (lAH-koo-ah)

Change the oil (please). Mi cambi l'olio, per favore. (mee kAHm-bee lOH-lee-oh pehr fah-vOH-reh)

Lubricate the car (please). Mi lubrifichi la macchina, per favore. (mee loo-brEE-fee-key lah mAHk-kee-nah pehr fah-vOH-reh)

Charge the battery. Mi carichi la batteria. (mee-kAH-ree-key lah baht-teh-rEE-ah)

Change this tire. Mi cambi questa ruota. (mee kAHm-bee koo-AY-stah roo-OH-tah)

Wash the car. Mi faccia il lavaggio alla macchina. (mee fAH-chee-ah eel lah-vAH-jee-oh AHl-lah mAHk-kee-nah)

Where are the restrooms? Dov'è sono i gabinetti? (dOH-veh sOH-noh ee gah-bee-nAYt-tee)

Where is my hotel on this map? Dov'è il mio albergo sulla cartina? (dov-vEH eel mEE-oh ahl-bEHr-goh sOO-lah khar-tEE-nah)

Drivers should be familiar with these universal road signs:

Guarded railroad crossing

Yield

Stop

Right of way

Dangerous intersection ahead

Gasoline (petrol) ahead

Parking

No vehicles allowed

Dangerous curve

Pedestrian crossing

Oncoming traffic
has right of way

No bicycles allowed

No parking allowed

No entry

No left turn

No U-turn

No passing

Border crossing

Traffic signal ahead

Speed limit

Traffic circle
(roundabout) ahead

Minimum speed limit

All traffic turns left

End of no passing zone

One-way street

Detour

Danger ahead

Entrance to expressway   Expressway ends

Where is the bus stop?/the bus terminal?	Dov'è la fermata dell'autobus/il capolinea? (dov-vEH lah fehr-mAH-tah dayl-lAH-oo-toh-boos/eel kah-poh-lEE-neh-ah)
In which direction do I have to go?	In quale direzione devo andare? (een koo-AH-leh dee-reh-tsee-neh dAY-voh ahn-dAH- reh)
Where is the subway station?	Dov'è la stazione della metropolitana? (doh-vEH lah stah-tsee-OH-nee dAYl-lah meh-troh-poh-lee-tAH-nah)
How much is the fare?	Quanto costa il biglietto? (koo-AHn-toh kOH-stah eel bee-ly-ee-AYt-toh)
Where can I buy a ticket?	Dov'è posso comprare un biglietto? (dOH-veh pOHs-soh kohm-prAH-reh oon bee-ly-ee-AYt-toh)
Which is the train that goes to _____ ?	Qual' é il treno che va a _____ ? (koo-ahl-lEH eel trEH-noh keh vah ah)
Does this train go to _____ ?	Questo treno va a _____ ? (koo-AYs-toh trEH-noh vAH ah)
Please tell me when we get there.	Può farmi sapere quando siamo arrivati. (poo-OH fAHr-mee sah-pAY-reh koo-AHn-doh see-AH-moh ahr-rEE-vah-tee)
Do I have to change trains?	Devo cambiare treno? (dAY-voh kahm-bee-AH-reh trEH-noh)
Is this seat taken?	È occupato questo posto? (EH oh-koo-pAH-toh koo-AYs-toh pOH-stoh)
Taxi! Are you free?	Tassì! È libero? (tahs-sEE EH lee-beh-roh)
Take me to this address.	Mi porti a questo indirizzo. (mee pOHr-tee ah koo-AYs-toh een-dee-rEE-tsoh)
How much is it?	Qual' è la tariffa? (koo-ah-lEH lah tah-rEE-fah)
Faster. I'm in a hurry.	Faccia presto. Ho fretta. (fAH-chea prEH-stoh. . .oh frAYt-tah)

Please drive slower.	Per cortesia guidi più piano lentamente. (pehr kohr-tay-sEE-ah goo-EE-dee pee-OO pee-AH-noh len-tAH-men-teh)
Where is there a flight to _____?	Quando c'é un volo per _____? (koo-AHn-doh chEH oon vOH-loh pehr)
I would like _____.	Vorrei _____. (vohr-rEH-ee)
• a round trip/one-way ticket.	• un biglietto di andata e ritorno/di andata (oon bee-ly-ee-AYt-toh dee ahn-dAH-tah ay ree-tOHr-noh/dee ahn-dAH-tah)
• in tourist class	• in classe turistica (een klAHs-seh too-rEE-stee-kah)
• in first class	• in prima classe (een prEE-mah klAHs-seh)
I would like a seat _____.	Vorrei un posto _____. (vohr-rEH-ee OOn pOH-stoh)
• in the non/smoking section	• tra i non/fumatori (trAH ee nohn/foo-mah-tOH-ree)
• next to the window	• accanto al finestrino (ah-kAHn-toh ahl fee-neh-strEE-noh)
• on the aisle	• vicino al corridoio (vee-chEE-noh ahl kohr-ree-dOH-ee-oh)
What is the fare?	Qual' è il prezzo del biglietto? (koo-ah-lEH eel prEH-tsoh dAYl bee-ly-ee-EHt-toh)
Are meals served?	Sono inclusi i pasti? (sOH-noh een-klOO-see ee pAH-stee)
When does the plane leave/arrive?	A che ora parte/arriva l'aereo? (ah kay OH-rah pAHr-teh/ahr-ree-vAH lah-EH-reh-oh)
When must I be at the airport?	Quando dovrò trovarmi all'aeroporto? (koo-AHn-doh doh-vrOH troh-vAHr-mee ahl-lah-eh-roh-pOHr-toh)
What is my flight number?	Qual' è il [mio] numero di volo? (koo-AH-lEH eel [mEE-oh] nOO-meh-roh dee vOH-loh)
What gate do we leave from?	Qual' è la nostra porta d'uscita? (koo-ah-lEH lah nOH-strah pOHr-tah doo-shEE-tah)
I want to confirm/cancel my reservation for flight _____.	Desidero confermare/cancellare la mia prenotazione per il volo _____. (day-sEE-deh-roh kohn-fayr-mAH-reh/kahn-chehl-lAH-reh lah mEE-ah preh-noh-tah-tsee-OH-neh pehr eel vOH-loh)

Leisure Time

Is there a discotheque here?	C'è una discoteca qui? (chEE OO-nah dee-skoh-tEH-kah koo-EE)
Is there one at the hotel?	C'è una in albergo? (chEE OO-nah een ahl-bEHr-goh)
I would like to make a reservation.	Vorrei fare una prenotazione. (vohr-rEH-ee fAH-reh OO-nah preh-noh-tah-tsee-OH-neh)

Where is the check-room?	Dov'è il guardaroba? (doh-vEH-eel goo-ahr-dah-rOH-bah)
Where can I find an English newspaper?	Dove posso trovare un giornale in inglese? (dOH-veh pOHs-soh troh-vAH-reh oon jee-ohr-nAH-leh een een-glAY-seh)
I would like to see a soccer match.	Vorrei vedere una partita di calcio. (vohr-rEH-ee veh-dAY-reh OO-nah pahr-tEE-tah dee kAHl-chee-oh)
Where can I buy the tickets?	Dove posso comprare dei biglietti? (dOH-veh pOHs-soh kohm-prAH-reh dAY bee-ly-ee AYt-tee)
Where is the stadium?	Dov'è lo stadio? (doh-vEH loh stAH-dee-oh)
What teams are going to play?	Quali squadre giocheranno? (koo-AH-lee skoo-AH-dreh jee-oh-keh-rAHn-noh)
Is there a pool near the hotel?	C'è una piscina nell'hotel? (chEE OO-nah pee-shEE-nah nAYl-loh-tEHl)
How far is _____ ?	Quanto dista _____? (koo-AHn-toh dEE-stah)

Restaurants

Breakfast	colazione (koh-lah-tsee-OH-neh)
Lunch	pranzo (prAHn-tsoh)
Dinner	cena (chEE-nah)
Excuse me, do you know a good restaurant?	Scusi, conosce un buon ristorante? (skOO-see koh-nOH-sheh OOn boo-OHN ree-stoh-rAHn-teh)
Is it very expensive?	É molto costoso? (eh mohl-toh koh-stOH-soh)
Waiter!	Cameriere! (kah-meh-ree-EH-reh)
We would like to have lunch.	Vorremmo pranzare. (vohr-rAYm-moh prahn-ts AH-reh)
The menu, please.	Il menu, per piacere. (eel may-noo pehr pee-ah-chAY-reh)
What's today special?	Qual' è il piatto del giorno? (koo-ah-lEH eel pee-AHt-toh dayl jee-OHr-noh)
What do you recommend?	Che cosa mi consiglia? (kay kOH-sah mee kohn-sEE-ly-ee-ah)
To begin with, bring us a cocktail.	Per cominciare, ci porti un cocktail. (pehr koh-meen-chee-AH-reh chee pOHr-tee oon kOHk-tayl)
A table for two, please.	Una tavola per due, per favore. (OO-nah tAH-voh-la pehr dOO-eh pehr feh-vOH-reh)
A bottle of	Una bottiglia d'acqua minerale
• mineral water.	• gassata. (oo-nah boht-tEE-ly-ee-ah dAH-koo-ah mee-neh-rAH-leh gahs-sAH-tah)
• a beer	• birra (bEEr-rah)
I would like to order now.	Vorrei ordinare adesso. (vohr-rEH-ee ohr-dee-nAH-reh ah-dEHs-soh)
Do you have a house wine?	Hanno il vino della casa? (AHn-noh eel vEE-noh dAYl-lah kAH-sah)

Waiter, we need _____ .

Cameriere/a, abbiamo bisogno di _____. (kah-meh-ree-EH-reh/ah ahb-bee-AH-moh bee-soH-ny-oh dee)

- a knife
  - un coltello (oon kohl-tEHl-loh)
- a fork
  - una forchetta (oo-nah fohr-kAYt-tah)
- a spoon
  - un cucchiaio (oon koo-key-AH-ee-oh)
- a teaspoon
  - un cucchiaino (oon koo-key-ah-EE-noh)
- a soup spoon
  - un cucchiaio per la minestra/il brodo (oon koo-key-AH-ee-oh pehr lah mee-nEHs-trah/eel brOH-doh)

- a glass
  - un bicchiere (oon bee-key-EH-reh)
- a cup
  - una tazza (oo-nah tAH-tsah)
- a saucer
  - un piattino (oon pee-aht-tEE-noh)
- a plate
  - un piatto (oon pee-AHt-toh)
- a napkin
  - un tovagliolo (oon tah-vah-ly-ee-OH-loh)
- toothpicks
  - gli stuzzicadenti (ly-ee stOO-tsee-kah-dEHn-tee)

I would like an expresso, please.

Vorrei un espresso, per favore. (vohr-rEH-ee oon ehs-prEHs-soh pehr fah-vOH-reh)

Do you mind if I smoke?

Le dispiace se fumo? (leh dee-spee-ah-cheh sey fOO-moh)

Do you have a light/ matches?

Ha un accendino/un fiammifero? (ah oon ah-chayn-dEE-noh/oon fee-ahm-mEE-feh-roh)

The check, please.

Il conto, per favore. (eel kOHn-toh pehr fah-vOH-reh)

Is the service included?

È incluso il servizio? (EH een-klOO-soh eel sehr-vEE-tsee-oh)

I don't think the bill is right.

Non penso che il conto sia corretto. (nohn pEHn-soh kay eel kOHn-toh sEE-ah kor-rEHt-toh)

Do you take credit cards?

Accettano carte di credito? (ah-chEHt-tah-noh kAHr-teh dee krEH-dee-toh)

Which one?

Quale? (koo-AH-leh)

We're in a hurry.

Abbiamo fretta. (ahb-bee-AH-moh frAYt-tah)

Do you have American cigarettes?

Ha sigarette americane? (AH see-gah-rAY-teh ah-meh-ree-kAH-neh)

What brand?

Di che marca? (dee kay mAHr-kah)

Where are the restrooms?

Dove sono i gabinetti? (dOH-veh sOH-noh ee gah-bee-nAYt-tee)

Shopping

Where can I find ____?

Dove si trova ____? (dOH-veh see trOH-vah)

Can you help me?

Lei può aiutarmi? (lay poo-OH ah-ee-oo-tAHr-mee)

I need ____.

Ho bisogno di ____. (oh bee-sOH-ny-oh dee)

Do you have any others?

Ci sono altri ____? (chee sOH-noh AHl-tree)

Do you take credit cards?

Accettano le carte di credito? (see ah-chEHt-tah-noh lay kAHr-teh dee krEH-dee-toh)

Can I pay with a traveler's check?	Posso pagare con un traveler's check? (pOHs-soh pah-gAH-reh kohn oon trAH-veh-lehs chEH-keh)
How much does ____ cost?	Quanto costa ____? (koo-AHn-toh kOHs-tah)
Do you have anything	Ha qualche cosa ____? (AH koo-AHl-keh kOH-sah)
• smaller	• più piccolo (pee-OO pEE-koh-loh)
• larger	• più grande (pee-OO grAHn-deh)

Medical Care

Where is the nearest pharmacy?	Dov'è la farmacia più vicina? (doh-vEH lah fahr-mah-chEE-ah pee-OO vee-chEE-nah)
I need something for a ____ .	Ho bisogno di qualche cosa per ____. (oh bee-sOH-ny-ee-oh dee koo-AHl-keh kOH-sah pehr)
• a cold	• il raffreddore (eel rah-frehd-dOH-reh)
• constipation	• la stitichezza (la stee-tee-kAY-tsah)
• a cough	• la tosse (lah tOH-seh)
• a headache	• il mal di testa (eel mAHl dee-tEH-stah)
• insomnia	• i'insonnia (leen-sOHn-nee-ah)
• a toothache	• il mal di denti (eel mAHl dee dEHn-tee)
• an upset stomach	• il mal di stomaco (eel mAHl dee-stOH-mah-koh)
I don't feel well.	Non mi sento bene. (nohn mee sEHn-toh bEH-neh)
I need a doctor right away.	Ho bisogno urgente di un medico. (oh bee-sOH-ny-ee-oh oor-jEHn-teh dee oon mEH-dee-koh)
Do you know a doctor who speaks English?	Conosce un dottore che parla inglese? (koh-nOH-sheh oon doht-tOH-reh kay pAHr-lah een-glAY-seh)
Where is his office/surgery?	Dov'è il suo ambulatorio? (doh-vEH eel sOO-oh ahm-boo-lah-tOH-ree-oh)
I have a pain in my chest.	Ho un dolore al petto. (oh oon doh-lOH-reh ahl pEHt-toh)
I had a heart attack.	Ho avuto un attacco cardiaco. (oh ah-vOO-toh oon ah-tAHk-koh kahr-dEE-ah-koh)
I am taking this medicine.	Sto prendendo questa medicina. (stOH prehn-dEHn-doh koo-AY-stah meh-dee-chEE-nah)
Do I have to go to the hospital?	Devo andare in ospedale? (dAY-voh ahn-dAH-reh een oh-speh-dAH-leh)
I have a toothache. Could you recommend a dentist?	Ho un mal di denti. Può raccomandarmi un dentista? (oh oon mAHl dee dEHn-tee. poo-OH rahk-koh-mahn-dAHr-mee oon dehn-tEE-stah)
I've broken these glasses.	Ho rotto questi occhiali. (HO rOHt-tah koo-AYs-tee oh-key-AH-lee.)

Can you replace them quickly?	Può darmene un'altro paio subito? (Poo-OH dAHr-meh-neh oon-nAHl-trah pah-yot sOO-bee-toh)

Telephones

Where is _____?	Dov'è _____? (doh-vEH)
• a public telephone	• un telefono pubblico? (oon teh-lEH-foh-noh pOOb-blee-koh)
• a telephone booth	• una cabina telefonica? (OO-nah kah-bEE-nah teh-leh-fOH-nee-kah)
• a telephone directory	• un elenco telefonico? (oon eh-lEHn-koh teh-leh-fOH nee-koh)
May l use your phone?	Posso usare il suo telefono? (pOHs-soh oo-sAH-reh eel sOO-oh teh-lEH-foh-noh)
Can I call direct?	Posso telefonare direttamente? (pOHs-soh teh-leh-foh-nAH-reh dee-reht-tah-mEHn-teh)
I want to reverse the charges.	Desidero fare una riversibile. (deh-sEE-deh-roh fAH-reh oo-nah ree-vehr-sEE-bee-leh)
Do I need tokens for the phone?	Occorrono i gettoni per il telefono? (ohk-kOHr-roh-noh ee jeht-tOH-nee pehr eel teh-lEH-foh-noh)
I want to make a ___ to ___ .	Vorrei fare una _____ a _____ . (vohr-rEH-ee fAH-reh OO-nah ah)
• local call	• telefonata urbana (teh-leh-foh-nAH-tah oor-bAH-nah)
• long-distance call	• una telefonata in teleselezione/interurbana, internazionale (OO-nah teh-leh-foh-nAH-tah een teh-leh-seh-leh-tsee-OH-neh/een-tehr-oor-bAH-nah, een-tehr-nah-tsee-oh-nAH-leh)
• person-to-person	• una telefonata diretta con preavviso (OO-nah teh-leh-foh-nAH-tah dee-rEHt-tah kohn preh-ahv-vEE-soh)
How do I get the operator?	Come si ottiene il centralino? (kOH-meh see oht-tee-EH-neh eel chehn-trah-lEE-noh)
Operator, can you give me _____?	Signorina (Signore) può darmi _____? (see-ny-oh-rEE-nah [see-ny-OH-reh] poo-OH dAHr-mee)
• number 23 345	• il ventitre trecentoquarantacinque (eel vayn-tee-trEH treh-chEHn-toh-koo-ah-rahn-tah-chEEn-koo-eh)
• extension 19	• interno diciannove (een-tEHr-noh dee-chee-ahn-nOH-veh)
• area code	• prefisso numero (preh-fEEs-soh nOO-meh-roh)
• country code	• prefisso internazionale (preh-fEEs-soh een-tehr-nah-tzee-oh-nAH-leh)

- city code
- prefisso interurbano (preh-fEEs-soh een-tehr-oor-bAH-noh)

My number is ____.

Il mio numero è ____. (eel mEE-oh nOO-meh-roh EH)

May I speak to ____?

Posso parlare con ____? (pOhs-soh pahr-lAH-reh kohn)

I want to leave a message.

Vorrei lasciare un messagio. (vohr-rEH-ee lah-shee-AH-re oon mehs-sAHjee-oh)

I was cut off.

È caduta la linea (ay kah-dOO-tah lah lEE-neh-ah)

Postal Service

servizio Postale (sehr-vEEh-tsyoh poh-stAH-leh)

Post Office

l'ufficio postale (loof-fEE-chee-oh poh-stAH-leh)

a post card

una cartolina postale (OO-nah kahr-toh-lEE-nah poh-stAl)

a letter

una lettera (OO-nah lAYt-teh-rah)

a telegram

un telegramma (oon teh-leh-grAHm-ah)

an airmail letter

una lettera via aerea (OO-nah lAYt-teh-rah vEE-ah ah-EH-reh-ah)

a registered letter

una lettera raccomandata (OO-nah lAYt-teh-rah rahk-koh-mahn-dAH-tah)

a package

un pacchetto (oon pah-kAYt-toh)

a special delivery letter

una lettera espresso (OO-nah lAYt-teh-rah ehs-prEHs-soh)

I would like to buy some stamps.

Vorrei comprare dei francobolli. (Vohr-rEH-ee kohm-prAH-reh day frahn-bOHl-lee)

Which is the window?

Qual' è lo sportello? (koo-ah-lEH loh spohr-tEHl-loh)

What is the postage to the United States/ Canada/ England/Australia?

Qual' è l'affrancatura per gli Stati Uniti/Canada/Inghilterra/Australia? (koo-ah-lEH lahf-frahn-kah-tOO-rah per ly-ee stAH-tee oo-nEE-tee/kah-nah-dAH/een-gheel-tEHr-rah/ahoo-strAH-lee-ah)

I would like to mail a letter.

Vorrei spedire una lettera (vohr-rEH-ee spay-dEE-reh OO-nah lAYt-teh-rah)

Where is a letterbox?

Dov'è una cassetta postale? (doh-vEH oo-nah kas-sAYt-tah poh-stAH-leh)

I would like to send a telegram.

Vorrei mandare un telegramma. (vohr-rEH-ee mahn-dAH-reh oon teh-leh-grAHm-mah)

How late is the office open?

L'ufficio sta aperto fino a tardi? (loof-fEE-che-oh stah ah-pEHr-toh fEE-noh ah tAHr-dee)

How much is it per word?

Quanto costa per parola? (koo-AHn-toh kOH-stah per pah-rOH-lah)

Signs

Acqua [non]potabile — (Not) potable water

Affitto, Affittasi — For rent

Alt	Stop
Aperto	Open
Ascensore	Elevator (Lift)
Attenzione	Caution, watch out
Avanti	Enter (come in, go, walk [at the lights])
Caldo or "C"	Hot
Cambio	Exchange
Cassiere	Cashier
Chiuso	Closed
Divieto di sosta	No parking
Divieto di transito	No entrance, keep out
Donne	Ladies' Entrance
Freddo or "F"	Cold
Gabinetti (WC)	Toilets
Informazione	Information
Ingresso	Entrance
Libero	Vacant
Non calpestare le aiuole	Keep off the grass
Non Entrate	Do Not Enter
Non Fumate	No Smoking
Non ostruiroa (bloccare) l'ingresso	Don't block entrance
Non toccare	Hands off, don't touch
Occupato	Occupied
Pericolo	Danger
Privato	Private
Riservato	Reserved
Scala mobile	Escalator
Loca si, affittasi	For rent
Si vende	For sale
Signore, Donne	Women's room
Signori, uomini	Men's room
Spingere	Push
Strada privata	Private road
Tirare	Pull
Uomini	Men
Uscita	Exit
Vendite	For sale
Vietato fumare	No smoking
Vietato nuotare	No bathing
Vietato sputare	No spitting

Numbers

Cardinal Numbers

0	zero (tsEH-roh)
1	uno (OO-noh)
2	due (dOO-eh)
3	tre (trEH)
4	quattro (koo-AHt-troh)

5	cinque (chEEn-koo-eh)
6	sei (sEH-ee)
7	sette (sEHt-teh)
8	otto (OHt-to)
9	nove (nOH-veh)
10	dieci (dee-EH-chee)
11	undici (OOn-dee-chee)
12	dodici (dOH-dee-chee)
13	tredici (trEH-dee-chee)
14	quattordici (koo-aht-tOHr-dee-chee)
15	quindici (koo-EEn-dee-chee)
16	sedici (sAY-dee-chee)
17	diciassette (dee-chee-ahs-sEHt-teh)
18	diciotto (dee-chee-OHt-toh)
19	diciannove (dee-chee-ahn-nOH-veh)
20	venti (vAYn-tee)
21	ventuno (vayn-tOO-noh)
22	ventidue (vayn-tee-dOO-eh)
23	ventitrè (vayn-tee-trEH)
24	ventiquattro (vayn-tee-koo-AHt-troh)
25	venticinque (vayn-tee-chEEn-koo-eh)
26	ventisei (vayn-tee-sEH-ee)
27	ventisette (vayn-tee-sEHt-teh)
28	ventotto (vayn-tOHt-toh)
29	ventinove (vayn-tee-nOH-veh)
30	trenta (trEHn-tah)
40	quaranta (koo-ah-rAHn-tah)
50	cinquanta (cheen-koo-AHn-tah)
60	sessanta (sehs-sAHn-tah)
70	settanta (seht-tAHn-tah)
80	ottanta (oht-tAHn-tah)
90	novanta (noh-vAHn-tah)
100	cento (chEHn-toh)
101	centouno (chEHn-toh OO-noh)
102	centodue (chEHn-toh dOO-eh)
200	duecento (doo-eh-chEHn-toh)
300	trecento (treh-chEHn-toh)
400	quattrocento (koo-aht-troh-chEHn-toh)
500	cinquecento (cheen-koo-eh-chEHn-toh)
600	seicento (seh-ee-chEHn-toh)
700	settecento (seht-teh-chEHn-toh)
800	ottocento (oht-toh-chEHn-toh)
900	novecento (noh-veh-chEHn-toh)
1,000	mille (mEEI-leh)
2,000	duemila (dOO-eh mEE-lah)
3,000	tremila (trEH-mEE-lah)
4,000	quattromila (koo-AHt-troh-mEE-lah)
5,000	cinquemila (chEEn-koo-eh-mEE-lah)
6,000	seimila (sEH-ee-mEE-lah)
7,000	settemila (seHt-teh-mEE-lah)

8,000	ottomila (OHt-toh-mEE-lah)
9,000	novemila (nOH-veh-mEE-lah)
10,000	diecimila (dee-EH-chee-mEE-lah)
20,000	ventimila (VAYn-tee-mEE-lah)
30,000	trentamila (trEHn-tah-mEE- lah)
40,000	quarantamila (koo-ah-rAHn-tah-mEE-lah)
50,000	cinquantamila (cheen-koo-AHn-tah-mEE-lah)
60,000	sessantamila (sehs-SAHn-tah-mEE-lah)
70,000	settantamila (seht-tAHn-tah-mEE-lah)
80,000	ottantamila (oht-tAHn-tah-mEE-lah)
90,000	novantamila (noh-vAHn-tah-mEE-lah)
100,000	centomila (chEHn-toh-mEE-lah)
200,000	duecentomila (doo-eh-cEHn-toh-mEE-lah)
300,000	trecentomila (treh-chEHn-toh-mEE-lah)
400,000	quattrocentomila (koo-aht-troh-chEHn-toh-mEE-lah)
500,000	cinquecentomila (cheen-koo-eh-chEHn-toh-mEE-lah)
600,000	seicentomila (seh-ee-chEHn-toh-mEE-lah)
700,000	settecentomila (seht-teh-chEHn-toh-mEE-lah)
800,000	ottocentomila (oht-toh-chEEn-toh-mEE-lah)
900,000	novecentomila (noh-veh-chEEn-toh-mEE-lah)
1,000,000	un milione (OOn mee-lee-OH-neh)
2,000,000	due milioni (dOO-eh mee-lee-OH-nee)
10,000,000	dieci milioni (dee-EH-chee mee-lee-OH-neh)
100,000,000	cento milioni (chEHn-toh mee-lee-OH-neh)
1,000,000,000	un miliardo (mee-lee-AHr-doh)

Ordinal Numbers

1°	primo (prEE-moh)
2°	secondo (seh-kOHn-doh)
3°	terzo (tEHr-tsoh)
4°	quarto (koo-AHr-toh)
5°	quinto (koo-EEn-toh)
6°	sesto (sEHs-toh)
7°	settimo (sEHt-tee-moh)
8°	ottavo (oht-tAH-voh)
9°	nono (nOH-noh)
10°	decimo (dEH-chee-moh)
the last one	l'ultimo (lOOl-tee-moh)
once	una volta (oo-nah vOHl-tah)
twice	due volte (dOO-eh vOHl-teh)
three times	tre volte (trEH-vOHl-teh)

Percentages

Apply the proper cardinal number (one, two, three, etc.) with the proper ordinal number (third, fourth, fifth, etc.). For example,

1/5	=	un quinto
3/16	=	tre sedicesimi
7/10	=	sette decimi

The major exception to this rule is 1/2, which is translated as mezzo.

Quantities

half of ____	la metà di ____ (lah meh-tAH dee)
half of the money	la metà dei soldi (lah meh-tAH day-ee sOHl-dee)
half a ____	mezzo ____ (mEH-tsoh)
half a kilo	mezzo chilo (mEH-tsoh kEE-loh)
a fourth (quarter)	un quarto (oon koo-AHr-toh)
a dozen	una dozzina (oo-nah doh-tsEE-nah)
a dozen oranges	una dozzina d'arance (oo-nah doh-tsEE-nah dah-rAHn-cheh)
100 grams	un etto (oon EHt-toh)
200 grams	due etti (dOO-eh EHt-tee)
350 grams	tre etti e mezzo (treh EHt-tee ay mEH-tsoh)
a pair/of	un paio/di (oon pAH-ee-oh/dee)
a pair of shoes	un paio di scarpe (oon pAH-ee-oh dee skAHr-peh)

Useful Italian Abbreviations

AA	Azienda Autonoma di Soggiorno e Turismo	Local Tourist Information Center
ACI	Automobile Club d'Italia	Automobile Club of Italy
Cap.	Capoluogo	Province
C.P.	Casella Postale	Post Office Box
CAP	Codice Postale	Zip Code
ENIT	Ente Nazionale per il Turismo	Italian State Tourist Office
EPT	Ente Provinciale per il Turismo	Provincial Tourist Information Center Inc.
F.lli.	Fratelli	Brothers
FS	Ferrovie dello Stato	Italian State Railways
IVA	Imposta sul Valore Aggiunto	Italian State Tax
L.	Lire	Italian currency
N., n°	Numero	Number
Pro Loco	Ente Locale per il Turismo	Local Tourist Information Office
Prov.	Provincia	Province
P.za	Piazza	(City)Square
S.	San, Santo(a)	Saint
S.A.	Società Anonima	Inc.
Sig.	Signor	Mr.
Sig.na	Signorina	Miss
Sig.ra	Signora	Mrs.
TCI	Touring Club Italiano	Italian Touring Club
v.	Via	Street
v.le	Viale	Boulevard
COM.	Comune	Municipality
REG.	Regione	Region

IV. BUSINESS DICTIONARY

A

abandon (v)	abbandonare	*(ahb-bahn-doh-nAh-reh)*
abandonment	l'abbandono	*(ahb-bahn-dOh-noh)*
abatement	lo sconto, la riduzione	*(skOhn-toh), (reeh-dooh-tsyOh-neh)*
ability-to-pay concept	il concetto di solvibilità	*(kohn-chEht-toh deeh sohl-veeh-beeh-leeh-tAh)*
above par	sopra la pari	*(sOh-prah lah pAh-reeh)*
above-mentioned	il summenzionato, il succitato	*(soohm-mehn-tsyoh-nAh-toh), (sooh-cheeh-tAh-toh)*
above-the-line	oltre la linea	*(Ohl-treh lah lEEh-neh-ah)*
absentee ownership	il proprietario assente	*(proh-pryeh-tAh-reeh-oh ahs-Sehn-teh)*
absenteeism	l'assenteismo	*(ahs-sehn-teh-EEhz-moh)*
absorb (v)	assorbire	*(ahs-sohr-bEEh-reh)*
absorb the loss (v)	assorbire la perdita	*(ahs-sohr-bEEh-reh lah pEhr-deeh-tah)*
absorption costing	la capitalizzazione dei costi fissi nel costo dell'inventario	*(kah-peeh-tah-leeh-tsah-tsyOh-neh dehee kOhs-teeh fEEhs-seeh nehl KoHs-toh dehl eehn-vehn-tAh-reeh-oh)*
abstract of title	il compendio del documento probatorio della titolarità di diritti	*(kohm-pEhn-deeh-oh dehl doh-kooh-mEhn-toh proh-bah-tOh-reeh-oh dehl-lah teeh-toh-lah-reeh-tAh deeh deeh-rEEht-teeh)*
accelerated depreciation	l'ammortamento accelerato	*(ahm-mohr-tah-mEhn-toh ahch-cheh-leh-rAh-toh)*
acceleration clause	la clausola d'accelerazione	*(klAhw-zoh-lah dahch-cheh-leh-rah-tsyOh-neh)*
acceleration premium	il premio d'accelerazione	*(prEh-meeh-oh dahch-cheh-leh-rah-tsyOh-neh)*
accept (v)	accettare	*(ahch-cheht-tAh-reh)*

A

acceptable quality level	il livello di qualità accettabile	*(leeh-vEhl-loh deeh kwah-leeh-tAh ahch-cheht-tAh-beeh-leh)*
acceptance agreement	l'accordo d'accettazione, convenzione d'accettazione	*(ahk-kOhr-doh dahch-chet-tah-tsyOh-neh), (kohn-vehn-tsyOh-neh dahch-chet-tah-tsyOh-neh)*
acceptance bill	l'accetazione cambiaria	*(ahch-chet-tah-tsyOh-neh kahm-byAh-reeh-ah)*
acceptance credit	il credito d'accettazione	*(krEh-deeh-toh dahch-chet-tah-tsyOh-neh)*
acceptance house	la casa di accettazione	*(kAh-zah dahch-chet-tah-tsyOh-neh)*
acceptance	l'accettazione	*(ahch-chet-tah-tsyOh-neh)*
acceptance sampling	la campionatura per accetta-zione	*(kahm-pyoh-nah-tOOh-rah pehr ahch-chet-tah-tsyOh-neh)*
acceptance test	l'esame d'accettazione	*(eh-zAh-meh dahch-chet-tah-tsyOh-neh)*
acceptor	l'accettante	*(ahch-cheht-tAhn-teh)*
accession rate	il tasso d'adesione	*(tAhs-soh dah-deh-zyOh-neh)*
accidental damage	il danno accidentale	*(dAhn-noh ahch-cheeh-dehn-tAh-leh)*
accommodation bill	la cambiale di comodo	*(kahm-byAh-leh deeh kOh-moh-doh)*
accommodation credit	la facilitazione d'appoggio creditizio	*(fah-cheeh-leeh-tah-tsyOh-neh dahp-pOhj-joh)*
accommodation endorsement	la girata di comodo	*(jeeh-rAh-tah deeh kOh-moh-doh)*
accommodation paper	la cambiale di comodo	*(kahm-byAh-leh deeh kOh-moh-doh)*
accommodation parity	la parità di comodo	*(pah-reeh-tAh deeh kOh-moh-doh)*
accommodation platform	la piattaforma di comodo	*(pyaht-tah-fOhr-mah deeh kOh-moh-doh)*
accompanied goods	i beni accompagnati	*(bEh-neeh ahk-kohm-pah-nyAh-teeh)*
accord and satisfaction	l'accordo e la soddisfazione	*(ahk-kOhr-doh eh lah sohd-deehs-fah-tsyOh-neh)*
account	il conto	*(kOhn-toh)*
account balance	il saldo contabile	*(sAhl-doh kohn-tAh-beeh-leh)*

account day	il giorno di liquidazione	*(jOhr-noh deeh leeh-kweeh-dah-tsyOh-neh)*
account executive	la persona responsabile per un prodotto e/o un cliente	*(pehr-sOh-nah rehs-pohn-sAh-beeh-leh pehr oohn proh-dOht-toh eh/oh oohn kleeh-Ehn-teh)*
account for (v)	essere responsabile per	*(Ehs-seh-reh rehs-pohn-sAh-beeh-leh pehr)*
account number	il numero di conto	*(nOOh-meh-roh deeh kOhn-toh)*
account period	la periodicità del conto	*(peh-ryoh-deeh-cheeh-tAh dehl kOhn-toh)*
account, current	il conto corrente	*(kOhn-toh kohr-rEhn-teh)*
accountability	la responsabilità	*(rehs-pohn-sah-beeh-leeh-tAh)*
accountant	il contabile	*(kohn-tAh-beeh-leh)*
accountant, chief	il capo contabile	*(kAh-poh kohn-tAh-beeh-leh)*
accounting department	la contabilità, il reparto contabilità	*(kohn-tah-beeh-leeh-tAh), (reh-pAhr-toh kohn-tah-beeh-leeh-tAh)*
accounting method	il sistema contabile, il sistema di contabilità	*(seehs-tEh-mah kohn-tAh-beeh-leh), (seehs-tEh-mah deeh kohn-tah-beeh-leeh-tAh)*
accounting period	il periodo contabile, il periodo di contabilità	*(peh-rEEh-oh-doh kohn-tAh-beeh-leh), (peh-rEEh-oh-doh deeh kohn-tah-beeh-leeh-tAh)*
accounting ratio	il rapporto di contabilità	*(rahp-pOhr-toh deeh kohn-tah-beeh-leeh-tAh)*
accounting, cost	la contabilità dei costi, la contabilità industriale	*(kohn-tah-beeh-leeh-tAh deh-eeh kOhs-teeh), (kohn-tah-beeh-leeh-tAh eehn-doohs-tryAh-leh)*
accounting, management	la contabilità amministrativa	*(kohn-tah-beeh-leeh-tAh ahm-meeh-neehs-trah-tEEh-vah)*
accounts payable	i conti debitori	*(kOhn-teeh deh-beeh-tOh-reeh)*
accounts receivable	i conti creditori	*(kOhn-teeh kreh-deeh-tOh-reeh)*
accounts, group	i conti di gruppo, il raggruppamento dei conti	*(kOhn-teeh deeh grOOhp-poh), (rahg-groohp-pah-mEhn-toh deeh-eeh kOhn-teeh)*

A

accounts, secured	i conti garantiti, i crediti garantiti	*(kOhn-teeh gah-rahn-tEEh-teeh), (kreh-dEEh-teeh gah-rahn-tEEh-teeh),*
accretion	l'accrescimento	*(ahk-kreh-sheeh-mEhn-toh)*
accrual	la maturazione	*(mah-tooh-rah-tsyOh-neh)*
accrual method	il sistema di competenza	*(seehs-tEh-mah deeh kohm-peh-tEhn-tsah)*
accrue (v)	derivare, maturare	*(deh-reeh-vAh-reh), (mah-tooh-rAh-reh)*
accrued assets	gli attivi maturati	*(aht-tEEh-veeh mah-tooh-rAh-teeh)*
accrued depreciation	l'ammortamento maturato	*(ahm-mohr-tah-mEhn-toh mah-tooh-rAh-toh)*
accrued expenses	le spese maturate	*(spEh-zeh mah-tooh-rAh-teh)*
accrued interest	l'interesse maturato	*(eehn-teh-rEhs-seh mah-tooh-rAh-toh)*
accrued revenue	il reddito maturato	*(rEhd-deeh-toh mah-tooh-rAh-toh)*
accrued taxes	le tasse maturate	*(tAhs-seh mah-tooh-rAh-teh)*
accumulated depreciation	il fondo ammortamento	*(fOhn-doh ahm-mohr-tah-mEhn-toh)*
acetate	l'acetato	*(ah-cheh-tAh-toh)*
acetic acid	l'acido acetico	*(Ah-ceeh-doh ah-chEh-teeh-koh)*
acetone	l'acetone	*(ah-cheh-tOh-neh)*
acid	l'acido	*(Ah-ceeh-doh)*
acid content	l'acidita	*(ah-cheeh-deeh-tAh)*
acid-test ratio	il rapporto di liquidità	*(rah-pOhr-toh deeh leeh-kweeh-deeh-tAh)*
acknowledge (v)	ammettere, riconoscere	*(ahm-mEht-teh-reh), (reeh-koh-nOh-sheh-reh)*
acknowledge receipt of (v)	accusiamo ricezione di	*(ahk-kooh-zyAh-moh reeh-cheh-tyOh-neh deeh)*
acoustic coupler	l'innesto acustico	*(eehn-nEhs-toh ah-kOOhs-teeh-koh)*
acquire (v)	ottenere, acquistare	*(oht-teh-nEh-reh), (ahk-kweehs-tAh-reh)*
acquired rights	i diritti acquisiti	*(deeh-rEEht-teeh ahk-kweeh-zEEh-teeh)*

acquisition	l'acquisto, la compra	*(ahk-kwEEhs-toh), (kOhm-prah)*
acquisition profile	il profilo di acquisizione, il profilo d'acquisto	*(proh-fEEh-loh deeh ahk-kweeh-zeeh-tsyOh-neh), (proh-fEEht-toh dahk-kwEEhs-toh)*
acre	l'acro	*(Ah-kroh)*
acreage allotment	l'allocazione del terreno	*(ahl-loh-kah-tsyOh-neh dehl tehr-rEh-noh)*
acronym	l'acronimo, la sigla	*(ah-krOh-neeh-moh), (sEEh-glah)*
across-the-board settlement	la risoluzione generale	*(reeh-soh-looh-tsyOh-neh jeh-neh-rAh-leh)*
across-the-board tariff negotiation	il negoziato tariffaro generale	*(neh-goh-tsyAh-toh tah-reehf-fAh-roh jeh-neh-rAh-leh)*
act of God	la forza maggiore	*(fOhr-zah mahj-jOh-reh)*
action plan	il piano d'azione	*(pyAh-noh dahts-tsyOh-neh)*
action research	la ricerca di azione	*(reeh-chEhr-kah deeh ah-tsyOh-neh)*
active account	il conto operativo	*(kOhn-toh oh-peh-rah-tEEh-voh)*
active assets	gli utili attivi	*(OOh-teeh-leeh aht-tEEh-veeh)*
active debt	il debito attivo	*(dEh-beeh-toh aht-tEEh-voh)*
active trust	il fondo d'investimento	*(fOhn-doh deehn-vehs-teeh-mEhn-toh)*
activity chart	il diagramma delle attività	*(deeh-ah-grAhm-mah dehl-leh aht-teeh-veeh-tAh)*
activity on arrow	il piano di immediata esecuzione	*(pyAh-noh deeh eehm-meh-dyAh-tah eh-zeh-kooh-tyOh-neh)*
actual	attuale, effettivo	*(aht-twAh-leh), (ehf-feht-tEEh-voh)*
actual cash value	il valore effettivo a pronti	*(vah-lOh-reh ehf-feht-tEEh-voh ah prOhn-teeh)*
actual costs	i costi effettivi, i costi reali	*(kOhs-teeh ehf-feht-tEEh-veeh), (kOhs-teeh reh-Ah-leeh)*
actual income	il reddito effettivo	*(rEhd-deeh-toh ehf-feht-tEEh-voh)*

actual liability	la passività effettiva, la responsabilità effettiva	*(pahs-seeh-teeh-veeh-tAh ehf-feht-tEEh-vah), (rehs-pohn-sah-beeh-leeh-tAh ehf-feht-tEEh-vah)*
actual market volume	il volume effettivo di merca-to	*(voh-lOOh-meh ehf-feht-tEEh-voh deeh mehr-kAh-toh)*
actual total loss	la perdita totale effettiva	*(pEhr-deeh-tah ehf-feht-tEEh-vah)*
actuary	l'attuario	*(aht-twAh-reeh-oh)*
add-on sales	le vendite aggiunte	*(vEhn-deeh-teh ahj-jOOhn-teh)*
addendum	l'aggiunta, l'appendice	*(ahj-jOOhn-tah), (ahp-pehn-dEEh-cheh)*
address commission	la commissione di racco-mandazione	*(kohm-meehs-syOh-neh deeh rahk-koh-mahn-dah-tsyOh-neh)*
adjudge (v)	aggiudicare	*(ahj-jooh-deeh-kAh-reh)*
adjudication	l'aggiudicazione	*(ahj-jooh-deeh-kah-tsyOh-neh)*
adjust (v)	aggiustare	*(ahj-jooh-stAh-reh)*
adjustable peg	il sistema di parità variabile	*(seehs-tEh-mah deeh pah-reeh-tAh vah-ryAh-beeh-leh)*
adjusted CIF price	il prezzo CIF rettificato	*(prEhts-tsoh reht-teeh-feeh-kAh-toh)*
adjusted earned income	l'introito rettificato	*(eehn-trOh-eeh-toh reht-teeh-feeh-kAh-toh)*
adjusted rate	il tasso rettificato	*(tAhs-soh reht-teeh-feeh-kAh-toh)*
adjusting entry	la scrittura contabile corretti-va	*(skreeht-tOOh-rah kohn-tAh-beeh-leh kohr-reht-tEEh-vah)*
adjustment process	la procedura di regolamento	*(proh-cheh-dOOh-rah deeh reh-goh-lah-mEhn-toh)*
adjustment trigger	l'evento determinante, lo scatto del processo di aggiustamento	*(eh-vEhn-toh deh-tehr-meeh-nAhn-teh), (loh skAht-toh dehl proh-chEhs-soh deeh ahj-joohs-tah-mEhn-toh)*
administration	l'amministrazione	*(ahm-meeh-neehs-trah-tsyOh-neh)*

administrative	amministrativo	*(ahm-meeh-neehs-trah-tEEh-voh)*
administrative expense	la spesa amministrativa	*(spEh-zah ahm-meeh-neehs-trah-tEEh-vah)*
administrator	l'amministratore	*(ahm-meeh-neeh-strah-tOh-reh)*
administratrix	l'amministratrice	*(ahm-meeh-neeh-strah-trEEh-cheh)*
advance (v)	avanzare, anticipare	*(ah-vahn-tsAh-reh), (ahn-teeh-cheeh-pAh-reh)*
advance freight	il nolo anticipato	*(nOh-loh ahn-teeh-cheeh-pAh-toh)*
advance notice	il preavviso	*(preh-ahv-vEEh-zoh)*
advance payments	i pagamenti anticipati	*(pah-gah-mEhn-teeh ahn-teeh-cheeh-pAh-teeh)*
advance refunding	il rimborso anticipato	*(reehm-bOhr-soh ahn-teeh-cheeh-pAh-toh)*
advantage, competitive	il vantaggio competitivo	*(vahn-tAhj-joh kohm-peh-teeh-tEEh-voh)*
adverse balance	il bilancio negativo	*(beeh-lAhn-choh neh-gah-tEEh-voh)*
advertisement (request) for bid	la richiesta d'appalto, il bando d'appalto	*(reeh-kyEhs-tah dahp-pAhl-toh) (bAhn-doh dahp-pAhl-toh)*
advertising agency	l'agenzia pubblicitaria	*(ah-jehn-tsEEh-ah poohb-bleeh-cheeh-tAh-reeh-ah)*
advertising budget	il preventivo pubblicitario	*(preh-vehn-tEEh-voh poohb-bleeh-cheeh-tAh-reeh-oh)*
advertising campaign	la campagna pubblicitaria	*(kahm-pAh-nyah poohb-bleeh-cheeh-tAh-reeh-ah)*
advertising drive	la spinta pubblicitaria	*(spEEhn-tah poohb-bleeh-cheeh-tAh-reeh-ah)*
advertising expenses	le spese pubblicitarie	*(spEh-zeh poohb-bleeh-cheeh-tAh-reeh-eh)*
advertising	la pubblicità	*(poohb-bleeh-cheeh-tAh)*
advertising manager	il direttore della pubblicità, il direttore pubblicitario	*(deeh-reht-tOh-reh dehl-lah poohb-bleeh-cheeh-tAh), (deeh-reht-tOh-reh poohb-bleeh-cheeh-tAh-reeh-oh)*
advertising media	i mezzi di pubblicità	*(mEhds-dseeh deeh poohb-bleeh-cheeh-tAh)*

advertising research	lo studio pubblicitario	*(stOOh-deeh-oh poohb-bleeh-cheeh-tAh-reeh-oh)*
advise (v)	avvisare	*(ahv-veeh-zAh-reh)*
advice note	la nota d'avviso	*(nOh-tah dahv-vEEh-zoh)*
advisory council	l'organo consultivo	*(Ohr-gah-noh kohn-soolh-tEEh-voh)*
advisory funds	la previsione di spese di consulenza	*(preh-veeh-zyOh-neh deeh spEh-zeh deeh kohn-sooh-lEhn-tsah)*
advisory service	il servizio consultivo	*(sehr-vEEh-tsyoh kohn-soolh-tEEh-voh)*
affidavit	la dichiarazione atto giurato	*(deeh-kyah-rah-tsyOh-neh Aht-toh jooh-rAH-toh)*
affiliate	la filiale	*(feeh-leeh-Ah-leh)*
affirmative action	l'azione contro la discriminazione	*(ah-tsyOh-neh kOhn-troh lah deehs-kreeh-meeh-nah-tsyOh-neh)*
afloat	a galla	*(ah gAhl-lah)*
after-hours trading	il commercio fuori orario	*(kohm-mEhrch-choh fwOh-reeh oh-rAh-reeh-oh)*
after-sales service	la manutenzione e servizio successivi alla vendita	*(mah-nooh-tehn-tsyOh-neh eh sehr-vEEh-tsyoh sooch-chehs-sEEh-veeh ahl-lah vEhn-deeh-tah)*
after-tax real rate of return	il rendimento reale al netto di tasse	*(rehn-deeh-mEhn-toh reh-Ah-leh ahl nEht-toh deeh tAhs-seh)*
afterdate (v)	postdatare	*(pohs-dah-tAh-reh)*
against all risks	contro qualsiasi rischio	*(kOhn-troh kwahl-sEEh-ah-seeh rEEhs-kyoh)*
agency	l'agenzia	*(ah-jehn-tsEEh-ah)*
agency bank	la banca d'agenzia	*(bAhn-kah dah-jehn-tsEEh-ah)*
agency fee	la commissione, la parcella dell'agenzia	*(kohm-meehs-syOh-neh), (pahr-chEhl-lah dehl ah-jehn-tsEEh-ah)*
agenda	l'agenda	*(ah-jEhn-dah)*
agent	l'agente	*(ah-jEhn-teh)*
agent bank	la banca agente	*(bAhn-kah ah-jEhn-teh)*
aggregate demand	la domanda aggregata	*(doh-mAhn-dah ahg-greh-gAh-tah)*

aggregate risk	il rischio cumulativo	*(rEEhs-kyoh kooh-mooh-lah-tEEh-voh)*
aggregate supply	l'offerta aggregata	*(ohf-fEhr-tah ahg-greh-gAh-tah)*
aging	l'invecchiamento	*(eehn-vehk-kyah-mEhn-toh)*
agreement	l'accordo, la convenzione	*(ahk-kOhr-doh), (kohn-vehn-tsyOh-neh)*
agricultural paper	la cambiale agraria	*(kahm-byAh-leh ah-grAh-reeh-ah)*
agricultural products	i prodotti agrari	*(proh-dOht-teeh ah-grAh-reeh)*
agriculture	l'agricoltura	*(ah-greeh-kohl-tOOh-rah)*
air express	l'espresso aereo	*(ehs-prEhs-soh ah-Eh-reh-oh)*
air filter	il filtro dell'aria	*(fEEhl-troh dehl Ah-reeh-ah)*
air freight	il trasporto via aerea	*(trahs-pOhr-toh vEEh-ah ah-Eh-reh-ah)*
air shipment	la spedizione aerea	*(speh-deeh-tsyOh-neh ah-Eh-reh-ah)*
alcohol	l'alcool	*(Ahl-kohl)*
alcoholic content	il contenuto alcoolico	*(kohn-teh-nOOh-toh ahl-kOh-leeh-koh)*
algorithm	l'algoritmo	*(ahl-goh-rEEht-moh)*
algorithmic language	il linguaggio algoritmico	*(leehn-gwAhj-joh ahl-goh-rEEht-meeh-koh)*
alien corporation	l'azienda straniera, la ditta straniera	*(ah-dsyEhn-dah strah-nyEh-rah), (dEEht-ah strah-nyEh-rah)*
all in cost	il costo complessivo	*(kOhs-toh kohm-plehs-sEEh-voh)*
all or none	tutto o niente	*(tOOht-toh oh nyEhn-teh)*
allergy	l'allergia	*(ahl-lehr-jEEh-ah)*
allocation of costs	l'allocazione dei costi	*(ahl-loh-kah-tsyOh-neh deh-eeh kOhs-teeh)*
allocation of responsibilities	l'allocazione di responsabilità	*(ahl-loh-kah-tsyOh-neh deeh rehs-pohn-sah-beeh-leeh-tAh)*
allocation, resources	l'allocazione delle risorse	*(ahl-loh-kah-tsyOh-neh deh-leh reeh-sOhr-seh)*

allonge (of a draft)	la coda (di cambiale)	*(kOh-dah deeh kahm-byAh-leh)*
allot (v)	allocare	*(ah-loh-kAh-reh)*
allotment	la ripartizione	*(reeh-pahr-teeh-tsyOh-neh)*
allotment letter	la lettera di ripartizione	*(lEht-teh-rah deeh reeh-pahr-teeh-tsyOh-neh)*
allow (v)	permettere	*(pehr-mEht-teh-reh)*
allowance	l'abbuono	*(ahb-bwOh-noh)*
allowance, depreciation	il fondo di ammortamento	*(fOhn-doh deeh ahm-mohr-tah-mEhn-toh)*
alloy steel	la lega d'acciaio	*(lEh-gah dahch-chAh-yoh)*
alongside	accanto	*(ahk-kAhn-toh)*
alteration	l'alterazione	*(ahl-teh-rah-tsyOh-neh)*
alternating current	la corrente alternata	*(kohr-rEhn-teh ahl-tehr-nAh-tah)*
alternative order	l'ordine alternativo	*(Ohr-deeh-neh ahl-tehr-nah-tEEh-voh)*
alternator	l'alternatore	*(ahl-tehr-nah-tOh-reh)*
aluminum	l'alluminio	*(ahl-looh-mEEh-nyoh)*
amalgamation	la fusione	*(fooh-zyOh-neh)*
amend (v)	emendare, revisionare	*(eh-mehn-dAh-reh), (reh-veeh-zyOh-nah-reh)*
amendment	l'emendamento	*(eh-mehn-dah-mEhn-toh)*
amine	l'amina	*(ah-mEEh-nah)*
ammonia	l'ammoniaca	*(ahm-moh-nEEh-ah-kah)*
amortization	l'ammortamento	*(ahm-mohr-tah-mEhn-toh)*
amount due	la somma dovuta	*(sOhm-mah doh-vOOh-tah)*
amount	la somma	*(sOhm-mah)*
ampere	l'ampere	*(ahm-pEh-reh)*
amphetamine	l'anfetamina	*(ahn-feh-tah-mEEh-nah)*
amplifier	l'amplificatore	*(ahm-pleeh-feeh-kah-tOh-reh)*
amplitude modulation (AM)	la modulazione di ampiezza	*(moh-dooh-lah-tsyOh-neh deeh ahm-pyEhts-tsah)*
anaesthetic	l'anestetico	*(ahn-ehs-tEh-teeh-koh)*
analgesic	l'analgesico	*(ahn-ahl-jEEh-zeeh-koh)*

analog computer	l'elaboratore a sistema analog	*(eh-lah-boh-rah-tOh-reh ah sees-tEh-mah Ah-nah-lohg)*
analysis	l'analisi	*(ah-nAh-leeh-zeeh)*
analysis, break-even	l'analisi di equilibrio tra i costi e i ricavi, il punto di pareggio	*(ah-nAh-leeh-zeeh deeh eh-kweeh-lEEh-breeh-oh trah eeh kOhs-teeh eh eeh reeh-kah-vAh-teeh), (pOOhn-toh deeh pah-rEhj-joh)*
analysis, competitor	l'analisi della concorrenza	*(ah-nAh-leeh-zeeh dehl-lah kohn-koh-rEhn-tsah)*
analysis, cost	l'analisi dei costi	*(ah-nAh-leeh-zeeh deh-eeh kOhs-teeh)*
analysis, cost-benefit	l'analisi del rapporto tra i costi ed i benefici	*(ah-nAh-leeh-zeeh dehl rahp-pOhr-toh trah eeh kOhs-teeh ed eeh beh-neeh-fEEh-cheeh)*
analysis, critical path	l'analisi del percorso critico	*(ah-nAh-leeh-zeeh dehl pehr-kOhr-soh krEEh-teeh-koh)*
analysis, financial	l'analisi finanziaria	*(ah-nAh-leeh-zeeh feeh-nahn-tsyAh-reeh-ah)*
analysis, functional	l'analisi funzionale	*(ah-nAh-leeh-zeeh foohn-tsyOh-nah-leh)*
analysis, input-output	l'analisi entrata/uscita, l'analisi dei fattori produttivi	*(ah-nAh-leeh-zeeh ehn-trAh-tah/ooh-shEEh-tah), (ah-nAh-leeh-zeeh deh-eeh faht-tOh-reeh proh-dooht-tEEh-veeh)*
analysis, investment	l'analisi d'investimento	*(ah-nAh-leeh-zeeh deehn-vehs-teeh-mEhn-toh)*
analysis, job	l'analisi del progetto, l'analisi dell'occupazione, l'analisi del lavoro	*(ah-nAh-leeh-zeeh dehl proh-jEht-toh), (ah-nAh-leeh-zeeh dehl ohk-kooh-pah-tsyOh-neh)*
analysis, needs	l'analisi delle esigenze	*(ah-nAh-leeh-zeeh dehl-leh eh-zeeh-jEhn-tseh)*
analysis, product	l'analisi del prodotto	*(ah-nAh-leeh-zeeh dehl proh-dOht-toh)*

A

analysis, profitability	l'analisi del rapporto tra costo e profitto, l'analisi dei profitti, lo studio sulla profittabilità	*(ah-nAh-leeh-zeeh dehl rahp-pOhr-toh trah kOhs-toh eh proh-fEEt-toh), (ah-nAh-leeh-zeeh deh-eeh proh-fEEt-teeh), (stOOh-deeh-oh soohl-lah proh-feet-teeh-beeh-leeh-tAh)*
analysis, risk	l'analisi del rischio	*(ah-nAh-leeh-zeeh dehl rEEhs-kyoh)*
analysis, sales	l'analisi delle vendite	*(ah-nAh-leeh-zeeh dehl-leh vEhn-deeh-teh)*
analysis, systems	l'analisi del sistema	*(ah-nAh-leeh-zeeh dehl seehs-tEh-mah)*
analyst	l'analista	*(ah-nah-lEEhs-tah)*
anchorage (dues)	gli oneri d'ancoraggio	*(Oh-neh-reeh dahn-koh-rAhj-joh)*
ancillary operations	le operazioni ausiliari	*(oh-peh-rah-tsyOh-neeh ah-ooh-zeeh-lyAh-reeh)*
angle of incidence	l'angolo d'incidenza	*(Ahn-goh-loh deen-cheeh-dEhn-tsah)*
angora	l'angora	*(Ahn-goh-rah)*
ankle boots	gli stivaletti	*(steeh-vah-lEht-teeh)*
annealing	la ricottura	*(reeh-koht-tOOh-rah)*
annual accounts	i conti annuali	*(kOhn-teeh ahn-nwAh-leeh)*
annual	annuale	*(ahn-nwAh-leh)*
annual audit	la revisione annuale dei conti	*(reh-veeh-zyOh-neh ahn-nwAh-leh deh-eeh kOhn-teeh)*
annual report	il rapporto annuale	*(rahp-pOhr-toh ahn-nwAh-leh)*
annuitant	il pensionante, il vitalizio	*(pehn-syoh-nAhn-teh) (veeh-tah-lEEh-tsyoh)*
annuity	la rendita	*(rEhn-deeh-tah)*
antacid	l'antacido	*(ahn-tAh-cheeh-doh)*
antenna	l'antenna	*(ahn-tEhn-nah)*
anti-dumping duty	la tariffa protettiva, la tariffa "anti-dumping"	*(tah-rEEhf-fah proh-teht-tEEh-vah)*
anti-inflammatory	l'antiflogistico	*(ahn-teeh-floh-jEEhs-teeh-koh)*
antibiotic	l'antibiotico	*(ahn-teeh-beeh-Oh-teeh-koh)*

A

anticoagulant	l'anticoagulante	*(ahn-teeh-koh-ah-gooh-lAhn-teh)*
antidepressant	l'antidepressivo	*(ahn-teeh-deh-prehs-sEEh-voh)*
antique authenticity certificate	il certificato antiquariale d'autenticità	*(chehr-teeh-feeh-kAh-toh ahn-teeh-kwah-ryAh-leh dah-ooh-tehn-teeh-cheeh-tAh)*
antiseptic	l'asettico	*(ah-sEht-teeh-koh)*
antitrust laws	le leggi anti-monopolistiche	*(lEhj-jeeh ahn-teeh moh-noh-poh-lEEhs-teeh-keh)*
apparel	l'abbigliamento	*(ahb-beeh-lyah-meHn-toh)*
application form	il modulo di richiesta	*(mOh-dooh-loh deeh reeh-kyEhs-tah)*
applied proceeds swap	il baratto, la permuta degli introiti	*(bah-rAht-toh) (pEhr-mooh-tah deh-lyeeh (eehn-trOh-eeh-teeh)*
appointment	l'appuntamento	*(ahp-poohn-tah-mEhn-toh)*
appraisal	la stima, la valutazione	*(stEEh-mah), (vah-looh-tah-tsyOh-neh)*
appraisal, capital expenditure	la stima delle spese capitali	*(stEEh-mah dehl-leh spEh-zeh kah-peeh-tAh-leeh)*
appraisal, financial	la valutazione finanziaria	*(vah-looh-tah-tsyOh-neh feeh-nahn-tsyAh-reeh-ah)*
appraisal, investment	la valutazione degli investimenti	*(vah-looh-tah-tsyOh-neh deh-lyeeh eehn-vehs-teeh-mEhn-teeh)*
appraisal, market	la valutazione di mercato	*(vah-looh-tah-tsyOh-neh deeh mehr-kAh-toh)*
appreciation	l'apprezzamento	*(ahp-prehts-tsah-mEhn-toh)*
apprentice	l'apprendista	*(ahp-prehn-dEEhs-tah)*
appropriation	lo stanziamento	*(stahn-tsyah-mEhn-toh)*
approval	l'approvazione	*(ahp-proh-vah-tsyOh-neh)*
approve (v)	approvare	*(ahp-proh-vAh-reh)*
approved delivery facility	lo stabilimento di consegna approvato	*(stah-beeh-leeh-mEhn-toh deeh kohn-sEh-nyah ahp-proh-vAh-toh)*
approved securities	i titoli mobiliari approvati	*(tEEh-toh-leeh moh-beeh-lyAh-reeh ahp-proh-vAh-teeh)*
arbitrage	l'arbitraggio	*(ahr-beeh-trAhj-joh)*

A

arbitration	l'arbitrato	*(ahr-beeh-trAh-toh)*
arbitration agreement	l'accordo d'arbitrato	*(ahk-kOhr-doh dahr-beeh-trAh-toh)*
arbitrator	l'arbitro	*(Ahr-beeh-troh)*
area manager	il direttore d'area	*(deeh-reht-tOh-reh dAh-reh-ah)*
area of origin guaranteed	la denominazione di origine controllata (D.O.C.)	*(deh-noh-meeh-nah-tsyOh-neh deeh oh-rEEh-jeeh-neh kohn-trohl-lAh-tah)*
arithmetic mean	la media aritmetica	*(mEh-deeh-ah ah-reeht-mEh-teeh-kah)*
arm's length	a distanza	*(ah deehs-tAhn-dsah)*
armaments	gli armamenti	*(ahr-mah-mEhn-teeh)*
around (exchange term)	circa	*(chEEhr-kah)*
arrears	gli arretrati	*(ahr-reh-trAh-teeh)*
as is goods	i beni nello stato attuale, i beni senza ricorso	*(bEh-neeh nehl-loh stAh-toh aht-twAh-leh)*
as per advice	come per nota informativa	*(kOh-meh pehr nOh-tah eehn-fohr-mah-tEEh-vah)*
as soon as possible	appena possibile	*(ahp-pEh-nah pohs-sEEh-beeh-leh)*
as, if and when	come, se e quando	*(kOh-meh), (seh eh kwAhn-doh)*
asking price	il prezzo richiesto	*(prEhts-tsoh reeh-kyEhs-toh)*
aspirin	l'aspirina	*(ahs-peeh-rEEh-nah)*
assay	l'analisi	*(ah-nAh-leeh-zeeh)*
assemble (v) (people)	riunire	*(reeh-ohh-nEEh-reh)*
assemble (v) (things)	montare	*(mohn-tAh-reh)*
assembly	il montaggio, l'assemblea	*(mohn-tAhj-joh), (ahs-sehm-blEh-ah)*
assembly line	la catena di montaggio, la linea di montaggio	*(kah-tEh-nah deeh mohn-tAhj-joh), (lEEh-neh-ah deeh mohn-tAhj-joh)*
assess (v)	valutare	*(vah-looh-tAh-reh)*

assessed valuation	la valutazione imponibile	*(vah-looh-tah-tsyOh-neh eehm-poh-nEEh-beeh-leh)*
assessment	la valutazione	*(vah-looh-tah-tsyOh-neh)*
asset	l'attivo, l'attività	*(aht-tEEh-voh) (aht-teeh-veeh-tAh)*
asset turnover	il giro d'attività, il movimento d'attività	*(jEEh-roh daht-teeh-veeh-tAh), (moh-veeh-mEhn-toh daht-teeh-veeh-tAh)*
asset value	il valore delle attività	*(vah-lOh-reh daht-teeh-veeh-tAh)*
assets, accrued	gli attivi maturati	*(aht-tEEh-veeh mah-tooh-rAh-teeh)*
assets, current	gli attivi correnti	*(aht-tEEh-veeh kohr-rEhn-teeh)*
assets, deferred	gli attivi differiti	*(aht-tEEh-veeh deehf-feh-rEEh-teeh)*
assets, fixed	gli attivi fissi, gli immobilizzi tecnici	*(aht-tEEh-veeh fEEhs-seeh), (eehm-moh-beeh-lEEhts-tseeh)*
assets, intangible	gli attivi intangibili	*(aht-tEEh-veeh eehn-tahn-jEEh-beeh-leeh)*
assets, liquid	gli attivi mobili, l'attivo circolante	*(aht-tEEh-veeh mOh-beeh-leeh), (aht-tEEh-voh cheehr-koh-lAhn-teh)*
assets, net	gli attivi netti	*(aht-tEEh-veeh nEht-teeh)*
assets, tangible	i beni reali	*(bEh-neeh reh-Ah-leeh)*
assign (v)	assegnare	*(ahs-seh-nyAh-reh)*
assignee	l'assegnatario	*(ahs-seh-nyah-tAh-reeh-oh)*
assignor	il cedente	*(cheh-dEhn-teh)*
assistant general manager	il vice direttore generale	*veeh-cheh deeh-reht-tOh-reh jeh-neh-rAh-leh)*
assistant	l'assistente	*(ahs-seehs-tEhn-teh)*
assistant manager	il vice direttore	*(veeh-cheh deeh-reht-tOh-reh)*
associate company	la società in accomandita, la ditta associata	*(soh-cheh-tAh eehn ahk-koh-mAhn-deeh-tah), (dEEt-tah ahs-soh-chAh-tah)*
assumed liability	la responsabilità presunta	*(rehs-pohn-sah-beeh-leeh-tAh preh-zOOhn-tah)*
astrakan	l'astrakan	*(ahs-trah-kAhn)*

at and from	a e da	*(ah eh dah)*
at best	al meglio	*(ahl mEh-lyoh)*
at call	a richiesta, a domanda	*(ah reeh-kyEhs-tah) (ah doh-mAhn-dah)*
at or better	a o superiore	*(ah oh soo-peh-ryOh-reh)*
at par	alla pari	*(ahl-lah pAh-reeh)*
at sight	a vista	*(ah vEEhs-tah)*
at the close	alla chiusura	*(ahl-lah kyooh-zOOh-rah)*
at the market	al mercato	*(ahl mehr-kAh-toh)*
at the opening	all'apertura	*(ahl ah-pehr-tOOh-rah)*
atom	l'atomo	*(Ah-toh-moh)*
atomic	atomico	*(ah-tOh-meeh-koh)*
attach (v)	allegare	*(ahl-leh-gAh-reh)*
attaché case	la cartella	*(kahr-tEhl-lah)*
attended time	il tempo presenziato	*(tEhm-poh preh-zen-tsyAh-toh)*
attestation	l'attestato	*(aht-tehs-tAh-toh)*
attorney	l'avvocato	*(ahv-voh-kAh-toh)*
attorney, power of	la procura	*(proh-kOOh-rah)*
attrition	l'attrito	*(aht-trEEh-toh)*
audit (v)	controllare, rivedere, verifi-care	*(kohn-trohl-lAh-reh), (reeh-veh-dEh-reh), (veh-reeh-feeh-kAh-reh)*
audit trail	il bilancio di revisione	*(beeh-lAhn-choh deeh reh-veeh-zyOh-neh)*
audit, internal	la revisione interna	*(reh-veeh-zyOh-neh eehn-tEhr-nah)*
auditing balance sheet	il foglio di revisione del bilancio contabile	*(fOh-lyoh deeh reh-veeh-zyOh-neh dehl beeh-lAhn-choh kohn-tAh-beeh-leh)*
auditor	il revisore	*(reh-veeh-zOh-reh)*
authenticity (gold)	l'autenticità, il titolo	*(ah-ooh-tehn-teehe-cheeh-tAh), (tEEh-toh-loh)*
authority, to have (v)	avere l'autorità	*(ah-vEh-reh ah-ooh-toh-reeh-tAh)*
authorize (v)	autorizzare	*(ah-ooh-toh-reehds-dsAh-reh)*

authorized dealer	il rivenditore autorizzato	*(reeh-vehn-deeh-tOh-reh ah-ooh-toh-reehds-dsAh-toh)*
authorized shares	le azioni autorizzate	*(ah-tsyOh-neeh ah-ooh-toh-reehds-dsAh-teh)*
authorized signature	la firma autorizzata	*(fEEhr-mah ah-ooh-toh-reehds-dsAh-tah)*
automatic	automatico	*(ah-ooh-toh-mAh-teeh-koh)*
automatic gearshift	il cambio automatico	*(kAhm-byoh ah-ooh-toh-mAh-teeh-koh)*
automation	l'automazione	*(ah-ooh-toh-mah-tsyOh-neh)*
automobile	l'automobile	*(ah-ooh-toh-mOh-beeh-leh)*
automotive worker	l' operaio	*(oh-peh-rAh-yoh)*
autonomous	autonomo	*(ah-ooh-tOh-noh-moh)*
availability, subject to	in base alla disponibilità	*(eehn bAh-zeh ahl-lah deehs-poh-neeh-beeh-leeh-tAh)*
average	la media	*(mEh-deeh-ah)*
average cost	il costo medio	*(kOhs-toh mEh-deeh-oh)*
average life	la vita media, la durata media	*(vEEh-tah mEh-deeh-ah), (dooh-rAh-tah mEh-deeh-ah)*
average price	il prezzo medio	*(prEhts-tsoh mEh-deeh-oh)*
average unit cost	il costo medio unitario	*(kOhs-toh mEh-deeh-oh ooh-neeh-tAh-reeh-oh)*
averaging	raggiungere una media, prendere la media	*(rahj-jOOhn-jeh-reh ooh-nah mEh-deeh-ah), (prEhn-deh-reh lah mEh-deeh-ah)*
avoidable costs	le spese evitabili	*(spEh-zeh eh-veeh-tAh-beeh-leeh)*

B

back date (v)	postdatare	*(pohs-dah-tAh-reh)*
back haul	il ritorno di una parte della merce sullo stesso percorso utilizzato per il trasporto originale	*(reeh-tOhr-noh deeh ooh-nah pAhr-teh deh-lah mEhr-cheh soohl-loh stEhs-soh pehr-kOhr-soh ooh-teeh-leehds-dsAh-toh pehr eehl tras-pOhr-toh oh-reeh-jeeh-nAh-leh)*

back order	l'ordine arretrato	*(Ohr-deeh-neh ahr-reh-trAh-toh)*
back selling	la rivendita del prodotto al fornitore originale	*(reeh-vEhn-deeh-tah dehl proh-dOht-toh ahl fohr-neeh-tOh-reh oh-reeh-jeeh-nAh-leh)*
back taxes	le imposte arretrate	*(eehm-pOhs-teh ahr-reh-trAh-teh)*
back-to-back credit	il credito documentario aperto sulla base di un altro credito originario, il credito disposto dal beneficiario di un credito	*(krEh-deeh-toh doh-kooh-mehn-tAh-reeh-oh ah-pEhr-toh soohl-lah bAh-zeh deeh oohn Ahl-troh krEh-deeh-toh oh-reeh-jeeh-nAh-reeh-oh), (krEh-deeh-toh deehs-pOhs-toh dahl beh-neh-feeh-chAh-reeh-oh deeh oohn krEh-deeh-toh)*
back-to-back loans	i prestiti erogati sulla base di una garanzia ricevuta	*(prEhs-teeh-teeh eh-roh-gAh-teeh soohl-lah bAh-zeh deeh ooh-nah gah-rahn-tsEEh-ah reeh-cheh-vOOh-tah)*
backed note	l'obbligazione garantita	*(ohb-bleeh-gah-tsyOh-neh gah-rahn-tEEh-tah)*
backing and filling	l'appoggio ed esecuzione	*(ahp-pOhj-joh ed eh-zeh-kooh-tsyOh-neh)*
backing support	il sostegno d'appoggio	*(sohs-tEh-nyoh dahp-pOhj-jo)*
backlog	gli ordini inevasi	*(Ohr-deeh-neeh eeh-neh-vAh-zeeh)*
backup bonds	i titoli obbligazionari dati in garanzia	*(tEEh-toh-leeh ohb-bleeh-gah-tsyoh-nAh-reeh)*
backwardation	il deporto	*(deh-pOhr-toh)*
backwash effect	l'effetto di risucchio	*(ehf-fEht-toh deeh reeh-sOOhk-kyoh)*
bad debt	il debito insolvibile	*(dEh-beeh-toh eehn-sohl-vEEh-beeh-leh)*
balance of payments	la bilancia dei pagamenti	*(beeh-lAhn-chah deh-eeh pah-gah-mEhn-teeh)*
balance of trade	la bilancia commerciale	*(beeh-lAhn-chah kohm-mehr-chAh-leh)*
balance ratios	gli indici di bilancio	*(EEhn-deeh-chee deeh beeh-lAhn-choh)*

balance sheet	il bilancio d'esercizio	*(beeh-lAhn-choh deh-zehr-chEEh-tsyoh)*
balance, bank	il bilancio bancario	*(beeh-lAhn-choh bahn-kAh-reeh-oh)*
balance, credit	il credito disponibile, il saldo e credito	*(krEh-deeh-toh deehs-poh-nEEh-beeh-leh), (sAhl-doh eh krEh-deeh-toh)*
bale capacity	la capacità in balle	*(kah-pah-cheeh-tAh eehn bAhl-leh)*
bale cargo	la merce imballata	*(mEhr-cheh eehm-bahl-lAh-tah)*
ballast bonus	il premio sulla zavorra	*(prEh-myoh soohl-lah dsah-vOhr-rah)*
balloon (payment)	l'ultimo pagamento rateale per un importo notevol-mente più alto dei prece-denti	*(OOhl-teeh-moh pah-gah-mEhn-toh rah-teh-Ah-leh pehr oohn eehm-pOhr-toh noh-teh-vohl-mEhn-teh pyOOh ahl-toh deh-eeh preh-cheh-dEhn-teeh)*
balloon note	l'obbligazione a rate con pagamento maggiorato alla maturità	*(ohb-bleeh-gah-tsyOh-neh ah rAh-teh kohn pah-gah-mEhn-toh mahj-joh-rAh-toh)*
bank	la banca	*(bAhn-kah)*
bank acceptance	l'accettazione bancaria	*(ahch-cheht-tah-tsyOh-neh bahn-kAh-reeh-ah)*
bank account	il conto bancario	*(kOhn-toh bahn-kAh-reeh-oh)*
bank balance	il bilancio bancario	*(beeh-lAhn-choh bahn-kAh-reeh-oh)*
bank carnet	il carnet bancario	*(kahr-nEh bahn-kAh-reeh-oh)*
bank charges	i costi bancari	*(kOhs-teeh bahn-kAh-reeh)*
bank check	l'assegno bancario	*(ahs-sEh-nyoh bahn-kAh-reeh-oh)*
bank deposit	il deposito bancario	*(deh-pOh-zeeh-toh bahn-kAh-reeh-oh)*
bank draft	la tratta bancaria	*(trAht-tah bahn-kAh-reeh-ah)*
bank examiner	il revisore bancario	*(reh-veeh-zOh-reh bahn-kAh-reeh-oh)*
bank exchange	il cambio bancario	*(kAhm-byoh bahn-kAh-reeh-oh)*

B

B

bank holiday	la festività legale	*(fehs-teeh-veeh-tAh leh-gAh-leh)*
bank letter of credit	la lettera di credito bancaria	*(lEht-teh-rah deeh krEh-deeh-toh bahn-kAh-reeh-oh)*
bank loan	il prestito bancario	*(prEhs-teeh-toh bahn-kAh-reeh-oh)*
bank money order	il vaglia bancario	*(vAh-lyah bahn-kAh-reeh-oh)*
bank note	la banconota	*(bahn-koh-nOh-tah)*
bank rate	il tasso bancario	*(tAhs-soh bahn-kAh-reeh-oh)*
bank release	il benestare bancario	*(beh-neh-stAh-reh bahn-kAh-reeh-oh)*
bank statement	il rendiconto bancario	*(rehn-deeh-kOhn-toh bahn-kAh-reeh-oh)*
bankruptcy	il fallimento	*(fahl-leeh-mEhn-toh)*
bar chart	il grafico a barra, il diagramma utilizzante barre	*(grAh-feeh-koh ah bAhr-rah), (deeh-ah-grAhm-mah ooh-teeh-leehds-dsAhn-teh bAhr-reh)*
barbiturates	i barbiturici	*(bahr-beeh-tOOh-reh-cheeh)*
bareboat charter	il noleggio a scafo nudo	*(noh-lEhj-joh ah skAh-foh nOOh-doh)*
bargain	l'affare	*(ahf-fAh-reh)*
bargaining power	il potere di negoziazione	*(poh-tEh-reh deeh neh-goh-tsyah-tsyOh-neh)*
bargaining, collective	la contrattazzione collettiva	*(kohn-traht-tah-tsyOh-neh kohl-leht-tEEh-vah)*
barratry	l'incitazione alla discordia	*(eehn-cheeh-tah-tsyOh-neh ahl-lah deehs-kOhr-deeh-ah)*
bars	le barre	*(bAhr-reh)*
barter (v)	barattare	*(bah-raht-tAh-reh)*
base	la base	*(bAh-zeh)*
base currency	la valuta di base	*(vah-lOOh-tah deeh bAh-zeh)*
base price	il prezzo di base	*(prEhts-tsoh deeh bAh-zeh)*
base rate	il tasso di base	*(tAhs-soh deeh bAh-zeh)*

base year	l'anno di base	*(Ahn-noh deeh bAh-zeh)*
basis point (1/100%)	il punto di base (centesimo di un percento)	*(pOOhn-toh deeh bAh-zeh), (chehn-tEh-zeeh-moh deeh oohn pehr-chEhn-toh)*
batch processing	l'elaborazione per gruppi	*(eh-lah-boh-rah-tsyOh-neh pehr grOOhp-peeh)*
batch production	la produzione in lotti	*(proh-dooh-tsyOh-neh eehn lOht-teeh)*
batiste	la batista	*(bah-tEEhs-tah)*
batten fitted	attrezzato con infissi per ancorare la merce	*(aht-trehts-tsAh-toh kohn eehn-fEEhs-seeh pehr lah mEhr-cheh)*
battery	la batteria	*(baht-teh-rEEh-ah)*
baud	il baud	*(bOhd)*
beam	il fascio	*(fAh-shoh)*
bear market	la borsa in fase negativa	*(bOhr-sah eehn fAh-zeh neh-gah-tEEh-vah)*
bearer bond	l'obbligazione al portatore	*(ohb-bleeh-gah-tsyOh-neh ahl pohr-tah-tOh-reh)*
bearer	il portatore	*(pohr-tah-tOh-reh)*
bearer security	il titolo al portatore	*(tEEh-toh-loh ahl pohr-tah-tOh-reh)*
beaver	il castoro	*(kahs-tOh-roh)*
bell-shaped curve	la curva a campana	*(kOOhr-vah ah kahm-pAh-nah)*
below par	sotto la pari	*(soht-toh lah pAh-reeh)*
below the line	capitalizzati	*(kah-peeh-tah-leehds-dsAh-teeh)*
belt	la cintura	*(cheehn-tOOh-rah)*
beneficiary	il beneficiario	*(beh-neh-feeh-chAh-reeh-oh)*
benzene	il benzolo	*(behn-dsOh-loh)*
bequest	il lascito	*(lAh-sheeh-toh)*
berth terms	i termini di ormeggio	*(tEhr-meeh-neeh deeh ohr-mEhj-joh)*
bid and asked	offerto e richiesto	*(ohf-fEhr-toh eh reeh-kyEhs-toh)*

bill broker	l'intermediario di obbliga-zioni	*(eehn-tehr-meh-dyAh-reeh-oh deeh ohb-bleeh-gah-tsyOh-neeh)*
bill	la fattura	*(faht-tOOh-rah)*
bill of exchange	la cambiale	*(kahm-byAh-leh)*
bill of lading	la polizza di carico	*(pOh-leehts-tsah deeh kAh-reeh-koh)*
bill of sale	l'atto di vendita	*(Aht-toh deeh vEhn-deeh-tah)*
bill of sight	il certificato d'ispezione	*(chehr-teeh-feeh-kAh-toh deehs-peh-tsyOh-neh)*
billboard	il cartellone	*(kahr-tehl-lOh-neh)*
billets	le billette	*(beehl-lEht-teh)*
billfold	il portafogli	*(pohr-tah-fOh-lyeeh)*
binary code	il codice binario	*(kOh-deeh-cheh beeh-nAh-reeh-oh)*
binary notation	la numerazione binaria, la notazione binaria	*(nooh-meh-rah-tsyOh-neh beeh-nAh-reeh-ah), (noh-tah-tsyOh-neh beeh-nAh-reeh-ah)*
binder	la caparra	*(kah-pAhr-rah)*
biochemistry	la biochimica	*(beeh-oh-kEEh-meeh-kah)*
biology	la biologia	*(beeh-oh-loh-jEEh-ah)*
bit	il bit	*(beeht)*
black and white	il bianco e nero	*(byAhn-koh eh nEh-roh)*
black market	il mercato nero	*(mehr-kAh-toh nEh-roh)*
blanket bond	l'obbligazione generale	*(ohb-bleeh-gah-tsyOh-neh jeh-neh-rAh-leh)*
blanket order	l'ordine generale	*(Ohr-deeh-neh jeh-neh-rAh-leh)*
blast furnace	l'altoforno	*(ahltoh-fOhr-noh)*
blazer	la giacca sportiva, il"blazer"	*(jAhk-kah spohr-tEEh-vah)*
bleed (v)	sanguinare	*(sahn-gweeh-nAh-reh)*
bleed	la pagina al vivo, smarginato	*(pAh-jeeh-nah ahl vEEh-voh), (zmahr-jeeh-nAh-toh)*
blend (v)	tagliare	*(tah-lyAh-reh)*
blockage of funds	il blocco dei fondi	*(blOhk-koh deh-eeh fOhn-deeh)*

blocked currency	la valuta bloccata	*(vah-lOOh-tah blohk-kAh-tah)*
blood	il sangue	*(sAhn-gweh)*
blotter	il tampone di carta assorbente	*(tahm-pOh-neh deeh kAhr-tah ahs-sohr-bEhn-teh)*
blouse	la camicetta	*(kah-meeh-chEht-tah)*
blowup	la gigantografia, l'ingrandimento	*(jeeh-gahn-toh-grah-fEEh-ah), (eehn-grahn-deeh-mEhn-toh)*
blue chip stock	le azioni pregiate	*(ah-tsyOh-neeh pre-jAh-teh)*
blue-collar worker	l'operaio	*(oh-peh-rAh-yoh)*
blueprint	la cianografia, il programma	*(chah-noh-grah-fEEh-ah), (proh-grAhm-mah)*
board meeting	la riunione del consiglio	*(reeh-ooh-nyOh-neh dehl kohn-sEEh-lyoh)*
board of directors	il consiglio di amministrazione	*(kohn-sEEh-lyoh deeh ahm-meeh-neehs-trah-tsyOh-neh)*
board of supervisors	il consiglio di sovrintendenza	*(kohn-sEEh-lyoh deeh sohv-reehn-tehn-dEhn-tsah)*
board, executive	il consiglio dirigenziale	*(kohn-sEEh-lyoh deeh-reeh-jehn-tsyAh-leh)*
boardroom	la sala del consiglio	*(sAh-lah dehl kohn-sEEh-lyoh)*
body	il corpo	*(kOhr-poh)*
boilerplate	il testo scritto senza particolare interesse	*(tEhs-toh skrEEt-toh sehn-tsah pahr-teeh-koh-lAh-reh eehn-teh-rEhs-seh)*
boldface	il neretto	*(neh-rEht-toh)*
bond areas	le aree delle obbligazioni	*(Ah-reh-eh deh-leh ohb-bleeh-gah-tsyOh-neeh)*
bond issue	l'emissione di buoni, le obbligazioni	*(eh-meehs-syOh-neh deeh bwOh-neeh), (ohb-bleeh-gah-tsyOh-neeh)*
bond	l'obbligazione	*(ohb-bleeh-gah-tsyOh-neh)*
bond power	il potere del buono, il potere di emettere obbligazioni	*(poh-tEh-reh dehl bwOh-noh) (poh-tEh-reh deeh eh-mEht-teh-reh ohb-bleeh-gah-tsyOh-neeh)*
bond rating	la valutazione dell'obbligazione	*(vah-looh-tah-tsyOh-neh dehl ohb-bleeh-gah-tsyOh-neh)*

B

bonded carrier	il portatore di obbligazioni	*(pohr-tah-tOh-reh deeh ohb-bleeh-gah-tsyOh-neeh)*
bonded goods	le merci vincolate	*(mEhr-cheeh veehn-koh-lAh-teh)*
bonded warehouse	il magazzino doganale	*(mah-gahds-dsEEh-noh doh-gah-nAh-leh)*
bone china	la porcellana "bone"	*(pohr-chehl-lAh-nah)*
bonus (premium)	il premio	*(prEh-myoh)*
book	il libro	*(lEEh-broh)*
book inventory	l'inventario registrato, l'inventario contabile	*(eehn-vehn-tAh-reeh-oh reh-jeehs-trAh-toh), (eehn-vehn-tAh-reeh-oh kohn-tAh-beeh-leh)*
book value	il valore registrato, il valore contabile	*(vah-lOh-reh reh-jeehs-trAh-toh), (vah-lOh-reh kohn-tAh-beeh-leh)*
book value per share	il valore registrato per azione	*(vah-lOh-reh reh-jeehs-trAh-toh pehr ah-tsyOh-neh)*
bookkeeping	la contabilità	*(kohn-tah-beeh-leeh-tAh)*
boom	l'espansione, il "boom"	*(ehs-pahn-syOh-neh)*
boot shop	la stivaleria	*(steeh-vah-leh-rEEh-ah)*
bootmaker	lo stivalaio	*(steeh-vah-lAh-yoh)*
boots	gli stivali	*(steeh-vAh-leeh)*
border	il confine	*(kohn-fEEh-neh)*
border tax adjustment	la correzione della tassa di confine	*(kohr-reh-tsyOh-neh deh-lah tAhs-sah deeh kohn-fEEh-neh)*
borrow (v)	prendere in prestito	*(prEhn-deh-reh eehn prEhs-teeh-toh)*
botanic	botanico	*(boh-tAh-neeh-koh)*
bottle (usually 75 centiliters)	la bottiglia	*(boht-tEEh-lyah)*
bouquet	il naso, il bouquet	*(nAh-zoh)*
bow tie	la cravatta a farfalla, papillion	*(krah-vAht-tah ah fahr-fAhl-lah), (pah-pee-'yohn)*
bowl	la scodella	*(skoh-dEhl-lah)*
boycott (v)	boicottare	*(boh-eeh-koht-tAh-reh)*

brainstorming	la conferenza-confronto idee, il dibattito costruttivo d'opinioni	*(kohn-feh-rEhn-zah kohn-frOhn-toh eeh-dEh-eh) (deeh-bAht-teeh-toh kohs-trooht-tEEh-voh)*
brake	il freno	*(frEh-noh)*
branch office	la filiale	*(feeh-lyAh-leh)*
brand acceptance	l'accettazione della marca	*(ahch-cheht-tah-tsyOh-neh dehl-lah mAhr-kah)*
brand image	l'immagine della marca	*(eehm-mAh-jeeh-neh dehl-lah mAhr-kah)*
brand	la marca	*(mAhr-kah)*
brand loyalty	la fedeltà alla marca	*(feh-dehl-tAh ahl-lah mAhr-kah)*
brand manager	il dirigente responsabile per la gestione della marca	*(deeh-reeh-jEhn-teh rehs-pohn-sAh-beeh-leh pehr lah jehs-tyOh-neh dehl-lah mAhr-kah)*
brand recognition	il riconoscimento della marca	*(reeh-koh-noh-sheeh-mEhn-toh dehl-lah mAhr-kah)*
breadbasket	il cestino per il pane	*(chehs-tEEh-noh pehr eehl pAh-neh)*
break even (v)	arrivare al punto di parità	*(ahr-reeh-vAh-reh ahl pOOhn-toh deeh pah-reeh-tAh)*
break-even analysis	l'analisi di equilibrio tra i costi e i ricavi, il punto di pareggio	*(ah-nAh-leeh-zeeh deeh eh-kweeh-lEEh-breeh-oh trah eeh kOhs-teeh eh eeh reeh-kAh-veeh), (pOOhn-toh deeh pah-rEhj-joh)*
break-even point	il punto della parità, il punto di pareggio, il volume di vendite al quale c'è equilibrio tra ricavi e costi	*(pOOhn-toh dehl-lah pah-reeh-tAh) (pOOhn-toh deeh pah-rEhj-joh), (voh-lOOh-meh deeh vEhn-deeh-teh ahl kwAh-leh cheh eh-kweeh-lEEh-breeh-oh trah reeh-kAh-veeh eh kOhs-teeh)*
briefcase	la borsa documenti	*(bOhr-sah doh-kooh-mEhn-teeh)*
broadcast (v)	trasmettere	*(trahz-mEht-teh-reh)*
broken lot	la partita divisa	*(pahr-tEEh-tah deeh-vEEh-zah)*
broken stowage	il carico frazionato	*(kAh-reeh-koh frah-tsyoh-nAh-toh)*

broker	l'intermediario	*(eehn-tehr-meh-dyAh-reeh-oh)*
broker, software	il mediatore di software	*(meh-dyah-tOh-reh deeh software)*
budget appropriation	lo stanziamento del preventivo	*(stahn-tsyah-mEhn-toh dehl preh-vehn-tEEh-voh)*
budget forecast	la previsione del preventivo	*(preh-veeh-zyOh-neh dehl preh-vehn-tEEh-voh)*
budget	il preventivo	*(preh-vehn-tEEh-voh)*
budget, advertising	il preventivo pubblicitario	*(preh-vehn-tEEh-voh poohb-bleeh-cheeh-tAh-reeh-oh)*
budget, cash	il preventivo di cassa, il preventivo in contanti	*(preh-vehn-tEEh-voh deeh kAhs-sah), (preh-vehn-tEEh-voh eehn kohn-tAhn-teeh)*
budget, investment	il preventivo d'investimento	*(preh-vehn-tEEh-voh deeh eehn-vehs-teeh-mEhn-toh)*
budget, marketing	il preventivo per il marketing	*(preh-vehn-tEEh-voh pehr eehl marketing)*
budget, sales	il preventivo per le spese di vendita	*(preh-vehn-tEEh-voh pehr leh spEh-zeh deeh vEhn-deeh-tah)*
bug (defect in computer program)	il difetto nel programma dell'elaboratore elettronico, il bug	*(deeh-fEht-toh nehl proh-grAhm-mah dehl eh-lah-boh-rah-tOh-reh eh-leht-trOh-neeh-koh)*
bull market	la borsa in fase di andamento positivo	*(bOhr-sah eehn fAh-zeh deeh ahn-dah-mEhn-toh poh-zeeh-tEEh-voh)*
bumper	il paraurti	*(pah-rah-OOhr-teeh)*
burden rate	il tasso dell'onere	*(tAhs-soh dehl Oh-neh-reh)*
bureaucrat	il burocrata	*(booh-rOh-krah-tah)*
business activity	l'attivita commerciale	*(aht-teeh-veeh-tAh kohm-mehr-chAh-leh)*
business card	il biglietto da visita	*(beeh-lyEht-toh dah vEEh-zeeh-tah)*
business cycle	il ciclo commerciale	*(chEEh-kloh kohm-mehr-chAh-leh)*

business management	l'amministrazione commerciale, la gestione commerciale	*(ahm-meeh-neehs-trah-tsyOh-neh kohm-mehr-chAh-leh), (jehs-tyOh-neh kohm-mehr-chAh-leh)*
business plan	il piano commerciale	*(pyAh-noh kohm-mehr-chAh-leh)*
business policy	la politica commerciale	*(poh-lEEh-teeh-kah kohm-mehr-chAh-leh)*
business strategy	la strategia commerciale	*(strah-teh-jEEh-ah kohm-mehr-chAh-leh)*
butter dish	il piattino per il burro	*(pyAht-teeh-noh pehr eehl bOOhr-roh)*
button	il bottone	*(boht-tOh-neh)*
buttonhole	l'occhiello, l'asola	*(ohk-kyEhl-loh), (Ah-zoh-lah)*
buy at best (v)	comprare al miglior prezzo	*(kohm-prAh-reh ahl meeh-lyOhr prEhts-tsoh)*
buy back (v)	riacquistare	*(reeh-ahk-kweehs-tAh-reh)*
buy on close (v)	comprare alla chiusura	*(kohm-prAh-reh ahl-lah kyooh-zOOh-rah)*
buy on opening (v)	comprare all'apertura	*(kohm-prAh-reh ahl ah-pehr-tOOh-rah)*
buyer	l'acquirente, il compratore	*(ahk-kweeh-rEhn-teh), (kohm-prah-tOh-reh)*
buyer's market	il mercato favorevole all'acquirente, il mercato propenso per gli acquirenti	*(mehr-kAh-toh fah-voh-rEh-voh-leh ahl ahk-kweeh-rEhn-teh), (mehr-kAh-toh poh-pEhn-soh pehr lyeeh ahk-kweeh-rEhn-teeh)*
buyer's option	all'opzione del compratore	*(ahl ohp-tsyOh-neh dehl kohm-prah-tOh-reh)*
buyer's premium	il premio del compratore	*(prEh-myoh dehl kohm-prah-tOh-reh)*
buyer's responsibility	la responsabilità dell'acquirente	*(rehs-pohn-sah-beeh-leeh-tAh dehl ahk-kweeh-rEhn-teh)*
buyer, chief	il compratore capo, il responsabile acquisti	*(kohm-prah-tOh-reh kAh-poh) (rehs-pohn-sAh-beeh-leh ahk-kwEEhs-teeh)*
buyer, credit	l'acquirente su credito	*(ahk-kweeh-rEhn-teh sooh krEh-deeh-toh)*

B

buyer, potential	l' acquirente potenziale, il compratore potenziale	*(ahk-kweeh-rEhn-teh poh-tehn-tsyAh-leh) (kohm-prah-tOh-reh poh-tehn-tsyAh-leh)*
buyout	la rilevazione delle quote dei soci liquidati	*(reeh-leh-vah-tsyOh-neh dehl-leh kwOh-teh deh-eeh sOh-chee leeh-kweeh-dAh-teeh)*
by-product	il prodotto derivato, il prodotto secondario	*(proh-dOht-toh deh-reeh-vAh-toh), (proh-dOht-toh seh-kohn-dAh-reeh-oh)*
bylaws	le normative, i regolamenti	*(norh-mah-tEEh-veh) (reh-goh-lah-mEhn-teeh)*
byte	il byte	

C

cable	il cavo	*(kAh-voh)*
cable television	la filodiffusione	*(feeh-loh-deehf-fooh-zyOh-neh)*
cable transfer	la bonifico elettronico	*(boh-nEEh-feeh-koh eh-leht-trOh-neeh-koh)*
calcium	il calcio	*(kAhlchoh)*
calculator	la calcolatrice	*(kahl-koh-lah-trEEh-cheh)*
calfskin	il vitello	*(veeh-tEhl-loh)*
call (v)	chiamare	*(kyah-mAh-reh)*
call feature	l'opzione di acquisto di valori mobiliari in qualsiasi momento a un certo prezzo	*(ohp-tsyOh-neh deeh ahk-kwEEhs-toh deeh vah-lOh-reeh moh-beeh-lyAh-reeh eehn kwahl-sEEh-ah-seeh moh-mEhn-toh ah oohn chEhr-toh prEhts-tsoh)*
call loan	il prestito rimborsabile a domanda	*(prEhs-teeh-toh reehm-bohr-sAh-beeh-leh ah doh-mAhn-dah)*
call money	il denaro investito a brevissima scadenza	*(deh-nAh-roh eehn-vehs-tEEh-toh ah breh-vEEhs-seeh-mah skah-dEhn-tsah)*

call option	l'opzione di acquistare delle azioni ad un dato prezzo entro un determinato periodo di tempo	(ohp-tsyOh-neh deeh ahk-kweehs-tAh-reh deh-leh ah-tsyOh-neeh Ehn-troh oohn deh-tehr-meeh-nAh-toh peh-rEEh-oh-doh deeh tEhm-poh)
call price	il prezzo al quale è redimibi-le un buono a richiesta	(prEhts-tsoh ahl kwAh-leh eh reh-deeh-mEEh-beeh-leh oohn bwOh-noh ah reeh-kyEhs-tah)
call protection	la protezione dalla richiesta di un rimborso immediato (obbligazioni)	(proh-teh-tsyOh-neh dahl-lah reeh-kyEhs-tah deeh oohn reehm-bOhr-soh eehm-meh-dyAh-toh ohb-bleeh-gah-tsyOh-neeh)
call rate	il tasso di interesse per rim-borsabile a brevissima scadenza	(tAhs-soh deeh eehn-teh-rEhs-seh pehr reehm-bohr-sAh-reh ah breh-vEEhs-seeh-mah skah-dEhn-tsah)
call rule	le norme per la richiesta di rimborso anticipato	(nOhr-meh pehr lah reeh-kyEhs-tah deeh reehm-bOhr-soh ahn-teeh-cheeh-pAh-toh)
callback	il richiamo (in genere per articoli difettosi)	(reeh-kyAh-moh eehn jEh-neh-reh pehr ahr-tEEh-koh-leeh deeh-feht-tOh-zeeh)
camera	la telecamera	(teh-leh-kAh-meh-rah)
campaign, advertising	la campagna pubblicitaria	(kahm-pAh-nyah poohb-bleeh-cheeh-tAh-reeh-ah)
campaign, productivity	la campagna di produttività	(kahm-pAh-nyah deeh proh-dooht-teeh-veeh-tAh)
camshaft	l'albero di distribuzione a camme	(Ahl-beh-roh deeh deehs-treeh-booh-tsyOh-neh ah kAhm-meh)
cancel (v)	cancellare	(kahn-chehl-lAh-reh)
cancelled check	l'assegno versato	(ahs-sEh-nyoh vehr-sAh-toh)
candlestick	il candeliere	(kahn-deh-lyEh-reh)
capacity	la capacità	(kah-pah-cheeh-tAh)
capacity, manufacturing	la capacità di produzione, la capacità produttiva	(kah-pah-cheeh-tAh deeh proh-dooh-tsyOh-neh), (kah-pah-cheeh-tAh proh-dooht-tEEh-vah)

C

capacity, plant	la capacità produttiva della fabbrica, il potenziale di capacità produttiva di un impianto	*(kah-pah-cheeh-tAh proh-dooht-tEEh-vah dehl-lah fAhb-breeh-kah), (poh-tehn-tsyAh-leh deeh kah-pah-cheeh-tAh proh-dooht-tEEh-vah deeh oohn eehm-pyAhn-toh)*
capacity, utilization	il livello d'utilizzo della capacità produttiva	*(leeh-vEhl-loh dooh-teeh-lEEhds-dsoh dehl-lah kah-pah-cheeh-tAh proh-dooht-tEEh-vah)*
cape	il mantello	*(mahn-tEhl-loh)*
capital	il capitale	*(kah-peeh-tAh-leh)*
capital account	il conto capitale	*(kOhn-toh kah-peeh-tAh-leh)*
capital allowance	la riserva capitale	*(reeh-zEhr-vah kah-peeh-tAh-leh)*
capital asset	gli attivi immobili	*(aht-tEEh-veeh eehm-mOh-beeh-leeh)*
capital budget	il preventivo capitale, il preventivo spese impianti e macchinari	*(preh-vehn-tEEh-voh kah-peeh-tAh-leh), (preh-vehn-tEEh-voh spEh-zeh eehm-pyAhn-teeh eh mahk-keeh-nAh-reeh)*
capital expenditure appraisal	la stima delle spese capitali	*(stEEh-mah deh-leh spEh-zeh kah-peeh-tAh-leeh)*
capital expenditure	l'investimento capitale	*(eehn-vehs-teeh-mEhn-toh kah-peeh-tAh-leh)*
capital exports (currency)	l'esportazione dei capitali	*(ehs-pohr-tah-tsyOh-neh deh-eeh kah-peeh-tAh-leeh)*
capital exports (goods)	l'esportazione di beni capitali	*(ehs-pohr-tah-tsyOh-neh deh-eeh bEh-neeh kah-peeh-tAh-leeh)*
capital gain/loss	gli utili di capitale/la perdita di capitale	*(OOh-teeh-leeh deeh kah-peeh-tAh-leh/pEhr-deeh-tah deeh kah-peeh-tAh-leh)*
capital goods	i beni capitali, i beni d'investimento	*(bEh-neeh kah-peeh-tAh-leeh), (bEh-neeh deehn-vehs-teeh-mEhn-toh)*
capital increase	l'aumento dei capitali	*(ah-ooh-mEhn-toh deh-eeh kah-peeh-tAh-leeh)*

capital market	il mercato dei capitali	*(mehr-kAh-toh deh-eeh kah-peeh-tAh-leeh)*
capital spending	la spesa dei capitali	*(spEh-zah deh-eeh kah-peeh-tAh-leeh)*
capital stock	il capitale azionario	*(kah-peeh-tAh-leeh ah-styoh-nAh-reeh-oh)*
capital structure	la struttura finanziaria	*(strooh-tOOh-rah feeh-nahn-tsyAh-reeh-ah)*
capital surplus	l'eccedenza dei capitali	*(ehch-cheh-dEhn-tsah deh-eeh kah-peeh-tAh-leeh)*
capital, raising	raccolta dei capitali	*(rahk-kOhl-tah deh-eeh kah-peeh-tAh-leeh)*
capital, return on	la resa sui capitali, i proventi sul capitale	*(rEh-zah sooh-eeh kah-peeh-tAh-leeh), (proh-vEhn-teeh soohl kah-peeh-tAh-leh)*
capital, risk	il capitale per finanziare nuove iniziative	*(kah-peeh-tAh-leh pehr feeh-nahn-tsyAh-reh nwOh-veh eeh-neeh-tsyah-tEEh-veh)*
capital, working	il capitale circolante, il capitale liquido	*(kah-peeh-tAh-leh cheehr-koh-lAhn-teh), (kah-peeh-tAh-leeh lEEh-kweeh-doh)*
capital-intensive	richiedente un notevole investimento di capitale	*(reeh-kyeh-dEhn-teh oohn noh-tEh-voh-leh eehn-vehs-teeh-mEhn-toh deeh kah-peeh-tAh-leh)*
capital-output ratio	il rapporto tra capitale e produzione	*(rahp-pOhr-toh trah kah-peeh-tAh-leh eh proh-dooh-tsyOh-neh)*
capitalism	il capitalismo	*(kah-peeh-tah-lEEhz-moh)*
capitalization	la capitalizzazione	*(kah-peeh-tah-leehds-dsah-tsyOh-neh)*
capsule	la capsula	*(kAhp-sooh-lah)*
car	la macchina	*(mAhk-keeh-nah)*
carbon	il carbonio	*(kahr-bOh-neeh-oh)*
carbon steel	l'acciaio al carbonio	*(ahch-chAh-yoh ahl kahr-bOh-nyoh)*
carburetor	il carburatore	*(kahr-booh-rah-tOh-reh)*
card case	il portabiglietti	*(pohr-tah-beeh-lyEht-teeh)*
cargo	la merce imbarcata	*(mEhr0cheh eehm-bahr-kAh-tah)*

C

carload	il carico di vettura	*(kAh-reeh-koh deeh veht-tOOh-rah)*
carnet	il carnet	*(kahr-nEh)*
carrier	il portatore	*(pohr-tah-tOh-reh)*
carrier's risk	a rischio del portatore	*(rEEhs-kyoh dehl pohr-tah-tOh-reh)*
carry forward (v)	portare a nuovo	*(pohr-tAh-reh ah nwOh-voh)*
carryback	la perdita detraibile dalle imposte	*(pEhr-deeh-tah deh-trah-EEh-beeh-leh dahl-leh eehm-pOhs-teh)*
carrying charges	le spese d'immobilizzo	*(spEh-zeh deehm-moh-beeh-lEEhts-tsoh)*
carrying value	il valore d'immobilizzo	*(vah-lOh-reh deehm-moh-beeh-lEEhts-tsoh)*
carryover	riportare	*(reeh-pohr-tAh-reh)*
cartel	il consorzio di industriali	*(kohn-sOhr-tsyoh deeh eehn-doohs-tryAh-leeh)*
carving knife	il trinciante	*(treehn-chAhn-teh)*
case	la cassa	*(kAhs-sah)*
cash	in contanti	*(eehn kohn-tAhn-teeh)*
cash balance	il saldo liquido	*(sAhl-doh lEEh-kweeh-doh)*
cash basis	in contanti	*(eehn kohn-tAhn-teeh)*
cash before delivery	il pagamento prima della consegna	*(pah-gah-mEhn-toh preeh-mah deh-lah kohn-sEh-nyah)*
cash book	il libro cassa	*(lEEh-broh kAhs-sah)*
cash budget	il preventivo di cassa, il preventivo in contanti	*(preh-vehn-tEEh-voh deeh kAhs-sah), (preh-vehn-tEEh-voh eehn kohn-tAhn-teeh)*
cash delivery	il pagamento alla consegna, la consegna in contanti	*(pah-gah-mEhn-toh preeh-mah ah-lah kohn-sEh-nyah) (kohn-sEh-nyah eehn kohn-tAhn-teeh)*
cash discount	lo sconto per contanti	*(skOh-ntoh pehr kohn-tAhn-teeh)*
cash dividend	il dividendo pagato in contanti	*(deeh-veeh-dEhn-doh pah-gAh-toh eehn kohn-tAhn-teeh)*

cash entry	l' annotazione di movimento di contanti, la registrazione del movimento di cassa	*(ahn-noh-tah-tsyOh-neh deeh moh-veeh-mEhn-toh deeh kohn-tAhn-teeh), (reh-jeehs-trah-tsyOh-neh dehl moh-veeh-mEhn-toh deeh kAhs-sah)*
cash flow	il movimento di cassa	*(moh-veeh-mEhn-toh deeh kAhs-sah)*
cash flow statement	la relazione del movimento di cassa	*(reh-lah-tsyOh-neh dehl moh-veeh-mEhn-toh deeh kAhs-sah)*
cash in advance	il pagamento anticipato	*(pah-gah-mEhn-toh ahn-teeh-cheeh-pAh-toh)*
cash management	l'amministrazione della cassa	*(ahm-meeh-neehs-trah-tsyOh-neh dehl-lah kAhs-sah)*
cash on delivery	il pagamento alla consegna	*(pah-gah-mEhn-toh ahl-lah kohn-sEh-nyah)*
cash surrender value	il valore in contanti alla resa	*(vah-lOh-reh eehn kohn-tAhn-teeh ahl-lah rEh-zah)*
cash-and-carry	il pagamento in contanti	*(pah-gah-mEhn-toh eehn kohn-tAhn-teeh)*
cashier's check	l'assegno bancario	*(ahs-sEh-nyoh bahn-kAh-reeh-oh)*
cashmere	il cachemire	*(bah-rEEh-leh)*
cask (225 liters)	il barile	*(kahs-sEht-tah)*
cassette	la cassetta	*(kahs-sEht-tah)*
cast iron	il ferro fuso, la ghisa di seconda fusione	*(fEhr-roh fOOh-zoh), (gEEh-zah deeh seh-kOhn-dah fooh-zyOh-neh)*
casualty insurance	l'assicurazione contro danni	*(ahs-seeh-kooh-rah-tsyOh-neh kohn-troh eeh dAhn-neeh)*
catalog	il catalogo	*(kah-tAh-loh-goh)*
catalyst	la catalisi	*(kah-tAh-leeh-zeeh)*
cathode	il catodo	*(kAh-toh-doh)*
ceiling	il soffitto	*(sohf-feeht-toh)*
centiliter	centilitro	*(chehn-tEEh-leeh-troh)*
central bank	la banca centrale	*(bAhn-kah chehn-trAh-leh)*

central processing unit (computers)	l'unità centrale per l'elaborazione dei dati	*(ooh-neeh-tAh chehn-trAh-leh pehr leh-lah-boh-rah-tsyOh-neh deh-eeh dAh-teeh)*
central rate	il tasso centrale	*(tAhs-soh chehn-trAh-leh)*
centralization	l'accentramento	*(ahch-chehn-trah-mEhn-toh)*
certificate	il certificato	*(chehr-teeh-feeh-kAh-toh)*
certificate of deposit	il certificato di deposito	*(chehr-teeh-feeh-kAh-toh deeh deh-pOh-zeeh-toh)*
certificate of incorporation	l'atto di costituzione	*(Aht-toh deeh kohs-teeh-tooh-tsyOh-neh)*
certificate of origin	il certificato d'origine	*(chehr-teeh-feeh-kAh-toh doh-rEEh-jeeh-neh)*
certified check	l'assegno garantito	*(ahs-sEH-nyoh gah-rahn-tEEh-toh)*
certified public accountant	il ragioniere diplomato dallo stato	*(rah-joh-nyEh-reh deeh-ploh-mAh-toh dahl-loh stAh-toh)*
chain (of stores)	la catena di negozi	*(kah-tEh-nah deeh neh-gOh-tseeh)*
chain of command	l'organigramma dirigenziale	*(ohr-gah-neeh-grAhm-mah deeh-reeh-gehn-tsyAh-leh)*
chain store group	il gruppo di grandi magazzini	*(grOOhp-poh deeh grAhn-deeh mah-gahds-dsEEh-neeh)*
chairman of the board	il presidente del consiglio	*(preh-zeeh-dEhn-teh dehl kohn-sEEh-lyoh)*
chamber of commerce	la camera di commercio	*(kAh-meh-rah deeh kohm-mEhr-choh))*
champagne glass	il flute, la coppa per lo spumante	*(kOhp-pah pehr- loh spooh-mAhn-teh)*
channel	il canale	*(kah-nAh-leh)*
channel of distribution	il canale di distribuzione	*(kah-nAh-leh deeh deehs-treeh-booh-tsyOh-neh)*
chapter	il capitolo	*(kah-pEEh-toh-loh)*
charge account	il conto aperto	*(kOhn-toh ah-pEhr-toh)*
chargeoff (v)	sgravare dalle tasse	*(zgrah-vAh-reh dahl-leh tAhs-seh)*
charges	gli oneri	*(Oh-neh-reeh)*

chart, activity	il diagramma delle attività	*(deeh-ah-grAhm-mah dehl-leh aht-teeh-veeh-tAh)*
chart, bar	il grafico a barra, il diagramma utilizzante barre	*(grAh-feeh-koh ah bAhr-rah), (deeh-ah-grAhm-mah ooh-teeh-leehds-dsAhn-teh bAhr-reh)*
chart, flow	il diagramma delle correnti	*(deeh-ah-grAhm-mah dehl-leh kohr-rEhn-teeh)*
chart, management	il quadro amministrativo, l'organigramma	*(kwAh-droh ahm-meeh-neehs-trah-tEEh-voh)*
charter	il documento costitutivo	*(doh-kooh-mEhn-toh kohs-teeh-tooh-tEEh-voh)*
chartered accountant	il ragioniere professionista	*(rah-joh-nyEh-reh proh-fehs-syoh-nEEhs-tah)*
charterparty agent	il mediatore per noleggio	*(meh-dyah-tOh-reh pehr noh-lEhj-joh)*
chassis	la carrozzeria	*(kahr-rohts-tseh-rEEh-ah)*
chattel	il bene mobile	*(bEh-neh mOh-beeh-leh)*
chattel mortgage	l'ipoteca su beni mobili	*(eeh-poh-tEh-kah sooh bEh-neeh mOh-beeh-leeh)*
cheap	a buon mercato	*(ah bwOhn mehr-kAh-toh)*
check	l'assegno	*(ahs-sEh-nyoh)*
check, counter	l'assegno bancario	*(ahs-sEh-nyoh bahn-kAh-reeh-oh)*
checking account	il conto corrente	*(kOhn-toh kohr-rEhn-teh)*
checklist	la lista di controllo	*(leehs-tah deeh kohn-trOhl-loh)*
cheese factory	il caseificio	*(kah-see-fehs-oh)*
cheese tray	il vassoio per formaggi	*(vahs-sOh-yoh pehr fohr-mAhj-jeeh)*
chemical	chimico	*(kEEh-meeh-koh)*
chemistry	la chimica	*(kEEh-meeh-kah)*
chief accountant	il capo contabile	*(kAh-poh kohn-tAh-beeh-leh)*
chief buyer	il compratore capo, il responsabile degli acquisti	*(kohm-prah-tOh-reh deh-lyeeh ahk-kwEEhs-teeh)*
chief executive	il direttore generale	*(deeh-reht-tOh-reh jeh-neh-rAh-leh)*
china	la porcellana fine	*(pohr-chehl-lAh-nah fEEh-neh)*

chip	il chip	*(chip)*
chloride	il cloruro	*(kloh-rOOh-roh)*
chloroform	il cloroformio	*(kloh-roh-fOhr-meeh-oh)*
chromium	il cromo	*(krOh-moh)*
cigarette case	il portasigarette	*(pohr-tah-seeh-gah-rEht-teh)*
circuit	il circuito	*(cheehr-kwEEh-toh)*
civil action	l'azione di parte civile	*(ah-tsyOh-neh deeh pAhr-teh cheeh-vEEh-leh)*
civil engineering	l'ingegneria civile	*(eehn-jeh-nyeh-rEEh-ah cheeh-vEEh-leh)*
claim	il reclamo	*(reh-klAh-moh)*
classified ad	la piccola pubblicità	*(pEEhk-koh-lah poohb-bleeh-cheeh-tAh)*
clean document	il documento pulito, il documento in ordine	*(doh-kooh-mEhn-toh pooh-lEEh-toh), (doh-kooh-mEhn-toh eehn Ohr-deeh-neh)*
clearinghouse	la stanza di compensazione	*(stAhn-tsah deeh kohm-pehn-sah-tsyOh-neh)*
climate	il clima	*(klEEh-mah)*
closed account	il conto chiuso	*(kOhn-toh kyOOh-zoh)*
closely held corporation	la ditta privata	*(dEEht-tah preeh-vAh-tah)*
closing entry	la scrittura di chiusura	*(skreeht-tOOh-rah deeh kyooh-zOOh-rah)*
closing price	il prezzo alla chiusura	*prEhts-tsoh ahl-lah kyooh-zOOh-rah)*
clutch	la frizione	*(freeh-tsyOh-neh)*
co-ownership	la comproprietà	*(kohm-proh-pryeh-tAh)*
coal	il carbone	*(kahr-bOh-neh)*
coat	il cappotto	*(kahp-pOht-toh)*
coated paper	la carta patinata	*(kAhr-tah pah-teeh-nAh-tah)*
coaxial cable	il cavo coassiale	*(kAh-voh koh-ahs-syAh-leh)*
codicil	il comma	*(kOhm-mah)*
coffee break	l'intervallo (per caffè)	*(een-tehr-vAhl-loh pehr kahf-fEh)*
coffeepot	la caffettiera	*(kahf-feht-tyEh-rah)*

coil	la serpentina, la bobina	(*sehr-pehn-tEEh-nah), (boh-bEEh-nah*)
coinsurance	la co-assicurazione	(*koh-ahs-seeh-kooh-rah-tsyOh-neh*)
coke	il coke	
cold call	la visita di vendita senza preavviso	(*vEEh-zeeh-tah deeh vEhn-deeh-tah sehn-tsah preh-ahv-vEEh-zoh*)
cold rolling	la laminatura a freddo	(*lah-meeh-nah-tOOh-rah ah frEhd-doh*)
collar	il colletto	(*kohl-lEht-toh*)
collateral	il collaterale	(*kohl-lah-teh-rAh-leh*)
colleague	il collega	(*kohl-lEh-gah*)
collect on delivery	il pagamento alla consegna	(*pah-gah-mEhn-toh ahl-lah kohn-sEh-nyah*)
collection period	il periodo di riscossione	(*peh-rEEh-oh-doh deeh reehs-kohs-syOh-neh*)
collective agreement	il patto collettivo	(*pAht-toh kohl-leht-teeh-voh*)
collective bargaining	la contrattazione collettiva	(*kohn-traht-tah-tsyOh-neh kohl-leht-tEEh-vah*)
collector of customs	l'esattore doganale, il doga-niere	(*eh-zaht-tOh-reh doh-gah-nAh-leh), (doh-gah-nyEh-reh*)
colloquium	il colloquio	(*kohl-lOh-kweeh-oh*)
color	il colore	(*koh-lOh-reh*)
color separation	la separazione dei colori	(*seh-pah-rah-tsyOh-neh deh-eeh koh-lOh-reeh*)
combination duty	il dazio combinato, la tariffa combinata	(*dAh-tsyoh kohm-beeh-nAh-toh), (tah-rEEhf-fah kohm-beeh-nAh-tah*)
combination	la combinazione	(*kohm-beeh-nah-tsyOh-neh*)
commerce	il commercio	(*kohm-mEhr-choh*)
commercial (advertisement)	l'avviso, l'avvertimento, l'annuncio	(*ahv-vEEh-zoh), (ahv-vehr-teeh-mEhn-toh), (ahn-nOOhn-choh*)
commercial bank	la banca commerciale	(*bAhn-kah kohm-mehr-chAh-leh*)
commercial grade	il livello commerciale, la qualità commerciale	(*leeh-vEhl-loh kohm-mehr-chAh-leh), (kwah-leeh-tAh kohm-mehr-chAh-leh*)

C

commercial invoice	la fattura commerciale	*(faht-tOOh-rah kohm-mehr-chAh-leh)*
commission (agency)	la parcella	*(pahr-chEhl-lah)*
commission (fee)	la provvigione	*(prohv-veeh-jOh-neh)*
commitment	l'impegno	*(eehm-pEh-nyoh)*
commodity exchange	la borsa (mercato) di beni di prima necessità	*(bOhr-sAh mehr-kAh-toh deeh bEh-neeh deeh prEEh-mah neh-chehs-seeh-tAh)*
commodity	l'oggetto di prima necessità, il bene	*(ohj-jEht-toh deeh prEEh-mah neh-chehs-seeh-tAh), (bEh-neh)*
common carrier	il vettore	*(veht-tOh-reh)*
common market	il mercato comune	*(mehr-kAh-toh koh-mOOh-neh)*
common stock	l'azione ordinaria	*(ah-tsyOh-neh ohr-deeh-nAh-reeh-ah)*
company	l'azienda	*(ah-dsyEhn-dah)*
company goal	l'obiettivo aziendale	*(ohb-byeht-tEEh-voh ah-dsyehn-dAh-leh)*
company policy	la politica aziendale	*(poh-lEEh-teeh-kah ah-dsyehn-dAh-leh)*
company, holding	la società finanziaria, la società madre	*(soh-cheh-tAh feeh-nahn-tsyAh-reeh-ah), (soh-cheh-tAh mAh-dreh)*
company, parent	la ditta madre, l'azienda madre	*(dEEht-tah mAh-dreh), (ah-dsyEhn-dah mAh-dreh)*
compensating balance	lasciare una certa somma di fondi nel conto corrente presso la istituzione	*(lahsh-shAh-reh ooh-nah chEhr-tah sOhm-mah deeh fOhn-doh nehl kOhn-toh kohr-rEhn-teh prEhs-soh lah eehs-teeh-tooh-tsyOh-neh)*
compensation	il compenso	*(kohm-pEhn-soh)*
compensation trade	il commercio compensativo	*(kohm-mEhr-choh kohm-pehn-sah-tEEh-voh)*
competition	la concorrenza, la competizione	*(kohn-kohr-rEhn-tsah), (kohm-peh-teeh-tsyOh-neh)*
competitive advantage	il vantaggio competitivo	*(vahn-tAhj-joh kohm-peh-teeh-tEEh-voh)*

competitive edge	il punto di vantaggio	*(pOOhn-toh deeh vahn-tAhj-joh)*
competitive price	il prezzo concorrenziale	*(prEhts-tsoh kohn-kohr-rehn-tsyAh-leh)*
competitive strategy	la strategia concorrenziale	*(strah-teh-jEEh-ah kohn-kohr-rehn-tsyAh-leh)*
competitor analysis	l'analisi del concorrente	*(ah-nAh-leeh-zeh dehl kohn-kohr-rEhn-teh)*
competitor	il concorrente	*(kohn-kohr-rEhn-teh)*
complimentary copy	la copia in omaggio	*(kOh-peeh-ah eehn oh-mAhj-joh)*
component	il componente	*(kohm-poh-nEhn-teh)*
composite index	l'indice composto	*(EEhn-deeh-cheh kohm-pOhs-toh)*
composition	la composizione	*(kohm-poh-zeeh-tsyOh-neh)*
compound	il composto	*(kohm-pOhst-oh)*
compound interest	l'interesse composto	*(eehn-teh-rEhs-seh kohm-pOhs-toh)*
compounds	i composti	*(kohm-pOhs-teeh)*
comptroller	il controllore	*(kohn-trohl-lOh-reh)*
computer	il cervello elettronico, il computer	*(chehr-vEhl-loh eh-leht-trOh-neeh-koh), (kumpyutor)*
computer bank	il computer bank	*(kumpyutor bahnk)*
computer center	il centro per elaborati elettronici	*(chEhn-troh pehr eh-lah-boh-rah-tOh-reeh eh-leht-trOh-neeh-cheeh)*
computer input	l'entrata dei dati nell'elaboratore elettronico (input)	*(ehn-trAh-tah deh-eeh dAh-teeh nehl eh-lah-boh-rah-tOh-reh eh-leht-trOh-neeh-koh)*
computer language	il linguaggio per elaboratori elettronici	*(leehn-gwAhj-joh pehr eh-lah-boh-rah-tOh-reeh eh-leht-trOh-neeh-cheeh)*
computer memory	la memoria dell'elaboratore	*(meh-mOh-reeh-ah dehl eh-lah-boh-rah-tOh-reh)*
computer output	la produzione del computer (computer output)	*(proh-dooh-tsyOh-neh dehl kumpyutor)*
computer program	il programma dell'elaboratore, il programma del computer	*(proh-grAhm-mah dehl eh-lah-boh-rah-tOh-reh dehl kumpyutor)*

C

C

computer storage	l'immagazzinaggio dei dati per il computer	*(eehm-mah-gahds-dseeh-nAhj-joh deh-eeh dAh-teeh pehr eel kumpyutor)*
computer terminal	il terminale dell'elaboratore, il terminale del computer	*(tehr-meeh-nAh-leh dehl eh-lah-boh-rah-tOh-reh)*
computer, analog	l'elaboratore a sistema analog	*(eh-lah-boh-rah-tOh-reh ah seehs-tEh-mah ah-nah-lOhg)*
computer, digital	l'elaboratore a sistema digitale, l'elaboratore digitale	*(eh-lah-boh-rah-tOh-reh ah seehs-tEh-mah deeh-jeeh-tAh-leh), (eh-lah-boh-rah-tOh-reh deeh-jeeh-tAh-leh)*
concentration	la concentrazione	*(kohn-cehn-trah-tsyOh-neh)*
condenser	il condensatore	*(kohn-dehn-sah-tOh-reh)*
conditional acceptance	l'accettazione condizionale	*(ahch-cheht-tah-tsyOh-neh kohn-deeh-tsyoh-nAh-leh)*
conditional sales contract	il contratto di vendita condizionata	*(kohn-trAht-toh deeh vEhn-deeh-tah kohn-deeh-tsyoh-nAh-tah)*
conductor	il conduttore	*(kohn-dooht-tOh-reh)*
conference room	la sala conferenze	*(sAh-lah kohn-feh-rEhn-tseh)*
confidential	confidenziale, riservato	*(kohn-feeh-dehn-tsyAh-leh), reeh-zehr-vAh-toh)*
confirmation of order	la conferma dell'ordine	*(kohn-fEhr-mah dehl Ohr-deeh-neh)*
conflict of interest	il conflitto d'interesse	*(kohn-flEEt-toh deen-teh-rEhs-seh)*
conglomerate	il conglomerato	*(kohn-gloh-meh-rAh-toh)*
connecting rod	la biella	*(byEhl-lah)*
consent	il consenso	*(kohn-cehn-sOh)*
consideration (bus. law)	il compenso, la considerazione	*(kohm-pEhn-soh), (kohn-seeh-deh-rah-tsyOh-neh)*
consignee	il destinatario	*dehs-teeh-nah-tAh-reeh-oh)*
consignment	la spedizione, la consegna	*(speh-deeh-tsyOh-neh), (kohn-sEh-nyah)*
consignment note	la nota di spedizione	*(nOh-tah deeh speh-deeh-tsyOh-neh)*
consolidated financial statement	il bilancio consolidato	*(beeh-lAhn-choh kohn-soh-leeh-dAh-toh)*

consolidation	il consolidamento	*(kohn-soh-leeh-dah-mEhn-toh)*
consortium	il consorzio	*(kohn-sOhr-tsyoh)*
consular invoice	la fattura consolare	*(faht-tOOh-rah kohn-soh-lAh-reh)*
consultant	il consulente	*(kohn-sooh-lEhn-teh)*
consultant, management	il consulente amministrativo	*(kohn-sooh-lEhn-teh ahm-meeh-neehs-trah-tEEh-voh)*
consumer	il consumatore	*(kohn-sooh-mah-tOh-reh)*
consumer acceptance	l'accettazione da parte del consumatore	*(ahch-cheht-tah-tsyOh-neh dah pAhr-teh dehl kohn-sooh-mah-tOh-reh)*
consumer credit	il credito al consumatore	*(krEh-deeh-toh ahl kohn-sooh-mah-tOh-reh)*
consumer goods	i beni di consumo	*(bEh-neeh deeh kohn-sOOh-moh)*
consumer price index	l'indice dei prezzi al consumo	*(EEhn-deeh-cheh deh-eeh prEhts-tseeh ahl kohn-sOOh-moh)*
consumer research	la ricerca sul consumatore	*(reeh-chEhr-kah soohl kohn-sooh-mah-tOh-reh)*
consumer satisfaction	la soddisfazione del consu-matore	*(sohd-deehs-fah-tsyOh-neh dehl kohn-sooh-mah-tOh-reh)*
container	il contenitore, il "container"	*(kohn-teh-neeh-tOh-reh)*
content	il contenuto	*(kohn-teh-nOOh-toh)*
contingencies	le contingenze	*(kohn-teehn-jEhn-tseh)*
contingent fund	il fondo di contingenza, il fondo di previdenza	*(fOhn-doh deeh kohn-teehn-jEhn-tsah), (fOhn-doh deeh preh-veeh-dEhn-dsah)*
contingent liability	la responsabilità contingente, la sopravvenienza passiva	*(rehs-pohn-sah-beeh-leeh-tAh kohn-teehn-jEhn-teh), (soh-prahv-veeh-vEhn-tsah pahs-sEEh-vah)*
contract	il contratto	*(kohn-trAht-toh)*
contract carrier	il vettore contrattuale	*(veht-tOh-reh kohn-traht-twAh-leh)*
contract month	il mese contrattuale	*(mEh-zeh kohn-traht-twAh-leh)*

C

control, cost	il controllo dei costi	*(kohn-trOhl-loh deh-eeh kOhs-teeh)*
control, financial	il controllo finanziario	*(kohn-trOhl-loh feeh-nahn-tsyAh-reeh-oh)*
control, inventory	il controllo dell'inventario	*(kohn-trOhl-loh dehl eehn-vehn-tAh-reeh-oh)*
control, manufacturing	il controllo della produzione	*(kohn-trOhl-loh deh-lah proh-dooh-tsyOh-neh)*
control, production	il controllo della produzione	*(kohn-trOhl-loh deh-lah proh-dooh-tsyOh-neh)*
control, quality	il controllo di qualita	*(kohn-trOhl-loh deeh kwah-leeh-tAh)*
control, stock	il controllo dei valori, il controllo delle azioni	*(kohn-trOhl-loh deh-eeh vah-lOh-reeh), (kohn-trOhl-loh dehl-leh ah-tsyOh-neeh)*
controllable costs	i costi controllabili	*(kOhs-teeh kohn-trohl-lAh-beeh-leeh)*
controller	il controllore	*(kohn-trohl-lOh-reh)*
controlling interest	l'interesse maggioritario	*(eehn-teh-rEhs-seh mahj-joh-reeh-tAh-reeh-oh)*
convertible debentures	le obbligazioni convertibili	*(ohb-bleeh-gah-tsyOh-neeh kohn-vehr-tEEh-beeh-leeh)*
convertible preferred stock	le azioni privilegiate convertibili	*(ah-tsyOh-neeh preeh-veeh-leh-jAh-teh kohn-vehr-tEEh-beeh-leeh)*
conveyor belt	il trasportatore a cinghia	*(trahs-pohr-tah-tOh-reh ah chEEhn-gyah)*
conveyor	il trasportatore	*(trahs-pohr-tah-tOh-reh)*
cooper	il bottaio	*(boht-tAh-yoh)*
cooperation agreement	la convenzione di cooperazione	*(kohn-vehn-tsyOh-neh deeh koh-oh-peh-rah-tsyOh-neh)*
cooperative advertising	la pubblicità cooperativa (in compartecipazione)	*(poohb-bleeh-cheeh-tAh koh-oh-peh-rah-tEEh-vah eehn kohm-pahr-teh-cheeh-pah-tsyOh-neh))*
cooperative	la cooperativa	*(koh-oh-peh-rah-tEEh-vah)*
copper	il rame	*(rAh-meh)*
copy (text)	il testo	*(tEhs-toh)*
copy	il materiale scritto	*(mah-teh-ryAh-leh skrEEht-toh)*

copy testing	l'esame di un testo pubblicitario	*(eh-zAh-meh deeh oohn tEhs-toh poohb-bleeh-cheeh-tAh-reeh-oh)*
copyright	i diritti d'autore	*(deeh-rEEht-teeh dah-ooh-tOh-reh)*
cork	il tappo	*(tAhp-poh)*
corkscrew	il cavatappi	*(kah-vah-tAhp-peeh)*
corporate growth	la crescita aziendale	*(krEh-sheeh-tah ah-dsyehn-dAh-leh)*
corporate image	l'immagine aziendale	*(eehm-mAh-jeeh-neh ah-dsyehn-dAh-leh)*
corporate income tax	l'imposta sul reddito delle persone giuridiche (IRPEG)	*(eehm-pOhs-tah soohl rEhd-deeh-toh deh-leh pehr-sOh-neh jooh-rEEh-deeh-keh)*
corporate planning	la pianificazione aziendale, la programmazione aziendale	*(pyah-neeh-feeh-kah-tsyOh-neh ah-dsyehn-dAh-leh), (proh-grahm-mah-tsyOh-neh ah-dsyehn-dAh-leh)*
corporate structure	la struttura aziendale	*(strooht-tOOh-rah ah-dsyehn-dAh-leh)*
corporation	la società per azioni, l'azienda, la ditta, la società	*(soh-cheh-tAh pehr ah-tsyOh-neeh), (ah-dsyEhn-dah), (dEEht-tah), (soh-cheh-tAh)*
corporation tax	l'imposta aziendale	*(eehm-pOhs-tah ah-dsyehn-dAh-leh)*
corpus	il corpo	*(kOhr-poh)*
correspondence	la corrispondenza	*(kohr-reehs-pohn-dEhn-tsah)*
correspondent bank	la banca corrispondente	*(bAhn-kah kohr-reehs-pohn-dEhn-teh)*
cortisone	il cortisone	*(kohr-teeh-zOh-neh)*
cost (v)	costare	*(kohs-tAh-reh)*
cost	il costo	*(kOhs-toh)*
cost accounting	la contabilità dei costi	*(kohn-tah-beeh-leeh-tAh deh-eeh kOhs-teeh)*
cost analysis	l'analisi dei costi	*(ah-nAh-leeh-zeeh deh-eeh kOhs-teeh)*
cost and freight	il costo e trasporto	*(kOhs-toh eh trahs-pOhr-toh)*

cost control	il controllo dei costi	*(kohn-trOhl-loh deh-eeh kOhs-teeh)*
cost effectiveness	l'efficienza dei costi	*(ehf-feeh-chEhn-tsah deh-eeh kOhs-teeh)*
cost factor	il fattore dei costi	*(faht-tOh-reh deh-eeh kOhs-teeh)*
cost of capital	il costo del capitale	*(kOhs-toh dehl kah-peeh-tAh-leh)*
cost of goods sold	il costo dei beni venduti	*(kOhs-toh deh-eeh bEh-neeh vehn-dOOh-teeh)*
cost of living	il costo della vita, il carovita	*(kOhs-toh dehl-lah vEEh-tah) (kah-roh-vEEh-tah)*
cost reduction	la riduzione dei costi	*(reeh-dooh-tsyOh-neh deh-eeh kOhs-teeh)*
cost, average	il costo medio	*(kOhs-toh mEh-dyoh)*
cost, direct	il costo diretto	*(kOhs-teeh deeh-rEht-toh*
cost, indirect	il costo indiretto	*(kOhs-toh eehn-deeh-rEht-toh)*
cost, replacement	il costo di ricambio	*(kOhs-toh deeh reeh-kAhm-byoh)*
cost-benefit analysis	l'analisi del rapporto tra i costi ed i benefici	*(ah-nAh-leeh-zeeh dehl rahp-pOhr-toh rah eeh kOhs-teeh ed eeh beh-neh-fEEh-cheeh)*
cost-plus contract	il contratto che garantisce un profitto in base al costo del prodotto	*(kohn-trAht-toh keh gah-rahn-tEEh-sheh oohn proh-fEEht-toh eehn bAh-zeh ahl kOhs-toh dehl proh-dOht-toh)*
cost-price squeeze	la riduzione del margin (di profitto)	*(reeh-dooh-tsyOh-neh dehl mAhr-jeeh-neh))*
costs, allocation of	l'allocazione dei costi	*(ahl-loh-kah-tsyOh-neh deh-eeh kOhs-teeh)*
costs, fixed	i costi fissi	*(kOhs-teeh fEEhs-seeh)*
costs, managed	i costi amministrati, i costi controllabili	*(kOhs-teeh ahm-meeh-neehs-trAh-teeh), (kOhs-teeh kohn-tohl-lAh-beeh-leeh)*
costs, production	i costi di produzione	*(kOhs-teeh deeh proh-dooh-tsyOh-neh)*
costs, set-up	i costi iniziali	*(kOhs-teeh eeh-neeh-tsyAh-leeh)*

costs, standard	i costi normali, i costi standard	*(kOhs-teeh nohr-mAh-leeh)*
costs, variable	i costi variabili	*(kOhs-teeh vah-ryAh-beeh-leeh)*
cotton	il cotone	*(koh-tOh-neh)*
cough (v)	tossire	*(tohs-sEEh-reh)*
cough drop	la pastiglia per la tosse	*(pahs-tEEh-lyah pehr-lah tOhs-seh)*
cough syrup	lo sciroppo per la tosse	*(sheeh-rOhp-poh pehr-lah tOhs-seh)*
counter check	l'assegno bancario	*(ahs-sEh-nyoh bahn-kAh-reeh-oh)*
counterfeit	il contraffatto	*(kohn-trahf-fAht-toh)*
countervailing duty	la tariffa controvalente	*(tah-rEEhf-fah kohn-troh-vah-lEhn-teh)*
country	il paese	*(pah-Eh-zeh)*
country of origin	il paese d'origine	*(pah-Eh-zeh doh-rEEh-jeeh-neh)*
country of risk	il paese a rischio	*(pah-Eh-zeh ah rEEhs-kyoh)*
coupon (bond interest)	la cedola di interesse su buoni, la cedola di interesse su obbligazioni	*(chEh-doh-lah deeh eehn-teh-rEhs-seh sooh bwOh-neeh) (hEh-doh-lah deeh eehn-teh-rEhs-seh sooh ohb-bleeh-gah-tsyOh-neeh)*
courier service	il servizio di corriere	*(sehr-vEEh-tsyoh deeh kohr-ryEh-reh)*
covenant	l'impegno, la promessa	*(eehm-pEh-nyoh), (proh-mEhs-sah)*
cover	la copertina	*(koh-pehr-tEEh-nah)*
cover charge	il coperto	*(koh-pEhr-toh)*
cover letter	la lettera di accompagnamento	*(lEht-teh-rah deeh ahk-kohm-pah-nyah-mEhn-toh)*
cover ratio	il rapporto di copertura	*(rahp-pOhr-toh deeh koh-pehr-tOOh-rah)*
coverage (insurance)	la copertura	*(koh-pehr-tOOh-rah)*
cowhide	il cuoio	*(kwOh-yoh)*
coyote	il coyote	*(koh-yOh-teh)*

cracking	la piroscissione	*(peeh-roh-sheehs-syOh-neh)*
crankshaft	l'albero a gomito	*(Ahl-beh-roh ah gOh-meeh-toh)*
crawling peg	la parità mobile	*(pah-reeh-tAh mOh-beeh-leh)*
credit (v)	accreditare	*(ahk-kreh-deeh-tAh-reh)*
credit	il credito	*(krEh-deeh-toh)*
credit balance	il credito disponibile, il saldo a credito	*(krEh-deeh-toh deehs-poh-nEEh-beeh-leh), (sAhl-doh ah krEh-deeh-toh)*
credit bank	la banca di credito	*(bAhn-kah deeh krEh-deeh-toh)*
credit bureau	l'ufficio di credito	*(ooh-fEEh-choh deeh krEh-deeh-toh)*
credit buyer	l'acquirente su credito	*(ahk-kweeh-rEhn-teh sooh krEh-deeh-toh)*
credit card	la carta di credito	*(kAhr-tah deeh krEh-deeh-toh)*
credit control	il controllo del credito	*(kohn-trOhl-loh dehl krEh-deeh-toh)*
credit insurance	l'assicurazione dei crediti	*(ahs-seeh-kooh-rah-tsyOh-neh deh-eeh krEh-deeh-teeh)*
credit line	la linea di credito	*(lEEh-neh-ah deeh krEh-deeh-toh)*
credit management	l'amministrazione del credito	*(ahm-meeh-neehs-trah-tsyOh-neh dehl krEh-deeh-toh)*
credit note	la nota di accredito	*(nOh-tah ahk-krEh-deeh-toh)*
credit rating	la valutazione del credito	*(vah-looh-tah-tsyOh-neh dehl krEh-deeh-toh)*
credit reference	la referenza bancaria, la referenza per ottenere credito	*(reh-feh-rEhn-tsah bahn-kAh-reeh-ah), (reh-feh-rEhn-tsah pehr oht-teh-nEh-reh krEh-deeh-toh)*
credit terms	i termini del credito	*(tEhr-meeh-neeh dehl krEh-deeh-toh)*
credit union	l'unione creditizia	*(ooh-nyOh-neh kreh-deeht-tEEh-tsyah)*
creditor	il creditore	*(kreh-deeh-tOh-reh)*

critical path analysis	l'analisi del percorso critico	*(ah-nAh-leeh-zeeh dehl pehr-kOhr-soh krEEh-teeh-koh)*
crop (v)	rifilare	*(reeh-feeh-lAh-reh)*
cross-licensing	le licenze accavallate	*(leeh-chEhn-tsheh ahk-kah-vahl-lAh-teh)*
crucible	il crogiuolo	*(kroh-jwOh-loh)*
crude	grezzo	*(grEhts-tsoh)*
crystal glass	il vetro di cristallo	*(vEh-troh- deeh kreehs-tAhl-loh)*
crystallization	la cristalizzazione	*(kreehs-tah-leehds-dsah-tsyOh-neh)*
cuff link	il gemello da camicia	*(jeh-mEhl-loh dah kah-mEEh-chah)*
cultural export permit	il permesso d'esportazione di beni culturali	*(pehr-mEhs-soh dehs-pohr-tah-tsyOh-neh)*
cultural property	il bene culturale	*(bEh-neh koohl-tooh-rAh-leh)*
cum dividend	con dividendo	*(kohn deeh-veeh-dEhn-doh)*
cumulative	cumulativo	*(kooh-mooh-lah-tEEh-voh)*
cumulative preferred stock	le azioni preferenziali cumulative	*(ah-tsyOh-neeh preh-feh-rehn-tsyAh-leeh kooh-mooh-lah-tEEh-veh)*
cup	la tazza	*(tAhts-tsah)*
cupola	la cupola	*(kOOh-poh-lah)*
currency	la valuta	*(vah-lOOh-tah)*
currency band	il serpente valutario (CEE)	*(sehr-pEhn-teh vah-looh-tAh-yoh)*
currency clause	il comma valutario	*(kOhm-mah vah-looh-tAh-yoh)*
currency conversion	la conversione di valuta	*(kohn-vehr-zyOh-neh deeh vah-lOOh-tah)*
currency exchange	il cambio valuta	*(kAhm-byoh vah-lOOh-tah)*
current	la corrente	*(kohr-rEhn-teh)*
current account	il conto corrente	*(kOhn-toh kohr-rEhn-teh)*
current assets	gli attivi correnti	*(aht-tEEh-veeh kohr-rEhn-teeh)*
current liabilities	gli impegni attuali, la responsabilità corrente	*(eehm-pEh-nyeeh aht-twAh-leeh), (rehs-pohn-sah-beeh-leeh-tAh kohr-rEhn-teh)*

current ratio	il rapporto corrente	*(rahp-pOhr-toh kohr-rEhn-teh)*
current yield	il rendimento corrente	*(rehn-deeh-mEhn-toh kohr-rEhn-teh)*
customer	il cliente	*(kleeh-Ehn-teh)*
customer service	il servizio reso al cliente	*(sehr-vEEh-tsyoh rEh-zoh ahl kleeh-Ehn-teh)*
customs	la dogana	*(doh-gAh-nah)*
customs broker	lo spedizioniere doganale	*(speh-deeh-tsyoh-nyEh-reh doh-dah-nAh-leh)*
customs duty	la tariffa doganale, il dazio	*(tah-rEEhf-fah doh-dah-nAh-leh), (dAh-tsyoh)*
customs entry	la dichiarazione doganale	*(deeh-kyah-rah-tsyOh-neh doh-dah-nAh-leh)*
customs union	l'unione doganale	*(ooh-nyOh-neh doh-dah-nAh-leh)*
cut (v)	tagliare	*(tah-lyAh-reh)*
cutback	la riduzione	*(reeh-dooh-tsyOh-neh)*
cutlery	la posateria	*(poh-zah-teh-rEEh-ah)*
cycle billing	la fatturazione a ciclo	*(faht-tooh-rah-tsyOh-neh ah chEEh-kloh)*
cycle, business	il ciclo commerciale	*(chEEh-kloh kohm-mehr-chAh-leh)*
cylinder	il cilindro	*(cheeh-lEEhn-droh)*

D

daily	giornaliero	*(johr-nah-lyEh-roh)*
dairy products	i prodotti lattiero-caseari	*(proh-dOht-teeh laht-tyEh-roh-kah-zeh-Ah-reeh)*
damage	il danno	*(dAhn-noh)*
dashboard	il cruscotto	*(krooh-kOht-toh)*
data	i dati	*(dah-teeh)*
data acquisition	l'acquisizione di dati	*(ahk-kweeh-zeeh-tsyOh-neh deeh dah-teeh)*
data bank	la banca dati	*(bAhn-kah dah-teeh)*

data base	il "data base," la base dei dati per elaboratori elettronici	*(bAh-zeh deh-eeh dah-teeh pehr eh-lah-boh-rah-tOh-reeh eh-leht-trOh-neeh-cheeh)*
date of delivery	la data di consegna	*(dAh-tah deeh kohn-sEh-nyah)*
day loan	il prestito giornaliero	*(prEhs-teeh-toh johr-nah-lyEh-roh)*
day order	l'ordine in giornata	*(Ohr-deeh-neh eehn johr-nAh-tah)*
dead freight	il nolo "vuoto per pieno"	*(nOh-loh vwOh-toh pehr pyEh-noh)*
dead rent	l'affitto morto	*(ahf-fEEht-toh mOhr-toh)*
deadline	la scadenza	*(skah-dEhn-tsah)*
deadlock	la situazione irresolubile, l'arresto, il punto morto	*(seeh-tooh-ah-tsyOh-neh eehr-reh-soh-lOOh-beeh-leh), (ahr-rEhs-toh), (pOOhn-toh mOhr-toh)*
deal	l'affare	*(ahf-fAh-reh)*
deal, package	la trattativa complessiva	*(traht-tah-tEEh-vah kohm-plehs-sEEh-vah)*
dealer	il commerciante	*(kohm-mehr-chAhn-teh)*
dealership	il licenziatario	*(leeh-chehn-tsyah-tAh-reeh-oh)*
debentures	le obbligazioni	*(ohb-bleeh-gah-tsyOh-neeh)*
debit	l'addebito	*(ahd-dEh-beeh-toh)*
debit entry	la nota di debito, la registrazione a debito	*(nOh-tah deeh dEh-beeh-toh)m (reh-jeehs-trah-tsyOh-neh ah dEh-beeh-toh)*
debit note	la nota di addebito	*(nOh-tah deeh ahd-dEh-beeh-toh)*
debt	il debito	*(dEh-beeh-toh)*
debug (v)	riparare il sistema nell'elaboratore	*(reeh-pah-rAh-reh eehl seehs-tEh-mah nehl eh-lah-boh-rah-tOh-reh)*
decanter	la caraffa	*(kah-rAhf-fah)*
deductible	il detraibile	*(deh-trah-EEh-beeh-leh)*
deduction	la detrazione	*(deh-trah-tsyOh-neh)*
deed	l'atto	*(Aht-toh)*

deed of sale	l'atto di vendita	*(Aht-toh deeh vEhn-deeh-tah)*
deed of transfer	l'atto di passaggio, l'atto di trasferimento	*(Aht-toh deeh pahs-sAhj-joh), (Aht-toh deeh trahs-feh-reeh-mEhn-toh)*
deed of trust	l'atto fiduciario	*(Aht-toh feeh-dooh-chAh-reeh-oh)*
default (v)	venire meno agli obblighi	*(veh-nEEh-reh mEh-noh ah-lyeeh Ohb-bleeh-geeh)*
defective	difettoso	*(deeh-feht-tOh-zoh)*
deferred annuities	le rendite differite	*(rEhn-deeh-teh deehf-feh-rEEh-teh)*
deferred assets	gli attivi differiti	*(aht-tEEh-veeh deehf-feh-rEEh-teeh)*
deferred charges	gli oneri differiti	*(Oh-neh-reeh deehf-feh-rEEh-teeh)*
deferred delivery	le consegne differite	*(kohn-sEh-nyeh deehf-feh-rEEh-teh)*
deferred income	il reddito differito	*(rEhd-deeh-toh deehf-feh-rEEh-toh)*
deferred liabilities	le responsabilità differite, le passività differite	*(rehs-pohn-sah-beeh-leeh-tAh deehf-feh-rEEh-teh), (pahs-seeh-veeh-tAh deehf-feh-rEEh-teh)*
deferred tax	le tasse differite	*(tAhs-seh deehf-feh-rEEh-teh)*
deficit	il deficit, il disavanzo, l'ammanco	*(dEh-feeh-cheeht), (deeh-zah-vAhn-tsoh)*
deficit financing	il ricorso al prestito per finanziare un'attività	*(reeh-kOhr-soh ahl prEhs-teeh-toh pehr feeh-nahn-tsyAh-reh oohn aht-teeh-veeh-Tah)*
deficit spending	la spesa fatta mentre la ditta è in passivo	*(spEh-zah fAht-tah mEhn-treh lah dEEht-tah eh eehn pahs-Seeh-voh)*
deflation	la deflazione	*(deh-flah-tsyOh-neh)*
defroster	lo sbrinatore	*(zbreeh-nah-tOh-reh)*
degree	il grado	*(grAh-doh)*
delay	il ritardo	*(reeh-tAhr-doh)*
delinquent account	il conto moroso	*(kOhn-toh moh-rOh-zoh)*

delivered price	il prezzo alla consegna	*(prEhts-tsoh ahl-lah kohn-sEh-nyah)*
delivery	la consegna	*(kohn-sEh-nyah)*
delivery date	la data di consegna	*(dAh-tah deeh kohn-sEh-nyah)*
delivery notice	la notifica di consegna	*(noh-tEEh-feeh-kah deeh kohn-sEh-nyah)*
delivery points	i punti di consegna	*(pOOhn-teeh deeh kohn-sEh-nyah)*
delivery price	il prezzo di consegna	*(prEhts-tsoh deeh kohn-sEh-nyah)*
demand (v)	richiedere	*(reeh-kyEh-deh-reh)*
demand	la richiesta	*(reeh-kyEhs-tah)*
demand deposit	il deposito a richiesta, il deposito in conto corrente	*(deh-pOh-zeeh-toh ah reeh-kyEhs-tah), (deh-pOh-zeeh-toh eehn kOhn-toh kohr-rEhn-teh)*
demand line of credit	la linea di credito a richiesta	*(lEEh-neh-ah deeh krEh-deeh-toh ah reeh-kyEhs-tah)*
demographic	il demografico	*(deh-moh-grAh-feeh-koh)*
demotion	la demozione	*(deh-moh-tsyOh-neh)*
demurrage (maritime)	la controstallia	*(kohn-troh-stAhl-lyah)*
demurrage	il ritardo	*(reeh-tAhr-doh)*
density	la densità	*(dehn-seeh-tAh)*
department	il reparto	*(reh-pAhr-toh)*
department store	il grande magazzino	*(grAhn-deh mah-gahds-dsEEh-noh)*
depletion accounting	la contabilità di riduzione	*(kohn-tah-beeh-leeh-tAh deeh reeh-dooh-tsyOh-neh)*
depletion control	il controllo della riduzione	*(kohn-trOhl-loh dehl-lah reeh-dooh-tsyOh-neh)*
deposit	il deposito	*(deh-pOh-zeeh-toh)*
deposit account	il conto di deposito	*(kOhn-toh deeh deh-pOh-zeeh-toh)*
deposit, bank	il deposito bancario	*(deh-pOh-zeeh-toh bahn-kAh-reeh-oh)*
depository	il deposito	*(deh-pOh-zeeh-toh)*

depreciation	il deprezzamento, l'ammortamento	*(deh-prehts-tsah-mEhn-toh), (ahm-mohr-tah-mEhn-toh)*
depreciation allowance	il fondo di ammortamento	*(fOhn-doh deeh ahm-mohr-tah-mEhn-toh)*
depreciation of currency	il deprezzamento della valuta	*(deh-prehts-tsah-mEhn-toh dehl-lah vah-lOOh-tah)*
depreciation, accelerated	l'ammortamento accelerato	*(ahm-mohr-tah-mEhn-toh ahch-cheh-leh-rAh-toh)*
depreciation, accrued	l'ammortamento maturato	*(ahm-mohr-tah-mEhn-toh mah-tooh-rAh-toh)*
depression	la depressione	*(deh-prehs-syOh-neh)*
deputy chairman	il vice presidente	*(vEEh-cheh preh-zeeh-dEhn-teh)*
deputy manager	il vice amministratore, il vice dirigente	*(vEEh-cheh ahm-meeh-neehs-trah-tOh-reh), (vEEh-cheh deeh-reeh-jEhn-teh)*
design (v)	disegnare	*(deeh-zeh-nyAh-reh)*
design engineering	la progettazione d'impianti, la progettazione industriale	*(proh-jeht-tah-tsyOh-neh deehm-pyAhnteeh), (proh-jeht-tah-tsyOh-neh eehn-doohs-tryAh-leh))*
designer	lo stilista	*(steeh-lEEhs-tah)*
dessert plate	il piatto per dolci	*(pyAht-toh pehr dOhl-cheeh)*
detector	la valvola rivelatrice	*(vAhlvoh-lah reeh-veh-lah-trEEh-cheh)*
devaluation	la svalutazione	*(zvah-looh-tah-tsyOh-neh)*
diabetes	il diabete	*(deeh-ah-bEh-teh)*
diesel	il diesel	*(dEE-zl)*
differential, price	la differenziale dei prezzi	*(deehf-feh-rehn-tsyAh-leh deh-eeh prEhts-tseeh)*
differential, tariff	la tariffa differenziale	*(tah-rEEhf-fah deehf-feh-rehn-tsyAh-leh)*
differential, wage	la differenza salariale, il differenziale di stipendio	*(deehf-feh-rEhn-tsah sah-lah-ryAh-leh), (deehf-feh-rehn-tsyAh-leh deeh steeh-pEhn-dyoh)*

digital	digitale	*(deeh-jeeh-tAh-leh)*
digital computer	l'elaboratore a sistema digitale, l'elaboratore digitale	*(eh-lah-boh-rah-tOh-reh ah seehs-tEh-mah deeh-jeeh-tAh-leh), (eh-lah-boh-rah-tOh-reh deeh-jeeh-tAh-leh)*
digitalis	il digitalis	*(deeh-jeeh-tAh-lees)*
dilution of equity	la diluizione del capitale azionario, la diluizione del capitale netto	*(deeh-looh-eeh-tsyOh-neh dehl kah-peeh-tAh-leh ah-tsyoh-nAh-reeh-oh), (deeh-looh-eeh-tsyOh-neh dehl kah-peeh-tAh-leh nEht-toh)*
dilution of labor	la diluizione della manodopera, l'assorbimento del personale non specializzato	*(deeh-looh-eeh-tsyOh-neh dehl-lah mah-noh-dOh-peh-rah), (ahs-sohr-beeh-mEhn-toh dehl pehr-soh-nAh-leh nohn speh-chah-leehds-dsAh-toh)*
diode	il diodo	*(dEEh-oh-doh)*
direct access storage	l'immagazzinaggio con accesso diretto	*(eehm-mah-gahds-dseeh-nAhj-joh kohn ahch-chEhs-soh deeh-rEht-toh)*
direct cost	il costo diretto	*(kOhs-toh deeh-rEht-toh)*
direct expenses	le spese dirette	*(spEh-zeh deeh-rEht-teh)*
direct investment	l'investimento diretto	*(eehn-vehs-teeh-mEhn-toh deeh-rEht-toh)*
direct labor	la manodopera diretta	*(mah-noh-dOh-peh-rah deeh-rEht-tah)*
direct mail	la pubblicità diretta	*(poohb-bleeh-cheeh-tAh deeh-rEht-tah)*
direct papers	le obbligazioni dirette	*(ohb-bleeh-gah-tsyOh-neeh deeh-rEht-teh)*
direct quotation	la citazione diretta	*(cheeh-tah-tsyOh-neh deeh-rEht-tah)*
direct selling	la vendita diretta	*(vEhn-deeh-tah deeh-rEht-tah)*
director	il direttore	*(deeh-reht-tOh-reh)*
disbursement	il pagamento	*(pah-gah-mEhn-toh)*
disc	il disco	*(dEEhs-koh)*
discharge (v)	scaricare	*(skah-reeh-kAh-reh)*
discount (v)	scontare	*(skohn-tAh-reh)*

D

discount	lo sconto	*(skOhn-toh)*
discount rate	tasso di sconto	*(tAhs-soh deeh skOhn-toh)*
discount securities	i titoli scontati	*(tEEh-toh-leeh skohn-tAh-teeh)*
discounted cash flow	il reddito futuro scontato al valore attuale	*(rEhd-deeh-toh fooh-tOOh-roh skohn-tAh-toh ahl vah-lOh-reh aht-twAh-leh)*
discretionary account	il fondo discrezionario	*(fOhn-doh deehs-kreh-tsyoh-nAh-reeh-oh)*
discretionary order	l'ordine discrezionale	*(Ohr-deeh-neh deehs-kreh-tsyoh-nAh-leh)*
disease	la malattia	*(mah-laht-tEEh-ah)*
dish	il piatto	*(pyAht-toh)*
disincentive	il disincentivo	*(deehs-eehn-chehn-tEEh-voh)*
disk	il dischetto	*(deehs-kEht-toh)*
dispatch	l'invio, la spedizione	*(eehn-vEEh-oh), (speh-deeh-tsyOh-neh)*
displacement	la cilindrata	*(cheeh-leehn-drAh-tah)*
disposable income	il reddito disponibile	*(rEhd-deeh-toh deehs-poh-nEEh-beeh-leh)*
dispute (v)	disputare	*(deehs-pooh-tAh-reh)*
dispute	la disputa	*(dEEhs-pooh-tah)*
dispute, labor	la disputa di lavoro, la disputa sindacale	*(dEEhs-pooh-tah deeh lah-vOh-roh), (dEEhs-pooh-tah seehn-dah-kAh-leh)*
distillation	la distillazione	*(deehs-teehl-lah-tsyOh-neh)*
distribution costs	i costi di distribuzione	*(kOhs-teeh deeh deehs-treeh-booh-tsyOh-neh)*
distribution network	la rete di distribuzione	*(rEh-teh deeh deehs-treeh-booh-tsyOh-neh)*
distribution policy	la politica di distribuzione	*(poh-lEEh-teeh-kah deeh deehs-treeh-booh-tsyOh-neh)*
distribution, channel of	il canale di distribuzione	*(kah-nAh-leh deeh deehs-treeh-booh-tsyOh-neh)*
distributor	il distributore	*(deehs-treeh-booh-tOh-reh)*
diuretic	il diuretico	*(deeh-ooh-rEh-teeh-koh)*

D

diversification	la diversificazione	*(deeh-vehr-seeh-feeh-kah-tsyOh-neh)*
divestment	la spogliazione, la vendita	*(spoh-lyah-tsyOh-neh), (vEhn-deeh-tah)*
dividend	il dividendo	*(deeh-veeh-dEhn-doh)*
dividend yield	il rendimento del dividendo	*(rehn-deeh-mEhn-toh dehl deeh-veeh-dEhn-doh)*
division of labor	la divisione del lavoro	*(deeh-veeh-zyOh-neh dehl lah-vOh-roh)*
dock (ship's receipt)	la ricevuta del custode del molo	*(reeh-cheh-vOOh-tah dehl koohs-tOh-deh dehl mOh-loh)*
dock handling charges	le spese di ormeggio	*(spEh-zeh dohr-mEhj-joh)*
document	il documento	*(doh-kooh-mEhn-toh)*
dollar cost averaging	la media del costo in dollari	*(mEh-deeh-ah dehl kOhs-toh eehn dOhl-lah-reeh)*
domestic bill	la fattura nazionale	*(faht-tOOh-rah nah-tsyoh-nAh-leh)*
domestic corporation	la ditta nazionale	*(dEEt-tah nah-tsyoh-nAh-leh)*
door-to-door (sales)	porta-a-porta (vendite)	*(pOhr-tah ah pOhr-tah vEhn-deeh-teh)*
dose	la dose	*(dOh-zeh)*
double dealing	l'inganno	*(eehn-gAhn-noh)*
double pricing	fissare due prezzi	*(feehs-sAh-reh dOOh-eh prEhts-tseeh)*
double taxation	la doppia tassazione	*(dOhp-pyah tahs-sah-tsyOh-neh)*
double time	il lavoro straordinario pagato il doppio, la doppia paga per gli straordinari	*(lah-vOh-roh strah-orh-deeh-nAh-reeh-oh pah-gAh-toh dOhp-pyoh), (dOhp-pyah pAh-gah pehr lyeeh strah-orh-deeh-nAh-reeh)*
double-entry bookkeeping	la contabilità a partita doppia	*(kohn-tah-beeh-leeh-tAh ah pahr-tEEh-tah dOhp-pyah)*
down payment	l'acconto, il deposito, la caparra	*(ahk-kOhn-toh), (deh-pOh-zeeh-toh), (kah-pAhr-rah)*

down period	il periodo di tempo inutiliz- zabile, la fase negativa	*(peh-rEEh-oh-doh deeh tEhm-poh eehn-ooh-teeh- leehds-dsAh-beeh-leh), (fAh-zeh neh-gah-tEEh- vah)*
down the line	in ogni caso	*(eehn Oh-nyeeh kAh-zoh)*
downswing	il ribasso	*(reeh-bAhs-soh)*
downtime	il periodo di tempo durante il quale l'elaboratore rimane inutilizzabile	*(peh-rEEh-oh-doh deeh tEhm-poh dooh-rAhn-teh eehl kwAh-leh leh-lah- boh-rah-tOh-reh reeh- mAh-neh eehn-ooh-teeh- leehds-dsAh-beeh-leh)*
downturn	il ribasso	*(reeh-bAhs-soh)*
draft	la tratta	*(trAht-tah)*
drape (v)	drappeggiare	*(drahp-pehj-jAh-reh)*
draw down (v)	ridurre l'inventario	*(reeh-dOOhr-reh leehn- vehn-tAh-reeh-oh)*
drawback	il ristorno, lo svantaggio	*(reehs-tOhr-noh), (zvahn- tAhj-joh)*
drawee	il trattario	*(traht-tAh-reeh-oh)*
drawer	il traente	*(trah-Ehn-teh)*
drayage	il trasporto	*(trahs-pOhr-toh)*
dregs	i rimasugli	*(reeh-mah-sOOh-lyeeh)*
dress	il vestito	*(vehs-tEEh-toh)*
drink	la bevanda	*(beh-vAhn-dah)*
driver	l'autista	*(ah-ooh-tEEhs-tah)*
drop	la goccia	*(gOhch-chah)*
drop shipment	la spedizione fatta diretta- mente al dettagliante	*(speh-deeh-tsyOh-neh fAht- tah deeh-reht-tah-mEhn- teh ahl deht-tah-lyAhn- teh)*
drug	il farmaco, la droga	*(fAhr-mah-koh), (drOh-gah)*
drugstore	la farmacia	*(fahr-mah-chEEh-ah)*
dry cargo	il carico secco	*(KAR-ee-ko sEhk-koh)*
dry goods	i beni solidi	*(beh-nee soh-lee-dee)*
dry wine	il vino secco	*(vEEh-noh sEhk-koh)*
dummy	il menabò	*(meh-nah-bOh)*

dumping (goods in foreign market)	il "dumping"	*(duhmpeeng)*
dun (v)	sollecitare pagamento	*(sohl-leh-cheeh-tAh-reh pah-gah-mEhn-toh)*
dunnage	il fondo della stiva	*(fOhn-doh dehl-lah stEEh-vah)*
duopoly	il duopolio	*(dooh-oh-pOh-leeh-oh)*
durable goods	i beni durevoli	*(bEh-neeh dooh-rEh-voh-leeh)*
duress	la pressione	*(prehs-syOh-neh)*
duty ad valorem	il dazio ad valorem	*(dAh-tsyoh ad vah-lOh-rehm)*
duty	il dazio	*(dAh-tsyoh)*
duty, anti-dumping	la tariffa protettiva, la tariffa "anti-dumping"	*(tah-rEEhf-fah proht-teht-tEEh-vah)*
duty, combination	il dazio combinato, la tariffa combinata	*(dAh-tsyoh kohm-beeh-nAh-toh), (tah-rEEhf-fah kohm-beeh-nAh-tah)*
duty, countervailing	la tariffa controvalente	*(tah-rEEhf-fah kohn-troh-vah-lEhn-teh)*
duty, export	la tariffa d'esportazione	*(tah-rEEhf-fah dehs-pohr-tah-tsyOh-neh)*
duty, remission	la remissione dell'imposta	*(reh-meehs-syOh-neh dehl-leehm-pOhs-tah)*
duty, specific	il dazio specifico, l'imposta specifica	*(dAh-tsyoh speh-chEEh-feeh-koh), (eehm-pOhs-tah speh-chEEh-feeh-kah)*
dutyfree	esente da dazio	*(eh-zEhn-teh dah dAh-tsyoh)*
dye (v)	tingere	*(tEEhn-jeh-reh)*
dynamics, group	la dinamica del gruppo	*(deeh-nAh-meeh-kah dehl grOOhp-poh)*
dynamics, market	la dinamica del mercato	*deeh-nAh-meeh-kah dehl mehr-kAh-toh)*
dynamics, product	la dinamica del prodotto	*(deeh-nAh-meeh-kah dehl proh-dOht-toh)*

E

earmark (v)	contrassegnare, specificare	*(kohn-trahs-seh-nyAh-reh), (speh-cheeh-feeh-kAh-reh)*
earnings	i guadagni	*(gwah-dAh-nyeeh)*
earnings on assets	gli utili sugli attivi	*(OOh-teeh-leeh sooh-lyeeh aht-tEEh-veeh)*
earnings per share	gli utili per azione	*(OOh-teeh-leeh pehr ah-tsyOh-neh)*
earnings performance	il rendimento sui guadagni	*(rehn-deeh-mEhn-toh sooh-eeh gwah-dAh-nyeeh)*
earnings report	la relazione sugli utili	*(reh-lah-tsyOh-neh sooh-lyeeh OOh-teeh-leeh)*
earnings yield	la rendita sui guadagni	*(rEhn-deeh-tah sooh-eeh gwah-dAh-nyeeh)*
earnings, retained	i profitti ritenuti, i guadagni ritenuti, gli utili ritenuti	*(proh-fEEht-teeh reeh-teh-nOOh-teeh), (gwah-dAh-nyeeh reeh-teh-nOOh-teeh), (OOh-teeh-leeh reeh-teh-nOOh-teeh)*
earthenware	la terraglia	*(tehr-rAh-lyah)*
econometrics	l'econometria	*(eh-koh-noh-meh-trEEh-ah)*
economic	economico	*(eh-koh-nOh-meeh-koh)*
economic indicators	gli indicatori economici	*(eehn-deeh-kah-tOh-reeh eh-koh-nOh-meeh-cheeh)*
economic life	la vita economica	*(vEEh-tah eh-koh-nOh-meeh-kah)*
economic order quantity	la quantità per un ordine economico	*(kwahn-teeh-tAh pehr oohn Ohr-deeh-neh eh-koh-nOh-meeh-koh)*
economics	l'economia	*(eh-koh-noh-mEEh-ah)*
economy of scale	l'economia di scala	*(eh-koh-noh-mEEh-ah deeh skAh-lah)*
edit (v)	redigere	*(reh-dEEh-jeh-reh)*
edition	il numero	*(nOOh-meh-roh)*
editor	il redattore	*(reh-daht-tOh-reh)*
effective yield	il rendimento effettivo	*(rehn-deeh-mEhn-toh ehf-feht-tEEh-voh)*
efficiency	l'efficienza	*(ehf-feeh-chEhn-tsah)*

elasticity (of supply or demand)	l'elasticità (dell'offerta e della domanda)	*(eh-lahs-teeh-cheeh-tAh dehl ohf-fEhr-tah eh dehl-lah doh-mAhn-dah)*
election	l'elezione	*(eh-leh-tsyOh-neh)*
electric arc furnace	l'altoforno ad arco elettrico	*(ahl-toh-fOhr-noh ad Ahr-koh eh-lEht-treeh-koh)*
electrical engineering	l'ingegneria elettrica	*(eehn-jeh-nyeh-rEEh-ah eh-lEht-treeh-kah)*
electricity	l'elettricità	*(eh-leht-treeh-cheeh-tAh)*
electrode	l'elettrodo	*(eh-lEht-troh-doh)*
electrodes	gli elettrodi	*(eh-lEht-troh-deeh)*
electrolysis	l'elettrolisi	*(eh-leht-trOh-leeh-zeeh)*
electrolytic process	la procedura elettrolitica	*(proh-cheh-dOOh-rah eh-leht-troh-lEEh-teeh-kah)*
electron	l'elettrone	*(eh-leht-trOh-neh)*
electronic	elettronico	*(eh-leht-trOh-neeh-koh)*
electronic whiteboard	la tavola elettronica per comandi	*(tAh-voh-la eh-leht-trOh-neeh-kah pehr koh-mAhn-deeh)*
electrostatic	elettrostatico	*(eh-leht-troh-stAh-teeh-koh)*
elegance	l'eleganza	*(eh-leh-gAhn-tsah)*
element	l'elemento	*(eh-leh-mEhn-toh)*
embargo	l'embargo	*(ehm-bAhr-goh)*
embezzlement	l'appropriazione indebita	*(ahp-proh-pryah-tsyOh-neh)*
employee	l'impiegato	*(eehm-pyeh-gAh-toh)*
employee counseling	l'assistenza al personale	*(ahs-seehs-tEhn-tsah ahl pehr-soh-nAh-leh)*
employee relations	le relazioni con il personale	*(reh-lah-tsyOh-neeh kohn eehl pehr-soh-nAh-leh)*
employment agency	l'agenzia per la ricerca del personale	*(ah-jehn-tsEEh-ah pehr lah reeh-chEhr-kah dehl pehr-soh-nAh-leh)*
encumbrances (liens, liabilities)	il gravame	*(grah-vAh-meh)*
end of period	la fine del periodo	*(fEEh-neh dehl peh-rEEh-oh-doh)*
end product	il prodotto finale	*(proh-dOht-toh feeh-nAh-leh)*

E

end-use certificate	il certificato attestante l'uso definitivo del prodotto	*(chehr-teeh-feeh-kAh-toh aht-tehs-tAhn-teh lOOh-zoh deh-feeh-neeh-tEEh-voh dehl proh-dOht-toh)*
endorsee	il giratario	*(geeh-rah-tAh-reeh-oh)*
endorsement	la girata	*(jeeh-rAh-tah)*
endorser	il girante	*(jeeh-rAhn-teh)*
endowment	la dotazione	*(doh-tah-tsyOh-neh)*
engine	il motore	*(moh-tOh-reh)*
engineer	l'ingegnere	*(eehn-jeh-nyEh-reh)*
engineering	l'ingegneria	*(eehn-jeh-nyeh-rEEh-ah)*
engineering and design department	il reparto progettazione e stilismo	*(reh-pAhr-toh proh-jeht-tah-tsyOh-neh eh steeh-lEEhz-moh)*
engineering, design	la progettazione d'impianti, la progettazione industriale	*(proh-jeht-tah-tsyOh-neh deehm-pyAhn-teeh) (proh-jeht-tah-tsyOh-neh eehn-doohs-tryAh-leh)*
engineering, industrial	l'ingegneria industriale, la progettazione industriale	*(eehn-jeh-nyeh-rEEh-ah eehn-doohs-tryAh-leh), (proh-jeht-tah-tsyOh-neh eehn-doohs-tryAh-leh)*
engineering, systems	la progettazione dei sistemi di elaborazione	*(proh-jeht-tah-tsyOh-neh deh-eeh seehs-tEh-meeh deeh eh-lah-boh-rah-tsyOh-neh)*
engineering, value	la progettazione utilizzante costi più bassi tra costi alternativi per espletare una certa attività	*(proh-jeht-tah-tsyOh-neh ooh-teeh-leehds-dsAhn-teh kOhs-teeh pyOOh bAhs-seeh trah kOsh-teeh ahl-tehr-nah-tEEh-veeh pehr ehs-pleh-tAh-reh ooh-nah chEhr-tah aht-teeh-veeh-tAh)*
engrave (v)	incidere	*(eehn-chEEh-deh-reh)*
enlarge (v)	ingrandire	*(eehn-grahn-dEEh-reh)*
enterprise	l'impresa	*(eehm-prEh-zah)*
entrepreneur	l'imprenditore	*(eehm-prehn-deeh-tOh-reh)*
entry permit	il permesso d'entrata, la dichiarazione d'entrata	*(pehr-mEhs-soh dehn-trAh-tah), (deeh-kyah-rah-tsyOh-neh dehn-trAh-tah)*

E

entry, cash	l'annotazione di movimento di contanti, la registrazione del movimento di cassa	*(ahn-noh-tah-tsyOh-neh deeh moh-veeh-mEhn-toh deeh kAhs-sah)*
entry, debit	la nota di debito, la registrazione a debito	*(nOh-tah deeh dEh-beeh-toh), (reh-jeehs-trah-tsyOh-neh ah dEh-beeh-toh)*
entry, ledger	l'entrata nel libro mastro, l'entrata sul registro	*(ehn-trAh-tah nehl lEEh-broh mAhs-troh), (ehn-trAh-tah soohl reh-jEEhs-troh)*
enzyme	l'enzima	*(ehn-dsEEh-mah)*
equal pay for equal work	la stessa paga per lo stesso lavoro	*(stEhs-sah pAh-gah pehr loh stEhs-soh lah-vOh-roh)*
equipment	gli attrezzi, l'attrezzatura, gli impianti e macchinari	*(aht-trEhts-tseeh), (aht-trehts-tsah-tOOh-rah), (eehm-pyAhn-teeh eh mahk-keeh-nAh-reeh)*
equipment leasing	l'affitto degli attrezzi	*(ahf-fEEt-toh deh-lyeeh aht-trEhts-tseeh)*
equity	l'equità, la giustizia, il capitale azionario	*(eh-kweeh-tAh), (joohs-tEEh-tsyah), (kah-peeh-tAh-leh ah-tsyoh-nAh-reeh-oh)*
equity investments	gli investimenti azionari	*(eehn-vehs-teeh-mEhn-teeh ah-tsyoh-nAh-reeh)*
equity share	la parte dovuta per il capitale netto	*(pAhr-teh doh-vOOh-tah pehr eehl kah-peeh-tAh-leh nEht-toh)*
equity, dilution of	la diluizione del capitale azionario, la diluizione del capitale netto	*(deeh-looh-eeh-tsyOh-neh dehl kah-peeh-tAh-leh ah-tsyoh-nAh-reeh-oh), (deeh-looh-eeh-tsyOh-neh dehl kah-peeh-tAh-leh nEht-toh)*
equity, return on	il reddito sul capitale netto	*(rEhd-deeh-toh soohl kah-peeh-tAh-leh nEht-toh)*
ergonomics	l'ergonometrica	*(ehr-goh-noh-mEh-treeh-kah)*
error	l'errore	*(ehr-rOh-reh)*
escalator clause	il comma della scala mobile	*(kOhm-mah dehl-lah skAh-lah mOh-beeh-leh)*

escape clause	la clausola d'uscita	*(klAhw-zoh-lah dooh-shEEh-tah)*
escheat	la proprietà incamerata	*(proh-pryeh-tAh eehn-kah-meh-rAh-tah)*
escrow	il deposito presso terzi	*(deh-pOh-zeeh-toh prEhs-soh tEhr-tseeh)*
escrow account	il conto depositato presso terzi	*(kOhn-toh deh-poh-zeeh-tAh-toh prEhs-soh tEhr-tseeh)*
espresso cup	la tazzina da espresso	*(tahts-tsEEh-nah dah ehs-prEhs-soh)*
estate	il patrimonio	*(pah-treeh-mOh-neeh-oh)*
estate (or chateau)	la fattoria	*(faht-toh-rEEh-ah)*
estate agent	l'agente patrimoniale	*(ah-jEhn-teh pah-treeh-mOh-nyAh-leh)*
estate bottled	imbottigliato all'origine	*(eehm-boht-teeh-lyAh-toh ahl oh-rEEh-jeeh-neh)*
estate tax	l'imposta patrimoniale	*(eehm-pOhs-tah pah-treeh-mOh-nyAh-leh)*
estimate (v)	stimare	*(steeh-mAh-reh)*
estimate	la stima	*(stEEh-mah)*
estimate, sales	la stima delle vendite	*(stEEh-mah dehl-leh vEhn-deeh-teh)*
estimated price	il prezzo previsto	*(prEhts-tsoh preh-vEEhs-toh)*
estimated time of arrival	l'ora d'arrivo prevista	*(Oh-rah dahr-rEEh-voh preh-vEEhs-tah)*
estimated time of departure	l'ora di partenza prevista	*(Oh-rah deeh pahr-tEhn-tsah preh-vEEhs-tah)*
ethane	l'etano	*(eh-tAh-noh)*
ether	l'etere	*(Eh-teh-reh)*
Eurobond	l'euro-obbligazione	*(eh-ooh-roh-ohb-bleeh-gah-tsyOh-neh)*
Eurocurrency	l'eurovaluta	*(eh-ooh-roh-vah-lOOh-tah)*
Eurodollar	l'eurodollaro	*(eh-ooh-roh-dOhl-lah-roh)*
evaluation	la valutazione	*(vah-looh-tah-tsyOh-neh)*
evaluation, job	la valutazione del lavoro	*(vah-looh-tah-tsyOh-neh dehl lah-vOh-roh)*
evaporation	l'evaporazione	*(eh-vah-poh-rah-tsyOh-neh)*

ex dividend	senza dividendo	*(sEhn-tsah deeh-veeh-dEhn-doh)*
ex dock	franco porto, ex molo	*(frAhn-koh pOhr-toh), (ex mOh-loh)*
ex factory	franco fabbrica	*(frAhn-koh fAhb-breeh-kah)*
ex mill	franco mulino	*(frAhn-koh mooh-lEEh-noh)*
ex mine	franco miniera	*(frAhn-koh meeh-nyEh-rah)*
ex rights	ex diritti	*(ex deeh-rEEht-teeh)*
ex ship	franco nave	*(frAhn-koh nAh-veh)*
ex warehouse	franco magazzino	*(frAhn-koh mah-gahds-dsEEh-noh)*
ex works	franco officina	*(frAhn-koh ohf-feeh-chEEh-nah)*
exchange (stock, commodity)	la borsa	*(bOhr-sah)*
exchange (v)	scambiare	*(skahm-byAh-reh)*
exchange control	il controllo valutario	*(kohn-tRohl-loh vah-looh-tAh-reeh-oh)*
exchange discount	lo sconto sul cambio	*(skOhn-toh soohl kAhm-byoh)*
exchange loss	la perdita sul cambio	*(pEhr-deeh-tah soohl kAhm-byoh)*
exchange rate	il tasso di cambio	*(tAhs-soh deeh kAhm-byoh)*
exchange risk	il rischio sul cambio	*(rEEhs-kyoh soohl kAhm-byoh)*
exchange value	il controvalore	*(kOhn-troh-vah-lOh-reh)*
excise duty	l'imposta sui consumi	*(eehm-pOhs-tah sooh-eeh kohn-sOOh-meeh)*
excise license	il permesso amministrativo per vendere beni di consumo	*(pehr-mEhs-soh ahm-meeh-neehs-trah-tEEh-voh pehr vEhn-deh-reh bEh-neeh deeh kohn-sOOh-moh)*
excise tax	l'imposta sui consumi, la tassa sul consumo	*(eehm-pOhs-tah sooh-eeh kohn-sOOh-meeh), (tAhs-sah soohl kohn-sOOh-moh)*
executive	il dirigente	*(deeh-reeh-jEhn-teh)*
executive board	il consiglio dirigenziale	*(kohn-sEEh-lyoh deeh-reeh-jehn-tsyAh-leh)*

E

executive committee	il comitato esecutivo	*(koh-meeh-tAh-toh eh-zeh-kooh-tEEh-voh)*
executive compensation	il compenso dirigenziale	*(kohm-pEhn-soh deeh-reeh-jehn-tsyAh-leh)*
executive director	il dirigente superiore	*(deeh-reeh-jEhn-teh sooh-peh-ryOh-reh)*
executive search	la ricerca di personale dirigenziale	*(reeh-chEhr-kah deeh pehr-soh-nAh-leh deeh-reeh-jehn-tsyAh-leh)*
executive secretary	la segretaria superiore	*(seh-greh-tAh-reeh-ah sooh-peh-ryOh-reh)*
executive, chief	il direttore generale	*(deeh-reht-tOh-reh jeh-neh-rAh-leh)*
executive, line	il dirigente di linea	*(deeh-reeh-jEhn-teh deeh lEEh-neh-ah)*
executor	l'esecutore, il testamentario	*(eh-zeh-kooh-tOh-reh), (tehs-tah-mEhn-tAh-reeh-oh)*
exemption	l'esenzione	*(eh-zehn-tsyOh-neh)*
exhaust	lo scarico, lo scappamento	*(skAh-reeh-koh), (skahp-pah-mEhn-toh)*
expected results	i risultati previsti	*(reeh-zoohl-tAh-teeh preh-vEEhs-teeh)*
expenditure	la spesa	*(spEh-zah)*
expense account	il listino di spese rimborsabili	*(leehs-tEEh-noh deeh spEh-zeh reehm-bohr-sAh-beeh-leeh)*
expenses	le spese	*(spEh-zeh)*
expenses, direct	le spese dirette	*(spEh-zeh deeh-rEht-teh)*
expenses, indirect	le spese indirette	*(spEh-zeh eehn-deeh-rEht-teh)*
expenses, running	le spese correnti, le spese operative	*(spEh-zeh kohr-rEhn-teeh), (spEh-zeh oh-peh-rah-tEEh-veh)*
expenses, shipping	le spese di spedizione, le spese di trasporto	*(spEh-zeh deeh speh-deeh-tsyOh-neh), (spEh-zeh deeh trahs-pOhr-toh)*
experiment	l'esperimento, la prova	*(ehs-peh-reeh-mEhn-toh), (prOh-vah)*
expiry date	la data di scadenza	*(dAh-tah deeh skah-dEhn-tsah)*
export (v)	esportare	*(ehs-pohr-tAh-reh)*

E

export agent	l'esportatore su commissione	*(ehs-pohr-tah-tOh-reh sooh kohm-meehs-syOh-neh)*
export credit	il credito all'esportazione	*(krEh-deeh-toh ahl ehs-pohr-tah-tsyOh-neh)*
export duty	la tariffa d'esportazione	*(tah-rEEhf-fah deeh ehs-pohr-tah-tsyOh-neh)*
export entry	la dichiarazione d'esportazione	*(deeh-kyah-rah-tsyOh-neh dehs-pohr-tah-tsyOh-neh)*
export house	la ditta che tratta esportazioni	*(dEEht-tah keh trAht-tah ehs-pohr-tah-tsyOh-neeh)*
export manager	il responsabile delle esportazioni	*(rehs-pohn-sAh-beeh-leh dehl-leh ehs-pohr-tah-tsyOh-neeh)*
export middleman	l'intermediario per l'esportazione	*(eehn-tehr-meh-dyAh-reeh-oh pehr lehs-pohr-tah-tsyOh-neh)*
export permit	il permesso d'esportazione	*(pehr-mEhs-soh dehs-pohr-tah-tsyOh-neh)*
export quota	la quota d'esportazione	*(kwOh-tah dehs-pohr-tah-tsyOh-neh)*
export regulations	le normative per l'esportazione	*(nohr-mah-tEEh-veh pehr ehs-pohr-tah-tsyOh-neh)*
export sales contract	il contratto di vendita per l'esportazione	*(kohn-trAht-toh deeh vEhn-deeh-tah pehr lehs-pohr-tah-tsyOh-neh)*
export tax	l'imposta d'esportazione	*(eehm-pOhs-tah dehs-pohr-tah-tsyOh-neh)*
export, for	per esportazione	*(pehr ehs-pohr-tah-tsyOh-neh)*
export-import bank	la banca import-export	*(bAhn-kah)*
expropriation	l'esproprio	*(ehs-prOh-prreeh-oh)*
extra dividend	il dividendo supplementare	*(deeh-veeh-dEhn-doh soohp-pleh-mehn-tAh-reh)*
eyedrop	il collirio	*(kohl-lEEh-reeh-oh)*
eyeglass case	il portaocchiali	*(pohr-tah-ohk-kyAh-leeh)*

E

F

fabric	il tessuto	*(tehs-sOOh-toh)*
face value	il valore dichiarato, il valore riportato	*(vah-lOh-reh deeh-kyah-rAh-toh), (vah-lOh-reh reeh-pohr-tAh-toh)*
facilities	i servizi, i facilitazione, gl'impianti	*(sehr-vEEhts-tseeh), (fah-cheeh-leeh-tah-tsyOh-neh), (eehm-pyAhn-teeh)*
fact sheet	il foglio di dati	*fOh-lyeeh deeh dAh-teeh)*
factor	il fattore, il "factor"	*(faht-tOh-reh)*
factor analysis	l'analisi dei fattori	*(ah-nAh-leeh-zeeh deh-eeh faht-tOh-reeh)*
factor rating	la stima da parte del factor	*(stEEh-mah dah pAhr-teh dehl faht-tOh-reh)*
factor, cost	il fattore dei costi	*(faht-tOh-reh deh-eeh kOhs-teeh)*
factor, load	il fattore del ricarico	*(faht-tOh-reh dehl reeh-kAh-reeh-koh)*
factor, profit	il fattore degli utili, il fattore dei profitti	*(faht-tOh-reh deh-lyeeh OOh-teeh-leeh), (faht-tOh-reh deh-eeh proh-fEEht-teeh)*
factory	la fabbrica	*(fAhb-breeh-kah)*
factory overhead	i costi fissi d'azienda	*(kOhs-teeh fEEhs-seeh dah-dsyEhn-dah)*
fail (v)	fallire	*(fahl-lEEh-reh)*
failure	il fallimento	*(fahl-leeh-mEhn-toh)*
fair market value	il valore di mercato	*(vah-lOh-reh deeh mehr-kAh-toh)*
fair return	il rendimento competitivo agli investimenti alternativi	*(rehn-deeh-mEhn-toh kohm-peh-teeh-tEEh-voh)*
fair trade	il commercio equo	*(kohm-mEhr-choh Eh-kwoh)*
farm out (v)	dare l'incarico a terzi	*(dAh-reh leehn-kAh-reeh-koh ah tEhr-tseeh)*
fashion	la moda	*(mOh-dah)*
fashionable	alla moda	*(ahl-lah mOh-dah)*
fee	la parcella	*(pah-che-lah)*

feed ratio	il rapporto d'alimentazione	*(rahp-pOhr-toh dah-leeh-mehn-tah-tsyOh-neh)*
feedback	la retroazione	*(reh-troh-ah-tsyOh-neh)*
fender	il parafango	*(pah-rah-fAhn-goh)*
ferment (v)	fermentare	*(fehr-mehn-tAh-reh)*
ferrite	la ferrite	*(feh-rEEh-teh)*
ferroalloys	le leghe di ferro	*(lEh-geh deeh fEhr-roh)*
ferromanganese	il ferromanganese	*(fehr-roh-mahn-gah-nEh-zeh)*
ferronickel	il ferronichel	*(fehr-roh-nee-kel)*
fiber optic	la fibra ottica	*(fEEh-brah Oht-teeh-kah)*
fidelity bond	l'obbligazione fiduciaria	*(ohb-bleeh-gah-tsyOh-neh)*
fiduciary	il fiduciario	*(feeh-dooh-chAh-reeh-oh)*
fiduciary issue	l'emissione fiduciaria	*(eh-meehs-syOh-neh feeh-dooh-chAh-reeh-ah)*
fiduciary loan	il prestito fiduciario	*(prEhs-teeh-toh feeh-dooh-chAh-reeh-oh)*
field warehousing	la cessione di garanzie per merci depositate in un magazzino	*(chehs-syOh-neh deeh gah-rahn-tsEEh-eh pehr mEhr-cheeh deh-poh-zeeh-tAh-teh eehn oohn mah-gahds-dsEEh-noh)*
filament	il filamento	*(feeh-lah-mEhn-toh)*
file	la cartella	*(kahr-tEhl-lah)*
filter	il filtro	*(fEEhl-troh)*
finalize (v)	finalizzare	*(feeh-nah-leehds-dsAh-reh)*
finance (v)	finanziare	*(feeh-nahn-tsyAh-reh)*
finance company	la società di finanziamento	*(soh-cheh-tAh deeh feeh-nahn-tsyah-mEhn-toh)*
financial analysis	l'analisi finanziaria	*(ah-nAh-leeh-zeeh feeh-nahn-tsyAh-reeh-ah)*
financial appraisal	la valutazione finanziaria	*(vah-looh-tah-tsyOh-neh feeh-nahn-tsyAh-reeh-ah)*
financial control	il controllo finanziario	*(kohn-trOhl-loh feeh-nahn-tsyAh-reeh-oh)*
financial director	il direttore finanziario	*(deeh-reht-tOh-reh feeh-nahn-tsyAh-reeh-oh)*

F

financial highlights	i punti di maggior interesse nel rapporto finanziario	*(pOOhn-teeh deeh mahj-johr eehn-teh-rEhs-seh nehl rahp-pOhr-toh feeh-nahn-tsyAh-reeh-oh)*
financial incentive	l'incentivo finanziario	*(eehn-chehn-tEEh-voh feeh-nahn-tsyAh-reeh-oh)*
financial management	l'amministrazione finanzia- ria	*(ahm-meeh-neehs-trah-tsyOh-neh feeh-nahn-tsyAh-reeh-ah)*
financial period	il periodo finanziario	*(peh-rEEh-oh-doh feeh-nahn-tsyAh-reeh-oh)*
financial planning	la pianificazione finanziaria	*(pyah-neeh-feeh-kah-tsyOh-neh feeh-nahn-tsyAh-reeh-ah)*
financial services	i servizi finanziari	*(sehr-vEEh-tseeh feeh-nahn-tsyAh-reeh)*
financial statement	il bilancio, la dichiarazione finanziaria	*(beeh-lAhn-choh), (deeh-kyah-rah-tsyOh-neh feeh-nahn-tsyAh-reeh-ah)*
financial year	l'anno fiscale	*(Ahn-noh feehs-kAhleh)*
fine (penalty)	la multa (l'ammenda)	*(mOOhl-tah), (ahm-mEhn-dah)*
finished goods inventory	l'inventario dei beni finiti	*(eehn-vehn-tAh-reeh-oh deh-eeh bEh-neeh feeh-nEEh-teeh)*
finished products	i prodotti finiti	*(proh-dOht-teeh feeh-nEEh-teeh)*
finishing mill	il laminatoio finitore	*(lah-meeh-nah-tO-yoh feeh-neeh-tOh-reh)*
fire (v)	licenziare	*(leeh-chehn-tsyAh-reh)*
firm	la ditta, l'azienda	*(dEEt-tah), (ah-dsyEhn-dah)*
first in-first out	la prima partita ad entrare-la prima partita ad uscire	*(prEEh-mah pahr-tEEh-tah ad ehn-trAh-reh lah prEEh-mah pahr-tEEh-tah ad ooh-shEEh-reh)*
first preferred stock	la prima azione privilegiata	*(prEEh-mah ah-tsyOh-neh preeh-veeh-leh-jAh-tah)*
fiscal agent	l'agente fiscale	*(ah-jEhn-teh feehs-kAh-leh)*
fiscal drag	il ritardo fiscale	*(reeh-tAhr-doh feehs-kAh-leh)*
fiscal year	l'anno fiscale	*(Ahn-noh feehs-kAh-leh)*

F

fishy-back service (container)	il trasporto di containers su navi	*(trahs-pOhr-toh deeh "containers" sooh nAh-veeh)*
fitch	la puzzola	*(pOOhts-tsoh-lah)*
fix the price (v)	fissare il prezzo	*(feehs-sAh-reh eehl prEhts-tsoh)*
fixed assets	gli attivi fissi, gli immobiliz-zi tecnici	*(aht-tEEh-veeh fEEhs-seeh), (eehm-moh-beeh-lEEhts-tseeh tEhk-neeh-cheeh)*
fixed capital	i capitali fissi	*(kah-peeh-tAh-leeh fEEhs-seeh)*
fixed charges	gli oneri fissi	*(Oh-neh-reeh fEEhs-seeh)*
fixed costs	i costi fissi	*(kOhs-teeh fEEhs-seeh)*
fixed expenses	le spese fisse, le spese costanti	*(spEh-zeh fEEhs-seh), (spEh-zeh kohs-tAhn-teeh)*
fixed income security	il titolo di mobiliare a reddi-to fisso	*(tEEh-toh-loh deeh moh-beeh-lyAh-reh ah rEhd-deeh-toh fEEhs-soh)*
fixed investment	l'investimento costante	*(eehn-vehs-teeh-mEhn-toh kohs-tAhn-teh)*
fixed liability	la responsabilità fissa	*(rehs-pohn-sah-beeh-leeh-tAh fEEhs-sah)*
fixed rate of exchange	il tasso di scambio fisso	*(tAhs-soh deeh skAhm-byoh fEEhs-soh)*
fixed term	il termine fisso	*(tEhr-meeh-neh fEEhs-soh)*
fixtures (on balance sheet)	gl'impianti fissi	*(eehm-pyAhn-teeh fEEhs-seeh)*
flannel	la flanella	*(flah-nEhl-lah)*
flat bond	il buono fisso, l'obbligazione	*(bwOh-noh fEEhs-soh), (ohb-bleeh-gah-tsyOh-neh)*
flat products	i prodotti piatti	*(proh-dOht-teeh pyAht-teeh)*
flat rate	l'importo fisso	*(eehm-pOhr-toh fEEhs-soh)*
flat yield	il rendimento piatto	*(rehn-deeh-mEhn-toh pyAht-toh)*
flatcar	il carro merci senza sponde	*(kAhr-roh mEhr-cheeh sEhn-tsah spOhn-deh)*

F

fleet policy	la polizza per un gruppo di automobili	*(pOh-leehts-tsah pehr oohn grOOhp-poh deeh ah-ooh-toh-mOh-beeh-lee)*
flexible tariff	l'imposta variabile	*(eehm-pOhs-tah vah-ryAh-beeh-leh)*
float (outstanding checks, stock)	il periodo di tempo durante il quale la banca usufruisce degli assegni depositati e non incassati	*(peh-rEEh-oh-doh deeh tEhm-poh dooh-rAhn-teh eehl kwAh-leh lah bAhn-kah ooh-zooh-frooh-EEh-sheh deh-lyeeh ahs-sEh-nyeeh deh-poh-zeeh-tAh-teeh eh nohn eehn-kahs-sAh-teeh)*
float (v) (issue stock)	lanciare (una nuova impresa)	*(lahn-chAh-reh ooh-nah nwOh-vah eehm-prEh-zah)*
floating asset	l'attivo variabile	*(aht-tEEh-voh vah-ryAh-beeh-leh)*
floating charge	l'onere variabile	*(Oh-neh-reh vah-ryAh-beeh-leh)*
floating debt	il debito fluttuante	*(dEh-beeh-toh flooh-tooh-Ahn-teh)*
floating exchange rate	il tasso di cambio variabile	*(tAhs-soh deeh kAhm-byoh vah-ryAh-beeh-leh)*
floating rate	il tasso fluttuante, il tasso variabile	*(tAhs-soh flooh-tooh-Ahn-teh), (tAhs-soh vah-ryAh-beeh-leh)*
floor (of exchange)	la sala delle contrattazioni	*(sAh-lah deeh kohn-traht-tah-tsyOh-neeh)*
floppy disk	il dischetto floppy, il "floppy disk"	*(deehs-kEht-toh)*
flow chart	il diagramma delle correnti	*(deeh-ah-grAhm-mah deh-leh kohr-rEhn-teeh)*
flute	il flute	
follow-up order	l'ordine successivo	*(Ohr-deeh-neh soohch-chehs-sEEh-voh)*
followup (v)	far seguito	*(fahr sEh-gweeh-toh)*
font	la serie completa di caratteri	*(sEh-ryeh kohm-plEh-tah deeh kah-rAht-teh-reeh)*
foodstuffs	gli alimentari	*(ah-leeh-mehn-tAh-reeh)*
footing (accounting)	l'addizione	*(ahd-deeh-tsyOh-neh)*

F

for export	per l'esportazione	*(pehr lehs-pohr-tah-tsyOh-neh)*
forecast (v)	prevedere	*(preh-veh-dEh-reh)*
forecast	la previsione	*(preh-veeh-zyOh-neh)*
forecast, budget	la previsione del preventivo	*(preh-veeh-zyOh-neh dehl preh-vehn-tEEh-voh)*
forecast, market	la previsione del mercato	*(preh-veeh-zyOh-neh dehl mehr-kAh-toh)*
forecast, sales	la previsione di vendite	*(preh-veeh-zyOh-neh deeh vEhn-deeh-teh)*
foreign bill of exchange	la cambiale emessa all'estero	*(kahm-byAh-leh eh-mEhs-sah ahl Ehs-teh-roh)*
foreign corporation	la ditta estera	*(dEEt-tah Ehs-teh-rah)*
foreign currency	la valuta estera	*(vah-lOOh-tah Ehs-teh-rah)*
foreign debt	il debito estero	*(dEh-beeh-toh Ehs-teh-roh)*
foreign exchange	il cambio estero	*(kAhm-byoh Ehs-teh-roh)*
foreign securities	i titoli mobiliari esteri	*(tEEh-toh-leeh moh-beeh-lyAh-reeh Ehs-teh-reeh)*
foreign tax credit	il credito sulle imposte estere	*(kReh-deeh-toh sohl-leh eehm-pOhs-teh Ehs-teh-reh)*
foreign trade	il commercio estero	*(kohm-mEhr-choh Ehs-teh-roh)*
foreman	il capo servizio	*(kAh-poh sehr-vEEh-tsyoh)*
forgery	la contraffazione	*(kohn-trahf-fah-tsyOh-neh)*
fork	la forchetta	*(for-kEht-tah)*
form	la forma	*(fOhr-mah)*
form letter	la lettera tipo, la lettera "standard"	*(lEht-teh-rah tEEh-poh)*
format	il formato	*(fohr-mAh-toh)*
formula	la formula	*(fOhr-mooh-lah)*
forward contract	il contratto a termine	*(kohn-trAht-toh ah tEhr-meeh-neh)*
forward cover	la copertura a termine	*(koh-pehr-tOOh-rah ah tEhr-meeh-neh)*
forward forward	il termine futuro	*(tEhr-meeh-neh fooh-tOOh-roh)*

F

forward margin	il margine a termine	*(mAhr-jeeh-neh ah tEhr-meeh-neh)*
forward market	il mercato a termine	*(mehr-kAh-toh ah tEhr-meeh-neh)*
forward purchase	l'acquisto a termine	*(ahk-kwEEhs-toh ah tEhr-meeh-neh)*
forward shipment	la spedizione a termine	*(speh-deeh-tsyOh-neh ah tEhr-meeh-neh)*
forwarding agent	lo spedizioniere	*(speh-deeh-tsyoh-nyEh-reh)*
foul bill of lading	la polizza di carico con riserve o eccezioni	*(pOh-leehts-tsah deeh kAh-reeh-koh kohn reeh-zEhr-veh oh ehch-cheh-tsyOh-neeh)*
foundry	la fonderia	*(fohn-deh-rEEh-ah)*
four colors	quattro colori	*(kwAht-troh koh-lOh-reeh)*
fox	la volpe	*(vOhl-peh)*
franchise	la concessione di appalto	*(kohn-chehs-syOh-deeh ahp-pAhl-toh)*
fraud	la frode	*(frOh-deh)*
free alongside ship	franco porto, F.A.S.	*(frAhn-koh pOhr-toh)*
free and clear	senza impegni	*(sEhn-tsah eehm-pEh-nyeeh)*
free enterprise	il liberismo economico	*(leeh-beh-rEEhz-moh eh-koh-nOh-meeh-koh)*
free list (commodities without duty)	le merci esentasse	*(mEhr-cheeh eh-zehn-tAhs-seh)*
free market	il mercato libero	*(mehr-kAh-toh lEEh-beh-roh)*
free market industry	l'industria di mercato libero	*(eehn-dOOhs-treeh-ah deeh mehr-kAh-toh lEEh-beh-roh)*
free of particular average	libero da medie particolari	*(lEEh-beh-roh dah mEh-deeh-eh pahr-teeh-koh-lAh-reeh)*
free on board (FOB)	franco bordo, F.O.B.	*(frAhn-koh bOhr-doh)*
free on rail	franco stazione ferroviaria	*(frAhn-koh stAh-tsyOh-neh fehr-roh-vyAh-reeh-ah)*
free port	il porto franco	*(pOhr-toh frAhn-koh)*
free time	il tempo libero	*(tEhm-poh lEEh-beh-roh)*

free trade	il commercio libero	*(kohm-mEhr-choh lEEh-beh-roh)*
free trade zone	la zona franca	*(dsOh-nah frAhn-kah)*
freelancer	il libero professionista	*(lEEh-beh-roh proh-fehs-syoh-nEEhs-tah)*
freight	le merci, il carico	*(mEhr-cheeh), (kAh-reeh-koh)*
freight all kinds	le merci di tutti i tipi	*(mEhr-cheeh deeh tOOht-teeh eeh tEEh-peeh)*
freight allowed	il carico permesso	*(kAh-reeh-koh pehr-mEhs-soh)*
freight collect	i costi di spedizione a carico del destinatario	*(kOhs-teeh deeh speh-deeh-tsyOh-neh ah kAh-reeh-koh dehl dehs-teeh-nah-tAh-reeh-oh)*
freight forwarder	lo spedizioniere	*(speh-deeh-tsyoh-nyEh-reh)*
freight included	compreso trasporto	*(kohm-prEh-soh trahs-pOhr-toh)*
freight prepaid	il trasporto prepagato	*(trahs-pOhr-toh preh-pah-gAh-toh)*
frequency curve	la curva di frequenza	*(kOOhr-vah deeh freh-kwEhn-tsah)*
frequency	la frequenza	*(freh-kwEhn-tsah)*
frequency modulation (FM)	la modulazione di frequenza	*(moh-dooh-lah-tsyOh-neh deeh freh-kwEhn-tsah)*
fringe benefits	gli addizionali	*(ahd-deeh-tsyoh-nAh-leeh)*
fringe market	il mercato marginale	*(mehr-kAh-toh mahr-jeeh-nAh-leh)*
front-end fee	l'onere anticipato, la commissione anticipata	*(Oh-neh-reh ahn-teeh-cheeh-pAh-toh), (kohm-meehs-syOh-neh ahn-teeh-cheeh-pAh-tah)*
front-end financing	il finanziamento anticipato	*(feeh-nahn-tsyah-mEhn-toh ahn-teeh-cheeh-pAh-toh)*
front-end loading	caricare i fondi all'inizio del contratto	*(kah-reeh-kAh-reh eeh fOhn-deeh ahl eeh-nEEh-tsyoh dehl kohn-trAht-toh)*
front-wheel drive	la trazione anteriore	*(trah-tsyOh-neh ahn-teh-ryOh-reh)*
frozen assets	gli attivi bloccati	*(aht-tEEh-veeh blohk-kAh-teeh)*

F

fruity	fruttato	*(frooht-tAh-toh)*
full settlement	il saldo completo	*(sAhl-doh kohm-plEh-toh)*
functional analysis	l'analisi funzionale	*(ah-nAh-leeh-zeeh foohn-tsyoh-nAh-leh)*
fund	il fondo	*(fOhn-doh)*
fund, contingent	il fondo di contingenza, il fondo di previdenza	*(fOhn-doh deeh kohn-teehn-jEhn-tsah), (fOhn-doh deeh preh-veeh-dEhn-tsah)*
fund, sinking	il fondo d'ammortamento per il ritiro di obbligazioni	*(fOhn-doh dahm-mohr-tah-mEhn-toh pehr eehl reeh-tEEh-roh deeh ohb-bleeh-gah-tsyOh-neeh)*
fund, trust	il fondo d'investimento fiduciario	*(fOhn-doh deehn-vehs-teeh-mEhntoh feeh-dooh-chyAh-reeh-oh)*
funded debt	il debito consolidato	*(dEh-beeh-toh kohn-soh-leeh-dAh-toh)*
funds, public	i fondi pubblici	*(fOhn-doh pOOhb-bleeh-cheeh)*
funds, working	il capitale liquido, i fondi attivi	*(kah-peeh-tAh-leh lEEh-kweeh-doh), (fOhn-deeh aht-tEEh-veeh)*
fungible goods	i beni fungibili	*(bEh-neeh foohn-jEEh-beeh-leeh)*
furnace	la fornace	*(fohr-nAh-cheh)*
futures	il contratto a futura consegna, il contratto a termine	*(kohn-trAht-toh ah fooh-tOOh-rah kohn-sEh-nyah), (kohn-trAht-toh ah tEhr-meeh-neh)*
futures option	l'opzione di acquisto o di vendita di un contratto a termine	*(ohp-tsyOh-neh deeh ahk-kwEEhs-toh oh deeh vEhn-deeh-tah deeh oohn kohn-trAht-toh ah tEhr-meeh-neh)*

G

gabardine	la gabardina	*(gah-bahr-dEEh-nah)*
galley proof	la bozza in colonna	*(bOhts-tsah eehn koh-lOhn-nah)*

galvanizing	la galvanizzazione, la zincatura	*(gahl-vah-neehds-dsah-tsyOh-neh), (dseehn-kah-tOOh-rah)*
garment bag	il portabiti	*(pohrt-Ah-beeh-teeh)*
garnishment	il precetto	*(preh-chEht-toh)*
gas chromatography	la gascromatografia	*(gahs-kroh-mah-toh-grah-fEEh-ah)*
gas consumption	il consumo di benzina	*(kohn-sOOh-moh dehl-lah behn-dsEEh-nah)*
gas pedal	l'acceleratore	*(ahch-cheh-leh-rah-tOh-reh)*
gasoline	la benzina	*(behn-dsEEh-nah)*
gasoline tank	il serbatoio della benzina	*(sehr-bah-tOh-yoh dehl-lah behn-dsEEh-nah)*
gearing	l'ingranaggio	*(eehn-grah-nAhj-joh)*
gearless	senza cambio	*(sehn-tsah kAhm-byoh)*
gearshift	il cambio	*(kAhm-byoh)*
general acceptance	l'accettazione generale	*(ah-cheht-tah-tsyOh-neh jeh-neh-rAh-leh)*
general average loss	la perdita media in genere	*(pEhr-deeh-tah mEh-dyah eehn jEh-neh-reh)*
general manager	l'amministratore generale	*(ahm-meeh-neehs-trah-tOh-reh jeh-neh-rAh-leh)*
general meeting	la riunione generale	*(reeh-ooh-nyOh-neh jeh-neh-rAh-leh)*
general partnership	la società in accomandita semplice (s.a.s.)	*(soh-cheh-tAh eehn ahk-koh-mAhn-deeh-tah)*
general strike	lo sciopero generale	*(shOh-peh-roh jeh-neh-rAh-leh)*
generator	il generatore	*(jeh-neh-rah-tOh-reh)*
gentleman's agreement	l'accordo sulla parola	*(ahk-kOhr-doh soohl-lah pah-rOh-lah)*
germanium	il germanio	*(jehr-mAh-neeh-oh)*
gilt (Brit. govt. security)	i titoli governativi, i buoni e obbligazioni del tesoro (Britannici)	*(tEEh-toh-leeh goh-vehr-nah-tEEh-veeh), (bwOh-neeh eh ohb-bleeh-gah-tsyOh-neeh dehl teh-Zoh-roh)*
glass	il bicchiere	*(beehk-kyEh-reh)*
glossy	lucido	*(lOOh-cheeh-doh)*
gloves	i guanti	*(gwAhn-teeh)*

G

glut	la sovvrabbondanza	*(sohv-vrahb-bohn-dAhn-dsah)*
go around (v)	fare il giro	*(fAh-reh eehl jEEh-roh)*
go public (v)	diventare una ditta per azioni	*(deeh-vehn-tAh-reh ooh-nah dEEht-tah pehr ah-tsyOh-neeh)*
go-go fund	il fondo d'investimento molto aggressivo	*(fOhn-doh deehn-vehs-teeh-mEhn-toh mOhl-toh ahg-grehs-sEEh-voh)*
godown	il magazzino commerciale nell'estremo oriente	*(mah-gahds-dsEEh-noh kohm-mehr-chAh-leh nehl ehs-trEh-moh oh-ryEhn-teh)*
going rate (or price)	il prezzo corrente	*(prEhts-tsoh kohr-rEhn-teh)*
going-concern value	il valore effettivo della ditta	*(vah-lOh-reh ehf-feht-tEEh-voh dehl-lah dEEht-tah)*
gold clause	la clausola d'oro	*(klAhw-zoh-lah dOh-roh)*
gold price	il prezzo dell'oro	*(prEhts-tsoh dehl Oh-roh)*
gold reserves	le riserve d'oro	*(reeh-zEhr-veh dOh-roh)*
good delivery (securities)	la buona consegna	*(bwOh-nah kohn-sEh-nyah)*
goods	i beni	*(bEh-neeh)*
goods, capital	i beni capitali, i beni d'investimento	*(bEh-neeh kah-peeh-tAh-leeh), (bEh-neeh deehn-vehs-teeh-mEhn-toh)*
goods, consumer	i beni di consumo	*(bEh-neeh deeh kohn-sOOh-moh)*
goods, durable	i beni durevoli	*(bEh-neeh dooh-rEh-voh-leeh)*
goods, industrial	i beni industriali	*(bEh-neeh eehn-doohs-tryAh-leeh)*
goodwill	la benevolenza	*(beh-neh-voh-lEhn-tsah)*
government	il governo	*(goh-vEhr-noh)*
government agency	l'ente governativo	*(Ehn-teh goh-vehr-nah-tEEh-voh)*
government bank	la banca governativa	*(bAhn-kah goh-vehr-nah-tEEh-vah)*
government bonds	i buoni governativi (del tesoro)	*(bwOh-neeh goh-vehr-nah-tEEh-veeh dehl teh-zOh-roh)*

G

grace period	il periodo di grazia	*(peh-rEEh-oh-doh deeh grAh-tsyah)*
grade, commercial	il livello commerciale, la qualità commerciale	*(leeh-vEhl-loh kohm-mehr-chAh-leh), (kwah-leeh-tAh kohm-mehr-chAh-leh)*
graft	la baratteria	*(bah-raht-teh-rEEh-ah)*
grain (m)	il grano	*(grAh-noh)*
grain (b)	la grana	*(grAh-nah)*
gram	il grammo	*(grAhm-moh)*
grant an overdraft (v)	concedere uno scoperto a fido	*(kohn-chEh-deh-reh ooh-nah skoh-pEhr-tah ah fEEh-doh)*
grantor	il donante	*(doh-nahn-tee)*
grape	l'uva	*(OOh-vah)*
grape bunch	il grappolo d'uva	*(grAhp-poh-loh dOOh-vah)*
grape harvest	la vendemmia	*(vehn-dEhm-myah)*
graph	il diagramma, il grafico	*(deeh-ah-grAhm-mah), (grAh-feeh-koh)*
gratuity	la gratifica	*(grah-tEEh-feeh-kah)*
gravy boat	la salsiera	*(sahl-syEh-rah)*
gray market	il mercato grigio	*(mehr-kAh-toh grEEh-joh)*
grid	la quadrettatura	*(kwah-dreht-tah-tOOh-rah)*
grievance procedure	la procedura per stabilire una lamentela	*(proh-cheh-dOOh-rah pehr stah-beeh-lEEh-reh ooh-nah lah-mehn-tEh-lah)*
grille	la cuffia del radiatore	*(kOOhf-fyah dehl rah-dyah-tOh-reh)*
grinding	la molatura	*(moh-lah-tOOh-rah)*
gross domestic product	il prodotto interno lordo	*(proh-dOht-toh eehn-tEhr-noh lOhr-doh)*
gross income	il reddito lordo	*(rEhd-deeh-toh lOhr-doh)*
gross investment	l'investimento lordo	*(eehn-vehs-teeh-mEhn-toh lOhr-doh)*
gross loss	la perdita lorda	*(pEhr-deeh-tah lOhr-dah)*
gross margin	il margine lordo	*(mAhr-jeeh-neh lOhr-doh)*
gross national product (GNP)	il prodotto nazionale lordo (Pnl)	*(proh-dOht-toh mahr-jeeh-nAh-leh lOhr-doh)*
gross price	il prezzo lordo	*(prEhts-tsoh lOhr-doh)*

G

gross profit	il profitto lordo, l'utile lordo	*(proh-fEEht-toh lOhr-doh)*
gross sales	le vendite lorde	*(vEhn-deeh-teh lOhr-deh)*
gross spread	la differenza tra il prezzo di vendita e i costi di produzione	*(deef-feh-rEhn-tsah trah eehl prEhts-tsoh deeh vEhn-deeh-tah eh eeh kOhs-teeh deeh proh-dooh-tsyOh-neh)*
gross weight	il peso lordo	*(pEh-zoh lOhr-doh)*
gross yield	il rendimento lordo	*(rehn-deeh-mEhn-toh lOhr-doh)*
group accounts	i conti di gruppo, il raggruppamento dei conti	*(kOhn-teeh deeh grOOhp-poh), (rahg-groohp-pah-mEhn-toh deh-eeh kOhn-teeh)*
group dynamics	la dinamica del gruppo	*(deeh-nAh-meeh-kah dehl grOOhp-poh)*
group insurance	la polizza d'assicurazione di gruppo	*(pOh-leehts-tsah dahs-seeh-kooh-rah-tsyOh-neh deeh grOOhp-poh)*
group training	l'istruzione in gruppo	*(eehs-trooh-tsyOh-neh eehn grOOhp-poh)*
group, product	il gruppo di prodotti	*(grOOhp-poh deeh proh-dOht-teeh)*
growth	la crescita	*(krEh-sheeh-tah)*
growth index	l'indice di crescita	*(EEhn-deeh-cheh deeh krEh-sheeh-tah)*
growth industry	l'industria in fase di crescita	*(eehn-dOOhs-treeh-ah eehn fAh-zeh deeh krEh-sheeh-tah)*
growth potential	il potenziale di crescita	*(poh-tehn-tsyAh-leh deeh krEh-sheeh-tah)*
growth rate	il tasso di crescita	*(tAhs-soh deeh krEh-sheeh-tah)*
growth stock	l'azione d'incremento	*(ah-tsyOh-neh deehn-kreh-mEhn-toh)*
growth, corporate	la crescita aziendale	*(krEh-sheeh-tah ah-dsyehn-dAh-leh)*
guarantee	la garanzia	*(gah-rahn-tsEEh-ah)*
guaranty bond	il buono garantito, l'obbligazione garantita	*(bwOh-noh gah-rahn-tEEh-toh), (ohb-bleeh-gah-tsyOh-neh bwOh-noh gah-rahn-tEEh-tah)*

G

guaranty company	la ditta di garanzia	*(dEEht-tah deeh gah-rahn-tsEEh-ah)*
guesstimate	la stima approssimativa	*(stEEh-mah ahp-prohs-seeh-mah-tEEh-vah)*
guidelines	i parametri	*(pah-rAh-meh-treeh)*

H

half-life (bonds)	la mezza scadenza (per buoni)	*(mEhds-dsah skah-dEhn-dsah pehr bwOh-neeh)*
hand-blown glass	il bicchiere soffiato a bocca	*(beehk-kyEh-reh sohf-fyAh-toh ah bOhk-kah)*
hand-embroidered napkins	i tovaglioli ricamati a mano	*(toh-vah-lyOh-leeh reeh-kah-mAh-teeeh ah mAh-noh)*
hand-painted	dipinto a mano	*(deeh-pEEhn-toh ah mAh-noh)*
handbag	la borsetta	*(bohr-sEht-tah)*
handicap	lo svantaggio	*(svahn-tAhj-joh)*
harbor dues	i diritti portuali	*(deeh-rEEht-teeh pohr-twAh-leeh)*
hard copy	la copia scritta	*(kOh-pyah skrEEht-tah)*
hard currency	la valuta pregiata	*(vah-lOOh-tah preh-jAh-tah)*
hard sell	la vendita aggressiva	*(vEhn-deeh-tah ahg-grehs-sEEh-vah)*
hardcover	la copertina a tela, la legatura cartonata	*(koh-pehr-tEEh-nah ah tEh-lah), (leh-gah-tOOh-rah kahr-toh-nAh-tah)*
hardware (computer)	il hardware	*(hahduehr)*
hardware	la ferramenta	*(fehr-rah-mEhn-tah)*
head office	la sede centrale	*(sEh-deh chehn-trAh-leh)*
headhunter	l'agente ricercatore di dirigenti	*(ah-jEhn-teh reeh-chehr-kah-tOh-reh deeh deeh-reeh-jEhn-teeh)*
headline	il titolo	*(tEEh-toh-loh)*
headload	il carico di testa	*(kAh-reeh-koh deeh tEhs-tah)*

H

headquarters	la sede	*(sEh-deh)*
heat	il calore	*(kah-lOh-reh)*
heavy industry	l'industria pesante	*(eehn-dOOhs-treeh-ah peh-zAhn-teh)*
heavy lift charges	gli oneri di sollevamento di carichi pesanti	*(Oh-neh-reeh deeh sohl-leh-vah-mEhn-toh deeh kAh-reeh-keeh peh-zAhn-teeh)*
hectare	l'ettaro	*(Eht-tah-roh)*
hedge (v)	essere elusivo, evitare di compromettersi, bilanciare	*(Ehs-seh-reh eh-looh-zEEh-voh), (eh-veeh-tAh-reh deeh kohm-proh-mEht-tehr-seeh), (beeh-lahn-chAh-reh)*
hem	l'orlo	*(Ohr-loh)*
hexachlorophene	l'esaclorofene	*(eh-zah-kloh-roh-fEh-neh)*
hidden assets	gli attivi nascosti	*(aht-tEEh-veeh nahs-kOhs-teeh)*
high fidelity	l'alta fedeltà	*(Ahl-tah feh-dehl-tAh)*
high technology	l'alta tecnologia	*(Ahl-tah tehk-noh-loh-jEEh-ah)*
highest bidder	il miglior offrente	*(meeh-lyOhr ohf-frEhn-teh)*
hire (v)	assumere	*(ahs-sOOh-meh-reh)*
hoard (v)	ammassare	*(ahm-mahs-sAh-reh)*
holder (negotiable instruments)	il detentore	*(deh-tehn-tOh-reh)*
holder in due course	il possessore in buona fede	*(pohs-sehs-sOh-reh eehn bwOh-nah fEh-deh)*
holding company	la società finanziaria, la società madre, il "holding"	*(soh-cheh-tAh feeh-nahn-tsyAh-reeh-ah), (soh-cheh-tAh mAh-dreh)*
holding period	il periodo di detenzione	*(peh-rEEh-oh-doh deeh deh-tehn-tsyOh-neh)*
holster	la fondina	*(fohn-dEEh-nah)*
home market	il mercato interno	*(mehr-kAh-toh eehn-tEhr-noh)*
homogeneity	l'omogeneità	*(oh-moh-geh-neh-eeh-tAh)*
hood	il cappuccio	*(kahp-pOOhch-choh)*
hormone	l'ormone	*(ohr-mOh-neh)*
horsepower	la potenza in cavalli	*(poh-tEhn-dsah eehn kah-vAhl-leeh)*

H

hot money	il denaro caldo	*(deh-nAh-roh kAhl-doh)*
hot rolling	la laminatura a caldo	*(lah-meeh-nah-tOOh-rah ah kAhl-doh)*
hourly earnings	i guadagni orari	*(gwah-dAh-nyeeh oh-rAh-reeh)*
housing authority	l'ente pubblico responsabile per gli alloggi	*(Ehn-teh pOOhb-bleeh-koh rehs-pohn-sAh-beeh-leh pehr lyeeh ahl-lOhj-jeeh)*
human resources	le risorse del personale	*(reeh-zOhr-seh dehl pehr-soh-nAh-leh)*
hybrid computer	l'elaboratore ibrido	*(eh-lah-boh-rah-tOh-reh EEh-breeh-doh)*
hydrocarbon	l'idrocarbonio	*(eeh-drohkahr-bOh-neeh-ohh)*
hydrochloric acid	l'acido cloridico	*(Ah-ceeh-doh kloh-rEEh-deeh-koh)*
hydrolysis	l'idrolisi	*(eeh-drOh-leeh-zeeh)*
hypertension	l'ipertensione	*(eeh-pehr-tehn-syOh-neh)*
hyphenate (v)	dividere una parola usando trattini, creare una parola composta di due nomi utilizzando un trattino	*(deeh-vEEh-deh-reh ooh-nah pah-rOh-lah ooh-zAhn-doh traht-tEEh-neeh), (kreh-Ah-reh ooh-nah pah-rOh-lah kohm-pOhs-tah deeh dOOh-eh nOh-meeh ooh-teeh-leehds-dsAhn-doh oohn traht-tEEh-noh)*
hypothecate	l'ipotecare	*(eeh-poh-teh-kAh-reh)*

I

idle capacity	la capacità produttiva inattiva	*(kah-pah-cheeh-tAh proh-dooht-tEEh-vah eehn-aht-tEEh-vah)*
ignition	l'accensione	*(ahch-chehn-syOh-neh)*
illegal	illegale	*(eehl-leh-gAh-leh)*
illegal shipments	le spedizioni illegali	*(speh-deeh-tsyOh-neeh eehl-leh-gAh-leeh)*
illustration	l'illustrazione	*(eehl-loohs-trah-tsyOh-neh)*
imitation	l'imitazione	*(eeh-meeh-tah-tsyOh-neh)*

impact, have an...on (v)	influenzare	*(eehn-flooh-ehn-tsAh-reh)*
impact, profit	l'impatto dei profitti, l'impatto sugli utili	*(eehm-pAht-toh deh-eeh proh-fEEht-teeh), (eehm-pAht-toh sooh-lyeeh OOh-teeh-leeh)*
impending changes	le modifiche incombenti	*(moh-dEEh-feeh-keh eehn-kohm-bEhn-teeh)*
implication	l'implicazione	*(eehm-pleeh-kah-tsyOh-neh)*
implied agreement	il patto implicito, la convenzione implicita	*(pAht-toh eehm-plEEh-cheeh-toh), (kohn-vehn-tsyOh-neh eehm-plEEh-cheeh-tah)*
import	l'importazione	*(eehm-pohr-tah-tsyOh-neh)*
import (v)	importare	*(eehm-pohr-tAh-reh)*
import declaration	la dichiarazione doganale	*(deeh-kyah-rah-tsyOh-neh doh-gah-nAh-leh)*
import deposits	i depositi d'importazione	*(deh-Poh-zeeh-teeh)*
import duty	il dazio	*(dAh-tsyoh)*
import entry	l'entrata d'importazione	*(ehn-trAh-tah deehm-pohr-tah-tsyOh-neh)*
import license	la licenza di importazione	*(leeh-chEhn-tsah deeh eehm-pohr-tah-tsyOh-neh)*
import quota	la quota d'importazione	*(kwOh-tah deehm-pohr-tah-tsyOh-neh)*
import regulations	le normative per l'importazione	*(nohr-mah-tEEh-veh pehr leehm-pohr-tah-tsyOh-neh)*
import tariff	la tariffa d'importazione	*(tah-rEEhf-fah deehm-pohr-tah-tsyOh-neh)*
import tax	l'imposta d'importazione	*(eehm-pOhs-tah deehm-pohr-tah-tsyOh-neh)*
importer of record	l'importatore registrato	*(eehm-pohr-tah-tOh-reh reh-jeehs-trAh-toh)*
impound (v)	sequestrare	*(seh-kwehs-trAh-reh)*
improve upon (v)	migliorare	*(meeh-lyoh-rAh-reh)*
improvements	i miglioramenti	*(meeh-lyoh-rah-mEhn-teeh)*
impulse buying	gli acquisti impulsivi	*(ahk-kwEEhs-teeh eehm-poohl-sEEh-veeh)*
impurity	l'impurezza	*(eehm-pooh-rEhts-tsah)*

I

imputed	l'imputato	*(eehm-pooh-tAh-toh)*
in the red	in passivo	*(eehn pahs-sEEh-voh)*
in transit	in transito	*(eehn trAhn-zeeh-toh)*
inadequate	inadeguato	*(eehn-ah-deh-gwAh-toh)*
incentive	l'incentivo	*(eehn-chehn-tEEh-voh)*
inch	il pollice	*(pOhl-leeh-cheh)*
inchoate interest	gl'interessi incipienti	*(eehn-teh-rEhs-seeh eehn-chee-pyEhn-teeh)*
incidental expenses	le spese incidentali	*(spEh-zeh eehn-cheeh-dehn-tAh-leeh)*
income	il reddito, il introito	*(rEhd-deeh-toh)*
income account	il conto redditizio	*(kOhn-toh rehd-deeh-tEEh-tsyoh)*
income bonds	i buoni redditizi	*(bwOh-neeh rehd-deeh-tEEh-tseeh*
income bracket	il livello di reddito	*(leeh-vEhl-loh deeh rEhd-deeh-toh)*
income statement	la dichiarazione del reddito	*(deeh-kyah-rah-tsyOh-neh dehl rEhd-deeh-toh)*
income tax, corporate	l'imposta sul reddito delle persone giuridiche (IRPEG)	*(eehm-pOhs-tah soohl rEhd-deeh-toh dehl-leh pehr-sOh-neh joo-rEEh-deeh-keh)*
income tax, personal	l'imposta sul reddito delle persone fisiche (IRPEF)	*(eehm-pOhs-tah soohl rEhd-deeh-toh dehl-leh pehr-sOh-neh fEEh-zeeh-keh)*
income yield	il rendimento	*(rehn-deeh-mEhn-toh)*
income, gross	il reddito lordo	*(rEhd-deeh-toh lOhr-doh)*
income, net	il reddito netto	*(rEhd-deeh-toh nEht-toh)*
incorporate (v)	incorporare	*(eehn-kohr-poh-rAh-reh)*
increase (v)	aumentare, incrementare	*(ahw-mehn-tAh-reh) (eehn-kreh-mehn-tAh-reh)*
increase	l'aumento, l'incremento	*(ahw-mEhn-toh), (eehn-kreh-mEhn-toh)*
increased costs	i costi incrementati	*(kOhs-teeh eehn-kreh-mehn-tAh-teeh)*
incremental cash flow	il movimento di cassa incrementale	*(moh-veeh-mEhn-toh deeh kAhs-sah eehn-kreh-mehn-tAh-leh)*

I

incremental costs	i costi incrementali	*(kOhs-teeh eehn-kreh-mehn-tAh-teeh)*
indebtedness	l'indebitamento	*(eehn-deh-beeh-tah-mEhn-toh)*
indemnity	l'indennità	*(eehn-dehn-neeh-tAh)*
indentured	legato con un contratto	*(leh-gAh-toh kohn oohn kohn-trAht-toh)*
index (indicator)	l'indice	*(EEhn-deeh-cheh)*
index (v)	indicizzare	*(eehn-deeh-cheehts-tsAh-reh)*
index linked guaranteed minimum wage	la paga base minima indicizzata	*(pAh-gah bAh-zeh mEEh-neeh-mah eehn-deeh-cheehts-tsAh-tah)*
index, growth	l'indice di crescita	*(EEhn-deeh-cheh deeh krEh-sheeh-tah)*
indexing	l'indicizzazione	*(eehn-deeh-cheehts-tsAh-tsyOh-neh)*
indirect claim	il reclamo indiretto	*(reh-klAh-moh eehn-deeh-rEht-toh)*
indirect cost	il costo indiretto	*(kOhs-toh eehn-deeh-rEht-toh)*
indirect expenses	le spese indirette	*(spEh-zeh eehn-deeh-rEht-teh)*
indirect labor	il lavoro indiretto	*(lah-vOh-roh eehn-deeh-rEht-toh)*
indirect tax	l'imposta indiretta	*(eehm-pOhs-tah eehn-deeh-rEht-tah)*
induction furnace	il forno ad induzione	*(fOh-rnoh ad eehn-dooh-tsyOh-neh)*
induction	l'induzione	*(eehn-dooh-tsyOh-neh)*
industrial accident	l'incidente industriale	*(eehn-cheeh-dEhn-teh eehn-doohs-tryAh-leh)*
industrial arbitration	l'arbitrato industriale	*(ahr-beeh-trAh-toh eehn-doohs-tryAh-leh)*
industrial engineering	l'ingegneria industriale, la progettazione industriale	*(eehn-jeh-nyeh-rEEh-ah eehn-doohs-tryAh-leh), (proh-jeht-tah-tsyOh-neh eehn-doohs-tryAh-leh)*
industrial goods	i beni industriali	*(bEh-neeh eehn-doohs-tryAh-leeh)*

I

industrial insurance	l'assicurazione industriale	*(ahs-seeh-kooh-rah-tsyOh-neh eehn-doohs-tryAh-leh)*
industrial planning	la pianificazione industriale	*pyah-neeh-feeh-kah-tsyOh-neh eehn-doohs-tryAh-leh)*
industrial relations	le relazioni industriali	*(reh-lah-tsyOh-neh eehn-doohs-tryAh-leeh)*
industrial union	il sindacato industriale	*(seehn-dah-kAh-toh eehn-doohs-tryAh-leh)*
industry	l'industria	*(eehn-dOOhs-treeh-ah)*
industrywide	a livello industriale	*(ah leeh-vEhl-loh eehn-doohs-tryAh-leh)*
inefficient	inefficiente	*(eehn-ehf-feeh-chEhn-teh)*
inelastic demand or supply	la domanda od offerta rigida o inelastica	*(doh-mAhn-dah od ohf-fEhr-tah rEEh-jeeh-dah oh eehn-eh-lAhs-teeh-kah)*
infant industry	l'industria nascente	*(eehn-dOOhs-tryeeh-ah nah-shEhn-teh)*
inflation	l'inflazione	*(eehn-flah-tsyOh-neh)*
inflationary	inflazionistico	*(eehn-flah-tsyoh-nEEhs-teeh-koh)*
infrastructure	l'infrastruttura	*(eehn-frahs-trooht-tOOh-rah)*
ingot mold	la lingottiera	*(leehn-goht-tyEh-rah)*
ingots	i lingotti	*(leehn-gOht-teeh)*
inheritance tax	l'imposta di successione	*(eehm-pOhs-tah deeh soohch-chehs-syOh-neh)*
injection	l'iniezione, la puntura	*(eehn-yeh-tsyOh-neh), (poohn-tOOh-rah)*
injector	l'iniettore	*(eeh-nyeht-tOh-reh)*
injunction	l'ingiunzione	*(eehn-joohn-tsyOh-neh)*
ink	l'inchiostro	*(eehn-kyOhs-troh)*
inland bill of lading	la polizza di carico nazionale	*(pOh-leehts-tsah deeh kAh-reeh-koh nah-tsyoh-nAh-leh)*
innovation	l'innovazione, la novità	*(eehn-noh-vah-tsyOh-neh), (noh-veeh-tAh)*
inorganic chemistry	la chimica inorganica	*(kEEh-meeh-kah eehn-ohr-gAh-neeh-kah)*

I

input	l'entrata, l'"input"	*(ehn-trAh-tah)*
input-output analysis	l'analisi entrata/uscita, l'analisi fattori produttivi	*(ah-nAh-leeh-zeeh ehn-trAh-tah/ooh-shEEh-tah), (ah-nAh-leeh-zeeh faht-tOh-reeh proh-dooht-tEEh-veeh)*
insert	il volantino	*(voh-lahn-tEEh-noh)*
insolvent	insolvente	*(eehn-sohl-vEhn-teh)*
inspection	l'ispezione	*(eehs-peh-tsyOh-neh)*
inspector	l'ispettore	*(eehs-peht-tOh-reh)*
instability	l'instabilità	*(eehn-stah-beeh-leeh-tAh)*
installment credit	il credito a rate	*(krEh-deeh-toh ah rAh-teh)*
installment plan	il sistema di vendita rateale	*(seehs-tEh-mah deeh vEhn-deeh-tah rah-teh-Ah-leh)*
institutional advertising	la pubblicità istituzionale	*(poohb-bleeh-cheeh-tAh eehs-teeh-tooh-tsyoh-nAh-leh)*
institutional investor	l'investitore istituzionale	*(eehn-vehs-teeh-tOh-reh eehs-teeh-tooh-tsyoh-nAh-leh)*
instruct (v)	istruire	*(eehs-trooh-EEh-reh)*
instrument	lo strumento	*(strooh-mEhn-toh)*
instrumental capital	il capitale industriale	*(kah-peeh-tAh-leh eehn-doohs-tryAh-leh)*
insulator	l'isolante	*(eeh-zoh-lAhn-teh)*
insulin	l'insulina	*(eehn-sooh-lEEh-nah)*
insurance	l'assicurazione	*(ahs-seeh-kooh-rah-tsyOh-neh)*
insurance broker	l'agente di assicurazione	*(ah-jEhn-teh deeh deeh ahs-seeh-kooh-rah-tsyOh-neh)*
insurance company	l'agenzia d'assicurazione	*(ah-jehn-tsEEh-ah dahs-seeh-kooh-rah-tsyOh-neh)*
insurance fund	il fondo di assicurazione	*(fOhn-doh deeh ahs-seeh-kooh-rah-tsyOh-neh)*
insurance policy	la polizza d'assicurazione	*(pOh-leehts-tsah dahs-seeh-kooh-rah-tsyOh-neh)*
insurance premium	il premio d'assicurazione	*(pReh-myoh dahs-seeh-kooh-rah-tsyOh-neh)*

insurance underwriter	il sottoscrittore dell'assicurazione	*(soht-toh-skreet-tOh-reh dehl ahs-seeh-kooh-rah-tsyOh-neh)*
intangible assets	gli attivi intangibili	*(aht-tEEh-veeh eehn-tahn-jEEh-beeh-leeh)*
integrated circuit	il circuito integrato	*(cheehr-kwEEh-toh eehn-teh-grAh-toh)*
integrated management system	il sistema di gestione integrato	*(seehs-tEh-mah deeh jehs-tyOh-neh eehn-teh-grAh-toh)*
intention	intenzione	*(eehn-tehn-seeh-oh-neh)*
interact (v)	iniziare un'azione reciproca	*(eeh-neeh-tsyAh-reh oohn ah-tsyOh-neh reh-chEEh-proh-kah)*
interbank	interbanca	*(eehn-tehr-bAhn-kah)*
interest	l'interesse	*(eehn-teh-rEhs-seh)*
interest arbitrage	l'arbitraggio d'interesse	*(ahr-beeh-trAhj-joh deehn-teh-rEhs-seh)*
interest expenses	le spese d'interesse	*(spEh-zeh deehn-teh-rEhs-seh)*
interest income	il reddito sugli interessi	*(rEhd-deeh-toh sooh-lyeeh eehn-teh-rEhs-seeh)*
interest parity	la parità d'interesse	*(pah-reeh-tAh deehn-teh-rEhs-seh)*
interest period	il periodo d'interesse	*(peh-rEEh-oh-doh deehn-teh-rEhs-seh)*
interest rate	il tasso d'interesse	*(tAhs-soh deehn-teh-rEhs-seh)*
interest, compound	l'interesse composto	*(eehn-teh-rEhs-seh kohm-pOhs-toh)*
interface	l'"interface"	*(eehn-tehr-fayse)*
interim	provvisorio	*(prohv-veeh-zOh-reeh-oh)*
interim budget	il preventivo provvisorio	*(preh-vehn-tEEh-voh prohv-veeh-zOh-reeh-oh)*
interim statement	la dichiarazione provvisoria	*(deeh-kyah-rah-tsyOh-neh prohv-veeh-zOh-reeh-ah)*
interlocking directorate	le direzioni congiunte	*(deeh-reh-tsyOh-neeh kohn-joohn-teh)*
intermediary goods	i beni intermediari	*(bEh-neeh eehn-tehr-meh-dyAh-reeh)*

I

intermediary	l'intermediario	*(eehn-tehr-meh-dyAh-reeh-oh)*
internal	interno	*(eehn-tEhr-noh)*
internal audit	la revisione interna	*(reh-veeh-zyOh-neh eehn-tEhr-nah)*
internal funding	i fondi interni	*(fOhn-deeh eehn-tEhr-neeh)*
internal rate of return	il rendimento interno	*(rehn-deeh-mEhn-toh eehn-tEhr-noh)*
internal revenue tax	le imposte indirette	*(eehm-pOhs-teh eehn-deeh-rEht-teh)*
International Date Line	la Linea lnternazionale di Demarcazione (dove il giorno cambia)	*(lEEh-neh-ah eehn-tehr-nah-tsyoh-nAh-leh deeh deh-mahr-kah-tsyOh-neh doh-beh eehl tEhm-poh kAhmb-yah)*
interstate commerce	il commercio interstatale	*(kohm-mEhr-choh eehn-tehr-stah-tAh-leh)*
intervene (v)	intervenire	*(eehn-tehr-veh-nEEh-reh)*
interview	l'intervista	*(eehn-tehr-vEEhs-tah)*
intestate	senza testamento	*(sEhn-tsah tehs-tah-mEhn-toh)*
intrinsic value	il valore intrinseco	*(vah-lOh-reh eehn-trEEhn-seh-koh)*
introduction	la premessa	*(preh-mEhs-sah)*
invalidate (v)	invalidare	*(eehn-vah-leeh-dAh-reh)*
inventory control	il controllo dell'inventario	*(kohn-trOhl-loh dehl eehn-vehn-tAh-reeh-oh)*
inventory	l'inventario	*(eehn-vehn-tAh-reeh-oh)*
inventory turnover	il giro dell'inventario	*(jEEh-roh dehl eehn-vehn-tAh-reeh-oh)*
inventory, perpetual	l'inventario perpetuo	*(eehn-vehn-tAh-reeh-oh pehr-pEh-tooh-oh)*
inventory, physical	l'inventario fisico	*(eehn-vehn-tAh-reeh-oh fEEh-zeeh-koh)*
inverted market	il mercato invertito, il mercato capovolto	*(mehr-kAh-toh eehn-vehr-tEEh-toh), (mehr-kAh-toh kah-poh-vOhl-toh)*
invest (v)	investire	*(eehn-vehs-tEEh-reh)*
invested capital	il capitale investito	*(kah-peeh-tAh-leh eehn-vehs-tEEh-toh)*

investment	l'investimento	*(eehn-vehs-teeh-mEhn-toh)*
investment adviser	il consulente sugli investimenti	*(kohn-sooh-lEhn-teh sooh-lyeeh eehn-vehs-teeh-mEhn-teeh)*
investment analysis	l'analisi d'investimento	*(ah-nAh-leeh-zeeh deehn-vehs-teeh-mEhn-toh)*
investment appraisal	la valutazione dell'investimento	*(vah-looh-tah-tsyOh-neh dehl eehn-vehs-teeh-mEhn-toh)*
investment bank	la banca d'investimento	*(bAhn-kah deehn-vehs-teeh-mEhn-toh)*
investment budget	il preventivo d'investimento	*(preh-vehn-tEEh-voh deehn-vehs-teeh-mEhn-toh)*
investment company	la compagnia d'investimento	*(kohm-pah-nyEEh-ah deehn-vehs-teeh-mEhn-toh)*
investment credit	il credito per investimento	*(krEh-deeh-toh deehn-vehs-teeh-mEhn-toh)*
investment criteria	i criteri d'investimento	*(kreeh-tEh-reeh deehn-vehs-teeh-mEhn-toh)*
investment grade	il livello di qualità per investimenti	*(leeh-vEhl-loh deeh kwah-leeh-tAh pehr eehn-vehs-teeh-mEhn-teeh)*
investment letter	la lettera d'investimento	*(lEht-teh-rah deehn-vehs-teeh-mEhn-toh)*
investment policy	la politica d'investimento	*(poh-lEEh-teeh-kah deehn-vehs-teeh-mEhn-toh)*
investment program	il programma d'investimento	*(proh-grAhm-mah deehn-vehs-teeh-mEhn-toh)*
investment strategy	la strategia d'investimento	*(strah-teh-jEEh-ah deehn-vehs-teeh-mEhn-toh)*
investment trust	il fondo comune d'investimento	*(fOhn-doh koh-mOOh-neh deehn-vehs-teeh-mEhn-toh)*
investment, return on	il ritorno sull'investimento, il profitto sull'investimento	*(reeh-tOhr-noh soohl eehn-vehs-teeh-mEhn-toh), (proh-fEEht-toh soohl eehn-vehs-teeh-mEhn-toh)*
investor relations	la relazioni con gli investitori	*(reh-lah-tsyOh-neeh kohn lyeeh eehn-vehs-teeh-tOh-reeh)*
invisibles	gli intangibili	*(eehn-tahn-jEEh-beeh-leeh)*

invitation to bid	la richiesta d'appalto, il bando d'appalto	*(reeh-kyEhs-tah dahp-pAhl-toh)*
invoice	la fattura	*(faht-tOOh-rah)*
invoice cost	il costo fatturato	*(kOhs-toh faht-tooh-rAh-toh)*
invoice, commercial	la fattura commerciale	*(faht-tOOh-rah kohm-mehr-chAh-leh)*
invoice, consular	la fattura consolare	*(faht-tOOh-rah kohn-soh-lAh-reh)*
invoice, pro forma	la fattura pro forma	*(faht-tOOh-rah proh fOhr-mah)*
iodine	lo iodio	*(yOh-deeh-oh)*
iron	il ferro	*(fEhr-roh)*
iron ore	il minerale ferroso	*(meeh-neh-rAh-leh fehr-rOh-zoh)*
isotope	l'isotopo	*(eeh-zOh-toh-poh)*
issue (stock)	l'emissione, il valore mobiliare	*(eh-meehs-syOh-neh), (vah-lOh-reh moh-beeh-lyAh-reh)*
issue (v)	emettere	*(eh-mEht-teh-reh)*
issue price	il prezzo d'emissione	*(prEhts-tsoh deh-meehs-syOh-neh)*
issued shares	le azioni emesse	*(ah-tsyOh-neeh eh-mEhs-seh)*
italic	il corsivo	*(kohr-sEEh-voh)*
item	la voce	*(vOh-cheh)*
itemize (v)	dettagliare	*(deht-tah-lyAh-reh)*
itemized account	il conto dettagliato	*(kOhn-toh deht-tah-lyAh-toh)*

I

J

jacket	la copertina di libro, la sopraccoperta	*(koh-pehr-tEEh-nah deeh lEEh-broh), (soh-prahk-koh-pEhr-tah)*
Jason clause	la clausola di negligenza	*(klAw-zoh-lah deeh neh-gleeh-jEhn-tsah)*
jawbone (v)	chiacchierare	*(kyahk-kyeh-rAh-reh)*
jet lag	il fuso orario	*(fOOh-zoh oh-rAh-reeh-oh)*

jewel	la gioiello	*(joh-yEhl-loh)*
jig (production)	il crivello	*(kreeh-vEhl-loh)*
job	il lavoro, la mansione	*(lah-vOh-roh), (mahn-syOh-neh)*
job analysis	l'analisi dell'occupazione, l'analisi del lavoro, l'analisi del progetto	*(ah-nAh-leeh-zeeh dehl ohk-kooh-pah-tsyOh-neh), (ah-nAh-leeh-zeeh dehl lah-vOh-roh), (ah-nAh-leeh-zeeh dehl dehl proh-jEht-toh)*
job description	la descrizione del lavoro	*(dehs-kreeh-tsyOh-neh dehl lah-vOh-roh)*
job evaluation	la valutazione del lavoro	*(vah-looh-tah-tsyOh-neh dehl lah-vOh-roh)*
job hopper	colui che cambia spesso il posto di lavoro	*(koh-lOOh-eeh keh kAhm-byah spEhs-soh eehl pOhs-toh deeh lah-vOh-roh)*
job lot	alla rinfusa	*(ah-lah reehn-fOOh-zah)*
job performance	la valutazione dell'adempimento del lavoro	*(vah-looh-tah-tsyOh-neh dehl ah-dehm-peeh-mEhn-toh dehl lah-vOh-roh)*
job security	la garanzia del posto di lavoro	*(jah-rahn-tsEEh-ah dehl pOhs-toh deeh lah-vOh-roh)*
jobber	il lavoratore a cottimo, il grossista	*(lah-voh-rah-tOh-reh ah kOht-teeh-moh), (grohs-sEEhs-tah)*
joint account	il conto congiunto	*(kOhn-toh kohn-jOOhn-toh)*
joint estate	il patrimonio congiunto	*(pah-treeh-mOh-neeh-oh kohn-jOOhn-toh)*
joint liability	la responsabilità congiunta	*(rehs-pohn-sah-beeh-leeh-tAh kohn-jOOhn-tah)*
joint owner	il comproprietario	*(kohm-proh-pryeh-tAh-reeh-oh)*
joint stock company	la ditta a capitale sociale	*(dEEt-tah ah kah-peeh-tAh-leh soh-chAh-leh)*
joint venture	il joint venture	*(johynt ventchuhr)*
journal	il giornale	*(johr-nAh-leh)*
journeyman	l'operaio a giornate	*(oh-peh-rAh-yoh ah johr-nAh-teh)*

joystick	il comando, il "joystick"	*(koh-mAhn-doh)*
judge	il giudice	*(gee-dee-chay)*
juice	il succo	*(sOOhk-koh)*
junior partner	il socio secondario	*(sOh-choh seh-kohn-dAh-reeh-oh)*
junior security	il titolo a garanzia seconda-ria	*(tEEh-toh-loh ah gah-rahn-tsEEh-ah seh-kohn-dAh-reeh-ah)*
jurisdiction	la giurisdizione	*(jooh-reehz-deeh-tsyOh-neh)*
justify (v)	giustificare	*(joohs-teeh-feeh-kAh-reh)*

K

keep posted (v)	tenere al corrente	*(teh-nEh-reh ahl kohr-rEhn-teh)*
key case	il portachiavi	*(pohr-tah-kyAh-veeh)*
key exports	le esportazioni chiave	*(ehs-pohr-tah-tsyOh-neeh kyAh-veh)*
key man insurance	l'assicurazione per il perso-nale indispensabile	*(ahs-seeh-kooh-rah-tyOh-neh pehr eehl pehr-soh-nAh-leh eehn-deehs-pehn-sAh-beeh-leh)*
Keynesian economics	l'economia keynesiana	*(eh-koh-noh-mEEh-ah kehn-syAh-nah)*
keypuncher	il perforatore	*(pehr-foh-rah-tOh-reh)*
kickback	la tangente	*(tahn-jAhn-teh)*
kidskin	il capretto	*(kah-prEht-toh)*
kilowatt	il kilowatt	*(kilohwaht)*
kiting (banking)	emettere un assegno scoper-to e poi depositare la somma necessaria per renderlo valido	*(eh-mEht-teh-reh oohn ahs-sEh-nyoh skoh-pEhr-toh eh pOh-eeh deh-poh-zeeh-tAh-reh lah sOhm-mah neh-chehs-sAh-reeh-ah pehr rEhn-dehr-loh vAh-leeh-doh)*
knife	il coltello	*(kohl-tEhl-loh)*
knot (nautical)	il nodo	*(nOh-doh)*
know-how	l'abilità, il "know-how"	*(ah-beeh-leeh-tAh)*

J

L

label	l'etichetta	*(eh-teeh-kEht-tah)*
labor	il lavoro	*(lah-vOh-roh)*
labor code	il codice del lavoro	*(kOh-deeh-cheh dehl lah-vOh-roh)*
labor dispute	la disputa di lavoro, la disputa sindacale	*(dEEhs-pooh-tah deeh lah-vOh-roh), (dEEhs-pooh-tah seehn-dah-kAh-leh)*
labor force	la forza lavoro	*(fOhr-tsah lah-vOh-roh)*
labor law	la normativa sul lavoro	*(nohr-mah-tEEh-vah soohl lah-vOh-roh)*
labor leader	il capo sindacale	*(kAh-poh seehn-dah-kAh-leh)*
labor market	il mercato del lavoro	*(mehr-kAh-toh dehl lah-vOh-roh)*
labor relations	i rapporti sindacali	*(rahp-pOhr-teeh seehn-dah-kAh-leeh)*
labor turnover	i ricambio della manodopera	*(reeh-kAhm-byoh dehl-lah mah-noh-dOh-peh-rah)*
labor union	il sindacato	*(seehn-dah-kAh-toh)*
labor-intensive industry	l'industria che dipende molto dal fattore della manodopera	*(eehn-dOOhs-treeh-ah keh deeh-pEhn-deh mOhl-toh dahl faht-tOh-reh dehl-lah mah-noh-dOh-peh-rah)*
labor-saving	gli accorgimenti che tendono a risparmiare sulla manodopera	*(ahk-kohr-jeeh-mEhn-teeh keh tEhn-doh-noh ah reehs-pahr-myAh-reh sohl-lah mah-noh-dOh-peh-rah)*
laboratory	il laboratorio	*(lah-boh-rah-tOh-reeh-oh)*
laboratory technician	il tecnico del laboratorio	*(tEhk-neeh-koh dehl lah-boh-rah-tOh-reeh-oh)*
laborer	il lavoratore	*(lah-voh-rah-tOh-reh)*
lace	il merletto	*(mehr-lEht-toh)*
lagging indicator	l'indicatore in ritardo	*(eehn-deeh-kah-tOh-reh eehn reeh-tAhr-doh)*
laissez-faire	laissez-faire	*(leh-sEh-fehr)*
lamb	l'agnello	*(ah-nyEhl-loh)*

L

land	la terra	*(tEhr-rah)*
land grant	la donazione di terra	*(doh-nah-tsyOh-neh deeh tEhr-rah)*
land reform	la riforma fondiaria	*(reeh-fOhr-mah fohn-dyAh-reeh-ah)*
land tax	l'imposta fondiaria	*(eehm-pOhs-tah fohn-dyAh-reeh-ah)*
landed cost	il costo alla destinazione	*(kOhs-toh ahl-lah dehs-teeh-nah-tsyOh-neh)*
landing certificate	il certificato per lo sbarco	*(chehr-teeh-feeh-kAh-toh pehr loh zbAhr-koh)*
landing charges	gli oneri di sbarco	*(Oh-neh-reeh deeh zbAhr-koh)*
landing costs	i costi di sbarco	*(kOhs-teeh deeh zbAhr-koh)*
landowner	il proprietario	*(proh-pryeh-tAh-reeh-oh)*
large-scale	grande scala	*(grAhn-deh skAh-lah)*
laser	il laser	*(lahyzehr)*
last in-first out	l'ultima partita consegnata-prima partita ad uscire	*(OOhl-teeh-mah pahr-tEEh-tah kohn-seh-nyAh-tah prEEh-mah pahr-tEEh-tah ad ooh-shEEh-reh)*
law	la legge	*(lEhj-jeh)*
law of diminishing returns	la legge dei rendimenti decrescenti	*(lEhj-jeh deh-eeh rehn-deeh-mEhn-teeh deh-kreh-shEhn-teeh)*
lawsuit	la causa	*(kAhw-zah)*
lawyer	l'avvocato	*(ahv-voh-kAh-toh)*
laxative	il lassativo, il purgante	*(lahs-sah-tEEh-voh), (poohr-gAhn-teh)*
lay time	il tempo di giacenza	*(tEhm-poh deeh jah-chEhn-tsah)*
lay up (v)	disarmare	*(deehz-ahr-mAh-reh)*
lay-off	il licenziamento	*(leeh-chehn-tsyah-mEhn-toh)*
laydays	le stallie	*(stAhl-leeh-eh)*
layout	la disposizione di una pagina	*(deehs-poh-zeeh-tsyOh-neh deeh ooh-nah pAh-jeeh-nah)*
layout	lo schema	*(skEh-mah)*

L

lead time	l'intervallo tra progettazione e produzione, il periodo di preparazione	*(eehn-tehr-vAhl-loh trah proh-jeht-tah-tsyOh-neh eh proh-dooh-tsyOh-neh)*
leader	il capo	*(kAh-poh)*
leading firm	la ditta primaria, la ditta "leader"	*(dEEht-tah preeh-mAh-reeh-ah)*
leading indicator	l'indicatore principale	*(eehn-deeh-kah-tOh-reh preehn-cheeh-pAh-leh)*
leads and lags	gli anticipi e ritardi	*(ahn-tEEh-cheeh-peeh eh reeh-tAhr-deeh)*
leakage	la dispersione, lo sconto	*(deehs-pehr-syOh-neh), (skOhn-toh)*
learning curve	la curva d'insegnamento	*(kOOhr-vah deehn-seh-nyah-mEhn-toh)*
lease (v)	affittare	*(ahf-feeht-tAh-reh)*
lease	il contratto d'affitto, il contratto di locazione	*(kohn-trAht-toh dahf-fEEht-toh), (kohn-trAht-toh deeh loh-kah-tsyOh-neh)*
leased department	il reparto affittato	*(reh-pAhr-toh ahf-feeht-tAh-toh)*
leather	la pelle	*(pEhl-leh)*
leather goods	la pelletteria	*(pehl-leht-teh-rEEh-ah)*
leather jacket	giubbotto di pelle	*(joohb-bOht-toh deeh pEhl-leh)*
leave of absence	l'aspettativa, la licenza	*(ahs-peht-tah-tEEh-vah), (leeh-chEhn-tsah)*
ledger	il libro mastro	*(lEEh-broh mAhs-troh)*
ledger account	il conto sul libro mastro	*(kOhn-toh dehl lEEh-broh mAhs-troh)*
ledger entry	l'entrata nel libro mastro, l'entrata sul registro	*(ehn-trAh-tah nehl lEEh-broh mAhs-troh), (ehn-trAh-tah soohl reh-jEEhs-troh)*
legacy	l'eredità	*(eh-reh-deeh-tAh)*
legal capital	il capitale sociale legale	*(kah-peeh-tAh-leh soh-chAh-leh leh-gAh-leh)*
legal entity	l'entità legale	*(ehn-teeh-tAh leh-gAh-leh)*
legal holiday	la festività legale	*(fehs-teeh-veeh-tAh leh-gAh-leh)*
legal list (fiduciary investments)	l'elenco legale	*(eh-lEhn-koh leh-gAh-leh)*

legal monopoly	il monopolio legale, il monopolio di stato	*(moh-noh-pOh-leeh-oh leh-gAh-leh), (moh-noh-pOh-leeh-oh deeh stAh-toh)*
legal tender	la valuta legale	*(vah-lOOh-tah leh-gAh-leh)*
legitimate	il legittimo	*(leeh-gEE-tee-moh)*
lending margin	il margine di prestito	*(mAhr-jeeh-neh deeh prEhs-teeh-toh)*
length	la lunghezza	*(loohn-gEhts-tsah)*
less-than-carload	il carico inferiore alla capacità di una vettura	*(kAh-reeh-koh eehn-feh-ryOh-reh ahl-lah kah-pah-cheeh-tAh deeh ooh-nah veht-tOOh-rah)*
less-than-truckload	il carico inferiore alla capacità di un camion	*(kAh-reeh-koh eehn-feh-ryOh-reh ahl-lah kah-pah-cheeh-tAh deeh oohn kAh-myohn)*
lessee	il locatario	*(loh-kah-tOh-reeh-oh)*
lessor	il locatore	*(loh-kah-tOh-reh)*
letter	la lettera	*(lEht-teh-rah)*
letter of credit	la lettera di credito	*(lEht-teh-rah deeh krEh-deeh-toh)*
letter of guaranty	la lettera di garanzia	*(lEht-teh-rah deeh gah-rahn-tsEEh-ah)*
letter of indemnity	la lettera d'indennità	*(lEht-teh-rah deehn-dehn-neeh-tAh)*
letter of introduction	la lettera di presentazione	*(lEht-teh-rah deeh preh-zehn-tah-tsyOh-neh)*
letterpress	la parte stampata	*(pAhr-teh stahm-pAh-tah)*
level out (v)	livellare	*(leeh-vehl-lAh-reh)*
leverage, financial	l'ammontare di passività nella struttura finanziara dell'impresa	*(ahm-mohn-tAh-reh deeh pahs-seeh-veeh-tAh nehl-lah strooht-tOOh-rah feeh-nahn-tsyAh-reeh-ah dehl eehm-prEh-zah)*
levy taxes (v)	imporre tasse	*(eehm-pOhr-reh tAhs-seh)*
liability insurance	l'assicurazione sulla responsabilità civile	*(ahs-seeh-kooh-rah-tsyOh-neh soohl-lah rehs-pohn-sah-beeh-leeh-tAh cheeh-vEEh-leh)*
liability	la responsabilità	*(rehs-pohn-sah-beeh-leeh-tAh)*

L

liability, actual	la responsabilità effettiva, la passività effettiva	*(rehs-pohn-sah-beeh-leeh-tAh ehf-feht-tEEh-vah), (pahs-seeh-veeh-tAh ehf-feht-tEEh-vah)*
liability, assumed	la responsabilità presunta	*(rehs-pohn-sah-beeh-leeh-tAh preh-zOOhn-tah)*
liability, contingent	la responsabilità contingente, la sopravvenienza passiva	*(rehs-pohn-sah-beeh-leeh-tAh kohn-teehn-jEhn-teh), (soh-prahv-veeh-vEhn-tsah pahs-sEEh-vah)*
liability, current	gli impegni attuali, la responsabilità corrente	*(eehm-pEh-nyeeh aht-twAh-leeh), (rehs-pohn-sah-beeh-leeh-tAh kohr-rEhn-teh)*
liability, fixed	la responsabilità fissa	*(rehs-pohn-sah-beeh-leeh-tAh fEEhs-sah)*
liability, unsecured	l'impegno senza garanzie, la passività senza garanzia	*(eehm-pEh-nyoh sEhn-tsah gah-rahn-tsEEh-eh), (pahs-seeh-veeh-tAh sEhn-tsah gah-rahn-tsEEh-eh)*
liable for tax	il responsabile per l'imposta	*(rehs-pohn-sAh-beeh-leeh pehr leehm-pOhs-tah)*
liable to	soggetto a	*(sohj-jEht-toh ah)*
liaison	il legame	*(leh-gAh-meh)*
libel	la diffamazione	*(deehf-fah-mah-tsyOh-neh)*
license	la licenza	*(leeh-chEhn-tsah)*
license fees	i costi di licenza	*(kOhs-teeh deeh leeh-chEhn-tsah)*
licensed warehouse	il deposito	*(deh-pOh-zeeh-toh)*
lien	il pegno	*(pEh-nyoh)*
life cycle of a product	la durata di un prodotto	*(dooh-rAh-tah deeh oohn proh-dOht-toh)*
life insurance policy	la polizza d'assicurazione sulla vita	*(pOh-leehts-tsah dahs-seeh-kooh-rah-tsyOh-neh)*
life member	il socio a vita	*(sOh-choh ah vEEh-tah)*
life of a patent	la durata di un brevetto	*(dooh-rAh-tah deeh oohn breh-vEht-toh)*
lighterage	lo scarico con chiatte	*(skAh-reeh-koh kohn kyAht-teh)*
limestone	il calce	*(kAhl-cheh)*

limit order (stock market)	l'ordine a termine	*(Ohr-deeh-neh ah tEhr-meeh-neh)*
limited liability	la responsabilità limitata	*(rehs-pohn-sah-beeh-leeh-tAh leeh-meeh-tAh-tah)*
limited partnership	la società a responsabilità limitata (s.r.l.)	*(soh-cheh-tAh ah rehs-pohn-sah-beeh-leeh-tAh leeh-meeh-tAh-tah)*
line	la linea	*(lEEh-neh-ah)*
line drawing	il disegno	*(deeh-zEh-nyoh)*
line executive	il dirigente di linea	*(deeh-reeh-jEhn-teh deeh lEEh-neh-ah)*
line management	l'amministrazione dirigen-ziale	*(ahm-meeh-neehs-trah-tsyOh-neh deeh-reeh-jehn-tsyAh-leh)*
line of business	l'attività commerciale	*(aht-teeh-veeh-tAh kohm-mehr-chAh-leh)*
line, product	la gamma di prodotti, la linea di prodotti	*(gAhm-mah deeh proh-dOht-teeh), (lEEh-neh-ah deeh proh-dOht-teeh)*
linear	lineare	*(leeh-neh-Ah-reh)*
linear estimation	la valutazione lineare	*(vah-looh-tah-tsyOh-neh leeh-neh-Ah-reh)*
linear programming	la programmazione lineare	*(proh-grahm-mah-tsyOh-neh leeh-neh-Ah-reh)*
linear terms	i termini lineari	*(tEhr-meeh-neeh leeh-neh-Ah-reeh)*
linen	la biancheria da tavola	*(byahn-keh-rEEh-ah dah tAh-voh-lah)*
lingerie	l'abbigliamento intimo	*(ahb-beeh-kyah-mEhn-toh EEhn-teeh-moh)*
lining	la foderatura	*(foh-deh-rah-tOOh-rah)*
liqueur	il liquore	*(leeh-kwOh-reh)*
liquid assets	gli attivi mobili, l'attivo cir-colante	*(aht-tEEh-veeh mOh-beeh-leeh), (aht-tEEh-voh cheehr-koh-lAhn-teh)*
liquidation	la liquidazione	*(leeh-kweeh-dah-tsyOh-neh)*
liquidation value	il valore liquidato	*(vah-lOh-reh leeh-kweeh-dAh-toh)*
liquidity	la liquidità	*(leeh-kweeh-deeh-tAh)*

liquidity preference (economics)	la preferenza per la liquidità	*(preh-feh-rEhn-tsah pehr lah leeh-kweeh-deeh-tAh)*
liquidity ratio	il rapporto di liquidità	*(rahp-pOhr-toh deeh leeh-kweeh-deeh-tAh)*
list (v)	elencare	*(eh-lehn-kAh-reh)*
list price	il prezzo di listino	*(prEhts-tsoh deeh leehs-tEEh-noh)*
listed securities	le azioni registrate presso la borsa	*(ah-tsyOh-neeh reh-jeehs-trAh-teh prEhs-soh lah bOhr-sah)*
liter	il litro	*(lEEh-troh)*
litigation	la lite	*(lEEh-teh)*
living trust	il fidecommisso vivente	*(feeh-deh-kohm-mEEhs-soh veeh-vEhn-teh)*
lizard skin	la pelle di lucertola	*(pEhl-leh deeh looh-chEhr-toh-lah)*
load (sales charge)	il carico, la commissione	*(kAh-reeh-koh), (kohm-meehs-syOh-neh)*
load factor	il fattore del ricarico	*(faht-tOh-reh dehl reeh-kAh-reeh-koh)*
loan	il prestito	*(prEhs-teeh-toh)*
loan stock	i titoli mobiliari prestati a un broker	*(tEEh-toh-leeh moh-beeh-lyAh-reeh prehs-tAh-teeh ah oohn broker)*
lobbying	i tentativi di influenzare atti governativi con pressioni varie	*(tehn-tah-tEEh-veeh deeh eehn-flooh-ehn-tsAh-reh Aht-teeh goh-vehr-nah-tEEh-veeh kohn prehs-syOh-neeh vAh-reeh-eh)*
local customs	le usanze locali	*(ooh-zAhn-tseh loh-kAh-leeh)*
local taxes	le imposte locali	*(eehm-pOhs-teh loh-kAh-leeh)*
lock in (v) (rate of interest)	bloccare, assicurare	*(blohk-kAh-reh), (ahs-seeh-kooh-rAh-reh)*
lock out	la serrata	*(sehr-rah-tOOh-rah)*
logistics	la logistica	*(loh-jEEhs-teeh-kah)*
logo	il marchio	*(mAhr-kyoh)*

long hedge	l'investimento di protezione a lunga scadenza	*(eehn-vehs-teeh-mEhn-toh deeh proh-teh-tsyOh-neh ah lOOhn-gah skah-dEhn-tsah)*
long interest	l'interesse lungo	*(eehn-teh-rEhs-seh lOOhn-goh)*
long sleeves	le maniche lunghe	*(mAh-neeh-keh lOOhn-geh)*
long ton	la tonnellata metrica	*(tohn-neh-lAh-tah mEh-treeh-kah)*
long-range planning	la pianificazione a lunga scadenza	*(pyah-neeh-feeh-kah-tsyOh-neh ah lOOhn-gah skah-dEhn-tsah)*
long-term capital account	il conto capitale a lungo termine	*(kOhn-toh kah-peeh-tAh-leh ah lOOhn-goh tEhr-meeh-neh)*
long-term debt	il debito a lungo termine	*(dEh-beeh-toh ah lOOhn-goh tEhr-meeh-neh)*
loss	le perdita	*(pEhr-deeh-tah)*
loss leader	l'articolo posto in vendita pubblicitaria al di sotto del prezzo necessario per guadagnare un profitto	*(ahr-tEEh-koh-loh pOhs-toh eehn vEhn-deeh-tah poohb-bleeh-cheeh-tAh-reeh-ah ahl deeh sOht-toh dehl prEhts-tsoh neh-chehs-sAh-reeh-oh pehr gwah-dah-nyAh-reh oohn proh-fEEht-toh)*
loss, gross	la perdita lorda	*(pEhr-deeh-tah lOhr-dah)*
loss, net	la perdita netta	*(pEhr-deeh-tah nEht-tah)*
loss-loss ratio	il rapporto perdita contro perdita	*(rahp-pOhr-toh pEhr-deeh-tah kOhn-troh pEhr-deeh-tah)*
lot	la partita, il lotto	*(pahr-tEEh-tah, lOht-toh)*
low income	il basso reddito	*(bAhs-soh rEhd-deeh-toh)*
low-interest loans	i prestiti con tasso d'interesse basso (favorevole)	*(prEhs-teeh-teeh kohn tAhs-soh deehn-teh-rEhs-seh bAhs-soh fah-voh-rEh-voh-leh)*
low-yield bonds	i buoni a basso rendimento	*(bwOh-neeh ah bAhs-soh rehn-deeh-mEhn-toh)*
lower case	il minuscolo	*(meeh-nOOhs-koh-loh)*
lump sum	la somma globale	*(sOhm-mah gloh-bAh-leh)*
luxury goods	i beni voluttuari	*(bEh-neeh voh-looht-twAh-reeh)*

L

luxury tax	l'imposta sui beni di lusso	*(eehm-pOhs-tah sooh-eeh bEh-neeh deeh lOOhs-soh)*
lynx	il lince	*(lEEhn-cheh)*

M

machinery	i macchinari	*(mahk-keeh-nAh-reeh)*
macroeconomics	la macroeconomia	*(mah-kroh-eh-koh-noh-mEEh-ah)*
magnetic memory	la memoria magnetica	*(meh-mOh-reeh-ah mah-nyEh-teeh-kah)*
magnetic tape	il nastro magnetico	*(nAhs-troh mah-nyEh-teeh-koh)*
magnum (2 bottles in one)	il bottiglione da due litri	*(boht-teeh-lyOh-neh dah dOOh-eh lEEh-treeh)*
mail order	l'ordine per corrispondenza	*(Ohr-deeh-neh pehr kohr-reehs-pohn-dEhn-tsah)*
mailing list	l'elenco di indirizzi per invio di materiali pubblicitari	*(eh-lEhn-koh deeh eehn-deeh-rEEhts-tseeh pehr eehn-vEEh-oh deeh mah-teh-ryAh-leeh poohb-bleeh-cheeh-tAh-reeh)*
mainframe computer	l'elaboratore centrale	*(eh-lah-boh-rah-tOh-reh chehn-trAh-leh)*
maintenance contract	il contratto di manutenzione	*(kohn-trAht-toh deeh mah-nooh-tehn-tsyOh-neh)*
maintenance	la manutenzione	*(mah-nooh-tehn-tsyOh-neh)*
maintenance margin	il margine di manutenzione	*(mAhr-jeeh-neh deeh mah-nooh-tehn-tsyOh-neh)*
maize	il mais, il granoturco	*(mah-EEhs), (grah-noh-tOOhr-koh)*
majority interest	l'interesse maggioritario	*(eehn-teh-rEhs-seh mahj-joh-reeh-tAh-reeh-oh)*
make available (v)	rendere disponibile	*(rEhn-deh-reh deehs-poh-nEEh-beeh-leh)*
make-or-buy decision	la decisione di fabbricare invece di comprare	*(deh-cheeh-zyOh-neh deeh fahb-breeh-kAh-reh eehn-vEh-cheh deeh kohm-prAh-reh)*

maker (of a check, draft, etc.)	il fattore	*(faht-tOh-reh)*
makeshift	di fortuna, di ripiego	*(deeh fohr-tOOh-nah), (deeh reeh-pyEh-goh)*
makeup case	il portatrucco	*(pohr-tah-trOOhk-koh)*
malleability	la malleabilità, la duttilità	*(mahl-leh-ah-beeh-leeh-tAh), (dooht-teeh-leeh-tAh)*
malolactic fermentation	la fermentazione malolattica	*(fehr-mehn-tah-tsyOh-neh mah-loh-lAht-teeh-kah)*
man (gal) Friday	il factotum	*(fahk-tOh-toohm)*
man hours	le ore lavorative	*(Oh-reh lah-voh-rah-tEEh-veh)*
man-made fibers	le fibre artificiali, le fibre sintetiche	*(fEEh-breh ahr-teeh-feeh-chAh-leeh), (fEEh-breh seehn-tEh-teeh-keh)*
manage (v)	amministrare	*(ahm-meeh-neehs-trAh-reh)*
managed costs	i costi amministrati, i costi controllabili	*(kOhs-teeh ahm-meeh-neehs-trAh-teeh)*
managed economy	l'economia controllata	*(eh-koh-noh-mEEh-ah kohn-trohl-lAh-tah)*
managed float	la variabilità amministrata o controllata	*(vah-ryah-beeh-leeh-tAh ahm-meeh-neehs-trAh-tah oh kohn-trohl-lAh-tah)*
management	l'amministrazione	*(ahm-meeh-neeh-strah-tsyOh-neh)*
management accounting	la contabilità amministrativa	*(kohn-tah-beeh-leeh-tAh ahm-meeh-neehs-trah-tEEh-vah)*
management by objectives	la gestione per obiettivi	*(jehs-tyOh-neh pehr oh-byeht-tEEh-veeh)*
management chart	il quadro amministrativo, l'organigramma	*(kwAh-droh ahm-meeh-neehs-trah-tEEh-voh), (ohr-gah-neeh-grAhm-mah)*
management consultant	il consulente amministrativo	*(kohn-sooh-lEhn-teh ahm-meeh-neehs-trah-tEEh-voh)*
management fee	l'onorario amministrativo	*(oh-noh-rAh-reeh-oh ahm-meeh-neehs-trah-tEEh-voh)*
management group	il gruppo amministrativo	*(grOOhp-poh ahm-meeh-neehs-trah-tEEh-voh)*

M

management team	l'équipe amministrativa	*(eh-kEEhp ahm-meeh-neehs-trah-tEEh-vah)*
management, business	l'amministrazione commerciale, la gestione commerciale	*(ahm-meeh-neeh-strah-tsyOh-neh kohm-mehr-chAh-leh), (jehs-tyOh-neh kohm-mehr-chAh-leh)*
management, credit	l'amministrazione del credito	*(ahm-meeh-neeh-strah-tsyOh-neh dehl krEh-deeh-toh)*
management, financial	l'amministrazione finanziaria	*(ahm-meeh-neeh-strah-tsyOh-neh feeh-nahn-tsyAh-reeh-ah)*
management, line	l'amministrazione dirigenziale	*(ahm-meeh-neeh-strah-tsyOh-neh deeh-reeh-jehn-tsyAh-leh)*
management, market	l'amministrazione del mercato, la gestione del mercato	*(ahm-meeh-neeh-strah-tsyOh-neh dehl mehr-kAh-toh), (jehs-tyOh-neh dehl mehr-kAh-toh)*
management, middle	l'amministrazione intermediaria	*(ahm-meeh-neeh-strah-tsyOh-neh eehn-tehr-meh-dyAh-reeh-ah)*
management, office	l'amministrazione dell'ufficio, la gestione dell'ufficio	*(ahm-meeh-neeh-strah-tsyOh-neh dehl oohf-fEEh-choh), (jehs-tyOh-neh)*
management, personnel	la gestione del personale	*(jehs-tyOh-neh dehl pehr-soh-nAh-leh)*
management, product	la gestione del prodotto	*(jehs-tyOh-neh dehl proh-dOht-toh)*
management, sales	l'amministrazione delle vendite, la gestione delle vendite	*(ahm-meeh-neeh-strah-tsyOh-neh dehl-leh vEhn-deeh-teh), (jehs-tyOh-neh dehl-leh vEhn-deeh-teh)*
management, top	il massimo livello amministrativo, la dirigenza	*(mAhs-seeh-moh leeh-vEhl-loh ahm-meeh-neehs-trah-tEEh-voh), (deeh-reeh-jEhn-tsah)*
manager	l'amministratore, il direttore	*(ahm-meeh-neehs-trah-tOh-reh), (deeh-reht-tOh-reh)*
mandate	il mandato	*(mahn-dAh-toh)*
mandatory redemption	l'estinzione obbligatoria	*(ehs-teehn-tsyOh-neh ohb-bleeh-gah-tOh-reeh-ah)*

manganese ore	il minerale manganese	*(meeh-neh-rAh-leh mahn-gah-nEh-zeh)*
manicuring kit	il completo per la manicure	*(kohm-plEh-toh pehr lah mah-neeh-kOOh-reh)*
manifest	il manifesto	*(mah-neeh-fEhs-toh)*
manpower	la manodopera	*(mah-noh-dOh-peh-rah)*
manual workers	gli operai	*(oh-peh-rAh-eeh)*
manufacturer	il fabbricante, il produttore	*(fahb-breeh-kAhn-teh), (proh-dooht-tOh-reh)*
manufacturer's agent	l'agente del produttore	*(ah-jEhn-teh dehl proh-dooht-tOh-reh)*
manufacturer's representative	il rappresentante del produttore	*(rahp-preh-zehn-tAhn-teh dehl proh-dooht-tOh-reh)*
manufacturing capacity	la capacità di produzione, la capacità produttiva	*(kah-pah-cheeh-tAh deeh proh-dooh-tsyOh-neh), kah-pah-cheeh-tAh proh-dooht-tEEh-vah)*
manufacturing control	il controllo della produzione	*(kohn-trOhl-loh dehl-lah proh-dooh-tsyOh-neh)*
margin call	richiedere il saldo del deposito per coprire perdite sulla borsa	*(reeh-kyEh-deh-reh eehl sAhl-doh dehl deh-pOh-zeeh-toh pehr koh-prEEh-reh pEhr-deeh-teh soohl-lah bOhr-sah)*
margin of safety	il margine di sicurezza	*(mAhr-jeeh-neh deeh seeh-kooh-rEhts-tsah)*
margin requirements	le esigenze di margine	*(eh-zeeh-jEhn-tseh deeh mAhr-jeeh-neh)*
margin, gross	il margine lordo	*(mAhr-jeeh-neh lOhr-doh)*
margin, net	il margine netto	*(mAhr-jeeh-neh nEht-toh)*
margin, profit	il margine di profitto	*(mAhr-jeeh-neh deeh proh-fEEht-toh)*
marginal account	il conto marginale	*(kOhn-toh mahr-jeeh-nAh-leh)*
marginal cost	il costo marginale	*(kOhs-toh mahr-jeeh-nAh-leh)*
marginal pricing	la determinazione del prezzo marginale	*(deh-tehr-meeh-nah-tsyOh-neh dehl prEhts-tsoh mahr-jeeh-nAh-leh)*
marginal productivity	la produttività marginale	*(proh-dooht-teeh-veeh-tAh mahr-jeeh-nAh-leh)*

M

marginal revenue	i ricavi marginali	*(reeh-kAhveeh mahr-jeeh-nAh-leeh)*
marine cargo insurance	l'assicurazione marittima	*(ahs-seeh-kooh-rah-tsyOh-neh mah-rEEht-teeh-mah)*
marine underwriter	l'assicuratore marino	*(ahs-seeh-kooh-rah-tOh-reh mah-rEEh-noh)*
maritime contract	il contratto marittimo	*(kohn-trAht-toh mah-rEEht-teeh-moh)*
mark down (v)	scontare	*(skohn-tAh-reh)*
market (v)	vendere, mettere sul merca-to, market	*(vEhn-deh-reh), (mEht-teh-reh soohl mehr-kAh-toh), (mahrket)*
market	il mercato	*(mehr-kAh-toh)*
market access	l'accesso al mercato	*(ahch-chEhs-soh ahl mehr-kAh-toh)*
market appraisal	la valutazione di mercato	*(vah-looh-tah-tsyOh-neh deeh mehr-kAh-toh)*
market concentration	la concentrazione di mercato	*(kohn-chehn-trah-tsyOh-neh deeh mehr-kAh-toh)*
market dynamics	la dinamica del mercato	*(deeh-nAh-meeh-kah dehl mehr-kAh-toh)*
market forces	le forze di mercato	*(fOhr-tseh deeh mehr-kAh-toh)*
market forecast	la previsione del mercato	*(preh-veeh-zyOh-neh dehl mehr-kAh-toh)*
market index	l'indice di mercato	*(EEhn-deeh-cheh deeh mehr-kAh-toh)*
market management	l'amministrazione del mer-cato, la gestione del mer-cato	*(ahm-meeh-neehs-trah-tsyOh-neh dehl mehr-kAh-toh), (jehs-tyOh-neh dehl mehr-kAh-toh)*
market penetration	la penetrazione commerciale	*(peh-neh-trah-tsyOh-neh kohm-mehr-chAh-leh)*
market plan	il piano di mercato, il pro-gramma di mercato	*(pyAh-noh deeh mehr-kAh-toh), (proh-grAhm-mah deeh mehr-kAh-toh)*
market position	la posizione di mercato	*(poh-zeeh-tsyOh-neh deeh mehr-kAh-toh)*
market potential	il potenziale di mercato	*(poh-tehn-tsyAh-leh deeh mehr-kAh-toh)*
market price	il prezzo di mercato	*(prEhts-tsoh deeh mehr-kAh-toh)*

market rating	la valutazione del mercato	*(vah-looh-tah-tsyOh-neh dehl mehr-kAh-toh)*
market report	il rapporto sul mercato	*(rahp-pOhr-toh soohl mehr-kAh-toh)*
market research	la ricerca di mercato	*(reeh-chEhr-kah deeh mehr-kAh-toh)*
market saturation	la saturazione del mercato	*(sah-tooh-rah-tsyOh-neh dehl mehr-kAh-toh)*
market share	la quota di mercato	*(kOh-tah deeh mehr-kAh-toh)*
market survey	l'indagine di mercato	*(eehn-dAh-jeeh-neh deeh mehr-kAh-toh)*
market trends	le tendenze del mercato	*(tehn-dEhn-tseh dehl mehr-kAh-toh)*
market value	il valore di mercato	*(vah-lOh-reh deeh mehr-kAh-toh)*
market, buyer's	il mercato favorevole all'acquirente, il mercato propenso per gli acquirenti	*(mehr-kAh-toh fah-voh-rEh-voh-leh ahl ahk-kweeh-rEhn-teh), (mehr-kAh-toh proh-pEhn-soh pehr lyeeh ahk-kweeh-rEhn-teeh)*
market, fringe	il mercato marginale	*(mehr-kAh-toh mahr-jeeh-nAh-leh)*
market-maker (securities)	il compratore e venditore di titoli mobiliari, colui che crea un mercato	*(kohm-prah-tOh-reh eh vehn-deeh-tOh-reh deeh tEEht-toh-leeh moh-beeh-lyAh-reeh), (koh-lOOh-eeh keh krEh-ah oohn mehr-kAh-toh)*
marketable securities	i titoli di sicura affidabilità che possono essere posti sul mercato, i titoli mobiliari	*(tEEh-toh-leeh deeh seeh-kOOh-rah ahf-feeh-dah-beeh-leeh-tAh keh pOhs-soh-noh Ehs-seh-reh soohl mehr-kAh-toh), (tEEh-toh-leeh moh-beeh-lyAh-reeh)*
marketing	il marketing	*(marketing)*
marketing budget	il preventivo per il marketing	*(preh-vehn-tEEh-voh eel marketing)*
marketing concept	il concetto di marketing	*(kohn-chEht-toh deeh marketing)*
marketing plan	la strategia di marketing	*(strah-teh-jEEh-ah deeh marketing)*
marketplace	il mercato	*(mehr-kAh-toh)*

M

markup	il ricarico	*(reeh-kAh-reeh-koh)*
marmot	la marmotta	*(mahr-mOht-tah)*
mass communications	le comunicazioni di massa	*(koh-mooh-neeh-kah-tsyOh-neeh deeh mAhs-sah)*
mass marketing	il marketing per il mercato di massa	*(mehr-kAh-toh deeh mAhs-sah)*
mass media	i mezzi di comunicazione, i "mass media"	*(mEhds-dseeh deeh koh-mooh-neeh-kah-tsyOh-neh)*
mass production	la produzione di serie	*(proh-dooh-tsyOh-neh deeh sEh-reeh-eh)*
matched samples	i campioni uniformi	*(kahm-pyOh-neeh ooh-neeh-fOhr-meeh)*
materials	i materiali	*(mah-teh-ryAh-leeh)*
maternity leave	il congedo di maternità	*(kohn-jEh-doh deeh mah-tehr-neeh-tAh)*
mathematical model	il modello matematico	*(moh-dEhl-loh mah-teh-mAh-teeh-koh)*
matrix	la matrice	*(mah-trEEh-cheh)*
matrix management	l'amministrazione a matrice	*(ahm-meeh-neehs-trah-tsyOh-neh ah mah-trEEh-cheh)*
matt	non lucido, opaco	*(nohn lOOh-cheeh-doh), (oh-pAh-koh)*
maturity date	la data di maturazione	*(dAh-tah deeh mah-tooh-rah-tsyOh-neh)*
maturity	la maturità	*(mah-tooh-reeh-tAh)*
maximize (v)	ottimizzare	*(oht-teeh-meehds-dsAh-reh)*
mean (average)	la media	*(mEh-deeh-ah)*
measure (v)	misurare	*(meeh-zooh-rAh-reh)*
mechanic	il meccanico	*(mehk-kAh-neeh-koh)*
mechanical	il montaggio	*(mohn-tAhj-joh)*
mechanical engineering	l'ingegneria meccanica	*(eehn-jeh-nyeh-rEEh-ah mehk-kAh-neeh-kah)*
mechanics' lien	il privilegio del fornitore	*(preeh-veeh-lEh-joh dehl fohr-nee-tOh-reh)*
median	il valore mediano	*(vah-lOh-reh meh-dyAh-noh)*
mediation	la mediazione	*(meh-dyah-tsyOh-neh)*

medicine	la medicina	*(meh-deeh-chEEh-nah)*
medium of exchange	il mezzo di scambio	*(mEhds-dsoh)*
medium term	il medio termine	*(mEh-deeh-oh tEhr-meeh-neh)*
meet the price (v)	venire incontro al prezzo	*(veh-nEEh-reh eehn-kOhn-troh ahl prEhts-tsoh)*
meeting	la riunione	*(reeh-ooh-nyOh-neh)*
meeting, board	la riunione del consiglio	*(reeh-ooh-nyOh-neh dehl kohn-sEEh-lyoh)*
member firm	la ditta associata	*(dEEht-tah ahs-soh-chAh-tah)*
member of firm	il socio	*(sOh-choh)*
memorandum	il memorandum, l'appunto	*(ahp-pOOhn-toh)*
mercantile	mercantile	*(mehr-kahn-tEEh-leh)*
mercantile agency	l'agenzia mercantile	*(ah-jehn-tsEEh-ah mehr-kahn-tEEh-leh)*
mercantile law	la legge mercantile	*(lEhj-jeh mehr-kahn-tEEh-leh)*
merchandise	i prodotti	*(proh-dOht-teeh)*
merchandising	la mercanzia	*(mehr-kahn-tsEEh-ah)*
merchant bank	la merchant bank	
merchant guild	l'associazione mercantile	*(ahs-soh-chah-tsyOh-neh mehr-kahn-tEEh-leh)*
merchant	il mercante	*(mehr-kAhn-teh)*
merger	la fusione	*(fooh-zyOh-neh)*
metals	i metalli	*(meh-tAhl-leeh)*
methane	il metano	*(meh-tAh-noh)*
method	il metodo	*(mEh-toh-doh)*
metrification	la metrificazione	*(meh-treeh-feeh-kah-tsyOh-neh)*
microchip	il microchip	*(meeh-kroh-chEEhp)*
microcomputer	il micro computer	*(meeh-kroh kohm-pyOOh-tehr)*
microfiche	la microfiche	*(meeh-kroh fEEsh)*
microfilm	il microfilm	*(meeh-kroh fEEhlm)*
microphone	il microfono	*(meeh-krOh-foh-noh)*

M

microprocessor	il micro elaboratore	*(meeh-kroh eh-lah-boh-rah-tOh-reh)*
microwave	la microonda	*(meeh-kroh-Ohn-dah)*
middle management	l'amministrazione intermediaria	*(ahm-meeh-neehs-trah-tsyOh-neh eehn-tehr-meh-dyAh-reeh-ah)*
middleman	l'intermediario	*(eehn-tehr-meh-dyAh-reeh-oh)*
mileage	il chilometraggio	*(keeh-loh-meh-trAhj-joh)*
milling	la macinatura, la fresatura	*(mah-cheeh-nah-tOOh-rah), (freh-zah-tOOh-rah)*
minicomputer	il mini computer, il mini elaboratore elettronico	*(mEEh-neeh kohm-pyOOh-tehr), (mEEh-neeh eh-lah-boh-rah-tOh-reh eh-leht-trOh-neeh-koh)*
minimum reserves	le riserve minime	*(reeh-zEhr-veh mEEh-neeh-meh)*
minimum wage	la paga minima, la paga base	*(pAh-gah mEEh-neeh-mah), (pAh-gah bAh-zeh)*
mink	il visone	*(veeh-zOh-neh)*
minority interest	l'interesse minoritario	*(eehn-teh-rEhs-seh meeh-noh-reeh-tAh-reeh-oh)*
mint	la zecca	*(dsEhk-kah)*
miscalculation	il calcolo errato	*(kAhl-koh-loh ehr-rAh-toh)*
miscellaneous	varie	*(vAh-reeh-eh)*
misleading	ingannevole	*(eehn-gahn-nEh-voh-leh)*
misunderstanding	malinteso	*(mah-leehn-tEh-zoh)*
mixed cost	il costo misto	*(kOhs-toh mEEhs-toh)*
mixed sampling	la campionatura mista	*(kahm-pyoh-nah-tOOh-rah mEEhs-tah)*
mixer	il miscelatore	*(meeh-sheh-lah-tOh-reh)*
mobility of labor	la mobilità della manodopera	*(moh-beeh-leeh-tAh dehl-lah dehl lah-vOh-roh)*
mock-up	il modello	*(mod-dEhl-loh)*
mode	la maniera	*(mah-nyEh-rah)*
model	il modello, la modella, il capo	*(moh-dEhl-loh), (moh-dEhl-lah), (kAh-poh)*

M

modem	il modulatore per la trasmissione di dati via cavo	*(moh-dooh-lah-tOh-reh pehr lah trahz-meehs-syOh-neh deeh dAh-teeh vEEh-ah kAh-voh)*
modular production	la produzione modulare	*(proh-dooh-tsyOh-neh moh-dooh-lAh-reh)*
molar	il molare	*(moh-lAh-reh)*
mole	il grammo molecola	*(grAhm-moh moh-lEh-koh-lah)*
molecule	la molecola	*(moh-lEh-koh-lah)*
molybdenum	il molibdeno	*(moh-leehb-dEh-noh)*
monetary base	la base monetaria	*(bAh-zeh moh-neh-tAh-reeh-ah)*
monetary credits	i crediti monetari	*(krEh-deeh-teeh moh-neh-tAh-reeh)*
monetary policy	la politica monetaria	*(poh-lEEh-teeh-kah moh-neh-tAh-reeh-ah)*
money	il denaro	*(deh-nAh-roh)*
money broker	il cambio valute, l'intermediario valutario	*(kAhm-byoh vah-lOOh-teh), (eehn-tehr-meh-dyAh-reeh-oh vah-looh-tAh-reeh-oh)*
money manager	l'amministratore finanziario	*(ahm-meeh-neehs-trah-tOh-reh feeh-nahn-tsyAh-reeh-oh)*
money market	il mercato monetario	*(mehr-kAh-toh moh-neh-tAh-reeh-ah)*
money order	il vaglia postale	*(vAh-lyah pohs-tAh-leh)*
money shop	il negozio di denaro	*(neh-gOh-tsyoh deeh deh-nAh-roh)*
money supply	la disponibilità dei capitali	*(deehs-poh-neeh-beeh-leeh-tAh deh-eeh kah-peeh-tAh-leeh)*
monitor	il monitor	
monopoly	il monopolio	*(moh-noh-pOh-leeh-oh)*
monopsony	il monopsonio	*(moh-nohp-sOh-neeh-oh)*
Monte Carlo technique	la tecnica di Monte Carlo	*(tEhk-neeh-kah)*
moonlighting	il lavoro nero	*(lah-vOh-roh nEh-roh)*
morale	il morale	*(moh-rAh-leh)*

moratorium	il moratorio	*(moh-rah-tOh-reeh-oh)*
Moroccan leather	il marocchino	*(mah-rohk-kEEh-noh)*
morphine	la morfina	*(mohr-fEEh-nah)*
mortgage	l'ipoteca	*(eeh-poh-tEh-kah)*
mortgage bank	la banca ipotecaria	*(bAhn-kah eeh-poh-teh-kAh-reeh-ah)*
mortgage bond	l'obbligazione garantita da ipoteca	*(ohb-bleeh-gah-tsyOh-neh gah-rahn-tEEh-tah dah eeh-poh-tEh-kah)*
mortgage certificate	il certificato ipotecario	*(chehr-teeh-feeh-kAh-toh eeh-poh-teh-kAh-reeh-oh)*
mortgage debenture	l'obbligazione ipotecaria	*(ohb-bleeh-gah-tsyOh-neh eeh-poh-teh-kAh-reeh-ah)*
most-favored nation	il paese con trattamento preferenziale	*(pah-Eh-zeh kohn traht-tah-mEhn-toh preh-feh-rehn-tsyAh-leh)*
motion	la mozione	*(moh-tsyOh-neh)*
motivation study	lo studio motivazionale	*(stOOh-deeh-oh moh-teeh-vah-tsyoh-nAh-leh)*
motor	il motore	*(moh-tOh-reh)*
movement of goods	lo spostamento dei beni	*(spohs-tah-mEhn-toh deh-eeh bEh-neeh)*
moving average	la media variabile	*(mEh-deeh-ah vah-ryAh-beeh-leh)*
moving expenses	le spese di trasloco	*(spEh-zeh deeh trahs-lOh-koh)*
moving parity	la parità variabile	*(pah-reeh-tAh vah-ryAh-beeh-leh)*
multicurrency	multivalutario	*(moohl-teeh-vah-looh-tAh-reeh-oh)*
multilateral agreement	la convenzione multilaterale	*(kohn-vehn-tsyOh-neh moohl-teeh-lah-teh-rAh-leh)*
multilateral trade	il commercio multilaterale	*(kohm-mEhr-choh moohl-teeh-lah-teh-rAh-leh)*
multinational corporation	la società multinazionale	*(soh-cheh-tAh moohl-teeh-nah-tsyoh-nAh-leh)*
multiple exchange rate	il tasso di cambio multiplo	*(tAhs-soh deeh kAhm-byoh mOOhl-teeh-ploh)*
multiple taxation	la tassazione multipla	*(tahs-sah-tsyOh-neh mOOhl-teeh-plah)*

multiples	i multipli	*(mOOhl-teeh-pleeh)*
multiplier	il moltiplicatore	*(mohl-teeh-pleeh-kah-tOh-reh)*
multiprogramming	multiprogrammato	*(moohl-teeh-proh-grahm-mAh-toh)*
municipal bond	l'obbligazione municipale	*(ohb-bleeh-gah-tsyOh-neh mooh-neeh-cheeh-pAh-leh)*
muslin	la mussola	*(mOohs-soh-lah)*
must	il mosto	*(mOhs-toh)*
mutual fund	il fondo d'investimento	*(fOhn-doh deehn-vehs-teeh-mEhn-toh)*
mutual savings bank	la cassa cooperativa di risparmio	*(kAhs-sah koh-oh-peh-rah-tEEh-vah deeh reehs-pAhr-myoh)*
mutually exclusive classes	le classi mutuamente esclusive	*(klAhs-seeh mooh-twah-mEhn-teh ehs-klooh-zEEh-veh)*

N

---

named inland point in country of origin	il punto interno denominato nel paese d'importazione	*(pOOhn-toh eehn-tEhr-noh deh-noh-meeh-nAh-toh nehl pah-Eh-zeh deehm-pohr-tah-tsyOh-neh)*
named point of destination	la destinazione indicata	*(dehs-teeh-nah-tsyOh-neh eehn-deeh-kAh-tah)*
named point of exportation	il punto d'esportazione indicato	*(pOOhn-toh dehs-pohr-tah-tsyOh-neh eehn-deeh-kAh-toh)*
named point of origin	il punto d'origine indicato	*(pOOhn-toh doh-rEEh-jeeh-neh eehn-deeh-kAh-toh)*
named port of importation	il porto d'importazione denominato	*(pOhr-toh deehm-pohr-tah-tsyOh-neh deh-noh-meeh-nAh-toh)*
named port of shipment	il porto di spedizione denominato	*(pOhr-toh deeh speh-deeh-tsyOh-neh deh-noh-meeh-nAh-toh)*
napkin	il tovagliolo	*(toh-vah-lyOh-loh)*
napkin ring	l'anello per tovagliolo	*(ah-nEhl-loh pehr toh-vah-lyOh-loh)*

narcotic	il narcotico	*(nahr-kOh-teeh-koh)*
national bank	la banca nazionale	*(bAhn-kah nah-tsyoh-nAh-leh)*
national debt	il debito nazionale	*(dEh-beeh-toh nah-tsyoh-nAh-leh)*
nationalism	il nazionalismo	*(nah-tsyoh-nah-lEEhz-moh)*
nationalization	la nazionalizzazione	*(nah-tsyoh-nah-leehds-dsah-tsyOh-neh)*
native produce	il prodotto locale	*(proh-dOht-toh loh loh-kAh-leh)*
natural gas	il gas naturale	*(gas nah-tooh-rAh-leh)*
natural resources	le risorse naturali	*(reeh-zOhr-seh nah-tooh-rAh-leeh)*
near money	l'attivita finanziaria a brevis-simo termine	*(aht-teeh-veeh-tAh ah breh-vEEhs-seeh-moh tEhr-meeh-neh)*
neck (of bottle)	il collo	*(kOhl-loh)*
needle	l'ago	*(Ah-goh)*
needs analysis	l'analisi delle esigenze	*(ah-nAh-leeh-zeeh dehl-leh eh-zeeh-jEhn-tseh)*
negative	il negativo	*(neh-gah-tEEh-voh)*
negative cash flow	il flusso di cassa negativo	*(flOOhs-soh deeh kAhs-sah neh-gah-tEEh-voh)*
negative pledge	il pegno negativo	*(pEh-nyoh neh-gah-tEEh-voh)*
negligent	negligente	*(neh-gleeh-jEhn-teh)*
negotiable	negoziabile	*(neh-goh-tsyAh-beeh-leh)*
negotiable securities	i titoli mobiliari negoziabili	*(tEEh-toh-leeh moh-beeh-lyAh-reeh neh-goh-tsyAh-beeh-leeh)*
negotiate (v)	negoziare, trattare	*(neh-goh-tsyAh-reh)*
negotiated sale	la vendita negoziata	*(vEhn-deeh-tah neh-goh-tsyAh-tah)*
negotiation	il negoziato	*(neh-goh-tsyAh-toh)*
net	netto	*(nEht-toh)*
net asset value	il valore netto degli attivi	*(vah-lOh-reh nEht-toh deh-lyeeh aht-tEEh-veeh)*
net asset worth	il valore netto degli attivi	*(vah-lOh-reh nEht-toh deh-lyeeh aht-tEEh-veeh)*

net assets	gli attivi netti	*(aht-tEEh-veeh nEht-teeh)*
net borrowed reserves	le riserve di capitali presi a prestito	*(reeh-zEhr-veh deeh kah-peeh-tAh-leeh prEh-zeeh ah prEhs-teeh-toh)*
net cash flow	il flusso netto di cassa	*(flOOhs-soh nEht-toh deeh kAhs-sah)*
net change	il cambio netto, il cambiamento netto	*(kAhm-byoh nEht-toh), (kahm-byah-mEhn-toh nEht-toh)*
net equity assets	gli attivi netti sulle azioni ordinarie	*(aht-tEEh-veeh nEht-teeh sohl-leh ah-tsyOh-neeh ohr-deeh-nAh-reeh-eh)*
net income	il reddito netto	*(rEhd-deeh-toh nEht-toh)*
net investment	l'investimento netto	*(eehn-vehs-teeh-mEhn-toh nEht-toh)*
net loss	la perdita netta	*(pEhr-deeh-tah nEht-tah)*
net margin	il margine netto	*(mAhr-jeeh-neh nEht-toh)*
net position (of a trader)	la posizione netta	*(poh-zeeh-tsyOh-neh nEht-tah)*
net present value	il valore attuale netto	*(vah-lOh-reh aht-twAh-leh nEht-toh)*
net profit	il profitto netto	*(proh-fEEht-toh nEht-toh)*
net sales	le vendite nette	*(vEhn-deeh-teh nEht-teh)*
net working capital	il capitale circolante al netto	*(kah-peeh-tAh-leh cheehr-koh-lAhn-teh ahl nEht-toh)*
net worth	il capitale azionario, il valore netto	*(kah-peeh-tAh-leh ah-tsyoh-nAh-reeh-oh), (vah-lOh-reh nEht-toh)*
network (v)	stabilire contatti capillari	*(stah-beeh-lEEh-reh kohn-tAht-teeh kah-peehl-lAh-reeh)*
neutral	neutro	*(nEh-ooh-troh)*
neutralization	la neutralizzazione	*(neh-ooh-trah-leehds-dsah-tsyOh-neh)*
neutron	il neutrone	*(neh-ooh-trOh-neh)*
new issue	la nuova emissione	*(nwOh-vah eh-meehs-syOh-neh)*
new money	l'infusione di fondi da nuove fonti	*(eehn-fooh-zyOh-neh deeh fOhn-deeh dah nwOh-veh fOhn-teeh)*

new product development	lo sviluppo di nuovi prodotti	*(zveeh-lOOhp-poh deeh nwOh-veeh proh-dOht-teeh)*
newsprint	la carta da giornale	*(kAhr-tah dah johr-nAh-leh)*
nickel	il nichelio	*(neeh-kEh-leeh-oh)*
night depositor	la cassa notturna	*(kAhs-sah noht-tOOhr-nah)*
nitrate	il nitrato	*(neeh-trAh-toh)*
nitric acid	acido nitrico	*(Ah-ceeh-doh nEEh-treeh-koh)*
nitrite	il nitrite	*(neeh-trEEt-teh)*
nitrogen	il nitrogeno	*(neeh-trOh-jeh-noh)*
no par value	senza valore alla pari	*(sEhn-tsah vah-lOh-reh ahl-lah pAh-reeh)*
no problem	nessun problema	*(nehs-sOOhn proh-blEh-mah)*
no-load fund	il fondo d'investimento senza provvigione	*(fOhn-doh deehn-vehs-teeh-mEhn-toh sEhn-tsah prohv-veeh-jOh-neh)*
nominal price	il prezzo nominale	*(prEhts-tsoh noh-meeh-nAh-leh)*
nominal yield	il reddito nominale	*(rEhd-deeh-toh noh-meeh-nAh-leh)*
noncumulative preferred stock	le azioni privilegiate non cumulative	*(ah-tsyOh-neeh preeh-veeh-leh-jAh-teh nohn kooh-mooh-lah-tEEh-veh)*
noncurrent assets	l'attività non a breve termine	*(aht-teeh-veeh-tAh nohn ah brEh-veh tEhr-meeh-neh)*
nondurable goods	i beni non durevoli	*(bEh-neeh nohn dooh-rEh-boh-leeh)*
nonfeasance	le trasgressione	*(trahs-grehs-syOh-neh)*
nonmember	il non associato, il non socio	*(nohn ahs-soh-chAh-toh), (nohn sOh-choh)*
nonprofit	senza fini di lucro	*(sEhn-tsah fEEh-neeh deeh lOOh-kroh)*
nonresident	il non residente, lo straniero	*(nohn reh-zeeh-dEhn-teh), (strah-nyEh-roh)*
nonvoting stock	le azioni senza diritto di voto	*(ah-tsyOh-neeh sEhn-tsah deeh-rEEht-toh deeh vOh-toh)*
norm	la norma	*(nOhr-mah)*

N

not otherwise indexed by name	non oltre indicato per nome	*(nohn Ohl-treh eehn-deeh-kAh-toh pehr nOh-meh)*
notary	il notaio	*(noh-tAh-yoh)*
note, credit	la nota di accredito	*(nOh-tah deeh ahk-krEh-deeh-toh)*
note, debit	la nota di addebito	*(nOh-tah deeh ahd-dEh-beeh-toh)*
note, promissory	la cambiale, il pagherò cambiario	*(kahm-byAh-leh), (pah-geh-rOh kahm-byAh-reeh-oh)*
notes receivable	le cambiali esigibili	*(kahm-byAh-leeh eh-zeeh-jEEh-beeh-leeh)*
novation	la novazione	*(noh-vah-tsyOh-neh)*
null and void	nullo a tutti gli effetti	*(nOOhl-loh ah tOOht-teeh lyeeh ehf-fEht-teeh)*
nullify (v)	annullare	*(ahn-noohl-lAh-reh)*
numerical control	il controllo numerico	*(kohn-trOhl-loh mooh-mEh-reeh-koh)*
nutria	il castorino	*(kahs-toh-rEEh-noh)*

O

obligation	l'obbligazione	*(ohb-bleeh-gah-tsyOh-neh)*
obsolescence	l'obsolescenza	*(ohb-soh-leh-shEhn-tsah)*
occupation	l'occupazione, l'impiego	*(ohk-kooh-pah-tsyOh-neh), (eehm-pyEh-goh)*
occupational hazard	il pericolo professionale	*(peh-rEEh-koh-loh proh-fehs-syoh-nAh-leh)*
odd lot broker	il mediatore di partite sparse	*(meh-dyah-tOh-reh deeh pahr-tEEh-teh spAhr-seh)*
odd lot	le rimanenze, la partita frazionata	*(reeh-mah-nEhn-tseh), (pahr-tEEh-tah frah-tsyoh-nAh-tah)*
odometer	il contachilometri	*(kohn-tah-keeh-lOh-meh-treeh)*
off board (stock market)	non ufficiale (borsa)	*(nohn oohf-feeh-chAh-leh [bohr-sah])*
off-line	inattivo, "off-line"	*(eeh-naht-tEEh-voh)*
off-the-books	non registrato, nero	*(nohn reh-jeehs-trAh-toh), (nEh-roh)*

offer (v)	offrire	*(ohf-frEEh-reh)*
offer for sale (v)	porre in vendita	*(pOhr-reh eehn vEhn-deeh-tah)*
offered price	il prezzo offerto	*(prEhts-tsoh ohf-fEhr-toh)*
offered rate	il tasso offerto	*(tAhs-soh ohf-fEhr-toh)*
office	l'ufficio	*(oohf-fEEh-choh)*
office management	l'amministrazione dell'ufficio, la gestione dell'ufficio	*(ahm-meeh-neehs-trah-tsyOh-neh dehl oohf-fEEh-choh), (jehs-tyOh-neh dehl oohf-fEEh-choh)*
office, branch	la filiale	*(feeh-lyAh-leh)*
office, head	la sede generale	*(sEh-deh jeh-neh-rAh-leh)*
offset printing	la fotolitografia	*(fOh-toh-leeh-toh-grah-fEEh-ah)*
offshore company	la ditta offshore	*(dEEht-tah)*
ohm	l'ohm	*(ohm)*
oil filter	il filtro dell'olio	*(fEEhl-troh dehl Oh-leeh-oh)*
oil pump	la pompa dell'olio	*(pOhm-pah dehl Oh-leeh-oh)*
oilcloth	la tela cerata	*(tEh-lah cheh-rAh-tah)*
ointment	l'unguento	*(oohn-gwEhn-toh)*
oligopoly	l'oligopolio	*(oh-leeh-goh-pOh-leeh-oh)*
oligopsony	l'oligopsonio	*(oh-leeh-gohp-sOh-neeh-oh)*
omit (v)	omettere	*(oh-mEht-teh-reh)*
on account	in conto	*(eehn kOhn-toh)*
on consignment	su rimessa	*(sooh reeh-mEhs-sah)*
on cost	su costo	*(sooh kOhs-toh)*
on demand	su richiesta	*(soh reeh-kyEhs-tah)*
on line (computer)	pronto per l'utilizzo, "on line"	*(prOhn-toh pehr looh-teeh-lEEhds-dsoh)*
on press	in stampa	*(eehn stAhm-pah)*
on the back	sul retro	*(soohl rEh-troh)*
on-the-job training	la formazione sul posto di lavoro	*(fohr-mah-tsyOh-neh soohl pOhs-toh deeh lah-vOh-roh)*
open account	il conto aperto	*(kOhn-toh ah-pEhr-toh)*

open cover	la copertura in abbonamento	*(koh-pehr-tOOh-rah eehn ahb-boh-nah-mEhn-toh)*
open door policy	la politica di apertura	*(poh-lEEh-teeh-kah deeh ah-pehr-tOOh-rah)*
open market	il mercato aperto	*(mehr-kAh-toh ah-pEhr-toh)*
open market operations	le operazioni di mercato aperto	*(oh-peh-rah-tsyOh-neeh deeh mehr-kAh-toh ah-pEhr-toh)*
open order	l'ordine continuo	*(Ohr-deeh-neh kohn-tEEh-nooh-oh)*
open shop	la fabbrica aperta anche ai non iscritti al sindacato	*(fAhb-breeh-kah ah-pEhr-tah Ahn-keh ah-eeh nohn eehs-krEEht-teeh ahl seehn-dah-kAh-toh)*
opening balance	il bilancio d'apertura	*(beeh-lAhn-choh dah-pehr-tOOh-rah)*
opening price	il prezzo iniziale, il prezzo di apertura del mercato	*(prEhts-tsoh eeh-neeh-tsyAh-leh), (prEhts-tsoh deeh h-pehr-tOOh-rah dehl mehr-kAh-toh)*
operating budget	il preventivo operativo	*(preh-vehn-tEEh-voh oh-peh-rah-tEEh-voh)*
operating expenses	le spese operative	*(spEh-zeh oh-peh-rah-tEEh-veh)*
operating income	il reddito operativo	*(rEhd-deeh-toh oh-peh-rah-tEEh-voh)*
operating profit	gli utili diretti	*(OOh-teeh-leeh deeh-rEht-teeh)*
operating statement	la dichiarazione operativa	*(deeh-kyah-rah-tsyOh-neh oh-peh-rah-tEEh-vah)*
operations audit	il controllo operativo	*(kohn-trOhl-loh oh-peh-rah-tEEh-voh)*
operations headquarters	la sede amministrativa	*(sEh-deh ahm-meeh-neehs-trah-tEEh-vah)*
operations management	la gestione delle operazioni	*(jehs-tyOh-neh dehl-leh oh-peh-rah-tsyOh-neeh)*
operator	l'operatore	*(oh-peh-rah-tOh-reh)*
opium	l'oppio	*(Ohp-pyoh)*
opossum	l'opossum	*(ohpahsuhm)*
opportunity costs	il costo dell'opportunità	*(kOhs-toh dehl ohp-pohr-tooh-neeh-tAh)*

optic	ottico	*(Oht-teeh-koh)*
option	l'opzione	*(ohp-tsyOh-neh)*
option index	l'indice delle opzioni	*(EEhn-deeh-cheh dehl-leh ohp-tsyOh-neeh)*
option, stock	l'opzione sulle azioni	*(ohp-tsyOh-neh soohl-leh ah-tsyOh-neeh)*
optional	opzionale, facoltativo	*(ohp-tsyoh-nAh-leh), (fah-kohl-tsah-tEEh-voh)*
oral bid	l'offerta a voce	*(ohf-fEhr-tah ah vOh-cheh)*
order (v)	ordinare	*(ohr-deeh-nAh-reh)*
order	l'ordine	*(Ohr-deeh-neh)*
order form	il modulo	*(mOh-dooh-loh)*
order number	il numero dell'ordine	*(nOOh-meh-roh dehl Ohr-deeh-neh)*
order of the day	l'ordine del giorno	*(Ohr-deeh-neh dehl jOhr-noh)*
order, to place an (v)	piazzare un ordine	*(pyahts-tsAh-reh oohn Ohr-deeh-neh)*
ordinance	la ordinanza	*(ohr-deeh-nAhn-zah)*
ordinary capital	il capitale ordinario	*(kah-peeh-tAh-leh ohr-deeh-nAh-reeh-oh)*
ore	il minerale	*(meeh-neh-rAh-leh)*
organic	organico	*(ohr-gAh-neeh-koh)*
organization chart	l'organigramma	*(ohr-gah-neeh-grAhm-mah)*
organization	l'organizzazione	*(ohr-gah-neehds-dsah-tsyOh-neh)*
original cost	il costo originale	*(kOhs-toh oh-reeh-jeeh-nAh-leh)*
original entry	l'entrata originale	*(ehn-trAh-tah oh-reeh-jeeh-nAh-leh)*
original maturity	la data originale di matura-zione	*(dAh-tah oh-reeh-jeeh-nAh-leh deeh mah-tooh-rah-tsyOh-neh)*
oscillator	l'oscillatore	*(oh-sheehl-lah-tOh-reh)*
ostrich skin	la pelle di struzzo	*(pEhl-leh deeh strOOhts-tsoh)*
other assets (and liabilities)	le altre attività (e passività)	*(Ahl-treh aht-teeh-veeh-tAh eh pahs-seeh-veeh-tAh)*
otter	la lontra	*(lOhn-trah)*

out of style	fuori moda	*(fWoh-reeh mOh-dah)*
out-of-pocket expenses	le spese di tasca propria	*(spEh-zeh deeh tAhs-kah prOh-preeh-ah)*
outbid (v)	offrire di più	*(ohf-frEEh-reh deeh pyOOh)*
outlay	lo sborsamento	*(zbohr-sah-mEhn-toh)*
outlet	lo sbocco	*(zbOhk-koh)*
outlook	la prospettiva	*(prohs-peht-tEEh-vah)*
output	la produzione	*(proh-dooh-tsyOh-neh)*
outsized articles	gli articoli fuori misura	*(ahr-tEEh-koh-leeh fwOh-reeh meeh-zOOh-rah)*
outstanding contract	il contratto insoluto	*(kohn-trAht-toh eehn-soh-lOOh-toh)*
outstanding debt	i debiti insoluti	*(dEh-beeh-teeh eehn-soh-lOOh-teeh)*
outstanding stock	le azioni in circolazione	*(ah-tsyOh-neeh eehn cheehr-koh-lah-tsyOh-neh)*
outturn	la produzione	*(proh-dooh-tsyOh-neh)*
over-the-counter quotation	le quotazione fuori borsa	*(kwoh-tah-tsyOh-neh fwOh-reeh bOhr-sah)*
overage	l'eccesso	*(ehch-chEhs-soh)*
overbuy (v)	acquistare in quantità eccesiva	*(ahk-kweehs-tAh-reh eehn kwahn-teeh-tAh ehch-chehs-sEEh-vah)*
overcapitalized	capitalizzato in eccesso	*(kah-peeh-tah-leehds-dsAh-toh eehn ehch-chEhs-soh)*
overcharge	il sovrapprezzo	*(soh-vrahp-prEhts-tsoh)*
overdraft	la somma in eccesso ai fondi disponibili, scoperto	*(sOhm-mah eehn ehch-chEhs-soh ah-eeh fOhn-deeh deehs-poh-nEEh-beeh-leeh), (skoh-pEhr-toh)*
overdue	scaduto	*(skah-dOOh-toh)*
overhang	la sporgenza	*(spohr-jEhn-tsah)*
overhead	le spese fisse generali	*(spEh-zeh fEEhs-seh jeh-neh-rAh-leeh)*
overlap	la sovrapposizione	*(soh-vrahp-poh-zeeh-tsyOh-neh)*

overnight	nel giro di una notte	*(nehl jEEh-roh deeh ooh-nah nOht-teh)*
overpaid	sovrappagato	*(soh-vrahp-pah-gAh-toh)*
overrun (in printing)	superare la giustezza	*(sooh-peh-rAh-reh lah joohs-tEhts-tsah)*
overseas common point	il punto comune oltremare	*(pOOhn-toh koh-mOOh-neh ohl-treh-mAh-reh)*
oversell (v)	vendere più di quanto si abbia	*(vEhn-deh-reh pyOOh deeh kwAhn-toh seeh Ahb-byah)*
overstock	il sovraccarico	*(soh-vrahk-kAh-reeh-koh)*
oversubscribed	sottoscritto oltre il necessario	*(soht-toh-skrEEht-toh Ohl-treh eehl neh-chehs-sAh-reeh-oh)*
oversupply	le forniture oltre il necessario	*(fohr-neeh-tOOh-reh Ohl-treh eehl neh-chehs-sAh-reeh-oh)*
overtime	il lavoro straordinario	*(lah-vOh-roh strah-ohr-deeh-nAh-ryoh)*
overvalued	sopravvalutato	*(soh-prahv-vah-looh-tAh-toh)*
owner	il proprietario	*(proh-preeh-eh-tAh-reeh-oh)*
owner's equity	l'interesse del proprietario	*(eehn-teh-rEhs-seh dehl proh-preeh-eh-tAh-reeh-oh)*
ownership	la proprietà	*(proh-preeh-eh-tAh)*
ownership, absentee	il proprietario assente	*(proh-preeh-eh-tAh-reeh-oh ahs-sEhn-teh)*
oxidation	l'ossidazione	*(ohs-seeh-dah-tsyOh-neh)*
oxygen	l'ossigeno	*(ohs-sEEh-jeh-noh)*

P

p/e ratio	il rapporto tra i prezzi ed i guadagni di un azione	*(rahp-pOhr-toh trah eeh prEhts-tseeh eh eeh gwah-dAh-nyeeh)*
package deal	la trattativa complessiva	*(traht-tah-tEEh-vah kohm-plehs-sEEh-vah)*
packaging	l'imballaggio	*(eehm-bahl-lAhj-joh)*
packing	l'imballo	*(eehm-bAhl-loh)*

packing case	la cassa d'imballo	*(kAhs-sah deehm-bAhl-loh)*
packing list	il listino d'imballaggio	*(leehs-tEEh-noh deehm-bahl-lAhj-joh)*
page	la pagina	*(pAh-jeeh-nah)*
page makeup	la composizione della pagina	*(kohm-poh-zeeh-tsyOh-neh dehl-lah pAh-jeeh-nah)*
pagination	l'impaginazione	*(eehm-pah-jeeh-nah-tsyOh-neh)*
paid holiday	il giorno festivo pagato	*(jOhr-noh fehs-tEEh-voh pah-gAh-toh)*
paid in full	completamente pagato	*(kohm-pleh-tah mEhn-teh pah-gAh-toh)*
paid-in surplus	l'eccedenza versata	*(ehch-cheh-dEhn-tsah vehr-sAh-tah)*
paid up capital	il capitale versato	*(kah-peeh-tAh-leh vehr-sAh-toh)*
paid up shares	le azioni liberate	*(ahts-tsyOh-neeh leeh-beh-rAh-teh)*
paint	la vernice	*(vehr-nEEh-cheh)*
pallet	il pallet	*(pahlet)*
palletized freight	la merce pallettizzata	*(mEhr-cheh pahl-leht-teehds-dsAh-tah)*
pamphlet	l'opuscolo	*(oh-pOOhs-koh-loh)*
panel	il pannello	*(pahn-nEhl-loh)*
paper	la carta	*(kAhr-tah)*
paper holder	il portacarta	*(pohr-tah-kAhr-teh)*
paper profit	il profitto su carta, gli utili su carta	*(proh-fEEht-toh sooh kAhr-tah), (OOh-teeh-leeh sooh kAhr-tah)*
paper tape	il nastro di carta	*(nAhs-troh deeh kAhr-tah)*
paperback	in brossura	*(brohs-sOOh-rah)*
par	pari	*(pAh-reeh)*
par value	il valore al pari	*(vah-lOh-reh ahl pAh-reeh)*
par, above	sopra la pari	*(sOh-prah lah pAh-reeh)*
par, below	sotto la pari	*(sOht-toh lah pAh-reeh)*
parallel circuit	il circuito in parallelo	*(cheehr-kwEEh-toh eehn pah-rahl-lEh-loh)*
parcel post	il pacco postale	*(pAhk-koh pohs-tAh-leh)*

parent company	la ditta madre, l'azienda madre	*(dEEht-tah mAh-dreh), (ah-dsyEhn-dah mAh-dreh)*
parity	la parità	*(pah-reeh-tAh)*
parity income ratio	il rapporto tra il reddito e la parità	*(rahp-pOhr-toh trah eehl rEhd-deeh-toh eh lah pah-reeh-tAh)*
parity price	il prezzo di parità	*(prEhts-tsoh deeh pah-reeh-tAh)*
part cargo	la parte della merce	*(pAhr-teh dehl-lah mEhr-cheh)*
partial payment	il pagamento parziale	*(pah-gah-mEhn-toh pahr-tsyAh-leh)*
participating preferred stock	le azioni preferenziali di partecipazione sugli utili	*(ah-tsyOh-neeh preh-feh-rehn-tsyAh-leeh deeh pahr-teh-cheeh-pah-tsyOh-neh sooh-lyeeh OOh-teeh-leeh)*
participation fee	la tariffa di partecipazione	*(tah-rEEhf-fah deeh pahr-teh-cheeh-pah-tsyOh-neh)*
participation loan	il prestito partecipato	*(prEhs-teeh-toh pahr-teh-cheeh-pAh-toh)*
particular average loss	la perdita media particolare	*(pEhr-deeh-tah mEh-deeh-ah pahr-teeh-koh-lAh-reh)*
partner	il socio	*(sOh-choh)*
partnership	la società di persone	*(soh-cheh-tAh deeh pehr-sOh-neh)*
parts	le parti	*(pAhr-teeh)*
passbook	il libretto di deposito bancario	*(leeh-brEht-toh deeh deh-pOh-see-toh bahn-kAh-ryoh)*
passed dividend	il dividendo eliminato	*(deeh-veeh-dEhn-doh eh-leeh-meeh-nAh-toh)*
passport case	il porta passaporto	*(pohr-tah-pahs-sah-pOhr-toh)*
past due	scaduto	*(skah-dOOh-toh)*
pasteurized	pastorizzato	*(pahs-toh-reehds-dsAh-toh)*
pastry server	la paletta	*(pah-lEht-tah)*
patent application	il modulo di richiesta per brevetto	*(mOh-dooh-loh deeh reeh-kyEhs-tah pehr breh-vEht-toh)*
patent	il brevetto	*(breh-vEht-toh)*

patent law	la legge sui brevetti	*(lEhj-jeh sooh-eeh breh-vEht-teeh)*
patent pending	il brevetto richiesto	*(breh-vEht-toh reeh-kyEhs-toh)*
patent royalty	i diritti di brevetto	*(deeh-rEEht-teeh deeh breh-vEht-toh)*
patented process	la procedura brevettata	*(proh-cheh-dOOh-rah breh-vEht-tah-tah)*
pattern	il modello, il disegno	*(moh-dEhl-loh), (deeh-zEh-nyoh)*
pay (v)	pagare	*(pah-gAh-reh)*
pay as you go	pagare in contanti	*(pah-gAh-reh eehn kohn-tAhn-teeh)*
pay up (v)	saldare	*(sahl-dAh-reh)*
payable on demand	pagabile su richiesta	*(pah-gAh-beeh-leh sooh reeh-kyEhs-tah)*
payable to bearer	pagabile al portatore	*(pah-gAh-beeh-leh ahl pohr-tah-tOh-reh)*
payable to order	pagabile all'ordine	*(pah-gAh-beeh-leh ahl Ohr-deeh-neh)*
payback period	il periodo di ripagamento	*(peh-rEEh-oh-doh deeh ree-pah-gah-mEhn-toh)*
payee	il creditore	*(kreh-deeh-tOh-reh)*
payer	il pagante	*(pah-gAhn-teh)*
payload	il carico effettivo	*(kAh-reeh-koh ehf-feht-tEEh-voh)*
paymaster	il preparatore delle paghe	*(preh-pah-rah-tOh-reh dehl-leh pAh-geh)*
payment	il pagamento	*(pah-gah-mEhn-toh)*
payment in full	il pagamento completo	*(pah-gah-mEhn-toh kohm-plEh-toh)*
payment in kind	il pagamento in natura	*(pah-gah-mEhn-toh eehn nah-tOOh-rah)*
payment refused	il pagamento rifiutato	*(pah-gah-mEhn-toh reeh-fyooh-tAh-toh)*
payoff	la liquidazione dei conti	*(leeh-kweeh-dah-tsyOh-neeh)*
payout period	il periodo di pagamento	*(peh-rEEh-oh-doh deeh pah-gah-mEhn-toh)*
payroll	il libro paga	*(leeh-broh pAh-gah)*

payroll tax	l'imposta sui salari	*(eehm-pOhs-tah sooh-eeh sah-lAh-reeh)*
peak load	il carico massimo	*(kAh-reeh-koh mAhs-seeh-moh)*
peg (v)	fissare	*(feehs-sAh-reh)*
pegged price	il prezzo fissato	*(prEhts-tsoh feehs-sAh-toh)*
pellet	la pallottolina	*(pahl-loht-toh-lEEh-nah)*
penalty clause	la clausola di penalità	*(klAhw-zoh-lah deeh peh-nah-leeh-tAh)*
penalty-fraud action	l'azione di penalità per azioni di frode	*(ah-tsyOh-neh deeh peh-nah-leeh-tAh pehr ah-tsyOh-neeh deeh frOh-deh)*
penicillin	la penicillina	*(peh-neeh-cheehl-lEEh-nah)*
penny stock	le azioni con un valore inferiore ad un dollaro	*(ah-tsyOh-neeh kohn oohn vah-lOh-reh eehn-feh-ryOh-reh ad oohn dOhl-lah-roh)*
pension fund	il fondo pensionistico	*(fOhn-doh pehn-syoh-nEEs-teeh-koh)*
pepper mill	il macinapepe	*(mAh-cheeh-nah pEh-peh)*
pepper shaker	il porta pepe	*(pOhr-tah pEh-peh)*
per capita	pro capite	*(proh kAh-peeh-teh)*
per diem	la diaria	*(deeh-Ah-reeh-ah)*
per share	per azione	*(pehr- ah-tsyOh-neh)*
percentage earnings	la percentuale di guadagni	*(pehr-chehn-twAh-leh deeh gwah-dAh-nyeeh)*
percentage of profits	la percentuale di profitti	*(pehr-chehn-twAh-leh deeh proh-fEEht-tteh)*
performance bond	l'assicurazione d'adempimento	*(ahs-seeh-kooh-rah-tsyOh-neh dah-dehm-peeh-mEhn-toh)*
periodic inventory	l'inventario periodico	*(eehn-vehn-tAh-ryoh peh-ryOh-deeh-koh)*
peripherals	le aggiunte	*(ahj-jOOhn-teh)*
perks	i benefici	*(beh-neh-fEEh-cheeh)*
permit	il permesso	*(pehr-mEhs-soh)*
perpetual inventory	l'inventario perpetuo	*(eehn-vehn-tAh-ryoh pehr-pEh-tooh-oh)*

P

personal deduction	la detrazione personale	*(deh-trah-tsyOh-neh pehr-soh-nAh-leh)*
personal exemption	l'esenzione personale	*(eh-zehn-tsyOh-neh pehr-soh-nAh-leh)*
personal income tax	l'imposta sul reddito delle persone fisiche (IRPEF)	*(eehm-pOhs-tah soohl rEhd-deeh-toh dehl-leh pehr-sOhn-eh fEEh-zeeh-keh)*
personal liability	la responsabilità personale	*(rehs-pohn-sah-beeh-leeh-tAh pehr-soh-nAh-leh)*
personal property	la proprietà personale	*(proh-pryeh-tAh pehr-soh-nAh-leh)*
personality test	l'esame della personalità	*(eh-sAh-meh dehl-lah pehr-soh-nah-leeh-tAh)*
personnel administration	l'amministrazione del perso-nale	*(ahm-meeh-neehs-trah-tsyOh-neh dehl pehr-soh-nAh-leh)*
personnel department	il reparto personale	*(reh-pAhr-toh pehr-soh-nAh-leh)*
personnel management	la gestione del personale	*(jehs-tyOh-neh dehl pehr-soh-nAh-leh)*
petrochemical	la petrochimica	*(peh-troh-kEEh-meeh-kah)*
petrodollars	i petrodollari	*(peh-troh-dOhl-lah-reeh)*
petroleum	il petrolio	*(peh-trOh-lyoh)*
pharmacist	il farmacista	*(fahr-mah-chEEhs-tah)*
phase in (v)	introdurre	*(eehn-troh-dOOhr-reh)*
phase out (v)	eliminare	*(eh-leeh-meeh-nAh-reh)*
phenol	il fenolo	*(feh-nOh-loh)*
phosphate	il fosfato	*(fohs-fAh-toh)*
physical inventory	l'inventario fisico	*(eehn-vehn-tAh-reeh-oh)*
physician	il medico	*(mEh-deeh-koh)*
phytosanitary regulations	le normative fitosanitarie	*(nohr-mah-tEEh-veh feeh-toh-sah-neeh-tAh-reeh-eh)*
picket line	la linea di picchettaggio	*(lEEh-neh-ah deeh peehk-keht-tAhj-joh)*
pickling	il decapaggio	*(deh-kah-pAhj-joh)*
pickup and delivery	il ritiro e la consegna	*(reeh-tEEh-roh eh lah kohn-sEh-nyah)*
pie chart	il grafico a fette	*(grAh-feeh-kof a fEht-teh)*

piecework	il lavoro a cottimo	*(lah-vOh-roh ah kOht-teeh-moh)*
pig iron	la ghisa, la ghisa di prima fusione	*(gEEh-zah), (gEEh-zah deeh prEEh-mah fooh-zyOh-neh)*
piggyback service	il trasporto di containers con camion	*(trahs-pOhr-toh deeh containers kohn kAh-myohn)*
pigment	il colore, il pigmento	*(koh-lOh-reh), (peehg-mEhn-toh)*
pigskin	la pelle di cinghiale	*(pEhl-leh deeh cheehn-gyAh-leh)*
pilferage	il piccolo furto	*(pEEhk-koh-loh fOOhr-toh)*
pill	la pillola	*(pEEhl-loh-lah)*
pilotage	il pilotaggio	*(peeh-loh-tAhj-joh)*
pinion	il pignone, il rocchetto	*(peeh-nyOh-neh), (rohk-kEht-toh)*
pipage	le tubazioni	*(tooh-bah-tsyOh-neeh)*
pipes and tubes	le condotte e i tubi	*(kohn-dOht-teh eh eeh tOOh-beeh)*
piston	il pistone	*(peehs-tOh-neh)*
pitcher	la caraffa, la brocca	*(kah-rAhf-fah), (brOhk-kah)*
place an order (v)	piazzare un ordine, ordinare	*(pyahts-tsAh-reh oohn Ohr-deeh-neh)*
place of business	il posto di lavoro	*(pOhs-toh deeh lah-vOh-roh)*
place setting	il coperto	*(koh-pEhr-toh)*
placement (personnel)	il collocamento	*(kohl-loh-kah-mEhn-toh)*
plan (v)	progettare	*(proh-jeht-tAh-reh)*
plan	il piano	*(pyAh-noh)*
plan, action	il piano d'azione	*(pyAh-noh dah-tsyOh-neh)*
plan, market	il piano di mercato, il programma di mercato	*(pyAh-noh deeh mehr-kAh-toh), (proh-grAhm-mah deeh mehr-kAh-toh)*
planned obsolescence	l'obsolescenza programmata	*(ohb-soh-leh-shEhn-tsah proh-gram-mAh-tah)*

P

plant capacity	la capacità produttiva della fabbrica, il potenziale di capacità produttiva di un impianto	*(kah-pah-cheeh-tAh proh-dooht-tEEh-vah dehl-lah fAhb-breeh-kah), (poh-tehn-tsyAh-leh deeh kah-pah-cheeh-tAh proh-dooht-tEEh-vah deeh oohn eehm-pyAhn-toh)*
plant location	la localizzazione degli impianti	*(loh-kah-leehds-dsah-tsyOh-neh deh-lyeeh eehm-pyAhn-teeh)*
plant manager	l'amministratore della fabbrica	*(ahm-meeh-neehs-trah-tOh-reh dehl-lah fAhb-breeh-kah)*
plants	le piante	*(pyAhn-teh)*
plate	il piatto, la lamiera, la piastra	*(pyAht-toh), (lah-myAh-rah), (pyAhs-trah)*
pleat	la piega	*(pyEh-gah)*
pleated	pieghettato	*(pyeh-geht-tAh-toh)*
pledge	l'impegno, la promessa	*(eehm-pEh-nyoh), (proh-mEhs-sah)*
plenary meeting	la riunione plenaria	*(reeh-ooh-nyOh-neh pleh-nAh-reeh-ah)*
plow back (v) (earnings)	reinvestire	*(reh-eehn-vehs-tEEh-reh)*
plus accrued interest	compreso interessi accumulati	*(kohm-prEh-zoh eehn-teh-rEhs-seeh ahk-kooh-mooh-lAh-teeh)*
pocketbook	la borsetta	*(bohr-sEht-tah)*
point (percentage, mortgage term)	i centesimi di percentuale per ipoteche	*(chehn-tEh-zeeh-meeh deeh pehr-chehn-twAh-leh pehr eeh-poh-tEh-keh)*
point	il punto tipografico	*(pOOhn-toh teeh-poh-grAh-feeh-koh)*
point of order	la questione di procedura	*(kwehs-tyOh-neh deeh proh-cheh-dOOh-rah)*
point of sale	il punto di vendita	*(pOOhn-toh deeh vEhn-deeh-tah)*

point, break-even	il punto di pareggio, il punto della parità, il volume di vendite al quale c'è equilibrio tra ricavi e costi	*(pOOhn-toh deeh pah-rEhj-joh), (pOOhn-toh dehl-lah pah-reeh-tAh), (voh-lOOh-meh deeh vEhn-deeh-teh ahl kwAh-leh chEh eh-kweeh-lEEh-breeh-oh trah reeh-kAh-veeh eh kOhs-teeh)*

pole	il polo	*(pOh-loh)*
policy	la polizza	*(pOh-leehts-tsah)*
policyholder	l'assicurato	*(ahs-seeh-kooh-rAh-toh)*
polyester	il poliestirolo	*(poh-leeh-ehs-teeh-rOh-loh)*
polymer	il polimero	*(poh-lEEh-meh-roh)*
pool (of funds)	il fondo monetario comune	*(fOhn-doh moh-neh-tAh-reeh-oh koh-mOOh-neh)*
pool (v)	mettere il fondo comune	*(mEht-teh-reh eehl fOhn-doh koh-mOOh-neh)*
pooling of interests	gli interessi in comune	*(eehn-teh-rEhs-seeh eehn koh-mOOh-neh)*
poplin	la poplina	*(poh-plEE-nah)*
portfolio	la cartella, il portafoglio	*(kahr-tEhl-lah), (pohr-tah-fOh-lyoh)*
portfolio management	l'amministrazione della cartella degli investimenti	*(ahm-meeh-neehs-trah-tsyOh-neh dehl-lah kahr-tEhl-lah)*
portfolio theory	la teoria d'azione relativa agli investimenti	*(teh-oh-rEEh-ah dah-tsyOh-neh reh-lah-tEEh-vah ah-lyeeh eehn-vehs-teeh-mEhn-teeh)*
portfolio, stock	la cartella d'azioni	*(kahr-tEhl-lah dah-tsyOh-neeh)*
position limit	il limite di perdita	*(lEEh-meeh-teh deeh pEhr-deeh-tah)*
positive	il positivo	*(poh-zeeh-tEEh-voh)*
positive cash flow	il movimento positivo dei fondi	*(moh-veeh-mEhn-toh poh-zeeh-tEEh-voh deh-eeh fOhn-deeh)*
possession	lo possesso	*(poh-zEEh-soh)*
post (v) (bookkeeping)	registrare	*(reh-jeehs-trAh-reh)*
postdated	postdatato	*(pohst-dah-tAh-toh)*
postpone (v)	posticipare	*(pohs-teeh-chee-pAh-reh)*

potential buyer	l'acquirente potenziale, il compratore potenziale	*(ahk-kweeh-rEhn-teh poh-tehn-tsyAh-leh)*
potential sales	le vendite potenziali	*(vEhn-deeh-teh poh-tehn-tsyAh-leeh)*
pottery	le stoviglie	*(stoh-vEEh-lyeh)*
powder	la polvere	*(pOhl-veh-reh)*
power	la potenza, il rendimento	*(poh-tEhn-dsah), (rehn-deeh-mEhn-toh)*
power of attorney	la procura	*(proh-kOOh-rah)*
power steering	il servosterzo	*(sehr-voh-stEhr-tsoh)*
practical	pratico	*(prAh-teeh-koh)*
preemptive right	il diritto di prelazione	*(deeh-rEEht-toh deeh preh-lah-tsyOh-neh)*
prefabrication	il prefabbricazione	*(preh-fahb-breeh-kah-tsyOh-neh)*
preface	la prefazione	*(preh-fah-tsyOh-neh)*
preferential debts	i debiti preferenziali	*(dEh-beeh-teeh preh-feh-rehn-tsyAh-leeh)*
preferred stock	l'azione preferenziale	*(ah-tsyOh-neh preh-feh-rehn-tsyAh-leh)*
preferred tariff	la tariffa preferenziale	*(tah-rEEhf-fah preh-feh-rehn-tsyAh-leh)*
preliminary prospectus	il prospetto preliminare	*(prohs-pEht-toh preh-leeh-meeh-nAh-reh)*
premises (location)	l'edificio	*(eh-deeh-fEEh-choh)*
premium offer	l'offerta premio	*(ohf-fEhr-tah prEh-myo)*
premium payment	il pagamento del premio	*(pah-gah-mEhn-toh deeh prEh-myo)*
premium price	il prezzo di premio	*(prEhts-tsoh deeh prEh-myo)*
premium, acceleration	il premio d'accelerazione	*(prEh-myoh dahch-cheh-leh-rah-tsyOh-neh)*
premium, insurance	il premio d'assicurazione	*(prEh-myo dahs-seeh-kooh-rah-tsyOh-neh)*
prepaid expenses (balance sheet)	le spese prepagate	*(spEh-zeh preh-pah-gAh-teh)*
prepay (v)	prepagare	*(preh-pah-gAh-reh)*
president	il presidente	*(preh-zeeh-dEhn-teh)*
press book	l'ultima bozza	*(OOhl-teeh-mah bohts-tsah)*

pressure	la pressione	*(prehs-syOh-neh)*
preventive maintenance	la manutenzione preventiva	*(mah-nooh-tehn-tsyOh-neh preh-vehn-tEEh-vah)*
price (v)	stabilire il prezzo	*(stah-beeh-lEEh-reh eehl prEhts-tsoh)*
price	il prezzo	*(prEhts-tsoh)*
price cutting	i tagli dei prezzi, la riduzione dei prezzi	*(tAh-lyeeh deh-eeh prEhts-tseeh)*
price differential	il differenziale dei prezzi	*(deef-feh-rehn-tsyAh-leh deh-eeh prEhts-tseeh)*
price elasticity	l'elasticità del prezzo	*(eh-lahs-teeh-cheeh-tAh dehl prEhts-tsoh)*
price index	l'indice dei prezzi	*(EEhn-deeh-cheh deh-eeh prEhts-tseeh)*
price limit	il prezzo limite	*(prEhts-tsoh lEEh-meeh-teh)*
price list	il listino prezzi	*(leehs-tEEh-noh prEhts-tseeh)*
price range	la gamma dei prezzi	*(gAhm-mah deh-eeh prEhts-tseeh)*
price support	il sostegno del prezzo	*(sohs-tEh-nyoh dehl prEhts-tsoh)*
price tick	lo sbalzo di prezzo	*(zbAhl-tsoh deeh prEhts-tsoh)*
price war	la guerra sui prezzi	*(gwEhr-rah sooh-eeh prEhts-tseeh)*
price, competitive	il prezzo concorrenziale	*(prEhts-tsoh kohn-kohr-rehn-tsyAh-leh)*
price, fix the (v)	fissare il prezzo	*(feehs-sAh-reh eehl prEhts-tsoh)*
price, market	il prezzo di mercato	*(prEhts-tsoh deeh mehr-kAh-toh)*
price/earnings ratio	il rapporto tra i prezzi ed i guadagni di un azione	*(rahp-pOhr-toh trah eeh prEhts-tseeh eh eeh gwah-dAh-nyeeh)*
primary market	il mercato primario	*(mehr-kAh-toh preeh-mAh-reeh-oh)*
primary reserves	le riserve primarie	*(reeh-zEhr-veh preeh-mAh-reeh-eh)*
prime cost	il costo primo	*(kOhs-toh prEEh-moh)*

P

prime time	le ore migliori per la pubblicità televisiva	*(Oh-reh meeh-lyOh-reeh pehr lah poohb-bleeh-cheeh-tAh teh-leh-veeh-zEEh-vah)*
principal	il principale	*(preehn-ceeh-pAh-leh)*
print	lo stampato	*(stahm-pAh-toh)*
printed circuit	il circuito stampato	*(cheehr-kwEEh-toh stahm-pAh-toh)*
printed matter	le stampe	*(stAhm-peh)*
printing	la stampa	*(stahm-pah)*
printing shop	la tipografia	*(teeh-poh-grah-fEEh-ah)*
printout	lo stampato	*(stahm-pAh-toh)*
priority	la priorità	*(preeh-oh-reeh-tAh)*
private fleet	la flotta privata	*(flOht-tah preeh-vAh-tah)*
private label (or brand)	la produzione per conto terzi	*(proh-dooh-tsyOh-neh pehr kOhn-toh tEhr-tseeh)*
private placement (finance)	la collocazione privata	*(kohl-loh-kah-tsyOh-neh preeh-vAh-tah)*
pro forma invoice	la fattura pro forma	*(faht-tOOh-rah proh fOhr-mah)*
pro forma statement	la dichiarazione pro forma	*(deeh-kyah-rah-tsyOh-neh proh fOhr-mah)*
probate	l'omologazione	*(oh-moh-loh-gah-tsyOh-neh)*
problem	il problema	*(proh-blEh-mah)*
problem analysis	l'analisi del problema	*(ah-nAh-leeh-zeeh dehl proh-blEh-mah)*
problem solving	la risoluzione di problemi	*(reeh-zoh-looh-tsyOh-neeh deeh proh-blEh-meeh)*
proceeds	i proventi	*(proh-vEhn-teeh)*
process (v)	trasformare, lavorare	*(trahs-fohr-mAh-reh), (lah-voh-rAh-reh)*
process	la procedura	*(proh-cheh-dOOh-rah)*
process, production	il procedimento di produzione, il processo produttivo	*(proh-cheh-deeh-mEhn-toh deeh proh-dooh-tsyOh-neh), (proh-chEhs-soh proh-dooht-tEEh-voh)*
processing error	l'errore di elaborazione	*(ehr-rOh-reh deeh eh-lah-boh-rah-tsyOh-neh)*
procurement	l'acquisto	*(ahk-kwEEhs-toh)*

product	il prodotto	*(proh-dOht-toh)*
product analysis	l'analisi del prodotto	*(ah-nAh-leeh-zeeh dehl proh-dOht-toh)*
product design	il disegno del prodotto	*(deeh-sEh-nyoh dehl proh-dOht-toh)*
product development	lo sviluppo del prodotto	*(sveeh-lOOhp-poh dehl proh-dOht-toh)*
product dynamics	la dinamica del prodotto	*(deeh-nAh-meeh-kah dehl proh-dOht-toh)*
product group	il gruppo di prodotti	*(grOOhp-poh deeh proh-dOht-teeh)*
product life	la durata del prodotto	*(ddoh-rAh-tah dehl proh-dOht-toh)*
product line	la gamma di prodotti, la linea di prodotti	*(gahm-mah deeh proh-dOht-teeh), (lEEh-neh-ah deeh proh-dOht-teeh)*
product management	la gestione del prodotto	*(jehs-tyOh-neh dehl proh-dOht-toh)*
product profitability	l'utile del prodotto	*(OOh-teeh-leh dehl proh-dOht-toh)*
production	la produzione	*(proh-dooh-tsyOh-neh)*
production control	il controllo della produzione	*(kohn-trOhl-loh dehl-lah proh-dooh-tsyOh-neh)*
production costs	i costi di produzione	*(Kohs-teeh deeh proh-dooh-tsyOh-neh)*
production line	la linea di produzione	*(lEEh-neh-ah deeh proh-dooh-tsyOh-neh)*
production process	il procedimento di produzio-ne, il processo produttivo	*(proh-cheh-deeh-mEhn-toh deeh proh-dooh-tsyOh-neh), (proh-chEhs-soh proh-dooht-tEEh-voh)*
production schedule	il programma di produzione	*(proh-grAhm-mah deeh proh-dooh-tsyOh-neh)*
productivity	la produttività	*(proh-dooht-teeh-veeh-tAh)*
productivity campaign	la campagna di produttività	*(kahm-pAh-nyah deeh proh-dooht-teeh-veeh-tA)*
profession	la professione	*(proh-fehs-syOh-neh)*
profit	il profitto, gli utili	*(proh-fEEht-toh), (OOh-teeh-leeh)*

P

profit and loss statement	la dichiarazione degli utili e delle perdite, il conto profitti e perdite	*(deeh-kyah-rah-tsyOh-neh deh-lyeeh OOh-teeh-leeh eh dehl-leh pEhr-deeh-teh), (kOhn-toh proh-fEEht-teeh eh pEhr-deeh-teh)*
profit factor	il fattore degli utili, il fattore dei profitti	*(faht-tOh-reh deh-lyeeh OOh-teeh-lee), (faht-tOh-reh deh-eeh proh-fEEht-teeh)*
profit impact	l'impatto dei profitti, l'impatto sugli utili	*(eehm-pAht-toh deh-eeh proh-fEEht-teeh), (eehm-pAht-toh sooh-lyeeh OOh-teeh-leeh)*
profit margin	il margine di profitto	*(mAhr-jeeh-neh deeh proh-fEEht-toh)*
profit projection	la proiezione degli utili	*(proh-yeh-tsyOh-neh deh-lyeeh OOh-teeh-leeh)*
profit sharing	la spartizione degli utili	*(spahr-teeh-tsyOh-neh deh-lyeeh OOh-teeh-leeh)*
profit taking	la vendita per la realizzazione di profitti	*(vEhn-deeh-tah pehr -lah reh-ah-leehds-dsah-tsyOh-neh deeh proh-fEEht-teeh)*
profit, gross	il profitto lordo, l'utile lordo	*(proh-fEEht-toh lOhr-doh) (OOh-teeh-leh lOhr-doh)*
profit, net	il profitto netto	*(proh-fEEht-toh nEht-toh)*
profitability analysis	l'analisi dei profitti, l'analisi del rapporto tra costo e profitto, lo studio sulla profittabilità	*(ah-nAh-leeh-zeeh deh-eeh proh-fEEht-teeh), (ah-nAh-leeh-zeeh trah kOhs-toh eh proh-fEEht-toh), (stOOh-dyoh sohl-lah proh-feeht-tah-beeh-leeh-tAh)*
profitability	la redditività	*(rehd-deeht-teeh-veeh-tAh)*
program (v)	programmare	*(proh-grahm-mAh-reh)*
program	il programma	*(proh-grAhm-mah)*
prohibited goods	i beni proibiti	*(bEh-neeh proh-eeh-bEEh-teeh)*
project (v)	proiettare, progettare	*(proh-yeht-tAh-reh), (proh-jeht-tAh-reh)*
project	il progetto	*(proh-jEht-toh)*
project planning	la pianificazione del progetto	*(pyah-neeh-feeh-kah-tsyOh-neh dehl proh-jEht-toh)*

promissory note	la cambiale, il pagherò cambiario	*(kahm-byAh-leh), (pah-geh-rOh kahm-byAh-reeh-oh)*
promotion	la promozione	*(proh-moh-tsyOh-neh)*
promotion, sales	la promozione delle vendite	*(proh-moh-tsyOh-ne dehl-leh vEhn-deeh-teh)*
prompt	pronto, sollecito	*(prOhn-toh), (sohl-lEh-cheeh-toh)*
proof of loss	la verifica della perdita	*(veh-rEEh-feeh-kah dehl-lah pEhr-deeh-tah)*
proofreading	la correzione delle bozza	*(kohr-reh-tsyOh-neh dehl-leh bOhts-tseh)*
property	la proprietà	*(proh-pryeh-tAh)*
proprietary	il diritto di proprietario	*(deeh-rEEht-toh proh-pryeh-tAh-reeh-oh)*
proprietor	il proprietario	*(proh-pryeh-tAh-reeh-oh)*
propulsion	la propulsione	*(proh-poohl-syOh-neh)*
prospectus	il prospetto	*(prohs-pEht-toh)*
protectionism	il protezionismo	*(proh-teh-tsyoh-nEEhz-moh)*
protest (banking; law) (v)	protestare	*(proh-tehs-tAh-reh)*
proton	il protone	*(proh-tOh-neh)*
prototype	il prototipo	*(proh-tOh-teeh-poh)*
proxy	la procura	*(proh-kOOh-rah)*
proxy statement	la dichiarazione per procura	*(deeh-kyah-rah-tsyOh-neh pehr proh-kOOh-rah)*
prudent man rule	la norma dell'uomo giudizioso	*(nOhr-mah dehl wOh-moh jooh-deeh-tsyOh-zoh)*
public auction	l'asta pubblica	*(Ahs-tah pOOhb-leeh-kah)*
public company	l'azienda pubblica	*(ah-dsyEhn-dah pOOhb-leeh-kah)*
public domain	il dominio pubblico	*(doh-meeh-neeh-oh pOOhb-leeh-koh)*
public funds	i fondi pubblici	*(fOhn-deeh pOOhb-leeh-cheeh)*
public offering	l'offerta al pubblico	*(ohf-fEhr-tah ahl pOOhb-leeh-koh)*
public opinion poll	il sondaggio della opinione pubblica	*(sohn-dAhj-joh dehl-lah oh-peeh-nyOh-neh pOOhb-leeh-kah)*

public property	la proprietà pubblica	*(proh-pryeh-tAh pOOhb-leeh-kah)*
public relations	le pubbliche relazioni	*(pOOhb-leeh-keh reh-lah-tsyOh-neeh)*
public sale	la vendita pubblica	*(vEhn-deeh-tah pOOhb-leeh-kah)*
public sector	il settore pubblico	*(seht-tOh-reh pOOhb-leeh-koh)*
public utilities	i servizi municipali	*(sehr-vEEh-tseeh mooh-neeh-cheeh-pAh-leeh)*
public works	i lavori pubblici	*(lah-vOh-reeh pOOhb-leeh-cheeh)*
publicity	la pubblicità	*(poohb-leeh-cheeh-tAh)*
publisher	l'editore	*(eh-deeh-tOh-reh)*
pump priming	l'investimento di fondi per iniziare l'attività	*(eehn-vehs-teeh-mEhn-toh deeh fOhn-deeh pehr eeh-neeh-tsyAh-reh laht-teeh-veeh-tAh)*
punch card	la scheda perforata	*(skEh-dah pehr-foh-rAh-tah)*
purchase (v)	acquistare, comprare	*(ahk-kweehs-tAh-reh), (kohm-prAh-reh)*
purchase money mortgage	l'ipoteca	*(eeh-poh-tEh-kah)*
purchase order	l'ordine d'acquisto	*(Ohr-deeh-neh dahk-kwEEhs-toh)*
purchase price	il prezzo d'acquisto	*(prEhts-tsoh dahk-kwEEhs-toh)*
purchasing agent	l'agente d'acquisto	*(ah-jEhn-teh dahk-kwEEhs-toh)*
purchasing manager	l'amministratore degli acquisti	*(ahm-meeh-neehs-trah-tOh-reh deh-lyeeh ahk-kwEEhs-teeh)*
purchasing power	il potere d'acquisto	*(poh-tEh-reh dahk-kwEEhs-toh)*
pure risk	il rischio puro	*(rEEhs-kyoh pOOh-roh)*
purgative	il purgante	*(poohr-gAhn-teh)*
purification	la purificazione	*(pooh-reeh-feeh-kah-tsyOh-neh)*
purse	la borsa	*(bOhr-sah)*

put and call	la compravendita di azioni sopra o sotto il prezzo attuale	*(kohm-prah-vEhn-deeh-tah deeh ah-tsyOh-neeh soh-prah eh sOht-toh eehl prEhts-tsoh aht-twAh-leh)*
put in a bid (v)	mettere in appalto	*(mEht-teh-reh eehn ahp-pAhl-toh)*
put option	l'opzione di vendita (di un'azione a un prezzo superiore a quello attuale)	*(ohp-tsyOh-neh deeh vEhn-deeh-tah deeh oohn ah-tsyOh-neh ah oohn prEhts-tsoh sooh-peh-ryOh-reh ah kwEhl-loh aht-twAh-leh)*
pyramid selling	la vendita piramidale	*(vEhn-deeh-tah peeh-rah-meeh-dAh-leh)*

Q

qualifications	le qualifiche	*(kwah-lEEh-feeh-keh)*
qualified acceptance endorsement	la girata d'accettazione qualificata	*(jeeh-rAh-tah dahch-cheht-tah-tsyOh-neh kwah-leeh-feeh-kAh-tah)*
quality control	il controllo di qualità	*(kohn-trOhl-loh deeh kwah-leeh-tAh)*
quality goods	i beni di qualità	*(bEh-neeh deeh kwah-leeh-tAh)*
quantity	la quantità	*(kwahn-teeh-tAh)*
quantity discount	lo sconto per quantità	*(skOhn-toh pehr kwahn-teeh-tAh)*
quasi-public company	l'azienda quasi pubblica	*(ah-dsyEhn-dah kwAh-zeeh pOOhb-leeh-kah)*
quick assets	le attività prontamente realizzabili	*(aht-teeh-veeh-tAh prohn-tah-mEhn-teh reh-ah-leehds-dsAh-beeh-leeh)*
quitclaim deed	la rinuncia ad un atto di proprietà	*(reeh-nOOhn-chah ad oohn Aht-toh deeh proh-pryeh-tAh)*
quorum	il quorum	*(kwOh-roohm)*
quota	la quota	*(kwOh-tah)*
quota, export	la quota d'esportazione	*(kwOh-tah dehs-pohr-tah-tsyOh-neh)*
quota, sales	la quota di vendita	*(kwOh-tah deeh vEhn-deeh-tah)*

quota system	il sistema di contingenta- mento	*(seehs-tEh-mah deeh kohn- teehn-jah-mEhn-toh)*
quotation	la quotazione, la citazione	*(kwoh-tah-tsyOh-neh), (cheeh-tah-tsyOh-neh)*

R

rabbit	il coniglio	*(koh-nEEh-lyoh)*
raccoon	il procione lavoratore	*(proh-chOh-neh lah-voh- rah-tOh-reh)*
rack jobber	la lavorazione su commessa	*(lah-voh-rah-tsyOh-neh sooh kohm-mEhs-sah)*
radar	il radar	*(raydahr)*
radial tire	il pneumatico radiale	*(pneh-ooh-mAh-teeh-koh rah-dyAh-leh)*
radio	la radio	*(rAh-deeh-oh)*
rail shipment	il trasporto ferroviario	*(trahs-pOhr-toh fehr-roh- vyAh-reeh-oh)*
rain check	l'abbuono per ricevere merce esaurita in un'altra data	*(ahb-bwOh-noh pehr reeh- chEh-veh-reh mEhr-cheh eh-zahw-rEEh-tah eehn oohn Ahl-trah dAh-tah)*
raincoat	l'impermeabile	*(eehm-pehr-meh-Ah-beeh- leh)*
raising capital	l'innalzamento dei capitali, il raccoglimento dei capi- tali	*(eehn-nahl-tsah-mEhn-toh deh-eeh kah-peeh-tAh- leeh), (rahk-koh-lyeeh- mEhn-toh deh-eeh kah- peeh-tAh-leeh)*
rally	il rafforzamento delle azioni	*(rahf-fohr-tsah-mEhn-toh dehl-leh ah-tsyOh-neeh)*
random access memory	la memoria d'accesso casua- le, il RAM	*(meh-mOh-reeh-ah dahc- chEhs-soh kah-zwAh-leh)*
random sample	il campione casuale	*(kahm-pyOh-neh kah-zwAh- leh)*
rate	il tasso	*(tAhs-soh)*
rate of growth	il tasso di crescita	*(tAhs-soh deeh krEh-sheeh- tah)*
rate of increase	il tasso d'incremento	*(tAhs-soh deehn-kreh- mEhn-toh)*

rate of interest	il tasso d'interesse	*(tAhs-soh deehn-teh-rEhs-seh)*
rate of return	il tasso di rimunerazione, il tasso di rendimento	*(tAhs-soh deeh reeh-mooh-neh-rah-tsyOh-neh), (tAhs-soh deeh rehn-deeh-mEhn-toh)*
rate, base	il tasso di base	*(tAhs-soh deeh bAh-zeh)*
rating, credit	la valutazione dei crediti	*(vah-looh-tah-tsyOh-neh deh-eeh krEh-deeh-teeh)*
rating, market	la valutazione del mercato	*(vah-looh-tah-tsyOh-neh dehl mehr-kAh-toh)*
ratio	la proporzione	*(proh-pohr-tsyOh-neh)*
ration (v)	razionare	*(rah-tsyoh-nAh-reh)*
raw materials	la materia prima	*(mah-tEh-reeh-ah prEEh-mah)*
rayon	il raion, la seta artificiale	*(rah-yOhn), (sEh-tah ahr-teeh-feeh-chAh-leh)*
re-export (v)	riesportare	*(reeh-ehs-pohr-tAh-reh)*
ready cash	il denaro disponibile	*(deh-nAh-roh deehs-poh-nEEh-beeh-leh)*
ready-to-wear	moda confezionata	*(mOh-dah kohn-feh-tsyoh-nAh-tah)*
reagent	il reagente, il reattivo	*(reh-ah-jEhn-teh), (reh-aht-tEEh-voh)*
real assets	gli attivi reali	*(aht-tEEh-veeh reh-Ah-leeh)*
real estate	gli immobili	*(eehm-mOh-beeh-leeh)*
real income	il reddito reale	*(rEhd-deeh-toh reh-Ah-leeh)*
real investment	l'investimento reale	*(eehn-vehs-teeh-mEhn-toh reh-Ah-leeh)*
real price	il prezzo reale	*(prEhts-tsoh reh-Ah-leeh)*
real time	il tempo reale	*(tEhm-poh reh-Ah-leeh)*
real wages	il salario reale	*(sah-lAh-reeh-oh reh-Ah-leeh)*
ream	la risma	*(rEEhz-mah)*
rear axle	l'asse posteriore	*(Ahs-seh pohs-teh-ryOh-reh)*
reasonable care	la cura ragionevole	*(kOOh-rah rah-joh-nEh-voh-leh)*
rebate	l'abbuono, lo sconto	*(ahb-bwOh-noh), (skOhn-toh)*

R

recapitalization	la ricapitalizzazione	*(reeh-kah-peeh-tah-leehds-dsah-tsyOh-neh)*
receipt	la ricevuta	*(reeh-cheh-vOOh-tah)*
receiver	custode	*(koohs-tOh-deh)*
recession	la recessione	*(reh-chehs-syOh-neh)*
reciprocal training	l'istruzione reciproca	*(eehs-trooh-tsyOh-neh reh-chEEh-proh-kah)*
record (v)	incidere, registrare	*(eehn-chEEh-deh-reh)*
record	il disco	*(dEEhs-koh)*
record date	la data di registrazione	*(dAh-tah deeh reh-jeehs-trah-tsyOh-neh)*
recourse	il ricorso	*(reeh-kOhr-soh)*
recovery	il ricovero	*(reeh-kOh-veh-roh)*
recovery of expenses	il rimborso delle spese	*(reehm-bOhr-soh dehl-leh spEh-zeh)*
red tape	la prassi burocratica	*(prAhs-seeh booh-roh-krAh-teeh-kah)*
redeemable bonds	le obbligazioni redimibili	*(ohb-bleeh-gah-tsyOh-neeh reh-deeh-mEEh-beeh-leeh)*
redemption allowance	la deduzione convertibile	*(deh-dooh-tsyOh-neh kohn-vehr-tEEh-beeh-leh)*
redemption fund	il fondo di investimento redimibile	*(fOhn-doh deeh eehn-vehs-teeh-mEhn-toh)*
redemption premium	il premio di redimibilità	*(prEh-myoh deeh reh-deeh-meeh-beeh-leeh-tAh)*
rediscount rate	il tasso di risconto	*(tAhs-soh deeh reeh-skOhn-toh)*
reduction	la riduzione	*(reeh-dooh-tsyOh-neh)*
reference number	il numero di riferimento	*(nOOh-meh-roh deeh reeh-feh-reeh-mEhn-toh)*
reference, credit	la referenza bancaria, la referenza per ottenere credito	*(reh-feh-rEhn-tsah bahn-kAh-reeh-ah), (reh-feh-rEhn-tsah pehr oht-teh-nEh-reh krEh-deeh-toh)*
refinancing	il rifinanziamento	*(reeh-feeh-nahn-tsyah-mEhn-toh)*
refine (v)	raffinare	*(rahf-feeh-nAh-reh)*
refinery	la raffineria	*(rahf-feeh-neh-rEEh-ah)*
reflation	la riflazione	*(reeh-flah-tsyOh-neh)*

refractories	i refrattari	*(reh-fraht-tAh-reeh)*
refund	il rimborso	*(reehm-bOhr-soh)*
refuse acceptance (v)	rifiutare l'accettazione	*(reeh-fyooh-tAh-reh lahch-cheht-tah-tsyOh-neh)*
refuse payment (v)	rifiutare il pagamento	*(reeh-fyooh-tAh-reh eehl pah-gah-mEhn-toh)*
regard (with regard to)	riguardo (al riguardo)	*(reeh-gwAhr-doh)*
register	il registro	*(reh-jEEhs-troh)*
registered check	l'assegno nominativo	*(ahs-sEh-nyoh noh-meeh-nah-tEEh-voh)*
registered mail	la raccomandata	*(rahk-koh-mahn-dAh-tah)*
registered representative	il rappresentante nominato	*(rahp-preh-zehn-tAhn-teh noh-meeh-nAh-toh)*
registered security	il titolo nominativo	*(tEEh-toh-loh noh-meeh-nah-tEEh-voh)*
registered trademark	il marchio registrato	*(mAhr-kyoh reh-jeehs-trAh-toh)*
regression analysis	l'analisi di regressione	*(ah-nAh-leeh-zeeh deeh reh-grehs-syOh-neh)*
regressive tax	l'imposta regressiva	*(eehm-pOhs-tah reh-grehs-sEEh-vah)*
regular warehouse	il magazzino regolare	*(mah-gahds-dsEEh-noh reh-goh-lAh-reh)*
regulation	la normativa	*(nohr-mah-tEEh-vah)*
reimburse (v)	rimborsare	*(reehm-bohr-sAh-reh)*
reinsurer	il riassicuratore	*(reeh-ahs-seeh-kooh-rah-tOh-reh)*
reliable source	la fonte attendibile	*(fOhn-teh aht-tehn-dEEh-beeh-leh)*
remainder (v)	liquidare	*(leeh-kweeh-dAh-reh)*
remedies	i rimedi	*(reeh-mEh-deeh)*
remedy (law)	il rimedio	*(reeh-mEh-dyoh)*
remission duty	la remissione dell'imposta	*(reh-meehs-syOh-neh dehl eehm-pOhs-tah)*
remission of a tax	la remissione di una tassa	*(reh-meehs-syOh-ne deeh ooh-nah tAhs-sah)*
remuneration	la rimunerazione	*(reeh-mooh-neh-rah-tsyOh-neh)*

renegotiate (v)	rinegoziare	*(reeh-neh-goh-tsyAh-reh)*
renew (v)	rinnovare	*(reehn-noh-vAh-reh)*
rent	l'affitto	*(ahf-fEEht-toh)*
reorder (v)	riordinare	*(reeh-ohr-deeh-nAh-reh)*
reorganize (v)	riorganizzare	*(reeh-ohr-gah-neehds-dsAh-reh)*
repay (v)	ripagare	*(reeh-pah-gAh-reh)*
repeat order	l'ordine ripetuto	*(Ohr-deeh-neh reeh-peh-tOOh-toh)*
replacement cost	il costo di ricambio	*(kOhs-toh deeh reeh-kAhm-byoh)*
replacement parts	le parti di ricambio	*(pAhr-teeh deeh reeh-kAhm-byoh)*
reply (v)	rispondere	*(reehs-pOhn-deh-reh)*
reply; in reply to	il riscontro; a riscontro di	*(reehs-kOhn-troh), (ah reehs-kOhn-troh deeh)*
report	la relazione	*(reh-lah-tsyOh-neh)*
repossession	il rientro in possesso	*(reeh-Ehn-troh eehn pohs-sEhs-soh)*
representative	il rappresentante	*(rahp-preh-zehn-tAhn-teh)*
reproduction costs	i costi d'riproduzione	*(kOhs-teeh deeh reeh-proh-dooh-tsyOh-neh)*
request for bid	il bando di appalto	*(bAhn-doh deeh ahp-pAhl-toh)*
requirements	le esigenze, le requisiti	*(eh-zeeh-jEhn-tseh), (reh-kweeh-zEEh-teeh)*
resale	la rivendita	*(reeh-vEhn-deeh-tah)*
research and development	la ricerca e lo sviluppo	*(reeh-chEhr-kah eh loh zveeh-lOOhp-poh)*
research	la ricerca	*(reeh-chEhr-kah)*
reserve	la riserva	*(reeh-zEhr-vah)*
resident buyer	il compratore in loco	*(kohm-prah-tOh-reh eehn lOh-koh)*
resistance	la resistenza	*(reh-zeehs-tEhn-tsah)*
resolution (legal document)	la risoluzione	*(reeh-zoh-looh-tsyOh-neh)*
resonance	la risonanza	*(reeh-soh-nAhn-tsah)*
resources allocation	l'allocazione delle risorse	*(ahl-loh-kah-tsyOh-neh dehl-leh reeh-zOhr-seh)*

restrictions on export	le restrizioni all'esportazione	*(rehs-treeh-tsyOh-neeh ahl ehs-pohr-tah-tsyOh-neh)*
restrictive labor practices	le procedure di lavoro restrittive	*(proh-cheh-dOOh-reh deeh lah-vOh-roh rehs-treet-tEEh-veh)*
restructure (v)	ristrutturare	*(reeh-strooht-tooh-rAh-reh)*
résumé	il curriculum vitae	*(koohr-rEEh-kooh-loohm veeh-teh-eeh)*
retail	al dettaglio	*(ahl deht-tAh-lyoh)*
retail bank	la banca al dettaglio, la banca per il consumatore	*(bAhn-kah ahl deht-tAh-lyoh), (bAhn-kah pehr eehl kohn-sooh-mah-tOh-reh)*
retail merchandise	i beni al dettaglio	*(bEh-neeh ahl deht-tAh-lyoh)*
retail outlet	il negozio al dettaglio	*(neh-gOh-tsyoh ahl deht-tAh-lyoh)*
retail price	il prezzo al dettaglio	*(prEhts-tsoh ahl deht-tAh-lyoh)*
retail sales tax	l'imposta sulla vendita al dettaglio	*(eehm-pOhs-tah soohl-lah vEhn-deeh-tah ahl deht-tAh-lyoh)*
retail trade	il commercio al dettaglio	*(kohm-mEhr-choh ahl deht-tAh-lyoh)*
retained earnings	i profitti ritenuti, i guadagni ritenuti, gli utili ritenuti	*(proh-fEEht-teeh reeh-teh-nOOh-teeh), (gwah-dAh-nyeeh reeh-teh-nOOh-teeh), (OOh-teeh-leeh reeh-teh-nOOh-teeh)*
retirement	il congedo, il pensionamento	*(kohn-jEh-doh), (pehn-syoh-nah-mEhn-toh)*
retroactive	arretrato	*(ahr-reh-trAh-toh)*
return on assets managed	il rendimento sulle attività amministrate	*(rehn-deeh-mEhn-toh soohl-leh aht-teeh-veeh-tAh ahm-meeh-neehs-trAh-teh)*
return on capital	i proventi sul capitale, il rendimento sul capitale	*(proh-vEhn-teeh soohl kah-peeh-tAh-leh), (rehn-deeh-mEhn-toh soohl kah-peeh-tAh-leh)*
return on equity	il reddito sul capitale netto	*(rEhd-deeh-toh soohl kah-peeh-tAh-leh nEht-toh)*

R

return on investment	il profitto sull'investimento, il ritorno sull'investimento	*(proh-fEEht-toh soohl eehn-vehs-teeh-mEhn-toh), (reeh-tOhr-noh soohl eehn-vehs-teeh-mEhn-toh)*
return on sales	la resa sulle vendite	*(rEh-zah sohl-leh vEhn-deeh-teh)*
return, rate of	il tasso di rimunerazione, il tasso di rendimento	*(tAhs-soh deeh reeh-mooh-neh-rah-tsyOh-neh), (tAhs-soh deeh rehn-deeh-mEhn-toh)*
revaluation	la rivalutazione	*(reeh-vah-looh-tah-tsyOh-neh)*
revenue	l'introito, il ricavo	*(eehn-trOhy-toh), (reeh-kAh-voh)*
revenue bond	l'obbligazione garantita dai ricavi dell'emittente	*(ohb-bleeh-gah-tsyOh-neh gah-rahn-tEEh-tah dah-eeh reeh-kAh-veeh dehl eh-meeht-tEhn-teh)*
reverse stock split	la riduzione nel numero delle azioni	*(reeh-dooh-tsyOh-neh nehl nOOh-meh-roh dehl-leh ah-tsyOh-neeh)*
revocable trust	il fondo d'investimento fiduciario revocabile	*(fOhn-deeh deehn-vehs-teeh-mEhn-toh feeh-dooh-chAh-reeh-oh reh-voh-kAh-beeh-leh)*
revolving credit	il credito rotativo	*(krEh-deeh-toh roh-tah-tEEh-voh)*
revolving fund	il fondo d'investimento rotativo	*(fOhn-doh deehn-vehs-teeh-mEhn-toh roh-tah-tEEh-voh)*
revolving letter of credit	la lettera di credito rotativa	*(lEht-teh-rah deeh krEh-deeh-tohroh-tah-tEEh-vah)*
reward	il premio	*(prEh-myoh)*
rider (contracts)	la postilla	*(pohs-tEEhl-lah)*
right of recourse	il diritto al ricorso	*(deeh-rEEht-toh ahl reeh-kOhr-soh)*
right of way	la precedenza	*(preh-cheh-dEhn-tsah)*
ring	l'anello	*(ah-nEhl-loh)*
ripe	maturo	*(mah-tOOh-roh)*
risk	il rischio	*(rEEhs-kyoh)*

risk analysis	l'analisi del rischio	*(ah-nAh-leeh-zeeh dehl rEEhs-kyoh)*
risk assessment	la valutazione del rischio	*(vah-looh-tah-tsyOh-neh dehl rEEhs-kyoh)*
risk capital	il capitale per finanziare nuove iniziative	*(kah-peeh-tAh-leh pehr feeh-nahn-tsyAh-reh nwOh-veh eeh-neeh-tsyah-tEEh-veh)*
robot	il robot	*(rohbaht)*
rod	l'asta, il ferro tondo	*(Ahs-tah), (fEhr-roh tOhn-doh)*
rollback	la riduzione	*(reeh-dooh-tsyOh-neh)*
rolling mill	il laminatoio	*(lah-meeh-nah-tOh-yoh)*
rolling stock	il materiale rotante	*(mah-teh-ryAh-leh roh-tAhn-teh)*
rollover	il rinvestimento degli utili di un investimento	*(reehn-vehs-teeh-mEhn-toh deh-lyĕeh OOh-teeh-leeh deeh oohn eehn-vehs-teeh-mEhn-toh)*
rough draft	la bozza	*(bOhts-tsah)*
rough estimate	la stima	*(stEEh-mah)*
round lot	la partita arrotondata, la partita intera	*(pahr-tEEh-tah ahr-roh-tohn-dAh-taha), (pahr-tEEh-tah eehn-tEh-rah)*
routine	la routine	*(ruhteen)*
royalty (payment)	i diritti d'autore	*(deeh-rEEht-teeh dahw-tOh-reh)*
running expenses	le spese correnti, le spese operative	*(spEh-zeh kohr-rEhn-teeh), (spEh-zeh oh-peh-rah-tEEh-veh)*
rush order	l'ordine urgente	*(Ohr-deeh-neh oohr-jEhn-teh)*

S

sable	lo zibellino	*(dseeh-behl-lEEh-noh)*
saccharin	la saccarina	*(sahk-kah-rEEh-nah)*
saddle	la sella	*(sEhl-lah)*
saddler	il sellaio	*(sehl-lAh-yoh)*
safe deposit box	la cassetta di sicurezza	*(kahs-sEht-tah deeh seeh-kooh-rEhts-tsah)*

safeguard	il salvaguardia	*(sahl-vah-gwAhr-dyah)*
salad plate	il piatto per l'insalata	*(pyAht-toh pehr leehn-sah-lAh-tah)*
salary	il salario	*(sah-lAh-reeh-oh)*
sale and leaseback	la vendita e il riaffitto	*(vEhn-deeh-tah eh eehl reeh-ahf-fEEht-toh)*
sales	le vendite	*(vEhn-deeh-teh)*
sales analysis	l'analisi delle vendite	*(ah-nAh-leeh-zeeh dehl-leh vEhn-deeh-teh)*
sales budget	il preventivo per le spese di vendita	*(preh-vehn-tEEh-voh pehr leh spEh-zeh deeh vEhn-deeh-tah)*
sales estimate	la stima delle vendite, le vendite previste	*(stEEh-mah dehl-leh vEhn-deeh-teh), (vEhn-deeh-teh preh-vEEhs-teh)*
sales force	il personale di vendita	*(pehr-soh-nAh-leh deeh vEhn-deeh-tah)*
sales forecast	le previsioni di vendita	*(preh-veeh-zyOh-neeh deeh vEhn-deeh-tah)*
sales management	l'amministrazione delle vendite, la gestione delle vendite	*(ahm-meeh-neehs-trah-tsyOh-neh dehl-leh vEhn-deeh-teh), (jehs-tyOh-neh dehl-leh vEhn-deeh-teh)*
sales promotion	la promozione delle vendite	*(proh-moh-tsyOh-neh dehl-leh vEhn-deeh-teh)*
sales quota	la quota di vendita	*(kwOh-tah deeh vEhn-deeh-tah)*
sales tax	l'imposta sulle vendite	*(eehm-pOhs-tah soohl-leh vEhn-deeh-teh)*
sales territory	il territorio di vendita	*(tehr-reeh-tOh-reeh-oh deeh vEhn-deeh-tah)*
sales turnover	il giro delle vendite	*(jEEh-roh dehl-leh vEhn-deeh-teh)*
sales volume	il volume delle vendite	*(voh-lOOh-meh dehl-leh vEhn-deeh-teh)*
salt	il sale	*(sAh-leh)*
salt shaker	la saliera	*(sah-lyEh-rah)*
salts	i sali	*(sAh-leeh)*
salvage (v)	recuperare	*(reh-kooh-peh-rAh-reh)*
salvage charges	le spese di recupero	*(spEh-zeh deeh reh-kOOh-peh-roh)*

salvage value	il valore di recupero	*(vah-lOh-reh deeh reh-kOOh-peh-roh)*
salve	l'unguento, la pomata	*(oohn-gwEhn-toh), (poh-mAh-tah)*
sample (v)	campionare	*(kahm-pyoh-nAh-reh)*
sample line	la linea campionaria	*(lEEh-neh-ah kahm-pyoh-nAh-reeh-ah)*
sample size	la misura del campione	*(meeh-zOOh-rah dehl kahm-pyOh-neh)*
saponification	la saponificazione	*(sah-poh-neeh-feeh-kah-tsyOh-neh)*
saucer	il piattino	*(pyaht-tEEh-noh)*
savings	i risparmi	*(reehs-pAhr-meeh)*
savings account	il conto di risparmio	*(kOhn-toh deeh reehs-pAhr-myoh)*
savings bank	la cassa di risparmio	*(kAhs-sah deeh reehs-pAhr-myoh)*
savings bond	il buono di risparmio	*(bwOh-noh deeh reehs-pAhr-myoh)*
scale	la scaglia, l'incrostatura	*(skAh-lyah), (eehn-krohs-tah-tOOh-rah)*
scalper	il bagarino	*(bah-gah-rEEh-noh)*
scanner	l'analizzatore di immagini, lo "scanner"	*(ah-nah-leehds-dsah-tOh-reh deeh eehm-mAh-jeeh-neeh)*
scanning	la scansione, l'esplorazione	*(skahn-syOh-neh), (ehs-ploh-rah-tsyOh-neh)*
scarf	la sciarpa, il foulard	*(shAhr-pah)*
schedule	l'orario	*(oh-rAh-reeh-oh)*
scissor case	il porta forbici	*(pohr-tah-fOhr-beeh-cheeh)*
scoring	la raschiatura	*(rahs-kyah-tOOh-rah)*
scrap	i rottami	*(roht-tAh-meeh)*
screen (v)	selezionare	*(seh-leh-tsyoh-nAh-reh)*
screen	lo schermo	*(skEhr-moh)*
script	il copione	*(koh-pyOh-neh)*
sealed bid	l'appalto sigillato	*(ahp-pAhl-toh seeh-jeehl-lAh-toh)*
sealskin	la pelle di foca	*(pEhl-leh deeh fOh-kah)*
seasonal	stagionale	*(stah-joh-nAh-leh)*

S

seat	il sedile	*(seh-dEEh-leh)*
seatbelt	la cintura di sicurezza	*(cheehn-tOOh-rah deeh seeh-kooh-rEhts-tsah)*
second mortgage	l'ipoteca secondaria	*(eeh-poh-tEh-kah seh-kohn-dAh-reeh-ah)*
second position	la posizione secondaria	*(poh-zeeh-tsyOh-neh seh-kohn-dAh-reeh-ah)*
secondary market (securities)	il mercato secondario per titoli mobiliari	*(mehr-kAh-toh seh-kohn-dAh-reeh-oh pehr tEEht-toh-leeh moh-beeh-lyAh-reeh)*
secondary offering (securities)	l'offerta secondaria di titoli di sicura affidabilità	*(ohf-fEhr-tah seh-kohn-dAh-reeh-ah deeh tEEht-toh-leeh deeh seeh-kOOh-rah ahf-feeh-dah-beeh-leeh-tAh)*
secretary	la/il segretaria/o	*(seh-greh-tAh-reeh-ah/oh)*
secured accounts	i conti garantiti, i crediti garantiti	*(kOhn-teeh gah-rahn-tEEh-teeh), (krEh-deeh-teeh gah-rahn-tEEh-teeh)*
secured liability	l'impegno garantito, la passività garantita	*(eehm-pEh-nyoh gah-rahn-tEEh-toh), (pahs-seeh-veeh-tAh gah-rahn-tEEh-tah)*
securities	i titoli di sicura affidabilità, i titoli mobiliari, le azioni, le obbligazioni	*(tEEht-toh-leeh deeh seeh-kOOh-rah ahf-feeh-deeh-beeh-leeh-tAh), (tEEht-toh-leeh moh-beeh-lyAh-reeh), (ah-tsyOh-neeh), (ohb-bleeh-gah-tsyOh-neeh)*
security	la sicurezza, la garanzia	*(seeh-kooh-rEhts-tsah)*
sedan	la berlina	*(behr-lEEh-nah)*
sedative	il calmante	*(kahl-mAhn-teh)*
self-appraisal	l'auto-critica	*(ah-ooh-toh-krEEh-teeh-kah)*
self-employed, be (v)	lavorare per conto proprio	*(lah-voh-rAh-reh pehr kOhn-toh prOh-preeh-oh)*
self-management	l'autogestione	*(ah-ooh-toh-jehs-tyOh-neh)*
self-service	il self-service	*(self-sehrvis)*
sell (v)	vendere	*(vEhn-deh-reh)*
sell direct (v)	vendita diretto	*(vEhn-deeh-tah deeh-rEht-toh)*

sell, hard	la vendita aggressiva	*(vEhn-deeh-tah ahg-grehs-sEEh-vah)*
sell, soft	la vendita non aggressiva	*(vEhn-deeh-tah nohn ahg-grehs-sEEh-vah)*
semi-variable costs	i costi semi-variabili	*(kOhs-teeh seh-meeh-vah-ryAh-beeh-leeh)*
semiconductor	il semiconduttore	*(seh-meeh-kohn-dooht-tOh-reh)*
senior issue	l'emissione primaria	*(eh-meehs-syOh-neh preeh-mAh-reeh-ah)*
seniority	l'anzianità	*(ahn-tsyah-neeh-tAh)*
separation	la separazione	*(seh-pah-rah-tsyOh-neh)*
serial bonds	le obbligazioni a scadenza periodica	*(ohb-bleeh-gah-tsyOh-neeh ah skah-dEhn-tsah peh-reeh-Oh-deeh-kah)*
serial storage	l'immagazzinaggio	*(eehm-mah-gahds-dseeh-nAhj-joh)*
serum	il siero	*(syEh-roh)*
service (v)	mantenere	*(mahn-teh-nEh-reh)*
service contract	il contratto di manutenzione	*(kohn-trAht-toh deeh mah-nooh-tehn-tsyOh-neh)*
service, advisory	il servizio consultivo	*(sehr-vEEh-tsyoh kohn-soohl-tEEh-voh)*
service, customer	il servizio reso al cliente	*(sehr-vEEh-tsyoh rEh-zoh ahl kleeh-Ehn-teh)*
set-up costs	i costi iniziali	*(kOhs-teeh eeh-neeh-tsyAh-leeh)*
settlement	la definizione	*(deh-feeh-neeh-tsyOh-neh)*
settlement, full	il saldo completo	*(sAhl-doh kohm-plEh-toh)*
severance pay	la bonuscita	*(bohn-ooh-shEEh-tah)*
sew (v)	cucire	*(kooh-chEEh-reh)*
sewing machine	la macchina da cucire	*(mAhk-keeh-nah dah kooh-chEEh-reh)*
sewn	rilegato	*(reeh-leh-gAh-toh)*
shareholder	l'azionista	*(ah-tsyoh-nEEhs-tah)*
shareholder's equity	il capitale netto dell'azionista	*(kah-peeh-tAh-leh nEht-toh dehl ah-tsyoh-nEEhs-tah)*
shareholders' meeting	la riunione degli azionisti	*(reeh-ooh-nyOh-neh deh-lyeeh ah-tsyoh-nEEhs-teeh)*

S

shares	le azioni	*(ah-tsyOh-neeh)*
sheet	il foglio, la lastra	*(fOh-lyoh), (lAhs-trah)*
sheets	le lastre, i fogli	*(lAhs-treh), (fOh-leeh)*
shift (labor)	il turno	*(tOOhr-noh)*
shipment	la spedizione, la consegna	*(speh-deeh-tsyOh-neh), (kohn-sEh-nyah)*
shipper	lo spedizioniere	*(speh-deeh-tsyoh-nyEh-reh)*
shipping agent	l'agente spedizioniere	*(ah-jEhn-teh speh-deeh-tsyoh-nyEh-reh)*
shipping charges	i costi di trasporto	*(kOhs-teeh deeh trahs-pOhr-toh)*
shipping expenses	le spese di spedizione, le spese di trasporto	*(spEh-zeh deeh speh-deeh-tsyOh-neh), (spEh-zeh deeh trahs-pOhr-toh)*
shipping instructions	le istruzioni per il trasporto	*(eehs-trooh-tsyOh-neeh pehr eehl trahs-pOhr-toh)*
shirt	la camicia	*(kah-mEEh-chah)*
shock absorber	gli ammortizzanti	*(ahm-mohr-teehds-dsAhn-teeh)*
shoe	la scarpa	*(skAhr-pah)*
shopping center	il centro acquisti fuori dall'area urbana	*(chEhn-troh ahk-kwEEhs-teeh fwOh-reeh dahl Ah-re-ah oohr-bAh-nah)*
short delivery	la consegna incompleta	*(kohn-sEh-nyah eehn-kohm-plEh-tah)*
short of, to be (v)	mancare	*(mahn-kAh-reh)*
short position	la posizione scoperta	*(poh-zeeh-tsyOh-neh skoh-pEhr-tah)*
short sale	la vendita allo scoperto	*(vEhn-deeh-tah ahl-loh skoh-pEhr-toh)*
short shipment	la spedizione incompleta	*(speh-deeh-tsyOh-neh eehn-kohm-plEh-tah)*
short sleeves	le maniche corte	*(mAh-neeh-keh kOhr-teh)*
short supply	le forniture carenti	*(fohr-neeh-tOOh-reh kah-rEhn-teeh)*
short wave	le onde corte	*(Ohn-deh kOhr-teh)*
short-term capital account	il conto capitale a breve termine	*(kOhn-toh kah-peeh-tAh-leh ah brEh-veh tEhr-meeh-neh)*

short-term debt	il debito a breve termine	*(dEh-beeh-toh ah brEh-veh tEhr-meeh-neh)*
short-term financing	il finanziamento a breve termine	*(feeh-nahn-tsyah-mEhn-toh ah brEh-veh tEhr-meeh-neh)*
shortage	la carenza, la mancanza	*(kah-rEhn-tsah), (mahn-kAhn-dsah)*
shrink-wrapping	l'imballaggio utilizzante pellicole di plastica ristretta	*(eehm-bahl-lAhj-joh ooh-teeh-llehds-dsAhn-teh pehl-leeh-koh-leh deeh plAhs-teeh-kah reehs-trEht-tah)*
sick leave	il congedo per malattia	*(kohn-jEh-doh pehr mah-laht-tEEh-ah)*
sight draft	la tratta a vista	*(trAht-tah ah vEEs-tah)*
signature	la firma	*(fEEhr-mah)*
silent partner	il socio accomandante	*(sOh-choh ahk-koh-moh-dAhn-teh)*
silicon	il silicone	*(seeh-leeh-kOh-neh)*
silk	la seta	*(sEh-tah)*
silk factory	il setificio	*(seh-teeh-fEEh-choh)*
silkworm	il baco di seta	*(bAh-koh deeh sEh-tah)*
silverware	l'argenteria	*(ahr-jehn-teh-rEEh-ah)*
simulate (v)	simulare	*(seeh-mooh-lAh-reh)*
sinking fund	il fondo d'ammortamento per il ritiro di obbligazioni	*(fOhn-doh dahm-mohr-tah-mEhn-toh pehr eehl reeh-tEEh-roh deeh ohb-bleeh-gah-tsyOh-neeh)*
sinus	la cavità	*(kah-veeh-tAh)*
sinusitis	la sinusite	*(seeh-nooh-sEEh-teh)*
size	il formato	*(fohr-mAh-toh)*
size	il numero, la taglia	*(nOOh-meh-roh), (tAh-lyah)*
skilled labor	la manodopera specializzata	*(mah-noh-dOh-eh-rah speh-chah-leehds-dsAh-tah)*
skin	la buccia	*(bOOhch-chah)*
skirt	la gonna	*(gOhn-nah)*
slabs	le sbarre	*(zbAhr-reh)*
slacks	i pantaloni, i calzoni	*(pahn-tah-lOOh-neeh), (kahl-tsOh-neeh)*

S

sleeping pill	il sonnifero	*(sohn-nEEh-feh-roh)*
sleeve	la manica	*(mAh-neeh-kah)*
sliding parity	la parità variabile	*(pah-reeh-tAh vah-ryAh-beeh-leh)*
sliding scale	la scala variabile, la scala mobile	*(skAh-lah vah-ryAh-beeh-leh), (skAh-lah mOh-beeh-leh)*
slippers	le pantofole	*(pahn-tOh-foh-leh)*
slump	la fase negativa	*(fAh-zeh neh-gah-tEEh-vah)*
small business	la piccola industria	*(pEEhk-koh-lah eehn-dOOhs-treeh-ah)*
snakeskin	la pelle di serpente	*(pEhl-leh deeh sehr-pEhn-teh)*
sneeze (v)	starnutire	*(stahr-nooh-tEEh-reh)*
socks	i calzini	*(kahl-tsEEh-neeh)*
soft cover	la copertina flessibile	*(koh-pehr-tEEh-nah flehs-sEEh-beeh-leh)*
soft currency	la valuta debole	*(vah-lOOh-tah dEh-boh-leh)*
soft goods	i beni non durevoli	*(bEh-neeh nohn dooh-rEh-voh-leeh)*
soft loan	il prestito con minor garanzia	*(prEhs-teeh-toh kohn meeh-nohr gah-rahn-tsEEh-ah)*
soft sell	la vendita non aggressiva	*(vEhn-deeh-tah nohn ahg-grehs-sEEh-vah)*
software	il software	*(sohftwahr)*
software broker	il mediatore di software	*(meh-dyah-tOh-reh)*
sole agent	l'agente esclusivo	*(ah-jEhn-teh ehs-klooh-zEEh-voh)*
sole proprietor	il proprietario unico	*(proh-pryeh-tAh-reeh-oh OOh-neeh-koh)*
sole rights	i diritti esclusivi	*(deeh-rEEht-teeh ehs-klooh-zEEh-veeh)*
solubility	la solubilità	*(soh-looh-beeh-leeh-tAh)*
solute	il soluto	*(soh-lOOh-toh)*
solution	la soluzione	*(soh-looh-tsyOh-neh)*
solvency	la liquidità	*(leeh-kweeh-deeh-tAh)*
solvent	il solvente	*(sohl-vEhn-teh)*
sound	il suono	*(sWoh-noh)*

S

soup dish	la zuppiera	*(dsoohp-pyEh-rah)*
sour	agro	*(Ah-groh)*
spare tire	la ruota di scorta	*(rwOh-tah deeh skOhr-tah)*
spark plug	la candela	*(kahn-dEh-lah)*
sparkling wine	il vino spumante	*(vEEh-noh spooh-mAhn-teh)*
speaker	l'altoparlante	*(ahl-toh-pahr-lAhn-teh)*
specialist (stock exchange)	lo specialista	*(speh-chah-lEEhs-tah)*
specialty goods	i beni specializzati	*(bEh-neeh speh-chah-leehds-dsAh-teeh)*
specialty steels	gli acciai con lavorazione particolare	*(ahch-chAh-eeh kohn lah-voh-rah-tsyOh-neh pahr-teeh-koh-lAh-reh)*
specific duty	il dazio specifico, l'imposta specifica	*(dAh-tsyoh speh-chEEh-feeh-koh) (eehm-pOhs-tah speh-chEEh-feeh-kah)*
spectrophotometry	la spettrofotometria	*(speht-troh-foh-toh-meh-trEEh-ah)*
spectrum	lo spettro	*(spEht-troh)*
speculator	lo speculatore	*(speh-kooh-lah-tOh-reh)*
speed up (v)	accelerare	*(ahch-eh-leh-rAh-reh)*
speedometer	l'indicatore di velocità, il tachimetro	*(eehn-deeh-kah-tOh-reh deeh veh-loh-cheeh-tAh), (tah-kEEh-meh-troh)*
spin off (v)	lanciare un nuovo prodotto sulla base di un altro pro-dotto	*(lahn-chAh-reh oohn nwOh-voh proh-dOht-toh soohl-lah bAh-zeh deeh oohn Ahl-troh proh-dOht-toh)*
spine	il dorso	*(dOhr-soh)*
spoilage	lo scarto	*(skAhr-toh)*
sponsor (of fund, partnership)	lo "sponsor"	*(spohnsuhr)*
spoon	il cucchiaio	*(koohk-kyAh-yoh)*
sportswear	l'abbigliamento sportivo	*(ahb-beeh-lyah-mEhn-toh spohr-tEEh-voh)*
spot delivery	la consegna immediata	*(kohn-sEh-nyah eehm-meh-dyAh-tah)*
spot market	il mercato a contanti	*(mehr-kAh-toh ah kohn-tAhn-teeh)*
spread	la variazione	*(vah-ryah-tsyOh-neh)*

S

spreadsheet	il modulo multiplo, lo "spreadsheet"	*(mOh-dooh-loh mOOhl-teeh-ploh)*
spring	la molla	*(mOhl-lah)*
staff	il personale	*(pehr-soh-nAh-leh)*
staff and line	il personale e i dirigenti	*(pehr-soh-nAh-leh eh eeh deeh-reeh-jEhn-teeh)*
staff assistant	l'assistente di servizio	*(ahs-seehs-tEhn-teh deeh sehr-vEEh-tsyoh)*
staff organization	l'organigramma di servizio	*(ohr-gah-neeh-grAhm-mah deeh sehr-vEEh-tsyoh)*
stagflation	la stagflazione	*(stahg-flah-tsyOh-neh)*
stainless steel	l'acciaio inossidabile	*(ahch-chAh-yoh eehn-ohs-seeh-dAh-beeh-leh)*
stale check	l'assegno vecchio	*(ahs-sEh-nyoh vEhk-kyoh)*
stand in line (v)	fare la coda	*(fAh-reh lah kOh-dah)*
stand-alone word processor	l'elaboratore del testo autonomo	*(eh-lah-boh-rah-tOh-reh dehl tEhs-toh ah-ooh-tOh-noh-moh)*
stand-alone workstation	il posto di lavoro autonomo	*(pOhs-toh deeh lah-vOh-roh ah-ooh-tOh-noh-moh)*
standard costs	i costi normali, i costi standard	*(kOhs-teeh nohr-mAh-leeh), (kOhs-teeh stahn-dahrd)*
standard deviation	lo scarto quadratico medio	*(skAhr-toh kwah-drAh-teeh-koh mEh-dyoh)*
standard of living	il tenore di vita	*(teh-nOh-reh deeh vEEh-tah)*
standard practice	le pratiche d'uso	*(prAh-teeh-keh dOOh-zoh)*
standard time	l'ora solare	*(Oh-rah soh-lAh-reh)*
standardization	la standardizzazione	*(stahn-dahr-deehds-dsah-tsyOh-neh)*
standing charges	la tariffa fissa	*(tah-rEEhf-fah fEEhs-sah)*
standing costs	i costi fissi	*(kOhs-teeh fEEhs-seeh)*
standing order	l'ordine fisso	*(Ohr-deeh-neh fEEhs-soh)*
starch	l'amido	*(Ah-meeh-doh)*
start-up cost	i costi iniziali	*(kOhs-teeh eeh-neeh-tsyAh-leeh)*
starter	il motorino d'avviamento	*(moh-toh-rEEh-noh dahv-veeh-ah-mEhn-toh)*
statement	la dichiarazione	*(deeh-kyah-rah-tsyOh-neh)*

S

statement of account	l'estratto conto	*(ehs-trAht-toh kOhn-toh)*
statement, financial	il bilancio, la dichiarazione finanziaria	*(beeh-lAhn-choh), (deeh-kyah-rah-tsyOh-neh feeh-nahn-tsyAh-reeh-ah)*
statement, pro forma	la dichiarazione pro forma	*(deeh-kyah-rah-tsyOh-neh proh-fOhr-mah)*
statement, profit and loss	la dichiarazione degli utili e delle perdite	*(deeh-kyah-rah-tsyOh-neh deh-lyeeh OOh-teeh-leeh eh dehl-leh pEhr-deeh-teh)*
statistics	le statistiche	*(stah-tEEhs-teeh-keh)*
statute	lo statuto	*(stah-tOOh-toh)*
statute of limitations	la scadenza oltre la quale non sono permesse azioni legali	*(skah-dEhn-tsah Ohl-treh lah kwAh-leh nohn sOh-noh pehr-mEhs-seh ah-tsyOh-neeh leh-gAh-leeh)*
steel mill	l'acciaieria	*(ahch-chah-yeh-rEEh-ah)*
steering	la guida	*(gwEEh-dah)*
steering wheel	lo sterzo, il volante	*(stEhr-tsoh), (voh-lAhn-teh)*
stereophonic	stereofonico	*(steh-reh-oh-fOh-neeh-koh)*
stimulant	lo stimolante	*(steeh-moh-lAhn-teh)*
stitch	il punto	*(pOOhn-toh)*
stock	il valore, il titolo, l'azione	*(vah-lOh-reh), (tEEh-toh-loh), (ah-tsyOh-neh)*
stock certificate	il certificato azionario	*(chEhr-teeh-feeh-kAh-toh ah-tsyoh-nAh-reeh-oh)*
stock control	il controllo dei valori, il controllo delle azioni	*(kohn-trOhl-loh deh-eeh vah-lOh-reeh), (kohn-trOhl-loh dehl-leh ah-tsyOh-neeh)*
stock exchange	la borsa	*(bOhr-sah)*
stock index	l'indice della borsa	*(EEhn-deeh-cheh dehl-lah bOhr-sah)*
stock market	la borsa	*(bOhr-sah)*
stock option	l'opzione sulle azioni	*(ohp-tsyOh-neh sohl-leh ah-tsyOh-neeh)*
stock portfolio	il portafoglio azionario	*(pohr-tah-fOh-lyoh ah-tsyoh-nAh-reeh-oh)*

S

stock power	il potere delle azioni, l'autorizzazione a collateralizzare azioni	*(poh-tEh-reh dehl-leh ah-tsyOh-neeh) (ah-ooh-toh-reehds-dsah-tsyOh-neh ah kohl-lah-teh-rah-leehds-dsAh-reh ah-tsyOh-neeh)*
stock profit	l'utile dalle azioni	*(OOh-teeh-leh dahl-leh ah-tsyOh-neeh)*
stock purchase	l'acquisto dei valori mobiliari	*(ahk-kwEEhs-toh deh-eeh vah-lOh-reeh moh-beeh-lyAh-reeh)*
stock split	il frazionamento delle azioni	*(frah-tsyoh-nah-mEhn-toh dehl-leh ah-tsyOh-neeh)*
stock takeover	l'insediamento tramite l'acquisto del controllo azionario	*(eehn-seh-dyah-mEhn-toh trAh-meeh-teh lahk-kwEEhs-toh dehl kohn-trOhl-loh ah-tsyoh-nAh-reeh-oh)*
stock turnover	il giro delle azioni, il ricambio delle azioni	*(jEEh-roh dehl-leh ah-tsyOh-neeh), (reeh-kAhm-byoh dehl-leh ah-tsyOh-neeh)*
stockbroker	il mediatore delle azioni	*(meh-dyah-tOh-reh dehl-leh ah-tsyOh-neeh)*
stockholder	l'azionista	*(ah-tsyoh-nEEhs-tah)*
stockholders' equity	il capitale degli azionisti, il capitale azionario	*(kah-peeh-tAh-leh deh-lyeeh ah-tsyoh-nEEhs-teeh), (kah-peeh-tAh-leh ah-tsyoh-nAh-reeh-oh)*
stockings	le calze	*(kAhl-tseh)*
stoneware	il grès	*(grEhs)*
stop-loss order	l'ordine di fermo perdita	*(Ohr-deeh-neh deeh fEhr-moh pEhr-deeh-tah)*
storage	l'immagazzinaggio	*(eehm-mah-gah-dseeh-nAhj-joh)*
store (v)	accumulare	*(ahk-kooh-moh-lAh-reh)*
stowage	lo stivaggio	*(steeh-vAhj-joh)*
stowage charges	i costi di stivaggio	*(kOhs-teeh deeh steeh-vAhj-joh)*

S

straddle	l'opzione col privilegio di acquistare o vendere un'azione allo stesso prezzo	*(ohp-tsyOh-neh kohl preeh-veeh-lEh-joh deeh ahk-kweehs-tAh-reh oh vEhn-deh-reh oohn ah-tsyOh-neh ahl-loh stEhs-soh prEhts-tsoh)*
strapping	l'azione che deriva dalla richiesta di esercitare due opzioni di acquisto ed una di vendita	*(ah-tsyOh-neeh keh deh-rEEh-vah dahl-lah reeh-kyEhs-tah deeh eh-zehr-cheeh-tAh-reh dooh-eh ohp-tsyOh-neeh deeh ahk-kwEEhs-toh ed ooh-nah deeh vEhn-deeh-tah)*
strategic articles	gli articoli strategici	*(ahr-tEEh-koh-leeh strah-tEh-jeeh-cheeh)*
streamline (v)	affusolare, scorrere in modo regolare	*(ahf-fooh-zoh-lAh-reh), (skOhr-reh-reh eehn mOh-doh reh-goh-lAh-reh)*
stress management	l'amministrazione della tensione	*(ahm-meeh-neehs-trah-tsyOh-neh dehl-lah tehn-syOh-neh)*
strike (v)	scioperare	*(shoh-peh-rAh-reh)*
strike, wildcat	lo sciopero selvaggio	*(shOh-peh-roh sehl-vAhj-joh)*
strikebreaker (scab)	il crumiro	*(krooh-mEEh-roh)*
stuffing	l'imbottitura	*(eehm-boht-teeh-tOOh-rah)*
style	lo stile	*(stEEh-leh)*
stylist	lo stilista	*(steeh-lEEhs-tah)*
subcontract (v)	subappaltare	*(soohb-ahp-pahl-tAh-reh)*
subcontractor	il subappaltatore	*(soohb-ahp-pahl-tah-tOh-reh)*
sublet	il subaffitto	*(soohb-ahf-fEEht-toh)*
subscription price	il prezzo di sottoscrizione	*(prEhts-tsoh deeh soht-toh-skreeh-tsyOh-neh)*
subsidiary	la filiale	*(feeh-lyAh-leh)*
subsidy	il sussidio	*(soohs-sEEh-deeh-oh)*
substandard	deficiente, sotto norma	*(deh-feeh-chEhn-teh), (sOht-toh fOhr-mah)*
suede	lo scamosciato	*(skah-moh-shAh-toh)*
suede jacket	il giubbotto di renna	*(joohb-bOht-toh deeh rEhn-nah)*

S

sugar bowl	la zuccheriera	*(dsoohk-kyeh-ryEh-rah)*
sugar content	il contenuto zuccherino	*(kohn-teh-nOOh-toh dsoohk-keh-rEEh-noh)*
suit	l'abito	*(Ah-beeh-toh)*
suitcase	la valigia	*(vah-lEEh-jah)*
sulfate	il solfato	*(sohl-fAh-toh)*
sulfuric acid	l'acido solforico	*(Ah-ceeh-doh sohl-fOh-reeh-koh)*
sulphamide	il sulfamide	*(soohl-fah-mEEh-deh)*
sum of the year's digits	la somma dei numeri dell'anno precedente, il sistema di ammortamento accelerato	*(sOhm-mah deh-eeh nOOh-meh-reeh dehl Ahn-noh preh-cheh-dEhn-teh), (seehs-tEh-mah deeh ahm-mohr-tah-mEhn-toh ahch-cheh-leh-rAh-toh)*
super alloys	la superleghe	*(sooh-pehr-lEh-geh)*
supersede (v)	sostituire	*(sohs-teeh-tooh-EEh-reh)*
supervisor	il supervisore	*(sooh-pehr-veeh-zOh-reh)*
supplier	il fornitore	*(fohr-neeh-tOh-reh)*
supply and demand	l'offerta e la domanda	*(ohf-fEhr-tah eh lah doh-mAhn-dah)*
support activities	le funzioni di sostegno	*(foohn-tsyOOh-neeh deeh sohs-tEh-nyoh)*
surcharge	il sovraccarico, il soprap-prezzo	*(soh-vrahk-kAh-reeh-koh), (soh-vrahp-prEhts-tsoh)*
surety company	la ditta garante	*(dEEht-tah gah-rAhn-teh)*
surplus capital	il capitale eccedente	*(kah-peeh-tAh-leh ehch-cheh-dEhn-teh)*
surplus goods	i beni eccedenti	*(bEh-neeh ehch-cheh-dEhn-teeh)*
surtax	la soprattassa	*(soh-praht-tAhs-sa)*
suspend payment (v)	sospendere il pagamento	*(sohs-pEhn-deh-reh eehl pah-gah-mEhn-toh)*
suspension	la sospensione	*(sohs-pehn-syOh-neh)*
sweater	il maglione	*(mah-lyOh-neh)*
switch	l'interruttore	*(eehn-tehr-rooht-tOh-reh)*
switching charges	le spese di scambio	*(spEh-zeh deeh skAhm-byoh)*

S

sworn statement	la dichiarazione sotto giura-mento	*(deeh-kyah-rah-tsyOh-neh soht-toh jooh-rah-mEhn-toh)*
syndicate (v)	costituire un sindacato	*(kohs-teeh-tooh-reh oon sin-dah-kah-toh)*
synthesis	la sintesi	*(sEEhn-teh-zeeh)*
synthetic	sintetico, artificiale	*(seehn-tEh-teeh-koh), (ahr-teeh-feeh-chAh-leh)*
syringe	la siringa	*(seeh-rEEhn-gah)*
systems analysis	l'analisi dei sistemi	*(ah-nAh-leeh-zeeh deh-eeh seehs-tEh-meeh)*
systems design	la progettazione dei sistemi d'elaborazione	*(proh-jeht-tah-tsyOh-neh deh-eeh seehs-tEh-meeh deh-lah-boh-rah-tsyOh-neh)*
systems engineering	la progettazione dei sistemi d'elaborazione	*(proh-jeht-tah-tsyOh-neh deh-eeh seehs-tEh-meeh deh-lah-boh-rah-tsyOh-neh)*
systems management	l'amministrazione dei siste-mi d'elaborazione	*(ahm-meeh-neehs-trah-tsyOh-neh deh-eeh seehs-tEh-meeh deh-lah-boh-rah-tsyOh-neh)*

T

T

table of contents	l'indice	*(EEhn-deeh-cheh)*
table wine	il vino da tavola	*(vEEh-noh dah tAh-voh-lah)*
tablecloth	la tovaglia	*(toh-vAh-lyah)*
tablespoon	il cucchiaio	*(koohk-kyAh-yoh)*
tablet	la compressa, la pastiglia	*(kohm-prEhs-sah), (pahs-tEEh-lyah)*
taffeta	il taffetà	*(tahf-feh-tAh)*
tailor	il sarto	*(sAhr-toh)*
take down (v)	smontare, ritirare	*(zmohn-tAh-reh), (reeh-teeh-rAh-reh)*
take off (v)	decollare	*(deh-kohl-lAh-reh)*
take out (v)	eliminare, togliere	*(eh-leeh-meeh-nAh-reh) (tOh-lyeh-reh)*
take-home pay	lo stipendio netto	*(steeh-pEhn-dyoh nEht-toh)*

takeover bid	l'offerta d'insediamento	*(ohf-fEhr-tah deehn-seh-dyah-mEhn-toh)*
takeover	l'insediamento	*(eehn-seh-dyah-mEhn-toh)*
tan (v)	conciare	*(kohn-chAh-reh)*
tangible assets	i beni reali	*(bEh-neeh reh-Ah-leeh)*
tanker	la petroliera	*(peh-troh-lyEh-rah)*
tanner	il conciatore	*(kohn-chah-tOh-reh)*
tannery	la concia	*(kOhn-chah)*
tannin	il tannino	*(tahn-nEEh-noh)*
tape	il nastro	*(nAhs-troh)*
target price	il prezzo indicativo	*(prEhts-tsoh eehndeeh-kah-tEEh-voh)*
tariff	la tariffa	*(tah-rEEhf-fah)*
tariff barriers	le barriere doganali, le barriere tariffarie	*(bahr-ryEh-reh doh-gah-nAh-leeh), (bahr-ryEh-reh tah-reehf-fAh-reeh-eh)*
tariff charges	i costi tariffari	*(kOhs-teeh tah-reehf-fAh-reeh)*
tariff classification	la classificazione doganale	*(klahs-seeh-feeh-kah-tsyOh-neh doh-gah-nAh-leh)*
tariff commodity	la voce tariffaria	*(vOh-cheh tah-reehf-fAh-reeh-ah)*
tariff differential	il differenziale tariffario	*(deef-feh-rehn-tsyAh-leh tah-reehf-fAh-reeh-oh)*
tariff war	la guerra tariffaria	*(gwEhr-rah tah-reehf-fAh-reeh-ah)*
task force	il gruppo di esperti	*(grOOhp-poh deeh ehs-pEhr-teeh)*
tasting (wine tasting)	la degustazione	*(deh-goohs-tah-tsyOh-neh)*
tax	la tassa, l'imposta	*(tAhs-sah), (eehm-pOhs-tah)*
tax allowance	lo sgravio fiscale	*(zgrah-vEEh-oh feehs-kAh-leh)*
tax base	la base delle tasse imponibili	*(bAh-zeh dehl-leh tAhs-seh eehm-poh-nEEh-beeh-leeh)*
tax burden	l'onere fiscale	*(Oh-neh-reh feehs-kAh-leh)*
tax collector	l'esattore delle tasse	*(eh-zaht-tOh-reh dehl-leh tAhs-seh)*

tax deduction	la detrazione dalle imposte	*(deh-trah-tsyOh-neh dahl-leh eehm-pOhs-teh)*
tax evasion	l'evasione fiscale	*(eh-vah-zyOh-neh feehs-kAh-leh)*
tax haven	il rifugio fiscale, il paradiso fiscale	*(reeh-fOOh-joh feehs-kAh-leh), (pah-rah-dEEh-zoh feehs-kAh-leh)*
tax relief	lo sgravio fiscale	*(zgrah-vEEh-oh feehs-kAh-leh)*
tax shelter	la riduzione delle tasse tramite facilitazioni permesse dal governo	*(reeh-dooh-tsyOh-neh dehl-leh tAhs-seh trAh-meeh-teh fah-cheeh-leeh-tah-tsyOh-neeh pehr-mEhs-seh dahl goh-vEhr-noh)*
tax, excise	l'imposta sui consumi, la tassa sul consumo	*(eehm-pOhs-tah sooh-eeh kohn-sOOh-meeh), (tAhs-sa soohl kohn-sOOh-moh)*
tax, export	l'imposta d'esportazione	*(eehm-pOhs-tah dehs-pohr-tah-tsyOh-neh)*
tax, import	l'imposta d'importazione	*(eehm-pOhs-tah deehm-pohr-tah-tsyOh-neh)*
tax, sales	l'imposta sulle vendite	*(eehm-pOhs-tah soohl-leh vEhn-deeh-teh)*
tax-free income	il reddito esentasse	*(rEhd-deeh-toh eh-zehn-tAhs-seh)*
taxation	la tassazione	*(tahs-sah-tsyOh-neh)*
team, management	l'équipe amministrativa	*(eh-eeh-kEEhp ahm-meeh-neehs-trah-tEEh-vah)*
teapot	la teiera	*(teh-yEh-rah)*
teaspoon	il cucchiaino da tè	*(koohk-kyah-EEh-noh dah tEh)*
telecommunications	le telecomunicazioni	*(teh-leh-koh-mooh-neeh-kah-tsyOh-neeh)*
telemarketing	il marketing telefonico	*(marketing teh-leh-fOh-neeh-koh)*
teleprocessing	la tele-elaborazione	*(teh-leh-eh-lah-boh-rah-tsyOh-neh)*
teller	il cassiere	*(kahs-syEh-reh)*
temper	il rinvenimento	*(reehn-veh-neeh-mEhn-toh)*
temperature	la temperatura	*(tehm-peh-rah-tOOh-rah)*
tender	l'offerta	*(ohf-fEhr-tah)*

T

tender offer	dare in appalto, offerta d'acquisto	*(dAh-reh eehn ahp-pAhl-toh), (ohf-fEhr-tah dahk-kwEEhs-toh)*
tender, legal	la valuta legale	*(vah-lOOh-tah leh-gAh-leh)*
term bond	il buono a termine	*(bwOh-noh ah tEhr-meeh-neh)*
term insurance	l'assicurazione a scadenza	*(ahs-seeh-kooh-rah-tsyOh-neh ah skah-dEhn-tsah)*
term loan	il prestito a termine	*(prEhs-teeh-toh ah tEhr-meeh-neh)*
terminal	il terminale	*(tehr-meeh-nAh-leh)*
terminate (v)	terminare	*(tehr-meeh-nAh-reh)*
terms of sale	le condizioni di vendita	*(kohn-deeh-tsyOh-neeh deeh vEhn-deeh-tah)*
terms of trade	le condizioni di commercio	*(kohn-deeh-tsyOh-neeh deeh kohm-mEhr-choh)*
territorial waters	le acque territoriali	*(ahk-kweh tehr-reeh-toh-ryAh-leeh)*
territory	il territorio	*(tehr-reeh-tOh-reeh-oh)*
thermometer	il termometro	*(tehr-mOh-meh-troh)*
thin market	il mercato debole, i pochi ordini di acquisto a un dato prezzo	*(mehr-kAh-toh dEh-boh-leh), (pOh-keeh Ohr-deeh-neeh deeh ahk-kwEEhs-toh ah oohn dAh-toh prEhts-tsoh)*
third window	la terza finestra, il terzo sbocco	*(tEhr-tsah feeh-nEhs-trah), ((tEhr-tsoh zbOhk-koh)*
third-party exporter	l'esportatore per conto terzi	*(ehs-pohr-tah-tOh-reh pehr kOhn-troh tEhr-tseeh)*
thread	il filo	*(fEEh-loh)*
through bill of lading	tramite polizza di carico	*(trAh-meeh-teh pOh-leehts-tsah deeh kAh-reeh-koh)*
throughput	la quantità di materiale messa in produzione durante un determinato periodo	*(kwahn-teeh-tAh deeh mah-tehryAh-leh mEhs-sah eehn proh-dooh-tsyOh-neh dooh-rAhn-teh oohn deh-tehr-meeh-nAh-toh peh-rEEh-oh-doh)*
tick, price	lo sbalzo di prezzo	*(zbAhl-tsoh deeh prEhts-tsoh)*
ticker tape	il nastro della telescrivente	*(nAhs-troh dehl-lah teh-leh-skreeh-vEhn-teh)*

tie	la cravatta	*(krah-vAht-tah)*
tied aid	l'assistenza vincolata	*(ahs-seehs-tEhn-dsah veehn-koh-lAh-tah)*
tied loan	il prestito vincolato	*(prEhs-teeh-toh veehn-koh-lAh-toh)*
tight market	il mercato ristretto	*(mehr-kAh-toh reehs-trEht-toh)*
time and motion study	lo studio del rapporto tra tempo e movimento	*(stOOh-dyoh dehl rahp-pOhr-toh trah tEhm-poh eh moh-veeh-mEhn-toh)*
time bill (of exchange)	la cambiale a termine	*(kahm-byAh-leh ah tEhm-poh)*
time deposit	il deposito a tempo	*(deh-pOh-zeeh-toh ah tEhm-poh)*
time order	l'ordine a scadenza	*(Ohr-deeh-neh ah skah-dEhn-tsah)*
time sharing	la multiproprietà	*(moohl-teeh-proh-pryeh-tAh)*
time zone	il fuso orario	*(fOOh-zoh oh-rAh-reeh-oh)*
time, lead	l'intervallo tra progettazione e produzione, il periodo di preparazione	*(eehn-tehr-vAhl-loh trah proh-jeht-tah-tsyOh-neh eh proh-dooh-tsyOh-neh), (peh-rEEh-oh-doh deeh preh-pah-rah-tsyOh-neh)*
timetable	l'orario, la tabella	*(oh-rAh-reeh-oh), (tah-bEhl-lah)*
tip (inside information)	l'informazione riservata	*(eehn-fohr-mah-tsyOh-neh reeh-zehr-vAh-tah)*
tire	il pneumatico	*(pneh-ooh-mAh-teeh-koh)*
titanium	il titanio	*(teeh-tAh-nyoh)*
title	il titolo	*(tEEh-toh-loh)*
title insurance	l'assicurazione del diritto di possesso	*(ahs-seeh-kooh-rah-tsyOh-neh dehl deeh-rEEht-toh deeh pohs-sEhs-soh)*
titration	la titolazione	*(teeh-toh-lah-tsyOh-neh)*
to the bearer	al portatore	*(ahl pohr-tah-tOh-reh)*

T

tombstone	il avviso al pubblico di sottoscrizione di azione o obbligazione su giornali finanziari	*(ahv-vEEh-zoh ahl pOOhb-leeh-koh deeh soht-toh-skreeh-tsyOh-neh deeh ah-tsyOh-neh oh ohb-bleeh-gah-tsyOh-neh sooh johr-nAh-leeh feeh-nahn-tsyAh-reeh)*
tonnage	la stazza	*(stAhts-tsah)*
tools	gli attrezzi, gli utensili	*(aht-trEhts-tseeh), (ooh-tEhn-seeh-leeh)*
top management	i dirigenti, il massimo livello amministrativo	*(deeh-reeh-jEhn-teeh), (mAhs-seeh-moh leeh-vEhl-looh ahm-meeh-neehs-trah-tEEh-voh)*
top price	il prezzo massimo	*(prEhts-tsoh mAhs-seeh-moh)*
top quality	la migliore qualità	*(meeh-lyOh-reh kwah-leeh-tAh)*
top up (v)	riempire	*(reeh-ehm-pEEh-reh)*
torque	la forza di torsione	*(fOhr-tsah deeh tohr-syOh-neh)*
tort	il torto	*(tOhr-toh)*
toughness	la durezza	*(dooh-rEhts-tsah)*
toxicology	la tossicologia	*(tohs-seeh-koh-loh-jEEh-ah)*
toxin	la tossina	*(tohs-sEEh-nah)*
trade (v)	commerciare	*(kohm-mehr-chAh-reh)*
trade	il commercio	*(kohm-mEhr-choh)*
trade acceptance	l'accettazione commerciale	*(ahch-cheht-tah-tsyOh-neh kohm-mehr-chAh-leh)*
trade agreement	il patto commerciale, la convenzione commerciale	*(pAht-toh kohm-mehr-chAh-leh), (kohn-vehn-tsyOh-neh kohm-mehr-chAh-leh)*
trade association	l'associazione settoriale, l'associazione commerciale	*(ahs-soh-chah-tsyOh-neh seht-toh-ryAh-leh), (ahs-soh-chah-tsyOh-neh kohm-mehr-chAh-leh)*
trade barrier	la barriera commerciale	*(bahr-ryEh-rah kohm-mehr-chAh-leh)*
trade commission	l'ufficio commerciale	*(oohf-fEEh-choh kohm-mehr-chAh-leh)*

trade credit	il credito commerciale	*(krEh-deeh-toh kohm-mehr-chAh-leh)*
trade date	il giorno di vendita per azioni	*(jOhr-noh deeh vEhn-deeh-tah pehr ah-tsyOh-neeh)*
trade discount	lo sconto agli operatori settoriali	*(skOhn-toh ah-lyeeh oh-peh-rah-tOh-reeh seht-toh-ryAh-leeh)*
trade house	la ditta che tratta scambi commerciali	*(dEEht-tah keh trAht-tah skAhm-beeh kohm-mehr-chAh-leeh)*
trade union	il sindacato	*(sin-dah-kAh-toh)*
trade, fair	il commercio equo, la fiera commerciale	*(kohm-mEhr-choh Eh-kwoh), (fyEh-rah kohm-mehr-chAh-leh)*
trade off	lo scambio	*(skAhm-byoh)*
trademark	il marchio registrato	*(mAhr-kyoh reh-jeehs-trAh-toh)*
trader	il commerciante	*(kohm-mehr-chAhn-teh)*
trading company	la ditta import/export, il "trading company"	*(dEEht-tah)*
trading floor (stock exchange)	la sala delle negoziazioni	*(sAh-lah dehl-leh neh-goh-tsyah-tsyOh-neeh)*
trading limit	il limite generalmente giornaliero dell'aumento o del decremento dei valori	*(lEEh-meeh-teh jeh-neh-rahl-mEhn-teh johr-nah-lyEh-roh dehl ah-ohh-mEhn-toh oh dehl deh-kreh-mEhn-toh deh-eeh vah-lOh-reeh)*
trainee	l'impiegato in fase d'addestramento	*(eehm-pyeh-gAh-toh eehn fAh-zeh dahd-dehs-trah-mEhn-toh)*
tranche	la tranche, la fetta	*(trAhnsh), (fEht-tah)*
tranquilizer	il tranquillante	*(trahn-kweehl-lAhn-teh)*
transaction	la transazione	*(trahn-sah-tsyOh-neh)*
transfer	la trasferta, il trasferimento	*(trahs-fEhr-tah), (trahs-feh-reeh-mEhn-toh)*
transfer agent	l'agente che effettua i trasferimenti dei titoli	*(ah-jEhn-teh keh ehf-fEht-tooh-ah eeh trahs-feh-reeh-mEhn-teeh deh-eeh tEEh-toh-leeh)*
transit, in	in transito	*(eehn trAhn-zeeh-toh)*
translator	il traduttore	*(trah-dooht-tOh-reh)*

T

transportation	il trasporto	*(trahs-pOhr-toh)*
traveler's check	l'assegno per il viaggiatore, il "traveler's check"	*(ahs-sEh-nyoh pehr eehl vyahj-jah-tOh-reh)*
treasurer	il tesoriere	*(teh-zoh-ryEh-reh)*
treasury bills	i buoni del tesoro a breve termine	*(bwOh-neeh dehl teh-zOh-roh ah brEh-veh tEhr-meeh-neh)*
treasury bonds	le obbligazioni del tesoro	*(ohb-bleeh-gah-tsyOh-neeh dehl teh-zOh-roh)*
treasury notes	le banconota	*(bahn-koh-nOh-tah)*
treasury stock	le azioni riacquistate	*(ah-tsyOh-neeh reeh-ahk-kweehs-tAh-teh)*
treaty	il trattato	*(traht-tAh-toh)*
trend	la tendenza	*(tehn-dEhn-tsah)*
trial balance	il bilancio provvisorio	*(beeh-lAhn-choh prohv-veeh-zOh-reeh-oh)*
troubleshoot (v)	scoprire e localizzare i guasti	*(skoh-prEEh-reh eh loh-kah-leehds-dsAh-reh eeh gwAhs-teeh)*
trousers	i calzoni, i pantaloni	*(kAhl-tsOOh-neeh), (pahn-tah-lOh-neeh)*
truckload	il carico di un camion	*(kAh-reeh-koh deeh oohn kAh-myon)*
trunk	il baule	*(bah-OOh-leh)*
trust	il fondo d'investimento	*(fOhn-doh deehn-vehs-teeh-mEhn-toh)*
trust company	la società per la gestione degli investimenti	*(soh-cheh-tAh pehr lah jehs-tyOh-neh deh-lyeeh eehn-vehs-teeh-mEhn-teeh)*
trust fund	il fondo d'investimento fiduciario	*(fOhn-doh deehn-vehs-teeh-mEhn-toh feeh-dooh-chAh-reeh-oh)*
trust receipt	la ricevuta fiduciaria	*(reeh-cheh-vOOh-tah feeh-dooh-chAh-reeh-ah)*
trustee	l'amministratore fiduciario	*(ahm-meeh-neehs-trah-tOh-reh feeh-dooh-chAh-reeh-oh)*
tube	il tubo	*(tOOh-boh)*
tune (v)	captare	*(kahp-tAh-reh)*
tungsten	il tungstenio	*(toohng-stEh-neeh-oh)*
tureen	la terrina	*(tehr-rEEh-nah)*

T

turnkey	le chiavi in mano	*(kyAh-veeh eehn mAh-noh)*
turnover, asset	il giro d'attivita, il movimento d'attività	*(jEEh-roh daht-teeh-veeh-tAh), (moh-veeh-mEhn-toh daht-teeh-veeh-tAh)*
turnover, inventory	il giro dell'inventario	*(jEEh-roh dehl eehn-vehn-tAh-reeh-oh)*
turnover, sales	il giro delle vendite	*(jEEh-roh dehl-leh vEhn-deeh-teh)*
turnover, stock	il giro delle azioni, il ricambio delle azioni	*(jEEh-roh dehl-leh ah-tsyOh-neeh), (reeh-kAhm-byoh dehl-leh ah-tsyOh-neeh)*
tuxedo	l'abito da sera, lo smoking	*(Ah-beeh-toh dah sEh-rah)*
two-name paper	il credito intestato a due	*(krEh-deeh-toh eehn-tahs-tAh-toh ah dOOh-eh)*
two-tiered market	il mercato a due livelli	*(mehr-kAh-toh ah dOOh-eh leeh-vEhl-leeh)*
type of vine	il vitigno	*(veeh-tEEh-nyoh)*

U

---

ultra vires acts	gli atti arbitrari	*(aht-teeh ahr-beeh-trAh-reeh)*
unaccompanied goods	i beni non accompagnati	*(bEh-neeh nohn ahk-kohm-pah-nyAh-teeh)*
unbleached linen	il lino grezzo	*(lEEh-noh grEhts-tsoh)*
uncollectible accounts	i conti inesigibili	*(kOhn-teeh eehn-eh-zeeh-jEEh-beeh-leeh)*
undercapitalized	sotto-capitalizzato	*(soht-toh-kah-peeh-tah-leehds-dsAh-toh)*
underdeveloped nations	i paesi in via di sviluppo	*(pah-Eh-zeeh eehn vEEh-ah deeh sveeh-lOOhp-poh)*
underestimate (v)	sottovalutare	*(soht-toh-vah-looh-tAh-reh)*
undercut (v)	vendere sotto il prezzo del concorrente	*(vEhn-deh-reh sOht-toh eehl prEhts-tsoh dehl kohn-kohr-rEhn-teh)*
underpaid	sottopagato	*(soht-toh-pah-gAh-toh)*
undersigned	il sottoscritto	*(soht-toh-skrEEht-toh)*
understanding (agreement)	l'accordo	*(ahk-kOhr-doh)*

undertake (v)	intraprendere	*(eehn-trah-prEhn-deh-reh)*
undervalue (v)	sottovalutare	*(soht-toh-vah-looh-tAh-reh)*
underwriter	l'assicuratore, il sottoscrittore	*(ahs-seeh-kooh-rah-tOh-reh), (soht-toh-skreeht-tOh-reh)*
undeveloped	non sviluppato	*(nohn sveeh-loohp-pAh-toh)*
unearned increment	il plusvalore	*(ploohs-vah-lOh-reh)*
unearned revenue	il reddito non da lavoro	*(rEhd-deeh-toh nohn dah lah-vOh-roh)*
unemployment	la disoccupazione	*(deehz-ohk-kooh-pah-tsyOh-neh)*
unemployment compensation	la cassa integrazione	*(kAhs-sah eehn-teh-grah-tsyOh-neh)*
unfair	non equo	*(nohn Eh-kwoh)*
unfavorable	sfavorevole	*(sfah-voh-rEh-voh-leh)*
unfeasible	inattuabile	*(eehn-aht-twAh-beeh-leh)*
unfermented grape juice	il succo d'uva non fermentato	*(sOOhk-koh dOOh-vah nohn fehr-mehn-tAh-toh)*
union contract	il contratto sindacale	*(kohn-trAht-toh seehn-dah-kAh-leh)*
union label	l'etichetta sindacale	*(eh-teeh-kEht-tah seehn-dah-kAh-leh)*
union, labor	il sindacato	*(seehn-dah-kAh-toh)*
unit cost	il costo unitario	*(kOhs-toh ooh-neeh-tAh-reeh-oh)*
unit load discount	lo sconto applicato sulle unità di carico	*(skOhn-toh ahp-pleeh-kAh-toh soohl-leh ooh-neeh-tAh deeh kAh-reeh-koh)*
unit price	il prezzo unitario	*(prEhts-tsoh ooh-neeh-tAh-reeh-oh)*
unlisted	non elencato	*(nohn eh-lehn-kAh-toh)*
unload (v)	scaricare	*(skah-reeh-kAh-reh)*
unsecured liability	l'impegno senza garanzie, la passività senza garanzia	*(eehm-pEh-nyoh sEhn-tsah gah-rahn-tsEEh-eh), (pahs-seeh-veeh-tAh sEhn-tsah gah-rahn-tsEEh-ah)*
unsecured loan	il prestito senza garanzia	*(prEhs-teeh-toh sEhn-tsah gah-rahn-tsEEh-ah)*

U

unskilled labor	il lavoro manuale, la manodopera non specializzata	*(lah-vOh-roh mah-nwAh-leh), (mah-noh-dOh-peh-rah nohn speh-chah-leehds-dsAh-tah)*
up to our expectations	alle nostre aspettative	*(ahl-leh nOhs-treh ahs-peht-tah-tEEh-veh)*
upmarket	il mercato privilegiato	*(mehr-kAh-toh preeh-veeh-leh-jAh-toh)*
upturn	la svolta positiva	*(svOhl-tah poh-zeeh-tEEh-vah)*
urban renewal	la ristrutturazione urbana	*(reeh-strooht-tooh-rah-tsyOh-neh oohr-bAh-nah)*
urban sprawl	la crescita incontrollata della zona urbana	*(krEh-sheeh-tah eehn-kohn-trohl-lAh-tah dehl-lah dsOh-nah oohr-bAh-nah)*
use tax	l'imposta sul consumo	*(eehm-pOhs-tah soohl kohn-sOOh-moh)*
useful life	la durata utile	*(dooh-rAh-tah OOh-teeh-leh)*
user-friendly	user friendly	*(yuzehr frehndlee)*
usury	l'usuria	*(ooh-zOOh-reeh-ah)*
utility	l'utilità	*(ooh-teeh-leeh-tAh)*

V

vaccine	il vaccino	*(vahch-chEEh-noh)*
vacuum	il vuoto	*(vwOh-toh)*
vacuum melting furnace	fornace per la colatura sotto vuoto	*(fohr-nAh-cheh pehr lah koht-tOOh-rah sOht-toh vwOh-toh)*
valid	valido	*(vAh-leeh-doh)*
validate (v)	validare	*(vah-leeh-dAh-reh)*
valuation	la valutazione	*(vah-looh-tah-tsyOh-neh)*
value	il valore	*(vah-lOh-reh)*

V

value engineering	la progettazione utilizzante costi più bassi tra costi alternativi per espletare una certa attività	*(proh-jeht-tah-tsyOh-neh ooh-teeh-leehds-dsAhn-teh kOhs-teeh pyOOh bAhs-seeh trah kOhs-teeh ahl-tehr-nah-tEEh-veeh pehr ehs-pleh-tAh-reh ooh-nah chEhr-tah aht-teeh-veeh-tAh)*
value for duty	il valore imponibile	*(vah-lOh-reh eehm-poh-nEEh-beeh-leh)*
value, asset	il valore delle attività	*(vah-lOh-reh deh-leh aht-teeh-veeh-tAh)*
value, book	il valore contabile	*(vah-lOh-reh kohn-tAh-beeh-leh)*
value, face	il valore dichiarato, il valore riportato	*(vah-lOh-reh deeh-kyah-rAh-toh), (vah-lOh-reh reeh-pohr-tAh-toh)*
value, market	il valore di mercato	*(vah-lOh-reh deeh mehr-kAh-toh)*
value-added tax	l'imposta sul valore aggiunto (IVA)	*(eehm-pOhs-tah soohl vah-lOh-reh ahj-jOOhn-toh)*
valve	la valvola	*(vAhl-voh-lah)*
vanadium	il vanadio	*(vah-nAh-dyoh)*
variable annuity	il reddito annuale variabile	*(rEhd-deeh-toh ahn-nwAh-leh vah-ryAh-beeh-leh)*
variable costs	i costi variabili	*(kOhs-teeh vah-ryAh-beeh-leh)*
variable import levy	l'imposta variabile di importazione	*(eehm-pOhs-tah vah-ryAh-beeh-leh deeh eehm-pohr-tah-tsyOh-neh)*
variable margin	il margine variabile	*(mAhr-jeeh-neh vah-ryAh-beeh-leh)*
variable rate	il tasso variabile	*(tAhs-soh vah-ryAh-beeh-leh)*
variable rate mortgage	l'ipoteca con tasso d'interesse variabile	*(eeh-poh-tEh-kah kohn tAhs-soh deehn-teh-rEhs-seh vah-ryAh-beeh-leh)*
variance	la variazione	*(vah-ryah-tsyOh-neh)*
vat	il tino, la tinozza	*(tEEh-noh) (teeh-nOhts-rsah)*
vector	il vettore	*(veht-tOh-reh)*
veil	il velo	*(vEh-loh)*

V

velocity of money	la velocità della circolazione monetaria	*(veh-loh-cheeh-tAh dehl-lah cheehr-koh-lah-tsyOh-neh moh-neh-tAh-reeh-ah)*
vendor	il venditore	*(vehn-deeh-tOh-reh)*
vendor's lien	il privilegio del venditore	*(preeh-veeh-lEh-joh dehl vehn-deeh-tOh-reh)*
venture capital	il capitale d'investimento in nuove iniziative	*(kah-peeh-tAh-leh deehn-vehs-teeh-mEhn-toh eehn nwOh-veh eeh-neeh-tsyah-tEEh-veh)*
vertical integration	l'integrazione verticale	*(eehn-teh-grah-tsyOh-neh vehr-teeh-kAh-leh)*
vest	il gilet	*(gee-lEh)*
vested interests	gli interessi acquisiti	*(eehn-teh-rEhs-seeh ahk-kweeh-zEEh-teeh)*
vested rights	i diritti acquisiti	*(deeh-rEEht-teeh ahk-kweeh-zEEh-teeh)*
veto	il veto	*(vEh-toh)*
vice-president	il vice-presidente	*(veeh-cheh-preh-zeeh-dEhn-teh)*
videocassette recorder (VCR)	il videoregistratore	*(veeh-deh-oh-reh-jeehs-trah-tOh-reh)*
vine	la vigna	*(vEEh-nyah)*
vineyard	il vigneto	*(veeh-nyEh-toh)*
vintage	la vendemmia	*(vehn-dEhm-myah)*
vintage year	l'annata	*(ahn-nAh-tah)*
vintner	il vinaio	*(veeh-nAh-yoh)*
vintry	la cantina	*(kahn-tEEh-nah)*
viscosity	la viscosità	*(veehs-koh-zeeh-tAh)*
visible balance of trade	il bilancio commerciale visibile	*(beeh-lAhn-choh kohm-mehr-chAh-leh veeh-zEEh-beeh-leh)*
vitamin	la vitamina	*(veeh-tah-mEEh-nah)*
voice-activated	attivato a voce	*(aht-teeh-vAh-toh ah vOh-cheh)*
voiced check	l'ispezione a voce	*(eehs-peh-tsyOh-neh ah vOh-cheh)*
void	invalido, nullo	*(eehn-vAh-leeh-doh), (nOOhl-loh)*

V

volatile market	il mercato instabile, il mercato volatile	*(mehr-kAh-toh eehn-stAh-beeh-leh), (mehr-kAh-toh voh-lAh-teeh-leh)*
volt	il volt	
voltage	il voltaggio	*(vohl-tAhj-joh)*
volume discount	lo sconto di volume	*(skOhn-toh deeh voh-lOOh-meh)*
volume	il volume, la mole	*(voh-lOOh-meh)*
volume, sales	il volume delle vendite	*(voh-lOOh-meh dehl-leh vEhn-deeh-teh)*
voting right	il diritto al voto	*(deeh-rEEht-toh ahl vOh-toh)*
voucher	la ricevuta	*(reeh-cheh-vOOh-tah)*

W

wage	lo stipendio, la paga	*(steeh-pEhn-deeh-oh), (pAh-gah)*
wage differential	la differenza salariale, il differenziale di stipendio	*(deehf-feh-rEhn-tsah sah-lah-ryAh-leh), (deehf-feh-rehn-tsyAh-leh deeh steeh-pEhn-deeh-oh)*
wage dispute	la disputa salariale	*(dEEhs-pooh-tah sah-lah-ryAh-leh)*
wage drift	lo slittamento salariale	*(zleeht-tah-mEhn-toh sah-lah-ryAh-leh)*
wage earner	il salariato	*(sah-lah-ryAh-toh)*
wage freeze	il blocco degli stipendi	*(blOhk-koh deh-lyeeh steeh-pEhn-deeh)*
wage level	il livello salariale	*(leeh-vEhl-loh sah-lah-ryAh-leh)*
wage scale	la scala salariale	*(skAh-lah sah-lah-ryAh-leh)*
wage structure	la struttura salariale	*(strooht-tOOh-rah sah-lah-ryAh-leh)*
wage-price spiral	la spirale dei salari e dei prezzi	*(speeh-rAh-leh deh-eeh sah-lAh-reeh eh deh-eeh prEhts-tseeh)*
wages	la paga, lo stipendio, il salario	*(pAh-gah), (steeh-pEhn-deeh-oh), (sah-lAh-reeh-oh)*

waist	la vita	*(vEEh-tah)*
waiver clause	la clausola di rinuncia	*(klAhw-zoh-lah deeh reeh-nOOhn-chah)*
walkout	lo sciopero	*(shee-oh-pEh-ro)*
wallet	il portafogli	*(pohr-tah-fOh-lyeeh)*
want ad	la piccola pubblicità	*(poohb-leeh-cheeh-tAh)*
warehouse	il magazzino	*(mah-gahds-dsEEh-noh)*
warehouseman	il magazziniere	*(mah-gah-dseeh-nyEh-reh)*
warrant (v)	garantire	*(gah-rahn-tEEh-reh)*
warranty	la garanzia	*(gah-rahn-tshEEh-ah)*
wasted asset	l'attivo sprecato, l'attività deperibile	*(aht-tEEh-voh spreh-kAh-toh), (aht-teeh-veeh-tAh deh-peh-rEEh-beeh-leh)*
watch strap	il cinturino per orologio	*(cheehn-tooh-rEEh-noh pehr oh-roh-lOh-joh)*
water pump	la pompa dell'acqua	*(pOhm-pah dehl Ahk-kwah)*
watt	il watt	*(uaht)*
wave	l'onda	*(Ohn-dah)*
waybill	la lettera di vettura	*(lEht-teh-rah deeh veht-tOOh-rah)*
wealth	la ricchezza	*(reehk-kEhts-tsah)*
wear and tear	l'usura	*(ooh-zOOh-rah)*
weaver	il tessitore	*(tehs-seeh-tOh-reh)*
web offset press	la macchina da stampa offset a bobina	*(mAhk-keeh-nah dah stAhm-pah offset ah boh-bEEh-nah)*
weekly return	la rendita settimanale	*(rEhn-deeh-tah seht-teeh-mah-nAh-leh)*
weight	il peso	*(pEh-zoh)*
weighted average	la media ponderata	*(mEh-dyah pohn-deh-rAh-tah)*
wharfage charges	gli oneri per l'uso del molo	*(Oh-neh-reeh pehr lOOh-zoh dehl mOh-loh)*
wheel	la ruota	*(rwOh-tah)*
when issued	quando emesso, a seguito dell'emmissione	*(kwAhn-doh eh-mEhs-soh), (ah sEh-gweeh-toh dehl eh-meehs-syOh-neh)*
whip	la frusta	*(frOOhs-tah)*

W

white-collar worker	l'impiegato	*(eehm-pyeh-gAh-toh)*
wholesale market	il mercato all'ingrosso	*(mehr-kAh-toh ahl eehn-grOhs-soh)*
wholesale price	il prezzo all'ingrosso	*(prEhts-tsoh ahl eehn-grOhs-soh)*
wholesale trade	il commercio all'ingrosso	*(kohm-mEhr-choh ahl eehn-grOhs-soh)*
wholesaler	il grossista	*(grohs-sEEhs-tah)*
width	la larghezza, l'ampiezza	*(lahr-gEhts-tsah), (ahm-pyEhts-tsah)*
wildcat strike	lo sciopero selvaggio	*(shOh-peh-roh sehl-vAhj-joh)*
will	il testamento	*(tehs-tah-mEhn-toh)*
windfall profits	i profitti inattesi	*(proh-fEEht-teeh eehn-aht-tEh-zeeh)*
window dressing (increase appeal) (v)	dare un miglior aspetto al prodotto	*(dAh-reh oohn meeh-lyOhr ahs-pEht-toh ahl proh-dOht-toh)*
windshield	il parabrezza	*(pah-rah-brEhts-tsah)*
wine cellar	la cantina, l'enoteca	*(kahn-tEEh-nah), (eh-noh-tEh-kah)*
wine cooperative	la cooperativa vinicola	*(koh-oh-peh-rah-tEEh-vah)*
wine growing areas	le zone di coltivazione delle vigne	*(dsOh-neh deeh kohl-teeh-vah-tsyOh-neh dehl-leh vEEh-nyeh)*
wine	il vino	*(vEEh-noh)*
wine steward	l'enologo, il sommelier	*(eh-nOh-loh-goh)*
winegrower	il viticultore	*(veeh-teeh-koohltOh-reh)*
winepress	il torchio da vino	*(tOhr-kyoh dah vEEh-noh)*
wire	il filo metallico	*(fEEh-loh meh-tAhl-leeh-koh)*
wire transfer	il trasferimento via cavo	*(trahs-feh-reeh-mEhn-toh vEEh-ah kAh-voh)*
with average	con una media	*(kohn ooh-nah mEh-dyah)*
withholding tax	l'imposta ritenuta alla fonte	*(eehm-pOhs-tah reeh-teh-nOOh-tah ahl-lah fOhn-teh)*
witness	il testimone	*(tehs-teeh-mOh-neh)*
wool	la lana	*(lAh-nah)*

W

word processor	il word processor	*(oord prahsehsor)*
work (v)	lavorare	*(lah-voh-rAh-reh)*
work committee	il comitato di lavoro	*(koh-meeh-tAh-toh deeh lah-vOh-roh)*
work council	il consiglio di lavoro	*(kohn-sEEh-lyoh deeh lah-vOh-roh)*
work cycle	il ciclo lavorativo	*(chEEh-kloh lah-voh-rah-tEEh-voh)*
work day	il giorno lavorativo	*(jOhr-noh lah-voh-rah-tEEh-voh)*
work in progress	il lavoro in corso	*(lah-vOh-roh eehn kOhr-soh)*
work load	la mole di lavoro, la quantità di lavoro	*(mOh-leh deeh lah-vOh-roh), (kwahn-teeh-tAh deeh lah-vOh-roh)*
work on contract	il lavoro per contratto	*(lah-vOh-roh pehr kohn-trAht-toh)*
work order	la commessa	*(kohm-mEhs-sah)*
work station	il posto di lavoro, il "work station"	*(pOhs-toh deeh lah-vOh-roh)*
workforce	la forza di lavoro	*(fOhr-tsah deeh lah-vOh-roh)*
working assets	le attività non di capitale, le attività liquide	*(aht-teeh-veeh-tAh nohn deeh kah-peeh-tAh-leh), (aht-teeh-veeh-tAh lEEh-kweeh-deh)*
working balance	il bilancio d'esercizio	*(beeh-lAhn-choh deh-zehr-chEEh-tsyoh)*
working capital	il capitale circolante, il capitale liquido	*(kah-peeh-tAh-leh cheehr-koh-lAhn-teh), (kah-peeh-tAh-leh lEEh-kweeh-doh)*
working class	la classe operaia	*(klAhs-seh oh-peh-rAh-yah)*
working contract	il contratto di lavoro	*(kohn-trAht-toh deeh lah-vOh-roh)*
working funds	il capitale liquido, i fondi attivi	*(kah-peeh-tAh-leh lEEh-kweeh-doh) (fOhn-deeh aht-tEEh-veeh)*
working hours	le ore di lavoro	*(Oh-reh deeh lah-vOh-roh)*
working papers	il permesso di lavoro	*(pehr-mEhs-soh deeh lah-vOh-roh)*
working tools	gli attrezzi per il lavoro	*(aht-trEhts-tseeh pehr eehl lah-vOh-roh)*

W

workplace	il posto di lavoro	*(pOhs-toh deeh lah-vOh-roh)*
workshop	il laboratorio	*(lah-boh-rah-tOh-reeh-oh)*
World Bank	la banca mondiale	*(bAhn-kah mohn-dyAh-leh)*
worth, net	il capitale azionario, il valore netto	*(kah-peeh-tAh-leh ah-tsyoh-nAh-reeh-oh), (vah-lOh-reh nEht-toh)*
worthless	senza valore	*(sEhn-tsah vah-lOh-reh)*
writ	il mandato	*(mahn-dAh-toh)*
write down (v)	svalutare	*(zvah-looh-tAh-reh)*
write off (v)	cancellare un'obbligazione dovuta	*(kahn-chehl-lAh-reh oohn ohb-bleeh-gah-tsyOh-neh doh-vOOh-tah)*
written agreement	la convenzione scritta	*(kohn-vehn-tsyOh-neh skrEEht-tah)*
written bid (stock exchange)	l'offerta scritta	*(ohf-fEhr-tah skrEEht-tah)*

Y

yardstick	il metro	*(mEh-troh)*
yarn	il filato	*(feeh-lAh-toh)*
year	l'anno	*(Ahn-noh)*
year, fiscal	l'anno fiscale	*(Ahn-noh feehs-kAh-leh)*
year-end	il fine anno	*(fEEh-neh Ahn-noh)*
yeast	il lievito	*(lyEh-veeh-toh)*
yield (v)	rendere	*(rEhn-deh-reh)*
yield	il reddito, il rendimento, la resa	*(rEhd-deeh-toh), (rehn-deeh-mEhn-toh), (rEh-zah)*
yield to maturity	il reddito alla maturita, il rendimento	*(rEhd-deeh-toh ahl-lah mah-tooh-reeh-tAh), (rehn-deeh-mEhn-toh)*

Z

zero coupon	l'obbligazione senza cedole per ricevere interessi	*(ohb-bleeh-gah-tsyOh-neh sEhn-tsah chEh-doh-leh pehr reeh-chEh-veh-reh eehn-teh-rEhs-seeh)*
zinc	lo zinco	*(dsEEhn-koh)*
zip code	il codice d'avviamento postale, C.A.P.	*(kOh-deeh-cheh dahv-vyah-mEhn-toh pohs-tAh-leh)*
zipper	la cerniera lampo	*(chehr-nyEh-rah lAhm-poh)*
zone	la zona	*(dsOh-nah)*
zoning law	la normativa per la costruzione in varie città	*(nohr-mah-tEEh-vah pehr lah kohs-trooh-tsyOh-neh dehl-lah cheeht-tAh)*

Z

a buon mercato	*(ah bwOhn mehr-kAh-toh)*	cheap
a distanza	*(ah deehs-tAhn-dsah)*	arm's length
a domanda	*(ah doh-mAhn-dah)*	at call
a e da	*(ah eh dah)*	at and from
a galla	*(ah gAhl-lah)*	afloat
a livello industriale	*(ah leeh-vEhl-loh eehndoohs-tryAh-leh)*	industrywide
a o superiore	*(sooh-peh-ryOh-reh))*	at or better
a richiesta	*(ah reeh-kyEhs-tah)*	at call
a rischio del portatore	*(ah rEEhs-kyoh dehl pohr-tah-tOh-reh)*	carrier's risk
a risconto di	*(ah reehs-kOhn-toh)*	in reply to
a seguito dell'emmissione	*(ah sEh-gweeh-toh dehl eh-meehs-syOh-neh)*	when issued
a vista	*(ah vEEhs-tah)*	at sight
abbandonare	*(ahb-bahn-doh-nAh-reh)*	abandon (v)
abbandono (m)	*(ahb-bahn-dOh-noh)*	abandonment
abbigliamento (m)	*(ahb-beeh-kyah-mEhn-toh)*	apparel
abbigliamento (m) intimo	*(ahb-beeh-kyah-mEhn-toh EEhn-teeh-moh)*	lingerie
abbigliamento sportivo	*(ahb-beeh-lyah-mEhn-toh spohr-tEEh-voh)*	sportswear
abbuono (m)	*(ahb-bwOh-noh)*	allowance, rebate
abbuono per ricevere merce esaurita in un'altra data	*(ahb-bwOh-noh pehr reeh-chEh-veh-reh mEhr-cheh eh-zahw-rEEh-tah eehn oohn Ahl-trah dAh-tah)*	rain check
abilità (f)	*(ah-beeh-leeh-tAh)*	know-how
abito (m)	*(Ah-beeh-toh)*	suit
abito da sera	*(Ah-beeh-toh dah sEh-rah)*	tuxedo
accanto	*(ahk-kAhn-toh)*	alongside
accelerare	*(ah-cheh-leh-rAh-reh)*	speed up (v)
acceleratore (m)	*(ahch-cheh-leh-rah-tOh-reh)*	gas pedal
accensione (f)	*(ahch-chehn-syOh-neh)*	ignition
accentramento (m)	*(ahch-chehn-trah-mEhn-toh)*	centralization

accesso (m) al mercato	*(ahch-chEhs-soh ahl mehr-kAh-toh)*	market access
accettante (f)	*(ahch-cheht-tAhn-teh)*	acceptor
accettare	*(ahch-cheht-tAh-reh)*	accept (v)
accettazione (f)	*(ahcheht-tah-tsyOh-neh)*	acceptance
accettazione bancaria	*(ahcheht-tah-tsyOh-neh bahn-kAh-reeh-ah)*	bank acceptance
accettazione cambiaria	*(ahcheht-tah-tsyOh-neh kahm-byAh-reeh-ah)*	acceptance bill
accettazione commerciale	*(ahcheht-tah-tsyOh-neh kohm-mehr-chAh-leh)*	trade acceptance
accettazione condizionale	*(ahcheht-tah-tsyOh-neh kohn-deeh-tsyoh-nAh-leh)*	conditional acceptance
accettazione da parte del consumatore	*(ahcheht-tah-tsyOh-neh dah pAhr-teh dehl kohn-soohmah-tOh-reh)*	consumer acceptance
accettazione della marca	*(ahcheht-tah-tsyOh-neh dehl-lah mAhr-kah)*	brand acceptance
accettazione generale	*(ahcheht-tah-tsyOh-neh jehneh-rAh-leh)*	general acceptance
acciai (m) con lavorazione particolare	*(ahch-chAh-eeh kohn lah-voh-rah-tsyOh-neh pahr-teeh-koh-lAh-reh)*	specialty steels
acciaieria (f)	*(ahch-chah-yeh-rEEh-ah)*	steel mill
acciaio (m) al carbonio	*(ahch-chAh-yoh ahl kahr-bOh-nyoh)*	carbon steel
acciaio (m) inossidabile	*(ahch-chAh-yoh eehn-ohs-seeh-dAh-beeh-leh)*	stainless steel
acconto (m)	*(ahk-kOhr-doh)*	down payment
accordo (m)	*(ahk-kOhr-doh)*	agreement, understanding
accordo d'accettazione	*(ahk-kOhr-doh dahcheht-tah-tsyOh-neh)*	acceptance agreement
accordo d'arbitrato	*(ahk-kOhr-doh dahr-beeh-trAh-toh)*	arbitration agreement
accordo e la soddisfazione	*(ahk-kOhr-doh eh lah sohd-deehs-fah-tsyOh-neh)*	accord and satisfaction
accordo sulla parola	*(ahk-kOhr-doh soohl-lah pah-rOh-lah)*	gentleman's agreement

A

accorgimenti (m) che tendono a risparmiare sulla manodopera	*(ahk-kohr-jeeh-mEhn-teeh keh tEhn-doh-noh ah reehs-pahr-myAh-reh soohl-lah mah-noh-dOh-peh-rah)*	labor-saving
accreditare	*(ahk-kreh-deeh-tAh-reh)*	credit (v)
accrescimento (m)	*(ahk-kreh-shee-mEhn-toh)*	accretion
accumulare	*(ahk-kooh-mooh-lAh-reh)*	store (v)
accusiamo ricezione di	*(ahk-kooh-zyAh-moh reeh-cheh-tsyOh-neh deeh)*	acknowledge receipt of (v)
acetato (m)	*(ah-cheh-tAh-toh)*	acetate
acetone (m)	*(ah-cheh-tOh-neh)*	acetone
acidità (f)	*(ah-cheeh-deeh-tAh)*	acid content
acido (m)	*(Ah-ceeh-doh)*	acid
acido acetico	*(Ah-ceeh-doh ah-chEh-teeh-koh)*	acetic acid
acido cloridico	*(Ah-ceeh-doh kloh-rEEh-deeh-koh)*	hydrochloric acid
acido nitrico	*(Ah-ceeh-doh nEEh-treeh-koh)*	nitric acid
acido solforico	*(Ah-ceeh-doh sohl-fOh-reeh-koh)*	sulfuric acid
acque (f) territoriali	*(Ahk-kweh tehr-reeh-toh-ryAh-leeh)*	territorial waters
acquirente (m/f)	*(ahk-kweeh-rEhn-teh)*	buyer
acquirente potenziale	*(ahk-kweeh-rEhn-teh poh-tehn-tsyAh-leh)*	potential buyer
acquirente su credito	*(ahk-kweeh-rEhn-teh sooh krEh-deeh-toh)*	credit buyer
acquisizione (f) di dati	*(ahk-kweeh-zeeh-tsyOh-neh deeh dAh-teeh)*	data acquisition
acquistare	*(ahk-kweehs-tAh-reh)*	acquire (v), purchase (v)
acquistare in quantità eccesiva	*(ahk-kweehs-tAh-reh eehn kwahn-teeh-tAh ehch-chehs-sEEh-vah)*	overbuy (v)
acquisti (m) impulsivi	*(ahk-kwEEhs-teeh eehm-poohl-sEEh-veeh)*	impulse buying
acquisto (m)	*(ahk-kwEEhs-toh)*	acquisition, procurement

acquisto a termine	*(ahk-kwEEhs-toh ah tEhr-meeh-neh)*	forward purchase
acquisto valori mobiliari	*(ahk-kwEEhs-toh vah-lOh-reeh moh-beeh-lyAh-reeh)*	stock purchase
acro (m)	*(Ah-kroh)*	acre
acronimo (m)	*(ah-krOh-neeh-moh)*	acronym
addebito (m)	*(ahd-dEh-beeh-toh)*	debit
addizionali (m)	*(ahd-deeh-tsyoh-nAh-leeh)*	fringe benefits
addizione (f)	*(ahd-deeh-tsyOh-neh)*	footing (accounting)
affare (m)	*(ahf-fAh-reh)*	bargain, deal
affittare	*(ahf-feeht-tAh-reh)*	lease (v)
affitto (m)	*(ahf-fEEht-toh)*	rent
affitto degli attrezzi	*(ahf-fEEht-toh deh-lyeeh aht-trEhts-tseeh)*	equipment leasing
affitto morto	*(ahf-fEEht-toh mOhr-toh)*	dead rent
affusolare	*(ahf-foohs-koh-lAh-reh)*	streamline (v)
agenda (f)	*(ah-jEhn-dah)*	agenda
agente (m/f)	*(ah-jEhn-teh)*	agent
agente che effettua i trasferimenti dei titoli	*(ah-jEhn-teh keh ehf-fEht-twah eeh trahs-feh-reeh-mEhn-teeh deh-eeh tEEht-toh-leeh)*	transfer agent
agente d'acquisto	*(ah-jEhn-teh dahk-kwEEhs-toh)*	purchasing agent
agente del produttore	*(ah-jEhn-teh dehl proh-dooht-tOh-reh)*	manufacturer's agent
agente di assicurazione	*(ah-jEhn-teh deeh ahs-seeh-kooh-rah-tsyOh-neh)*	insurance broker
agente esclusivo	*(ah-jEhn-teh ehs-klooh=zEEh-voh)*	sole agent
agente fiscale	*(ah-jEhn-teh feehs-kAh-leh)*	fiscal agent
agente patrimoniale	*(ah-jEhn-teh pah-treeh-moh-nyAh-leh)*	estate agent
agente ricercatore di dirigenti	*(ah-jEhn-teh reeh-chehr-kah-tOh-reh deeh deeh-reeh-jEhn-teeh)*	headhunter
agente spedizioniere	*(ah-jEhn-teh peh-deeh-tsyoh-nyEh-reh)*	shipping agent
agenzia (f)	*(ah-jehn-tsEEh-ah)*	agency

agenzia d'assicurazione	*(ah-jehn-tsEEh-ah dahs-seeh-kooh-rah-tsyOh-neh)*	insurance company
agenzia mercantile	*(ah-jehn-tsEEh-ah mehr-kahn-tEEh-leh)*	mercantile agency
agenzia per la ricerca del personale	*(ah-jehn-tsEEh-ah pehr-lah reeh-chEhr-kah dehl pehr-soh-nAh-leh)*	employment agency
agenzia pubblicitaria	*(ah-jehn-tsEEh-ah poohb-leeh-cheeh-tAh-reeh-ah)*	advertising agency
aggiudicare	*(ahj-jooh-deeh-kAh-reh)*	adjudge (v)
aggiudicazione (f)	*(ahj-jooh-deeh-kah-tsyOh-neh)*	adjudication
aggiunta (f)	*(ahj-jOOhn-tah)*	addendum, (pl) peripherals
aggiustare	*(ahj-joohs-tAh-reh)*	adjust (v)
agnello (m)	*(ah-nyEhl-loh)*	lamb
ago (m)	*(Ah-goh)*	needle
agricoltura (f)	*(ah-greeh-kohl-tOOh-rah)*	agriculture
agro	*(Ah-groh)*	sour
al dettaglio	*(ahl-deht-tAh-lyoh)*	retail
al meglio	*(ahl mEh-lyoh)*	at best
al mercato	*(ahl mehr-kAh-toh)*	at the market
al portatore	*(ahl pohs-tah-tOh-reh)*	to the bearer
albero (m) a gomito	*(Ahl-beh-roh ah gOh-meeh-toh)*	crankshaft
albero di distribuzione a camme	*(Ahl-beh-roh deeh deehs-treeh-booh-tsyOh-neh ah kAhm-meh)*	camshaft
alcool (m)	*(Ahl-kohl)*	alcohol
algoritmo (m)	*(ahl-goh-rEEht-moh)*	algorithm
alimentari (m)	*(ah-leeh-mehn-tAh-reh)*	foodstuffs
all'apertura	*(ahl ah-pehr-tOOh-rah)*	at the opening
all'opzione del compratore	*(ahl ohp-tsyOh-neh dehl kohm-prah-tOh-reh)*	buyer's option
alla chiusura	*(ahl-lah kyooh-zOOh-rah)*	at the close
alla moda	*(Ahl-lah mOh-dah)*	fashionable
alla pari	*(ahl-lah pAh-reeh)*	at par
alla rinfusa	*(ahl-lah reehn-fOOh-zah)*	job lot

alle nostre aspettative	*(ahl-leh nOhs-treh ahs-peht-tah-tEEh-veh)*	up to our expectations
allegare	*(ahl-leh-gAh-reh)*	attach (v)
allergia (f)	*(ahl-lehr-jEEh-ah)*	allergy
allocare	*(ah-loh-kAh-reh)*	allot (v)
allocazione (f) dei costi	*(ahl-loh-kah-tsyOh-neh deh-eeh kOhs-teeh)*	allocation of costs
allocazione del terreno	*(ahl-loh-kah-tsyOh-neh dehl tehr-rEh-noh)*	acreage allotment
allocazione delle risorse	*(ahl-loh-kah-tsyOh-neh dehl-leh reeh-sOhr-seh)*	resources allocation
allocazione di responsabilità	*(ahl-loh-kah-tsyOh-neh deeh rehs-pohn-sah-beeh-leeh-tAh)*	allocation of responsibilities
alluminio (m)	*(ahl-looh-mEEh-nyoh)*	aluminum
alta fedeltà (f)	*(Ahl-tah feh-dehl-tAh)*	high fidelity
alta tecnologia (f)	*(Ahl-tah tehk-noh-loh-jEEh-ah)*	high technology
alterazione (f)	*(ahl-teh-rah-tsyOh-neh)*	alteration
alternatore (m)	*(ahl-tehr-nah-tOh-reh)*	alternator
altoforno (m)	*(ahltoh-fOhr-noh)*	blast furnace
altoforno ad arco elettrico	*(ahl-toh-fOhr-noh ad Ahr-koh eh-lEht-treeh-koh)*	electric arc furnace
altoparlante (m)	*(ahl-toh-pahr-lAhn-teh)*	speaker
altre attività (f) (e passività)	*(Ahl-treh aht-teeh-veeh-tAh eh pahs-seeh-veeh-tAh)*	other assets (and liabilities)
amido (m)	*(Ah-meeh-doh)*	starch
amina (f)	*(ah-mEEh-nah)*	amine
ammanco (m)	*(ahm-mAhn-koh)*	deficit
ammassare	*(ahm-mahs-sAh-reh)*	hoard (v)
ammettere	*(ahm-mEht-teh-reh)*	acknowledge (v)
amministrare	*(ahm-meeh-neehs-trAh-reh)*	manage (v)
amministrativo	*(ahm-meeh-neehs-trah-tEEh-voh)*	administrative
amministratore (m)	*(ahm-meeh-neehs-trah-tOh-reh)*	administrator, manager
amministratore degli acquisti	*(ahm-meeh-neehs-trah-tOh-reh deh-lyeeh ahk-kwEEhs-teeh}*	purchasing manager

amministratore della fabbrica	*(ahm-meeh-neehs-trah-tOh-reh dehl-lah fAhb-breeh-kah)*	plant manager
amministratore fiduciario	*(ahm-meeh-neehs-trah-tOh-reh feeh-dooh-chAh-reeh-oh)*	trustee
amministratore finanziario	*(ahm-meeh-neehs-trah-tOh-reh feeh-nahn-tsyAh-reeh-oh)*	money manager
amministratore generale	*(ahm-meeh-neehs-trah-tOh-reh jeh-neh-rAh-leh)*	general manager
amministratrice (f)	*(ahm-meeh-neehs-trah-trEEh-cheh)*	administratrix
amministrazione (f)	*(ahm-meeh-neehs-trah-tsyOh-neh)*	administration, management
amministrazione a matrice	*(ahm-meeh-neehs-trah-tsyOh-neh ah mahtrEEh-cheh)*	matrix management
amministrazione commerciale	*(ahm-meeh-neehs-trah-tsyOh-neh kohm-mehr-chAh-leh)*	business management
amministrazione dei sistemi di elaborazione	*(ahm-meeh-neehs-trah-tsyOh-neh deh-eeh seehs-tEh-meeh deeh eh-lah-boh-rah-tsyOh-neh)*	systems management
amministrazione del credito	*(ahm-meeh-neehs-trah-tsyOh-neh dehl krEh-deeh-toh)*	credit management
amministrazione del mercato	*(ahm-meeh-neehs-trah-tsyOh-neh dehl mehr-kAh-toh)*	market management
amministrazione del personale	*(ahm-meeh-neehs-trah-tsyOh-neh dehl pehr-soh-nAh-leh)*	personnel administration
amministrazione dell'ufficio	*(ahm-meeh-neehs-trah-tsyOh-neh dehl oohf-fEEh-choh)*	office management
amministrazione della cartella degli investimenti	*(ahm-meeh-neehs-trah-tsyOh-neh dehl-lah kahr-tEhl-lah deh-lyeeh eehn-vehs-teeh-mEhn-teeh)*	portfolio management
amministrazione della cassa	*(ahm-meeh-neehs-trah-tsyOh-neh dehl-lah kAhs-sah)*	cash management

amministrazione della tensione	*(ahm-meeh-neehs-trah-tsyOh-neh dehl-lah tehn-syOh-neh)*	stress management
amministrazione delle vendite	*(ahm-meeh-neehs-trah-tsyOh-neh dehl-leh vEhn-deeh-teh)*	sales management
amministrazione dirigenziale	*(ahm-meeh-neehs-trah-tsyOh-neh deeh-reeh-jehn-tsyAh-leh)*	line management
amministrazione finanziaria	*(ahm-meeh-neehs-trah-tsyOh-neh feeh-nahn-tsyAh-reeh-ah)*	financial management
amministrazione intermediaria	*(ahm-meeh-neehs-trah-tsyOh-neh eehn-tehr-mEh-dyah)*	middle management
ammoniaca (f)	*(ahm-moh-nEEh-ah-kah)*	ammonia
ammontare (m) di passività nella struttura finanziara dell'impresa	*(ah-mohn-tAh-reh deeh pah-seeh-veeh-tAh neh-lah strooht-tOOh-rah feeh-nahn-tsyAh-reeh-ah dehl-eehm-prEh-zah)*	leverage (financial)
ammortamento (m)	*(ahm-mohr-tah-mEhn-toh)*	amortization, depreciation
ammortamento accelerato	*(ahm-mohr-tah-mEhn-toh ahch-cheh-leh-rAh-toh)*	accelerated depreciation
ammortamento maturato	*(ahm-mohr-tah-mEhn-toh mah-tooh-rAh-toh)*	accrued depreciation
ammortizzatore (m)	*(ahm-mohr-teehds-dsAh-tOh-reh)*	shock absorber
ampere (m)	*(ahm-pEh-reh)*	ampere
ampiezza (f)	*(ahm-pyEhts-tsah)*	width
amplificatore (m)	*(ahm-pleeh-feeh-kah-tOh-reh)*	amplifier
analgesico (m)	*(ahn-ahl-jEEh-zeeh-koh)*	analgesic
analisi (f)	*(ah-nAh-leeh-zeeh)*	analysis, assay
analisi d'investimento	*(ah-nAh-leeh-zeeh deehn-vehs-teeh-mEhn-toh)*	investment analysis
analisi dei costi	*(ah-nAh-leeh-zeeh deh-eeh kOhs-teh)*	cost analysis
analisi dei fattori	*(ah-nAh-leeh-zeeh deh-eeh faht-tOh-reeh)*	factor analysis

A

analisi dei fattori produttivi	*(ah-nAh-leeh-zeeh deh-eeh faht-tOh-reeh proh-dooht-tEEh-veeh)*	input-output analysis
analisi dei profitti	*(ah-nAh-leeh-zeeh deh-eeh proh-fEEht-teeh)*	profitability analysis
analisi dei sistemi	*(ah-nAh-leeh-zeeh deh-eeh seehs-tEh-meeh)*	systems analysis
analisi della concorrenza	*(ah-nAh-leeh-zeeh dehl-lah kohn-kohr-rEhn-tsah)*	competitor analysis
analisi del lavoro	*(ah-nAh-leeh-zeeh dehl lah-vOh-roh)*	job analysis
analisi del percorso critico	*(ah-nAh-leeh-zeeh dehl pehr-kOhr-soh krEEh-teeh-koh)*	critical path analysis
analisi del problema	*(ah-nAh-leeh-zeeh dehl proh-blEh-mah)*	problem analysis
analisi del prodotto	*(ah-nAh-leeh-zeeh dehl proh-dOht-toh)*	product analysis
analisi del progetto	*(ah-nAh-leeh-zeeh dehl proh-jEht-toh)*	job analysis
analisi del rapporto tra costo e profitto	*(ah-nAh-leeh-zeeh dehl rahp-pOhr-toh trah kOhs-toh eh proh-fEEht-toh)*	profitability analysis
analisi del rapporto tra i costi ed i benefici	*(ah-nAh-leeh-zeeh dehl rahp-pOhr-toh trah eeh kOhs-teeh eh eeh beh-neeh-fEEh-cheeh)*	cost-benefit analysis
analisi del rischio	*(ah-nAh-leeh-zeeh dehl rEEhs-kyoh)*	risk analysis
analisi delle esigenze	*(ah-nAh-leeh-zeeh dehl-leh eh-zeeh-jEhn-tseh)*	needs analysis
analisi delle vendite	*(ah-nAh-leeh-zeeh dehl-leh vEhn-deeh-teh)*	sales analysis
analisi di equilibrio tra i costi e i ricavi	*(ah-nAh-leeh-zeeh deeh eh-kweeh-lEEh-breeh-oh trah eeh kOhs-teeh eh eeh reeh-kAh-veeh)*	break-even analysis
analisi di regressione	*(ah-nAh-leeh-zeeh deeh reh-grehs-syOh-neh)*	regression analysis
analisi entrata/uscita	*(ah-nAh-leeh-zeeh ehn-trAh-tah/ooh-shEEh-tah)*	input-output analysis
analisi finanziaria	*(ah-nAh-leeh-zeeh feeh-nahn-tsyAh-reeh-ah)*	financial analysis

analisi funzionale	*(ah-nAh-leeh-zeeh foohn-tsyoh-nAh-leh)*	functional analysis
analista (m/f)	*(ah-nah-lEEhs-tah)*	analyst
analizzatore (m) di immagini	*(ah-nah-leehds-dsah-tOh-reh deeh eehm-mAh-jeeh-neeh)*	scanner
anello (m)	*(ah-nEhl-loh)*	ring
anello (m) per tovagliolo	*(ah-nEhl-loh pehr toh-vah-lyOh-loh)*	napkin ring
anestetico (m)	*(ah-nehs-tEh-teeh-koh)*	anaesthetic
anfetamina (m)	*(Ahn-feh-tah-mEEh-nah)*	amphetamine
angolo (m) d'incidenza	*(Ahn-goh-loh deehn-cheeh-dEhn-tsah)*	angle of incidence
annata (f)	*(ahn-nAh-tah)*	vintage year
anno (m)	*(Ahn-noh)*	year
anno di base	*(Ahn-noh deeh bAh-zeh)*	base year
anno finanziario	*(Ahn-noh feeh-nahn-tsyAh-reeh-oh)*	financial year
anno fiscale	*(Ahn-noh feehs-kAh-leh)*	fiscal year
annotazione (f) di movimento di contanti	*(ahn-noh-tah-tsyOh-neh deeh moh-veeh-mEhn-toh deeh kohn-tAhn-teeh)*	cash entry
annuale	*(ahn-nwAh-leh)*	annual
annullare	*(ahn-noohl-lAh-reh)*	nullify (v)
annuncio (m)	*(ahn-nOOhn-choh)*	commercial (advertisement)
antacido (m)	*(ahnt-Ah-cheeh-doh)*	antacid
antenna (f)	*(ahn-tEhn-nah)*	antenna
antibiotico (m)	*(ahn-teeh-beeh-Oh-teeh-koh)*	antibiotic
anticipare	*(ahn-teeh-cheeh-pAh-reh)*	advance (v)
anticipi (m) e ritardi	*(ahn-tEEh-cheeh-peeh eh reeh-tAhr-deeh)*	leads and lags
anticoagulante (m)	*(ahn-teeh-koh-ah-gooh-lAhn-teh)*	anticoagulant
antidepressivo (m)	*(ahn-teeh-deh-prehs-sEEh-voh)*	antidepressant
antiflogistico (m)	*(ahn-teeh-floh-jEEhs-teeh-koh)*	anti-inflammatory

A

anzianità (f)	*(ahn-tsyah-neeh-tAh)*	seniority
appalto (m) sigillato	*(ahp-pAhl-toh seeh-jeehl-lAh-toh)*	sealed bid
appena possibile	*(ahp-pEh-nah pohs-sEEh-beeh-leh)*	as soon as possible
appendice (f)	*(ahp-pehn-dEEh-cheh)*	addendum
appoggio (m) ed esecuzione	*(ahp-pOhj-joh eh eh-zeh-kooh-tsyOh-neh)*	backing and filling
apprendista (m/f)	*(ahp-prehn-dEEhs-tah)*	apprentice
apprezzamento (m)	*(ahp-prehts-tsah-mEhn-toh)*	appreciation
appropriazione (m) indebita	*(ahp-proh-pryah-tsyOh-neh eehn-dEh-beeh-tah)*	embezzlement
approvare	*(ahp-proh-vAh-reh)*	approve (v)
approvazione (f)	*(ahp-proh-vah-tsyOh-neh)*	approval
appuntamento (m)	*(ahp-poohn-tah-mEhn-toh)*	appointment
appunto (m)	*(ahp-pOOhn-toh)*	memorandum
arbitraggio (m)	*(ahr-beeh-trAhj-joh)*	arbitrage
arbitraggio d'interesse	*(ahr-beeh-trAhj-joh deehn-teh-rEhs-seh)*	interest arbitrage
arbitrato (m)	*(ahr-beeh-trAh-toh)*	arbitration
arbitrato industriale	*(ahr-beeh-trAh-toh eehn-doohs-tryAh-leh)*	industrial arbitration
arbitro (m)	*(Ahr-beeh-troh)*	arbitrator
aree (f) delle obbligazioni	*(Ah-reh-eh dehl-leh ohb-bleeh-gah-tsyOh-neeh)*	bond areas
argenteria (m)	*(ahr-jehn-teh-rEEh-ah)*	silverware
armamenti (m)	*(ahr-mah-mEhn-teeh)*	armaments
arresto (m)	*(ahr-rEhs-toh)*	deadlock
arretrati (m)	*(ahr-reh-trAh-teeh)*	arrears
arretrato	*(ahr-reh-trAh-toh)*	retroactive
arrivare al punto di parità	*(ahr-reeh-vAh-reh ahl pOOhn-toh deeh pah-reeh-tAh)*	break even (v)
articoli (m) fuori misura	*(ahr-tEEh-koh-leeh fwOh-reeh meeh-zOOh-rah)*	outsized articles
articoli strategici	*(ahr-tEEh-koh-leeh strah-tEh-jeeh-cheeh)*	strategic articles

articolo (m) posto in vendita pubblicitaria al di sotto del prezzo necessario per guadagnare un profitto	*(ahr-tEEh-koh-loh pOhs-toh eehn vEhn-deeh-tah poohb-leeh-cheeh-tAh-reeh-ah ahl deeh sOht-toh dehl prEhts-tsoh neh-chehs-sAh-reeh-oh pehr gwah-dah-nyAh-reh oohn proh-fEEht-toh)*	oss leader
artificiale	*(ahr-teeh-feeh-chAh-leh)*	synthetic
asettico (m)	*(ah-sEht-teeh-koh)*	antiseptic
asola (f)	*(Ah-zoh-lah)*	buttonhole
aspettativa (f)	*(ahs-peht-tah-tEEh-vah)*	leave of absence
aspirina (f)	*(ahs-peeh-rEEh-nah)*	aspirin
asse (m) posteriore	*(Ahs-seh pohs-teh-ryOh-reh)*	rear axle
assegnare	*(ahs-seh-nyAh-reh)*	assign (v)
assegnatario/a (m/f)	*(ahs-seh-nyah-tAh-reeh-oh/ah)*	assignee
assegno (m)	*(ahs-sEh-nyoh)*	check
assegno bancario	*(ahs-sEh-nyoh bahn-kAh-reeh-oh)*	bank check, cashier's check, counter check
assegno garantito	*(ahs-sEh-nyoh gah-rahn-tEEh-toh)*	certified check
assegno nominativo	*(ahs-sEh-nyoh noh-meeh-nah-tEEh-voh)*	registered check
assegno per il viaggiatore	*(ahs-sEh-nyoh pehr eehl vyahj-jah-tOh-reh)*	traveler's check
assegno vecchio	*(ahs-sEh-nyoh vEhk-kyoh)*	stale check
assegno versato	*(ahs-sEh-nyoh vehr-sAh-toh)*	canceled check
assemblea (f)	*(ahs-sehm-blEh-ah)*	assembly
assenteismo (m)	*(ahs-sehn-teh-EEhz-moh)*	absenteeism
assicurare	*(ahs-seeh-kooh-rAh-reh)*	lock in (v) (rate of interest)
assicurato/a (m/f)	*(ahs-seeh-kooh-rAh-toh)*	policyholder
assicuratore marino	*(ahs-seeh-kooh-rah-tOh-reh mah-rEEh-noh)*	marine underwriter
assicuratore/trice (m/f)	*(ahs-seeh-kooh-rah-tOh-reh)*	underwriter
assicurazione (f)	*(ahs-seeh-kooh-rah-tsyOh-neh)*	insurance

assicurazione a scadenza	*(ahs-seeh-kooh-rah-tsyOh-neh ah skah-dEhn-tsah)*	term insurance
assicurazione contro danni	*(ahs-seeh-kooh-rah-tsyOh-neh kOhn-troh eeh dAhn-neeh)*	casualty insurance
assicurazione d'adempimento	*(ahs-seeh-kooh-rah-tsyOh-neh dah-dehm-peeh-mEhn-toh)*	performance bond
assicurazione dei crediti	*(ahs-seeh-kooh-rah-tsyOh-neh deh-eeh krEh-deeh-teeh)*	credit insurance
assicurazione del diritto di possesso	*(ahs-seeh-kooh-rah-tsyOh-neh dehl deeh-rEEht-toh deeh pohs-sEhs-soh)*	title insurance
assicurazione industriale	*(ahs-seeh-kooh-rah-tsyOh-neh eehn-doohs-tryAh-leh)*	industrial insurance
assicurazione marittima	*(ahs-seeh-kooh-rah-tsyOh-neh mah-rEEht-teeh-mah)*	marine cargo insurance
assicurazione per il personale indispensabile	*(ahs-seeh-kooh-rah-tsyOh-neh pehr eehl pehr-soh-nAh-leh eehn-deehs-pehn-sAh-beeh-leh)*	key man insurance
assicurazione sulla responsabilità civile	*(ahs-seeh-kooh-rah-tsyOh-neh soohl-lah rehs-pohn-sah-beeh-leeh-tAh cheeh-vEEh-leh)*	liability insurance
assistente (m/f)	*(ahs-seehs-tEhn-teh)*	assistant
assistente di servizio	*(ahs-seehs-tEhn-teh deeh sehr-vEEh-tsyoh)*	staff assistant
assistenza (f) al personale	*(ahs-seehs-tEhn-dsah)*	employee counseling
assistenza vincolata	*(ahs-seehs-tEhn-dsah veehn-koh-lAh-tah)*	tied aid
associazione (f) commerciale	*(ahs-soh-chah-tsyOh-neh kohm-mehr-chAh-leh)*	trade association
associazione mercantile	*(ahs-soh-chah-tsyOh-neh mehr-kah-ntEEh-leh)*	merchant guild
associazione settoriale	*(ahs-soh-chah-tsyOh-neh seht-toh-ryAh-leh)*	trade association
assorbimento (m) del personale non specializzato	*(ahs-sohr-beeh-mEhn-toh dehl pehr-soh-nAh-leh nohn speh-chah-leehds-dsAh-toh)*	dilution of labor

assorbire	*(ahs-sohr-bEEh-reh)*	absorb (v)
assorbire la perdita	*(ahs-sohr-bEEh-reh lah pEhr-deeh-tah)*	absorb the loss (v)
assumere	*(ahs-sOOh-neh-reh)*	hire (v)
asta (f)	*(Ahs-tah)*	rod
asta (f) pubblica	*(Ahs-tah pOOhb-leeh-kah)*	public auction
astrakan (m)	*(ahs-trah-kAhn)*	astrakan
atomica	*(ah-tOh-meeh-kah)*	atomic
atomo (m)	*(Ah-toh-moh)*	atom
attestato (m)	*(aht-tehs-tah-tsyOh-neh)*	attestation
atti (m) arbitrari	*(Aht-teeh ahr-beeh-trAh-reeh)*	ultra vires acts
attivato a voce	*(aht-teeh-vAh-toh ah vOh-cheh)*	voice-activated
attivi (m) bloccati	*(aht-tEEh-veeh)*	frozen assets
attivi correnti	*(aht-tEEh-veeh kohr-rEhn-teeh)*	current assets
attivi differiti	*(aht-tEEh-veeh deehf-feh-rEEh-teeh)*	deferred assets
attivi fissi	*(aht-tEEh-veeh fEEhs-seeh)*	fixed assets
attivi immobili	*(aht-tEEh-veeh eehm-mOh-beeh-leeh)*	capital asset
attivi intangibili	*(aht-tEEh-veeh eehn-tahn-jEEh-beeh-leeh)*	intangible assets
attivi maturati	*(aht-tEEh-veeh mah-tooh-rAh-teeh)*	accrued assets
attivi mobili	*(aht-tEEh-veeh mOh-beeh-leeh)*	liquid assets
attivi nascosti	*(aht-tEEh-veeh nahs-kOhs-teeh)*	hidden assets
attivi netti	*(aht-tEEh-veeh nEht-teeh)*	net assets
attivi netti sulle azioni ordinarie	*(aht-tEEh-veeh nEht-teeh sohl-leh ah-tsyOh-neeh)*	net equity assets
attivi reali	*(aht-tEEh-veeh reh-Ah-leeh)*	real assets
attività (f)	*(aht-teeh-veeh-tAh)*	asset
attività commerciale	*(aht-teeh-veeh-tAh kohm-mehr-chAh-leh)*	business activity, line of business
attività deperibile	*(aht-teeh-veeh-tAh deh-peh-rEEh-beeh-leh)*	wasted asset

attività finanziaria a brevissimo termine	*(aht-teeh-veeh-tAh feeh-nahn-tsyAh-reeh-ah ah breh-vEEhs-seeh-moh tEhr-meeh-neh)*	near money
attività liquide	*(aht-teeh-veeh-tAh lEEh-kweeh-deh)*	working assets
attività non a breve termine	*(aht-teeh-veeh-tAh nohn ah brEh-veh tEhr-meeh-neh)*	noncurrent assets
attività non di capitale	*(aht-teeh-veeh-tAh nohn deeh kah-peeh-tAh-leh)*	working assets
attività prontamente realizzabili	*(aht-teeh-veeh-tAh prohn-tah-mEhn-teh reh-ah-leehds-dsAh-beeh-leeh)*	quick assets
attivo (m)	*(aht-tEEh-voh)*	asset
attivo circolante	*(aht-tEEh-voh cheehr-koh-lAhn-teh)*	liquid assets
attivo sprecato	*(aht-tEEh-voh spreh-kAh-toh)*	wasted asset
attivo variabile	*(aht-tEEh-voh vah-ryAh-beeh-leh)*	floating asset
atto (m)	*(Aht-toh)*	deed
atto di costituzione	*(Aht-toh deeh kohs-teeh-tooh-tsyOh-neh)*	certificate of incorporation
atto di passaggio	*(Aht-toh deeh pahs-sAhj-joh)*	deed of transfer
atto di trasferimento	*(Aht-toh deeh trahs-feh-reeh-mEhn-toh)*	deed of transfer
atto di vendita	*(Aht-toh deeh vEhn-deeh-tah)*	bill of sale, deed of sale
atto fiduciario	*(Aht-toh feeh-dooh-chAh-reeh-oh)*	deed of trust
attrezzato con infissi per ancorare la merce	*(ahtreh-tsAh-toh kohn eehn-fEEhs-seeh pehr ahn-koh-rAh-reh lah mEhr-cheh)*	batten fitted
attrezzatura (f)	*(aht-trehts-tsah-tOOh-rah)*	equipment
attrezzi (m)	*(aht-trEhts-tseeh)*	equipment, tools
attrezzi per il lavoro	*(aht-trEhts-tseeh pehr eehl lah-vOh-roh)*	working tools
attrito (m)	*(aht-trEEh-toh)*	attrition
attuale	*(aht-twAh-leh)*	actual
attuario (m)	*(aht-twAh-reeh-oh)*	actuary

aumentare	*(ah-ooh-mehn-tAh-reh)*	increase (v)
aumento (m)	*(ah-ooh-mEhn-toh)*	increase
aumento dei capitali	*(ah-ooh-mEhn-toh deh-eeh kah-peeh-tAh-leeh)*	capital increase
autista (m)	*(ah-ooh-tEEhs-tah)*	driver
auto-critica (f)	*(ah-ooh-toh-krEEh-teeh-kah)*	self-appraisal
autogestione (f)	*(ah-ooh-toh-jehs-tyOh-neh)*	self-management
automatico	*(ah-ooh-toh-mAh-teeh-koh)*	automatic
automazione (f)	*(ah-ooh-toh-mah-tsyOh-neh)*	automation
automobile (f)	*(ah-ooh-toh-mOh-beeh-leh)*	automobile
autonomo	*(ah-ooh-tOh-noh-moh)*	autonomous
autorizzare	*(ah-ooh-toh-reehds-dsAh-reh)*	authorize (v)
autorizzazione (f) a collateralizzare azioni	*(ah-ooh-toh-reehds-dsah-tsyOh-neh ah kohl-lah-teh-rah-leehds-dsAh-reh ah-tsyOh-neeh)*	stock power
avanzare	*(ah-vahn-tsAh-reh)*	advance (v)
avere l'autorità	*(ah-vEh-reh lah-ooh-toh-reeh-tAh)*	authority, to have (v)
avvertimento (m)	*(ahv-vehr-teeh-mEhn-toh)*	commercial (advertisement)
avvisare	*(ahv-veeh-zAh-reh)*	advise (v)
avviso (m)	*(ahv-vEEh-zoh)*	commercial (advertisement)
avviso al pubblico di sottoscrizione di azione o obbligazione su giornali finanziari	*(ahv-vEEh-zoh ahl pOOhb-bleeh-koh deeh soht-toh-skreeh-tsyOh-neh deeh ah-tsyOh-neh oh ohb-bleeh-gah-tsyOh-neh sooh johr-nAh-leeh feeh-nahn-tsyAh-reeh)*	tombstone
avvocato (m)	*(ahv-voh-kAh-toh)*	attorney, lawyer
azienda (f)	*(ah-dsyEhn-dah)*	company, corporation, firm
azienda madre	*(ah-dsyEhn-dah mAh-dreh)*	parent company
azienda pubblica	*(ah-dsyEhn-dah pOOhb-leeh-kah)*	public company

A

azienda quasi pubblica	*(ah-dsyEhn-dah kwAh-seeh pOOhb-leeh-kah)*	quasi-public company
azienda straniera	*(ah-dsyEhn-dah strah-nyEh-rah)*	alien corporation
azione (f)	*(ah-tsyOh-neh)*	action, stock
azione che deriva dalla richiesta di esercitare due opzioni di acquisto ed una di vendita	*(ah-tsyOh-neh keh deh-rEEh-vah dahl-lah reeh-kyEhs-tah deeh eh-zehr-cheeh-tAh-reh dooh-eh ohp-tsyOh-neeh deeh ahk-kwEEhs-toh eh ooh-nah deeh vEhn-deeh-tah)*	strapping
azione contro la discriminazione	*(ah-tsyOh-neh kOhn-troh lah deehs-kreeh-meeh-nah-tsyOh-neh)*	affirmative action
azione d'incremento	*(ah-tsyOh-neh deehn-kreh-mEhn-toh)*	growth stock
azione di parte civile	*(ah-tsyOh-neh deeh pAhr-teh cheeh-cEEh-leh)*	civil action
azione di penalità per azioni di frode	*(ah-tsyOh-neh deeh peh-nah-leeh-tAh pehr (ah-tsyOh-neeh deeh frOh-deh)*	penalty-fraud action
azione ordinaria	*(ah-tsyOh-neh ohr-deeh-nAh-reeh-ah)*	common stock
azione preferenziale	*(ah-tsyOh-neh preh-feh-rehn-tsyAh-leh)*	preferred stock
azioni (f)	*(ah-tsyOh-neeh)*	securities, shares
azioni autorizzate	*(ah-tsyOh-neeh ah-ooh-toh-reehds-dsAh-teh)*	authorized shares
azioni con un valore inferiore ad un dollaro	*(ah-tsyOh-neeh kohn oohn vah-lOh-reh eehn-feh-ryOh-reh ad oohn dOhl-lah-roh)*	penny stock
azioni emesse	*(ah-tsyOh-neeh eh-mEhs-seh)*	issued shares
azioni in circolazione	*(ah-tsyOh-neeh eehn cheehr-koh-lah-tsyOh-neh)*	outstanding stock
azioni liberate	*(ah-tsyOh-neeh leeh-beh-rAh-teh)*	paid up shares
azioni preferenziali cumulative	*(ah-tsyOh-neeh preh-feh-rehn-tsyAh-leeh kooh-mooh-lah-tEEh-veh)*	cumulative preferred stock

azioni preferenziali di partecipazione sugli utili	*(ah-tsyOh-neeh preh-feh-rehn-tsyAh-leeh deeh pahr-teh-ceeh-pah-tsyOh-neh sooh-lyeeh OOh-teeh-leeh)*	participating preferred stock
azioni pregiate	*(ah-tsyOh-neeh preh-jAh-teh)*	blue chip stock
azioni privilegiate convertibili	*(ah-tsyOh-neeh preeh-veeh-leh-jAh-teh kohn-vehr-tEEh-beeh-leeh)*	convertible preferred stock
azioni privilegiate non cumulative	*(ah-tsyOh-neeh preeh-veeh-leh-jAh-teh nohn kooh-mooh-lah-tEEh-veh)*	noncumulative preferred stock
azioni registrate presso la borsa	*(ah-tsyOh-neeh reh-jeehs-trAh-teh prEhs-soh lah bOhr-sah)*	listed securities
azioni riacquistate	*(ah-tsyOh-neeh reeh-ahk-kweehs-tAh-teh)*	treasury stock
azioni senza diritto di voto	*(ah-tsyOh-neeh sEhn-tsah deeh-rEEht-toh deeh vOh-toh)*	nonvoting stock
azionista (m/f)	*(ah-tsyoh-nEEhs-tah)*	shareholder, stockholder

B

baco (m) di seta	*(bAh-koh deeh sEh-tah)*	silkworm
bagarino (m)	*(bah-gah-rEEh-noh)*	scalper
banca (f)	*(bAhn-kah)*	bank
banca agente	*(bAhn-kah ah-jEhn-teh)*	agent bank
banca al dettaglio	*(bAhn-kah ahl-deht-tAh-lyoh)*	retail bank
banca centrale	*(bAhn-kah chehn-trAh-leh)*	central bank
banca commerciale	*(bAhn-kah kohm-mehr-chAh-leh)*	commercial bank
banca corrispondente	*(bAhn-kah kohr-reehs-pohn-dEhn-teh)*	correspondent bank
banca d'agenzia	*(bAhn-kah dah-jehn-tsEEh-ah)*	agency bank
banca d'investimento	*(bAhn-kah deehn-vehs-teeh-mEhn-toh)*	investment bank

banca dati	*(bAhn-kah dAh-teeh)*	data bank
banca di credito	*(bAhn-kah deeh krEh-deeh-toh)*	credit bank
banca governativa	*(bAhn-kah goh-vehr-nah-tEEh-vah)*	government bank
banca import-export	*(bAhn-kah)*	export-import bank
banca ipotecaria	*(bAhn-kah eeh-poh-teh-kAh-reeh-ah)*	mortgage bank
banca mondiale	*(bAhn-kah mohn-dyAh-leh)*	World Bank
banca nazionale	*(bAhn-kah nah-tsyoh-nAh-leh)*	national bank
banca per il consumatore	*(bAhn-kah pehr eehl kohn-sooh-mah-tOh-reh)*	retail bank
banconota (f)	*(bahn-koh-nOh-tah)*	bank note, treasury note
bando (m) d'appalto	*(bAhn-doh dahp-pAhl-toh)*	advertisement for bid (request), invitation to bid
barattare	*(bah-raht-tAh-reh)*	barter (v)
baratteria (f)	*(bah-raht-teh-rEEh-ah)*	graft
baratto (m)	*(bah-rAht-toh)*	applied proceeds swap
barbiturici (m)	*(bahr-beeh-tOOh-reh-cheeh)*	barbiturates
barile (m)	*(bah-rEEh-leh)*	cask (225 liters)
barre (f)	*(bAhr-reh)*	bars
barriera (f) commerciale	*(bah-ryEh-rah kohm-mehr-chAh-leh)*	trade barrier
barriere doganali	*(bah-ryEh-reh doh-gah-nAh-leeh)*	tariff barriers
barriere tariffarie	*(bah-ryEh-reh tah-reehf-fAh-reeh-eh)*	tariff barriers
base (f)	*(bAh-zeh)*	base
base (f) dei dati per elaboratori elettronici	*(bAh-zeh deh-eeh dAh-teeh pehr eh-lah-boh-rah-tOh-reeh eh-leht-trOh-neeh-cheeh)*	data base
base delle tasse imponibili	*(bAh-zeh dehl-leh tAhs-seh eehm-poh-nEEh-beeh-leeh)*	tax base

base monetaria	*(bAh-zeh moh-neh-tAh-reeh-ah)*	monetary base
basso (m) reddito	*(bAhs-soh rEhd-deeh-toh)*	low income
batista (f)	*(bah-tEEhs-tah)*	batiste
batteria (f)	*(baht-teh-rEEh-ah)*	battery
baud (m)	*(bohd)*	baud
baule (m)	*(bah-OOh-leh)*	trunk
bene (m)	*(bEh-neh)*	commodity
bene culturale	*(bEh-neh koohl-tooh-rAh-leh)*	cultural property
bene mobile	*(bEh-neh mOh-beeh-leh)*	chattel
benefici (m)	*(beh-neh-fEEh-cheeh)*	perks
beneficiario (m)	*(beh-neh-feeh-chAh-reeh-oh)*	beneficiary
benestare (m) bancario	*(beh-neh-stAh-reh)*	bank release
benevolenza (f)	*(beh-neh-voh-lEhn-tsah)*	goodwill
beni (m)	*(bEh-neeh)*	goods
beni accompagnati	*(bEh-neeh ahk-kohm-pah-nyAh-teeh)*	accompanied goods
beni al dettaglio	*(bEh-neeh ahl-deht-tAh-lyoh)*	retail merchandise
beni capitali	*(bEh-neeh kah-peeh-tAh-leeh)*	capital goods
beni d'investimento	*(bEh-neeh deehn-vehs-teeh-mEhn-toh)*	capital goods
beni di consumo	*(bEh-neeh deeh kohn-sOOh-moh)*	consumer goods
beni di qualità	*(bEh-neeh deeh kwah-leeh-tAh)*	quality goods
beni durevoli	*(bEh-neeh dooh-rEh-voh-leeh)*	durable goods
beni eccedenti	*(bEh-neeh ehch-cheh-dEhn-teeh)*	surplus goods
beni fungibili	*(bEh-neeh foohn-jEEh-beeh-leeh)*	fungible goods
beni industriali	*(bEh-neeh eehn-doohs-tryAh-leeh)*	industrial goods
beni intermediari	*(bEh-neeh eehn-tehr-meh-dyAh-reeh)*	intermediary goods

B

beni nello stato attuale	*(bEh-neeh nehl-loh stAh-toh aht-twAh-leh)*	as is goods
beni non accompagnati	*(bEh-neeh nohn ahk-kohm-pah-nyAh-teeh)*	unaccompanied goods
beni non durevoli	*(bEh-neeh nohn dooh-rEh-voh-leeh)*	nondurable goods, soft goods
beni proibiti	*(bEh-neeh prohy-bEEh-teeh)*	prohibited goods
beni reali	*(bEh-neeh reh-Ah-leeh)*	tangible assets
beni senza ricorso	*(bEh-neeh sEhn-tsah reeh-kOhr-soh)*	as is goods
beni solidi	*(bEh-neeh sOh-leeh-deeh)*	dry goods
beni specializzati	*(bEh-neeh speh-chah-leehds-dsAh-teeh)*	specialty goods
beni voluttuari	*(bEh-neeh voh-looht-tAh-reeh)*	luxury goods
benzina (f)	*(behn-dsEEh-nah)*	gasoline
benzolo (f)	*(behn-dsOh-loh)*	benzene
berlina (f)	*(behr-lEEh-nah)*	sedan
bevanda	*(beh-vAhn-dah)*	drink
biancheria (f) da tavola	*(byahn-keh-rEEh-ah dah tAh-voh-lah)*	linen
bianco e nero (m)	*(byAhn-koh eh nEh-roh)*	black and white
bicchiere (m)	*(beehk-kyEh-reh)*	glass
bicchiere soffiato a bocca	*(beehk-kyEh-reh sohf-fyAh-toh ah bOhk-kah)*	hand-blown glass
biella (f)	*(byEhl-lah)*	connecting rod
biglietto (m) da visita	*(beeh-lyEht-toh dah vEEh-zeeh-tah)*	business card
bilancia (f) commerciale	*(beeh-lAhn-chah kohm-mehr-chAh-leh)*	balance of trade
bilancia dei pagamenti	*(beeh-lAhn-chah deh-eeh pah-gah-mEhn-teeh)*	balance of payments
bilanciare	*(beeh-lahn-chAh-reh)*	hedge (v)
bilancio (m)	*(beeh-lAhn-choh)*	financial statement
bilancio bancario	*(beeh-lAhn-choh bahn-kAh-reeh-oh)*	bank balance
bilancio commerciale visibile	*(beeh-lAhn-choh kohm-mehr-chAh-leh eh veeh-zEEh-beeh-leh)*	visible balance of trade

bilancio consolidato	*(beeh-lAhn-choh kohn-soh-leeh-dAh-toh)*	consolidated financial statement
bilancio d'apertura	*(beeh-lAhn-choh dah-pehr-tOOh-rah)*	opening balance
bilancio d'esercizio	*(beeh-lAhn-choh deh-zehr-chEEh-tsyoh)*	balance sheet, working balance
bilancio di revisione	*(beeh-lAhn-choh deeh reh-veeh-zyOh-neh)*	audit trail
bilancio negativo	*(beeh-lAhn-choh neh-gah-tEEh-voh)*	adverse balance
bilancio provvisorio	*(beeh-lAhn-choh prohv-veeh-zOh-reeh-oh)*	trial balance
billette (f)	*(beehl-lEht-teh)*	billets
biochimica (f)	*(beeh-oh-kEEh-meeh-kah)*	biochemistry
biologia (f)	*(beeh-oh-loh-jEEh-ah)*	biology
bit (m)	*(bit)*	bit
bloccare	*(blohk-kAh-reh)*	lock in (v) (rate of interest)
blocco (m) degli stipendi	*(blOhk-koh deh-lyeeh steeh-pEhn-deeh)*	wage freeze
blocco dei fondi	*(blOhk-koh deh-eeh fOhn-deeh)*	blockage of funds
bobina (f)	*(boh-bEEh-nah)*	coil
boicottare	*(bohy-koht-tAh-reh)*	boycott (v)
bonifico elettronico	*(boh-neeh-fi-koh eh-leht-trOh-neeh-koh)*	cable transfer
borsa	*(bOhr-sah)*	stock exchange, stock market
borsa (f)	*(bOhr-sah)*	purse
borsa (mercato) di beni di prima necessità	*(bOhr-sah mehr-kAh-toh deeh bEh-neeh deeh prEEh-mah neh-chehs-seeh-tAh)*	commodity exchange
borsa documenti	*(bOhr-sah doh-kooh-mEhn-teeh)*	briefcase
borsa in fase di andamento positivo	*(bOhr-sah eehn fAh-zeh deeh ahn-dah-mEhn-toh poh-zeeh-tEEh-voh)*	bull market
borsa in fase negativa	*(bOhr-sah eehn fAh-zeh neh-gah-tEEh-vah)*	bear market

B

borsetta (f)	*(bohr-sEht-tah)*	handbag, pocketbook
botanico	*(boh-tAh-neeh-koh)*	botanic
bottaio (m)	*(boht-tAh-yoh)*	cooper
bottiglia (f)	*(boht-tEEh-lyah)*	bottle (usually 75 centiliters)
bottiglione da due litri (m)	*(boht-teeh-lyOh-neh dah dOOh-eh lEEh-treeh)*	magnum (2 bottles in one)
bottone (m)	*(boh-tOh-neh)*	button
bouquet (m)	*(boo-kEh)*	bouquet
bozza (f)	*(bOhts-tsah)*	rough draft
bozza (f) in colonna	*(bOhts-tsah eehn koh-lOhn-nah)*	galley proof
brevetto (m)	*(breh-vEht-toh)*	patent
brevetto richiesto	*(breh-vEht-toh reeh-kyEhs-toh)*	patent pending
brocca (f)	*(brOhk-kah)*	pitcher
buccia (f)	*(bOOhch-chah)*	skin
bug (m)	*(bug)*	bug (defect in computer program)
buona consegna (f)	*(bwOh-nah kohn-sEh-nyah)*	good delivery (securities)
buoni (m) a basso rendimento	*(bwOh-neeh ah bAhs-soh rehn-deeh-mEhn-toh)*	low-yield bonds
buoni del tesoro a breve termine	*(bwOh-neeh dehl teh-zOh-roh ah brEh-veh tEhr-meeh-neh)*	treasury bills
buoni e obbligazioni del tesoro (Britannici)	*(bwOh-neeh eh ohb-bleeh-gah-tsyOh-neeh dehl teh-zOh-roh)*	gilt (Brit. govt. security)
buoni governativi (del tesoro)	*(bwOh-neeh goh-vehr-nah-tEEh-veeh dehl eh-zOh-roh)*	government bonds
buoni redditizi	*(bwOh-neeh rehd-deeh-tEEh-tseeh)*	income bonds
buono (m) a termine	*(bwOh-noh ah tEhr-meeh-neh)*	term bond
buono di risparmio	*(bwOh-noh deeh reehs-pAhr-myoh)*	savings bond

buono fisso	*(bwOh-noh fEEhs-soh)*	flat bond
buono garantito	*(bwOh-noh gah-rahn-tEEh-toh)*	guaranty bond
buonuscita (f)	*(bohn-ooh-shEEh-tah)*	severance pay
burocrata (m)	*(booh-rOh-krah-tah)*	bureaucrat
byte (m)	*(bahyt)*	byte

C

cachemire (m)	*(ca-che-mEE-reh)*	cashmere
caffettiera (f)	*(kahf-feht-tyEh-rah)*	coffeepot
calce (m)	*(kAhl-cheh)*	limestone
calcio (m)	*(kAhl-choh)*	calcium, soccer
calcolatrice (f)	*(kahl-koh-lah-trEEh-cheh)*	calculator
calcolo (m) errato	*(kAhl-koh-loh ehr-rAh-toh)*	miscalculation
calmante (m)	*(kahl-mAhn-teh)*	sedative
calore (m)	*(kah-lOh-reh)*	heat
calze (f)	*(kAhl-tseh)*	stockings
calzini (m)	*(kahl-tsEEh-neeh)*	socks
calzoni (m)	*(kahl-tsOh-neeh)*	slacks, trousers
cambiale (f)	*(kahm-byAh-leh)*	bill of exchange, promissory note
cambiale a termine	*(kahm-byAh-leh ah tEhr-meeh-neh)*	time bill (of exchange)
cambiale agraria	*(kahm-byAh-leh ah-grAh-reeh-ah)*	agricultural paper
cambiale di comodo	*(kahm-byAh-leh deeh kOh-moh-doh)*	accommodation bill, accommodation paper
cambiale emessa all'estero	*(kahm-byAh-leh eh-mEhs-sah ahl Ehs-teh-roh)*	foreign bill of exchange
cambiali (f) esigibili	*(kahm-byAh-leeh eh-zeeh-jEEh-beeh-leeh)*	notes receivable
cambio (m)	*(kAhm-byoh)*	gearshift
cambio (m) bancario	*(kAhm-byoh bahn-kAh-reeh-oh)*	bank exchange
cambio (m) valute	*(kAhm-byoh vah-lOOh-teh)*	money broker

cambio automatico	*(kAhm-byoh ah-ooh-toh-mAh-teeh-koh)*	automatic gearshift
cambio estero	*(kAhm-byoh Ehs-teh-roh)*	foreign exchange
cambio netto, il cambiamento netto	*(kAhm-byoh nEht-toh), (kahm-byah-mEhn-toh nEht-toh)*	net change
cambio valuta	*(kAhm-byoh vah-lOOh-tah)*	currency exchange
camera (f) di commercio	*(kAh-meh-rah deeh kohm-mEhr-choh)*	chamber of commerce
camicetta (f)	*(kah-meeh-chEht-tah)*	blouse
camicia (f)	*(kah-mEEh-chah)*	shirt
campagna (f) di produttività	*(kahm-pAh-nyah deeh proh-dooh-teeh-veeh-tAh)*	productivity campaign
campagna pubblicitaria	*(kahm-pAh-nyah poohb-leeh-cheeh-tAh-reeh-ah)*	advertising campaign
campionare	*(kahm-pyoh-nAh-reh)*	sample (v)
campionatura (f) mista	*(kahm-pyoh-nah-tOOh-rah mEEhs-tah)*	mixed sampling
campionatura per accettazione	*(kahm-pyoh-nah-tOOh-rah pehr ahcheht-tah-tsyOh-neh)*	acceptance sampling
campione (m) casuale	*(kahm-pyOh-neh kah-zwAh-leh)*	random sample
campioni uniformi	*(kahm-pyOh-neeh ooh-neeh-fOhr-meeh)*	matched samples
canale (m)	*(kah-nAh-leh)*	channel
canale (m) di distribuzione	*(kah-nAh-leh deeh deeh deehs-treeh-booh-tsyOh-neh)*	channel of distribution
cancellare	*(kahn-chehl-lAh-reh)*	cancel (v)
cancellare un'obbligazione dovuta	*(kahn-chehl-lAh-reh oohn ohb-bleeh-gah-tsyOh-neh doh-vOOh-tah)*	write off (v)
candela (f)	*(kahn-dEh-lah)*	spark plug
candeliere (m)	*(kahn-deh-lyEh-reh)*	candlestick
cantina (f)	*(kahn-tEEh-nah)*	wine cellar
capacità (f)	*(kah-pah-cheeh-tAh)*	capacity

capacità di produzione, capacità produttiva	*(kah-pah-cheeh-tAh deeh proh-dooh-tsyOh-neh), (kah-pah-cheeh-tAh proh-dooht-tEEh-vah)*	manufacturing capacity
capacità in balle	*(kah-pah-cheeh-tAh eehn bAhl-leh)*	bale capacity
capacità produttiva della fabbrica	*(kah-pah-cheeh-tAh proh-dooht-tEEh-vah dehl-lah fAhb-breeh-kah)*	plant capacity
capacità produttiva inattiva	*(kah-pah-cheeh-tAh proh-dooht-tEEh-vah eehn-aht-tEEh-vah)*	idle capacity
caparra (f)	*(kah-pAhr-rah)*	binder, down payment
capitale (m)	*(kah-peeh-tAh-leh)*	capital
capitale azionario	*(kah-peeh-tAh-leh ah-tsyoh-nAh-reeh-oh)*	capital stock, equity, net worth
capitale circolante al netto	*(kah-peeh-tAh-leh cheehr-koh-lAhn-teh ahl nEht-toh)*	net working capital
capitale d'investimento in nuove iniziative	*(kah-peeh-tAh-leh deehn-vehs-teeh-mEhn-toh eehn nwOh-veh eeh-neeh-tsyah-tEEh-veh)*	venture capital
capitale degli azionisti	*(kah-peeh-tAh-leh deh-lyeeh ah-tsyoh-nEEhs-teeh)*	stockholders' equity
capitale eccedente	*(kah-peeh-tAh-leh ehch-cheh-dEhn-teh)*	surplus capital
capitale industriale	*(kah-peeh-tAh-leh eehn-doohs-tryAh-leh)*	instrumental capital
capitale investito	*(kah-peeh-tAh-leh eehn-vehs-tEEh-toh)*	invested capital
capitale liquido	*(kah-peeh-tAh-leh lEEh-kweeh-doh)*	working capital, working funds
capitale ordinario	*(kah-peeh-tAh-leh ohr-deeh-nAh-reeh-oh)*	ordinary capital
capitale per finanziare nuove iniziative	*(kah-peeh-tAh-leh pehr feeh-nahn-tsyAh-reh nwOh-veh eeh-neeh-tsyah-tEEh-veh)*	risk capital
capitale sociale legale	*(kah-peeh-tAh-leh soh-chAh-leh leh-gAh-leh)*	legal capital
capitale versato	*(kah-peeh-tAh-leh vehr-sAh-toh)*	paid up capital

capitali fissi	(kah-peeh-tAh-leeh fEEhs-seeh)	fixed capital
capitalismo (m)	(kah-peeh-tah-lEEhz-moh)	capitalism
capitalizzati	(kah-peeh-tahl-leehds-dsAh-teeh)	below the line
capitalizzato in eccesso	(kah-peeh-tahl-leehds-dsAh-toh eehn ehch-chEhs-soh)	overcapitalized
capitalizzazione (f)	(kah-peeh-tah-leehds-dsah-tyOh-neh)	capitalization
capitalizzazione dei costi fissi nel costo dell'inventario	(kah-peeh-tah-leehds-dsah-tyOh-neh deh-eeh kOhs-teeh fEEhs-seeh nehl kOhs-toh dehl eehn-vehn-tAh-reeh-oh)	absorption costing
capitolo	(kah-pEEh-toh-loh)	chapter
capo (m)	(kAh-poh)	leader
capo (m)	(kAh-poh)	model
capo contabile	(kAh-poh kohn-tAh-beeh-leh)	chief accountant
capo servizio	(kAh-poh sehr-vEEh-tsyoh)	foreman
capo sindacale	(kAh-poh seehn-dah-kAh-leh)	labor leader
cappotto (m)	(kahp-pOht-toh)	coat
cappuccio (m)	(kahp-pOOhch-choh)	hood
capretto (m)	(kah-prEht-toh)	kidskin
capsula (f)	(kAhp-sooh-lah)	capsule
captare	(kahp-tAh-reh)	tune (v)
caraffa (f)	(kah-rAhf-fah)	decanter, pitcher
carbone (m)	(kahr-bOh-ne)	coal
carbonio (m)	(kahr-bOh-neeh-oh)	carbon
carburatore (m)	(kahr-booh-rah-tOh-reh)	carburetor
carenza (f)	(kah-rEhn-tsah)	shortage
caricare i fondi all'inizio del contratto	(kah-reeh-kAh-reh eeh fOhn-deeh ahl eeh-nEEh-tsyoh dehl kohn-trAht-toh)	front-end loading
carico (m)	(kAh-reeh-koh)	freight, load (sales charge)

carico di testa	*(kAh-reeh-koh deeh tEhs-tah)*	headload
carico di un camion	*(kAh-reeh-koh deeh oohn kAh-myohn)*	truckload
carico di un camion inferiore alla capacità	*(kAh-reeh-koh deeh oohn kAh-myohn eehn-feh-ryOh-reh ahl-lah kah-pah-cheeh-tAh)*	less-than-truckload
carico di una vettura inferiore alla capacità	*(kAh-reeh-koh deeh ooh-nah veh-tOOh-rah eehn-feh-ryOh-reh ahl-lah kah-pah-cheeh-tAh)*	less-than-carload
carico di vettura	*(kAh-reeh-koh deeh veht-tOOh-rah)*	carload
carico effettivo	*(kAh-reeh-koh ehf-feht-tEEh-voh)*	payload
carico frazionato	*(kAh-reeh-koh frah-tsyoh-nAh-toh)*	broken stowage
carico massimo	*(kAh-reeh-koh mAhs-seeh-moh)*	peak load
carico permesso	*(kAh-reeh-koh pehr-mEhs-soh)*	freight allowed
carico secco	*(kAh-reeh-koh sEhk-koh)*	dry cargo
carnet (m)		carnet
carnet bancario	*(carnet bahn-kAh-reeh-oh)*	bank carnet
carovita (m)	*(kah-roh-vEEh-tah)*	cost of living
carro (m) merci senza sponde	*(kAhr-roh mEhr-cheeh sEhn-tsah spOhn-deh)*	flatcar
carrozzeria (f)	*(kahr-rohts-tseh-rEEh-ah)*	chassis
carta (f)	*(kAhr-tah)*	paper
carta da giornale	*(kAhr-tah dah johr-nAh-leh)*	newsprint
carta di credito	*(kAhr-tah deeh krEh-deeh-toh)*	credit card
carta patinata	*(kAhr-tah pah-teeh-nAh-tah)*	coated paper
cartella (f)	*(kahr-tEhl-lah)*	attaché case, portfolio
cartella d'azioni	*(kahr-tEhl-lah deeh ah-tsyOh-neeh)*	portfolio, stock
cartellone (m)	*(kahr-tehl-lOh-neh)*	billboard

C

casa (f) di accettazione	*(kAh-zah deeh ahcheht-tah-tsyOh-neh)*	acceptance house
caseificio (m)	*(kAh-see-feek-oh)*	cheese factory
cassa (f)	*(kAhs-sah)*	case
cassa cooperativa di risparmio	*(kAhs-sah koh-oh-peh-rah-tEEh-vah deeh reehs-pAhr-myoh)*	mutual savings bank
cassa d'imballo	*(kAhs-sa deehm-bAhl-loh)*	packing case
cassa di risparmio	*(kAhs-sah deeh reehs-pAhr-myoh)*	savings bank
cassa integrazione	*(kAhs-sa eehn-teh-grah-tsyOh-neh)*	unemployment compensation
cassa notturna	*(kAhs-sa noht-tOOhr-nah)*	night depository
cassetta (f)	*(kahs-sEht-tah)*	cassette
cassetta di sicurezza	*(kahs-sEht-tah deeh seeh-kooh-rEhts-tsah)*	safe deposit box
cassiere (m)	*(kahs-syEh-reh)*	teller
castorino (m)	*(kahs-toh-rEEh-noh)*	nutria
castoro (m)	*(kahs-tOh-roh)*	beaver
catalisi (f)	*(kah-tAh-leeh-zeeh)*	catalyst
catalogo (m)	*(kah-tAh-loh-goh)*	catalog
catena (f) di montaggio	*(kah-tEh-nah deeh mohn-tAhj-joh)*	assembly line
catena di negozi	*(kah-tEh-nah deeh neh-gOh-tseeh)*	chain (of stores)
catodo (m)	*(kAh-toh-doh)*	cathode
causa (f)	*(kAhw-zah)*	lawsuit
cavatappi (m)	*(kah-vah-tAhp-peeh)*	corkscrew
cavità (f)	*(kah-veeh-tAh)*	sinus
cavo (m)	*(kAh-voh)*	cable
cavo (m) coassiale	*(kAh-voh koh-ahs-syAh-leh)*	coaxial cable
cedente (m)	*(cheh-dEhn-teh)*	assignor
cedola (f) di interesse su obbligazioni	*(chEh-doh-lah deeh eehn-teh-rEhs-seh sooh ohb-bleeh-gah-tsyOh-neeh)*	coupon (bond interest)
cedola di interesse su buoni	*(chEh-doh-lah deeh eehn-teh-rEhs-seh sooh bwOh-neeh)*	coupon (bond interest)

centesimi (m) di percentuale per ipoteche	*(chEhn-tEh-zeeh-meeh deeh pehr-chehn-twAh-leh pehr eeh-poh-tEh-keh)*	point (percentage, mortgage term)
centilitro (m)	*(chehn-tEEh-leeh-troh)*	centiliter
centro (m) acquisti fuori dall'area urbana	*(chEhn-troh ahk-kwEEhs-teeh fwOh-reeh dahl Ah-reh-ah oohr-bAh-nah)*	shopping center
centro per elaborati elettronici	*(chEhn-troh pehr eh-lah-boh-rAh-teeh eh-leht-trOh-neeh-cheeh)*	computer center
cerniera (f) lampo	*(chehr-nyEh-rah lAhm-poh)*	zipper
certificato (m)	*(chehr-teeh-feeh-kAh-toh)*	certificate
certificato antiquariale d'autenticità	*(chehr-teeh-feeh-kAh-toh ahn-teeh-kwah-ryAh-leh dah-ooh-tehn-teeh-cheeh-tAh)*	antique authenticity certificate
certificato attestante l'uso definitivo del prodotto	*(chehr-teeh-feeh-kAh-toh aht-tehs-tAhn-teh lOOh-zoh deh-feeh-neeh-tEEh-voh dehl proh-dOht-toh)*	end-use certificate
certificato azionario	*(chehr-teeh-feeh-kAh-toh ahtsyoh-nAh-reeh-oh)*	stock certificate
certificato d'ispezione	*(chehr-teeh-feeh-kAh-toh deehs-peh-tsyOh-neh)*	bill of sight
certificato d'origine	*(chehr-teeh-feeh-kAh-toh doh-rEEh-jeeh-neh)*	certificate of origin
certificato di deposito	*(chehr-teeh-feeh-kAh-toh deeh deh-pOh-zeeh-toh)*	certificate of deposit
certificato ipotecario	*(chehr-teeh-feeh-kAh-toh eeh-poh-teh-kAh-reeh-oh)*	mortgage certificate
certificato per lo sbarco	*(chehr-teeh-feeh-kAh-toh pehr loh zbAhr-koh)*	landing certificate
cervello (m) elettronico	*(chehr-vEhl-loh eh-leht-trOh-neeh-koh)*	computer
cessione (f) di garanzie per merci depositate in un magazzino	*(chehs-syOh-neh deeh gah-rahn-tsEEh-eh pehr mEhr-cheeh deh-poh-zeeh-tAh-teh eehn -oohn mah-gahds-dsEEh-noh)*	field warehousing
cestino (m) per il pane	*(chehs-tEEh-noh pehr eehl pAh-neh)*	breadbasket
chiacchierare	*(kyahk-kyeh-rAh-reh)*	jawbone (v)

chiamare	*(kyah-mAh-reh)*	call (v)
chiavi (f) in mano	*(kyAh-veeh eehn mAh-noh)*	turnkey
chilometraggio (m)	*(keeh-loh-meh-trAhj-joh)*	mileage
chimica (f)	*(kEEh-meeh-kah)*	chemistry
chimica inorganica	*(kEEh-meeh-kah eehn-ohr-gAh-neeh-kah)*	inorganic chemistry
chimico	*(kEEh-meeh-koh)*	chemical
chip (m)	*(chip)*	chip (computer)
cianografia (f)	*(chah-noh-grah-fEEh-ah)*	blueprint
ciclo (m) commerciale	*(chEEh-kloh kohm-mehr-chAh-leh)*	business cycle
ciclo lavorativo	*(chEEh-kloh lah-voh-rah-tEEh-voh)*	work cycle
cilindrata	*(cheeh-leehn-drAh-tah)*	displacement
cilindro (m)	*(cheeh-lEEhn-droh)*	cylinder
cintura (f)	*(chEEhn-tOOh-rah)*	belt
cintura (f) di sicurezza	*(cheehn-tOOh-rah deeh seeh-kooh-rEhts-tsah)*	seatbelt
cinturino (m) per orologio	*(cheehn-tooh-rEEh-noh pehr oh-roh-lOh-joh)*	watch strap
circa	*(chEEhr-kah)*	around (exchange term)
circuito (m)	*(cheehr-kwEEh-toh)*	circuit
circuito in parallelo	*(cheehr-kwEEh-toh eehn pah-rahl-lEh-loh)*	parallel circuit
circuito integrato	*(cheehr-kwEEh-toh eehn-teh-grAh-toh)*	integrated circuit
circuito stampato	*(cheehr-kwEEh-toh stahm-pAh-toh)*	printed circuit
citazione (f)	*(cheeh-tah-tsyOh-neh)*	quotation
citazione diretta	*(cheeh-tah-tsyOh-neh deeh-rEht-tah)*	direct quotation
classe (f) lavorativa	*(klAhs-seh lah-voh-rah-tEEh-vah)*	working class
classi mutualmente esclusive	*(klAhs-seeh mooh-twahl-mEhn0teh ehs-klooh-zEEh-veh)*	mutually exclusive classes
classificazione (f) doganale	*(klahs-seeh-feeh-kah-tsyOh-neh doh-gah-nAh-leh)*	tariff classification

clausola (f) d'accelerazione	*(klAhw-zoh-lah dahch-cheh-leh-rah-tsyOh-neh)*	acceleration clause
clausola d'oro	*(klAhw-zoh-lah dOh-roh)*	gold clause
clausola d'uscita	*(klAhw-zoh-lah dooh-shEEh-tah)*	escape clause
clausola di negligenza	*(klAhw-zoh-lah deeh neh-gleeh-jEhn-tsah)*	Jason clause
clausola di penalità	*(klAhw-zoh-lah deeh peh-nah-leeh-tAh)*	penalty clause
clausola di rinuncia	*(klAhw-zoh-lah deeh reeh-nOOhn-chah)*	waiver clause
cliente (m)	*(kleeh-Ehn-teh)*	customer
clima (m)	*(klEEh-mah)*	climate
cloroformio (m)	*(kloh-roh-fOhr-meeh-oh)*	chloroform
cloruro (m)	*(kloh-rOOh-roh)*	chloride
co-assicurazione (f)	*(koh-ahs-seeh-kooh-rah-tsyOh-neh)*	coinsurance
coda (di cambiale) (f)	*(kOh-dah deeh kahm-byAh-leh)*	allonge (of a draft)
codice (m) binario	*(kOh-deeh-cheh beeh-nAh-reeh-oh)*	binary code
codice (m) d'avviamento postale, C.A.P.	*(kOh-deeh-cheh dahv-vyah-mEhn-toh pohs-tAh-leh)*	zip code
codice del lavoro	*(kOh-deeh-cheh dehl lah-vOh-roh)*	labor code
coke (m)	*(kohk)*	coke
collaterale (m)	*(kohl-lah-teh-rAh-leh)*	collateral
collega (m)	*(kohl-lEh-gah)*	colleague
colletto (m)	*(kohl-lEht-toh)*	collar
collirio (m)	*(kohl-lEEh-reeh-oh)*	eyedrop
collo (m)	*(kOhl-loh)*	neck (of bottle)
collocamento (m)	*(kohl-loh-kah-mEhn-toh)*	placement (personnel)
collocazione (f) privata	*(kohl-loh-kah-tsyOh-neh preeh-vAh-tah)*	private placement (finance)
colloquio (m)	*(kohl-lOh-kweeh-oh)*	colloquium
colore (m)	*(koh-lOh-reh)*	color
colore (m)	*(koh-lOh-reh)*	pigment

⌐ (m)	*(kohl-tEhl-loh)*	knife
⌐i che cambia spesso il posto di lavoro	*(koh-lOOh-eeh keh kAhm-byah spEhs-soh eehl pOhs-toh deeh lah-vOh-roh)*	job hopper
colui che crea un mercato	*(koh-lOOh-eeh keh krEh-ah oohn mehr-kAh-toh)*	market-maker (securities)
comando (m), "joystick" (m)	*(koh-mAhn-doh)*	joystick
combinazione (f)	*(kohm-beeh-nah-tsyOh-neh)*	combination
come per nota informativa	*(kOh-meh pehr nOh-tah eehn-fohr-mah-tEEh-vah)*	as per advice
come se e quando	*(kOh-meh seh eh kwAhn-doh)*	as, if and when
comitato (m) di lavoro	*(koh-meeh-tAh-toh deeh lah-vOh-roh)*	work committee
comitato esecutivo	*(koh-meeh-tAh-toh eh-zeh-kooh-tEEh-voh)*	executive committee
comma (m)	*(kOhm-mah)*	codicil
comma della scala mobile	*(kOhm-mah dehl-lah skAh-lah mOh-beeh-leh)*	escalator clause
comma valutaria	*(kOhm-mah vah-looh-tAh-reeh-ah)*	currency clause
commerciante (m)	*(kohm-mehr-chAhn-teh)*	dealer, trader
commerciare	*(kohm-mehr-chAh-reh)*	trade (v)
commercio (m)	*(kohm-mEhr-choh)*	commerce, trade
commercio al dettaglio	*(kohm-mEhr-choh ahl-deht-tAh-lyoh)*	retail trade
commercio all'ingrosso	*(kohm-mEhr-choh ahl eehn-grOhs-soh)*	wholesale trade
commercio compensativo	*(kohm-mEhr-choh kohm-pehn-sah-tEEh-voh)*	compensation trade
commercio equo	*(kohm-mEhr-choh Eh-kwoh)*	fair trade
commercio estero	*(kohm-mEhr-choh Ehs-teh-roh)*	foreign trade
commercio fuori orario	*(kohm-mEhr-choh fwOh-reeh oh-rAh-reeh-oh)*	after-hours trading
commercio interstatale	*(kohm-mEhr-choh eehn-tehr-stah-tAh-leh)*	interstate commerce

commercio libero	*(kohm-mEhr-choh lEEh-beh-roh)*	free trade
commercio multilaterale	*(kohm-mEhr-choh moohl-teeh-lah-teh-rAh-leh)*	multilateral trade
commessa (f)	*(kohm-mEhs-sah)*	work order, female clerk
commissione (f)	*(kohm-meehs-syOh-neh)*	agency fee, load (sales charge)
commissione anticipata	*(kohm-meehs-syOh-neh ahn-teeh-chee-pAh-tah)*	front-end fee
commissione di raccomanda-zione	*(kohm-meehs-syOh-neh deeh rahk-koh-mahn-dah-tsyOh-neh)*	address commission
compagnia (f) d'investimento	*(kohm-pah-nyEEh-ah deehn-vehs-teeh-mEhn-toh)*	investment company
compendio (m) del documento probatorio della titolarità di diritti	*(kohm-pEhn-dyoh dehl doh-kooh-mEhn-toh proh-bah-tOh-reeh-oh dehl-lah teeh-toh-lah-reeh-tAh deeh deeh-rEEht-teeh)*	abstract of title
compenso (m)	*(kohm-pEhn-soh)*	compensation, consideration (bus. law)
compenso dirigenziale	*(kohm-pEhn-soh deeh-reeh-jehn-tsyAh-leh)*	executive compensation
competizione (f)	*(kohm-peh-teeh-tsyOh-neh)*	competition
completamente pagato	*(kohm-pkeh-tah-mEhn-teh pah-gAh-toh)*	paid in full
completo (m) per la manicure	*(kohm-plEh-toh pehr lah mah-neeh-kOOh-reh)*	manicuring kit
componente (m)	*(kohm-poh-nEhn-teh)*	component
composizione (f)	*(kohm-poh-zeeh-tsyOh-neh)*	composition
composizione della pagina	*(kohm-poh-zeeh-tsyOh-neh dehl-lah pAh-jeeh-nah)*	page makeup
composti (m)	*(kohm-pOhs-teeh)*	compounds
composto (m)	*(kohm-pOhst-oh)*	compound
compra (f)	*(kOhm-prah)*	acquisition
comprare	*(kohm-prAh-reh)*	purchase (v)
comprare al miglior prezzo	*(kohm-prAh-reh ahl meeh-lyoh prEhts-tsoh)*	buy at best (v)

re all'apertura	*(kohm-prAh-reh ahl ah-pehr-toOh-rah)*	buy on opening (v)
mprare alla chiusura	*(kohm-prAh-reh ahl-lah kyooh-zOOh-rah)*	buy on close (v)
compratore (m)	*(kohm-prah-tOh-reh)*	buyer
compratore capo	*(kohm-prah-tOh-reh kAh-poh)*	chief buyer
compratore e venditore di titoli mobiliari	*(kohm-prah-tOh-reh eh vehn-deeh-tOh-reh deeh tEEh-toh-leeh moh-beeh-kyAh-reeh)*	market-maker (securities)
compratore in loco	*(kohm-prah-tOh-reh eehn lOh-koh)*	resident buyer
compratore potenziale	*(kohm-prah-tOh-reh poh-tehn-tsyAh-leh)*	potential buyer
compravendita (f) di azioni sopra o sotto il prezzo attuale	*(kohm-prah-vEhn-deeh-tah deeh ah-tsyOh-neeh sOh-prah oh sOht-toh eehl prEhts-tsoh aht-twAh-leh)*	put and call
compreso interessi accumulati	*(kohm-prEh-zeeh eehn-teh-rEhs-seeh ahk-kooh-mooh-lAh-teeh)*	plus accrued interest
compreso trasporto	*(kohm-prEh-zoh trahs-pOhr-toh)*	freight included
compressa (f)	*(kohm-prEhs-sah)*	tablet
comproprietà (f)	*(kohm-proh-pryeh-tAh)*	co-ownership
comproprietario (m)	*(kohm-proh-pryeh-tAh-reeh-oh)*	joint owner
computer (m)	*(kumpyutor)*	computer
comunicazioni (f) di massa	*(koh-mooh-neeh-kah-tsyOh-neeh deeh mAhs-sah)*	mass communications
con dividendo	*(kOhn deeh-veeh-dEhn-doh)*	cum dividend
con una media	*(kohn ooh-nah mEh-dyah)*	with average
concedere uno scoperto a fido	*(kohn-chEh-deh-reh ooh-noh skoh-pEhr-toh ah fEEh-doh)*	grant an overdraft (v)
concentrazione (f)	*(kohn-cehn-trah-tsyOh-neh)*	concentration
concentrazione (f) di mercato	*(kohn-chehn-trah-tsyOh-neh deeh mehr-kAh-toh)*	market concentration
concessione (f) di appalto	*(kohn-chehs-syOh-neh deeh ahp-pAhl-toh)*	franchise

concetto (m) di marketing	*(kohn-chEht-toh deeh marketing)*	marketing concept
concetto di solvibilità	*(kohn-chEht-toh deeh sohl-veeh-beeh-leeh-tAh)*	ability-to-pay concept
concia (f)	*(kOhn-chah)*	tannery
conciare	*(kohn-chAh-reh)*	tan (v)
conciatore (m)	*(kohn-chah-tOh-reh)*	tanner
concorrente (m)	*(kohn-kohr-rEhn-teh)*	competitor
concorrenza (f)	*(kohn-kohr-rEhn-tsah)*	competition
condensatore (m)	*(kohn-dehn-sah-tOh-reh)*	condenser
condizioni (f) di commercio	*(kohn-deeh-tsyOh-neeh deeh kohm-mEhr-choh)*	terms of trade
condizioni di vendita	*(kohn-deeh-tsyOh-neeh deeh vEhn-deeh-tah)*	terms of sale
condotte (f) e tubi (m)	*(kohn-dOht-teh eh tOOh-beeh)*	pipes and tubes
conduttore (m)	*(kohn-dooht-tOh-reh)*	conductor
conferenza-confronto (f) idee	*(kohn-feh-rEhn-tsah kohn-frOhn-toh eeh-dEh-eh)*	brainstorming
conferma (f) dell'ordine	*(kohn-fEhr-mah dehl Ohr-deeh-neh)*	confirmation of order
confidenziale	*(kohn-feeh-dehn-tsyAh-leh)*	confidential
confine (m)	*(kohn-fEEh-neh)*	border
conflitto (m) d'interesse	*(kohn-flEEht-toh deehn-teh-rEhs-seh)*	conflict of interest
congedo (m)	*(kohn-jEh-doh)*	retirement
congedo di maternità	*(kohn-jEh-doh deeh mah-tehr-neeh-tAh)*	maternity leave
congedo per malattia	*(kohn-jEh-doh pehr mah-laht-tEEh-ah)*	sick leave
conglomerato (m)	*(kohn-gloh-meh-rAh-toh)*	conglomerate
coniglio (m)	*(koh-nEEh-lyoh)*	rabbit
consegna (f)	*(kohn-sEh-nyah)*	consignment, delivery, shipment
consegna immediata	*(kohn-sEh-nyah eehm-meh-dyAh-tah)*	spot delivery
consegna in contanti	*(kohn-sEh-nyah eehn kohn-tAhn-teeh)*	cash delivery

C

...a incompleta	*(kohn-sEh-nyah eehn-kohm-plEh-tah)*	short delivery
...segne differite	*(kohn-sEh-nyeh deehf-feh-rEEh-teh)*	deferred delivery
consenso (m)	*(kohn-sEhn-zoh)*	consent
considerazione (f)	*(kohn-seeh-deh-rah-tsyOh-neh)*	consideration (bus. law)
consiglio (m) di amministrazione	*(kohn-sEEh-lyoh deeh ahm-meeh-neehs-trah-tsyOh-neh)*	board of directors
consiglio di lavoro	*(kohn-sEEh-lyoh deeh lah-vOh-roh)*	work council
consiglio di sovrintendenza	*(kohn-sEEh-lyoh deeh soh-vreehn-tehn-dEhn-tsah)*	board of supervisors
consiglio dirigenziale	*(kohn-sEEh-lyoh deeh-reeh-jehn-tsyAh-leh)*	executive board
consolidamento (m)	*(kohn-seeh-lyah-mEhn-toh)*	consolidation
consorzio (m)	*(kohn-sOhr-tsyoh)*	consortium
consorzio di industriali	*(kohn-sOhr-tsyoh deeh eehn-doohs-tryAh-leeh)*	cartel
consulente (m)	*(kohn-sooh-lEhn-teh)*	consultant
consulente amministrativo	*(kohn-sooh-lEhn-teh ahm-meeh-neehs-trah-tEEh-voh)*	management consultant
consulente sugli investimenti	*(kohn-sooh-lEhn-teh sooh-lyeeh eehn-vehs-teeh-mEhn-teeh)*	investment adviser
consumatore (m)	*(kohn-sooh-mah-tOh-reh)*	consumer
consumo (m) di benzina	*(kohn-sOOh-moh dehl-lah behn-dsEEh-nah)*	gas consumption
contabile (m)	*(kohn-tAh-beeh-leh)*	accountant
contabilità (f)	*(kohn-tah-beeh-leeh-tAh)*	accounting department, bookkeeping
contabilità a partita doppia	*(kohn-tah-beeh-leeh-tAh ah pahr-tEEh-tah dOhp-pyah)*	double-entry bookkeeping
contabilità amministrativa	*(kohn-tah-beeh-leeh-tAh ahm-meeh-neehs-trah-tEEh-vah)*	management accounting

contabilità dei costi, contabilità industriale	*(kohn-tah-beeh-leeh-tAh deh-eeh kOhs-teeh), (kohn-tah-beeh-leeh-tAh eehn-doohs-tryAh-leh)*	cost accounting
contabilità di riduzione	*(kohn-tah-beeh-leeh-tAh deeh reeh-dooh-tsyOh-neh)*	depletion accounting
contachilometri (m)	*(kohn-tah-keeh-lOh-meh-treeh)*	odometer
contanti (m)	*(kohn-tAhn-teeh)*	cash
contenitore (m)	*(kohn-teh-neeh-tOh-reh)*	container
contenuto (m)	*(kohn-teh-nOOh-toh)*	content
contenuto (m) alcoolico	*(kohn-teh-nOOh-toh ahl-kOOh-leeh-koh)*	alcoholic content
contenuto zuccherino	*(kohn-teh-nOOh-toh dsoohk-keh-rEEh-noh)*	sugar content
conti (m) annuali	*(kOhn-teeh ahn-nwAh-leeh)*	annual accounts
conti creditori	*(kOhn-teeh kreh-deeh-tOh-reeh)*	accounts receivable
conti debitori	*(kOhn-teeh deh-beeh-tOh-reeh)*	accounts payable
conti di gruppo	*(kOhn-teeh deeh grOOhp-poh)*	group accounts
conti garantiti	*(kOhn-teeh gah-rahn-tEEh-teeh)*	secured accounts
conti inesigibili	*(kOhn-teeh eehn-eh-zeeh-jEEh-beeh-leeh)*	uncollectible accounts
contingenze (f)	*(kohn-teehn-jEhn-tseh)*	contingencies
conto (m)	*(kOhn-toh)*	account
conto aperto	*(kOhn-toh ah-pEhr-toh)*	charge account, open account
conto bancario	*(kOhn-toh bahn-kAh-reeh-oh)*	bank account
conto capitale	*(kOhn-toh kah-peeh-tAh-leh)*	capital account
conto capitale a breve termine	*(kOhn-toh kah-peeh-tAh-leh ah-brEh-veh tEhr-meeh-neh)*	short-term capital account
conto capitale a lungo termine	*(kOhn-toh kah-peeh-tAh-leh ah lOOhn-goh tEhr-meeh-neh)*	long-term capital account
conto chiuso	*(kOhn-toh kyOOh-zoh)*	closed account

...giunto	*(kOhn-toh kohn-jOOhn-toh)*	joint account, joint cost
... corrente	*(kOhn-toh kohr-rEhn-teh)*	checking account, current account
conto depositato presso terzi	*(kOhn-toh deh-poh-zeeh-tAh-toh prEhs-soh tEhr-tseeh)*	escrow account
conto dettagliato	*(kOhn-toh deht-tah-lyAh-toh)*	itemized account
conto di deposito	*(kOhn-toh deeh deh-pOh-zeeh-toh)*	deposit account
conto di risparmio	*(kOhn-toh deeh reehs-pAhr-myoh)*	savings account
conto marginale	*(kOhn-toh mahr-jeeh-nAh-leh)*	marginal account
conto moroso	*(kOhn-toh moh-rOh-zoh)*	delinquent account
conto operativo	*(kOhn-toh oh-peh-rah-tEEh-voh)*	active account
conto profitti e perdite	*(kOhn-toh proh-fEEht-teeh eh pEhr-deeh-teh)*	profit and loss statement
conto redditizio	*(kOhn-toh rehd-deeh-tEEh-tseeh-oh)*	income account
conto sul libro mastro	*(kOhn-toh soohl lEEh-broh mAhs-troh)*	ledger account
contraffatto (m)	*(kohn-trahf-fAht-toh)*	counterfeit
contraffazione (f)	*(kohn-trahf-fah-tsyOh-neh)*	forgery
contrassegnare	*(kohn-trahs-seh-nyAh-reh)*	earmark (v)
contrattazione (f) collettiva	*(kohn-traht-tah-tsyOh-neh kohl-leht-tEEh-vah)*	collective bargaining
contratto (m)	*(kohn-trAht-toh)*	contract
contratto a futura consegna	*(kohn-trAht-toh ah fooh-tOOh-rah kohn-sEh-nyah)*	futures
contratto a termine	*(kohn-trAht-toh ah tEhr-meeh-neh)*	forward contract, futures
contratto che garantisce un profitto in base al costo del prodotto	*(kohn-trAht-toh keh gah-rahn-tEEh-sheh oohn proh-fEEht-toh eehn bAh-zeh ahl kOhs-toh dehl proh-dOht-toh)*	cost-plus contract
contratto d'affitto	*(kohn-trAht-toh dahf-fEEht-toh)*	lease

contratto di lavoro	*(kohn-trAht-toh deeh lah-vOh-roh)*	working contract
contratto di locazione	*(kohn-trAht-toh deeh loh-kah-tsyOh-neh)*	lease
contratto di manutenzione	*(kohn-trAht-toh deeh mah-nooh-tehn-tsyOh-neh)*	maintenance contract, service contract
contratto di vendita condizionata	*(kohn-trAht-toh deeh vEhn-deeh-tah kohn-deeh-tsyoh-nAh-tah)*	conditional sales contract
contratto di vendita per l'esportazione	*(kohn-trAht-toh deeh vEhn-deeh-tah pehr lehs-pohr-tah-tsyOh-neh)*	export sales contract
contratto insoluto	*(kohn-trAht-toh eehn-soh-lOOh-toh)*	outstanding contract
contratto marittimo	*(kohn-trAht-toh mah-rEEht-teeh-moh)*	maritime contract
contratto sindacale	*(kohn-trAht-toh seehn-dah-kAh-leh)*	union contract
contro qualsiasi rischio	*(kOhn-troh kwahl-sEEh-ah-seeh rEEhs-kyoh)*	against all risks
controllare	*(kohn-trohl-lAh-reh)*	audit (v)
controllo (m) dei costi	*(kohn-trOhl-loh deh-eeh kOhs-teeh)*	cost control
controllo dei valori	*(kohn-trOhl-loh deh-eeh vah-lOh-reeh)*	stock control
controllo del credito	*(kohn-trOhl-loh dehl krEh-deeh-toh)*	credit control
controllo dell'inventario	*(kohn-trOhl-loh dehl eehn-vehn-tAh-reeh-oh)*	inventory control
controllo della produzione	*(kohn-trOhl-loh dehl-lah proh-dooh-tsyOh-neh)*	manufacturing control, production control
controllo della riduzione	*(kohn-trOhl-loh dehl-lah reeh-dooh-tsyOh-neh)*	depletion control
controllo delle azioni	*(kohn-trOhl-loh dehl-leh ah-tsyOh-neeh)*	stock control
controllo di qualita	*(kohn-trOhl-loh deeh kwah-leeh-tAh)*	quality control
controllo finanziario	*(kohn-trOhl-loh feeh-nahn-tsyAh-reeh-oh)*	financial control

controllo numerico	*(kohn-trOhl-loh nooh-mEh-reeh-koh)*	numerical control
controllo operativo	*(kohn-trOhl-loh oh-peh-rah-tEEh-voh)*	operations audit
controllo valutario	*(kohn-trOhl-loh vah-looh-tAh-reeh-oh)*	exchange control
controllore (m)	*(kohn-trohl-lOh-reh)*	comptroller, controller
controstallia (f) (maritime)	*(kohn-troh-stAhl-leeh-ah)*	demurrage
controvalore (m)	*(kohn-troh-vah-lOh-reh)*	exchange value
convenzione (f)	*(kohn-vehn-tsyOh-neh)*	agreement
convenzione commerciale	*(kohn-vehn-tsyOh-neh kohm-mehr-chAh-leh)*	trade agreement
convenzione d'accettazione	*(kohn-vehn-tsyOh-neh dahcheht-tah-tsyOh-neh)*	acceptance agreement
convenzione implicita	*(kohn-vehn-tsyOh-neh eehm-plEEh-cheeh-tah)*	implied agreement
convenzione multilaterale	*(kohn-vehn-tsyOh-neh moohl-teeh-lah-teh-rAh-leh)*	multilateral agreement
convenzione scritta	*(kohn-vehn-tsyOh-neh skrEEht-tah)*	written agreement
conversione (f) di valuta	*(kohn-vehr-zyOh-neh deeh vah-lOOh-tah)*	currency conversion
cooperativa (f)	*(ko-oh-peh-rah-tEEh-vah)*	cooperative
cooperativa (f) vinicola	*(koh-oh-peh-rah-tEEh-vah)*	wine cooperative
cooperazione	*(koh-oh-peh-rah-tsyOh-neh)*	cooperation agreement
copertina (f)	*(koh-pehr-tEEh-nah)*	cover
copertina a tela	*(koh-pehr-tEEh-nah ah tEh-lah)*	hardcover
copertina di libro	*(koh-pehr-tEEh-nah deeh lEEh-broh)*	jacket
copertina flessibile	*(koh-pehr-tEEh-nah flehs-sEEh-beeh-leh)*	soft cover
coperto (m)	*(koh-pEhr-toh)*	cover charge
coperto (m)	*(koh-pEhr-toh)*	place setting
copertura (f)	*(koh-pehr-tOOh-rah)*	coverage (insurance)

copertura a termine	*(koh-pehr-tOOh-rah ah tEhr-meeh-neh)*	forward cover
copertura in abbonamento	*(koh-pehr-tOOh-rah eehn ahb-boh-nah-mEhn-toh)*	open cover
copia (f) in omaggio	*(kOh-pyah eehn oh-mAhj-joh)*	complimentary copy
copia scritta	*(kOh-pyah skrEEht-tah)*	hard copy
copiare	*(koh-oyAh-reh)*	copy (v)
copione (m)	*(koh-pyOh-neh)*	script
coppa (f) per lo spumante	*(kOhp-pah pehr- loh spooh-mAhn-teh)*	champagne glass
corpo (m)	*(kOhr-poh)*	body
corpo (m)	*(kOhr-poh)*	corpus
corrente (f)	*(kohr-rEhn-teh)*	current
corrente alternata	*(kohr-rEhn-teh ahl-tehr-nAh-tah)*	alternating current
correzione (f) della tassa di confine	*(kohr-reh-tsyOh-neh dehl-lah tAhs-sah deeh kohn-fEEh-neh)*	border tax adjustment
correzione (f) delle bozza	*(koh-rehts-tsyOh-neh dehl-leh bOhts-tseh)*	proofreading
corrispondenza (f)	*(kohr-reehs-pohn-dEhn-tsah)*	correspondence
corsivo (m)	*(kohr-sEEh-voh)*	italic
cortisone (m)	*(kohr-teeh-zOh-neh)*	cortisone
costare	*(kohs-tAh-reh)*	cost (v)
costi (m) amministrati	*(kOhs-teeh ahm-meeh-neehs-trAh-teeh)*	managed costs
costi bancari	*(kOhs-teeh bahn-kAh-reeh)*	bank charges
costi controllabili	*(kOhs-teeh kohn-trohl-lAh-beeh-leeh)*	controllable costs, managed costs
costi di distribuzione	*(kOhs-teeh deeh deehs-treeh-booh-tsyOh-neh)*	distribution costs
costi di licenza	*(kOhs-teeh deeh leeh-chEhn-tsah)*	license fees
costi di produzione	*(kOhs-teeh deeh proh-dooh-tsyOh-neh)*	production costs
costi di riproduzione	*(kOhs-teeh deeh reeh-proh-dooh-tsyOh-neh)*	reproduction costs

costi di sbarco	*(kOhs-teeh deeh zbAhr-koh)*	landing costs
costi di spedizione a carico del destinatario	*(kOhs-teeh deeh speh-deeh-tsyOh-neh ah kAh-reeh-koh dehl dehs-teeh-nah-tAh-ryoh)*	freight collect
costi di stivaggio	*(kOhs-teeh deeh steeh-vAhj-joh)*	stowage charges
costi di trasporto	*(kOhs-teeh deeh trahs-pOhr-toh)*	shipping charges
costi effettivi	*(kOhs-teeh ehf-feht-tEEh-veeh)*	actual costs
costi fissi	*(kOhs-teeh fEEhs-seeh)*	fixed costs, standing costs
costi fissi d'azienda	*(kOhs-teeh fEEhs-seeh dah-dsyEhn-dah)*	factory overhead
costi incrementali	*(kOhs-teeh eehn-kreh-mehn-tAh-leeh)*	incremental costs, increased costs
costi iniziali	*(kOhs-teeh eeh-neeh-tsyAh-leeh)*	set-up costs, start-up cost
costi normali	*(kOhs-teeh nohr-mAh-leeh)*	standard costs
costi reali	*(kOhs-teeh reh-Ah-leeh)*	actual costs
costi semi-variabili	*(kOhs-teeh seh-meeh vah-ryAh-beeh-leeh)*	semi-variable costs
costi standard	*(kOhs-teeh standard)*	standard costs
costi tariffari	*(kOhs-teeh tah-reehf-fAh-reeh)*	tariff charges
costi variabili	*(kOhs-teeh vah-ryAh-beeh-leeh)*	variable costs
costituire un sindacato	*(kohs-teeh-tooh-EEh-reh oohn seehn-dah-kAh-toh)*	syndicate (v)
costo (m)	*(kOhs-toh)*	cost
costo alla destinazione	*(kOhs-toh ahl-lah dehs-teeh-nah-tsyOh-neh)*	landed cost
costo complessivo	*(kOhs-toh kohm-plehs-sEEh-voh)*	all in cost
costo congiunto	*(kOhs-toh kohn-jOOhn-toh)*	joint cost
costo dei beni venduti	*(kOhs-toh deh-eeh bEh-neeh vehn-dOOh-teeh)*	cost of goods sold
costo del capitale	*(kOhs-toh dehl kah-peeh-tAh-leh)*	cost of capital

costo dell'opportunità	*(kOhs-toh dehl ohp-pohr-tooh-neeh-tAh)*	opportunity costs
costo di ricambio	*(kOhs-toh deeh reeh-kAhm-byoh)*	replacement cost
costo diretto	*(kOhs-toh dee-reh-toh)*	direct cost
costo e trasporto	*(kOhs-toh eh trahs-pOhr-toh)*	cost and freight
costo fatturato	*(kOhs-toh faht-tooh-rAh-toh)*	invoice cost
costo indiretto	*(kOhs-toh eehn-deeh-rEht-toh)*	indirect cost
costo marginale	*(kOhs-toh mahr-jeeh-nAh-leh)*	marginal cost
costo medio	*(kOhs-toh mEh-dyoh)*	average cost
costo medio unitario	*(kOhs-toh mEh-dyoh ooh-neeh-tAh-reeh-oh)*	average unit cost
costo misto	*(kOhs-toh mEEhs-toh)*	mixed cost
costo originale	*(kOhs-toh oh-reeh-jeeh-nAh-leh)*	original cost
costo primo	*(kOhs-toh prEEh-moh)*	prime cost
costo unitario	*(kOhs-toh ooh-neeh-tAh-reeh-oh)*	unit cost
cotone (m)	*(koh-tOh-neh)*	cotton
coyote (m)	*(kayohtee)*	coyote
cravatta (f)	*(krah-vAht-tah)*	tie
cravatta a farfalla	*(krah-vAht-tah ah fahr-fAhl-lah)*	bow tie
creare una parola composta di due nomi utilizzante un trattino	*(kreh-Ah-reh ooh-nah pah-rOh-lah kohm-pOhs-tah deeh dOOh-eh nOh-meeh ooh-teeh-leehds-dsAhn-teh oohn traht-tEEh-noh)*	hyphenate (v)
crediti (m) garantiti	*(krEh-deeh-teeh gah-rahn-tEEh-teeh)*	secured accounts
crediti monetari	*(krEh-deeh-teeh moh-neh-tAh-reeh)*	monetary credits
credito (m)	*(krEh-deeh-toh)*	credit
credito a rate	*(krEh-deeh-toh ah rAh-teh)*	installment credit
credito al consumatore	*(krEh-deeh-toh ahl kohn-sooh-mah-tOh-reh)*	consumer credit

credito all'esportazione	*(krEh-deeh-toh ahl ehs-pohr-tah-tsyOh-neh)*	export credit
credito commerciale	*(krEh-deeh-toh kohm-mehr-chAh-leh)*	trade credit
credito d'accettazione	*(krEh-deeh-toh dahcheht-tah-tsyOh-neh)*	acceptance credit
credito disponibile	*(krEh-deeh-toh deehs-poh-nEEh-beeh-leh)*	credit balance
credito disposto dal beneficiario di un credito	*(krEh-deeh-toh deehs-pOhs-toh dahl beh-neh-feeh-chAh-reeh-oh deeh oohn krEh-deeh-toh)*	back-to-back credit
credito documentario aperto sulla base di un altro credito originario	*(krEh-deeh-toh doh-kooh-mehn-tAh-reeh-oh ah-pEhr-toh soohl-lah bAh-zeh deeh oohn Ahl-troh krEh-deeh-toh oh-reeh-jeeh-nAh-reeh-oh)*	back-to-back credit
credito intestato a due	*(krEh-deeh-toh eehn-tehs-tAh-toh ah dOOh-eh)*	two-name paper
credito per investimento	*(krEh-deehe-toh pehr eehn-vehs-teeh-mEhn-toh)*	investment credit
credito rotativo	*(krEh-deeh-toh roh-tah-tEEh-voh)*	revolving credit
credito sulle imposte estere	*(krEh-deeh-toh soohl-leh eehm-pOhs-teh Ehs-teh-reh)*	foreign tax credit
creditore (m)	*(kreh-deeh-tOh-reh)*	creditor, payee
crescita (f)	*(krEh-sheeh-tah)*	growth
crescita aziendale	*(krEh-sheeh-tah ah-dsyehn-dAh-leh)*	corporate growth
crescita incontrollata della zona urbana	*(krEh-sheeh-tah eehn-kohn-trohl-lAh-tah)*	urban sprawl
cristalizzazione (f)	*(kreehs-tah-leehds-dsah-tsyOh-neh)*	crystallization
criteri (m) d'investimento	*(kreeh-tEh-reeh deehn-vehs-teeh-mEhn-toh)*	investment criteria
crivello (m)	*(kreeh-vEhl-loh)*	jig (production)
crogiuolo (m)	*(kroh-jwOh-loh)*	crucible
cromo (m)	*(krOh-moh)*	chromium
crumiro (m)	*(krroh-mEEh-roh)*	strikebreaker (scab)

C

cruscotto (m)	*(kroohs-kOht-toh)*	dashboard
cucchiaino (m) da tè	*(koohk-kyah-EEh-noh dah tEh)*	teaspoon
cucchiaio (m)	*(koohk-kyAh-yoh)*	spoon
cucire	*(kooh-chEEh-reh)*	sew (v)
cuffia (f) del radiatore	*(kOOhf-fyah dehl rah-dyah-tOh-reh)*	grille
cumulativo	*(kooh-mooh-lah-tEEh-voh)*	cumulative
cuoio (m)	*(kwOh-yoh)*	cowhide
cupola (f)	*(kOOh-poh-lah)*	cupola
cura (f)	*(kOOh-rah)*	medication
cura (f) ragionevole	*(kOOh-rah rah-joh-nEh-voh-leh)*	reasonable care
curriculum (m) vitae	*(koohr-rEEh-kooh-loohm vEE-teh)*	resume
curva (f) a campana	*(kOOhr-vah ah cahmp-ahna)*	bell-shaped curve
curva d'insegnamento	*(kOOhr-vah ah kahm-pAh-nah)*	learning curve
curva di frequenza	*(kOOhr-vah deeh freh-kwEhn-tsah)*	frequency curve

D

danno (m)	*(dAhn-noh)*	damage
danno accidentale	*(dAhn-noh ahch-cheeh-dehn-tAh-leh)*	accidental damage
dare in appalto	*(dAh-reh eehn ahp-pAhl-toh)*	tender offer
dare l'incarico a terzi	*(dAh-reh leehn-kAh-reeh-koh ah tEhr-tseeh)*	farm out (v)
dare un miglior aspetto al prodotto	*(dAh-reh oohn meeh-lyOhr ahs-pEht-toh ahl proh-dOht-toh)*	window dressing (increase appeal) (v)
data (f) di consegna	*(dAh-tah deeh kohn-sEh-nyah)*	date of delivery
data di maturazione	*(dAh-tah deeh mah-tooh-rah-tsyOh-neh)*	maturity date

data di registrazione	*(dAh-tah deeh reh-jeehs-trah-tsyOh-neh)*	record date
data di scadenza	*(dAh-tah deeh skah-dEhn-tsah)*	expiry date
data originale di maturazione	*(dAh-tah oh-reeh-jeeh-nAh-leh)*	original maturity
dati (m)	*(dAh-teeh)*	data
dazio (m)	*(dAh-tsyoh)*	duty (customs, import)
dazio ad valorem	*(dAh-tsyoh ad vah-lOh-rehm)*	duty ad valorem
dazio combinato	*(dAh-tsyoh kohm-beeh-nAh-toh)*	combination duty
dazio specifico	*(dAh-tsyoh speh-chEEh-feeh-koh)*	specific duty
debiti (m) insoluti	*(dEh-beeh-teeh eehn-soh-lOOh-teeh)*	outstanding debt
debiti preferenziali	*(dEh-beeh-teeh preh-feh-rehn-tsyAh-leeh)*	preferential debts
debito (m)	*(dEh-beeh-toh)*	debt
debito a breve termine	*(dEh-beeh-toh ah brEh-veh tEhr-meeh-neh)*	short-term debt
debito a lungo termine	*(dEh-beeh-toh ah lOOhn-goh tEhr-meeh-neh)*	long-term debt
debito attivo	*(dEh-beeh-toh aht-tEEh-voh)*	active debt
debito consolidato	*(dEh-beeh-toh kohn-soh-leeh-dAh-toh)*	debt
debito estero	*(dEh-beeh-toh Ehs-teh-roh)*	foreign debt
debito fluttuante	*(dEh-beeh-toh flooht-twAhn-teh)*	floating debt
debito insolvibile	*(dEh-beeh-toh eehn-sohl-vEEh-beeh-leh)*	bad debt
debito nazionale	*(dEh-beeh-toh nah-tsyoh-nAh-leh)*	national debt
decapaggio (m)	*(deh-kah-pAhj-joh)*	pickling
decisione (f) di fabbricare invece di comprare	*(deh-cheeh-zyOh-neh deeh fahb-breeh-kAh-reh eehn-vEh-cheh deeh kohm-prAh-reh)*	make-or-buy decision
decollare	*(deh-kohl-lAh-reh)*	take off (v)

deduzione (f) convertibile	*(deh-dooh-tsyOh-neh kohn-vehr-tEEh-beeh-leh)*	redemption allowance
deficiente	*(deh-feeh-chEhn-teh)*	substandard
deficit (m)	*(deh-feeh-chEEht)*	deficit
definizione (f)	*(deh-feeh-neeh-tsyOh-neh)*	settlement
deflazione (f)	*(deh-flah-tsyOh-neh)*	deflation
degustazione (f)	*(deh-goohs-tah-tsyOh-neh)*	tasting (wine tasting)
demografico (m)	*(deh-moh-grAh-feeh-koh)*	demographic
demozione (f)	*(deh-moh-tsyOh-neh)*	demotion
denaro (m)	*(deh-nAh-roh)*	money
denaro caldo	*(deh-nAh-roh kAhl-doh)*	hot money
denaro disponibile	*(deh-nAh-roh deehs-poh-nEEh-beeh-leh)*	ready cash
denaro investito a brevissima scadenza	*(deh-nAh-roh eehn-vehs-tEEh-toh ah breh-vEEhs-seeh-mah skah-dEhn-tsah)*	call money
denominazione di origine controllata (D.O.C.) (f)	*(deh-noh-meeh-nah-tsyOh-neh deeh oh-rEEh-jeeh-neh kohn-trohl-lAh-tah)*	area of origin guaranteed
densità (f)	*(dehn-seeh-tAh)*	density
deporto (m)	*(deh-pOhr-toh)*	backwardation
depositi (m) d'importazione	*(deh-pOs-eeteeh)*	import deposits
deposito (m)	*(deh-pOh-zeeh-toh)*	deposit, depository, down payment, licensed warehouse
deposito a richiesta	*(dEh-pOh-zeeh-toh ah reeh-kyEhs-tah)*	demand deposit
deposito a tempo	*(deh-pOh-zeeh-toh ah tEhm-poh)*	time deposit
deposito bancario	*(deh-pOh-zeeh-toh bahn-kAh-reeh-oh)*	bank deposit
deposito in conto corrente	*(deh-pOh-zeeh-toh eehn kOhn-toh kohr-rEhn-teh)*	demand deposit
deposito presso terzi	*(deh-pOh-zeeh-toh prEhs-soh tEhr-tseeh)*	escrow
depressione (f)	*(deh-prehs-syOh-neh)*	depression

D

deprezzamento (m)	*(deh-prehts-tsah-mEhn-toh)*	depreciation
deprezzamento della valuta	*(deh-prehts-tsah-mEhn-toh dehl-lah vah-lOOh-tah)*	depreciation of currency
derivare	*(deh-reeh-vAh-reh)*	accrue (v)
descrizione (f) del lavoro	*(dehs-kreeh-tsyOh-neh deeh lah-vOh-roh)*	job description
destinatario (m)	*(dehs-teeh-nah-tAh-reeh-oh)*	consignee
destinazione (f) indicata	*(dehs-teeh-nah-tsyOh-neh)*	named point of destination
detentore (m)	*(deh-tehn-tOh-reh)*	holder (negotiable instruments)
determinazione (f) del prezzo marginale	*(deh-tehr-meeh-nah-tsyOh-neh dehl prEhts-tsoh mahr-jeeh-nAh-leh)*	marginal pricing
detraibile (m)	*(deh-trah-EEh-beeh-leh)*	deductible
detrazione (f)	*(deh-trah-tsyOh-neh)*	deduction
detrazione dalle imposte	*(deh-trah-tsyOh-neh dahl-leh eehm-pOhs-teh)*	tax deduction
detrazione personale	*(deh-trah-tsyOh-neh pehr-soh-nAh-leh)*	personal deduction
dettagliare	*(deht-tah-lyAh-reh)*	itemize (v)
di fortuna	*(deeh fohr-tOOh-nah)*	makeshift
di ripiego	*(deeh reeh-pyEh-goh)*	makeshift
diabete (m)	*(deeh-ah-bEh-teh)*	diabetes
diagramma (m)	*(deeh-ah-grAhm-mah)*	graph
diagramma delle attività	*(deeh-ah-grAhm-mah dehl-leh aht-teeh-veeh-tAh)*	activity chart
diagramma delle correnti	*(deeh-ah-grAhm-mah dehl-leh kohr-rEhn-teeh)*	flow chart
diagramma utilizzante barre	*(deeh-ah-grAhm-mah ooh-teeh-leehds-dsAhn-teh bAhr-reh)*	bar chart
diaria (f)	*(deeh-Ah-reeh-ah)*	per diem
dibattito (m) costruttivo d'opinioni	*(deeh-bAht-teeh-toh kohs-trooht-tEEh-voh doh-peeh-nyOh-neeh)*	brainstorming
dichiarazione (f)	*(deeh-kyah-rah-tsyOh-neh)*	statement
dichiarazione atto giurato	*(deeh-kyah-rah-tsyOh-neh Aht-toh jooh-rAh-tohl)*	affidavit

dichiarazione d'entrata	*(deeh-kyah-rah-tsyOh-neh dehn-trAh-tah)*	entry permit
dichiarazione d'esportazione	*(deeh-kyah-rah-tsyOh-neh dehs-pohr-tah-tsyOh-neh)*	export entry
dichiarazione degli utili e delle perdite	*(deeh-kyah-rah-tsyOh-neh deh-lyeeh OOh-teeh-leeh eh dehl-leh pEhr-deeh-teh)*	profit and loss statement
dichiarazione del reddito	*(deeh-kyah-rah-tsyOh-neh dehl rEhd-deeh-toh)*	income statement
dichiarazione di conto	*(deeh-kyah-rah-tsyOh-neh deeh kOhn-toh)*	statement of account
dichiarazione doganale	*(deeh-kyah-rah-tsyOh-neh doh-gah-nAh-leh)*	customs entry, import declaration
dichiarazione finanziaria	*(deeh-kyah-rah-tsyOh-neh feeh-nahn-tsyAh-reeh-ah)*	financial statement
dichiarazione operativa	*(deeh-kyah-rah-tsyOh-neh oh-peh-rah-tEEh-vah)*	operating statement
dichiarazione per procura	*(deeh-kyah-rah-tsyOh-neh pehr proh-kOOh-rah)*	proxy statement
dichiarazione pro forma	*(deeh-kyah-rah-tsyOh-neh proh fOhr-mah)*	pro forma statement
dichiarazione provvisoria	*(deeh-kyah-rah-tsyOh-neh prohv-veeh-zOh-reeh-ah)*	interim statement
dichiarazione scritta e giurata	*(deeh-kyah-rah-tsyOh-neh skrEEht-tah eh jooh-rAh-tah)*	affidavit
dichiarazione sotto giuramento	*(deeh-kyah-rah-tsyOh-neh sOht-toh jooh-rah-mEhn-toh)*	sworn statement
diesel (m)	*(dEE-zl)*	diesel
difetto (m) nel programma dell'elaboratore elettronico	*(deeh-fEht-toh nehl proh-grAhm-mah dehl eh-lah-boh-rah-tOh-reh eh-leht-trOh-neeh-koh)*	bug (defect in computer program)
difettoso	*(deeh-feht-tOh-soh)*	defective
diffamazione (f)	*(deef-fah-mah-tsyOh-neh)*	libel
differenza (f) salariale	*(deehf-feh-rEhn-tsah sah-lah-ryAh-leh)*	wage differential

D

differenza tra il prezzo di vendita e i costi di produzione	*(deehf-feh-rEhn-tsah trah eehl prEhts-tsoh deeh vEhn-deeh-tah eh eeh kOhs-teeh deeh proh-dooh-tsyOh-neh)*	gross spread
differenziale (m) dei prezzi	*(deehf-feh-rehn-tsyAh-leh deh-eeh prEhts-tseeh)*	price differential
differenziale di stipendio	*(deehf-feh-rehn-tsyAh-leh deeh steeh-pEhn-deeh-oh)*	wage differential
differenziale tariffario	*(deehf-feh-rehn-tsyAh-leh tah-reehf-fAh-reeh-oh)*	tariff differential
digitale	*(deeh-jeeh-tAh-leh)*	digital
digitalis (m)	*(deeh-jeeh-tAh-lees)*	digitalis
diluizione (f) del capitale azionario	*(deeh-lweeh-tsyOh-neh dehl kah-peeh-tAh-leh ah-tsyoh-nAh-reeh-oh)*	dilution of equity
diluizione del capitale netto	*(deeh-lweeh-tsyOh-neh dehl kah-peeh-tAh-leh nEht-toh)*	dilution of equity
diluizione della manodopera	*(deeh-lweeh-tsyOh-neh dehl-lah mah-noh-dOh-peh-rah)*	dilution of labor
dinamica (f) del gruppo	*(deeh-nAh-meeh-kah dehl grOOhp-poh)*	group dynamics
dinamica del mercato	*(deeh-nAh-meeh-kah dehl mehr-kAh-toh)*	market dynamics
dinamica del prodotto	*(deeh-nAh-meeh-kah dehl proh-dOht-toh)*	product dynamics
diodo (m)	*(dEEh-oh-doh)*	diode
dipinto a mano	*(deeh-pEEhn-toh ah mAh-noh)*	hand-painted
direttore (m)	*(deeh-rEht-toh-reh)*	director, manager
direttore d'area	*(deeh-rEht-toh-reh dAh-reh-ah)*	area manager
direttore della pubblicità, direttore pubblicitario	*(deeh-rEht-toh-reh dehl-lah poohb-leeh-cheeh-tAh), (deeh-reht-tOh-reh poohb-leeh-cheeh-tAh-reeh-oh)*	advertising manager
direttore finanziario	*(deeh-rEht-toh-reh feeh-nahn-tsyAh-reeh-oh)*	financial director
direttore generale	*(deeh-rEht-toh-reh jeh-neh-rAh-leh)*	chief executive

direzioni congiunte	*(deeh-reh-tsyOh-neeh kohn-jOOhn-teh)*	interlocking directorate
dirigente (m)	*(deeh-reeh-jEhn-teh)*	executive
dirigente di linea	*(deeh-reeh-jEhn-teh deeh lEEh-neh-ah)*	line executive
dirigente responsabile per la gestione della marca	*(deeh-reeh-jEhn-teh rehs-pohn-sAh-beeh-leh pehr lah jehs-tyOh-neh dehl-lah mAhr-kah)*	brand manager
dirigente superiore	*(deeh-reeh-jEhn-teh sooh-peh-ryOh-reh)*	executive director
dirigenti (m), dirigenza (f)	*(deeh-reeh-jEhn-teh), (deeh-reeh-jEhn-tsah)*	top management
diritti (m) acquisiti	*(deeh-rEEht-teeh ahk-kweeh-zEEh-teeh)*	acquired rights, vested rights
diritti (m) d'autore	*(deeh-rEEht-toh dah-ooh-tOh-reh)*	copyright
diritti di brevetto	*(deeh-rEEht-teeh deeh breh-vEht-toh)*	patent royalty
diritti esclusivi	*(deeh-rEEht-teeh ehs-klooh-zEEh-veeh)*	sole rights
diritti portuali	*(deeh-rEEht-teeh pohr-twAh-leeh)*	harbor dues
diritto al ricorso	*(deeh-rEEht-toh ahl reeh-kOhr-soh)*	right of recourse
diritto al voto	*(deeh-rEEht-toh ahl vOh-toh)*	voting right
diritto di prelazione	*(deeh-rEEht-toh deeh preh-lah-tsyOh-neh)*	preemptive right
diritto di proprietario	*(deeh-rEEht-toh deeh proh-pryeh-tAh-reeh-oh)*	proprietary
disarmare	*(deeh-zahr-mAh-reh)*	lay up (v)
disavanzo (m)	*(deeh-zah-vAhn-tsoh)*	deficit
dischetto (m)	*(deehs-kEht-toh)*	disk
dischetto floppy	*(deehs-kEht-toh floppy)*	floppy disk
disco (m)	*(dEEhs-koh)*	disc
disco (m)	*(dEEhs-koh)*	record
disegnare	*(deeh-zeh-nyAh-reh)*	design (v)
disegno (m)	*(deeh-zEh-nyoh)*	line drawing
disegno (m)	*(deeh-zEh-nyoh)*	pattern

D

disegno del prodotto	*(deeh-zEh-nyoh dehl proh-dOht-toh)*	product design
disincentivo (m)	*(deeh-zeehn-chehn-tEEh-voh)*	disincentive
disoccupazione (f)	*(deeh-zohk-kooh-pah-tsyOh-neh)*	unemployment
dispersione (f)	*(deehs-pehr-syOh-neh)*	leakage
disponsibilità (f) dei capitali	*(deehs-poh-neeh-beeh-leeh-tAh deh-eeh kah-peeh-tAh-leeh)*	money supply
disposizione (f) di una pagina	*(deehs-poh-zeeh-tsyOh-neh deeh ooh-nah pAh-jeeh-nah)*	layout
disputa (f)	*(dEEhs-pooh-tah)*	dispute
disputa di lavoro	*(dEEhs-pooh-tah deeh lah-vOh-roh)*	labor dispute
disputa salariale	*(dEEhs-pooh-tah sah-lah-ryAh-leh)*	wage dispute
disputa sindacale	*(dEEhs-pooh-tah seehn-dah-kAh-leh)*	labor dispute
disputare	*(deehs-pooh-tAh-reh)*	dispute (v)
distillazione (f)	*(deehs-teehl-lah-tsyOh-neh)*	distillation
distributore (m)	*(deehs-treeh-booh-tOh-reh)*	distributor
ditta (f)	*(dEEht-tah)*	corporation, firm
ditta a capitale sociale	*(dEEht-tah ah kah-peeh-tAh-leh soh-chAh-leh)*	joint stock company
ditta associata	*(dEEht-tah ahs-soh-chAh-tah)*	associate company, member firm
ditta che tratta esportazioni	*(dEEht-tah keh trAht-tah ehs-pohr-tah-tsyOh-neeh)*	export house
ditta che tratta scambi commerciali	*(dEEht-tah keh trAht-tah skAhm-beeh kohm-mehr-chAh-leeh)*	trade house
ditta di garanzia	*(dEEht-tah deeh gah-rahn-tsEEh-ah)*	guaranty company
ditta estera	*(dEEht-tah Ehs-teh-rah)*	foreign corporation
ditta garante	*(dEEht-tah Ehs-teh-rah)*	surety company
ditta import/export	*(dEEht-tah import-export)*	trading company
ditta madre	*(dEEht-tah mAh-dreh)*	parent company

D

ditta nazionale	*(dEEht-tah nah-tsyoh-nAh-leh)*	domestic corporation
ditta offshore	*(dEEht-tah offshore)*	offshore company
ditta primaria, ditta "leader"	*(dEEht-tah preeh-mAh-reeh-ah)*	leading firm
ditta privata	*(dEEht-tah preeh-vAh-tah)*	closely held corporation
ditta straniera	*(dEEht-tah strah-nyEh-rah)*	alien corporation
diuretico (m)	*(deeh-ooh-rEh-teeh-koh)*	diuretic
diventare una ditta per azioni	*(deeh-vehn-tAh-reh ooh-nah dEEht-tah pehr ah-tsyOh-neeh)*	go public (v)
diversificazione (f)	*(deeh-vehr-seeh-feeh-kah-tsyOh-neh)*	diversification
dividendo (m)	*(deeh-veeh-dEhn-doh)*	dividend
dividendo eliminato	*(deeh-veeh-dEhn-doh eh-leeh-meeh-nAh-toh)*	passed dividend
dividendo pagato in contanti	*(deeh-veeh-dEhn-doh pah-gAh-toh eehn kohn-tAhn-teeh)*	cash dividend
dividendo supplementare	*(deeh-veeh-dEhn-doh soohp-pleh-mehn-tAh-reh)*	extra dividend
dividere una parola usando trattini	*(deeh-vEEh-deh-reh ooh-nah pahr-rOh-lah ooh-zAhn-do traht-tEEh-neeh)*	hyphenate (v)
divisione (f) del lavoro	*(deeh-veeh-zyOh-neh deeh lah-vOh-roh)*	division of labor
documento (m)	*(doh-kooh-mEhn-toh)*	document
documento costitutivo	*(doh-kooh-mEhn-toh kohs-teeh-tooh-tEEh-voh)*	charter
documento in ordine	*(doh-kooh-mEhn-toh eehn Ohr-deeh-neh)*	clean document
documento pulito	*(doh-kooh-mEhn-toh pooh-lEEh-toh)*	clean document
dogana (f)	*(doh-gAh-nah)*	customs
doganiere (m)	*(doh-gah-nyEh-reh)*	collector of customs
domanda (f) aggregata	*(doh-mAhn-dah ahg-greh-gAh-tah)*	aggregate demand
domanda od offerta rigida o inelastica	*(doh-mAhn-dah od ohf-fEhr-tah rEEh-jeeh-dah oh eeh-neh-lAhs-teeh-kah)*	inelastic demand or supply

D

dominio (m) pubblico	*(doh-mEEh-neeh-oh pOOhb-leeh-koh)*	public domain
donante (m)	*(doh-nahn-teay)*	grantor
donazione (f) di terra	*(doh-nah-tsyOh-neh deeh tEhr-rah)*	land grant
doppia (f) tassazione	*(dOhp-pyah tahs-sah-tsyOh-neh)*	double taxation
doppia paga per gli straordinari	*(dOhp-pyah pAh-gah pehr-lyeeh strah-nyEh-reeh)*	double time
dorso (m)	*(dOhr-soh)*	spine
dose (f)	*(dOh-zeh)*	dose
dotazione (f)	*(doh-tah-tsyOh-neh)*	endowment
drappeggiare	*(drahp-pehj-jAh-reh)*	drape (v)
droga (m)	*(drOh-gah)*	drug
dumping (m)	*(duhmpeeng)*	dumping (goods in foreign market)
duopolio (m)	*(dooh-oh-pOh-leeh-oh)*	duopoly
durata (f) del prodotto	*(dooh-rAh-tah dehl proh-dOht-toh)*	product life
durata di un brevetto	*(dooh-rAh-tah deeh oohn breh-vEht-toh)*	life of a patent
durata di un prodotto	*(dooh-rAh-tah deeh oohn proh-dOht-toh)*	life cycle of a product
durata media	*(dooh-rAh-tah mEh-dyah)*	average life
durata utile	*(dooh-rAh-tah OOh-teeh-leh)*	useful life
durezza (f)	*(dooh-rEhts-tsah)*	toughness
duttilità (f)	*(dooht-teeh-leeh-tAh)*	malleability

E

eccedenza (f) dei capitali	*(ehch-cheh-dEhn-tsah deh-eeh kah-peeh-tAh-leeh)*	capital surplus
eccedenza versata	*(ehch-cheh-dEhn-tsah vehr-sAh-tah)*	paid-in surplus
eccesso (m)	*(ehch-chEhs-soh)*	overage
econometria (f)	*(eh-koh-noh-meh-trEEh-ah)*	econometrics
economia (f)	*(eh-koh-noh-mEEh-ah)*	economics

economia controllata	*(eh-koh-noh-mEEh-ah kohn-trohl-lAh-tah)*	managed economy
economia di scala	*(eh-koh-noh-mEEh-ah deeh skAh-lah)*	economy of scale
economia keynesiana	*(eh-koh-noh-mEEh-ah kehn-syAh-nah)*	Keynesian economics
economico	*(eh-koh-nOh-meeh-koh)*	economic
edificio (m)	*(eh-deeh-fEEh-choh)*	premises (location)
editore/trice (m/f)	*(eh-deeh-tOh-reh/trEEh-cheh)*	publisher
effettivo	*(ehf-feht-tEEh-voh)*	actual
effetto (m) di risucchio	*(ehf-fEht-toh deeh reeh-sOOhk-kyoh)*	backwash effect
efficienza (f)	*(ehf-feeh-chEhn-tsah)*	efficiency
efficienza dei costi	*(ehf-feeh-chEhn-tsah deh-eeh kOhs-teeh)*	cost effectiveness
elaboratore (m) a sistema analog	*(eh-lah-boh-rah-tOh-reh ah seehs-tEh-mah ah-nahy-lOhg)*	analog computer
elaboratore a sistema digitale, elaboratore digitale	*(eh-lah-boh-rah-tOh-reh ah seehs-tEh-mah deeh-jeeh-tAh-leh), (eh-lah-boh-rah-tOh-reh deeh-jeeh-tAh-leh)*	digital computer
elaboratore centrale	*(eh-lah-boh-rah-tOh-reh chehn-trAh-leh)*	mainframe computer
elaboratore del testo autonomo	*(eh-lah-boh-rah-tOh-reh dehl tEhs-toh ah-ooh-tOh-noh-moh)*	stand-alone word processor
elaboratore ibrido	*(eh-lah-boh-rah-tOh-reh EEh-breeh-doh)*	hybrid computer
elaborazione (f) per gruppi	*(eh-lah-boh-rah-tsyOh-neh pehr grOOhp-peeh)*	batch processing
elasticità (f) (dell'offerta e della domanda)	*(eh-lahs-teeh-cheeh-tAh dehl ohf-fEhr-tah eh dehl-lah doh-mAhn-dah)*	elasticity (of supply or demand)
elasticità del prezzo	*(eh-lahs-teeh-cheeh-tAh dehl prEhts-tsoh)*	price elasticity
eleganza (f)	*(eh-leh-gAhn-dsah)*	elegance
elemento (m)	*(eh-leh-mEhn-toh)*	element
elencare	*(eh-lehn-kAh-reh)*	list (v)

E

elenco (m) di indirizzi per invio di materiali pubblicitari	*(eh-lEhn-koh deeh eehn-deeh-rEEhts-tseeh pehr eehn-vEEh-oh deeh mah-teh-ryAh-leeh poohb-leeh-cheeh-tAh-reeh)*	mailing list
elenco legale	*(eh-lEhn-koh leh-gAh-leh)*	legal list (fiduciary investments)
elettricità (f)	*(eh-leht-treeh-cheeh-tAh)*	electricity
elettrodi (m)	*(eh-lEht-troh-deeh)*	electrodes
elettrodo (m)	*(eh-lEht-troh-doh)*	electrode
elettrolisi (f)	*(eh-leht-trOh-leeh-zeeh)*	electrolysis
elettrone (m)	*(eh-leht-trOh-neh)*	electron
elettronico	*(eh-leht-trOh-neeh-koh)*	electronic
elettrostatico	*(eh-leht-troh-stAh-teeh-koh)*	electrostatic
elezione	*(eh-lehs-ee-Ohn)*	election
eliminare	*(eh-leeh-meeh-nAh-reh)*	phase out (v), take out (v)
embargo (m)	*(ehm-bAhr-goh)*	embargo
emendamento (m)	*(Eh-mehn-dah-mEhn-toh)*	amendment
emendare	*(eh-mehn-dAh-reh)*	amend (v)
emettere	*(eh-mEht-teh-reh)*	issue (v)
emettere un assegno scoperto e poi depositare la somma necessaria per renderlo valido	*(eh-mEht-teh-reh oohn ahs-sEh-nyoh skoh-pEhr-toh eh pOh-eeh deh-poh-zeeh-tAh-reh lah sOhm-mah neh-chehs-sAh-reeh-ah pehr rEhn-dehr-loh vAh-leeh-doh)*	kiting (banking)
emissione (f)	*(eh-meehs-syOh-neh)*	issue (stock)
emissione di buoni	*(eh-meehs-syOh-neh deeh bwOh-neeh)*	bond issue
emissione fiduciaria	*(eh-meehs-syOh-neh feeh-dooh-chAh-reeh-ah)*	fiduciary issue
emissione primaria	*(eh-meehs-syOh-neh preeh-mAh-reeh-ah)*	senior issue
enologo (m)	*(eh-nOh-loh-goh)*	wine steward
enoteca (f)	*(eh-noh-tEh-kah)*	wine cellar
ente (m) governativo	*(Ehn-teh goh-vehr-nah-tEEh-voh)*	government agency

ente pubblico responsabile per gli alloggi	*(Ehn-teh pOOhb-leeh-koh rehs-pohn-sAh-beeh-leh pehr lyeeh ahl-lOhj-jeeh)*	housing authority
entità (f) legale	*(ehn-teeh-tAh)*	legal entity
entrata (f)	*(ehn-trAh-tah)*	input
entrata d'importazione	*(ehn-trAh-tah deehm-pohr-tah-tsyOh-neh)*	import entry
entrata dei dati nell'elaboratore elettronico	*(ehn-trAh-tah nehl eh-lah-boh-rah-tOh-reh eh-leht-trOh-neeh-koh)*	computer input
entrata nel libro mastro	*(ehn-trAh-tah nehl lEEh-broh mAhs-troh)*	ledger entry
entrata originale	*(ehn-trAh-tah oh-reeh-jeeh-nAh-leh)*	original entry
entrata sul registro	*(ehn-trAh-tah soohl-reh-jEEhs-troh)*	ledger entry
enzima (m)	*(ehn-dsEEh-mah)*	enzyme
équipe (f) amministrativa	*(eh-kEEhp ahm-meeh-neehs-trah-tEEh-vah)*	management team
equità (m)	*(eh-kweeh-tAh)*	equity
eredità (f)	*(eh-reh-deeh-tAh)*	legacy
ergonometrica (f)	*(ehr-goh-noh-mEh-treeh-kah)*	ergonomics
errore (m)	*(ehr-rOh-reh)*	error
errore di elaborazione	*(ehr-rOh-reh deeh eh-lah-boh-rah-tsyOh-neh)*	processing error
esaclorofene (m/f)	*(eh-zah-kloh-roh-fEh-neh)*	hexachlorophene
esame (m) d'accettazione	*(eh-zAh-meh dahcheht-tah-tsyOh-neh)*	acceptance test
esame della personalità	*(eh-zAh-meh dehl-lah pehr-soh-nah-leeh-tAh)*	personality test
esame di un testo pubblicitario	*(eh-zAh-meh deeh oohn tEhs-toh poohb-leeh-cheeh-tAh-reeh-oh)*	copy testing
esattore (m) delle tasse	*(eh-zaht-tOh-reh dehl-leh tAhs-seh)*	tax collector
esattore doganale	*(eh-zaht-tOh-reh doh-gah-nAh-leh)*	collector of customs
esecutore/trice (m/f)	*Eh-seh-kooh-tOh-reh/trEEh-cheh)*	executor

E

esente da dazio	*(eh-zEhn-teh dah dAh-tsyoh)*	dutyfree
esenzione (f)	*(eh-zehn-tsyOh-neh)*	exemption
esenzione personale	*(eh-zehn-tsyOh-neh pehr-soh-nAh-leh)*	personal exemption
esigenze (f)	*(eh-zeeh-jEhn-tseh)*	requirements
esigenze di margine	*(eh-zeeh-jEhn-tseh deeh mAhr-jeeh-neh)*	margin requirements
espansione (f)	*(ehs-pahn-syOh-neh)*	boom
esperimento (m)	*(ehs-peh-reeh-mEhn-toh)*	experiment
esplorazione (f)	*(eh-leht-troh-stAh-teeh-koh)*	scanning
esportare	*(ehs-pohr-tAh-reh)*	export (v)
esportatore su commissione	*(ehs-pohr-tah-tOh-reh sooh kohm-meehs-syOh-neh)*	export agent
esportatore/trice (m/f) per conto terzi	*(ehs-pohr-tah-tOh-reh/trEEh-cheh pehr kOhn-toh tEhr-tseeh)*	third-party exporter
esportazione (f) dei capitali	*(ehs-pohr-tah-tsyOh-neh deh-eeh kah-peeh-tAh-leeh)*	capital exports (currency)
esportazione di beni capitali	*(ehs-pohr-tah-tsyOh-neh deh-eeh bEh-neeh kah-peeh-tAh-leeh)*	capital exports (goods)
esportazioni chiave	*(ehs-pohr-tah-tsyOh-neh kyAh-veh)*	key exports
espresso (m) aereo	*(ehs-rEhs-soh)*	air express
esproprio (m)	*(ehs-prOh-preeh-oh)*	expropriation
essere elusivo	*(Ehs-seh-reh eh-looh-zEEh-voh)*	hedge (v)
essere responsabile per	*(Ehs-seh-reh rehs-pohn-sAh-beeh-leh)*	account for (v)
estinzione (f) obbligatoria	*(ehs-teehn-tsyOh-neh ohb-bleeh-gah-tOh-reeh-ah)*	mandatory redemption
etano (m)	*(eh-tAh-noh)*	ethane
etere (m)	*(Eh-teh-reh)*	ether
etichetta (f)	*(eh-teeh-kEht-tah)*	label
etichetta (f) sindacale	*(eh-teeh-kEht-tah seehn-dah-kAh-leh)*	union label
ettaro (m)	*(Eht-tah-roh)*	hectare

euro-obbligazione (f)	*(eh-ooh-roh-ohb-bleeh-gah-tsyOh-neeh)*	Eurobond
eurodollaro (m)	*(eh-ooh-roh-dOhl-lah-roh)*	Eurodollar
eurovaluta (f)	*(eh-ooh-roh-vah-lOOh-tah)*	Eurocurrency
evaporazione (f)	*(eh-vah-poh-rah-tsyOh-neh)*	evaporation
evasione (f) fiscale	*(eh-vah-zyOh-neh feehs-kAh-leh)*	tax evasion
evento (m) determinante lo scatto del processo di aggiustamento	*(eh-vEhn-toh deh-tehr-meeh-nAhn-teh loh skAht-toh dehl proh-chEhs-soh deeh ahj-joohs-tah-mEhn-toh)*	adjustment trigger
evitare di compromettersi	*(eh-veeh-tAh-reh deeh kohm-proh-mEht-tehr-seeh)*	hedge (v)
ex diritti	*(ex deeh-rEEht-teeh)*	ex rights
ex molo	*(ex mOh-loh)*	ex dock

F

| | **F** | |

fabbrica (f)	*(fAhb-breeh-kah)*	factory
fabbrica aperta anche ai non iscritti al sindacato	*(fAhb-breeh-kah ah-pEhr-tah ahn-keh ah-eeh nohn eehs-krEEht-teeh ahl seehn-dah-kAh-toh)*	open shop
fabbricante (m)	*(fahb-breeh-kAhn-teh)*	manufacturer
facilitazione (f)	*(fah-cheeh-leeh-tah-tsyOh-neh)*	facilities
facilitazione d'appoggio creditizio	*(fah-cheeh-leeh-tah-tsyOh-neh dahp-pOhj-joh kreh-deeh-tEEh-tsyoh)*	accommodation credit
facoltativo	*(fah-kohl-tah-tEEh-voh)*	optional
factotum (m)	*(fahk-tOh-toohm)*	man/gal Friday
fallimento (m)	*(fahl-leeh-mEhn-toh)*	bankruptcy, failure
fallire	*(fahl-lEEh-reh)*	fail (v)
far seguito	*(fahr sEh-gweeh-toh)*	followup (v)
fare il giro	*(fAh-reh eehl jEEh-roh)*	go around (v)
fare la coda	*(fAh-reh lah kOh-dah)*	stand in line (v)
farmacia (f)	*(fahr-mah-chEEh-ah)*	drugstore

farmacista (m/f)	*(fahr-mah-chEEhs-tah)*	pharmacist
farmaco (m)	*(fAhr-mah-koh)*	drug
fascio (m)	*(fEEh-brah)*	beam
fase (f) negativa	*(fAh-zeh neh-gah-tEEh-vah)*	down period, slump
fattore (m)	*(faht-tOh-reh)*	factor, maker (of a check, draft, etc.)
fattore degli utili	*(faht-tOh-reh deh-lyeeh OOh-teeh-leeh)*	profit factor
fattore dei costi	*(faht-tOh-reh deh-eeh kOhs-teeh)*	cost factor
fattore dei profitti	*(faht-tOh-reh deh-eeh proh-fEEht-teeh)*	profit factor
fattore del ricarico	*(faht-tOh-reh deeh reeh-kAh-reeh-koh)*	load factor
fattoria (f)	*(faht-toh-rEEh-ah)*	estate (or chateau)
fattura (f)	*(faht-tOOh-rah)*	bill, invoice
fattura commerciale	*(faht-tOOh-rah kohm-mehr-chAh-leh)*	commercial invoice
fattura consolare	*(faht-tOOh-rah kohn-soh-lAh-reh)*	consular invoice
fattura nazionale	*(faht-tOOh-rah nah-tsyoh-nAh-leh)*	domestic bill
fattura pro forma	*(faht-tOOh-rah proh-fOhr-mah)*	pro forma invoice
fatturazione (f) a ciclo	*(faht-tooh-rah-tsyOh-neh ah chEEh-kloh)*	cycle billing
fedeltà (f) alla marca	*(feh-dehl-tAh ahl-lah mAhr-kah)*	brand loyalty
fenolo (m)	*(feh-nOh-loh)*	phenol
fermentare	*(fehr-mehn-tAh-reh)*	ferment (v)
fermentazione malolattica (f)	*(fehr-mehn-tah-tsyOh-neh mah-loh-lAht-teeh-kah)*	malolactic fermentation
ferramenta (f)	*(feh-rah-mEhn-tah)*	hardware
ferrite (f)	*(feh-rEEh-teh)*	ferrite
ferro (m)	*(fEhr-roh)*	iron
ferro (m) fuso	*(fEhr-roh fOOh-zoh)*	cast iron
ferro tondo	*(fEhr-roh tOhn-doh)*	rod
ferromanganese (m)	*(fehr-roh-mahn-gah-nEh-zeh)*	ferromanganese

F

ferronichel	*(feh-roh-nee-kel*	ferronickel
festività (f) legale	*(fehs-teeh-veeh-tAh leh-gAh-leh)*	bank holiday, legal holiday
fetta (f)	*(fEht-tah)*	tranche
fibra ottica (f)	*(fEEh-brah Oht-teeh-kah)*	fiber optic
fibre (f) artificiali, fibre sintetiche	*(fEEh-breh ahr-teeh-feeh-chAh-leeh), (fEEh-breh seehn-tEh-teeh-keh)*	man-made fibers
fidecommisso (m) vivente	*(feeh-deh-kohm-mEEhs-soh veeh-vEhn-teh)*	living trust
fiduciario (m)	*(feeh-dooh-chAh-reeh-oh)*	fiduciary
fiera (f) commerciale	*(fyEh-rah kohm-mehr-chAh-leh)*	fair trade
filamento (m)	*(feeh-lah-mEhn-toh)*	filament
filato (m)	*(feeh-lAh-toh)*	yarn
filiale (f)	*(feeh-lyAh-leh)*	affiliate, branch office, subsidiary
filo (m)	*(fEEh-loh)*	thread
filo (m) metallico	*(fEEh-loh meh-tAhl-leeh-koh)*	wire
filodiffusione (f)	*(feeh-loh-deehf-fooh-zyOh-neh)*	cable television
filtro (m)	*(fEEhl-troh)*	filter
filtro (m) dell'olio	*(fEEhl-troh dehl Oh-leeh-oh)*	oil filter
filtro dell'aria (m)	*(fEEhl-troh dehl Ah-reeh-ah)*	air filter
finalizzare	*(feeh-nah-leehds-dsAh-reh)*	finalize (v)
finanziamento (m) a breve termine	*(feeh-nahn-tsyah-mEhn-toh ah brEh-veh tEhr-meeh-neh)*	short-term financing
finanziamento anticipato	*(feeh-nahn-tsyah-mEhn-toh ahn-teeh-chee-pAh-toh)*	front-end financing
finanziare	*(feeh-nahn-tsyAh-reh)*	finance (v)
fine (f) del periodo	*(fEEh-neh dehl peh-rEEh-oh-doh)*	end of period
fine anno (m)	*(fEEh-neh Ahn-noh)*	year-end
firma (f)	*(fEEhr-mah)*	signature

F

firma autorizzata	*(fEEhr-mah ah-ooh-toh-reehds-dsAh-tah)*	authorized signature
fissare	*(feehs-sAh-reh)*	peg (v)
fissare due prezzi	*(feehs-sAh-reh dOOh-eh prEhts-tseeh)*	double pricing
fissare il prezzo	*(feehs-sAh-reh eehl prEhts-tsoh)*	fix the price (v)
flanella (f)	*(flah-nEhl-lah)*	flannel
flotta (f) privata	*(flOht-tah preeh-vAh-tah)*	private fleet
flusso (m) di cassa negativo	*(flOOhs-soh deeh kAhs-sah neh-gah-tEEh-voh)*	negative cash flow
flusso netto di cassa	*(flOOhs-soh nEht-toh deeh kAhs-sah)*	net cash flow
flute (m)	*(floot)*	champagne glass, flute
foderatura (f)	*(foh-deh-rah-tOOh-rah)*	lining
foglio (m)	*(fOh-lyoh)*	sheet
foglio (m) di dati	*(fOh-lyoh deeh dAh-teeh)*	fact sheet
foglio di revisione del bilancio contabile	*(fOh-lyoh deeh reh-veeh-zyOh-neh dehl beeh-lAhn-choh kohn-tAh-beeh-leh)*	auditing balance sheet
fonderia (f)	*(fohn-deh-rEEh-ah)*	foundry
fondi attivi	*(fOhn-deeh (aht-tEEh-veeh)*	working funds
fondi interni	*(fOhn-deeh eehn-tEhr-neeh)*	internal funding
fondi pubblici	*(fOhn-deeh pOOhb-leeh-cheeh)*	public funds
fondina (f)	*(fohn-dEEh-nah)*	holster
fondo (m)	*(fOhn-doh)*	fund
fondo ammortamento	*(fOhn-doh ahm-mohr-tah-mEhn-toh)*	accumulated depreciation
fondo comune d'investimento	*(fOhn-doh koh-mOOh-neh deehn-vehs-teeh-mEhn-toh)*	investment trust
fondo d'ammortamento per il ritiro di obbligazioni	*(fOhn-doh dahm-mohr-tah-mEhn-toh pehr-eehl reeh-tEEh-roh deeh ohb-bleeh-gah-tsyOh-neeh)*	sinking fund
fondo d'investimento	*(fOhn-doh deehn-vehs-teeh-mEhn-toh)*	active trust, mutual fund

F

fondo d'investimento fiduciario	(fOhn-doh deehn-vehs-teeh-mEhn-toh feeh-dooh-chAh-reeh-oh)	trust fund
fondo d'investimento fiduciario revocabile	(fOhn-doh deehn-vehs-teeh-mEhn-toh feeh-dooh-chAh-reeh-oh reh-voh-kAh-beeh-leh)	revocable trust
fondo d'investimento molto aggressivo	(fOhn-doh deehn-vehs-teeh-mEhn-toh mOhl-toh ahg-grehs-sEEh-voh)	go-go fund
fondo d'investimento rotativo	(fOhn-doh deehn-vehs-teeh-mEhn-toh roh-tah-tEEh-voh)	revolving fund
fondo d'investimento senza commissioni	(fOhn-doh deehn-vehs-teeh-mEhn-toh sEhn-tsah kohm-meehs-syOh-neeh)	no-load fund
fondo della stiva	(fOhn-doh dehl-lah stEEh-vah)	dunnage
fondo di ammortamento	(fOhn-doh deeh ahm-mohr-tah-mEhn-toh)	depreciation allowance
fondo di assicurazione	(fOhn-doh deeh ahs-seeh-kooh-rah-tsyOh-neh)	insurance fund
fondo di contingenza	(fOhn-doh deeh kohn-teehn-jEhn-tsah)	contingent fund
fondo di investimento redimibile	(fOhn-doh deehn-vehs-teeh-mEhn-toh reh-deeh-mEEh-beeh-leh)	redemption fund
fondo di previdenza	(fOhn-doh deeh prohv-veeh-dEhn-dsah)	contingent fund
fondo discrezionario	(fOhn-doh deehs-kreh-tsyoh-nAh-reeh-oh)	discretionary account
fondo monetario comune	(fOhn-doh moh-neh-tAh-reeh-oh koh-mOOh-neh)	pool (of funds)
fondo pensionistico	(fOhn-doh pehn-syoh-nEEhs-teeh-koh)	pension fund
fonte (f) attendibile	(fOhn-teh aht-tehn-dEEh-beeh-leh)	reliable source
forchetta (f)	(for-kEht-tah)	fork
forma (f)	(fOhr-mah)	form
formato (m)	(fohr-mAh-toh)	format
formula (f)	(fOhr-mooh-lah)	formula
fornace (f)	(fohr-nAh-cheh)	furnace

F

fornace per la colatura sotto vuoto	*(fohr-nAh-cheh pehr lah koht-tOOh-rah sOht-toh vwOh-toh)*	vacuum melting furnace
fornitore (m)	*(fohr-neeh-tOh-reh)*	supplier
forniture (f) carenti	*(fohr-neeh-tOOh-reh kah-rEhn-teeh)*	short supply
forniture oltre il necessario	*(fohr-neeh-tOOh-reh Ohl-treh eehl neh-chehs-sAh-reeh-oh)*	oversupply
forno (m) ad induzione	*(fOh-rnoh ad eehn-dooh-tsyOh-neh)*	induction furnace
forza (f) di lavoro	*(fOhr-tsah deeh lah-vOh-roh)*	workforce, labor force
forza (f) di torsione	*(fOhr-tsah deeh tohr-syOh-neh)*	torque
forza maggiore	*(fOhr-tsah mahj-jOh-reh)*	act of God
forze di mercato	*(fOhr-tseh deeh mehr-kAh-toh)*	market forces
fosfato (m)	*(fohs-fAh-toh)*	phosphate
fotolitografia (f)	*(foh-toh-leeh-toh-grah-fEEh-ah)*	offset printing
foulard (m)	*(phoo-lAhrd)*	scarf
franco fabbrica	*(frAhn-koh fAhb-breeh-kah)*	ex factory
franco magazzino	*(frAhn-koh mah-gahds-dsEEh-noh)*	ex warehouse
franco miniera	*(frAhn-koh meeh-nyEh-rah)*	ex mine
franco mulino	*(frAhn-koh mooh-lEEh-noh)*	ex mill
franco nave	*(frAhn-koh nAh-veh)*	ex ship
franco officina	*(frAhn-koh ohf-feeh-chEEh-nah)*	ex works
franco porto	*(frAhn-koh pOhr-toh)*	ex dock, free alongside ship
franco stazione ferroviaria	*(frAhn-koh stah-tsyOh-neh fehr-roh-vyAh-reeh-ah)*	free on rail
frazionamento (m) delle azioni	*(frah-tsyoh-nah-mEhn-toh dehl-leh ah-tsyOh-neeh)*	stock split
freno (m)	*(frEh-noh)*	brake
frequenza (f)	*(freh-kwEhn-tsah)*	frequency
fresatura (f)	*(freh-zah-tOOh-rah)*	milling

F

frizione (f)	*(freeh-tsyOh-neh)*	clutch
frode (f)	*(frOh-deh)*	fraud
frusta (f)	*(frOOhs-tah)*	whip
fruttato	*(frooht-tAh-toh)*	fruity
funzioni (f) di sostegno	*(foohn-tsyOh-neeh deeh sohs-tEh-nyoh)*	support activities
fuori moda	*(fwOh-reeh mOh-dah)*	out of style
fusione (f)	*(fooh-zyOh-neh)*	amalgamation, merger
fuso (m) orario	*(fOOh-zoh oh-rAh-ryoh)*	jet lag, time zone

G

gabardina (f)	*(gah-bahr-dEEh-nah)*	gabardine
galvanizzazione (f)	*(gahl-vah-neehds-dsah-tsyOh-neh)*	galvanizing
gamma (f) dei prezzi	*(gAhm-mah deh-eeh prEhts-tseeh)*	price range
gamma dei prodotti	*(gAhm-mah deeh proh-dOht-teeh)*	product line
garantire	*(gah-rahn-tEEh-reh)*	warrant (v)
garanzia (f)	*(gah-rahn-tsEEh-ah)*	guarantee, security, warranty
garanzia del posto di lavoro	*(gah-rahn-tsEEh-ah dehl pOhs-toh deeh lah-vOh-roh)*	job security
gas (m) naturale	*(gas nah-tooh-rAh-leh)*	natural gas
gascromatografia (f)	*(gas-kroh-mah-toh-grah-fEEh-ah)*	gas chromatography
gemello (m) da camicia	*(jeh-mEhl-loh dah kah-mEEh-chah)*	cuff link
generatore (m)	*(jeh-neh-rah-tOh-reh)*	generator
germanio (m)	*(jehr-mAh-neeh-oh)*	germanium
gestione (f) commerciale	*(jehs-tyOh-neh kohm-mehr-chAh-leh)*	business management
gestione del mercato	*(jehs-tyOh-neh dehl mehr-kAh-toh)*	market management

gestione del personale	*(jehs-tyOh-neh dehl pehr-soh-nAh-leh)*	personnel management
gestione del prodotto	*(jehs-tyOh-neh deeh oohn proh-dOht-toh)*	product management
gestione dell'ufficio	*(jehs-tyOh-neh dehl oohf-fEEh-choh)*	office management
gestione delle operazioni	*(jehs-tyOh-neh dehl-leh oh-peh-rah-tsyOh-neeh)*	operations management
gestione delle vendite	*(jehs-tyOh-neh dehl-leh vEhn-deeh-teh)*	sales management
gestione per obiettivi	*(jehs-tyOh-neh pehr oh-byeht-tEEh-veeh)*	management by objectives
ghisa (f)	*(gEEh-zah)*	pig iron
ghisa di prima fusione	*(gEEh-zah deeh prEEh-mah fooh-zyOh-neh)*	pig iron
ghisa di seconda fusione	*(gEEh-zah deeh seh-kOhn-dah fooh-zyOh-neh)*	cast iron
giacca (f) sportiva	*(jAhk-kah spohr-tEEh-vah)*	blazer
gigantografia (f)	*(jeeh-gahn-toh-grah-fEEh-ah),*	blowup
gilet (m)	*(jee-lEh)*	vest
gioiello (f)	*(joh-yEhl-loh)*	jewel
giornale (m)	*(johr-nAh-leh)*	journal
giornaliero (m)	*(johr-nah-lyEh-roh)*	daily
giorno (m) di liquidazione	*(jOhr-noh deeh leeh-kweeh-dah-tsyOh-neh)*	account day
giorno di vendita per azioni	*(jOhr-noh deeh vEhn-deeh-tah pehr ah-tsyOh-neeh)*	trade date
giorno festivo pagato	*(jOhr-noh fehs-tEEh-voh pah-gAh-toh)*	paid holiday
giorno lavorativo	*(jOhr-noh lah-voh-rah-tEEh-voh)*	work day
giratario (m)	*(jeeh-rah-fAh-reeh-oh)*	endorsee
girante (m)	*(jeeh-rAhn-teh)*	endorser
girata (f)	*(jeeh-rAh-tah)*	endorsement
girata d'accettazione qualificata	*(jeeh-rAh-tah dahcheht-tah-tsyOh-neh kwah-leeh-feeh-kAh-tah)*	qualified acceptance endorsement
girata di comodo	*(jeeh-rAh-tah deeh kOh-moh-doh)*	accommodation endorsement

giro (m) d'attività	*(jEEh-roh deeh aht-teeh-veeh-tAh)*	asset turnover
giro dell'inventario	*(jEEh-roh dehl eehn-vehn-tAh-reeh-oh)*	inventory turnover
giro delle azioni	*(jEEh-roh dehl-leh ah-tsyOh-neeh)*	stock turnover
giro delle vendite	*(jEEh-roh dehl-leh vEhn-deeh-teh)*	sales turnover
giubbotto (m) di pelle	*(joohb-bOht-toh deeh pEhl-leh)*	leather jacket
giubbotto di renna	*(joohb-bOht-toh deeh rEhn-nah)*	suede jacket
giudice (m)	*(jooh-dee-cheh)*	judge
giurisdizione (f)	*(jooh-reehz-deeh-tsyOh-neh)*	jurisdiction
giustificare	*(joohs-teeh-feeh-kAh-reh)*	justify (v)
giustizia (f)	*(joohs-tEEh-tsyah)*	equity
goccia (f)	*(gOhch-chah)*	drop
gonna (f)	*(gOhn-nah)*	skirt
governo (m)	*(goh-vEhr-noh)*	government
grado (m)	*(grAh-doh)*	degree
grafico (m)	*(grAh-feeh-koh)*	graph
grafico a barra	*(grAh-feeh-ko ah bAhr-rah)*	bar chart
grafico a fette	*(grAh-feeh-ko ah fEht-teh)*	pie chart
grammo (m)	*(grAhm-moh)*	gram
grammo molecola	*(grAhm-moh moh-lEh-koh-lah)*	mole
grana (f)	*(grAh-nah)*	grain (of something)
grande (m) magazzino	*(grAhn-deh mah-gahds-dsEEh-noh)*	department store
grande scala	*(grAhn-deh skAh-lah)*	large-scale
grano (m)	*(grAh-noh)*	grain (food)
granoturco (m)	*(grah-noh-tOOhr-koh)*	maize
grappolo d'uva (m)	*(grAhp-poh-loh dOOh-vah)*	grape bunch
gratifica (f)	*(grah-tEEh-feeh-kah)*	gratuity
gravame (m)	*(grah-vAh-meh)*	encumbrances (liens, liabilities)

G

grès (m)	*(grehs)*	stoneware
grezzo	*(grEhts-tsoh)*	crude
grossista (m)	*(grohs-sEEhs-tah)*	jobber, wholesaler
gruppo (m) amministrativo	*(grOOhp-poh ahm-meeh-neehs-trah-tEEh-voh)*	management group
gruppo di esperti	*(grOOhp-poh deeh ehs-pEhr-teeh)*	task force
gruppo di grandi magazzini	*(grOOhp-poh deeh grAhn-deeh mah-gahds-dsEEh-neeh)*	chain store group
gruppo di prodotti	*(grOOhp-poh deeh proh-dOht-teeh)*	product group
guadagni (m)	*(gwah-dAh-nyeeh)*	earnings
guadagni orari	*(gwah-dAh-nyeeh oh-rAh-reeh)*	hourly earnings
guadagni ritenuti	*(gwah-dAh-nyeeh reeh-teh-nOOh-teeh)*	retained earnings
guanti (m)	*(gwAhn-teeh)*	gloves
guerra (m) sui prezzi	*(gwEhr-rah sooh-eeh prEhts-tseeh)*	price war
guerra tariffaria	*(gwEhr-rah tah-reehf-fAh-reeh-ah)*	tariff war
guida (f)	*(gwEEh-dah)*	steering

H

---

hardware (m)		hardware (computer)

I

---

idrocarbonio (m)	*(eeh-droh-kahr-bOh-neeh-oh)*	hydrocarbon
idrolisi (f)	*(eeh-drOh-leeh-zeeh)*	hydrolysis
illegale	*(eehl-leh-gAh-leh)*	illegal
illustrazione (f)	*(eehl-loohs-trah-tsyOh-neh)*	illustration
imballaggio (m)	*(eehm-bahl-lAhj-joh)*	packaging

G

imballaggio utilizzante pellicole di plastica ristretta	*(eehm-bahl-lAhj-joh ooh-teeh-leehds-dsAhn-teh pehl-lEEh-koh-leh deeh plAhs-teeh-kah reehs-trEht-tah)*	shink-wrapping
imballo (m)	*(eehm-bAhl-loh)*	packing
imbottigliato all'origine	*(eehm-boht-teeh-lyAh-toh ahl oh-rEEh-jeeh-neh)*	estate bottled
imbottitura (f)	*(eehm-boht-teeh-tOOh-rah)*	stuffing
imitazione (f)	*(eeh-mah-tsyOh-neh)*	imitation
immagazzinaggio (m)	*(eehm-mah-gahds-dseeh-nAhj-joh)*	storage, serial storage
immagazzinaggio con accesso diretto	*(eehm-mah-gahds-dseeh-nAhj-joh kohn ahch-chEhs-soh)*	direct access storage
immagazzinaggio dei dati per il computer	*(eehm-mah-gahds-dseeh-nAhj-joh deh-eeh dAh-teeh pehr eehl computer)*	computer storage
immagine (f) aziendale	*(eehm-mAh-jeeh-neh ah-dsyehn-dAh-leh)*	corporate image
immagine della marca	*(eehm-mAh-jeeh-neh dehl-lah mAhr-kah)*	brand image
immobili (m)	*(eehm-mOh-beeh-leeh)*	real estate
immobilizzi (m) tecnici	*(eehm-moh-beeh-EEhts-tseeh)*	fixed assets
impaginazione (f)	*(eehm-pah-jeeh-nah-tsyOh-neh)*	pagination
impatto (m) dei profitti	*(eehm-pAht-toh deh-eeh proh-fEEht-teeh)*	profit impact
impatto sugli utili	*(eehm-pAht-toh sooh-lyeeh OOh-teeh-leeh)*	profit impact
impegni (m) attuali	*(eehm-pEh-nyeeh aht-twAh-leeh)*	current liabilities
impegno (m)	*(eehm-pEh-nyoh)*	commitment, covenant, pledge
impegno garantito	*(eehm-pEh-nyoh gah-rahn-tEEh-toh)*	secured liability
impegno senza garanzie	*(eehm-pEh-nyoh sEhn-tsah gah-rahn-tsEEh-ah)*	unsecured liability
impermeabile (m)	*(eehm-pehr-meh-Ah-beeh-leh)*	raincoat

I

impianti (m)	*(eehm-pyAhn-teeh)*	facilities
impianti e macchinari	*(eehm-pyAhn-teeh eh mahk-keeh-nAh-reeh)*	equipment
impianti fissi	*(eehm-pyAhn-teeh fEEhs-seeh)*	fixtures (on balance sheet)
impiegato (m)	*(eehm-pyeh-gAh-toh)*	employee, white-collar worker
impiegato in fase d'addestramento	*(eehm-pyeh-gAh-toh eehn fAh-zeh dahd-dehs-trah-mEhn-toh)*	trainee
implicazione (f)	*(eehm-pleeh-kah-tsyOh-neh)*	implication
imporre tasse	*(eehm-pOhr-reh tAhs-seh)*	levy taxes (v)
importare	*(eehm-pohr-tAh-reh)*	import (v)
importatore/trice (m/f) registrato	*(eehm-pohr-tah-tOh-reh)*	importer of record
importazione (f)	*(eehm-pohr-tah-tsyOh-neh)*	import
importo (m) fisso	*(eehm-pOhr-toh fEEhs-soh)*	flat rate
imposta (f)	*(eehm-pOhs-tah)*	tax
imposta aziendale	*(eehm-pOhs-tah ah-dsyehn-dAh-leh)*	corporation tax
imposta d'esportazione	*(eehm-pOhs-tah dehs-pohr-tah-tsyOh-neh)*	export tax
imposta d'importazione	*(eehm-pOhs-tah deehm-pohr-tah-tsyOh-neh)*	import tax
imposta di successione	*(eehm-pOhs-tah deeh soohch-chehs-syOh-neh)*	inheritance tax
imposta fondiaria	*(eehm-pOhs-tah fohn-dyAh-reeh-ah)*	land tax
imposta indiretta	*(eehm-pOhs-tah eehn-deeh-rEht-tah)*	indirect tax
imposta patrimoniale	*(eehm-pOhs-tah pah-treeh-moh-nyAh-leh)*	estate tax
imposta regressiva	*(eehm-pOhs-tah reh-grehs-sEEh-vah)*	regressive tax
imposta ritenuta alla fonte	*(eehm-pOhs-tah reeh-teh-nOOh-tah ahl-lah fOhn-teh)*	withholding tax
imposta specifica	*(eehm-pOhs-tah speh-chEEh-feeh-kah)*	specific duty

I

imposta sui beni voluttari	*(eehm-pOhs-tah sooh-eeh bEh-neeh voh-looht-tAh-reeh)*	luxury tax
imposta sui consumi	*(eehm-pOhs-tah sooh-eeh kohn-sOOh-meeh)*	excise tax, excise duty
imposta sui salari	*(eehm-pOhs-tah sooh-eeh sah-lAh-reeh)*	payroll tax
imposta sul consumo	*(eehm-pOhs-tah soohl kohn-sOOh-moh)*	use tax
imposta sul reddito delle persone fisiche (IRPEF)	*(eehm-pohs-tah-tsyOh-neh doohl rEhd-deeh-toh dehl-leh pehr-sOh-neh fEEh-zeeh-keh)*	personal income tax
imposta sul reddito delle persone giuridiche (IRPEG)	*(eehm-pohs-tah-tsyOh-neh doohl rEhd-deeh-toh dehl-leh pehr-sOh-neh jooh-rEEh-deeh-keh)*	corporate income tax
imposta sul valore aggiunto (IVA)	*(eehm-pOhs-tah soohl vah-lOh-reh ahj-jOOhn-toh)*	value-added tax
imposta sulla vendita al dettaglio	*(eehm-pOhs-tah soohl-lah vEhn-deeh-tah ahl-deht-tAh-lyoh)*	retail sales tax
imposta sulle vendite	*(eehm-pOhs-tah soohl-leh vEhn-deeh-teh)*	sales tax
imposta variabile	*(eehm-pOhs-tah vah-ryAh-beeh-leh)*	flexible tariff
imposta variabile di importazione	*(eehm-pOhs-tah vah-ryAh-beeh-leh deeh eehm-pohr-tah-tsyOh-neh)*	variable import levy
imposte arretrate	*(eehm-pOhs-teh ahr-reh-trAh-teh)*	back taxes
imposte indirette	*(eehm-pOhs-teh eehn-deeh-rEht-teh)*	internal revenue tax
imposte locali	*(eehm-pOhs-teh loh-kAh-leeh)*	local taxes
imprenditore/trice (m/f)	*(eehm-prehn-deeh-tOh-reh)*	entrepreneur
impresa (f)	*(eehm-prEh-zah)*	enterprise
impurezza (f)	*(eehm-pooh-rEhts-tsah)*	impurity
imputato (m)	*(eehm-pooh-tAh-toh)*	imputed
in base alla disponibilità	*(eehn bAh-zeh ahl-lah deehs-poh-neeh-beeh-leeh-tAh)*	availability, subject to

in brossura	*(eehn brohs-sOOh-rah)*	paperback
in contanti	*(eehn kohn-tAhn-teeh)*	cash basis
in conto	*(eehn kOhn-toh)*	on account
in ogni caso	*(eehn Oh-nyeeh kAh-zoh)*	down the line
in passivo	*(eehn pahs-sEEh-voh)*	in the red
in stampa	*(eehn stAhm-pah)*	on press
in transito	*(eehn trAhn-zeeh-toh)*	in transit
inadeguato	*(eehn -ah-deh-gwAh-toh)*	inadequate
inattivo	*(eehn -aht-tEEh-voh)*	off-line
inattuabile	*(eehn -aht-twAh-beeh-leh)*	unfeasible
incentivo (m)	*(eehn -chehn-tEEh-voh)*	incentive
incentivo finanziario	*(eehn -chehn-tEEh-voh feeh-nahn-tsyAh-reeh-oh)*	financial incentive
inchiostro (m)	*(eehn-kyOhs-troh)*	ink
incidente (m) industriale	*(eehn-cheeh-dEhn-teh eehn-doohs-tryAh-leh)*	industrial accident
incidere	*(eehn-chEEh-deh-reh)*	engrave (v)
incidere	*(eehn-chEEh-deh-reh)*	record (v)
incitazione (f) alla discordia	*(eehn-cheeh-tah-tsyOh-neh ahl-lah deehs-kOhr-dyah)*	barratry
incorporare	*(eehn-kohr-poh-rAh-reh)*	incorporate (v)
incrementare	*(eehn-kreh-mehn-tAh-reh)*	increase (v)
incremento (m)	*(eehn-kreh-mEhn-toh)*	increase
incrostatura (f)	*(eehn-krohs-tah-tOOh-rah)*	scale
indagine (f) di mercato	*(eehn-dAh-jeeh-neh deeh mehr-kAh-toh)*	market survey
indebitamento (m)	*(eehn-deh-beeh-tah-mEhn-toh)*	indebtedness
indennità (f)	*(eehn-dehn-neeh-tAh)*	indemnity
indicatore (m) di velocità	*(eehn-deeh-kah-tOh-reh deeh veh-loh-cheeh-tAh)*	speedometer
indicatore (m) in ritardo	*(eehn-deeh-kah-tOh-reh)*	lagging indicator
indicatore principale	*(eehn-deeh-kah-tOh-reh preehn-ceeh-pAh-leh)*	leading indicator
indicatori economici	*(eehn-deeh-kah-tOh-reeh eh-koh-nOh-meeh-cheeh)*	economic indicators

I

indice (m)	(EEhn-deeh-cheh)	index (indicator), table of contents
indice (m)	(EEhn-deeh-cheh)	table of contents
indice composto	(EEhn-deeh-cheh kohm-pOhs-toh)	composite index
indice dei prezzi	(EEhn-deeh-cheh deh-eeh prEhts-tseeh)	price index
indice dei prezzi al consumo	(EEhn-deeh-cheh deh-eeh prEhts-tseeh ahl kohn-sOOh-moh)	consumer price index
indice della borsa	(EEhn-deeh-cheh dehl-lah bOhr-sah)	stock index
indice delle opzioni	(EEhn-deeh-cheh dehl-leh ohp-tsyOh-neeh)	option index
indice di crescita	(EEhn-deeh-cheh deeh krEh-sheeh-tah)	growth index
indice di mercato	(EEhn-deeh-cheh deeh mehr-kAh-toh)	market index
indici di bilancio	(EEhn-deeh-cheeh deeh beeh-lAhn-choh)	balance ratios
indicizzare	(eehn-deeh-cheehds-dsAh-reh)	index (v)
indicizzazione (f)	(eehn-deeh-cheehds-dsah-tsyOh-neh)	indexing
industria (f)	(eehn-dOOhs-tryah)	industry
industria che dipende molto dal fattore della manodopera	(eehn-dOOhs-tryah keh deeh-pEhn-deh mOhl-toh dahl faht-tOh-reh dehl-lah mah-noh-dOh-peh-rah)	labor-intensive industry
industria di mercato libero	(eehn-dOOhs-treeh-ah deeh mehr-kAh-toh lEEh-beh-roh)	free market industry
industria in fase di crescita	(eehn-dOOhs-tryah eehn fAh-zeh deeh krEh-scheeh-tah)	growth industry
industria nascente	(eehn-dOOhs-tryah nah-shEhn-teh)	infant industry
industria pesante	(eehn-dOOhs-tryah peh-zAhn-teh)	heavy industry
induzione (f)	(eehn-dooh-tsyOh-neh)	induction
inefficiente	(eehn-ehf-feeh-chEhn-teh)	inefficient

I

inflazione (f)	*(eehn-flah-tsyOh-neh)*	inflation
inflazionistico	*(eehn-flah-tsyoh-nEEhs-teeh-koh)*	inflationary
influenzare	*(eehn-flooh-ehn-tsAh-reh)*	impact, have an...on (v)
informazione (f) riservata	*(eehn-fohr-mah-tsyOh-neh reeh-zehr-vAh-tah)*	tip (inside information)
infrastruttura (f)	*(eehn-frah-strooht-tOOh-rah)*	infrastructure
infusione (f) di fondi da nuove fonti	*(eehn-fooh-zyOh-neh deeh fOhn-deeh dah nwOh-veh fOhn-teeh)*	new money
ingannevole	*(eehn-gahn-nEh-voh-leh)*	misleading
inganno (m)	*(eehn-gAhn-noh)*	double dealing
ingegnere (m)	*(eehn-jeh-nyEh-reh)*	engineer
ingegneria (f)	*(eehn-jeh-nyeh-rEEh-ah)*	engineering
ingegneria civile	*(eehn-jeh-nyeh-rEEh-ah cheeh-vEEh-leh)*	civil engineering
ingegneria elettrica	*(eehn-jeh-nyeh-rEEh-ah eh-lEht-treeh-kah)*	electrical engineering
ingegneria industriale	*(eehn-jeh-nyeh-rEEh-ah eehn-doohs-tryAh-leh)*	industrial engineering
ingegneria meccanica	*(eehn-jeh-nyeh-rEEh-ah mehk-kAh-neeh-kah)*	mechanical engineering
ingiunzione (f)	*(eehn-joohn-tsyOh-neh)*	injunction
ingranaggio (f)	*(eehn-grah-nAhj-joh)*	gearing
ingrandimento (m)	*(eehn-grahn-deeh-mEhn-toh)*	blowup
ingrandire	*(eehn-grahn-dEEh-reh)*	enlarge (v)
iniettore (m)	*(eeh-nyeht-tOh-reh)*	injector
iniezione (f)	*(eeh-nyeh-tsyOh-neh)*	injection
iniziare un'azione reciproca	*(eehn- oohn ah-tsyOh-neh reh-chEEh-proh-kah)*	interact (v)
innalzamento (m) dei capitali	*(eehn-nahl-tsah-mEhn-toh deh-eeh kah-peeh-tAh-leeh)*	raising capital
innesto (m) acustico	*(eehn-nEhs-toh ah-kOOhs-teeh-koh)*	acoustic coupler
innovazione (f)	*(eehn-noh-vah-tzee-Oh-ne)*	innovation

I

insediamento (f)	*(eeh-seh-dyah-mEhn-toh)*	takeover
insediamento tramite acquisto del controllo azionario	*(eehn-seh-dyah-mEhn-toh trAh-meeh-teh ahk-kwEEhs-toh dehl kohn-trOhl-loh ah-tsyoh-nAh-reeh-oh)*	stock takeover
insolvente	*(eehn-sohl-vEhn-teh)*	insolvent
instabilità (f)	*(eehn-stah-beeh-leeh-tAh)*	instability
insulina (f)	*(eehn-sooh-lEEh-nah)*	insulin
intangibili (m)	*(eehn-tahn-jEEh-beeh-leeh)*	invisibles
integrazione (f) verticale	*(eehn-teh-grah-tsyOh-neh vehr-teeh-kAh-leh)*	vertical integration
intenzione	*(eehn-tehn-see-Oh-neh)*	intention
interbanca	*(eehn-tehr-bAhn-kah)*	interbank
interesse (m)	*(eehn-teh-rEhs-seh)*	interest
interesse composto	*(eehn-teh-rEhs-seh kohm-pOhs-toh)*	compound interest
interesse del proprietario	*(eehn-teh-rEhs-seh dehl proh-pryeh-tAh-reeh-oh)*	owner's equity
interesse lungo	*(eehn-teh-rEhs-seh lOOhn-goh)*	long interest
interesse maggioritario	*(eehn-teh-rEhs-seh mahj-joh-reeh-tAh-reeh-oh)*	controlling interest, majority interest
interesse maturato	*(eehn-teh-rEhs-seh mah-tooh-rAh-toh)*	accrued interest
interesse minoritario	*(eehn-teh-rEhs-seh meeh-noh-reeh-tAh-reeh-oh)*	minority interest
interessi acquisiti	*(eehn-teh-rEhs-seeh ahk-kweeh-zEEh-teeh)*	vested interests
interessi in comune	*(eehn-teh-rEhs-seeh eehn koh-mOOh-neh)*	pooling of interests
interessi incipienti	*(eehn-teh-rEhs-seh eehn-chee-pyEhn-teeh)*	inchoate interest
interface (m)	*(intehrfahys)*	interface
intermediario (m)	*(eehn-tehr-meh-dyAh-reeh-oh)*	broker, intermediary, middleman
intermediario di obbligazioni	*(eehn-tehr-meh-dyAh-reeh-oh deeh ohb-bleeh-gah-tsyOh-neeh)*	bill broker

intermediario per l'esportazione	*(eehn-tehr-meh-dyAh-reeh-oh pehr lehs-pohr-tah-tsyOh-neh)*	export middleman
intermediario valutario	*(eehn-tehr-meh-dyAh-reeh-oh vah-looh-tAh-reeh-oh)*	money broker
interno	*(eehn-tEhr-noh)*	internal
interruttore (m)	*(eehn-tehr-rooht-tOh-reh)*	switch
intervallo (m) (per caffè)	*(eehn-tehr-vAhl-loh pehr kahf-fEh)*	coffee break
intervallo tra progettazione e produzione	*(eehn-tehr-vAhl-loh trah proh-jeht-tah-tsyOh-neh eh proh-dooh-tsyOh-neh)*	lead time
intervenire	*(eehn-tehr-veh-nEEh-reh)*	intervene (v)
intervista (f)	*(eehn-tehr-vEEhs-tah)*	interview
intraprendere	*(eehn-trah-prEhn-deh-reh)*	undertake (v)
introdurre	*(eehn-troh-dOOhr-reh)*	phase in (v)
introito (m)	*(eehn-trOy-toh)*	income, revenue
introito rettificato	*(eehn-trOy-toh reht-teeh-feeh-kAh-toh)*	adjusted earned income
invalidare	*(eehn-vah-leeh-dAh-reh)*	invalidate (v)
invalido	*(eehn-vAh-leeh-doh)*	void
invecchiamento (m)	*(eehn-vehk-kyah-mEhn-toh)*	aging
inventario (m)	*(eehn-vehn-tAh-reeh-oh)*	inventory
inventario contabile	*(eehn-vehn-tAh-reeh-oh kohn-tAh-beeh-leh)*	book inventory
inventario dei beni finiti	*(eehn-vehn-tAh-reeh-oh deh-eeh bEh-neeh feeh-nEEh-teeh)*	finished goods inventory
inventario fisico	*(eehn-vehn-tAh-reeh-oh fEEh-zeeh-koh)*	physical inventory
inventario periodico	*(eehn-vehn-tAh-reeh-oh peh-ryOh-deeh-koh)*	periodic inventory
inventario perpetuo	*(eehn-vehn-tAh-reeh-oh pehr-pEh-twoh)*	perpetual inventory
inventario registrato	*(eehn-vehn-tAh-reeh-oh reh-jeehs-trAh-toh)*	book inventory
investimenti (m) azionari	*(eehn-vehs-teeh-mEhn-teeh ah-tsyoh-nAh-reeh)*	equity investments
investimento (m)	*(eehn-vehs-teeh-mEhn-toh)*	investment

I

investimento capitale	*(eehn-vehs-teeh-mEhn-toh kah-peeh-tAh-leh)*	capital expenditure
investimento costante	*(eehn-vehs-teeh-mEhn-toh kohs-tAhn-teh)*	fixed investment
investimento di fondi per iniziare l'attività	*(eehn-vehs-teeh-mEhn-toh deeh fOhn-deeh pehr eehn-eeh-tsyAh-reh laht-teeh-veeh-tAh)*	pump priming
investimento di protezione a lunga scadenza	*(eehn-vehs-teeh-mEhn-toh deeh proh-teh-tsyOh-neh ah lOOhn-gah skah-dEhn-tsah)*	long hedge
investimento diretto	*(eehn-vehs-teeh-mEhn-toh deeh-rEht-toh)*	direct investment
investimento lordo	*(eehn-vehs-teeh-mEhn-toh lOhr-doh)*	gross investment
investimento netto	*(eehn-vehs-teeh-mEhn-toh nEht-toh)*	net investment
investimento reale	*(eehn-vehs-teeh-mEhn-toh reh-Ah-leh)*	real investment
investire	*(eehn-vehs-tEEh-reh)*	invest (v)
investitore/trice (m/f) istituzionale	*(eehn-vehs-teeh-tOh-reh)*	institutional investor
invio (m)	*(eehn-vEEh-oh)*	dispatch
iodio (m)	*(yOh-deeh-oh)*	iodine
ipertensione (f)	*(eeh-pehr-tehn-syOh-neh)*	hypertension
ipoteca (f)	*(eeh-poh-tEh-kah)*	mortgage, purchase money mortgage
ipoteca con tasso d'interesse variabile	*(eeh-poh-tEh-kah kohn tAhs-soh deehn-teh-rEhs-seh vah-ryAh-beeh-leh)*	variable rate mortgage
ipoteca secondaria	*(eeh-poh-tEh-kah seh-kohn-dAh-reeh-ah)*	second mortgage
ipoteca su beni mobili	*(eeh-poh-tEh-kah sooh bEh-neeh mOh-beeh-leeh)*	chattel mortgage
ipotecare (v)	*(eeh-poh-teh-kAh-reh)*	hypothecate
isolante (m)	*(eeh-zoh-lAhn-teh)*	insulator
isotopo (m)	*(eeh-zOh-toh-poh)*	isotope
ispettore/trice (m/f)	*(eehs-peht-tOh-reh)*	inspector
ispezione (f)	*(eehs-peh-tsyOh-neh)*	inspection

ispezione a voce	*(eehs-peh-tsyOh-neh ah vOh-cheh)*	voiced check
istruire	*(eehs-trooh-EEh-reh)*	instruct (v)
istruzione (f) in gruppo	*(eehs-trooh-tsyOh-neh eehn grOOhp-poh)*	group training
istruzione reciproca	*(eehs-trooh-tsyOh-neh reh-chEEh-proh-kah)*	reciprocal training
istruzione sul posto di lavoro	*(eehs-trooh-tsyOh-neh soohl pOhs-toh deeh lah-vOh-roh)*	on-the-job training
istruzioni (f) per il trasporto	*(eehs-trooh-tsyOh-neeh pehr eehl trahs-pOhr-toh)*	shipping instructions

---

J

joint venture (m)	*(johynt ventchuhr)*	joint venture

K

kilowatt (m)	*(kilohwaht)*	kilowatt

L

laboratorio (m)	*(lah-boh-rah-tOh-reeh-oh)*	laboratory
laboratorio (m)	*(lah-boh-rah-tOh-reeh-oh)*	workshop
laissez-faire	*(leh-sEh fehr)*	laissez-faire
lamiera (f)	*(lah-myEh-rah)*	plate
laminatoio (m)	*(lah-meeh-nah-tOh-yoh)*	rolling mill
laminatoio finitore	*(lah-meeh-nah-tO-yoh feeh-neeh-tOh-reh)*	finishing mill
laminatura a caldo (f)	*(lah-meeh-nah-tOOh-rah ah kAhl-doh)*	hot rolling
laminatura a freddo	*(lah-meeh-nah-tOOh-rah ah frEhd-doh)*	cold rolling
lana (f)	*(lAh-nah)*	wool
lana d'angora	*(lAh-nah Ahn-goh-rah)*	angora

I

lanciare (una nuova impresa)	*(lahn-chAh-reh ooh-nah nwOh-vah eehm-prEh-zah)*	float (v) (issue stock)
lanciare un nuovo prodotto sulla base di un altro prodotto	*(lahn-chAh-reh oohn nwOh-voh proh-dOht-toh soohl-lah bAh-zeh deeh oohn Ahl-troh proh-dOht-toh)*	spin-off (v)
larghezza (f)	*(lahr-gEhts-tsah)*	width
lasciare una certa somma di fondi nel conto corrente presso la istituzione	*(lah-shAh-reh ooh-nah chEhr-tah deeh fOhn-deeh nehl kOhn-toh kohr-rEhn-teh prEhs-soh lah eehs-teeh-tooh-tsyOh-neh)*	compensating balance
lascito (m)	*(lAh-sheeh-toh)*	bequest
laser (m)	*(layzuhr)*	laser
lassativo (m)	*(lahs-sah-tEEh-voh)*	laxative
lastre (f)	*(lAhs-treh)*	sheets
lavorare	*(lah-voh-rAh-reh)*	process (v), work (v)
lavorare per conto proprio	*(lah-voh-rAh-reh pehr kOhn-toh prOh-preeh-oh)*	self-employed, be (v)
lavoratore (m)	*(lah-voh-rah-tOh-reh)*	laborer
lavoratore a cottimo (m)	*(lah-voh-rah-tOh-reh ah kOht-teeh-moh)*	jobber
lavorazione (f) su commessa	*(lah-voh-rah-tsyOh-neh sooh kohm-mEhs-sah)*	rack jobber
lavori (m) pubblici	*(lah-vOh-reeh pOOhb-leeh-cheeh)*	public works
lavoro (m)	*(lah-vOh-roh)*	job, labor
lavoro a cottimo	*(lah-vOh-roh ah kOht-teeh-moh)*	piecework
lavoro in corso	*(lah-vOh-roh eehn kOhr-soh)*	work in progress
lavoro indiretto	*(lah-vOh-roh eehn-deeh-rEht-toh)*	indirect labor
lavoro manuale	*(lah-vOh-roh mah-nwAh-leh)*	unskilled labor
lavoro nero	*(lah-vOh-roh nEh-roh)*	moonlighting

lavoro per contratto	*(lah-vOh-roh pehr kohn-trAht-toh)*	work on contract
lavoro straordinario	*(lah-vOh-roh strah-ohr-deeh-nAh-reeh-oh)*	overtime
lavoro straordinario pagato il doppio	*(lah-vOh-roh strah-ohr-deeh-nAh-reeh-oh pah-gAh-toh eehl dOhp-pyoh)*	double time
lega d'acciaio (f)	*(lEh-gah dahch-chAh-yoh)*	alloy steel
legame (m)	*(leh-gAh-meh)*	liaison
legato con un contratto	*(leh-gAh-toh kohn oohn kohn-trAht-toh)*	indentured
legatura cartonata (f)	*(leh-gah-tOOh-rah kahr-toh-nAh-tah)*	hardcover
legge (f)	*(lEhj-jeh)*	law
legge dei rendimenti decrescenti	*(lEhj-jeh deh-eeh rehn-deeh-mEhn-teeh deh-kreh-shEhn-teeh)*	law of diminishing returns
legge mercantile	*(lEhj-jeh mehr-kah-ntEEh-leh)*	mercantile law
legge sui brevetti	*(lEhj-jeh sooh-eeh breh-vEht-teeh)*	patent law
leggi anti-monopolistiche	*(lEhj-jeeh ahn-teeh-moh-noh-poh-lEEhs-teeh-keh)*	antitrust laws
leghe (f) di ferro	*(lEh-geh deeh fEhr-roh)*	ferroalloys
legittimo (m)	*(leeh-gEE-teeh-moh)*	legitimate
lettera (f)	*(lEht-teh-rah)*	letter
lettera d'indennità	*(lEht-teh-rah deehn-dehn-neeh-tAh)*	letter of indemnity
lettera d'investimento	*(lEht-teh-rah deehn-vehs-teeh-mEhn-toh)*	investment letter
lettera di accompagna-mento	*(lEht-teh-rah dahk-kohm-pah-nyah-mEhn-toh)*	cover letter
lettera di credito	*(lEht-teh-rah deeh krEh-deeh-toh)*	letter of credit
lettera di credito bancaria	*(lEht-teh-rah deeh krEh-deeh-toh bahn-kAh-reeh-ah)*	bank letter of credit
lettera di credito rotativa	*(lEht-teh-rah deeh krEh-deeh-toh roh-tah-tEEh-vah)*	revolving letter of credit

lettera di garanzia	*(lEht-teh-rah deeh gah-rahn-tsEEh-ah)*	letter of guaranty
lettera di presentazione	*(lEht-teh-rah deeh preh-zehn-tah-tsyOh-neh)*	letter of introduction
lettera di ripartizione	*(lEht-teh-rah deeh reeh-pahr-teeh-tsyOh-neh)*	allotment letter
lettera di vettura	*(lEht-teh-rah deeh veht-tOOh-rah)*	waybill
lettera tipo, lettera "standard"	*(lEht-teh-rah tEEh-poh)*	form letter
liberismo (m) economico	*(leeh-beh-rEEhz-moh eh-koh-nOh-meeh-koh)*	free enterprise
libero da medie particolari	*(lEEh-beh-roh dah mEh-dyeh pahr-teeh-koh-lAh-reeh)*	free of particular average
libero professionista (m/f)	*(lEEh-beh-roh proh-fehs-syoh-nEEhs-tah)*	freelancer
libretto (m) di deposito bancario	*(leeh-brEht-toh deeh deh-pOh-zeeh-toh bahn-kAh-reeh-oh)*	passbook
libro (m)	*(lEEh-broh)*	book
libro (m) cassa	*(lEEh-broh deeh kAhs-sah)*	cash book
libro mastro	*(lEEh-broh mAhs-troh)*	ledger
libro paga	*(lEEh-broh pAh-gah)*	payroll
licenza (f)	*(leeh-chEhn-tsah)*	leave of absence, license
licenza di importazione	*leeh-chEhn-tsah deehm-pohr-tah-tsyOh-neh)*	import license
licenze accavallate	*leeh-chEhn-tseh ahk-kah-vahl-lAh-teh)*	cross-licensing
licenziamento (m)	*(leeh-chehn-tsyah-mEhn-toh)*	lay-off
licenziare	*(leeh-chehn-tsyAh-reh)*	fire (v)
licenziatario (m)	*(leeh-chehn-tsyah-tAh-reeh-oh)*	dealership
lievito (f)	*(lyEh-veeh-toh)*	yeast
limite (m) di perdita	*(lEEh-meeh-teh deeh pEhr-deeh-tah)*	position limit

limite generalmente giornaliero dell'aumento o decremento dei valori	*(lEEh-meeh-teh jeh-neh-rahl-mEhn-teh johr-nah-lyAh-roh dehl ah-ooh-mEhn-toh oh deh-kreh-mEhn-toh deh-eeh vah-lOh-reeh)*	trading limit
lince (m)	*(lEEhn-cheh)*	lynx
Linea Internazionale di Demarcazione (dove il giorno cambia)	*(leeh-nah-ah eehn-tehr-nah-tsyoh-nAh-leh deeh deh-mahr-kah-tsyOh-neh/dOh-veh eehl jOhr-noh kAhm-byah)*	International Date Line
linea (f)	*(lEEh-neh-ah)*	line
linea (f) campionaria	*(lEEh-neh-ah kahm-pyoh-nAh-reeh-ah)*	sample line
linea di credito	*(lEEh-neh-ah deeh krEh-deeh-toh)*	credit line
linea di credito a richiesta	*(lEEh-neh-ah deeh krEh-deeh-toh ah reeh-kyEhs-tah)*	demand line of credit
linea di montaggio	*(lEEh-neh-ah deeh mohn-tAhj-joh)*	assembly line
linea di picchettaggio	*(lEEh-neh-ah deeh peehk-keh-tAh-joh)*	picket line
linea di produzione	*(lEEh-neh-ah deeh proh-dooh-tsyOh-neh)*	production line
lineare	*(leeh-neh-Ah-reh)*	linear
lingotti (m)	*(leehn-gOht-teeh)*	ingots
lingottiera (f)	*(leehn-goht-tyEh-rah)*	ingot mold
linguaggio (m) algoritmico	*(leehn-gwAhj-joh ahl-goh-rEEht-meeh-koh)*	algorithmic language
linguaggio per elaboratori elettronici	*(leehn-gwAhj-joh pehr eh-lah-boh-rah-tOh-reeh eh-leht-trOh-neeh-cheeh)*	computer language
lino (m) grezzo	*(lEEh-noh grEhts-tsoh)*	unbleached linen
liquidare	*(leeh-kweeh-dAh-reh)*	remainder (v)
liquidazione (f)	*(leeh-kweeh-dah-tsyOh-neh)*	liquidation
liquidazione dei conti	*(leeh-kweeh-dah-tsyOh-neh deh-eeh kOhn-teeh)*	payoff
liquidita (f)	*(leeh-kweeh-deeh-tAh)*	liquidity, solvency
liquore (m)	*(leeh-kwOh-reh)*	liqueur

lista (f) di controllo	*(lEEhs-tah)*	checklist
listino (m) d'imballaggio	*(leehs-tEEh-noh)*	packing list
listino di spese rimborsabili	*(leehs-tEEh-noh deeh spEh-zeh reehm-bohr-sAh-beeh-leeh)*	expense account
listino prezzi	*(leehs-tEEh-noh prEhts-tseeh)*	price list
lite (f)	*(lEEh-teh)*	litigation
litro (m)	*(lEEh-troh)*	liter
livellare	*(leeh-vehl-lAh-reh)*	level out (v)
livello (m) commerciale	*(leeh-vEhl-loh kohm-mehr-chAh-leh)*	commercial grade
livello d'utilizzo della capacità produttiva	*(leeh-vEhl-loh dooh-teeh-lEEhds-dsoh dehl-lah kah-pah-cheeh-tAh proh-dooht-tEEh-vah)*	capacity, utilization
livello di qualità per investimenti	*(leeh-vEhl-loh deeh kwah-leeh-tAh pehr eehn-vehs-teeh-mEhn-teeh)*	investment grade
livello di qualità accettabile	*(leeh-vEhl-loh deeh kwah-leeh-tAh ahch-cheht-tAh-beeh-leh)*	acceptable quality level
livello di reddito	*(leeh-vEhl-loh deeh rEhd-deeh-toh)*	income bracket
livello salariale	*(leeh-vEhl-loh sah-lah-ryAh-leh)*	wage level
localizzazione (f) degli impianti	*(loh-kah-leehds-dsah-tsyOh-neh deh-lyeeh eehm-pyAhn-teeh)*	plant location
locatario (m)	*(loh-kah-tAh-reeh-oh)*	lessee
locatore/trice (m/f)	*(loh-kah-tOh-reh/trEE-che)*	lessor
logistica (f)	*(loh-jEEhs-teeh-kah)*	logistics
lontra (f)	*(lOhn-trah)*	otter
lotto (m)	*(lOht-toh)*	lot
lucido	*(lOOh-cheeh-doh)*	glossy
lunghezza (f)	*(loohn-gEhts-tsah)*	length

M

macchina (f)	*(mAhk-keeh-nah)*	car
macchina (f) da cucire	*(mAhk-keeh-nah dah kooh-chEEh-reh)*	sewing machine
macchina (f) da stampa offset a bobina	*(mAhk-keeh-nah dah stAhm-pah offset ah boh-bEEh-nah)*	web offset press
macchinari (m)	*(mahk-keeh-nAh-reeh)*	machinery
macinapepe (m)	*(mAh-cheeh-nah pEh-peh)*	pepper mill
macinatura (f)	*(mah-cheeh-nah-tOOh-rah)*	milling
macroeconomia (f)	*(mah-kroh-eh-koh-noh-mEEh-ah)*	macroeconomics
magazziniere (m)	*(mah-gahds-dseeh-nyEh-reh)*	warehouseman
magazzino (m)	*(mah-gahds-dsEEh-noh)*	warehouse
magazzino commerciale nell'estremo oriente	*(mah-gahds-dsEEh-noh kohm-mehr-chAh-leh nehl ehs-trEh-moh oh-ryEhn-teh)*	godown
magazzino doganale	*(mah-gahds-dsEEh-noh doh-gah-nAh-leh)*	bonded warehouse
magazzino regolare	*(mah-gahds-dsEEh-noh reh-goh-lAh-reh)*	regular warehouse
maglione (m)	*(mah-lyOh-neh)*	sweater
mais (m)	*(mah-EEhs)*	maize
malattia (f)	*(mah-laht-tEEh-ah)*	disease
malinteso	*(mah-leehn-tEh-zoh)*	misunderstanding
malleabilità (f)	*(mah-leh-ah-beeh-leeh-tAh)*	malleability
mancanza (f)	*(mahn-kAhn-tsah)*	shortage
mancare	*(mahn-kAh-reh)*	short of, to be (v)
mandato (m)	*(mahn-dAh-toh)*	mandate, writ
manica (f)	*(mAh-neeh-kah)*	sleeve
maniche (f) corte	*(mAh-neeh-keh kOhr-teh)*	short sleeves
maniche lunghe	*(mAh-neeh-keh lOOhn-geh)*	long sleeves
maniera (f)	*(mah-nyEh-rah)*	mode
manifesto (m)	*(mah-neeh-fEhs-toh)*	manifest
manodopera (f)	*(mah-noh-dOh-peh-rah)*	manpower

M

manodopera diretta	*(mah-noh-dOh-peh-rah deeh-rEht-tah)*	direct labor
manodopera specializzata	*(mah-noh-dOh-peh-rah speh-chah-leehds-dsAh-tah)*	skilled labor
mansione (f)	*(mahn-syOh-neh)*	job
mantello (m)	*(mahn-tEhl-loh)*	cape
mantenere	*(mahn-teh-nEh-reh)*	service (v)
manutenzione (f)	*(mah-nooh-tah-tsyOh-neh)*	maintenance
manutenzione e servizio successivi alla vendita	*(mah-nooh-tah-tsyOh-neh eh sehr-vEEh-tsyoh soohch-chehs-sEEh-veeh ahl-lah vEhn-deeh-tah)*	after-sales service
manutenzione preventiva	*(mah-nooh-tah-tsyOh-neh preh-vehn-tEEh-vah)*	preventive maintenance
marca (f)	*(mAhr-kah)*	brand
marchio (m)	*(mAhr-kyoh)*	logo
marchio registrato	*(mAhr-kyoh reh-jeehs-trAh-toh)*	trademark, registered trademark
margine (m) a termine	*(mAhr-jeeh-neh ah tEhr-meeh-neh)*	forward margin
margine di manutenzione	*(mAhr-jeeh-neh deeh mah-nooh-tehn-tsyOh-neh)*	maintenance margin
margine di prestito	*(mAhr-jeeh-neh deeh prEhs-teeh-toh)*	lending margin
margine di profitto	*(mAhr-jeeh-neh deeh proh-fEEht-toh)*	profit margin
margine di sicurezza	*(mAhr-jeeh-neh seeh-kooh-rEhts-tsah)*	margin of safety
margine lordo	*(mAhr-jeeh-neh lOhr-doh)*	gross margin
margine netto	*(mAhr-jeeh-neh nEht-toh)*	net margin
margine variabile	*(mAhr-jeeh-neh vah-ryAh-beeh-leh)*	variable margin
market	*(mahrket)*	market (v)
marketing (m)	*(marketing)*	marketing
marketing per il mercato di massa	*(marketing pehr eehl mehr-kAh-toh deeh mAhs-sah)*	mass marketing
marketing telefonico	*(marketing teh-leh-fOh-neeh-koh)*	telemarketing

marmotta (f)	*(mahr-mOht-tah)*	marmot
marocchino (m)	*(mah-rohk-kEEh-noh)*	Moroccan leather
massimo (m) livello amministrativo	*(mAhs-seeh-moh leeh-vEhl-loh ahm-meeh-neehs-trah-tEEh-voh)*	top management
materia (f) prima	*(mah-tEh-reeh-ah prEEh-mah)*	raw materials
materiale (m) rotante	*(mah-teh-ryAh-leh roh-tAhn-teh)*	rolling stock
materiale scritto (m)	*(mah-teh-ryAh-leh skrEEht-toh)*	copy
materiali	*(mah-teh-ryAh-leeh)*	materials
matrice (f)	*(mah-trEEh-cheh)*	matrix
maturare	*(mah-tooh-rAh-reh)*	accrue (v)
maturazione (f)	*(mah-tooh-rah-tsyOh-neh)*	accrual
maturità (f)	*(mah-tooh-reeh-tAh)*	maturity
maturo	*(mah-tOOh-roh)*	ripe
meccanico (m)	*(mehk-kAh-neeh-koh)*	mechanic
media (f)	*(mEh-dyah)*	average, mean
media aritmetica	*(mEh-dyah ah-reeht-mEh-teeh-kah)*	arithmetic mean
media del costo in dollari	*(mEh-dyah dehl kOhs-toh eehn dOhl-lah-reeh)*	dollar cost averaging
media ponderata	*(mEh-dyah pohn-deh-rAh-tah)*	weighted average
media variabile	*(mEh-dyah vah-ryAh-beeh-leh)*	moving average
mediatore (m) delle azioni	*(meh-dyah-tOh-reh dehl-leh ah-tsyOh-neeh)*	stockbroker
mediatore di partite sparse	*(meh-dyah-tOh-reh deeh pahr-tEEh-teh spAhr-seh)*	odd lot broker
mediatore di software	*(meh-dyah-tOh-reh deeh software)*	software broker
mediatore per noleggio	*(meh-dyah-tOh-reh pehr noh-lEhj-joh)*	charterparty agent
mediazione (f)	*(meh-dyah-tsyOh-neh)*	mediation
medicina (f)	*(meh-deeh-chEEh-nah)*	medicine
medico (m)	*(mEh-deeh-koh)*	physician
medio termine (m)	*(mEh-dyoh tEhr-meeh-neh)*	medium term

M

memorandum (m)		memorandum
memoria (f) d'accesso casuale	*(meh-mOh-reeh-ah dahch-Ehs-soh kah-zwAh-leh)*	random access memory
memoria dell'elaboratore	*(meh-mOh-reeh-ah dehl eh-lah-boh-rah-tOh-reh)*	computer memory
memoria magnetica	*(meh-mOh-reeh-ah mah-nyEh-teeh-kah)*	magnetic memory
menabò (m)	*(meh-nah-bOh)*	dummy
mercante (m)	*(mehr-kAhn-teh)*	merchant
mercantile	*(mehr-kah-ntEEh-leh)*	mercantile
mercanzia (f)	*(mehr-kAhn-tsyah)*	merchandising
mercato (m)	*(mehr-kAh-toh)*	market, marketplace
mercato a contanti	*(mehr-kAh-toh ah kohn-tAhn-teeh)*	spot market
mercato a due livelli	*(mehr-kAh-toh ah dOOh-eh leeh-vEhl-leeh)*	two-tiered market
mercato a termine	*(mehr-kAh-toh ah tEhr-meeh-neh)*	forward market
mercato all'ingrosso	*(mehr-kAh-toh ahl eehn-grOhs-soh)*	wholesale market
mercato aperto	*(mehr-kAh-toh ah-pEhr-toh)*	open market
mercato capovolto	*(mehr-kAh-toh kah-poh-vOhl-toh)*	inverted market
mercato comune	*(mehr-kAh-toh koh-mOOh-neh)*	common market
mercato debole	*(mehr-kAh-toh dEh-boh-leh)*	thin market
mercato dei capitali	*(mehr-kAh-toh deh-eeh kah-peeh-tAh-leeh)*	capital market
mercato del lavoro	*(mehr-kAh-toh dehl lah-vOh-roh)*	labor market
mercato favorevole all'acquirente	*(mehr-kAh-toh fah-voh-rEh-voh-leh ahl ahk-kweeh-rEhn-teh)*	buyer's market
mercato grigio	*(mehr-kAh-toh grEEh-joh)*	gray market
mercato instabile	*(mehr-kAh-toh eehn-stAh-beeh-leh)*	volatile market
mercato interno	*(mehr-kAh-toh eehn-tEhr-noh)*	home market
mercato invertito	*(mehr-kAh-toh eehn-vehr-tEEh-toh)*	inverted market

mercato libero	*(mehr-kAh-toh lEEh-beh-roh)*	free market
mercato marginale	*(mehr-kAh-toh mahr-jeeh-nAh-leh)*	fringe market
mercato monetario	*(mehr-kAh-toh moh-neh-tAh-reeh-oh)*	money market
mercato nero	*(mehr-kAh-toh nEh-roh)*	black market
mercato primario	*(mehr-kAh-toh preeh-mAh-reeh-oh)*	primary market
mercato privilegiato	*(mehr-kAh-toh preeh-veeh-leh-jAh-toh)*	upmarket
mercato propenso per gli acquirenti	*(mehr-kAh-toh proh-pEhn-soh pehr- lyeeh ahk-kweeh-rEhn-teeh)*	buyer's market
mercato ristretto	*(mehr-kAh-toh reehs-trEht-toh)*	tight market
mercato secondario per titoli mobiliari	*(mehr-kAh-toh seh-kohn-dAh-reeh-oh pehr tEEh-toh-leeh moh-beeh-lyAh-reeh)*	secondary market (securities)
mercato volatile	*(mehr-kAh-toh voh-lAh-teeh-leh)*	volatile market
merce (f) imballata	*(mEhr-cheh eehm-bahl-lAh-tah)*	bale cargo
merce imbarcata	*(mEhr-cheh eehm-bahr-kAh-tah)*	cargo
merce pallettizzata	*(mEhr-cheh pahl-leht-teehds-dsAh-tah)*	palletized freight
merchant (f) bank	*(muhrchent baynk)*	merchant bank
merci (f)	*(mEhr-cheeh)*	freight
merci di tutti i tipi	*(mEhr-cheeh deeh tOOht-teeh eeh tEEh-peeh)*	freight all kinds
merci esentasse	*(mEhr-cheeh eh-zehn-tAhs-seh)*	free list (commodities without duty)
merci vincolate	*(mEhr-cheeh veehn-koh-lAh-teh)*	bonded goods
merletto (m)	*(mehr-lEht-toh)*	lace
mese (m) contrattuale	*(mEh-zeh kohn-traht-twAh-leh)*	contract month
metalli (m)	*(meh-tAhl-leeh)*	metals

metano (m)	*(meh-tAh-noh)*	methane
metodo (m)	*(mEh-toh-doh)*	method
metodo di ammortamento accelerato	*(mEh-toh-doh deeh ahm-mohr-tah-mEhn-toh ahch-cheh-leh-rAh-toh)*	sum of the year's digits
metrificazione (f)	*(meh-treeh-feeh-kah-tsyOh-neh)*	metrification
metro (m)	*(mEh-troh)*	yardstick
mettere in appalto	*(mEht-teh-reh eehn ahp-pAhl-toh)*	put in a bid (v)
mettere in fondo comune	*(mEht-teh-reh eehn fOhn-doh koh-mOOh-neh)*	pool (v)
mettere sul mercato	*(mEht-teh-reh soohl mehr-kAh-toh)*	market (v)
mezza (f) scadenza (per buoni)	*(mEhds-dsah skah-dEhn-tsah pehr bwOh-neeh)*	half-life (bonds)
mezzi di communicazione	*(mEhds-dseh deeh koh-mooh-neeh-kah-tsyOh-neh)*	mass media
mezzi di pubblicità	*(mEhds-dseeh deeh poohb-bleeh-cheeh-tAh)*	advertising media
mezzo di scambio	*(mEhds-dsoh deeh skAhm-byoh)*	medium of exchange
micro computer (m)	*(meeh-kroh computer)*	microcomputer
micro elaboratore (m)	*(meeh-kroh eh-lah-boh-rah-tOh-reh)*	microprocessor
microchip (m)	*(meeh-kroh chip)*	microchip
microfiche (f)	*(meehkrohfeesh))*	microfiche
microfilm (m)	*(meehkrohfilm)*	microfilm
microfono (m)	*(meeh-krOh-foh-noh)*	microphone
microonda (f)	*(meeh-kroh-Ohn-dah)*	microwave
modificare	*(moh-deeh-feeh-kAh-reh)*	amend (v)
miglior offrente (m)	*(meeh-lyOhr ohf-frEhn-teh)*	highest bidder
miglioramenti (m)	*(meeh-lyoh-rah-mEhn-teeh)*	improvements
migliorare	*(meeh-lyoh-rAh-reh)*	improve upon (v)
migliore qualità (f)	*(meeh-lyOh-reh)*	top quality
minerale (m)	*(meeh-neh-rAh-leh)*	ore
minerale ferroso	*(meeh-neh-rAh-leh fehr-rOh-zoh)*	iron ore

minerale manganese	*(meeh-neh-rAh-leh mahn-gah-nEh-zeh)*	manganese ore
mini computer (m)	*(meeh-neeh computer)*	minicomputer
mini elaboratore elettronico (m)	*(meeh-neeh eh-lah-boh-rah-tOh-reh eh-leht-trOh-neeh-koh)*	minicomputer
minuscolo (m)	*(meeh-nOOhs-koh-loh)*	lower case
miscelatore (m)	*(meeh-sheh-lah-tOh-reh)*	mixer
misura (f) del campione	*(meeh-zOOh-rah dehl kahm-pyOh-neh)*	sample size
misurare	*(meeh-zooh-rAh-reh)*	measure (v)
mobilità (f) della manodopera	*(moh-beeh-leeh-tAh dehl-lah mah-noh-dOh-peh-rah)*	mobility of labor
moda (f)	*(mOh-dah)*	fashion
moda confezionata	*(mOh-dah kohn-feh-tsyoh-nAh-tah*	ready-to-wear
modello matematico	*(moh-dEhl-loh mah-teh-mAh-teeh-koh)*	mathematical model
modello/a (m/f)	*(moh-dEhl-loh/ah)*	model, pattern
modificare	*(moh-deeh-feeh-kAH-reh)*	amend (v)
modifiche (f) incombenti	*(moh-dEEh-feeh-keh eehn-kohm-bEhn-teeh)*	impending changes
modulatore (m) per la trasmissione di dati via cavo	*(moh-dooh-lah-tOh-reh pehr lah trahs-meehs-syOh-neh deeh dAh-teeh vEEh-ah kAh-voh)*	modem
modulazione (f) di ampiezza	*(moh-dooh-lah-tsyOh-neh deeh ahm-pyEhts-tsah)*	amplitude modulation (AM)
modulazione di frequenza	*(moh-dooh-lah-tsyOh-neh deeh freh-kwEhn-tsah)*	frequency modulation (FM)
modulo (m)	*(mOh-dooh-loh)*	order form
modulo di richiesta	*(mOh-dooh-loh deeh reeh-kyEhs-tah)*	application form
modulo di richiesta per brevetto	*(mOh-dooh-loh deeh reeh-kyEhs-tah pehr breh-vEht-toh)*	patent application
modulo multiplo	*(mOh-dooh-loh mOOhl-teeh-ploh)*	spreadsheet
molare (m)	*(moh-lAh-reh)*	molar
molatura (f)	*(moh-lah-tOOh-rah)*	grinding

M

mole (f)	*(mOh-leh)*	volume
molecola (f)	*(moh-lEh-koh-lah)*	molecule
molibdeno (m)	*(moh-leehb-dEh-noh)*	molybdenum
molla (f)	*(mOhl-lah)*	spring
moltiplicatore (m)	*(mohl-teeh-pleeh-kah-tOh-reh)*	multiplier
monitor (m)	*(mahnitehr)*	monitor
monopolio (m)	*(moh-noh-pOh-leeh-oh)*	monopoly
monopolio di stato	*(moh-noh-pOh-leeh-oh deeh stAh-toh)*	legal monopoly
monopolio legale	*(moh-noh-pOh-leeh-oh leh-gAh-leh)*	legal monopoly
monopsonio (m)	*(moh-nohp-sOh-neeh-oh)*	monopsony
montaggio (m)	*(mohn-tAhj-joh)*	assembly
montaggio (m)	*(mohn-tAhj-joh)*	mechanical
montare	*(mohn-tAh-reh)*	assemble (v) (things)
morale (m)	*(moh-rAh-leh)*	morale
moratorio (m)	*(moh-rah-tOh-reeh-oh)*	moratorium
morfina (f)	*(mohr-fEEh-nah)*	morphine
mosto (m)	*(mOhs-toh)*	must
motore (m)	*(moh-tOh-reh)*	engine
motore (m)	*(moh-tOh-reh)*	motor
motorino (m) d'avviamento	*(moh-toh-rEEh-noh dahv-veeh-ah-mEhn-toh)*	starter
movimento (m) d'attività	*(moh-veeh-mEhn-toh daht-teeh-veeh-tAh)*	asset turnover
movimento di cassa	*(moh-veeh-mEhn-toh deeh kAhs-sah)*	cash flow
movimento di cassa incrementale	*(moh-veeh-mEhn-toh deeh kAhs-sah eehn-kreh-mehn-tAh-leh)*	incremental cash flow
movimento positivo dei fondi	*(moh-veeh-mEhn-toh poh-zeeh-tEEh-voh deh-eeh fOhn-deeh)*	positive cash flow
mozione (f)	*(mOh-tsyOh-neh)*	motion
multa (f) (l'ammenda)	*(mOOhl-tah/ahm-mEhn-dah)*	fine (penalty)
multipli (m)	*(mOOhl-teeh-pleeh)*	multiples

multiprogrammato	*(moohl-teeh-proh-grahm-mAh-toh)*	multiprogramming
multiproprietà (f)	*(moohl-teeh-proh-pryeh-tAh)*	time sharing
multivalutario (m)	*(moohl-teeh-vah-looh-tAh-reeh-oh)*	multicurrency
mussola (f)	*(mOohs-soh-lah)*	muslin

N

narcotico (m)	*(nahr-kOh-teeh-koh)*	narcotic
naso (m)	*(nAh-zoh)*	bouquet, nose
nastro (m)	*(nAhs-troh)*	tape
nastro (m) della telescrivente	*(nAhs-troh dehl-lah teh-lehskreeh-vEhn-teh)*	ticker tape
nastro di carta	*(nAhs-troh deeh kAhr-tah)*	paper tape
nastro magnetico	*(nAhs-troh mah-nyEh-teeh-koh)*	magnetic tape
nazionalismo (m)	*(nah-tsyoh-nah-lEEhz-moh)*	nationalism
nazionalizzazione (f)	*(nah-tyoh-nah-leehds-dsah-tsyOh-neh)*	nationalization
negativo (m)	*(neh-gah-tEEh-voh)*	negative
negligente	*(neh-gleeh-jEhn-teh)*	negligent
negoziabile	*(neh-goh-tsyAh-beeh-leh)*	negotiable
negoziare	*(neh-goh-tsyAh-reh)*	negotiate (v)
negoziato (m)	*(neh-goh-tsyAh-toh)*	negotiation
negoziato tariffaro generale	*(neh-goh-tsyAh-toh tah-reehf-fAh-roh jeh-neh-rAh-leh)*	across-the-board tariff negotiation
negozio (m) al dettaglio	*(neh-gOh-tsyoh ahl-deht-tAh-lyoh)*	retail outlet
negozio di denaro	*(neh-gOh-tsyoh deeh deh-nAh-roh)*	money shop
nel giro di una notte	*(nehl jEEh-roh deeh ooh-nah nOht-teh)*	overnight
neretto (m)	*(neh-rEht-toh)*	boldface
nessun problema	*(nehs-sOOhn proh-blEh-mah)*	no problem

M

netto	*(nEht-toh)*	net
neutralizzazione (f)	*(neh-ooh-trah-leehds-dsah-tsyOh-neh)*	neutralization
neutro	*(nEh-ooh-troh)*	neutral
neutrone (m)	*(neh-ooh-trOh-neh)*	neutron
nichelio (m)	*(neeh-kEh-leeh-oh)*	nickel
nitrato (m)	*(neeh-trAh-toh)*	nitrate
nitrite (m)	*(neeh-trEEh-teh)*	nitrite
nitrogeno (m)	*(neeh-trOh-jeh-noh)*	nitrogen
nodo (m)	*(nOh-doh)*	knot (nautical)
noleggio a scafo nudo	*(noh-lEhj-joh ah skAh-foh nOOh-doh)*	bareboat charter
nolo "vuoto per pieno"	*(nOh-loh vwOh-toh pehr pyEh-noh)*	dead freight
nolo (m) anticipato	*(nOh-loh ahn-teeh-chee-pAh-toh)*	advance freight
non associato (m)	*(nohn ahs-soh-chAh-toh)*	nonmember
non elencato	*(nohn eh-lehn-kAh-toh)*	unlisted
non equo	*(nohn Eh-kwoh)*	unfair
non lucido	*(nohn lOOh-cheeh-doh)*	matt
non oltre indicato per nome	*(nohn Ohl-treh eehn-deeh-kAh-toh pehr nOh-meh)*	not otherwise indexed by name
non registrato	*(nohn reh-jeehs-trAh-toh)*	off-the-books
non residente (m)	*(nohn reh-zeeh-dEhn-teh)*	nonresident
non socio (m)	*(nohn sOh-choh)*	nonmember
non sviluppato	*(nohn sveeh-loohp-pAh-toh)*	undeveloped
non ufficiale	*(nohn oohf-feeh-chAh-leh)*	off board (stock market)
norma (f)	*(nOhr-mah)*	norm
norma dell'uomo giudizioso	*(nOhr-mah dehl wOh-moh jooh-deeh-tsyOh-zoh)*	prudent man rule
normativa (f)	*(nohr-mah-tEEh-vah)*	regulation
normativa per la costruzione in varie città	*(nohr-mah-tEEh-vah pehr-lah kohs-trooh-tsyOh-neh)*	zoning law
normativa sul lavoro	*(nohr-mah-tEEh-vah soohl lah-vOh-roh)*	labor law

normative	*(nohr-mah-tEEh-veh)*	bylaws
normative fitosanitarie	*(nohr-mah-tEEh-veh feeh-toh-sah-neeh-tAh-reeh-eh)*	phytosanitary regulations
normative per l'esportazione	*(nohr-mah-tEEh-veh pehr lehs-pohr-tah-tsyOh-neh)*	export regulations
normative per l'importazione	*(nohr-mah-tEEh-veh pehr leehm-pohr-tah-tsyOh-neh)*	import regulations
norme (f) per la richiesta di rimborso anticipato	*(nOhr-meh pehr lah reeh-kyEhs-tah deeh reehm-bOhr-soh ahn-teeh-cheeh-pAh-toh)*	call rule
nota (f) d'avviso	*(nOh-tah deeh ahv-vEEh-zoh)*	advice note
nota di accredito	*(nOh-tah deeh krEh-deeh-toh)*	credit note
nota di addebito	*(nOh-tah deeh ahd-dEh-beeh-toh)*	debit note
nota di debito	*(nOh-tah deeh dEh-beeh-toh)*	debit entry
nota di spedizione	*(nOh-tah deeh speh-deeh-tsyOh-neh)*	consignment note
notaio (m)	*(noh-tAh-yoh)*	notary
notazione (f) binaria	*(noh-tah-tsyOh-neh)*	binary notation
notifica (f) di consegna	*(noh-tEEh-feeh-kah)*	delivery notice
novazione (f)	*(noh-vah-tsyOh-neh)*	novation
novità (f)	*(noh-veeh-tAh)*	innovation
nullo	*(noohl-loh)*	void
nullo a tutti gli effetti	*(noohl-loh ah tOOht-teeh lyeeh ehf-fEht-teeh)*	null and void
numerazione (f) binaria	*(nooh-meh-rah-tsyOh-neh beeh-nAh-reeh-ah)*	binary notation
numero (m)	*(nOOh-meh-roh)*	edition
numero (m)	*(nOOh-meh-roh)*	size
numero (m) dell'ordine	*(nOOh-meh-roh dehl Ohr-deeh-neh)*	order number
numero di conto	*(nOOh-meh-roh deeh kOhn-toh)*	account number

numero di riferimento	*(nOOh-meh-roh deeh reeh-feh-reeh-mEhn-toh)*	reference number
nuova (f) emissione	*(nwOh-vah eh-meehs-syOh-neh)*	new issue

O

obbligazione (f)	*(ohb-bleeh-gah-tsyOh-neh)*	bond, flat bond, obligation
obbligazione a rate con pagamento maggiorato alla maturità	*(ohb-bleeh-gah-tsyOh-neh ah rAh-teh kohn pah-gah-mEhn-toh mahj-joh-rAh-toh ahl-lah mah-tooh-reeh-tAh)*	balloon note
obbligazione al portatore	*(ohb-bleeh-gah-tsyOh-neh ahl pohr-tah-tOh-reh)*	bearer bond
obbligazione fiduciaria	*(ohb-bleeh-gah-tsyOh-neh feeh-dooh-chAh-reeh-ah)*	fidelity bond
obbligazione garantita	*(ohb-bleeh-gah-tsyOh-neh gah-rahn-tEEh-tah)*	backed note, guaranty bond
obbligazione garantita da ipoteca	*(ohb-bleeh-gah-tsyOh-neh gah-rahn-tEEh-tah dah eeh-poh-tEh-kah)*	mortgage bond
obbligazione garantita dai ricavi dell'emittente	*(ohb-bleeh-gah-tsyOh-neh gah-rahn-tEEh-tah dah-eeh reeh-kAh-veeh dehl eh-meeht-tEhn-teh)*	revenue bond
obbligazione generale	*(ohb-bleeh-gah-tsyOh-neh jeh-neh-rAh-leh)*	blanket bond
obbligazione ipotecaria	*(ohb-bleeh-gah-tsyOh-neh eeh-poh-teh-kAh-reeh-ah)*	mortgage debenture
obbligazione municipale	*(ohb-bleeh-gah-tsyOh-neh mooh-neeh-chee-pAh-leh)*	municipal bond
obbligazione senza cedole per ricevere interessi	*(ohb-bleeh-gah-tsyOh-neh sEhn-tsah chEh-doh-leh pehr reeh-chEh-veh-reh eehn-teh-rEhs-seeh)*	zero coupon
obbligazioni	*(ohb-bleeh-gah-tsyOh-neeh)*	bond issue, debentures, securities
obbligazioni a scadenza periodica	*(ohb-bleeh-gah-tsyOh-neeh ah skah-dEhn-tsah peh-reeh-Oh-deeh-kah)*	serial bonds

obbligazioni convertibili	*(ohb-bleeh-gah-tsyOh-neeh kohn-vehr-tEEh-beeh-leeh)*	convertible debentures
obbligazioni del tesoro	*(ohb-bleeh-gah-tsyOh-neeh dehl teh-zOh-roh)*	treasury bonds
obbligazioni dirette	*(ohb-bleeh-gah-tsyOh-neeh deeh-rEht-teh)*	direct papers
obbligazioni redimibili	*(ohb-bleeh-gah-tsyOh-neeh reh-deeh-mEEh-beeh-leeh)*	redeemable bonds
obiettivo (m) aziendale	*(ohb-byeht-tEEh-voh ah-dsyehn-dAh-leh)*	company goal
obsolescenza (f)	*(ohb-soh-leh-shEhn-tsah)*	obsolescence
obsolescenza programmata	*(ohb-soh-leh-shEhn-tsah proh-grahm-mAh-tah)*	planned obsolescence
occhiello (m)	*(ohk-kyEhl-loh)*	buttonhole
occupazione (f)	*(ohk-kooh-pah-tsyOh-ne)*	occupation
offerta (f)	*(ohf-fEhr-tah)*	tender
offerta a voce	*(ohf-fEhr-tah ah vOh-cheh)*	oral bid
offerta aggregata	*(ohf-fEhr-tah ahg-greh-gAh-tah)*	aggregate supply
offerta al pubblico	*(ohf-fEhr-tah ahl pOOhb-leeh-koh)*	public offering
offerta d'acquisto	*(ohf-fEhr-tah dahk-kwEEhs-toh)*	tender offer
offerta d'insediamento	*(ohf-fEhr-tah deehn-seh-dyah-mEhn-toh)*	takeover bid
offerta e la domanda	*(ohf-fEhr-tah eh lah doh-mAhn-dah)*	supply and demand
offerta premio	*(ohf-fEhr-tah prEh-myoh)*	premium offer
offerta scritta	*(ohf-fEhr-tah skrEEht-tah)*	written bid (stock exchange)
offerta secondaria di titoli di sicura affidabilità	*(ohf-fEhr-tah seh-kohn-dAh-reeh-ah deeh tEEh-toh-leeh deeh seeh-kOOh-rah ahf-feeh-dah-beeh-leeh-tAh)*	secondary offering (securities)
offerto e richiesto	*(ohf-fEhr-toh eh reeh-kyEhs-toh)*	bid and asked
offrire	*(ohf-frEEh-reh)*	offer (v)

offrire di più	*(ohf-frEEh-reh deeh pyOOh)*	outbid (v)
oggetto di prima necessità	*(ohj-jEht-toh deeh prEEh-mah neh-chehs-seeh-tAh)*	commodity
ohm (m)		ohm
oligopolio	*(oh-leeh-goh-pOh-leeh-oh)*	oligopoly
oligopsonio	*(oh-leeh-gohp-sOh-neeh-oh)*	oligopsony
oltre la linea	*(Ohl-treh lah lEEh-neh-ah)*	above-the-line
omettere	*(oh-mEht-teh-reh)*	omit (v)
omogeneità (f)	*(oh-moh-geh-neh-eeh-tAh)*	homogeneity
omologazione (f)	*(oh-moh-loh-gah-tsyOh-neh)*	probate
onda (f)	*(Ohn-dah)*	wave
onde corte	*(Ohn-deh kOhr-teh)*	short wave
onere (m) anticipato	*(Oh-neh-reh ahn-teeh-chee-pAh-toh)*	front-end fee
onere fiscale	*(Oh-neh-reh feehs-kAh-leh)*	tax burden
onere variabile	*(Oh-neh-reh vah-ryAh-beeh-leh)*	floating charge
oneri	*(Oh-neh-reeh)*	charges
oneri d'ancoraggio	*(Oh-neh-reeh dahn-koh-rAhj-joh)*	anchorage (dues)
oneri di sbarco	*(Oh-neh-reeh deeh zbAhr-koh)*	landing charges
oneri di sollevamento di carichi pesanti	*(Oh-neh-reeh deeh sohl-leh-vah-mEhn-toh)*	heavy lift charges
oneri differiti	*(Oh-neh-reeh deehf-feh-rEEh-teeh)*	deferred charges
oneri fissi	*(Oh-neh-reeh fEEhs-seeh)*	fixed charges
oneri per l'uso del molo	*(Oh-neh-reeh pehr lOOh-zoh dehl mOh-loh)*	wharfage charges
onorario (m) amministrativo	*(oh-noh-rAh-reeh-oh ahm-meeh-neehs-trah-tEEh-voh)*	management fee
opaco	*(oh-pAh-koh)*	matte
operai (m)	*(oh-peh-rAh-eeh)*	manual workers, blue-collar worker
operaio a giornate	*(oh-peh-rAh-yoh ah johr-nAh-teh)*	journeyman
operaio/a (m/f)	*(oh-peh-rAh-yoh)*	blue-collar worker

operatore (m)	*(oh-peh-rah-tOh-reh)*	operator
operazioni (f) ausiliari	*(oh-peh-rah-tsyOh-neeh ah-ooh-zeeh-lyAh-reeh)*	ancillary operations
operazioni di mercato aperto	*(oh-peh-rah-tsyOh-neeh deeh mehr-kAh-toh ah-pEhr-toh)*	open market operations
opossum (m)	*(oh-pah-suhm)*	opossum
oppio (m/f)	*(Ohp-pyoh)*	opium
opuscolo (m)	*(oh-pOOhs-koh-loh)*	pamphlet
opzionale	*(ohp-tsyoh-nAh-leh)*	optional
opzione (f)	*(ohp-tsyOh-neh)*	option
opzione col privilegio di acquistare o vendere un'azione allo stesso prezzo	*(ohp-tsyOh-neh kohl preeh-veeh-lEh-joh deeh ahk-kweehs-tAh-reh oh vEhn-deh-reh oohn ah-tsyOh-neh ahl-loh stEhs-soh prEhts-tsoh)*	straddle
opzione di acquistare delle azioni ad un dato prezzo entro un determinato periodo di tempo	*(ohp-tsyOh-neh deeh ahk-kweehs-tAh-reh dehl-leh ah-tsyOh-neeh ad oohn dAh-toh prEhts-tsoh Ehn-troh oohn deh-tehr-meeh-nAh-toh peh-rEEh-oh-doh deeh tEhm-poh)*	call option
opzione di acquisto di valori mobiliari in qualsiasi momento a un certo prezzo	*(ohp-tsyOh-neh deeh ahk-kwEEhs-toh deeh vah-lOh-reeh moh-beeh-lyAh-reeh eehn kwahl-sEEh-ah-seeh moh-mEhn-toh ah oohn chEhr-toh prEhts-tsoh)*	call feature
opzione di acquisto o di vendita di un contratto a termine	*(ohp-tsyOh-neh deeh ahk-kwEEhs-toh oh deeh vEhn-deeh-tah deeh oohn kohn-trAht-toh ah tEhr-meeh-neh)*	futures option
opzione di vendita (di un'azione a un prezzo superiore a quello attuale)	*(ohp-tsyOh-neh deeh vEhn-deeh-tah deeh oohn ah-tsyOh-neh ah oohn prEhts-tsoh sooh-peh-ryOh-reh ah kwEhl-loh aht-twAh-leh)*	put option
opzione sulle azioni	*(ohp-tsyOh-neh sohl-leh ah-tsyOh-neeh)*	stock option

ora (f) d'arrivo prevista	*(Oh-rah dahr-rEEh-voh preh-vEEhs-tah)*	estimated time of arrival
ora di partenza prevista	*(Oh-rah deeh pahr-tEhn-tsah preh-vEEhs-tah)*	estimated time of departure
ora solare	*(Oh-rah soh-lAh-reh)*	standard time
orario (m)	*(oh-rAh-reeh-oh)*	schedule, timetable
orario di lavoro (m)	*(oh-rAh-reeh-oh deeh lah-voh-roh)*	working hours
ordinanza (f)	*(ohr-deen-Ahn-sah)*	ordinance
ordinare	*(ohr-deeh-nAh-reh)*	order (v), place, an order (v)
ordine (m)	*(Ohr-deeh-neh)*	order
ordine a scadenza	*(Ohr-deeh-neh ah skah-dEhn-tsah)*	time order
ordine a termine	*(Ohr-deeh-neh ah tEhr-meeh-neh)*	limit order (stock market)
ordine alternativo	*(Ohr-deeh-neh ahl-tehr-nah-tEEh-voh)*	alternative order
ordine arretrato	*(Ohr-deeh-neh ahr-reh-trAh-toh)*	back order
ordine continuo	*(Ohr-deeh-neh kohn-tEEh-nooh-oh)*	open order
ordine d'acquisto	*(Ohr-deeh-neh dahk-kwEEhs-toh)*	purchase order
ordine del giorno	*(Ohr-deeh-neh dehl jOhr-noh)*	order of the day
ordine di fermo perdita	*(Ohr-deeh-neh deeh fEhr-moh pEhr-deeh-tah)*	stop-loss order
ordine discrezionale	*(Ohr-deeh-neh deehs-kreh-tsyoh-nAh-leh)*	discretionary order
ordine fisso	*(Ohr-deeh-neh fEEhs-soh)*	standing order
ordine generale	*(Ohr-deeh-neh jeh-neh-rAh-leh)*	blanket order
ordine in giornata	*(Ohr-deeh-neh eehn johr-nAh-tah)*	day order
ordine per corrispondenza	*(Ohr-deeh-neh pehr kohr-reehs-pohn-dEhn-tsah)*	mail order
ordine ripetuto	*(Ohr-deeh-neh reeh-peh-tOOh-toh)*	repeat order
ordine successivo	*(Ohr-deeh-neh soohch-chehs-sEEh-voh)*	follow-up order

O

O

ordine urgente	*(Ohr-deeh-neh oohr-jEhn-teh)*	rush order
ordini inevasi	*(Ohr-deeh-neh eehn-eh-vAh-zeeh)*	backlog
ore lavorative	*(Oh-reh lah-voh-rah-tEEh-veh)*	man hours
ore migliori per la pubblicità televisiva	*(Oh-reh meeh-lyOh-reeh pehr lah poohb-bleeh-cheeh-tAh)*	prime time
organico	*(ohr-gAh-neeh-koh)*	organic
organigramma (f)	*(ohr-gah-neeh-grAhm-mah)*	management chart, organization chart
organigramma di servizio	*(ohr-gah-neeh-grAhm-mah deeh sehr-vEEh-tsyoh)*	staff organization
organigramma dirigenziale	*(ohr-gah-neeh-grAhm-mah deeh-reeh-jehn-tsyAh-leh)*	chain of command
organizzazione (f)	*(ohr-gah-neehds-dsah-ttsyOh-neh)*	organization
organo (f) consultivo	*(Ohr-gah-noh kohn-soohl-tEEh-voh)*	advisory council
orlo (m)	*(Ohr-loh)*	hem
ormone (m)	*(ohr-mOh-neh)*	hormone
oscillatore (m)	*(oh-sheehl-lah-tOh-reh)*	oscillator
ossidazione (f)	*(ohs-seeh-dah-tsyOh-neh)*	oxidation
ossigeno (m)	*(ohs-sEEh-jeh-noh)*	oxygen
ottenere	*(oht-teh-nEh-reh)*	acquire (v)
ottico	*(Oht-teeh-koh)*	optic
ottimizzare	*(oht-teeh-meehds-dsAh-reh)*	maximize (v)

P

pacco (m) postale	*(pAhk-koh)*	parcel post
paese (m)	*(pah-Eh-zeh)*	country
paese (m) a rischio	*(pah-Eh-zeh ah rEEhs-kyoh)*	country of risk
paese con trattamento preferenziale	*(pah-Eh-zeh kohn traht-tah-mEhn-toh preh-feh-rehn-tsyAh-leh)*	most-favored nation

paese d'origine	*(pah-Eh-zeh doh-rEEh-jeeh-neh)*	country of origin
paesi in via di sviluppo	*(pah-Eh-zeeh eehn vEEh-ah deeh zveeh-lOOhp-poh)*	underdeveloped nations
paga (f)	*(pAh-gah)*	wage, wages
paga base	*(pAh-gah bAh-zeh)*	minimum wage
paga base minima indicizzata	*(pAh-gah bAh-zeh mEEh-neeh-mah eehn-deeh-cheehds-dsAh-tah)*	index linked guaranteed minimum wage
paga minima	*(pAh-gah mEEh-neeh-mah)*	minimum wage
pagabile al portatore	*(pah-gAh-beeh-leh ahl pohr-tah-tOh-reh)*	payable to bearer
pagabile all'ordine	*(pah-gAh-beeh-leeh ahl Ohr-deeh-neh)*	payable to order
pagabile su richiesta	*(pah-gAh-beeh-leh sooh reeh-kyEhs-tah)*	payable on demand
pagamenti (m) anticipati	*(pah-gah-mEhn-teeh ahn-teeh-chee-pAh-teeh)*	advance payments
pagamento (m)	*(pah-gah-mEhn-toh)*	disbursement, payment
pagamento alla consegna	*(pah-gah-mEhn-toh ahl-lah kohn-sEh-nyah)*	cash delivery, collect on delivery
pagamento anticipato	*(pah-gah-mEhn-toh ahn-teeh-chee-pAh-toh)*	cash in advance
pagamento completo	*(pah-gah-mEhn-toh kohm-plEh-toh)*	payment in full
pagamento del premio	*(pah-gah-mEhn-toh dehl prEh-myoh)*	premium payment
pagamento in contanti	*(pah-gah-mEhn-toh eehn kohn-tAhn-teeh)*	cash-and-carry
pagamento in natura	*(pah-gah-mEhn-toh eehn nah-tOOh-rah)*	payment in kind
pagamento parziale	*(pah-gah-mEhn-toh pahr-tsyAh-leh)*	partial payment
pagamento prima della consegna	*(pah-gah-mEhn-toh prEEh-mah dehl-lah kohn-sEh-nyah)*	cash before delivery
pagamento rifiutato	*(pah-gah-mEhn-toh reeh-fyooh-tAh-toh)*	payment refused
pagante (m)	*(pah-gAhn-teh)*	payer

P

pagare	*(pah-gAh-reh)*	pay (v)
pagare in contanti	*(pah-gAh-reh eehn kohn-tAhn-teeh)*	pay as you go
pagherò (m) cambiario	*(pah-geh-rOh)*	promissory note
pagina (f)	*(pAh-jeeh-nah)*	page
pagina al vivo	*(pAh-jeeh-nah ahl vEEh-voh)*	bleed
paletta (f)	*(pah-lEht-tah)*	pastry server
pallet (m)	*(pahlet)*	pallet
pallottolina (f)	*(pahl-loht-toh-lEEh-nah)*	pellet
pannello (m)	*(pahn-nEhl-loh)*	panel
pantaloni (m)	*(pahn-tah-lOh-neeh)*	slacks, trousers
pantofole (f)	*(pahn-tOh-foh-leh)*	slippers
papillion	*(pah-pee-yohn)*	bow tie
parabrezza (m)	*(pah-rah-brEhts-tsah)*	windshield
paradiso (m) fiscale	*(pah-rah-dEEh-zoh)*	tax haven
parafango (m)	*(pah-rah-fAhn-goh)*	fender
parametri (m)	*(pah-rAh-meh-treeh)*	guidelines
paraurti (m)	*(pah-rah-OOhr-teeh)*	bumper
parcella (f)	*(pahr-chEhl-lah)*	(agency) commission, fee
parcella dell'agenzia	*(pahr-chEhl-lah dehl ah-jehn-tsEEh-ah)*	agency fee
pari	*(pAh-reeh)*	par
parità (f)	*(pah-reeh-tAh)*	parity, sliding parity
parità d'interesse	*(pah-reeh-tAh deehn-teh-rEhs-seh)*	interest parity
parità di comodo	*(pah-reeh-tAh deeh kOh-moh-doh)*	accommodation parity
parità mobile	*(pah-reeh-tAh mOh-beeh-leh)*	crawling peg
parità variabile	*(pah-reeh-tAh vah-ryAh-beeh-leh)*	moving parity
parte (f) stampata	*(pAhr-teh stahm-pAh-tah)*	letterpress
parte della merce	*(pAhr-teh dehl-lah mEhr-cheh)*	part cargo

parte dovuta per il capitale netto	*(pAhr-teh doh-vOOh-tah pehr eehl kah-peeh-tAh-leh nEht-toh)*	equity share
parti	*(pAhr-teeh)*	parts
parti di ricambio	*(pAhr-teeh deeh reeh-kAhm-byoh)*	replacement parts
partita (f)	*(pahr-tEEh-tah)*	lot
partita arrotondata	*(pahr-tEEh-tah ahr-roh-tohn-dAh-tah)*	round lot
partita divisa	*(pahr-tEEh-tah deeh-vEEh-zah)*	broken lot
partita frazionata	*(pahr-tEEh-tah frah-tsyoh-nAh-tah)*	odd lot
partita intera	*(pahr-tEEh-tah eehn-tEh-rah)*	round lot
partita variabile	*(pahr-tEEh-tah vah-ryAh-beeh-leh)*	sliding parity
passività differite	*(pahs-seeh-veeh-tAh deehf-feh-rEEh-teh)*	deferred liabilities
passività garantita	*(pahs-seeh-veeh-tAh gah-rahn-tEEh-tah)*	secured liability
passività senza garanzia	*(pahs-seeh-veeh-tAh sEhn-tsah gah-rahn-tsEEh-ah)*	unsecured liability
pastiglia (f)	*(pahs-tEEh-lyah)*	tablet
pastiglia per la tosse	*(pahs-tEEh-lyah pehr-lah tOhs-seh)*	cough drop
pastorizzato	*(pahs-toh-reehds-dsAh-toh)*	pasteurized
patrimonio (m)	*(pah-treeh-mOh-nyoh)*	estate
patrimonio congiunto	*(pah-treeh-mOh-nyoh kohn-jOOhn-toh)*	joint estate
patto (m) collettivo	*(pAht-toh kohl-leht-tEEh-voh)*	collective agreement
patto commerciale	*(pAht-toh kohm-mehr-chAh-leh)*	trade agreement
patto implicito	*(pAht-toh eehm-plEEh-cheeh-toh)*	implied agreement
pegno (m)	*(pEh-nyoh)*	lien
pegno negativo	*(pEh-nyoh neh-gah-tEEh-voh)*	negative pledge

pegno per il mercato	*(pEh-nyoh pehr eehl mehr-kAh-toh)*	mechanics' lien
pelle (f)	*(pEhl-leh)*	leather
pelle di cinghiale	*(pEhl-leh deeh cheehn-gyAh-leh)*	pigskin
pelle di foca	*(pEhl-leh deeh fOh-kah)*	sealskin
pelle di lucertola	*(pEhl-leh deeh looh-chEhr-toh-lah)*	lizard skin
pelle di serpente	*(pEhl-leh deeh sehr-pEhn-teh)*	snakeskin
pelle di struzzo	*(pEhl-leh deeh strOOhts-tsoh)*	ostrich skin
pelletteria (f)	*(pehl-leht-teh-rEEh-ah)*	leather goods
penetrazione (f) commerciale	*(peh-neh-trah-tsyOh-neh kohm-mehr-chAh-leh)*	market penetration
penicillina	*(peh-neeh-chehl-lEEh-nah)*	penicillin
pensionamento (m)	*(pehn-syoh-nah-mEhn-toh)*	retirement
pensionante (m/f)	*(pehn-syoh-nAhn-teh)*	annuitant
per azione	*(pehr ah-tsyOh-neh)*	per share
per esportazione	*(pehr ehs-pohr-tah-tsyOh-neh)*	for export
percentuale (f) di profitti	*(pehr-chehn-twAh-leh deeh proh-fEEht-teeh)*	percentage of profits
percentuale di guadagni	*(pehr-chehn-twAh-leh deeh gwah-dAh-nyeeh)*	percentage earnings
perdita (f)	*(pEhr-deeh-tah)*	loss
perdita detraibile dalle imposte	*(pEhr-deeh-tah deh-trah-EEh-beeh-leh dahl-leh eehm-pOhs-teh)*	carryback
perdita lorda	*(pEhr-deeh-tah lOhr-dah)*	gross loss
perdita media in genere	*(pEhr-deeh-tah mEh-dyah eehn jEh-neh-reh)*	general average loss
perdita media particolare	*(pEhr-deeh-tah mEh-dyah pahr-teeh-koh-lAh-reh)*	particular average loss
perdita netta	*(pEhr-deeh-tah nEht-tah)*	net loss
perdita sul cambio	*(pEhr-deeh-tah soohl kAhm-byoh)*	exchange loss
perdita totale effettiva	*(pEhr-deeh-tah toh-tAh-leh ehf-feht-tEEh-vah)*	actual total loss

perforatore (m)	*(pehr-foh-rah-tOh-reh)*	keypuncher
pericolo (m) professionale	*(peh-rEEh-koh-loh proh-fehs-syoh-nAh-leh)*	occupational hazard
periodicità (f) del conto	*(peh-ryoh-deeh-cheeh-tAh dehl kOhn-toh)*	account period
periodo (m) contabile, il periodo di contabilità	*(peh-rEEh-oh-doh kohn-tAh-beeh-leh), (peh-rEEh-oh-doh deeh kohn-tah-beeh-leeh-tAh)*	accounting period
periodo d'interesse	*(peh-rEEh-oh-doh deehn-teh-rEhs-seh)*	interest period
periodo di detenzione	*(peh-rEEh-oh-doh deeh deh-tehn-tsyOh-neh)*	holding period
periodo di grazia	*(peh-rEEh-oh-doh deeh grAh-tsyah)*	grace period
periodo di pagamento	*(peh-rEEh-oh-doh deeh pah-gah-mEhn-toh)*	payout period
periodo di preparazione	*(peh-rEEh-oh-doh deeh preh-pah-rah-tsyOh-neh)*	lead time
periodo di ripagamento	*(peh-rEEh-oh-doh deeh reeh-pah-gah-mEhn-toh)*	payback period
periodo di riscossione	*(peh-rEEh-oh-doh deeh reehs-kohs-syOh-neh)*	collection period
periodo di tempo durante il quale l'elaboratore rimane inutilizzabile	*(peh-rEEh-oh-doh deeh tEhm-poh dooh-rAhn-teh eehl kwAh-leh leh-lah-boh-rah-tOh-reh reeh-mAh-neh eehn-ooh-teeh-leehds-dsAh-beeh-leh)*	downtime
periodo di tempo durante il quale la banca usufruisce degli assegni depositati e non incassati	*(peh-rEEh-oh-doh deeh tEhm-poh dooh-rAhn-teh eehl kwAh-leh lah bAhn-kah oohzooh-frooh-EEh-sdheh deh-lyeeh ahs-sEh-nyeeh deh-poh-zeeh-tAh-teeh eh nohn eehn-kahs-sAh-teeh)*	float (outstanding checks, stock)
periodo di tempo inutilizzabile	*(peh-rEEh-oh-doh deeh tEhm-poh eehn-ooh-teeh-leehds-dsAh-beeh-leh)*	down period
periodo finanziario	*(peh-rEEh-oh-doh feeh-nahn-tsyAh-reeh-oh)*	financial period
permesso (m)	*(pehr-mEhs-soh)*	permit

permesso amministrativo per vendere beni di consumo	*(pehr-mEhs-soh ahm-meeh-neehs-trah-tEEh-voh pehr vEhn-deh-reh bEh-neeh deeh kohn-sOOh-moh)*	excise license
permesso d'entrata	*(pehr-mEhs-soh dehn-trAh-tah)*	entry permit
permesso d'esportazione	*(pehr-mEhs-soh dehs-pohr-tah-tsyOh-neh)*	export permit
permesso d'esportazione di beni culturali	*(pehr-mEhs-soh dehs-pohr-tah-tsyOh-neh deeh bEh-neeh koohl-tooh-rAh-leeh)*	cultural export permit
permesso di lavoro	*(pehr-mEhs-soh deeh lah-vOh-roh)*	working papers
permettere	*(pehr-mEht-teh-reh)*	allow (v)
permuta (f) degli introiti	*(pEhr-mooh-tah deh-lyeeh eehn-trOhy-teeh)*	applied proceeds swap
persona (f) responsabile per un prodotto e/o un cliente	*(pehr-sOh-nah rehs-pohn-sAh-beeh-leh pehr oohn proh-dOht-toh eh/oh oohn kleeh-Ehn-teh)*	account executive
personale (m)	*(pehr-soh-nAh-leh)*	staff
personale di vendita	*(pehr-soh-nAh-leh deeh vEhn-deeh-tah)*	sales force
personale e i dirigenti	*(pehr-soh-nAh-leh deeh vEhn-deeh-tah)*	staff and line
peso (m)	*(pEh-zoh)*	weight
peso lordo	*(pEh-zoh lOhr-doh)*	gross weight
petrochimica (f)	*(peh-troh-kEEh-meeh-kah)*	petrochemical
petrodollari (m)	*(peh-troh-dOhl-lah-reeh)*	petrodollars
petroliera (f)	*(peh-troh-lyEh-rah)*	tanker
petrolio (m)	*(peh-trOh-lyoh)*	petroleum
pianificazione (f) a lunga scadenza	*(pyah-neeh-feeh-kah-tsyOh-neh ah lOOhn-gah skah-dEhn-tsah)*	long-range planning
pianificazione aziendale	*(pyah-neeh-feeh-kah-tsyOh-neh ah-dsyehn-dAh-leh)*	corporate planning
pianificazione del progetto	*(pyah-neeh-feeh-kah-tsyOh-neh dehl proh-jEht-toh)*	project planning
pianificazione finanziaria	*(pyah-neeh-feeh-kah-tsyOh-neh feeh-nahn-tsyAh-reeh-ah)*	financial planning

pianificazione industriale	*(pyah-neeh-feeh-kah-tsyOh-neh eehn-doohs-tryAh-leh)*	industrial planning
piano (m)	*(pyAh-noh*	plan
piano commerciale	*(pyAh-noh kohm-mehr-chAh-leh)*	business plan
piano d'azione	*(pyAh-noh dah-tsyOh-neh)*	action plan
piano di immediata esecuzione	*(pyAh-noh deeh eehm-meh-dyAh-tah eh-zeh-koohtsyOh-neh)*	activity on arrow
piano di mercato	*(pyAh-noh deeh mehr-kAh-toh)*	market plan
piante (f)	*(pyAhn-teh)*	plants
piastra (f)	*(pyAhs-trah)*	plate
piattaforma (f) di comodo	*(pyaht-tah-fOhr-mah deeh kOh-moh-doh)*	accommodation platform
piattino (m)	*(pyaht-tEEh-noh)*	saucer
piattino per il burro	*(pyAht-teeh-noh pehr eehl bOOhr-roh)*	butter dish
piatto (m)	*(pyAht-toh)*	dish, plate
piatto per dolci	*(pyAht-toh pehr dOhl-cheeh)*	dessert plate
piatto per insalata	*(pyAht-toh pehr leehn-sah-lAh-tah)*	salad plate
piazzare un ordine	*(pyahts-tsAh-reh oohn Ohr-deeh-neh))*	place an order (v)
piccola industria (f)	*(pEEhk-koh-lah eehn-dOOhs-treeh-ah)*	small business
piccola pubblicita (f)	*(pEEhk-koh-lah poohb-bleeh-cheeh-tAh)*	classified ad, want ad
piccolo furto (m)	*(pEEhk-koh-loh fOOhr-toh)*	pilferage
piega (f)	*(pyEh-gah)*	pleat
pieghettato	*(pyeh-geht-tAh-toh)*	pleated
pigmento (m)	*(peehg-mEhn-toh)*	pigment
pignone (m)	*(peeh-nyOh-neh)*	pinion
pillola (f)	*(pEEhl-loh-lah)*	pill
pilotaggio (m)	*(peeh-loh-tAhj-joh)*	pilotage
piroscissione (f)	*(peeh-roh-sheehs-syOh-neh)*	cracking
pistone (m)	*(ppehs-tOh-neh)*	piston

P

plusvalore (m)	*(ploohs-vah-lOh-reh)*	unearned increment
pneumatico (m)	*(pneh-ooh-mAh-teeh-koh)*	tire
pneumatico radiale	*(pneh-ooh-mAh-teeh-koh rah-dyAh-leh)*	radial tire
pochi (m) ordini di acquisto a un dato prezzo	*(pOh-keeh Ohr-deeh-neeh deeh ahk-kwEEhs-toh ah oohn dAh-toh prEhts-tsoh)*	thin market
poliestirolo (m)	*(poh-leeh-ehs-teeh-rOh-loh)*	polyester
polimero (m)	*(poh-lEEh-meh-roh)*	polymer
politica (f) aziendale	*(poh-lEEh-teeh-kah ah-dsyehn-dAh-leh)*	company policy
politica commerciale	*(poh-lEEh-teeh-kah kohm-mehr-chAh-leh)*	business policy
politica d'investimento	*(poh-lEEh-teeh-kah deehn-vehs-teeh-mEhn-toh)*	investment policy
politica di apertura	*(poh-lEEh-teeh-kah deeh ah-pehr-tOOh-rah)*	open door policy
politica di distribuzione	*(poh-lEEh-teeh-kah deeh deehs-treeh-booh-tsyOh-neh)*	distribution policy
politica monetaria	*(poh-lEEh-teeh-kah moh-neh-tAh-reeh-ah)*	monetary policy
polizza (f)	*(pOh-leehts-tsah)*	policy
polizza d'assicurazione	*(pOh-leehts-tsah dahs-seeh-kooh-rah-tsyOh-neh)*	insurance policy
polizza d'assicurazione di gruppo	*(pOh-leehts-tsah deeh ahs-seeh-kooh-rah-tsyOh-neh deeh grOOhp-poh)*	group insurance
polizza d'assicurazione sulla vita	*(pOh-leehts-tsah dahs-seeh-kooh-rah-tsyOh-neh soohl-lah vEEh-tah)*	life insurance policy
polizza di carico	*(pOh-leehts-tsah deeh kAh-reeh-koh)*	bill of lading
polizza di carico con riserve o eccezioni	*(pOh-leehts-tsah deeh kAh-reeh-koh kohn reeh-zEhr-veh oh ehch-cheh-tsyOh-neeh)*	foul bill of lading
polizza di carico nazionale	*(pOh-leehts-tsah deeh kAh-reeh-koh nah-tsyoh-nAh-leh)*	inland bill of lading

polizza per un gruppo di automobili	*(pOh-leehts-tsah pehr oohn grOOhp-poh deeh ah-ooh-toh-mOh-beeh-leeh)*	fleet policy
pollice (m)	*(pOhl-leeh-cheh)*	inch
polo (m)	*(pOh-loh)*	pole
polvere (f)	*(pOhl-veh-reh)*	powder
pomata (f)	*(poh-mAh-tah)*	salve
pompa (f) dell'acqua	*(pOhm-pah dehl Ahk-kwah)*	water pump
pompa dell'olio	*(pOhm-pah dehl Oh-leeh-oh)*	oil pump
poplina (f)	*(poh-plEE-nah)*	poplin
porcellana (f) "bone"	*(pohr-chehl-lAh-nah)*	bone china
porcellana	*(pohr-chehl-lAh-nah fEEh-neh)*	fine china
porre in vendita	*(pOhr-reh eehn vEhn-deeh-tah)*	offer for sale (v)
porta (m) pepe	*(pOhr-tah pEh-peh)*	pepper shaker
porta-a-porta (vendite)	*(pOhr-tah ah pOhr-tah/vEhn-deeh-teh)*	door-to-door (sales)
portabiglietti (m)	*(pohr-tah-beeh-lyEht-teeh)*	card case
portabiti (m)	*(pohrt-Ah-beeh-teeh)*	garment bag
portacarta (m)	*(pohr-tah-kAhr-tah)*	paper holder
portachiavi (m)	*(pohr-tah-kyAh-veeh)*	key case
portafogli (m)	*(pohr-tah-fOh-lyeeh)*	billfold, wallet
portafoglio (m)	*(pohr-tah-fOh-lyoh)*	portfolio
portafoglio azionario	*(pohr-tah-fOh-lyoh ah-tsyoh-nAh-reeh-oh)*	stock portfolio
portaforbici (m)	*(pohr-tah-fOhr-beeh-cheeh)*	scissor case
portaocchiali (m)	*(pohr-tah-ohk-kyAh-leeh)*	eyeglass case
portapassaporto (m)	*(pohr-tah-pahs-sah-pOhr-toh)*	passport case
portare a nuovo	*(pohr-tAh-reh)*	carry forward (v)
portasigarette (m)	*(pohr-tah-seeh-gah-rEht-teh)*	cigarette case
portatore (m)	*(pohr-tah-tOh-reh)*	bearer, carrier
portatore di obbligazioni	*(pohr-tah-tOh-reh deeh ohb-bleeh-gah-tsyOh-neeh)*	bonded carrier

portatrucco (m)	*(pohr-tah-trOOhk-koh)*	makeup case
porto (m) d'importazione denominato	*(pOhr-toh deehm-pohr-tah-tsyOh-neh deh-noh-meeh-nAh-toh)*	named port of importation
porto di spedizione denominato	*(pOhr-toh deeh speh-deeh-tsyOh-neh deh-noh-meeh-nAh-toh)*	named port of shipment
porto franco	*(pOhr-toh frAhn-koh)*	free port
posateria (f)	*(poh-zah-teh-rEEh-ah)*	cutlery
positivo (m)	*(poh-zeeh-tEEh-voh)*	positive
posizione (f) di mercato	*(poh-zeeh-tsyOh-neh deeh mehr-kAh-toh)*	market position
posizione netta	*(poh-zeeh-tsyOh-neh nEht-tah)*	net position, (of a trader)
posizione scoperta	*(poh-zeeh-tsyOh-neh skoh-pEhr-tah)*	short position
posizione secondaria	*(poh-zeeh-tsyOh-neh seh-kohn-dAh-reeh-ah)*	second position
possesso (m)	*(poh-sehs-Oh)*	possession
possessore in buona fede	*(pohs-sehs-sOh-reh eehn bwOh-nah fEh-deh)*	holder in due course
postdatare	*(post-dah-tAh-reh)*	afterdate (v), back date (v)
postdatato	*(post-dah-tAh-toh)*	postdated
posticipare	*(post-teeh-cheeh-pAh-reh)*	postpone (v)
postilla (f)	*(pohs-tEEh-lah)*	(contracts) rider
posto (m) di lavoro	*(pOhs-toh deeh lah-vOh-roh)*	place of business, work station, workplace
posto di lavoro autonomo	*(pOhs-toh deeh lah-vOh-roh ah-ooh-tOh-noh-moh)*	stand-alone work station
potenza (f)	*(poh-tEhn-dsah)*	power
potenza (f) in cavalli	*(poh-tEhn-dsah eehn kah-vAhl-leeh)*	horsepower
potenziale (m) di capacità produttiva di un impianto	*(poh-tehn-tsyAh-leh deeh kah-pah-cheeh-tAh proh-dooht-tEEh-vah deeh oohn eehm-pyAhn-toh)*	plant capacity
potenziale di crescita	*(poh-tehn-tsyAh-leh deeh krEh-sheeh-tah)*	growth potential

potenziale di mercato	*(poh-tehn-tsyAh-leh deeh mehr-kAh-toh)*	market potential
potere (m) d'acquisto	*(poh-tEh-reh dahk-kwEEhs-toh)*	purchasing power
potere del buono	*(poh-tEh-reh dehl bwOh-noh)*	bond power
potere delle azioni	*(poh-tEh-reh dehl-leh ah-tsyOh-neeh)*	stock power
potere di emettere obbligazioni	*(poh-tEh-reh deeh eh-mEht-teh-reh ohb-bleeh-gah-tsyOh-neeh)*	bond power
potere di negoziazione	*(poh-tEh-reh deeh neh-goh-tsyah-tsyOh-neh)*	bargaining power
prassi (f) burocratica	*(prAhs-seeh booh-roh-krAh-teeh-kah)*	red tape
pratiche (f) d'uso	*(prAh-teeh-keh dOOh-zoh)*	standard practice
pratico	*(prAh-teeh-koh)*	practical
preavviso (m)	*(preh-ahv-vEEh-zoh)*	advance notice
precedenza (f)	*(preh-cheh-dEhn-tsah)*	right of way
precetto (m)	*(preh-chEht-toh)*	garnishment
prefabbricazione (m)	*(preh-fahb-breeh-kah-tsyOh-neh)*	prefabrication
prefazione (f)	*(preh-fah-tsyOh-neh)*	preface
preferenza (f) per la liquidità	*(preh-feh-rEhn-tsah pehr la leeh-kweeh-deeh-tAh)*	liquidity preference, (economics)
premessa (m)	*(preh-mEhs-sah)*	introduction
premio (m)	*(prEh-myoh)*	bonus, (premium), reward
premio d'accelerazione	*(prEh-myoh dahch-cheh-leh-rah-tsyOh-neh)*	acceleration premium
premio d'assicurazione	*(prEh-myoh dahs-seeh-kooh-rah-tsyOh-neh)*	insurance premium
premio d'assicurazione	*(prEh-myoh dahs-seeh-kooh-rah-tsyOh-neh)*	premium, insurance
premio del compratore	*(prEh-myoh dehl kohm-prah-tOh-reh)*	buyer's premium
premio di redimibilità	*(prEh-myoh deeh reh-deeh-meeh-beeh-leeh-tAh)*	redemption premium
premio sulla zavorra	*(prEh-myoh sohl-lah dsah-vOhr-rah)*	ballast bonus

P

prendere in prestito	*(prEhn-deh-reh eehn prEhs-teeh-toh)*	borrow (v)
prendere la media	*(prEhn-deh-reh lah mEh-dyah)*	averaging
prepagare	*(preh-pah-gAh-reh)*	prepay (v)
preparatore (m) delle paghe	*(preh-pah-rah-tOh-reh)*	paymaster
presidente (m)	*(preh-zeeh-dEhn-teh)*	president
presidente del consiglio	*(preh-zeeh-dEhn-teh dehl kohn-sEEh-lyoh)*	chairman of the board
pressione (f)	*(prehs-syOh-neh)*	duress
pressione (f)	*(prehs-syOh-neh)*	pressure
prestiti (m) con tasso d'interesse basso (favorevole)	*(prEhs-teeh-teeh kohn tAhs-soh deehn-teh-rEhs-seh bAhs-soh/fah-voh-rEh-voh-leh)*	low-interest loans
prestiti erogati sulla base di una garanzia ricevuta	*(prEhs-teeh-teeh eh-roh-gAh-teeh soohl-lah bAh-zeh deeh ooh-nah gah-rahn-tsEEh-ah reeh-cheh-vOOh-tah)*	back-to-back loans
prestito (m)	*(prEhs-teeh-toh)*	loan
prestito a termine	*(prEhs-teeh-toh ah tEhr-meeh-neh)*	term loan
prestito bancario	*(prEhs-teeh-toh bahn-kAh-reeh-oh)*	bank loan
prestito con minor garanzia	*(prEhs-teeh-toh kohn meeh-nOhr gah-rahn-tsEEh-ah)*	soft loan
prestito fiduciario	*(prEhs-teeh-toh feeh-dooh-chAh-reeh-oh)*	fiduciary loan
prestito giornaliero	*(prEhs-teeh-toh johr-nah-lyEh-roh)*	day loan
prestito partecipato	*(prEhs-teeh-toh pahr-teh-cheeh-pAh-toh)*	participation loan
prestito rimborsabile a domanda	*(prEhs-teeh-toh reehm-bohr-sAh-beeh-leh ah doh-mAhn-dah)*	call loan
prestito senza garanzia	*(prEhs-teeh-toh sEhn-tsah gah-rahn-tsEEh-ah)*	unsecured loan
prestito vincolato	*(prEhs-teeh-toh veehn-koh-lAh-tah)*	tied loan

prevedere	*(preh-veh-dEh-reh)*	forecast (v)
preventivo (m) capitale	*(preh-vehn-tEEh-voh kah-peeh-tAh-leh)*	capital budget
preventivo d'investimento	*(preh-vehn-tEEh-voh deehn-vehs-teeh-mEhn-toh)*	investment budget
preventivo di cassa	*(preh-vehn-tEEh-voh deeh kAhs-sah)*	cash budget
preventivo in contanti	*(preh-vehn-tEEh-voh eehn kohn-tAhn-teeh)*	cash budget
preventivo operativo	*(preh-vehn-tEEh-voh oh-peh-rah-tEEh-voh)*	operating budget
preventivo per il marketing	*(preh-vehn-tEEh-voh pehr eehl marketing)*	marketing budget
preventivo per le spese di vendita	*(preh-veh-ntEEh-voh pehr leh spEh-zeh deeh vEhn-deeh-tah)*	sales budget
preventivo provvisorio	*(preh-vehn-tEEh-voh prohv-veeh-zOh-reeh-oh)*	interim budget
preventivo pubblicitario	*(preh-vehn-tEEh-voh poohb-leeh-cheeh-tAh-reeh-oh)*	advertising budget
preventivo spese impianti e macchinari	*(preh-vehn-tEEh-voh spEh-zeh eehm-pyAhn-teeh eh mahk-keeh-nAh-reeh)*	capital budget
previsione (f)	*(preh-veeh-zyOh-neh)*	forecast
previsione del bilancio	*(preh-veeh-zyOh-neh dehl beeh-lAhn-choh)*	budget forecast
previsione del mercato	*(preh-veeh-zyOh-neh dehl mehr-kAh-toh)*	market forecast
previsione di spese di consulenza	*(preh-veeh-zyOh-neh deeh spEh-zeh deeh kohn-sooh-lEhn-tsah)*	advisory funds
previsioni di vendita	*(preh-veeh-zyOh-neeh deeh vEhn-deeh-tah)*	sales forecast
prezzo (m)	*(prEhts-tsoh)*	price
prezzo al dettaglio	*(prEhts-tsoh ahl-deht-tAh-lyoh)*	retail price
prezzo al quale è redimibile un buono a richiesta	*(prEhts-tsoh ahl kwAh-leh eh reh-deeh-mEEh-beeh-leh oohn bwOh-noh ah reeh-kyEhs-tah)*	call price
prezzo all'ingrosso	*(prEhts-tsoh ahl eehn-grOhs-soh)*	wholesale price

prezzo alla chiusura	*(prEhts-tsoh ahl-lah kyooh-zOOh-rah)*	closing price
prezzo alla consegna	*(prEhts-tsoh ahl-lah kohn-sEh-nyah)*	delivered price
prezzo CIF rettificato	*(prEhts-tsoh reht-teeh-feeh-kAh-toh)*	adjusted CIF price
prezzo concorrenziale	*(prEhts-tsoh kohn-kohr-rehn-tsyAh-leh)*	competitive price
prezzo corrente	*(prEhts-tsoh kohr-rEhn-teh)*	going rate, (or price)
prezzo d'acquisto	*(prEhts-tsoh dahk-kwEEhs-toh)*	purchase price
prezzo d'emissione	*(prEhts-tsoh deh-meehs-syOh-neh)*	issue price
prezzo dell'oro	*(prEhts-tsoh dehl Oh-roh)*	gold price
prezzo di apertura del mercato	*(prEhts-tsoh deeh ah-pehr-tOOh-rah dehl mehr-kAh-toh)*	opening price
prezzo di base	*(prEhts-tsoh deeh bAh-zeh)*	base price
prezzo di consegna	*(prEhts-tsoh deeh kohn-sEh-nyah)*	delivery price
prezzo di listino	*(prEhts-tsoh deeh leehs-tEEh-noh)*	list price
prezzo di mercato	*(prEhts-tsoh deeh mehr-kAh-toh)*	price, market
prezzo di parità	*(prEhts-tsoh deeh pah-reeh-tAh)*	parity price
prezzo di premio	*(prEhts-tsoh deeh prEh-myoh)*	premium price
prezzo di sottoscrizione	*(prEhts-tsoh deeh soht-toh-skreeh-tsyOh-neh)*	subscription price
prezzo di una opzione di acquisto	*(prEhts-tsoh deeh ooh-nah ohp-tsyOh-neh deeh ahk-kwEEhs-toh)*	call price
prezzo fissato	*(prEhts-tsoh feehs-sAh-toh)*	pegged price
prezzo indicativo	*(prEhts-tsoh eehn-deeh-kah-tEEh-voh)*	target price
prezzo iniziale	*(prEhts-tsoh eeh-neeh-tsyAh-leh)*	opening price
prezzo limite	*(prEhts-tsoh lEEh-meeh-teh)*	price limit
prezzo lordo	*(prEhts-tsoh lOhr-doh)*	gross price

prezzo massimo	*(prEhts-tsoh mAhs-seeh-moh)*	top price
prezzo medio	*(prEhts-tsoh mEh-dyoh)*	average price
prezzo nominale	*(prEhts-tsoh noh-meeh-nAh-leh)*	nominal price
prezzo offerto	*(prEhts-tsoh ohf-fEhr-toh)*	offered price
prezzo previsto	*(prEhts-tsoh preh-vEEhs-toh)*	estimated price
prezzo reale	*(prEhts-tsoh reh-Ah-leh)*	real price
prezzo richiesto	*(prEhts-tsoh reeh-kyEhs-toh)*	asking price
prezzo unitario	*(prEhts-tsoh ooh-neeh-tAh-reeh-oh)*	unit price
prima azione (f) privilegiata	*(prEEh-mah ah-tsyOh-neh preeh-veeh-leh-jAh-tah)*	first preferred stock
prima partita ad entrare/la prima partita ad uscire	*(prEEh-mah pahr-tEEh-tah ad ehn-trAh-reh/prEEh-mah pahr-tEEh-tah ad ooh-shEEh-reh)*	first in-first out
principale (m)	*(preehn-cheeh-pAh-leh)*	principal
priorità (f)	*(preeh-oh-reeh-tAh)*	priority
privilegio (m) del venditore	*(preeh-veeh-lEEh-joh dehl vehn-deeh-tOh-reh)*	vendor's lien
pro capite	*(proh kAh-peeh-teh)*	per capita
problema (m)	*(proh-blEh-mah)*	problem
procedimento di produzione	*(proh-cheh-deeh-mEhn-toh deeh proh-dooh-tsyOh-neh)*	production process
procedura (f)	*(proh-cheh-dOOh-rah)*	process
procedura (f) brevettata	*(proh-cheh-dOOh-rah breh-veht-tAh-tah)*	patented process
procedura di regolamento	*(proh-cheh-dOOh-rah deeh reh-goh-lah-mEhn-toh)*	adjustment process
procedura elettrolitica	*(proh-cheh-dOOh-rah eh-leht-troh-lEEh-teeh-kah)*	electrolytic process
procedura per stabilire una lamentela	*(proh-cheh-dOOh-rah pehr stah-beeh-lEEh-reh ooh-nah lah-mehn-tEh-lah)*	grievance procedure
procedure restrittive di lavoro	*(proh-cheh-dOOh-reh rehs-treeht-tEEh-veh deeh lah-vOh-roh)*	restrictive labor practices

processo produttivo	*(proh-chEhs-soh proh-dooht-tEEh-voh)*	production process
procione (m) lavoratore	*(proh-chOh-neh lah-voh-rah-tOh-reh)*	raccoon
procura (f)	*(proh-kOOh-rah)*	power of attorney, proxy
prodotti (m)	*(proh-dOht-teeh)*	merchandise
prodotti (m) finiti	*(proh-dOht-teeh feeh-nEEh-teeh)*	finished products
prodotti agrari	*(proh-dOht-teeh ah-grAh-reeh)*	agricultural products
prodotti lattiero-caseari	*(proh-dOht-teeh laht-tyEh-roh kah-ẓeh-Ah-reeh)*	dairy products
prodotti piatti	*(proh-dOht-teeh pyAht-teeh)*	flat products
prodotto (m)	*(proh-dOht-toh)*	product
prodotto derivato	*(proh-dOht-toh deh-reeh-vAh-toh)*	by-product
prodotto finale	*(proh-dOht-toh feeh-nAh-leh)*	end product
prodotto interno lordo	*(proh-dOht-toh eehn-tEhr-noh lOhr-doh)*	gross domestic product
prodotto locale	*(proh-dOht-toh loh-kAh-leh)*	native produce
prodotto nazionale lordo (Pnl)	*(proh-dOht-toh nah-tsyoh-nAh-leh lOhr-doh)*	gross national product, (GNP)
prodotto secondario	*(proh-dOht-toh seh-kohn-dAh-ryoh)*	by-product
produttività (f)	*(proh-dooh-teeh-veeh-tAh)*	productivity
produttività marginale	*(proh-dooh-teeh-veeh-tAh mahr-jeeh-nAh-leh)*	marginal productivity
produttore (m)	*(proh-dooht-tOh-reh)*	manufacturer
produzione (f)	*(proh-dooh-tsyOh-neh)*	output, outturn, production
produzione del computer	*(proh-dooh-tsyOh-neh dehl computer)*	computer output
produzione di serie	*(proh-dooh-tsyOh-neh deeh sEh-reeh-eh)*	mass production
produzione in lotti	*(proh-dooh-tsyOh-neh eehn lOht-teeh)*	batch production

produzione modulare	*(proh-dooh-tsyOh-neh moh-dooh-lAh-reh)*	modular production
produzione per conto terzi	*(proh-dooh-tsyOh-neh pehr kOhn-toh tEhr-tseeh)*	private label, (or brand)
professione (f)	*(proh-fehs-syOh-neh)*	profession
profilo (m) di acquisizione, profilo d'acquisto	*(proh-fEEh-loh deeh ahk-kweeh-zeeh-tsyOh-neh), (proh-fEEh-loh dahk-kwEEhs-toh)*	acquisition profile
profitti (m) inattesi	*(proh-fEEht-teeh eehn-aht-tEh-zeeh)*	windfall profits
profitti ritenuti	*(proh-fEEht-teeh reeh-teh-nOOh-teeh)*	retained earnings
profitto (m)	*(proh-fEEht-toh)*	profit
profitto lordo	*(proh-fEEht-toh lOhr-doh)*	gross profit
profitto netto	*(proh-fEEht-toh nEht-toh)*	net profit
profitto su carta	*(proh-fEEht-toh sooh kAhr-tah)*	paper profit
profitto sull'investimento	*(proh-fEEht-toh soohl eehn-vehs-teeh-mEhn-toh)*	return on investment
progettare	*(proh-jeht-tAh-reh)*	plan (v)
progettare	*(proh-jeht-tAh-reh)*	project (v)
progettazione (f) d'impianti	*(proh-jeht-tah-tsyOh-neh deehm-pyAhn-teeh)*	design engineering
progettazione (f) dei sistemi di elaborazione	*(proh-jeht-tah-tsyOh-neh deh-eeh seehs-tEh-meeh deeh eh-lah-boh-rah-tsyOh-neh)*	systems design, systems engineering
progettazione industriale	*(proh-jeht-tah-tsyOh-neh eehn-doohs-tryAh-leh)*	design engineering
progettazione industriale	*(proh-jeht-tah-tsyOh-neh eehn-doohs-tryAh-leh)*	industrial engineering
progettazione utilizzante costi più bassi tra costi alternativi per espletare una certa attività	*(proh-jeht-tah-tsyOh-neh ooh-teeh-leehds-dsAhn-teh kOhs-teeh pyOOh bAhs-seeh trah kOhs-teeh ahl-tehr-nah-tEEh-veeh pehr ehs-pleh-tAh-reh ooh-nah chEhr-tah aht-teeh-veeh-tAh)*	value engineering
progetto (m)	*(proh-jEht-toh)*	project
programma (m)	*(proh-grAhm-mah)*	program

programma d'investimento	*(proh-grAhm-mah deehn-vehs-teeh-mEhn-toh)*	investment program
programma del computer	*(proh-grAhm-mah dehl computer)*	computer program
programma dell'elaboratore	*(proh-grAhm-mah dehl eh-lah-boh-rah-tOh-reh)*	computer program
programma di mercato	*(proh-grAhm-mah deeh mehr-kAh-toh)*	market plan
programma di produzione	*(proh-grAhm-mah deeh proh-dooh-tsyOh-neh)*	production schedule
programmare	*(proh-grahm-mAh-reh)*	program (v)
programmazione (f) aziendale	*(proh-grahm-mah-tsyOh-neh ah-dsyehn-dAh-leh)*	corporate planning
programmazione lineare	*(proh-grahm-mah-tsyOh-neh leeh-neh-Ah-reh)*	linear programming
proiettare	*(proh-yeht-tAh-reh)*	project (v)
proiezione (f) degli utili	*(proh-yeh-tsyOh-neh deh-lyeeh OOh-teeh-leeh)*	profit projection
promessa (f)	*(proh-mEhs-sah)*	covenant, pledge
promozione (f)	*(proh-moh-tsyOh-neh)*	promotion
promozione delle vendite	*(proh-moh-tsyOh-neh dehl-leh vEhn-deeh-teh)*	sales promotion
pronto	*(prOhn-toh)*	prompt
pronto per l'utilizzo	*(prOhn-toh pehr looh-teeh-lEEhds-dsoh)*	(computer) on line
proporzione (f)	*(proh-pohr-tsyOh-neh)*	ratio
proprietà (f)	*(proh-pryeh-tAh)*	ownership, property
proprietà incamerata	*(proh-pryeh-tAh eehn-kah-meh-rAh-tah)*	escheat
proprietà personale	*(proh-pryeh-tAh pehr-soh-nAh-leh)*	personal property
proprietà pubblica	*(proh-preyh-tAh pOOhb-leeh-kah)*	public property
proprietario (m)	*(proh-pryeh-tAh-reeh-oh)*	landowner, owner, proprietor
proprietario assente	*(proh-pryeh-tAh-reeh-oh ahs-sEhn-teh)*	absentee ownership
proprietario unico	*(proh-pryeh-tAh-reeh-oh OOh-neeh-koh)*	sole proprietor

propulsione (f)	*(proh-poohl-syOh-neh)*	propulsion
prospettiva (f)	*(prohs-peht-tEEh-vah)*	outlook
prospetto (m)	*(prohs-pEht-toh)*	prospectus
prospetto preliminare	*(prohs-pEht-toh preh-leeh-meeh-nAh-reh)*	preliminary prospectus
protestare	*(proh-tehs-tAh-reh)*	protest (banking; law) (v)
protezione (f) dalla richiesta di un rimborso immediato (obbligazioni)	*(proh-teh-tsyOh-neh dahl-lah reeh-kyEhs-tah deeh oohn reehm-bOhr-soh eehm-meh-dyAh-toh ohb-bleeh-gah-tsyOh-neeh)*	call protection
protezionismo (m)	*(proh-teh-tsyoh-nEEhz-moh)*	protectionism
protone (m)	*(proh-tOh-neh)*	proton
prototipo (m)	*(proh-tOh-teeh-poh)*	prototype
prova (f)	*(prOh-vah)*	experiment
proventi (m)	*(proh-vEhn-teeh)*	proceeds
proventi sul capitale	*(proh-vEhn-teeh soohl kah-peeh-tAh-leh)*	return on capital
provvigione (f)	*(prohv-veeh-jOh-neh)*	(fee) commission
provvisorio	*(prohv-veeh-zOh-reeh-oh)*	interim
pubbliche (f) relazioni	*(pOOhb-leeh-keh reh-lah-tsyOh-neeh)*	public relations
pubblicità (f)	*(poohb-leeh-cheeh-tAh)*	advertising, publicity
pubblicità cooperativa (in compartecipa-zione)	*(poohb-leeh-cheeh-tAh koh-ohpeh-rah-tEEh-cah eehn kohm-pahr-teh-ceeh-pah-tsyOh-neh)*	cooperative advertising
pubblicità diretta	*(poohb-leeh-cheeh-tAh deeh-rEht-tah)*	direct mail
pubblicità istituzionale	*(poohb-leeh-cheeh-tAh eehs-teeh-tooh-tsyoh-nAh-leh)*	institutional advertising
punti (m) di consegna	*(pOOhn-teeh deeh kohn-sEh-nyah)*	delivery points
punti di maggior interesse nel rapporto finanziario	*(pOOhn-teeh deeh mahj-jOhr eehn-teh-rEhs-seh nehl rahp-pOhr-toh feeh-nahn-tsyAh-reeh-oh)*	financial highlights

punto (centesimo di un percento di base)	*(pOOhn-toh chehn-tEh-zeeh-moh deeh oohn peh-chEhn-toh deeh bAh-zeh)*	basis point, (¹⁄₁₀₀%)
punto (m)	*(pOOhn-toh)*	stitch
punto (m) comune oltremare	*(pOOhn-toh koh-mOOh-neh ohl-treh-mAh-reh)*	overseas common point
punto (m) tipografico	*(pOOhn-toh teeh-poh-grAh-feeh-koh)*	point
punto d'esportazione indicato	*(pOOhn-toh dehs-pohr-tah-tsyOh-neh eehn-deeh-kAh-toh)*	named point of exportation
punto d'origine indicato	*(pOOhn-toh doh-rEEh-jeeh-neh eehn-deeh-kAh-toh)*	named point of origin
punto della parità	*(pOOhn-toh deeh pah-reeh-tAh)*	break-even point
punto di pareggio	*(pOOhn-toh deeh pah-rEhj-joh)*	break-even point
punto di vantaggio	*(pOOhn-toh deeh vahn-tAhj-joh)*	competitive edge
punto di vendita	*(pOOhn-toh deeh vEhn-deeh-tah)*	point of sale
punto interno denominato nel paese d'importazione	*(pOOhn-toh eehn-tEhr-noh deh-noh-meeh-nAh-toh nehl pah-Eh-zeh deehm-pohr-tah-tsyOh-neh)*	named inland point in country of origin
punto morto	*(pOOhn-toh mOhr-toh)*	deadlock
puntura (f)	*(poohn-tOOh-rah)*	injection
purgante (m)	*(poohr-gAhn-teh)*	laxative, purgative
purificazione (f)	*(pooh-reeh-feeh-kah-tsyOh-neh)*	purification
puzzola (f)	*(pOOhts-tsoh-lah)*	fitch

Q

quadrettatura (f)	*(kwah-dreht-tah-tOOh-rah)*	grid
quadro (m) amministrativo	*(kwAh-droh ahm-meeh-neehs-trah-tEEh-voh)*	management chart
qualifiche (f)	*(kwah-lEEh-feeh-keh)*	qualifications
qualità (f) commerciale	*(kwah-leeh-tAh kohm-mehr-chAh-leh)*	commercial grade

quando emesso	*(kwAhn-doh eh-mEhs-soh)*	when issued
quantità (f)	*(kwahn-teeh-tAh)*	quantity
quantità di lavoro	*(kwahn-teeh-tAh deeh lah-vOh-roh)*	work load
quantità di materiale messa in produzione durante un determinato periodo	*(kwahn-teeh-tAh deeh mah-teh-ryAh-leh mEhs-sah eehn proh-dooh-tsyOh-neh dooh-rAhn-teh oohn deh-tehr-meeh-nAh-toh peh-rEEh-oh-doh)*	throughput
quantità per un ordine economico	*(kwahn-teeh-tAh pehr oohn Ohr-deeh-neh eh-koh-nOh-meeh-koh)*	economic order quantity
quattro colori	*(kwAht-troh koh-lOh-reeh)*	four colors
questione (f) di procedura	*(kwehs-tyOh-neh deeh proh-cheh-dOOh-rah)*	point of order
quorum (m)	*(koo-Oh-room)*	quorum
quota (f)	*(kwOh-tah)*	quota
quota d'esportazione	*(kwOh-tah dehs-pohr-tah-tsyOh-neh)*	export quota
quota d'importazione	*(kwOh-tah deehm-pohr-tah-tsyOh-neh)*	import quota
quota di mercato	*(kwOh-tah deeh mehr-kAh-toh)*	market share
quota di vendita	*(kwOh-tah deeh vEhn-deeh-tah)*	sales quota
quotazione (f)	*(kwoh-tah-tsyOh-neh)*	quotation
quotazione fuori borsa	*(kwoh-tah-tsyOh-neh fwOh-reeh bOhr-sah)*	over-the-counter quotation

R

raccoglimento (m) dei capitali	*(rahk-koh-lyeeh-mEhn-toh deh-eeh kah-peeh-tAh-leeh)*	raising capital
raccolta dei capitali	*(rahk-kOhl-tah deh-eeh kah-peeh-tAh-leeh)*	capital, raising
raccomandata (f)	*(rahk-koh-mahn-dAh-tah)*	registered mail
radar (m)	*(raydahr)*	radar
radio (f)	*(rAh-deeh-oh)*	radio

raffinare	*(rahf-feeh-nAh-reh)*	refine (v)
raffineria (f)	*(rahf-feeh-neh-rEEh-ah)*	refinery
rafforzamento (m) delle azioni	*(rahf-fohr-tsah-mEhn-toh dehl-leh ah-tsyOh-neeh)*	rally
raggiungere una media	*(rahj-jOOhn-jeh-reh ooh-nah mEh-dyah)*	averaging
raggrupamento (m) dei conti	*(rahg-groohp-pah-mEhn-toh)*	group accounts
ragioniere (m) diplomato dallo stato	*(rah-joh-nyEh-reh deeh-ploh-mAh-toh dehl-loh stAh-toh)*	certified public accountant
ragioniere professionista	*(rah-joh-nyEh-reh proh-fehs-syoh-nEEhs-tah)*	chartered accountant
raion (m)	*(rah-yOhn)*	rayon
rame (m)	*(rAh-meh)*	copper
rapporti (m) sindacali	*(rahp-pOhr-teeh seehn-dah-kAh-leeh)*	labor relations
rapporto (m) annuale	*(rahp-pOhr-toh ahn-nwAh-leh)*	annual report
rapporto corrente	*(rahp-pOhr-toh kohr-rEhn-teh)*	current ratio
rapporto d'alimentazione	*(rahp-pOhr-toh dah-leeh-mehn-tah-tsyOh-neh)*	feed ratio
rapporto di contabilità	*(rahp-pOhr-toh deeh kohn-tah-beeh-leeh-tAh)*	accounting ratio
rapporto di copertura	*(rahp-pOhr-toh deeh koh-pehr-tOOh-rah)*	cover ratio
rapporto di liquidità	*(rahp-pOhr-toh deeh leeh-kweeh-deeh-tAh)*	acid-test ratio
rapporto di liquidità	*(rahp-pOhr-toh deeh leeh-kweeh-deeh-tAh)*	liquidity ratio
rapporto perdita contro perdita	*(rahp-pOhr-toh pEhr-deeh-tah kOhn-troh pEhr-deeh-tah)*	loss-loss ratio
rapporto sul mercato	*(rahp-pOhr-toh soohl mehr-kAh-toh)*	market report
rapporto tra capitale e produzione	*(rahp-pOhr-toh trah kah-peeh-tAh-leh eh proh-dooh-tsyOh-neh)*	capital-output ratio

R

rapporto tra i prezzi ed i guadagni di un azione	*(rahp-pOhr-toh trah eeh (prEhts-tseeh eh eeh gwah-dAh-nyeeh deeh oohn ah-tsyOh-neh)*	price/earnings ratio, p/e ratio
rapporto tra il reddito e la parità	*(rahp-pOhr-toh trah eehl rEhd-deeh-toh eh lah pah-reeh-tAh)*	parity income ratio
rappresentante (m)	*(rahp-preh-zehn-tAhn-teh)*	representative
rappresentante del produttore	*(rahp-preh-zehn-tAhn-teh dehl proh-dooht-tOh-reh)*	manufacturer's representative
rappresentante nominato	*(rahp-preh-zehn-tAhn-teh noh-meeh-nAh-toh)*	registered representative
raschiatura (f)	*(rahs-kyah-tOOh-rah)*	scoring
razionare	*(rah-tsyoh-nAh-reh)*	ration (v)
reagente (m)	*(reh-ah-jEhn-teh)*	reagent
reattivo (m)	*(reh-aht-tEEh-voh)*	reagent
recessione (f)	*(reh-chehs-syOh-neh)*	recession
reclamo (m)	*(reh-klAh-moh)*	claim
reclamo indiretto	*(reh-klAh-moh eehn-deeh-rEht-toh)*	indirect claim
recuperare	*(reh-kooh-peh-rAh-reh)*	salvage (v)
redattore (m)	*(reh-daht-tOh-reh)*	editor
redditività (f)	*(rehd-deeht-teeh-veeh-tAh)*	profitability
reddito (m)	*(rEhd-deeh-toh)*	income, yield
reddito alla maturità	*(rEhd-deeh-toh ahl-lah mah-tooh-reeh-tAh)*	yield to maturity
reddito annuale variabile	*(rEhd-deeh-toh ahn-nwAh-leh vah-ryAh-beeh-leh)*	variable annuity
reddito differito	*(rEhd-deeh-toh deehf-feh-rEEh-toh)*	deferred income
reddito disponibile	*(rEhd-deeh-toh deehs-poh-nEEh-beeh-leh)*	disposable income
reddito effettivo	*(rEhd-deeh-toh ehf-feht-tEEh-voh)*	actual income
reddito esentasse	*(rEhd-deeh-toh eh-zehn-tAhs-seh)*	tax-free income
reddito futuro scontato al valore attuale	*(rEhd-deeh-toh fooh-tOOh-roh skohn-tAh-toh ahl vah-lOh-reh aht-twAh-leh)*	discounted cash flow

R

reddito lordo	*(rEhd-deeh-toh lOhr-doh)*	gross income
reddito maturato	*(rEhd-deeh-toh mah-tooh-rAh-toh)*	accrued revenue
reddito netto	*(rEhd-deeh-toh nEht-toh)*	net income
reddito nominale	*(rEhd-deeh-toh noh-meeh-nAh-leh)*	nominal yield
reddito non da lavoro	*(rEhd-deeh-toh nohn dah lah-vOh-roh)*	unearned revenue
reddito operativo	*(rEhd-deeh-toh oh-peh-rah-tEEh-voh)*	operating income
reddito reale	*(rEhd-deeh-toh reh-Ah-leh)*	real income
reddito sugli interessi	*(rEhd-deeh-toh sooh-lyeeh eehn-teh-rEhs-seeh)*	interest income
reddito sul capitale netto	*(rEhd-deeh-toh soohl kah-peeh-tAh-leh nEht-toh)*	return on equity
redigere	*(reh-dEEh-jeh-reh)*	edit (v)
referenza (f) bancaria	*(reh-feh-rEhn-tsah bahn-kAh-reeh-sh)*	credit reference
referenza per ottenere credito	*(reh-feh-rEhn-tsah pehr oht-teh-nEh-reh krEh-deeh-toh)*	credit reference
refrattari (m)	*(reh-fraht-tAh-reeh)*	refractories
registrare	*(reh-jeehs-trah-tsyOh-neh)*	post (v) (bookkeeping)
registrazione (f) a debito	*(reh-jeehs-trah-tsyOh-neh ah dEh-beeh-toh)*	debit entry
registrazione del movimento di cassa	*(reh-jeehs-trah-tsyOh-neh dehl moh-veeh-mEhn-toh deeh kAhs-sah)*	cash entry
registro (m)	*(reh-jEEhs-troh)*	register
regolamenti (m)	*(reh-goh-lah-mEhn-teeh)*	bylaws
reinvestire	*(reh-eehn-vehs-tEEh-reh)*	plow back (v) (earnings)
relazione (f)	*(reh-lah-tsyOh-neh)*	report
relazione del movimento di cassa	*(reh-lah-tsyOh-neh dehl moh-veeh-mEhn-toh deeh kAhs-sah)*	cash flow statement
relazione sugli utili	*(reh-lah-tsyOh-neh sooh-lyeeh OOh-teeh-leeh)*	earnings report

relazioni con gli investitori	*(reh-lah-tsyOh-neeh kohn lyeeh eehn-vehs-teeh-tOh-reeh)*	investor relations
relazioni con il personale	*(reh-lah-tsyOh-neeh kohn eehl pehr-soh-nAh-leh)*	employee relations
relazioni industriali	*(reh-lah-tsyOh-neeh eehn-doohs-tryAh-leeh)*	industrial relations
remissione (f) dell'imposta	*(reh-meehs-syOh-neh dehl eehm-pOhs-tah)*	remission duty
remissione di una tassa	*(reh-meehs-syOh-neh deeh ooh-nah tAhs-sah)*	remission of a tax
rendere	*(rEhn-deh-reh)*	yield (v)
rendere disponibile	*(rEhn-deh-reh deehs-poh-nEEh-beeh-leh)*	make available (v)
rendiconto (m) bancario	*(rehn-deeh-kOhn-toh bahn-kAh-reeh-oh)*	bank statement
rendimento (m)	*(rehn-deeh-mEhn-toh)*	income yield, yield, yield to maturity
rendimento (m)	*(rehn-deeh-mEhn-toh)*	power
rendimento competitivo agli investimenti alternativi	*(rehn-deeh-mEhn-toh kohm-peh-teeh-tEEh-voh ah-lyeeh eehn-vehs-teeh-mEhn-teeh ahl-tehr-nah-tEEh-veeh)*	fair return
rendimento corrente	*(rehn-deeh-mEhn-toh kohr-rEhn-teh)*	current yield
rendimento del dividendo	*(rehn-deeh-mEhn-toh dehl deeh-veeh-dEhn-doh)*	dividend yield
rendimento effettivo	*(rehn-deeh-mEhn-toh ehf-feht-tEEh-voh)*	effective yield
rendimento interno	*(rehn-deeh-mEhn-toh eehn-tOhr-noh)*	internal rate of return
rendimento lordo	*(rehn-deeh-mEhn-toh lOhr-doh)*	gross yield
rendimento piatto	*(rehn-deeh-mEhn-toh pyAht-toh)*	flat yield
rendimento reale al netto di tasse	*(rehn-deeh-mEhn-toh reh-Ah-leh ahl nEht-toh deeh tAhs-seh)*	after-tax real rate of return
rendimento sui guadagni	*(rehn-deeh-mEhn-toh sooh-eeh gwah-dAh-nyeeh)*	earnings performance

rendimento sul capitale	*(rehn-deeh-mEhn-toh soohl kah-peeh-tAh-leh)*	return on capital
rendimento sulle attività amministrate	*(rehn-deeh-mEhn-toh soohl-leh aht-teeh-veeh-tAh ahm-meeh-neehs-trAh-teh)*	return on assets managed
rendita (f)	*(rEhn-deeh-tah)*	annuity
rendita settimanale	*(rEhn-deeh-tah seht-teeh-mah-nAh-leh)*	weekly return
rendita sui guadagni	*(rEhn-deeh-tah sooh-eeh gwah-dAh-nyeeh)*	earnings yield
rendite differite	*(rEhn-deeh-teh deehf-feh-rEEh-teh)*	deferred annuities
reparto (m)	*(reh-pAhr-toh)*	department
reparto affittato	*(reh-pAhr-toh ahf-feeht-tAh-toh)*	leased department
reparto contabilità	*(reh-pAhr-toh kohn-tah-beeh-leeh-tAh)*	accounting department
reparto personale	*(reh-pAhr-toh pehr-soh-nAh-leh)*	personnel department
reparto progettazione e stilismo	*(reh-pAhr-toh proh-jeht-tah-tsyOh-neh eh steeh-lEEhz-moh)*	engineering and design department
requisiti (f)	*(reh-kweeh-zEEh-teeh)*	requirements
resa (f)	*(rEh-zah)*	yield
resa (f) sui capitali	*(rEh-zah sooh-eeh kah-peeh-tAh-leeh)*	return on capital
resa sulle vendite	*(rEh-zah sohl-leh vEhn-deeh-teh)*	return on sales
resistenza (f)	*(reh-zeehs-tEhn-tsah)*	resistance
responsabile (m) degli acquisti	*(rehs-pohn-sAh-beeh-leh deh-lyeeh ahk-kwEEhs-teeh)*	chief buyer
responsabile delle esportazioni	*(rehs-pohn-sAh-beeh-leh dehl-leh ehs-pohr-tah-tsyOh-neeh)*	export manager
responsabile per l'imposta	*(rehs-pohn-sAh-beeh-leh pehr leehm-pOhs-tah)*	liable for tax
responsabilità (f)	*(rehs-pohn-sah-beeh-leeh-tAh)*	accountability, liability
responsabilità assunta	*(rehs-pohn-sAh-beeh-leh ahs-soohn-tah)*	assumed liability

R

responsabilità congiunta	*(rehs-pohn-sah-beeh-leeh-tAh kohn-jOOhn-tah)*	joint liability
responsabilità contingente	*(rehs-pohn-sah-beeh-leeh-tAh kohn-teehn-jEhn-teh)*	contingent liability
responsabilità corrente	*(rehs-pohn-sah-beeh-leeh-tAh kohr-rEhn-teh)*	current liabilities
responsabilità dell'acquirente	*(rehs-pohn-sah-beeh-leeh-tAh dehl ahk-kweeh-rEhn-teh)*	buyer's responsibility
responsabilità differite	*(rehs-pohn-sah-beeh-leeh-tAh deef-feh-rEEh-teh)*	deferred liabilities
responsabilità effettiva	*(rehs-pohn-sah-beeh-leeh-tAh ehf-feht-tEEh-vah)*	actual liability
responsabilità fissa	*(rehs-pohn-sah-beeh-leeh-tAh fEEhs-sah)*	fixed liability
responsabilità limitata	*(rehs-pohn-sah-beeh-leeh-tAh leeh-meeh-tAh-tah)*	limited liability
responsabilità personale	*(rehs-pohn-sah-beeh-leeh-tAh pehr-soh-nAh-leh)*	personal liability
restrizioni (f) all'esportazione	*(rehs-treeh-tsyOh-neeh ahl ehs-pohr-tah-tsyOh-neh)*	restrictions on export
rete (f) di distribuzione	*(rEh-teh deeh deehs-treeh-booh-tsyOh-neh)*	distribution network
retroazione (f)	*(reh-troh-ah-tsyOh-neh)*	feedback
revisione (f) annuale dei conti	*(reh-veeh-zyOh-neh ahn-nwAh-leh deh-eeh kOhn-teeh)*	annual audit
revisione interna	*(reh-veeh-zyOh-neh eehn-tEhr-nah)*	internal audit
revisore (m)	*(reh-veeh-zOh-reh)*	auditor
revisore bancario	*(reh-veeh-zOh-reh bahn-kAh-reeh-oh)*	bank examiner
riacquistare	*(reeh-ahk-kweehs-tAh-reh)*	buy back (v)
riassicuratore (m)	*(reeh-ahs-seeh-kooh-rah-tOh-reh)*	reinsurer
ribasso (m)	*(reeh-lAhs-soh)*	downswing, downturn
ricambio (m) della manodopera	*(reeh-kAhm-byoh dehl-lah mah-noh-dOh-peh-rah)*	labor turnover
ricambio delle azioni	*(reeh-kAhm-byoh dehl-leh ah-tsyOh-neeh)*	stock turnover

R

ricapitalizzazione (f)	*(reeh-kah-peeh-tah-leehds-dsah-tsyOh-neh)*	recapitalization
ricarico (m)	*(reeh-kAh-reeh-koh)*	markup
ricavi (m) marginali	*(reeh-kAh-veeh mahr-jeeh-nAh-leeh)*	marginal revenue
ricavo (m)	*(reeh-kAh-voh)*	revenue
ricchezza (f)	*(reehk-kEhts-tsah)*	wealth
ricerca (f)	*(reeh-chEhr-kah)*	research
ricerca di azione	*(reeh-chEhr-kah deeh ah-tsyOh-neh)*	action research
ricerca di mercato	*(reeh-chEhr-kah deeh mehr-kAh-toh)*	market research
ricerca di personale dirigenziale	*(reeh-chEhr-kah deeh pehr-soh-nAh-leh deeh-jeeh-rehn-tsyAh-leh)*	executive search
ricerca e lo sviluppo	*(reeh-chEhr-kah eh loh zveeh-lOOhp-poh)*	research and development
ricerca sul consumatore	*(reeh-chEhr-kah soohl kohn-sooh-mah-tOh-reh)*	consumer research
ricevuta (f)	*(reeh-cheh-vOOh-tah)*	receipt, voucher
ricevuta del custode del molo	*(reeh-cheh-vOOh-tah dehl koohs-tOh-deh dehl mOh-loh)*	dock, (ship's receipt)
ricevuta fiduciaria	*(reeh-cheh-vOOh-tah feeh-dooh-chAh-reeh-ah)*	trust receipt
richiamo (m) (in genere per articoli difettosi)	*(reeh-kyAh-moh eehn jEh-neh-reh pehr ahr-tEEh-koh-leeh deeh-feht-tOh-zeeh)*	callback
richiedente un notevole investimento di capitale	*(reeh-kyeh-dEhn-teh oohn noh-tEh-voh-leh eehn-vehs-teeh-mEhn-toh deeh kah-peeh-tAh-leh)*	capital-intensive
richiedere	*(reeh-kyEh-deh-reh)*	demand (v)
richiedere il saldo del deposito per coprire perdite sulla borsa	*(reeh-kyEh-deh-reh eehl sAhl-doh dehl deh-pOh-zeeh-toh pehr koh-prEEh-reh pEhr-deeh-teh soohl-lah bOhr-sah)*	margin call
richiesta (f)	*(reeh-kyEhs-tah)*	demand
richiesta d'appalto	*(reeh-kyEhs-tah dahp-pAhl-toh)*	advertisement, (request) for bid

R

richiesta d'appalto	*(reeh-kyEhs-tah dahp-pAhl-toh)*	invitation to bid
riconoscere	*(reeh-koh-nOh-sheh-reh)*	acknowledge (v)
riconoscimento (m) della marca	*(reeh-koh-noh-sheeh-mEhn-toh dehl-lah mAhr-kah)*	brand recognition
ricorso (m)	*(reeh-kOhr-soh)*	recourse
ricorso al prestito per finanziare un'attività	*(reeh-kOhr-soh ahl prEhs-teeh-toh pehr feeh-nahn-tsyAh-reh oohn aht-teeh-veeh-tAh)*	deficit financing
ricottura (f)	*(reeh-koht-tOOh-rah)*	annealing
ricovero (m)	*(reeh-kOh-veh-roh)*	recovery
ridurre l'inventario	*(reeh-dOOhr-reh leehn-vehn-tAh-ryoh)*	draw down (v)
riduzione (f)	*(reeh-dooh-tsyOh-neh)*	abatement, cutback, rollback
riduzione (f)	*(reeh-dooh-tsyOh-neh)*	reduction
riduzione dei costi	*(reeh-dooh-tsyOh-neh deh-eeh kOhs-teeh)*	cost reduction
riduzione dei prezzi	*(reeh-dooh-tsyOh-neh deh-eeh prEhts-tseeh)*	price cutting
riduzione del margine (di profitto)	*(reeh-dooh-tsyOh-neh dehl mAhr-jee-neh)*	cost-price squeeze
riduzione delle tasse tramite facilitazioni permesse dal governo	*(reeh-dooh-tsyOh-neh dehl-leh tAhs-seh trAh-meeh-teh fah-cheeh-leeh-tah-tsyOh-neeh pehr-mEhs-seh dahl goh-vEhr-noh)*	tax shelter
riduzione nel numero delle azioni	*(reeh-dooh-tsyOh-neh nehl nOOh-meh-roh dehl-leh ah-tsyOh-neeh)*	reverse stock split
riempire	*(reeh-ehm-pEEh-reh)*	top up (v)
rientro (m) in possesso	*(reeh-Ehn-troh)*	repossession
riesportare	*(reeh-ehs-pohr-tAh-reh)*	re-export (v)
rifilare	*(reeh-feeh-lAh-reh)*	crop (v)
rifinanziamento (m)	*(reeh-feeh-nahn-tsyah-mEhn-toh)*	refinancing
rifiutare accettazione	*(reeh-fyooh-tAh-reh ahcheht-tah-tsyOh-neh)*	refuse acceptance (v)
rifiutare pagamento	*(reeh-fyooh-tAh-reh pah-gah-mEhn-toh)*	refuse payment (v)

R

riflazione (f)	*(reeh-flah-tsyOh-neh)*	reflation
riforma (f) fondiaria	*(reeh-fOhr-mah fohn-dyAh-reeh-ah)*	land reform
riguardo (al riguardo)	*(reeh-gwAhr-doh)*	regard (with regard to)
rilegato	*(reeh-leh-gAh-toh)*	sewn
rilevazione (f) delle quote dei soci liquidati	*(reeh-leh-vah-tsyOh-neh dehl-leh kwOh-teh deh-eeh sOh-cheeh leeh-kweeh-dAh-teeh)*	buyout
rimanenze (f)	*(reeh-mah-nEhn-tseh)*	odd lot
rimasugli (m)	*(reeh-mah-sOOh-lyeeh)*	dregs
rimborsare	*(reehm-bohr-sAh-reh)*	reimburse (v)
rimborso (m)	*(reehm-bOhr-soh)*	refund
rimborso anticipato	*(reehm-bOhr-soh ahn-teeh-chee-pAh-toh)*	advance refunding
rimborso delle spese	*(reehm-bOhr-soh dehl-leh spEh-zeh)*	recovery of expenses
rimedi (m)	*(reeh-mEh-deeh)*	remedies
rimedio (m)	*(reeh-mEh-dyoh)*	remedy, (law)
rimunerazione (f)	*(reeh-mooh-neh-rah-tsyOh-neh)*	remuneration
rinegoziare	*(reeh-neh-goh-tsyAh-reh)*	renegotiate (v)
rinnovare	*(reehn-noh-vAh-reh)*	renew (v)
rinuncia (f) ad un atto di proprietà	*(reeh-nOOhn-chah ad oohn Aht-toh deeh propryeh-tAh)*	quitclaim deed
rinvenimento (m)	*(reehn-veh-neeh-mEhn-toh)*	temper
rinvestimento (m) degli utili di un investimento	*(reehn-vehs-teeh-mEhn-toh deh-lyeeh OOh-teeh-leeh deeh oohn eehn-vehs-teeh-mEhn-toh)*	roll-over
riordinare	*(reeh-ohr-deeh-nAh-reh)*	reorder (v)
riorganizzare	*(reeh-ohr-gah-neehds-dsAh-reh)*	reorganize (v)
ripagare	*(reeh-pah-gAh-reh)*	repay (v)
riparare il sistema nell'elaboratore	*(reeh-pah-rAh-reh eehl seehs-tEh-mah nehl eh-lah-boh-rah-tOh-reh)*	debug (v)

R

ripartizione (f)	*(reeh-pahr-teeh-tsyOh-neh)*	allotment
riportare	*(reeh-pohr-tAh-reh)*	carryover
rischio (m)	*(rEEhs-kyoh*	risk
rischio cumulativo	*(rEEhs-kyoh kooh-mooh-lah-tEEh-voh)*	aggregate risk
rischio puro	*(rEEhs-kyoh pOOh-roh)*	pure risk
rischio sul cambio	*(rEEhs-kyoh soohl kAhm-byoh)*	exchange risk
riscontro (m)	*(reehs-kOhn-troh)*	reply
riserva (f)	*(reeh-zEhr-vah)*	reserve
riserva capitale	*(reeh-zEhr-vah kah-peeh-tAh-leh)*	capital allowance
riservato	*(reeh-zehr-vAh-toh)*	confidential
riserve (f) d'oro	*(reeh-zEhr-veh)*	gold reserves
riserve di capitali presi a prestito	*(reeh-zEhr-veh deeh kah-peeh-tAh-leeh prEh-zeeh ah prEhs-teeh-toh)*	net borrowed reserves
riserve minime	*(reeh-zEhr-veh mEEh-neeh-meh)*	minimum reserves
riserve primarie	*(reeh-zEhr-veh preeh-mAh-reeh-eh)*	primary reserves
risma (f)	*(rEEhz-mah)*	ream
risoluzione (f)	*(reeh-soh-looh-tsyOh-neh)*	resolution, (legal document)
risoluzione di problemi	*(reeh-soh-looh-tsyOh-neh deeh proh-blEh-meeh)*	problem solving
risoluzione generale	*(reeh-soh-looh-tsyOh-neh jeh-neh-rAh-leh)*	across-the-board settlement
risonanza (f)	*(reeh-soh-nAhn-tsah)*	resonance
risorse (f) del personale	*(reeh-sOhr-seh dehl pehr-soh-nAh-leh)*	human resources
risorse naturali	*(reeh-sOhr-seh nah-tooh-rAh-leeh)*	natural resources
risparmi (m)	*(reehs-pAhr-meeh)*	savings
rispondere	*(reehs-Pohn-deh-reh)*	reply (v)
ristorno (m)	*(reehs-tOhr-noh)*	drawback
ristrutturare	*(reehs-trooht-tooh-rAh-reh)*	restructure (v)

R

ristrutturazione (f) urbana	*(reehs-trooht-tooh-rah-tsyOh-neh)*	urban renewal
risultati (m) previsti	*(reeh-zoohl-tAh-teeh)*	expected results
ritardo (m)	*(reeh-tAhr-doh)*	delay, demurrage
ritardo fiscale	*(reeh-tAhr-doh feehs-kAh-leh)*	fiscal drag
ritirare	*(reeh-teeh-rAh-reh)*	take down (v)
ritiro (m) e la consegna	*(reeh-tEEh-roh)*	pickup and delivery
ritorno (m) di una parte della merce sullo stesso percorso utilizzato per il trasporto originale	*(reeh-tOhr-noh deeh ooh-nah pAhr-teh dehl-lah mEhr-cheh soohl-loh stEhs-soh pehr-kOhr-soh ooh-teeh-leehds-dsAh-toh pehr eehl trahs-pOhr-toh oh-reeh-jeeh-nAh-leh)*	back haul
ritorno sull'investimento	*(reeh-tOhr-noh soohl eehn-vehs-teeh-mEhn-toh)*	return on investment
riunione (f)	*(reeh-ooh-nyOh-neh)*	meeting
riunione degli azionisti	*(reeh-ooh-nyOh-neh deh-lyeeh ah-tsyoh-nEEhs-teeh)*	shareholders' meeting
riunione del consiglio	*(reeh-ooh-nyOh-neh dehl kohn-sEEh-lyoh)*	board meeting
riunione generale	*(reeh-ooh-nyOh-neh jeh-neh-rAh-leh)*	general meeting
riunione plenaria	*(reeh-ooh-nyOh-neh pleh-nAh-reeh-ah)*	plenary meeting
riunire	*(reeh-ooh-nEEh-reh)*	assemble (v) (people)
rivalutazione (f)	*(reeh-vah-looh-tah-tsyOh-neh)*	revaluation
rivedere	*(reeh-veh-dEh-reh)*	audit (v)
rivendita (f)	*(reeh-vEhn-deeh-tah)*	resale
rivendita del prodotto al fornitore originale	*(reeh-vEhn-deeh-tah dehl proh-dOht-toh ahl fohr-neeh-tOh-reh oh-reeh-jeeh-nAh-leh)*	back selling
rivenditore (m) autorizzato	*(reeh-vehn-deeh-tOh-reh ah-ooh-toh-reehds-dsAh-toh)*	authorized dealer
robot (m)	*(rohbaht)*	robot
rocchetto (m)	*(rohk-kEht-toh)*	pinion

rottami (m)	*(roht-tAh-meeh)*	scrap
routine (f)	*(rooteen)*	routine
ruota (f)	*(rwOh-tah)*	wheel
ruota di scorta	*(rwOh-tah deeh skOhr-tah)*	spare tire

S

saccarina (f)	*(sahk-kah-rEEh-nah)*	saccharin
sala (f) conferenze	*(sAh-lah kohn-feh-rEhn-tseh)*	conference room
sala del consiglio	*(sAh-lah dehl kohn-sEEh-lyoh)*	boardroom
sala delle contrattazioni	*(sAh-lah dehl-leh kohn-traht-tah-tsyOh-neeh)*	floor, (of exchange)
sala delle negoziazioni	*(sAh-lah dehl-leh neh-goh-tsyah-tsyOh-neeh)*	trading floor, (stock exchange)
salariato (m)	*(sah-lah-ryAh-toh)*	wage earner
salario (m)	*(sah-lAh-reeh-oh)*	salary, wages
salario reale	*(sah-lAh-reeh-oh reh-Ah-leh)*	real wages
saldare	*(sahl-dAh-reh)*	pay up (v)
saldo (m) a credito	*(sAhl-doh a krEh-deeh-toh)*	credit balance
saldo completo	*(sAhl-doh kohm-plEh-toh)*	full settlement
saldo contabile	*(sAhl-doh kohn-tAh-beeh-leh)*	account balance
saldo e credito	*(sAhl-doh eh krEh-deeh-toh)*	balance, credit
saldo liquido	*(sAhl-doh lEEh-kweeh-doh)*	cash balance
sale (m)	*(sAh-leh)*	salt
sali (m)	*(sAh-leeh)*	salts
saliera (f)	*(sah-lyEh-rah)*	salt shaker
salsiera (f)	*(sahl-syEh-rah)*	gravy boat
salvaguardia (m)	*(sahl-vah-gwAh-rdyah)*	safeguard
sangue (m)	*(sAhn-gweh)*	blood
sanguinare	*(sahn-gweeh-nAh-reh)*	bleed (v)
saponificazione (f)	*(sah-poh-neeh-feeh-kah-tsyOh-neh)*	saponification

S

sarto (m)	*(sAhr-toh)*	tailor
saturazione (f) del mercato	*(sah-tooh-rah-tsyOh-neh deeh mehr-kAh-toh)*	market saturation
sbalzo (m) di prezzo	*(zbAhl-tsoh deeh prEhts-tsoh)*	price tick
sbarre (f)	*(zbAhr-reh)*	slabs
sbocco (m)	*(zbOhk-koh)*	outlet
sborsamento (m)	*(zbohr-sah-mEhn-toh)*	outlay
sbrinatore (m)	*(zbreeh-nah-tOh-reh)*	defroster
scadenza (f)	*(skah-dEhn-tsah)*	deadline
scadenza oltre la quale non sono permesse azioni legali	*(skah-dEhn-tsah Ohl-treh lah kwAh-leh nohn sOh-noh pehr-mEhs-seh ah-tsyOh-neeh leh-gAh-leeh)*	statute of limitations
scaduto	*(skah-dOOh-toh)*	overdue, past due
scaglia (f)	*(skAh-lyah)*	scale
scala (f) salariale	*(skAh-lah sah-lah-ryAh-leh)*	wage scale
scala variabile, scala mobile	*(skAh-lah vah-ryAh-beeh-leh), (skAh-lah mOh-beeh-leh)*	sliding scale
scambiare	*(skahm-byAh-reh)*	exchange (v)
scambio (m)	*(skAhm-byoh)*	trade-off
scamosciato (m)	*(skah-moh-shAh-toh)*	suede
scansione (f)	*(skahn-syOh-neh)*	scanning
scappamento (m)	*(skahp-pah-mEhn-toh)*	exhaust
scaricare	*(skAh-reeh-kAh-reh)*	discharge (v), unload (v)
scarico (m)	*(skAh-reeh-koh)*	exhaust
scarico (m) con chiatte	*(skAh-reeh-koh kohn kyAht-teh)*	lighterage
scarpa (f)	*(skAhr-pah)*	shoe
scarto (m)	*(skAhr-toh)*	spoilage
scarto quadratico medio	*(skAhr-toh kwah-drAh-teeh-koh mEh-dyoh)*	standard deviation
scheda (f) perforata	*(skEh-dah pehr-fohr-Ah-tah)*	punch card
schema (m)	*(skEh-mah)*	layout
schermo (m)	*(skEhr-moh)*	screen
sciarpa (f)	*(shAhr-pah)*	scarf

S

scioperare	*(shoh-peh-rAh-reh)*	strike (v)
sciopero (m)	*(shOh-peh-roh)*	walkout
sciopero generale	*(shOh-peh-roh jeh-neh-rAh-leh)*	general strike
sciopero selvaggio	*(shOh-peh-roh sehl-vAhj-joh)*	wildcat strike
sciroppo (m) per la tosse	*(sheeh-rOhp-poh pehr-lah tOhs-seh)*	cough syrup
scodella (f)	*(skoh-dEhl-lah)*	bowl
scontare	*(skohn-tAh-reh)*	discount (v), mark down (v)
sconto (m)	*(skOhn-toh)*	abatement, discount, leakage, rebate
sconto agli operatori settoriali	*(skOhn-toh ah-lyeeh oh-peh-rah-tOh-reeh seht-toh-ryAh-leh)*	trade discount
sconto applicato sulle unità di carico	*(skOhn-toh ahp-pleeh-kAh-toh sohl-leh ooh-neeh-tAh deeh kAh-reeh-koh)*	unit loan discount
sconto di volume	*(skOhn-toh deeh voh-lOOh-meh)*	volume discount
sconto per contanti	*(skOhn-toh pehr kohn-tAhn-teeh)*	cash discount
sconto per quantità	*(skOhn-toh pehr kwahn-teeh-tAh)*	quantity discount
sconto sul cambio	*(skOhn-toh soohl kAhm-byoh)*	exchange discount
scoprire e localizzare i guasti	*(skoh-prEEh-reh)*	troubleshoot (v)
scorrere in modo regolare	*(skOhr-reh-reh)*	streamline (v)
scrittura (f) contabile correttiva	*(skreeht-tOOh-rah)*	adjusting entry
scrittura di chiusura	*(skreeht-tOOh-rah deeh kyooh-zOOh-rah)*	closing entry
sede (f)	*(sEh-deh)*	headquarters
sede amministrativa	*(sEh-deh ahm-meeh-neehs-trah-tEEh-vah)*	operations headquarters
sede centrale	*(sEh-deh chehn-trAh-leh)*	head office
sedile (m)	*(seh-dEEh-leh)*	seat
segnatura (f)	*(seh-nyah-tOOh-rah)*	signature

S

segretario (m) superiore	*(seh-greh-tAh-reeh-oh sooh-peh-ryOh-reh)*	executive secretary
selezionare	*(seh-leh-tsyoh-nAh-reh)*	screen (v)
self-service (m)	*(self-sehrvis)*	self-service
sella (f)	*(sEhl-lah)*	saddle
sellaio (m)	*(sehl-lAh-yoh)*	saddler
semiconduttore (m)	*(seh-meeh-kohn-dooht-tOh-reh)*	semiconductor
senza cambio	*(sEhn-tsah kAhm-byoh)*	gearless
senza dividendo	*(sEhn-tsah deeh-veeh-dEhn-doh)*	ex dividend
senza fini di lucro	*(sEhn-tsah fEEh-neeh deeh lOOh-kroh)*	nonprofit
senza impegni	*(sEhn-tsah eehm-pEh-nyeeh)*	free and clear
senza testamento	*(sEhn-tsah tehs-tah-mEhn-toh)*	intestate
senza valore	*(sEhn-tsah vah-lOh-reh)*	worthless
senza valore alla pari	*(sEhn-tsah vah-lOh-reh ahl-lah pAh-reeh)*	no par value
separazione (f)	*(seh-pah-rah-tsyOh-neh)*	separation
separazione (f) dei colore	*(seh-pah-rah-tsyOh-neh deh-eeh koh-lOh-reeh)*	color separation
sequestrare	*(seh-kehs-tAh-reh)*	impound (v)
serbatoio (m) della benzina	*(sehr-bah-tOh-yoh dehl-lah behn-dsEEh-nah)*	gasoline tank
serie completa (f) di caratteri	*(sEh-ryeh kohm-plEh-tah deeh kah-rAht-teh-reeh)*	font
serpente (m) valutario (CEE)	*(sehr-pEhn-teh vah-looh-tAh-reeh-oh)*	currency band
serpentina (f)	*(sehr-pehn-tEEh-nah)*	coil
serrata (f)	*(sehr-rAh-tah)*	lock out
servizi (m)	*(sehr-vEEhts-tseeh)*	facilities
servizi finanziari	*(sehr-vEEhts-tseeh feeh-nahn-tsyAh-reeh)*	financial services
servizi municipali	*(sehr-vEEhts-tseeh mooh-neeh-cheeh-pAh-leeh)*	public utilities
servizio consultivo	*(sehr-vEEh-tsyoh kohn-soohl-tEEh-voh)*	service advisory

servizio di corriere	*(sehr-vEEh-tsyoh deeh kohr-ryEh-reh)*	courier service
servizio reso al cliente	*(sehr-vEEh-tsyoh rEh-zoh ahl kleeh-Ehn-teh)*	customer service
servosterzo (m)	*(sehr-voh-stEhr-tsoh)*	power steering
seta (f)	*(sEh-tah)*	silk
seta artificiale, raion	*(sEh-tah ahr-teeh-feeh-chAh-leh), (rAh-yohn)*	rayon
setificio (m)	*(seh-teeh-fEEh-choh)*	silk factory
settore (m) pubblico	*(seht-tOh-reh pOOhb-leeh-koh)*	public sector
sfavorevole	*(sfah-voh-rEh-voh-leh)*	unfavorable
sgravare dalle tasse	*(zgrah-vAh-reh dahl-leh tAhs-seh)*	chargeoff (v)
sgravio (m) fiscale	*(zgrah-vEEh-oh feehs-kAh-leh)*	tax allowance, tax relief
sicurezza (f)	*(seeh-kooh-rEhts-tsah)*	security
siero (m)	*(syEh-roh)*	serum
sigla (f)	*(sEEh-glah)*	acronym
silicone (m)	*(seeh-leeh-kOh-neh)*	silicon
simulare	*(seeh-mooh-lAh-reh)*	simulate (v)
sindacato (m)	*(seehn-dah-kAh-toh)*	labor union, trade union
sindacato industriale	*(seehn-dah-kAh-toh eehn-doohs-tryAh-leh)*	industrial union
sintesi (f)	*(sEEhn-teh-zeeh)*	synthesis
sintetico	*(seehn-tEh-teeh-koh)*	synthetic
sinusite (f)	*(seeh-nooh-zEEh-teh)*	sinusitis
siringa (f)	*(seeh-rEEhn-gah)*	syringe
sistema (m) contabile, sistema di contabilità	*(seehs-tEh-mah kohn-tAh-beeh-leh), (seehs-tEh-mah deeh kohn-tah-beeh-leeh-tAh)*	accounting method
sistema di competenza	*(seehs-tEh-mah deeh kohm-peh-tEhn-tsah)*	accrual method
sistema di contingenta-mento	*(seehs-tEh-mah deeh kohn-teehn-jah-mEhn-toh)*	quota system

sistema di gestione integrato	*(seehs-tEh-mah deeh jehs-tyOh-neh eehn-teh-grAh-toh)*	integrated management system
sistema di parità variabile	*(seehs-tEh-mah deeh pah-reeh-tAh vah-ryAh-beeh-leh)*	adjustable peg
sistema di vendita rateale	*(seehs-tEh-mah deeh vEhn-deeh-tah rah-teh-Ah-leh)*	installment plan
situazione irresolubile	*(seeh-twah-tsyOh-neh eehr-reh-soh-lOOh-beeh-leh)*	deadlock
slittamento (m) salariale	*(zleeht-tah-mEhn-toh sah-lah-ryAh-leh)*	wage drift
smarginato	*(zmahr-jeeh-nAh-toh)*	bleed
smoking (m)	*(smokkeeng)*	tuxedo
smontare	*(zmohn-tAh-reh)*	take down (v)
società (f)	*(soh-cheh-tAh)*	corporation
società a responsabilità limitata (s.r.l.)	*(soh-cheh-tAh ah rehs-pohn-sah-beeh-leeh-tAh leeh-meeh-tAh-tah)*	limited partnership
società di finanziamento	*(soh-cheh-tAh deeh feeh-nahn-tsyah-mEhn-toh)*	finance company
società di persone	*(soh-cheh-tAh deeh pehr-sOh-neh)*	partnership
società finanziaria	*(soh-cheh-tAh feeh-nahn-tsyAh-reeh-ah)*	holding company
società in accomandita	*(soh-cheh-tAh eehn ahk-koh-mAhn-deeh-tah)*	associate company
società in accomandita semplice (s.a.s.)	*(soh-cheh-tAh eehn ahk-koh-mAhn-deeh-tah sEhm-pleeh-cheh)*	general partnership
società madre	*(soh-cheh-tAh mAh-dreh)*	holding company
società multinazionale	*(soh-cheh-tAh moohl-teeh-nah-tsyoh-nAh-leh)*	multinational corporation
società per azioni	*(soh-cheh-tAh pehr ah-tsyOh-neeh)*	corporation
società per la gestione degli investimenti	*(soh-cheh-tAh pehr lah jehs-tyOh-neh deh-lyeeh eehn-vehs-teeh-mEhn-teeh)*	trust company
socio	*(sOh-choh)*	member of firm, partner
socio a vita	*(sOh-choh ah vEEh-tah)*	life member

S

socio accommandante	*(sOh-choh ahk-koh-mahn-dAhn-teh)*	silent partner
socio secondario	*(sOh-choh seh-kohn-dAh-reeh-oh)*	junior partner
soddisfazione (f) del consumatore	*(sohd-deehs-fah-tsyOh-neh dehl kohn-sooh-mah-tOh-reh)*	consumer satisfaction
soffitto (m)	*(sohf-fEEht-toh)*	ceiling
software (m)	*(sohftwahr)*	software
soggetto a	*(sohj-jEht-toh ah)*	liable to
solfato (m)	*(sohl-fAh-toh)*	sulfate
sollecitare pagamento	*(sohl-leh-cheeh-tAh-reh pah-gah-mEhn-toh)*	dun (v)
sollecito	*(sohl-lEh-cheeh-toh)*	prompt
solubilità (f)	*(soh-looh-beeh-leeh-tAh)*	solubility
soluto (f)	*(soh-lOOh-toh)*	solute
soluzione (f)	*(soh-looh-tsyOh-neh)*	solution
solvente (m)	*(sohl-vEhn-teh)*	solvent
somma (f)	*(sOhm-mah)*	amount
somma dei numeri dell'anno precedente	*(sOhm-mah deh-eeh nOOh-meh-reeh dehl Ahn-noh preh-cheh-dEhn-teh)*	sum of the year's digits
somma dovuta	*(sOhm-mah doh-vOOh-tah)*	amount due
somma globale	*(sOhm-mah gloh-bAh-leh)*	lump sum
somma in eccesso ai fondi disponibili, scoperto	*(sOhm-mah eehn ehch-chEhs-soh ah-eeh fOhn-deeh deehs-poh-nEEh-beeh-leeh)*	overdraft
sommelier (m)	*(soh-meh-lee-Eh)*	wine steward
sondaggio (m) della opinione pubblica	*(sohn-dAhj-joh dehl-lah oh-peeh-nyOh-neh pOOhb-leeh-kah)*	public opinion poll
sonnifero (m)	*(sohn-nEEh-feh-roh)*	sleeping pill
sopra la pari	*(sOh-prah lah pAh-reeh)*	above par
sopraccoperta (f)	*(soh-prahk-koh-pEhr-tah)*	jacket
soprapprezzo (m)	*(soh-prahp-prEhts-tsoh)*	surcharge
soprattassa (f)	*(soh-praht-tAhs-sah)*	surtax
sopravvalutato	*(soh-prahv-vah-looh-tAh-toh)*	overvalued

S

sopravvenienza (f) passiva	*(soh-prahv-veeh-vEhn-tsah)*	contingent liability
sospendere il pagamento	*(sohs-pEhn-deh-reh pah-gah-mEhn-toh)*	suspend payment (v)
sospensione (f)	*(sohs-pehn-syOh-neh)*	suspension
sostegno (m) d'appoggio	*(sohs-tEh-nyoh dahp-pOhj-joh)*	backing support
sostegno del prezzo	*(sohs-tEh-nyoh dehl prEhts-tsoh)*	price support
sostituire	*(sohs-teeh-tooh-EEh-reh)*	supersede (v)
sotto la pari	*(sOht-toh lah pAh-reeh)*	below par
sotto norma	*(sOht-toh nOhr-mah)*	substandard
sotto-capitalizzato	*(sOht-toh-kah-peeh-tahl-leehds-dsAh-toh)*	undercapitalized
sottopagato	*(sOht-toh-pah-gAh-toh)*	underpaid
sottoscritto (m)	*(soht-toh-skrEEht-toh)*	undersigned
sottoscritto oltre il necessario	*(soht-toh-skrEEht-toh Ohl-treh eehl neh-chehs-sAh-reeh-oh)*	oversubscribed
sottoscrittore (m)	*(soht-toh-skreeht-tOh-reh)*	underwriter
sottoscrittore dell'assicurazione	*(soht-toh-skreeht-tOh-reh dehl ahs-seeh-kooh-rah-tsyOh-neh)*	insurance underwriter
sottovalutare	*(soht-toh-vah-looh-tAh-reh)*	underestimate (v), undervalue (v)
sovrabbondanza (f)	*(soh-vrahb-bohn-dAhn-dsah)*	glut
sovraccarico (m)	*(soh-vrahk-kAh-reeh-koh)*	overstock, surcharge
sovrappagato	*(soh-vrahp-pah-gAh-toh)*	overpaid
sovrapposizione (f)	*(soh-vrahp-poh-zeeh-tsyOh-neh)*	overlap
sovrapprezzo (m)	*(soh-vrahp-prEhts-tsoh)*	overcharge
spartizione (f) degli utili	*(spahr-teeh-tsyOh-neh deh-lyeeh OOh-teeh-leeh)*	profit sharing
specialistà (m)	*(speh-chah-lEEhs-tah)*	specialist, (stock exchange)
specificare	*(speh-cheeh-feeh-kAh-reh)*	earmark (v)
speculatore (m)	*(speh-kooh-lah-tOh-reh)*	speculator
spedizione (f)	*(speh-deeh-tsyOh-neh)*	consignment

spedizione (f)	*(speh-deeh-tsyOh-neh)*	dispatch, shipment
spedizione a termine	*(speh-deeh-tsyOh-neh ah tEhr-meeh-neh)*	forward shipment
spedizione aerea	*(speh-deeh-tsyOh-neh ah-Eh-reh-ah)*	air shipment
spedizione fatta direttamente al dettagliante	*(speh-deeh-tsyOh-neh fAht-tah deeh-rEht-tah-mEhn-teh ahl deht-tah-lyAhn-teh)*	drop shipment
spedizione incompleta	*(speh-deeh-tsyOh-neh eehn-kohm-plEh-tah)*	short shipment
spedizioni illegali	*(speh-deeh-tsyOh-neeh eehl-leh-gAh-leeh)*	illegal shipments
spedizioniere (f)	*(speh-deeh-tsyoh-nyEh-reh)*	forwarding agent, freight forwarder, shipper
spedizioniere doganale	*(speh-deeh-tsyoh-nyEh-reh doh-gah-nAh-leh)*	customs broker
spesa (f)	*(spEh-zah)*	expenditure
spesa amministrativa	*(spEh-zah ahm-meeh-neehs-trah-tEEh-vah)*	administrative expense
spesa dei capitali	*(spEh-zah deh-eeh kah-peeh-tAh-leeh)*	capital spending
spesa fatta mentre la ditta è in passivo	*(dpEh-zah fAht-tah mEhn-treh lah dEEht-tah eh eehn pahs-sEEh-voh)*	deficit spending
spese (f) correnti	*(spEh-zeh kohr-rEhn-teeh)*	running expenses
spese	*(spEh-zeh)*	expenses
spese costanti	*(spEh-zeh kohs-tAhn-teeh)*	fixed expenses
spese d'immobilizzo	*(spEh-zeh deehm-moh-beeh-lEEhts-tsoh)*	carrying charges
spese d'interesse	*(spEh-zeh deehn-teh-rEhs-seh)*	interest expenses
spese di ormeggio	*(spEh-zeh deeh ohr-mEhj-joh)*	dock handling charges
spese di recupero	*(spEh-zeh deeh reh-kOOh-peh-roh)*	salvage charges
spese di scambio	*(spEh-zeh deeh skAhm-byoh)*	switching charges
spese di spedizione	*(spEh-zeh deeh speh-deeh-tsyOh-neh)*	shipping expenses

S

spese di tasca propria	*(spEh-zeh deeh tAhs-kah prOh-pryah)*	out-of-pocket expenses
spese di trasloco	*(spEh-zeh deeh trahs-lOh-koh)*	moving expenses
spese di trasporto	*(spEh-zeh deeh trahs-pOhr-toh)*	shipping expenses
spese dirette	*(spEh-zeh deeh-rEht-teh)*	direct expenses
spese evitabili	*(spEh-zeh eh-veeh-tAh-beeh-leeh)*	avoidable costs
spese fisse	*(spEh-zeh fEEhs-seh)*	fixed expenses
spese fisse generali	*(spEh-zeh fEEhs-seh jeh-neh-rAh-leeh)*	overhead
spese incidentali	*(spEh-zeh jeh-neh-rAh-leeh)*	incidental expenses
spese indirette	*(spEh-zeh eehn-deeh-rEht-teh)*	indirect expenses
spese maturate	*(spEh-zeh mah-tohh-rAh-teh)*	accrued expenses
spese operative	*(spEh-zeh oh-peh-rah-tEEh-veh)*	operating expenses, running expenses
spese prepagate	*(spEh-zeh preh-pah-gAh-teh)*	prepaid expenses, (balance sheet)
spese pubblicitarie	*(spEh-zeh poohb-leeh-cheeh-tAh-reeh-eh)*	advertising expenses
spettro (m)	*(spEht-troh)*	spectrum
spettrofotometria (f)	*(speht-troh-foh-toh-meh-trEEh-ah)*	spectrophotometry
spia	*(spEE-ah)*	detector
spinta pubblicitaria	*(spEEhn-tah poohb-leeh-cheeh-tAh-reeh-ah)*	advertising drive
spirale (f) dei salari e dei prezzi	*(speeh-rAh-leh deh-eeh sah-lAh-reeh eh deh-eeh prEhts-tseeh)*	wage-price spiral
spogliazione (f)	*(spoh-lyah-tsyOh-neh)*	divestment
sponsor (m)	*(spohnsuhr))*	sponsor, (of fund, partnership)
sporgenza (f)	*(spohr-jEhn-tsah)*	overhang
spostamento (m) dei beni	*(spohs-tah-mEhn-toh)*	movement of goods
stabilimento (m) di consegna approvato	*(stah-beeh-leeh-mEhn-toh)*	approved delivery facility
stabilire contatti capillari	*(stah-beeh-lEEh-reh kohn-tAht-teeh kah-peehl-lAh-reeh)*	network (v)

stabilire il prezzo	*(stah-beeh-lEEh-reh eehl prEhts-tsoh)*	price (v)
stagflazione (f)	*(stahg-flah-tsyOh-neh)*	stagflation
stagionale	*(stah-joh-nAh-leh)*	seasonal
stallie (f)	*(stahl-lEEh-eh)*	laydays
stampa (f)	*(stahm-pah)*	printing
stampato (m)	*(stahm-pAh-toh)*	print
stampato (m)	*(stahm-pAh-toh)*	printout
stampe (f)	*(stAhm-peh)*	printed matter
standardizzazione (f)	*(stahn-dahr-deehds-dsah-tsyOh-neh)*	standardization
stanza (f) di compensazione	*(stAhn-dsah)*	clearinghouse
stanziamento (m)	*(stahn-tsyah-mEhn-toh)*	appropriation
stanziamento (m) del preventivo	*(stahn-tsyah-mEhn-toh dehl preh-vehn-tEEh-voh)*	budget appropriation
starnutire	*(stahr-nooh-tEEh-reh)*	sneeze (v)
statistiche (f)	*(stah-tEEhs-teeh-keh)*	statistics
statuto (m)	*(stah-tOOh-toh)*	statute
stazza (f)	*(stAhts-tsah)*	tonnage
stereofonico	*(steh-reh-oh-fOh-neeh-koh)*	stereophonic
sterzo (m)	*(stEhr-tsoh)*	steering wheel
stessa paga (f) per lo stesso lavoro	*(stEhs-sah pAh-gah pehr loh-stEhs-soh lah-vOh-roh)*	equal pay for equal work
stile (m)	*(stEEh-leh)*	style
stilista (m)	*(steeh-lEEhs-tah)*	designer
stima (f)	*(stEEh-mah)*	appraisal, estimate, rough estimate
stima approssimativa	*(stEEh-mah ahp-prohs-seeh-mah-tEEh-vah)*	guesstimate
stima da parte del factor	*(stEEh-mah dah-pAhr-teh dehl factor)*	factor rating
stima delle spese capitali	*(stEEh-mah dehl-leh spEh-zeh kah-peeh-tAh-leeh)*	capital expenditure appraisal
stima delle vendite	*(stEEh-mah dehl-leh vEhn-deeh-teh)*	sales estimate
stimare	*(steeh-mAh-reh)*	estimate (v)

stimolante (m)	*(steeh-moh-lAhn-teh)*	stimulant
stipendio (m)	*(steeh-pEhn-deeh-oh)*	salary, wage, wages
stipendio netto	*(steeh-pEhn-deeh nEht-toh)*	take-home pay
stivaggio (m)	*(steeh-vAhj-joh)*	stowage
stivalaio (m)	*(steeh-vah-kAh-yoh)*	bootmaker
stivaleria (f)	*Steeh-vah-leh-rEEh-ah)*	boot shop
stivaletti (m)	*(steeh-vah-lEht-teeh)*	ankle boots
stivali (m)	*(steeh-vAh-leeh)*	boots
stoviglie (f)	*(stoh-vEEh-lyeh)*	pottery
straniero (m)	*(strah-nyEh-roh)*	nonresident
strategia (f) commerciale	*(strah-teh-jEEh-ah kohm-mehr-chAh-leh)*	business strategy
strategia concorrenziale	*(strah-teh-jEEh-ah kohn-kohr-rehn-tsyAh-leh)*	competitive strategy
strategia d'investimento	*(strah-teh-jEEh-ah deehn-vehs-teeh-mEhn-toh)*	investment strategy
strategia di marketing	*(strah-teh-jEEh-ah deeh marketing)*	marketing plan
strumento (m)	*(strooh-mEhn-toh)*	instrument
struttura aziendale	*(strooht-tOOh-rah ah-dsyehn-dAh-leh)*	corporate structure
struttura finanziaria	*(strooht-tOOh-rah feeh-nahn-tsyAh-reeh-ah)*	capital structure
struttura salariale	*(strooht-tOOh-rah sah-lah-ryAh-leh)*	wage structure
studio (m) del rapporto tra tempo e movimento	*(stOOh-dyoh dehl rahp-pOhr-toh trah tEhm-poh eh moh-veeh-mEhn-toh)*	time and motion study
studio motivazionale	*(stOOh-dyoh moh-teeh-vah-tsyoh-nAh-leh)*	motivation study
studio pubblicitario	*(stOOh-dyoh poohb-leeh-cheeh-tAh-reeh-oh)*	advertising research
studio sulla profittabilità	*(stOOh-dyoh sohl-lah proh-feeht-tah-beeh-leeh-tAh)*	profitability analysis
su costo	*(sooh kOhs-toh)*	on cost
su richiesta	*(sooh reeh-kyEhs-tah)*	on demand
su rimessa	*(sooh reeh-mEhs-sah)*	on consignment
subaffitto (m)	*(soohb-ahf-fEEht-toh)*	sublet

subappaltare	*(soohb-ahp-pahl-tAh-reh)*	subcontract (v)
subappaltatore (m)	*(soohb-ahp-pahl-tah-tOh-reh)*	subcontractor
succitato (m)	*(soohch-cheeh-tAh-toh)*	above-mentioned
succo (m)	*(sOOhk-koh)*	juice
succo d'uva non fermentato	*(sOOhk-koh dOOh-vah nohn fehr-mehn-tAh-toh)*	unfermented grape juice
sul retro	*(soohl rEh-troh)*	on the back
sulfamide (m)	*(sohl-fah-mEEh-deh)*	sulphamide
summenzionato (m)	*(soohm-mehn-tsyoh-nAh-toh)*	above-mentioned
suono (m)	*(swOh-noh)*	sound
superare (f) giustezza	*(sooh-peh-rAh-reh lah joohs-tEhts-tsah)*	overrun (in printing)
superleghe (f)	*(sooh-pehr-lEh-geh)*	super alloys
supervisore (m)	*(sooh-pehr-veeh-zOh-reh)*	supervisor
sussidio (m)	*(soohs-sEEh-dyoh)*	subsidy
svalutare	*(zvah-looh-tAh-reh)*	write down (v)
svalutazione (f)	*(zvah-looh-tah-tsyOh-neh)*	devaluation
svantaggio (m)	*(zvahn-tAhj-joh)*	drawback, handicap
sviluppo (m) del prodotto	*(zveeh-lOOhp-poh dehl proh-dOht-toh)*	product development
sviluppo di prodotti nuovi	*(zveeh-lOOhp-poh deeh proh-dOht-teeh nwOh-veeh)*	new product development
svolta (f) positiva	*(zvOhl-tah)*	upturn

T

tabella (f)	*(tah-bEhl-lah)*	timetable
taffetà (m)	*(tahf-feh-tAh)*	taffeta
tagli (m) dei prezzi	*(tAh-lyeeh deh-eeh prEhts-tseeh)*	price cutting
taglia (f)	*(tAh-lyah)*	size
tagliare	*(tah-lyAh-reh)*	cut (v)
tagliare	*tah-lyAh-reh)*	blend (v)
tampone (m) di carta assorbente (m)	*(tahm-pOh-neh deeh kAhr-tah ahs-sohr-bEhn-teh)*	blotter

tangente (f)	*(tahn-jEhn-teh)*	kickback
tannino (m)	*(tahn-nEEh-noh)*	tannin
tappo (m)	*(tAhp-poh)*	cork
tariffa (f)	*(tah-rEEhf-fah)*	tariff
tariffa combinata	*(tah-rEEhf-fah kohm-beeh-nAh-tah)*	combination duty
tariffa controvalente	*(tah-rEEhf-fah kohn-troh-vah-lEhn-teh)*	countervailing duty
tariffa d'esportazione	*(tah-rEEhf-fah dehs-pohr-tah-tsyOh-neh)*	export duty
tariffa d'importazione	*(tah-rEEhf-fah deehm-pohr-tah-tsyOh-neh)*	import tariff
tariffa di partecipazione	*(tah-rEEhf-fah deeh pahr-teh-ceeh-pah-tsyOh-neh)*	participation fee
tariffa differenziale	*(tah-rEEhf-fah deehf-feh-rehn-tsyAh-leh)*	differential tariff
tariffa doganale	*(tah-rEEhf-fah doh-gah-nAh-leh)*	customs duty
tariffa fissa	*(tah-rEEhf-fah fEEhs-sah)*	standing charges
tariffa preferenziale	*(tah-rEEhf-fah preh-feh-rehn-tsyAh-leh)*	preferred tariff
tariffa protettiva, tariffa "anti-dumping"	*(tah-rEEhf-fah proh-teht-tEEh-vah)*	anti-dumping duty
tassa (f)	*(tAhs-sah)*	tax
tassa sul consumo	*(tAhs-sah soohl kohn-sOOh-moh)*	excise tax
tassazione (f)	*(tahs-sah-tsyOh-neh)*	taxation
tassazione multipla	*(tahs-sah-tsyOh-neh mOOhl-teeh-plah)*	multiple taxation
tasse differite	*(tAhs-seh deehf-feh-rEEh-teh)*	deferred tax
tasse maturate	*(tAhs-seh mah-tooh-rAh-teh)*	accrued taxes
tasso (m)	*(tAhs-soh)*	rate
tasso bancario	*(tAhs-soh bahn-kAh-reeh-oh)*	bank rate
tasso centrale	*(tAhs-soh chehn-trAh-leh)*	central rate
tasso d'adesione	*(tAhs-soh dah-deh-zyOh-neh)*	accession rate

T

tasso d'incremento	*(tAhs-soh deehn-kreh-mEhn-toh)*	rate of increase
tasso d'interesse	*(tAhs-soh deehn-teh-rEhs-seh)*	interest rate
tasso dell'onere	*(tAhs-soh dehl Oh-neh-reh)*	burden rate
tasso di base	*(tAhs-soh deeh bAh-zeh)*	base rate
tasso di cambio	*(tAhs-soh deeh kAhm-byoh)*	exchange rate
tasso di cambio multiplo	*(tahs-soh deeh kAhm-byoh mOOhl-teeh-ploh)*	multiple exchange rate
tasso di cambio variabile	*(tAhs-soh deeh kAhm-byoh vah-ryAh-beeh-leh)*	floating exchange rate
tasso di crescita	*(tAhs-soh deeh krEh-sheeh-tah)*	rate of growth
tasso di interesse rimborsabile a brevissima scadenza	*(tAhs-soh deeh eehn-teh-rEhs-seh reehm-bohr-sAh-beeh-leh ah breh-vEEhs-seeh-mah skah-dEhn-tsah)*	call rate
tasso di rendimento	*(tAhs-soh deeh rehn-deeh-mEhn-toh)*	rate of return
tasso di rimunerazione	*(tAhs-soh deeh reeh-mooh-neh-rah-tsyOh-neh)*	rate of return
tasso di risconto	*(tAhs-soh deeh reehs-kOhn-toh)*	rediscount rate
tasso di scambio fisso	*(tAhs-soh deeh skAhm-byoh fEEhs-soh)*	fixed rate of exchange
tasso di sconto	*(tAhs-soh deeh skOhn-toh)*	discount rate
tasso fluttuante	*(tAhs-soh flooht-tooh-Ahn-teh)*	floating rate
tasso offerto	*(tAhs-soh ohf-fEhr-toh)*	offered rate
tasso rettificato	*(tAhs-soh reht-teeh-feeh-kAh-toh)*	adjusted rate
tasso variabile	*(tAhs-soh vah-ryAh-beeh-leh)*	floating rate, variable rate
tavola (f) elettronica per comandi	*(tAh-voh-lah eh-leht-trOh-neeh-kah pehr koh-mAhn-deeh)*	electronic whiteboard
tazza (f)	*(tAhts-tsah)*	cup
tazzina (f) da espresso	*(tahts-tsEEh-nah dah ehs-prEhs-soh)*	espresso cup

T

tecnica (f) di Monte Carlo	*(tEhk-neeh-kah)*	Monte Carlo technique
tecnico (m) del laboratorio	*(tEhk-neeh-koh dehl lah-boh-rah-tOh-reeh-oh)*	laboratory technician
teiera (f)	*(teh-yEh-rah)*	teapot
tela cerata (f)	*(tEh-lah cheh-rAh-tah)*	oilcloth
tele-elaborazione (f)	*(teh-leh-eh-lah-boh-rah-tsyOh-neh)*	teleprocessing
telecamera (f)	*(teh-leh-kAh-meh-rah)*	camera
telecomunicazioni (f)	*(teh-leh-koh-mooh-neeh-kah-tsyOh-neeh)*	telecommunications
temperatura (f)	*(tehm-peh-rah-tOOh-rah)*	temperature
tempo (m) di giacenza	*(tEhm-poh)*	lay time
tempo libero	*(tEhm-poh lEEh-beh-roh)*	free time
tempo presenziato	*(tEhm-poh preh-zehn-tsyAh-toh)*	attended time
tempo reale	*(tEhm-poh reh-Ah-leh)*	real time
tendenza (f)	*(tehn-dEhn-tsah)*	trend
tendenze del mercato	*(tehn-dEhn-tseh deeh mehr-kAh-toh)*	market trends
tenere al corrente	*(teh-nEh-reh ahl kohr-rEhn-teh)*	keep posted (v)
tenore (m) di vita	*(teh-nOh-reh deeh vEEh-tah)*	standard of living
tentativi (m) di influenzare atti governativi con pressioni varie	*(tehn-tah-tEEh-veeh deeh eehn-flooh-ehn-tsAh-reh Aht-teeh goh-vehr-nah-tEEh-veeh kohn prehs-syOh-neeh vAh-ryeh)*	lobbying
teoria (f) d'azione relativa agli investimenti	*(teh-oh-rEEh-ah dah-tsyOh-neh reh-lah-tEEh-vah ah-lyeeh eehn-vehs-teeh-mEhn-teeh)*	portfolio theory
terminale (m)	*(tehr-meeh-nAh-leh)*	terminal
terminale del computer	*(tehr-meeh-nAh-leh dehl computer)*	computer terminal
terminale dell'elaboratore	*(tehr-meeh-nAh-leh dehl eh-lah-boh-rah-tOh-reh)*	computer terminal
terminare	*(tehr-meeh-nAh-reh)*	terminate (v)
termine (m) fisso	*(tEhr-meeh-neh fEEhs-soh)*	fixed term

T

termine futuro	*(tEhr-meeh-neh fooh-tOOh-roh)*	forward forward
termini del credito	*(tEhr-meeh-neeh dehl krEh-deeh-toh)*	credit terms
termini di ormeggio	*(tEhr-meeh-neeh deeh ohr-mEhj-joh)*	berth terms
termini lineari	*(tEhr-meeh-neeh leeh-neh-Ah-reeh)*	linear terms
terra (f)	*(tEhr-rah)*	land
terraglia (f)	*(tehr-rAh-lyah)*	earthenware
terrina (f)	*(teh-rEEh-nah)*	tureen
territorio (m)	*(tehr-reeh-tOh-reeh-oh)*	territory
territorio di vendita	*(tehr-reeh-tOh-reeh-oh deeh vEhn-deeh-tah)*	sales territory
terza (f) finestra	*(tEhr-tsah feeh-nEhs-trah)*	third window
terzo sbocco	*(tEhr-tsoh zbOhk-koh)*	third window
tesoriere (m)	*(teh-zoh-ryEh-reh)*	treasurer
tessitore (m)	*(tehs-seeh-tOh-reh)*	weaver
tessuto (m)	*(tehs-sOOh-toh)*	fabric
testamentario (m)	*(tehs-tah-mEhn-toh)*	executor
testamento (m)	*(tehs-tah-mEhn-toh)*	will
testimone (m)	*(tehs-teeh-mOh-neh)*	witness
testo (m) (text)	*(tEhs-toh)*	copy
testo scritto senza particolare interesse	*(tEhs-toh skrEEht-toh sEhn-tsah pahr-teeh-koh-lAh-reh eehn-teh-rEhs-seh)*	boilerplate
tingere	*(tEEhn-jeh-reh)*	dye (v)
tino (m)	*(tEEh-noh)*	vat
tinozza (f)	*(teeh-nOhts-tsah)*	vat
tipografia (f)	*(teeh-pioh-grah-fEEh-ah)*	printing shop
titanio (m)	*(teeh-tAh-nyoh)*	titanium
titolazione (f)	*(teeh-toh-lah-tsyOh-neh)*	titration
titoli (m) di sicura affidabilità	*(tEEh-toh-leeh deeh seeh-kOOh-rah ahf-feeh-dah-beeh-leeh-tAh)*	securities

T

titoli di sicura affidabilità che possono essere posti sul mercato	*(tEEh-toh-leeh deeh seeh-kOOh-rah ahf-feeh-dah-beeh-leeh-tAh keh pOhs-soh-noh Ehs-seh-reh pOhs-teeh soohl mehr-kAh-toh)*	marketable securities
titoli governativi	*(tEEh-toh-leeh goh-vehr-nah-tEEh-veeh)*	gilt, (Brit. govt. security)
titoli mobiliari	*(tEEh-toh-leeh moh-beeh-lyAh-reeh)*	marketable securities, securities
titoli mobiliari approvati	*(tEEh-toh-leeh moh-beeh-lyAh-reeh ahp-proh-vAh-teeh)*	approved securities
titoli mobiliari esteri	*(tEEh-toh-leeh moh-beeh-lyAh-reeh Ehs-teh-reeh)*	foreign securities
titoli mobiliari negoziabili	*(tEEh-toh-leeh moh-beeh-lyAh-reeh neh-goh-tsyAh-beeh-leeh)*	negotiable securities
titoli mobiliari prestati a un broker	*(tEEh-toh-leeh moh-beeh-lyAh-reeh prehs-tAh-teeh ah oohn broker)*	loan stock
titoli obbligazionari dati in garanzia	*(tEEh-toh-leeh ohb-bleeh-gah-tsyoh-nAh-reeh dAh-teeh eehn gah-rahn-tsEEh-ah)*	backup bonds
titoli scontati	*(tEEh-toh-leeh skohn-tAh-teeh)*	discount securities
titolo (m)	*(tEEh-toh-loh)*	headline, title
titolo a garanzia secondaria	*(tEEh-toh-loh ah gah-rahn-tsEEh-ah seh-kohn-dAh-reeh-ah)*	junior security
titolo al portatore	*(tEEh-toh-loh ahl pohs-tah-tOh-reh)*	bearer security
titolo di mobiliare a reddito fisso	*(tEEh-toh-loh deeh moh-beeh-lyAh-reh ah rEhd-deeh-toh fEEhs-soh)*	fixed income security
titolo nominativo	*(tEEh-toh-loh noh-meeh-nah-tEEh-voh)*	registered security
titulo	*(tEEl-toh-loh)*	authenticity (gold)
togliere	*(tOh-lyeh-reh)*	take out (v)
tonnellata (f) metrica	*(tohn-nehl-lAh-toh mEh-tree-kah)*	long ton

torchio da vino (m)	*(tOhr-kyoh dah vEEh-noh)*	winepress
torto (m)	*(tOhr-toh)*	tort
tossicologia (f)	*(tohs-seeh-koh-loh-jEEh-ah)*	toxicology
tossina (f)	*(tohs-sEEh-nah)*	toxin
tossire	*(tohs-sEEh-reh)*	cough (v)
tovaglia (f)	*(toh-vAh-lyah)*	tablecloth
tovaglioli (m) ricamati a mano	*(toh-vah-lyOh-leeh reeh-kah-mAh-teeeh ah mAh-noh)*	hand-embroidered napkins
tovagliolo (m)	*(toh-vah-lyOh-loh)*	napkin
traduttore (m)	*(trah-dooht-tOh-reh)*	translator
traente (m)	*(trah-Ehn-teh)*	drawer
tramite (f) polizza di carico	*(trAh-meeh-teh pOh-leehts-tsah deeh kAh-reeh-koh)*	through bill of lading
tranche (f)		tranche
tranquillante (m)	*(trahn-kweehl-lAhn-teh)*	tranquilizer
transazione (f)	*(trahn-sah-tsyOh-neh)*	transaction
trasferimento (m)	*(trahs-feh-reeh-mEhn-toh)*	transfer
trasferimento via cavo	*(trahs-feh-reeh-mEhn-toh vEEh-ah kAh-voh)*	wire transfer
trasferta (f)	*(trahs-fEhr-tah)*	transfer
trasformare	*(trahs-fohr-mAh-reh)*	process (v)
trasgressione (f)	*(trahs-grehs-syOh-neh)*	nonfeasance
trasmettere	*(trahz-mEht-teh-reh)*	broadcast (v)
trasportatore (m)	*(trahs-pohr-tah-tOh-reh)*	conveyor
trasportatore a cinghia	*(trahs-pohr-tah-tOh-reh ah chEEhn-gyah)*	conveyor belt
trasporto (m)	*(trahs-pOhr-toh)*	drayage, transportation
trasporto di containers con camion	*(trahs-pOhr-toh deeh containers kohn kAh-myohn)*	piggyback service
trasporto di containers su navi	*(trahs-pOhr-toh deeh containers sooh nAh-veeh)*	fishy-back service, (container)
trasporto ferroviario	*(trahs-pOhr-toh fehr-roh-vyAh-reeh-oh)*	rail shipment
trasporto prepagato	*(trahs-pOhr-toh preh-pah-gAh-toh)*	freight prepaid

T

trasporto via aerea	*(trahs-pOhr-toh vEEh-ah ah-Eh-reh-ah)*	air freight
tratta (f)	*(trAht-tah)*	draft
tratta a vista	*(trAht-tah ah vEEhs-tah)*	sight draft
tratta bancaria	*(trAht-tah bahn-kAh-reeh-ah)*	bank draft
trattare	*(traht-tAh-reh)*	negotiate (v)
trattario (m)	*(traht-tAh-reeh-oh)*	drawee
trattativa (f) complessiva	*(traht-tah-tEEh-vah kohm-plehs-sEEh-vah)*	package deal
trattato (m)	*(traht-tAh-toh)*	treaty
trazione (f) anteriore	*(trah-tsyOh-neh ahn-teh-ryOh-reh)*	front-wheel drive
trinciante (m)	*(treehn-chAhn-teh)*	carving knife
tubazioni (f)	*(tooh-bah-tsyOh-neeh)*	pipage
tubo (m)	*(tOOh-boh)*	tube
tungstenio (m)	*(toohng-stEh-neeh-oh)*	tungsten
turno (m)	*(tOOhr-noh)*	(labor) shift
tutto o niente	*(tOOht-toh oh nyEhn-teh)*	all or none

U

ufficio (m)	*(oohf-fEEh-choh)*	office
ufficio commerciale	*(oohf-fEEh-choh kohm-mehr-chAh-leh)*	trade commission, commercial office
ufficio di credito	*(oohf-fEEh-choh deeh krEh-deeh-toh)*	credit bureau
ultima bozza (f)	*(OOhl-teeh-mah bOhts-tsah)*	press book
ultima partita consegnata-prima partita ad uscire	*(OOhl-teeh-mah pahr-tEEh-tah kohn-seh-nyAh-tah prEEh-mah pahr-tEEh-tah ad ooh-shEEh-reh)*	last in-first out
ultimo pagamento (m) rateale per un importo notevolmente più alto dei precedenti	*(OOhl-teeh-moh pah-gah-mEhn-toh rah-teh-Ah-leh pehr oohn eehm-pOhr-toh noh-teh-vohl-mEhn-teh pyOOh Ahl-toh deh-eeh preh-cheh-dEhn-teeh)*	balloon (payment)

T

unguento (m)	*(oohn-gwEhn-toh)*	salve, ointment
unione (f) creditizia	*(ooh-nyOh-neh kreh-deeh-tEEh-tsyah)*	credit union
unione doganale	*(ooh-nyOh-neh doh-gah-nAh-leh)*	customs union
unità (f) centrale per l'elaborazione dei dati	*(ooh-neeh-tAh chehn-trAh-leh pehr leh-lah-boh-rah-tsyOh-neh deh-eeh dAh-teeh)*	central processing unit, (computers)
usanze (f) locali	*(ooh-zAhn-tseh)*	local customs
user friendly	*(yuzehr frehndlee)*	user-friendly
usura (f)	*(ooh-zOOh-rah)*	wear and tear
usuria (f)	*(ooh-zOOh-ryah)*	usury
utensili (m)	*(ooh-tEhn-seeh-leh)*	tools
utile (m)	*(OOh-teeh-leh)*	profit
utile dalle azioni	*(OOh-teeh-leh dahl-leh ah-tsyOh-neeh)*	stock profit
utile del prodotto	*(OOh-teeh-leh dehl proh-dOht-toh)*	product profitability
utile lordo	*(OOh-teeh-leh lOhr-doh)*	gross profit
utili attivi	*(OOh-teeh-leeh aht-tEEh-veeh)*	active assets
utili di capitale/la perdita di capitale	*(OOh-teeh-leh deeh kah-peeh-tAh-leh)/pEhr-deeh-tah deeh kah-peeh-tAh-leh)*	capital gain/loss
utili diretti	*(OOh-teeh-leeh deeh-rEht-teeh)*	operating profit
utili per azione	*(OOh-teeh-leeh pehr ah-tsyOh-neh)*	earnings per share
utili ritenuti	*(OOh-teeh-leeh reeh-teh-nOOh-teh)*	retained earnings
utili su carta	*(OOh-teeh-leeh sooh kAhr-tah)*	paper profit
utili sugli attivi	*(OOh-teeh-leeh sooh-lyeeh aht-tEEh-veeh)*	earnings on assets
utilità (f)	*(ooh-teeh-leeh-tAh)*	utility
uva (m)	*(OOh-vah)*	grape

U

vaccino (m)	*(vahch-chEEh-noh)*	vaccine
vaglia (m) bancario	*(vAh-lyah bahn-kAh-reeh-oh)*	bank money order
vaglia postale	*(vAh-lyah pohs-tAh-leh)*	money order
validare	*(vah-leeh-dAh-reh)*	validate (v)
valido	*(vAh-leeh-doh)*	valid
valigia (f)	*(vah-lEEh-jah)*	suitcase
valore (m)	*(vah-lOh-reh)*	stock, value
valore al pari	*(vah-lOh-reh ahl pAh-reeh)*	par value
valore attuale netto	*(vah-lOh-reh aht-twAh-leh nEht-toh)*	net present value
valore daziabile	*(vah-lOh-reh dah-tsyAh-beeh-leh)*	value for duty
valore delle attività	*(vah-lOh-reh dehl-leh aht-teeh-veeh-tAh)*	asset value
valore di mercato	*(vah-lOh-reh deeh mehr-kAh-toh)*	fair market value, market value
valore di recupero	*(vah-lOh-reh deeh reh-kOOh-eh-roh)*	salvage value
valore dichiarato	*(vah-lOh-reh deeh-kyah-rAh-toh)*	face value
valore effettivo a pronti	*(vah-lOh-reh ehf-feht-tEEh-voh ah prOhn-teeh)*	actual cash value
valore effettivo della ditta	*(vah-lOh-reh ehf-feht-tEEh-voh dehl-lah dEEht-tah)*	going-concern value
valore in contanti alla resa	*(vah-lOh-reh eehn kohn-tAhn-teeh ahl-lah rEh-zah)*	cash surrender value
valore intrinseco	*(vah-lOh-reh eehn-trEEhn-zeh-koh)*	intrinsic value
valore liquidato	*(vah-lOh-reh leeh-kweeh-dAh-toh)*	liquidation value
valore mediano	*(vah-lOh-reh meh-dyAh-noh)*	median
valore mobiliare	*(vah-lOh-reh moh-beeh-lyAh-reh)*	issue (stock)
valore netto	*(vah-lOh-reh nEht-toh)*	net worth

valore netto degli attivi	*(vah-lOh-reh nEht-toh deh-lyeeh aht-tEEh-veeh)*	net asset value
valore registrato	*(vah-lOh-reh reh-keehs-trAh-toh)*	book value
valore registrato per azione	*(vah-lOh-reh reh-jeehs-trAh-toh pehr ah-tsyOh-neh)*	book value per share
valore riportato	*(vah-lOh-reh reeh-pohr-tAh-toh)*	face, value
valuta (f)	*(vah-lOOh-tah)*	currency
valuta bloccata	*(vah-lOOh-tah blohk-kAh-tah)*	blocked currency
valuta debole	*(vah-lOOh-tah dEh-boh-leh)*	soft currency
valuta di base	*(vah-lOOh-tah deeh bAh-zeh)*	foreign currency
valuta legale	*(vah-lOOh-tah leh-gAh-leh)*	legal tender
valuta pregiata	*(vah-lOOh-tah preh-jAh-tah)*	hard currency
valutare	*(vah-looh-tAh-reh)*	assess (v)
valutazione (f)	*(vah-looh-tah-tsyOh-neh)*	appraisal, assessment, evaluation
valutazione degli investimenti	*(vah-looh-tah-tsyOh-neh deh-lyeeh eehn-vehs-teeh-mEhn-teeh)*	investment, appraisal
valutazione del credito	*(vah-looh-tah-tsyOh-neh dehl krEh-deeh-toh)*	credit rating
valutazione del lavoro	*(vah-looh-tah-tsyOh-neh dehl lah-vOh-roh)*	job evaluation
valutazione del mercato	*(vah-looh-tah-tsyOh-neh deeh mehr-kAh-toh)*	market rating
valutazione del rischio	*(vah-looh-tah-tsyOh-neh dehl rEEhs-kyoh)*	risk assessment
valutazione dell'adempimento del lavoro	*(vah-looh-tah-tsyOh-neh dehl ah-dehm-peeh-mEhn-toh dehl lah-vOh-roh)*	job performance rating
valutazione dell'investimento	*(vah-looh-tah-tsyOh-neh dehl eehn-vehs-teeh-mEhn-toh)*	investment appraisal

valutazione dell'obbligazione	*(vah-looh-tah-tsyOh-neh dehl ohb-bleeh-gah-tsyOh-neh)*	bond rating
valutazione di mercato	*(vah-looh-tah-tsyOh-neh deeh mehr-kAh-toh)*	market appraisal
valutazione finanziaria	*(vah-looh-tah-tsyOh-neh feeh-nahn-tsyAh-reeh-ah)*	financial appraisal
valutazione imponibile	*(vah-looh-tah-tsyOh-neh eehm-poh-nEEh-beeh-leh)*	assessed valuation
valutazione lineare	*(vah-looh-tah-tsyOh-neh leeh-neh-Ah-reh)*	linear estimation
valvola (f)	*(vAhl-voh-lah)*	valve
vanadio (m)	*(vah-nAh-dyoh)*	vanadium
vantaggio (m) competitivo	*(vahn-tAhj-joh kohm-peh-teeh-tEEh-voh)*	competitive advantage
variabilità (f) amministrata o controllata	*(vah-ryah-beeh-leeh-tAh ahm-meeh-neehs-trAh-tah oh kohn-trohl-lAh-tah)*	managed float
variazione (f)	*(vah-ryah-tsyOh-neh)*	spread, variance
varie	*(vAh-ryeh)*	miscellaneous
vassoio (m) per formaggi	*(vah-sO-yo pehr fohr-mAh-jee)*	cheese tray
velo (m)	*(vEh-loh)*	veil
velocità (f) della circolazione monetaria	*(veh-loh-cheeh-tAh dehl-lah cheehr-koh-lah-tsyOh-neh moh-neh-tAh-reeh-ah)*	velocity of money
vendemmia (f)	*(vehn-dEhm-myah)*	grape harvest, vintage
vendere	*(vEhn-deh-reh)*	market (v), sell (v)
vendere più di quanto si abbia	*(vEhn-deh-reh pyOOh deeh kwAhn-toh seeh Ahb-byah)*	oversell (v)
vendere sotto il prezzo del concorrente	*(vEhn-deh-reh sOht-toh eehl prEhts-tsoh dehl kohn-kohr-rEhn-teh)*	undercut (v)
vendita (f)	*(vEhn-deeh-tah)*	divestment, sale
vendita aggressiva	*(vEhn-deeh-tah ahg-grehs-sEEh-vah)*	hard sell

V

vendita allo scoperto	*(vEhn-deeh-tah ahl-loh skoh-pEhr-toh)*	short sale
vendita diretta	*(vEhn-deeh-tah deeh-rEht-tah)*	direct selling
vendita e il riaffitto	*(vEhn-deeh-tah eh eehl reeh-ahf-fEEht-toh)*	sale and leaseback
vendita negoziata	*(vEhn-deeh-tah neh-goh-tsyAh-tah)*	negotiated sale
vendita non aggressiva	*(vEhn-deeh-tah nohn ahg-grehs-sEEh-vah)*	soft sell
vendita per la realizzazione di profitti	*(vEhn-deeh-tah pehr lah reh-ah-leehds-dsah-tsyOh-neh deeh proh-fEEht-teeh)*	profit taking
vendita piramidale	*(vEhn-deeh-tah peeh-rah-meeh-dAh-leh)*	pyramid selling
vendita pubblica	*(vEhn-deeh-tah pOOhb-leeh-kah)*	public sale
vendite (f)	*(vEhn-deeh-teh)*	sales
vendite aggiunte	*(vEhn-deeh-teh ahj-jOOhn-teh)*	add-on sales
vendite lorde	*(vEhn-deeh-teh lOhr-deh)*	gross sales
vendite nette	*(vEhn-deeh-teh nEht-teh)*	net sales
vendite potenziali	*(vEhn-deeh-teh poh-tehn-tsyAh-leeh)*	potential sales
vendite previste	*(vEhn-deeh-teh preh-vEEhs-teh)*	sales estimate
venditore (m)	*(vehn-deeh-tOh-reh)*	vendor
venire incontro al prezzo	*(veh-nEEh-reh eehn-kOhn-troh ahl prEhts-tsoh)*	meet the price (v)
venire meno agli obblighi	*(veh-nEEh-reh mEh-noh ah-lyeeh Ohb-bleeh-geeh)*	default (v)
verifica (f) della perdita	*(veh-rEEh-feeh-kah dehl-lah pEhr-deeh-tah)*	proof of loss
verificare	*(veh-reeh-feeh-kAh-reh)*	audit (v)
vernice (f)	*(vehr-nEEh-cheh)*	paint
vestito (m)	*(vehs-tEEh-toh)*	dress
veto (m)	*(vEh-toh)*	veto
vetro (m) di cristallo	*(vEh-troh- deeh kreehs-tAhl-loh)*	crystal glass

vettore (m)	*(veht-tOh-reh)*	common carrier
vettore (m)	*(veht-tOh-reh)*	vector
vettore contrattuale	*(veht-tOh-reh kohn-traht-twAh-leh)*	contract carrier
vice amministratore/trice (m/f)	*(vEEh-cheh ahm-meeh-neehs-trah-tOh-reh/trEEh-cheh)*	deputy manager
vice direttore generale	*(vEEh-cheh deeh-reht-tOh-reh jeh-neh-rAh-leh)*	assistant general manager
vice direttore/trice (m/f)	*(vEEh-cheh deeh-reht-tOh-reh/trEEh-cheh)*	assistant manager
vice dirigente (m/f)	*(vEEh-cheh deeh-reeh-jEhn-teh)*	deputy manager
vice-presidente/essa (m/f)	*(vEEh-cheh preh-zeeh-dEhn-teh/Ehs-sah)*	vice-president
videoregistratore (m)	*(veeh-deh-oh-reh-jeehs-trah-tOh-reh)*	videocassette recorder (VCR)
vigna (f)	*(vEEh-nyah)*	vine
vigneto (m)	*(veeh-nyEh-toh)*	vineyard
vinaio (m)	*(veeh-nAh-yoh)*	vintner
vino (m)	*(vEEh-noh)*	wine
vino da tavola	*(vEEh-noh dah tAh-voh-lah)*	table wine
vino secco	*(vEEh-noh sEh-koh)*	dry wine
vino spumante	*(vEEh-noh spooh-mAhn-teh)*	sparkling wine
viscosità (f)	*(veehs-koh-zeeh-tAh)*	viscosity
visita (f) di vendita senza preavviso	*(vEEh-zeeh-tah deeh vEhn-deeh-tah sEhn-tsah preh-ahv-vEEh-zoh)*	cold call
visone (m)	*(veeh-zOh-neh)*	mink
vita (f) economica	*(vEEh-tah eh-koh-nOh-meeh-kah)*	economic life
vita media	*(vEEh-tah mEh-dyah)*	average life
vitalizio (m)	*(veeh-tah-lEEh-tsyoh)*	annuitant
vitamina (f)	*(veeh-tah-mEEh-nah)*	vitamin
vite (f)	*(vEEh-tah)*	waist
vitello (m)	*(veeh-tEhl-loh)*	calfskin
viticultore (m)	*(veeh-teeh-koohl-tOh-reh)*	winegrower
vitigno (m)	*(veeh-tEEh-nyoh)*	type of vine

V

voce (f)	*(vOh-cheh)*	item
voce tariffaria	*(vOh-cheh tah-reehf-fAh-reeh-ah)*	tariff commodity
volante (m)	*(voh-lAhn-teh)*	steering wheel
volantino (m)	*(voh-lahn-tEEh-noh)*	insert
volpe (f)	*(vOhl-peh)*	fox
volt (m)		volt
voltaggio (m)	*(vohl-tAhj-joh)*	voltage
volume (m)	*(voh-lOOh-meh)*	volume
volume delle vendite	*(voh-lOOh-meh dehl-leh vEhn-deeh-teh)*	sales volume
volume di vendite al quale c'è equilibrio tra ricavi e costi	*(voh-lOOh-meh deeh vEhn-deeh-teh ahl kwAh-leh cheh eh-kweeh-lEEh-breeh-oh trah reeh-kAh-veeh eh kOhs-teeh)*	break-even point
volume effettivo di mercato	*(voh-lOOh-meh ehf-feht-tEEh-voh deeh mehr-kAh-toh)*	actual market volume
vuoto (m)	*(vwOh-toh)*	vacuum

W

watt (m)	*(waht)*	watt
word processor (m)	*(wuhrd prahsesohr)*	word processor

Z

zecca (f)	*(dsEhk-kah)*	mint
zibellino (m)	*(dseeh-behl-lEEh-noh)*	sable
zincatura (f)	*(dseehn-kah-tOOh-rah)*	galvanizing
zinco (m)	*(dsEEhn-koh)*	zinc
zona (f)	*(dsOh-nah)*	zone
zona franca	*(dsOh-nah frAhn-kah)*	free trade zone

Z

zone (f) di coltivazione delle vigne	*(dsOh-neh deeh kohl-teeh-vah-tsyOh-neh dehl-leh vEEh-nyeh)*	wine growing areas
zuccheriera (f)	*(dsoohk-kyeh-ryEh-rah)*	sugar bowl
zuppiera (f)	*(dsoohp-pyEh-rah)*	soup dish

KEY WORDS FOR KEY INDUSTRIES

The dictionary that forms the centerpiece of *Italian for the Business Traveler* is a compendium of some 3,000 words that you are likely to use or encounter as you do business abroad. It will greatly facilitate fact-finding about the business possibilities that interest you, and will help guide you through negotiations as well as reading documents. To supplement the dictionary, we have added a special feature—groupings of key terms about ten industries. As you explore any of these industries, you'll want to have *Italian for the Business Traveler* at your fingertips to help make sure you don't misunderstand or overlook an aspect that could have a material effect on the outcome of your business decision. The industries covered in the vocabulary lists are the following:

- chemicals
- chinaware and tableware
- electronics
- fashion
- iron and steel
- leather goods
- motor vehicles
- pharmaceuticals
- printing and publishing
- winemaking

	CHEMICALS	

English to Italian

acetate	l'acetato	*(ah-cheh-tAh-toh)*
acetic acid	l'acido acetico	*(Ah-ceeh-doh ah-chEh-teeh-koh)*
acetone	l'acetone	*(ah-cheh-tOh-neh)*
acid	l'acido	*(Ah-ceeh-doh)*
amine	l'amina	*(ah-mEEh-nah)*
ammonia	l'ammoniaca	*(ahm-moh-nEEh-ah-kah)*
analysis	l'analisi	*(ah-nAh—leeh-zeeh)*
atom	l'atomo	*(Ah-toh-moh)*
atomic	atomico	*(ah-tOh-meeh-koh)*
base	la base	*(bAh-zeh)*
benzene	il benzolo	*(behn-dsOh-loh)*
biochemistry	la biochimica	*(beeh-oh-kEEh-meeh-kah)*
biology	la biologia	*(beeh-oh-loh-jEEh-ah)*
carbon	il carbonio	*(kahr-bOh-neeh-oh)*
catalyst	la catalisi	*(kah-tAh-leeh-zeeh)*
chemistry	la chimica	*(kEEh-meeh-kah)*
chloride	il cloruro	*(kloh-rOOh-roh)*
chloroform	il cloroformio	*(kloh-roh-fOhr-meeh-oh)*
composition	la composizione	*(kohm-poh-zeeh-tsyOh-neh)*
compound	il composto	*(kohm-pOhst-oh)*
concentration	la concentrazione	*(kohn-cehn-trah-tsyOh-neh)*
cracking	la piroscissione	*(peeh-roh-sheehs-syOh-neh)*
crystallization	la cristalizzazione	*(kreehs-tah-leehds-dsah-tsyOh-neh)*
degree	il grado	*(grAh-doh)*
density	la densità	*(dehn-seeh-tAh)*
distillation	la distillazione	*(deehs-teehl-lah-tsyOh-neh)*
electrolysis	l'elettrolisi	*(eh-leht-trOh-leeh-zeeh)*
electron	l'elettrone	*(eh-leht-trOh-neh)*
element	l'elemento	*(eh-leh-mEhn-toh)*

engineer	l'ingegnere	*(eehn-jeh-nyEh-reh)*
enzyme	l'enzima	*(ehn-dsEEh-mah)*
ethane	l'etano	*(eh-tAh-noh)*
ether	l'etere	*(Eh-teh-reh)*
evaporation	l'evaporazione	*(eh-vah-poh-rah-tsyOh-neh)*
experiment	l'esperimento, la prova	*(ehs-peh-reeh-mEhn-toh), (prOh-vah)*
formula	la formula	*(fOhr-mooh-lah)*
gas chromatography	la gascromatografia	*(gahs-kroh-mah-toh-grah-fEEh-ah)*
gram	il grammo	*(grAhm-moh)*
homogeneity	l'omogeneità	*(oh-moh-geh-neh-eeh-tAh)*
hydrocarbon	l'idrocarbonio	*(eeh-drohkahr-bOh-neeh-ohh)*
hydrochloric acid	l'acido cloridico	*(Ah-ceeh-doh kloh-rEEh-deeh-koh)*
hydrolysis	l'idrolisi	*(eeh-drOh-leeh-zeeh)*
impurity	l'impurezza	*(eehm-pooh-rEhts-tsah)*
inorganic chemistry	la chimica inorganica	*(kEEh-meeh-kah eehn-ohr-gAh-neeh-kah)*
isotope	l'isotopo	*(eeh-zOh-toh-poh)*
laboratory	il laboratorio	*(lah-boh-rah-tOh-reeh-oh)*
methane	il metano	*(meh-tAh-noh)*
molar	il molare	*(moh-lAh-reh)*
mole	il grammo molecola	*(grAhm-moh moh-lEh-koh-lah)*
molecule	la molecola	*(moh-lEh-koh-lah)*
natural gas	il gas naturale	*(gas nah-tooh-rAh-leh)*
neutral	neutro	*(nEh-ooh-troh)*
neutralization	la neutralizzazione	*(neh-ooh-trah-leehds-dsah-tsyOh-neh)*
neutron	il neutrone	*(neh-ooh-trOh-neh)*
nitrate	il nitrato	*(neeh-trAh-toh)*
nitric acid	acido nitrico	*(Ah-ceeh-doh nEEh-treeh-koh)*
nitrite	il nitrito	*(neeh-trEEh-toh)*
oxidation	l'ossidazione	*(ohs-seeh-dah-tsyOh-neh)*

oxygen	l'ossigeno	*(ohs-sEEh-jeh-noh)*
petroleum	il petrolio	*(peh-trOh-lyoh)*
phosphate	il fosfato	*(fohs-fAh-toh)*
polymer	il polimero	*(poh-lEEh-meh-roh)*
product	il prodotto	*(proh-dOht-toh)*
proton	il protone	*(proh-tOh-neh)*
purification	la purificazione	*(pooh-reeh-feeh-kah-tsyOh-neh)*
reagent	il reagente, il reattivo	*(reh-ah-jEhn-teh), (reh-aht-tEEh-voh)*
reduction	la riduzione	*(reeh-dooh-tsyOh-neh)*
refine (v)	raffinare	*(rahf-feeh-nAh-reh)*
refinery	la raffineria	*(rahf-feeh-neh-rEEh-ah)*
research	la ricerca	*(reeh-chEhr-kah)*
salt	il sale	*(sAh-leh)*
saponification	la saponificazione	*(sah-poh-neeh-feeh-kah-tsyOh-neh)*
solubility	la solubilità	*(soh-looh-beeh-leeh-tAh)*
solute	il soluto	*(soh-lOOh-toh)*
solution	la soluzione	*(soh-looh-tsyOh-neh)*
solvent	il solvente	*(sohl-vEhn-teh)*
spectrophotometry	la spettrofotometria	*(speht-troh-foh-toh-meh-trEEh-ah)*
spectrum	lo spettro	*(spEht-troh)*
sulfate	il solfato	*(sohl-fAh-toh)*
sulfuric acid	l'acido solforico	*(Ah-ceeh-doh sohl-fOh-reeh-koh)*
titration	la titolazione	*(teeh-toh-lah-tsyOh-neh)*
viscosity	la viscosità	*(veehs-koh-zeeh-tAh)*
yield	la resa	*(rEh-sah)*
yield (v)	rendere	*(rEhn-deh-reh)*

Italian to English

acetato (m)	*(ah-cheh-tAh-toh)*	acetate
acetone (m)	*(ah-cheh-tOh-neh)*	acetone
acido (m)	*(Ah-ceeh-doh)*	acid

acido acetico	*(Ah-ceeh-doh ah-chEh-teeh-koh)*	acetic acid
acido cloridico	*(Ah-ceeh-doh kloh-rEEh-deeh-koh)*	hydrochloric acid
acido nitrico	*(Ah-ceeh-doh nEEh-treeh-koh)*	nitric acid
acido solforico	*(Ah-ceeh-doh sohl-fOh-reeh-koh)*	sulfuric acid
amina (f)	*(ah-mEEh-nah)*	amine
ammoniaca (f)	*(ahm-moh-nEEh-ah-kah)*	ammonia
analisi (f)	*(ah-nAh—leeh-zeeh)*	analysis
atomica	*(ah-tOh-meeh-koh)*	atomic
atomo (m)	*(Ah-toh-moh)*	atom
base (f)	*(bAh-zeh)*	base
benzolo (f)	*(behn-dsOh-loh)*	benzene
biochimica (f)	*(beeh-oh-kEEh-meeh-kah)*	biochemistry
biologia (f)	*(beeh-oh-loh-jEEh-ah)*	biology
carbonio (m)	*(kahr-bOh-neeh-oh)*	carbon
catalisi (f)	*(kah-tAh-leeh-zeeh)*	catalyst
chimica (f)	*(kEEh-meeh-kah)*	chemistry
chimica inorganica	*(kEEh-meeh-kah eehn-ohr-gAh-neeh-kah)*	inorganic chemistry
cloroformio (m)	*(kloh-roh-fOhr-meeh-oh)*	chloroform
cloruro (m)	*(kloh-rOOh-roh)*	chloride
composizione (f)	*(kohm-poh-zeeh-tsyOh-neh)*	composition
composto (m)	*(kohm-pOhst-oh)*	compound
concentrazione (f)	*(kohn-cehn-trah-tsyOh-neh)*	concentration
cristalizzazione (f)	*(kreehs-tah-leehds-dsah-tsyOh-neh)*	crystallization
densità (f)	*(dehn-seeh-tAh)*	density
distillazione (f)	*(deehs-teehl-lah-tsyOh-neh)*	distillation
elemento (m)	*(eh-leh-mEhn-toh)*	element
elettrolisi (f)	*(eh-leht-trOh-leeh-zeeh)*	electrolysis
elettrone (m)	*(eh-leht-trOh-neh)*	electron
enzima (m)	*(ehn-dsEEh-mah)*	enzyme
esperimento (m)	*(ehs-peh-reeh-mEhn-toh)*	experiment

etano (m)	*(eh-tAh-noh)*	ethane
etere (m)	*(Eh-teh-reh)*	ether
evaporazione (f)	*(eh-vah-poh-rah-tsyOh-neh)*	evaporation
formula (f)	*(fOhr-mooh-lah)*	formula
fosfato (m)	*(fohs-fAh-toh)*	phosphate
gas metano	*(gas mEh-tah-noh)*	natural gas
gascromatografia (f)	*(gas-kroh-mah-toh-grah-fEEh-ah)*	gas chromatography
grado (m)	*(grAh-doh)*	degree
grammo (m)	*(grAhm-moh)*	gram
grammo molecola	*(grAhm-moh moh-lEh-koh-lah)*	mole
idrocarbonio (m)	*(eeh-droh-kahr-bOh-neeh-oh)*	hydrocarbon
idrolisi (f)	*(eeh-drOh-leeh-zeeh)*	hydrolysis
impurezza (f)	*(eehm-pooh-rEhts-tsah)*	impurity
ingegnere (m)	*(eehn-jeh-nyEh-reh)*	engineer
isotopo (m)	*(eeh-zOh-toh-poh)*	isotope
laboratorio (m)	*(lah-boh-rah-tOh-reeh-oh)*	laboratory
metano (m)	*(meh-tAh-noh)*	methane
molare (m)	*(moh-lAh-reh)*	molar
molecola (f)	*(moh-lEh-koh-lah)*	molecule
neutralizzazione (f)	*(neh-ooh-trah-leehds-dsah-tsyOh-neh)*	neutralization
neutro	*(nEh-ooh-troh)*	neutral
neutrone (m)	*(neh-ooh-trOh-neh)*	neutron
nitrato (m)	*(neeh-trAh-toh)*	nitrate
nitrito (m)	*(neeh-trEEh-toh)*	nitrite
omogeneità (f)	*(oh-moh-geh-neh-eeh-tAh)*	homogeneity
ossidazione (f)	*(ohs-seeh-dah-tsyOh-neh)*	oxidation
ossigeno (m)	*(ohs-sEEh-jeh-noh)*	oxygen
petrolio (m)	*(peh-trOh-lyoh)*	petroleum
piroscissione (f)	*(peeh-roh-sheehs-syOh-neh)*	cracking
polimero (m)	*(poh-lEEh-meh-roh)*	polymer
prodotto (m)	*(proh-dOht-toh)*	product

protone (m)	*(proh-tOh-neh)*	proton
prova (f)	*(prOh-vah)*	experiment
purificazione (f)	*(pooh-reeh-feeh-kah-tsyOh-neh)*	purification
raffinare	*(rahf-feeh-nAh-reh)*	refine (v)
raffineria (f)	*(rahf-feeh-neh-rEEh-ah)*	refinery
reagente (m)	*(reh-ah-jEhn-teh)*	reagent
reattivo (m)	*(reh-aht-tEEh-voh)*	reagent
rendere	*(rEhn-deh-reh)*	yield (v)
resa (f)	*(rEh-zah)*	yield
ricerca (f)	*(reeh-chEhr-kah)*	research
riduzione (f)	*(reeh-dooh-tsyOh-neh)*	reduction
sale (m)	*(sAh-leh)*	salt
saponificazione (f)	*(sah-poh-neeh-feeh-kah-tsyOh-neh)*	saponification
solfato (m)	*(sohl-fAh-toh)*	sulfate
solubilità (f)	*(soh-looh-beeh-leeh-tAh)*	solubility
soluto (f)	*(soh-lOOh-toh)*	solute
soluzione (f)	*(soh-looh-tsyOh-neh)*	solution
solvente (m)	*(sohl-vEhn-teh)*	solvent
spettro (m)	*(spEht-troh)*	spectrum
spettrofotometria (f)	*(speht-troh-foh-toh-meh-trEEh-ah)*	spectrophotometry
titolazione (f)	*(teeh-toh-lah-tsyOh-neh)*	titration
viscosità (f)	*(veehs-koh-zeeh-tAh)*	viscosity

CHINAWARE AND TABLEWARE

English to Italian

bone china	la porcellana "bone"	*(pohr-chehl-lAh-nah)*
bowl	la scodella	*(skoh-dEhl-lah)*
breadbasket	il cestino per il pane	*(chehs-tEEh-noh pehr eehl pAh-neh)*
butter dish	il piattino per il burro	*(pyAht-teeh-noh pehr eehl bOOhr-roh)*
candlestick	il candeliere	*(kahn-deh-lyEh-reh)*
carving knife	il trinciante	*(treehn-chAhn-teh)*
champagne glass	il flute, la coppa per lo spumante	*(kOhp-pah pehr- loh spooh-mAhn-teh)*
cheese tray	il vassoio per formaggi	*(vahs-sOh-yoh pehr fohr-mAhj-jeeh)*
china	la porcellana fine	*(pohr-chehl-lAh-nah fEEh-neh)*
coffeepot	la caffettiera	*(kahf-feht-tyEh-rah)*
crystal glass	il vetro di cristallo	*(vEh-troh- deeh kreehs-tAhl-loh)*
cup	la tazza	*(tAhts-tsah)*
cutlery	la posateria	*(poh-zah-teh-rEEh-ah)*
decanter	la caraffa	*(kah-rAhf-fah)*
dessert plate	il piatto per dolci	*(pyAht-toh pehr dOhl-cheeh)*
dish	il piatto	*(pyAht-toh)*
earthenware	la terraglia	*(tehr-rAh-lyah)*
espresso cup	la tazzina da espresso	*(tahts-tsEEh-nah dah ehs-prEhs-soh)*
flute	il flute	*(floot)*
fork	la forchetta	*(for-kEht-tah)*
glass	il bicchiere	*(beehk-kyEh-reh)*
gravy boat	la salsiera	*(sahl-syEh-rah)*
hand-painted	dipinto a mano	*(deeh-pEEhn-toh ah mAh-noh)*
hand-blown glass	il bicchiere soffiato a bocca	*(beehk-kyEh-reh sohf-fyAh-toh ah bOhk-kah)*

hand-embroidered napkins	i tovaglioli ricamati a mano	*(toh-vah-lyOh-leeh reeh-kah-mAh-teeeh ah mAh-noh)*
knife	il coltello	*(kohl-tEhl-loh)*
lace	il merletto	*(mehr-lEht-toh)*
linen	la biancheria da tavola	*(byahn-keh-rEEh-ah dah tAh-voh-lah)*
napkin	il tovagliolo	*(toh-vah-lyOh-loh)*
napkin ring	l'anello per tovagliolo	*(ah-nEhl-loh pehr toh-vah-lyOh-loh)*
oilcloth	la tela cerata	*(tEh-lah cheh-rAh-tah)*
pastry server	la paletta	*(pah-lEht-tah)*
pepper mill	il macinapepe	*(mAh-cheeh-nah pEh-peh)*
pepper shaker	il porta pepe	*(pOhr-tah pEh-peh)*
pitcher	la caraffa, la brocca	*(kah-rAhf-fah), (brOhk-kah)*
place setting	il coperto	*(koh-pEhr-toh)*
plate	il piatto	*(pyAht-toh)*
pottery	le stoviglie	*(stoh-vEEh-lyeh)*
salad plate	il piatto per l'insalata	*(pyAht-toh pehr leehn-sah-lAh-tah)*
salt shaker	la saliera	*(sah-lyEh-rah)*
saucer	il piattino	*(pyaht-tEEh-noh)*
silverware	l'argenteria	*(ahr-jehn-teh-rEEh-ah)*
soup dish	la zuppiera	*(dsoohp-pyEh-rah)*
spoon	il cucchiaio	*(koohk-kyAh-yoh)*
stainless steel	l'acciaio inossidabile	*(ahch-chAh-yoh eehn-ohs-seeh-dAh-beeh-leh)*
stoneware	il grès	*(grehs)*
sugar bowl	la zuccheriera	*(dsoohk-kyeh-ryEh-rah)*
tablecloth	la tovaglia	*(toh-vAh-lyah)*
tablespoon	il cucchiaio	*(koohk-kyAh-yoh)*
teapot	la teiera	*(teh-yEh-rah)*
teaspoon	il cucchiaino da tè	*(koohk-kyah-EEh-noh dah tEh)*
thread	il filo	*(fEEh-loh)*
tureen	la terrina	*(tehr-rEEh-nah)*
unbleached linen	il lino grezzo	*(lEEh-noh grEhts-tsoh)*

Italian to English

acciaio (m) inossid-abile	*(ahch-chAh-yoh eehn-ohs-seeh-dAh-beeh-leh)*	stainless steel
anello (m) per tovagliolo	*(ah-nEhl-loh pehr toh-vah-lyOh-loh)*	napkin ring
argenteria (m)	*(ahr-jehn-teh-rEEh-ah)*	silverware
biancheria (f) da tavola	*(byahn-keh-rEEh-ah dah tAh-voh-lah)*	linen
bicchiere (m)	*(beehk-kyEh-reh)*	glass
bicchiere soffiato a bocca	*(beehk-kyEh-reh sohf-fyAh-toh ah bOhk-kah)*	hand-blown glass
brocca (f)	*(brOhk-kah)*	pitcher
caffettiera (f)	*(kahf-feht-tyEh-rah)*	coffeepot
candeliere (m)	*(kahn-deh-lyEh-reh)*	candlestick
caraffa (f)	*(kah-rAhf-fah)*	decanter, pitcher
cestino (m) per il pane	*(chehs-tEEh-noh pehr eehl pAh-neh)*	breadbasket
coltello (m)	*(kohl-tEhl-loh)*	knife
coperto (m)	*(koh-pEhr-toh)*	place setting
coppa (f) per lo spumante	*(kOhp-pah pehr- loh spooh-mAhn-teh)*	champagne glass
cucchiaino (m) da tè	*(koohk-kyah-EEh-noh dah tEh)*	teaspoon
cucchiaio (m)	*(koohk-kyAh-yoh)*	spoon
dipinto a mano	*(deeh-pEEhn-toh ah mAh-noh)*	hand-painted
filo (m)	*(fEEh-loh)*	thread
flute (m)	*(floot)*	champagne glass, flute
forchetta (f)	*(for-kEht-tah)*	fork
grès (m)	*(grehs)*	stoneware
lino (m) grezzo	*(lEEh-noh grEhts-tsoh)*	unbleached linen
macinapepe (m)	*(mAh-cheeh-nah pEh-peh)*	pepper mill
merletto (m)	*(mehr-lEht-toh)*	lace
paletta (f)	*(pah-lEht-tah)*	pastry server
piattino (m)	*(pyaht-tEEh-noh)*	saucer
piattino per il burro	*(pyAht-teeh-noh pehr eehl bOOhr-roh)*	butter dish

piatto (m)	*(pyAht-toh)*	dish, plate
piatto per dolci	*(pyAht-toh pehr dOhl-cheeh)*	dessert plate
piatto per insalata	*(pyAht-toh pehr leehn-sah-lAh-tah)*	salad plate
porcellana (f) "bone"	*(pohr-chehl-lAh-nah)*	bone china
porcellana fine	*(pohr-chehl-lAh-nah fEEh-neh)*	fine china
porta (m) pepe	*(pOhr-tah pEh-peh)*	pepper shaker
posateria (f)	*(poh-zah-teh-rEEh-ah)*	cutlery
saliera (f)	*(sah-lyEh-rah)*	salt shaker
salsiera (f)	*(sahl-syEh-rah)*	gravy boat
scodella (f)	*(skoh-dEhl-lah)*	bowl
stoviglie (f)	*(stoh-vEEh-lyeh)*	pottery
tazza (f)	*(tAhts-tsah)*	cup
tazzina (f) da espresso	*(tahts-tsEEh-nah dah ehs-prEhs-soh)*	espresso cup
teiera (f)	*(teh-yEh-rah)*	teapot
tela cerata (f)	*(tEh-lah cheh-rAh-tah)*	oilcloth
terraglia (f)	*(tehr-rAh-lyah)*	earthenware
terrina (f)	*(teh-rEEh-nah)*	tureen
tovaglia (f)	*(toh-vAh-lyah)*	tablecloth
tovaglioli (m) ricamati a mano	*(toh-vah-lyOh-leeh reeh-kah-mAh-teeeh ah mAh-noh)*	hand-embroidered napkins
tovagliolo (m)	*(toh-vah-lyOh-loh)*	napkin
trinciante (m)	*(treehn-chAhn-teh)*	carving knife
vassoio (m) per formaggi	*(vah-sO-yo pehr fohr-mAh-jee)*	cheese tray
vetro (m) di cristallo	*(vEh-troh- deeh kreehs-tAhl-loh)*	crystal glass
zuccheriera (f)	*(dsoohk-kyeh-ryEh-rah)*	sugar bowl
zuppiera (f)	*(dsoohp-pyEh-rah)*	soup dish

ELECTRONICS

English to Italian

alternating current	la corrente alternata	*(kohr-rEhn-teh ahl-tehr-nAh-tah)*
ampere	l'ampere	*(ahm-pEh-reh)*
amplifier	l'amplificatore	*(ahm-pleeh-feeh-kah-tOh-reh)*
amplitude modulation (AM)	la modulazione di ampiezza	*(moh-dooh-lah-tsyOh-neh deeh ahm-pyEhts-tsah)*
antenna	l'antenna	*(ahn-tEhn-nah)*
beam	il fascio	*(fAh-shoh)*
binary code	il codice binario	*(kOh-deeh-cheh beeh-nAh-reeh-oh)*
broadcast (v)	trasmettere	*(trahz-mEht-teh-reh)*
cable television	la filodiffusione	*(feeh-loh-deehf-fooh-zyOh-neh)*
camera	la telecamera	*(teh-leh-kAh-meh-rah)*
cassette	la cassetta	*(kahs-sEht-tah)*
cathode	il catodo	*(kAh-toh-doh)*
channel	il canale	*(kah-nAh-leh)*
circuit	il circuito	*(cheehr-kwEEh-toh)*
coaxial cable	il cavo coassiale	*(kAh-voh koh-ahs-syAh-leh)*
computer	l'elaboratore elettronico, il "computer"	*(eh-lah-boh-rah-tOh-reh eh-leht-trOh-neeh-koh), (kumpyutor)*
condenser	il condensatore	*(kohn-dehn-sah-tOh-reh)*
conductor	il conduttore	*(kohn-dooht-tOh-reh)*
current	la corrente	*(kohr-rEhn-teh)*
detector	la valvola rivelatrice	*(vAhlvoh-lah reeh-veh-lah-trEEh-cheh)*
digital	digitale	*(deeh-jeeh-tAh-leh)*
diode	il diodo	*(dEEh-oh-doh)*
electricity	l'elettricità	*(eh-leht-treeh-cheeh-tAh)*
electrode	l'elettrodo	*(eh-lEht-troh-doh)*
electron	l'elettrone	*(eh-leht-trOh-neh)*
electronic	elettronico	*(eh-leht-trOh-neeh-koh)*

electrostatic	elettrostatico	*(eh-leht-troh-stAh-teeh-koh)*
fiber optic	la fibra ottica	*(fEEh-brah Oht-teeh-kah)*
filament	il filamento	*(feeh-lah-mEhn-toh)*
filter	il filtro	*(fEEhl-troh)*
frequency	la frequenza	*(freh-kwEhn-tsah)*
frequency modula- tion (FM)	la modulazione di frequenza	*(moh-dooh-lah-tsyOh-neh deeh freh-kwEhn-tsah)*
generator	il generatore	*(jeh-neh-rah-tOh-reh)*
germanium	il germanio	*(jehr-mAh-neeh-oh)*
high fidelity	l'alta fedeltà	*(Ahl-tah feh-dehl-tAh)*
induction	l'induzione	*(eehn-dooh-tsyOh-neh)*
insulator	l'isolante	*(eeh-zoh-lAhn-teh)*
integrated circuit	il circuito integrato	*(cheehr-kwEEh-toh eehn- teh-grAh-toh)*
kilowatt	il kilowatt	*(kilohwaht)*
laser	il laser	*(lahyzehr)*
microphone	il microfono	*(meeh-krOh-foh-noh)*
microwave	la microonda	*(meeh-kroh-Ohn-dah)*
mixer	il miscelatore	*(meeh-sheh-lah-tOh-reh)*
motor	il motore	*(moh-tOh-reh)*
negative	il negativo	*(neh-ha-tEEh-voh)*
ohm	l'ohm	*(ohm)*
optic	ottico	*(Oht-teeh-koh)*
oscillator	l'oscillatore	*(oh-sheehl-lah-tOh-reh)*
panel	il pannello	*(pahn-nEhl-loh)*
parallel circuit	il circuito in parallelo	*(cheehr-kwEEh-toh eehn pah-rahl-lEh-loh)*
pole	il polo	*(pOh-loh)*
positive	il positivo	*(poh-zeeh-tEEh-voh)*
power	la potenza, il rendimento	*(poh-tEhn-dsah), (rehn- deeh-mEhn-toh)*
printed circuit	il circuito stampato	*(cheehr-kwEEh-toh stahm- pAh-toh)*
program	il programma	*(proh-grAhm-mah)*
radar	il radar	*(raydahr)*
radio	la radio	*(rAh-deeh-oh)*

receiver	il ricevitore	*(reeh-cheh-veeh-tOh-reh)*
record	il disco	*(dEEhs-koh)*
record (v)	incidere	*(eehn-chEEh-deh-reh)*
resistance	la resistenza	*(reh-zeehs-tEhn-tsah)*
resonance	la risonanza	*(reeh-soh-nAhn-tsah)*
scanning	la scansione, l'esplorazione	*(skahn-syOh-neh), (ehs-ploh-rah-tsyOh-neh)*
screen	lo schermo	*(skEhr-moh)*
semiconductor	il semiconduttore	*(seh-meeh-kohn-dooht-tOh-reh)*
short wave	le onde corte	*(Ohn-deh kOhr-teh)*
silicon	il silicone	*(seeh-leeh-kOh-neh)*
sound	il suono	*(sWoh-noh)*
speaker	l'altoparlante	*(ahl-toh-pahr-lAhn-teh)*
stereophonic	stereofonico	*(steh-reh-oh-fOh-neeh-koh)*
switch	l'interruttore	*(eehn-tehr-rooht-tOh-reh)*
tape	il nastro	*(nAhs-troh)*
telecommunica-tions	le telecomunicazioni	*(teh-leh-koh-mooh-neek-kah-tsyOh-neeh)*
tube	il tubo	*(tOOh-boh)*
tune (v)	captare	*(kahp-tAh-reh)*
vacuum	il vuoto	*(vwOh-toh)*
vector	il vettore	*(veht-tOh-reh)*
videocassette recorder (VCR)	il videoregistratore	*(veeh-deh-oh-reh-jeehs-trah-tOh-reh)*
volt	il volt	*(vohlt)*
voltage	il voltaggio	*(vohl-tAhj-joh)*
watt	il watt	*(waht)*
wave	l'onda	*(Ohn-dah)*
wire	il filo	*(fEEh-loh)*

Italian to English

alta fedeltà (f)	*(Ahl-tah feh-dehl-tAh)*	high fidelity
altoparlante (m)	*(ahl-toh-pahr-lAhn-teh)*	speaker
ampere (m)	*(ahm-pEh-reh)*	ampere

amplificatore (m)	*(ahm-pleeh-feeh-kah-tOh-reh)*	amplifier
antenna (f)	*(ahn-tEhn-nah)*	antenna
canale (m)	*(kah-nAh-leh)*	channel
captare	*(kahp-tAh-reh)*	tune (v)
cassetta (f)	*(kahs-sEht-tah)*	cassette
catodo (m)	*(kAh-toh-doh)*	cathode
cavo (m) coassiale	*(kAh-voh koh-ahs-syAh-leh)*	coaxial cable
circuito (m)	*(cheehr-kwEEh-toh)*	circuit
circuito in parallelo	*(cheehr-kwEEh-toh eehn pah-rahl-lEh-loh)*	parallel circuit
circuito integrato	*(cheehr-kwEEh-toh eehn-teh-grAh-toh)*	integrated circuit
circuito stampato	*(cheehr-kwEEh-toh stahm-pAh-toh)*	printed circuit
codice (m) binario	*(kOh-deeh-cheh beeh-nAh-reeh-oh)*	binary code
condensatore (m)	*(kohn-dehn-sah-tOh-reh)*	condenser
conduttore (m)	*(kohn-dooht-tOh-reh)*	conductor
corrente (f)	*(kohr-rEhn-teh)*	current
corrente alternata	*(kohr-rEhn-teh ahl-tehr-nAh-tah)*	alternating current
digitale	*(deeh-jeeh-tAh-leh)*	digital
diodo (m)	*(dEEh-oh-doh)*	diode
disco (m)	*(dEEhs-koh)*	record
elaboratore (m) elettronico	*(eh-lah-boh-rah-tOh-reh eh-leht-trOh-neeh-koh)*	computer
elettricità (f)	*(eh-leht-treeh-cheeh-tAh)*	electricity
elettrodo (m)	*(eh-lEht-troh-doh)*	electrode
elettrone (m)	*(eh-leht-trOh-neh)*	electron
elettronico	*(eh-leht-trOh-neeh-koh)*	electronic
elettrostatico	*(eh-leht-troh-stAh-teeh-koh)*	electrostatic
esplorazione (f)	*(eh-leht-troh-stAh-teeh-koh)*	scanning
fascio (m)	*(fEEh-brah)*	beam
fibra ottica (f)	*(fEEh-brah Oht-teeh-kah)*	fiber optic
filamento (m)	*(feeh-lah-mEhn-toh)*	filament
filo (m)	*(fEEh-loh)*	wire

filodiffusione (f)	*(feeh-loh-deehf-fooh-zyOh-neh)*	cable television
filtro (m)	*(fEEhl-troh)*	filter
frequenza (f)	*(freh-kwEhn-tsah)*	frequency
generatore (m)	*(jeh-neh-rah-tOh-reh)*	generator
germanio (m)	*(jehr-mAh-neeh-oh)*	germanium
incidere	*(eehn-chEEh-deh-reh)*	record (v)
induzione (f)	*(eehn-dooh-tsyOh-neh)*	induction
interruttore (m)	*(eehn-tehr-rooht-tOh-reh)*	switch
isolante (m)	*(eeh-zoh-lAhn-teh)*	insulator
kilowatt (m)	*(kilowaht)*	kilowatt
laser (m)	*(lahyzuhr)*	laser
microfono (m)	*(meeh-krOh-foh-noh)*	microphone
microonda (f)	*(meeh-kroh-Ohn-dah)*	microwave
miscelatore (m)	*(meeh-sheh-lah-tOh-reh)*	mixer
modulazione (f) di ampiezza	*(moh-dooh-lah-tsyOh-neh deeh ahm-pyEhts-tsah)*	amplitude modulation (AM)
modulazione di fre- quenza	*(moh-dooh-lah-tsyOh-neh deeh freh-kwEhn-tsah)*	frequency modulation (FM)
motore (m)	*(moh-tOh-reh)*	motor
nastro (m)	*(nAhs-troh)*	tape
negativo (m)	*(neh-gah-tEEh-voh)*	negative
ohm (m)	*(ohm)*	ohm
onda (f)	*(Ohn-dah)*	wave
onde corte	*(Ohn-deh kOhr-teh)*	short wave
oscillatore (m)	*(oh-sheehl-lah-tOh-reh)*	oscillator
ottico	*(Oht-teeh-koh)*	optic
pannello (m)	*(pahn-nEhl-loh)*	panel
polo (m)	*(pOh-loh)*	pole
positivo (m)	*(poh-zeeh-tEEh-voh)*	positive
potenza (f)	*(poh-tEhn-dsah)*	power
programma (m)	*(proh-grAhm-mah)*	program
radar (m)		radar
radio (f)	*(rAh-deeh-oh)*	radio
rendimento (m)	*(rehn-deeh-mEhn-toh)*	power

resistenza (f)	*(reh-zeehs-tEhn-tsah)*	resistance
ricevitore (m)	*(reeh-cheh-veeh-tOh-reh)*	receiver
risonanza (f)	*(reeh-soh-nAhn-tsah)*	resonance
scansione (f)	*(skahn-syOh-neh)*	scanning
schermo (m)	*(skEhr-moh)*	screen
semiconduttore (m)	*(seh-meeh-kohn-dooht-tOh-reh)*	semiconductor
silicone (m)	*(seeh-leeh-kOh-neh)*	silicon
stereofonico	*(steh-reh-oh-fOh-neeh-koh)*	stereophonic
suono (m)	*(swOh-noh)*	sound
telecamera (f)	*(teh-leh-kAh-meh-rah)*	camera
telecomunicazioni (f)	*(teh-leh-koh-mooh-neek-kah-tsyOh-neeh)*	telecommunications
trasmettere	*(trahz-mEht-teh-reh)*	broadcast (v)
tubo (m)	*(tOOh-boh)*	tube
valvola (f) rivelatrice	*(vAhlvoh-lah reeh-veh-lah-trEEh-cheh)*	detector
vettore (m)	*(veht-tOh-reh)*	vector
videoregistratore (m)	*(veeh-deh-oh-reh-jeehs-trah-tOh-reh)*	videocassette recorder (VCR)
volt (m)	*(vohlt)*	volt
voltaggio (m)	*(vohl-tAhj-joh)*	voltage
vuoto (m)	*(vwOh-toh)*	vacuum
watt (m)	*(waht)*	watt

FASHION

English to Italian

angora	l'angora	*(Ahn-goh-rah)*
blazer	la giacca sportiva, il "blazer"	*(jAhk-kah spohr-tEEh-vah)*
batiste	la batista	*(bah-tEEhs-tah)*
belt	la cintura	*(cheehn-tOOh-rah)*
blouse	la camicetta	*(kah-meeh-chEht-tah)*
bow tie	la cravatta a farfalla	*(krah-vAht-tah ah fahr-fAhl-lah)*
button	il bottone	*(boht-tOh-neh)*
buttonhole	l'occhiello, l'asola	*(ohk-kyEhl-loh), (Ah-zoh-lah)*
cape	il mantello	*(mahn-tEhl-loh)*
cashmere	il cachemire	*(cah-che-mEE-reh)*
coat	il cappotto	*(kahp-pOht-toh)*
collar	il colletto	*(kohl-lEht-toh)*
color	il colore	*(koh-lOh-reh)*
cuff link	il gemello da camicia	*(jeh-mEhl-loh dah kah-mEEh-chah)*
cut (v)	tagliare	*(tah-lyAh-reh)*
design (v)	disegnare	*(deeh-zeh-nyAh-reh)*
designer	lo stilista, il "designer"	*(steeh-lEEhs-tah)*
drape (v)	drappeggiare	*(drahp-pehj-jAh-reh)*
dress	il vestito	*(vehs-tEEh-toh)*
elegance	l'eleganza	*(eh-leh-gAhn-tsah)*
fabric	il tessuto	*(tehs-sOOh-toh)*
fashion	la moda	*(mOh-dah)*
fashionable	alla moda	*(ahl-lah mOh-dah)*
flannel	la flanella	*(flah-nEhl-lah)*
gabardine	la gabardina	*(gah-bahr-dEEh-nah)*
hem	l'orlo	*(Ohr-loh)*
hood	il cappuccio	*(kahp-pOOhch-choh)*
jewel	la gioiello	*(joh-yEhl-loh)*

length	la lunghezza	*(loohn-gEhts-tsah)*
lingerie	l'abbigliamento intimo	*(ahb-beeh-kyah-mEhn-toh EEhn-teeh-moh)*
lining	la foderatura	*(foh-deh-rah-tOOh-rah)*
long sleeves	le maniche lunghe	*(mAh-neeh-keh lOOhn-geh)*
model	il modello, il capo, la model-la	*(moh-dEhl-loh), (kAh-poh), (moh-dEhl-lah)*
muslin	la mussola	*(mOohs-soh-lah)*
needle	l'ago	*(Ah-goh)*
out of style	fuori moda	*(fWoh-reeh mOh-dah)*
pattern	il modello	*(moh-dEhl-loh),*
pleat	la piega	*(pyEh-gah)*
pleated	pieghettato	*(pyeh-geht-tAh-toh)*
polyester	il poliestere	*(poh-leeh-ehs-teh-reh)*
poplin	la poplina	*(poh-plEEh-nah)*
print	lo stampato	*(stahm-pAh-toh)*
raincoat	l'impermeabile	*(eehm-pehr-meh-Ah-beeh-leh)*
rayon	il raion, la seta artificiale	*(rah-yOhn), (sEh-tah ahr-teeh-feeh-chAh-leh)*
ready-to-wear	moda confezionata	*(mOh-dah kohn-feh-tsyoh-nAh-tah)*
scarf	la sciarpa, il foulard	*(shAhr-pah)*
sew (v)	cucire	*(kooh-chEEh-reh)*
sewing machine	la macchina da cucire	*(mAhk-keeh-nah dah kooh-chEEh-reh)*
shirt	la camicia	*(kah-mEEh-chah)*
shoe	la scarpa	*(skAhr-pah)*
short sleeves	le maniche corte	*(mAh-neeh-keh kOhr-teh)*
silk	la seta	*(sEh-tah)*
silkworm	il baco di seta	*(bAh-koh deeh sEh-tah)*
silk factory	il setificio	*(seh-teeh-fEEh-choh)*
size	il numero, la taglia	*(nOOh-meh-roh), (tAh-lyah)*
skirt	la gonna	*(gOhn-nah)*
sleeve	la manica	*(mAh-neeh-kah)*
slacks	i pantaloni, i calzoni	*(pahn-tah-lOOh-neeh), (kahl-tsOh-neeh)*

socks	i calzini	*(kahl-tsEEh-neeh)*
sportswear	l'abbigliamento sportivo	*(ahb-beeh-lyah-mEhn-toh spohr-tEEh-voh)*
stitch	il punto	*(pOOhn-toh)*
stockings	le calze	*(kAhl-tseh)*
style	lo stile	*(stEEh-leh)*
stylist	lo stilista	*(steeh-lEEhs-tah)*
suede	lo scamosciato	*(skah-moh-shAh-toh)*
suit	l'abito	*(Ah-beeh-toh)*
sweater	il maglione	*(mah-lyOh-neh)*
synthetic	sintetico, artificiale	*(seehn-tEh-teeh-koh), (ahr-teeh-feeh-chAh-leh)*
taffeta	il taffetà	*(tahf-feh-tAh)*
tailor	il sarto	*(sAhr-toh)*
thread	il filo	*(fEEh-loh)*
tie	la cravatta	*(krah-vAht-tah)*
trousers	i calzoni, i pantaloni	*(kAhl-tsOOh-neeh), (pahn-tah-lOh-neeh)*
tuxedo	l'abito da sera, lo smoking	*(Ah-beeh-toh dah sEh-rah)*
veil	il velo	*(vEh-loh)*
vest	il gilet	*(gee-lEh)*
waist	la vita	*(vEEh-tah)*
weaver	il tessitore	*(tehs-seeh-tOh-reh)*
width	la larghezza, l'ampiezza	*(lahr-gEhts-tsah), (ahm-pyEhts-tsah)*
wool	la lana	*(lAh-nah)*
yarn	il filato	*(feeh-lAh-toh)*
zipper	la cerniera lampo	*(chehr-nyEh-rah lAhm-poh)*

Italian to English

abbigliamento (m) intimo	*(ahb-beeh-kyah-mEhn-toh EEhn-teeh-moh)*	lingerie
abbigliamento sportivo	*(ahb-beeh-lyah-mEhn-toh spohr-tEEh-voh)*	sportswear
abito (m)	*(Ah-beeh-toh)*	suit
abito da sera	*(Ah-beeh-toh dah sEh-rah)*	tuxedo

ago (m)	*(Ah-goh)*	needle
alla moda	*(Ahl-lah mOh-dah)*	fashionable
ampiezza (f)	*(ahm-pyEhts-tsah)*	width
artificiale	*(ahr-teeh-feeh-chAh-leh)*	synthetic
asola (f)	*(Ah-zoh-lah)*	buttonhole
baco (m) di seta	*(bAh-koh deeh sEh-tah)*	silkworm
batista (f)	*(bah-tEEhs-tah)*	batiste
bottone (m)	*(boh-tOh-neh)*	button
cachemire (m)	*(cah-che-mEE-reh)*	cashmere
calze (f)	*(kAhl-tseh)*	stockings
calzini (m)	*(kahl-tsEEh-neeh)*	socks
calzoni (m)	*(kahl-tsOh-neeh)*	slacks, trousers
camicetta (f)	*(kah-meeh-chEht-tah)*	blouse
camicia (f)	*(kah-mEEh-chah)*	shirt
capo (m)	*(kAh-poh)*	model
cappotto (m)	*(kahp-pOht-toh)*	coat
cappuccio (m)	*(kahp-pOOhch-choh)*	hood
cerniera (f) lampo	*(chehr-nyEh-rah lAhm-poh)*	zipper
cintura (f)	*(cheehn-tOOh-rah)*	belt
colletto (m)	*(kohl-lEht-toh)*	collar
colore (m)	*(koh-lOh-reh)*	color
cravatta (f)	*(krah-vAht-tah)*	tie
cravatta a farfalla	*(krah-vAht-tah ah fahr-fAhl-lah)*	bow tie
cucire	*(kooh-chEEh-reh)*	sew (v)
disegnare	*(deeh-zeh-nyAh-reh)*	design (v)
drappeggiare	*(drahp-pehj-jAh-reh)*	drape (v)
eleganza (f)	*(eh-leh-gAhn-dsah)*	elegance
filato (m)	*(feeh-lAh-toh)*	yarn
filo (m)	*(fEEh-loh)*	thread
flanella (f)	*(flah-nEhl-lah)*	flannel
foderatura (f)	*(foh-deh-rah-tOOh-rah)*	lining
foulard (m)	*(phoo-lAhrd)*	scarf
fuori moda	*(fwOh-reeh mOh-dah)*	out of style

gabardina (f)	*(gah-bahr-dEEh-nah)*	gabardine
gemello (m) da camicia	*(jeh-mEhl-loh dah kah-mEEh-chah)*	cuff link
giacca (f) sportiva	*(jAhk-kah spohr-tEEh-vah)*	blazer
gilet (m)	*(jee-lEh)*	vest
gioiello (f)	*(joh-yEhl-loh)*	jewel
gonna (f)	*(gOhn-nah)*	skirt
impermeabile (m)	*(eehm-pehr-meh-Ah-beeh-leh)*	raincoat
lana (f)	*(lAh-nah)*	wool
lana d'angora	*(lAh-nah Ahn-goh-rah)*	angora
larghezza (f)	*(lahr-gEhts-tsah)*	width
lunghezza (f)	*(loohn-gEhts-tsah)*	length
macchina (f) da cucire	*(mAhk-keeh-nah dah kooh-chEEh-reh)*	sewing machine
maglione (m)	*(mah-lyOh-neh)*	sweater
manica (f)	*(mAh-neeh-kah)*	sleeve
maniche (f) corte	*(mAh-neeh-keh kOhr-teh)*	short sleeves
maniche lunghe	*(mAh-neeh-keh lOOhn-geh)*	long sleeves
mantello (m)	*(mahn-tEhl-loh)*	cape
moda (f)	*(mOh-dah)*	fashion
moda confezionata	*(mOh-dah kohn-feh-tsyoh-nAh-tah*	ready-to-wear
modello/a (m/f)	*(moh-dEhl-loh/ah)*	model, pattern
mussola (f)	*(mOohs-soh-lah)*	muslin
numero (m)	*(nOOh-meh-roh)*	size
occhiello (m)	*(ohk-kyEhl-loh)*	buttonhole
orlo (m)	*(Ohr-loh)*	hem
pantaloni (m)	*(pahn-tah-lOh-neeh)*	slacks, trousers
piega (f)	*(pyEh-gah)*	pleat
pieghettato	*(pyeh-geht-tAh-toh))*	pleated
poliestere	*(poh-leeh-Ehs-teh-reh)*	polyester
poplina (f)	*(poh-plEE-nah)*	poplin
punto (m)	*(pOOhn-toh)*	stitch
raion (m)	*(rah-yOhn)*	rayon

sarto (m)	*(sAhr-toh)*	tailor
scamosciato (m)	*(skah-moh-shAh-toh)*	suede
scarpa (f)	*(skAhr-pah)*	shoe
sciarpa (f)	*(shAhr-pah)*	scarf
seta (f)	*(sEh-tah)*	silk
seta artificiale	*(sEh-tah ahr-teeh-feeh-chAh-leh)*	rayon
setificio (m)	*(seh-teeh-fEEh-choh)*	silk factory
sintetico	*(seehn-tEh-teeh-koh)*	synthetic
smoking (m)	*(smokkeeng)*	tuxedo
stampato (m)	*(stahm-pAh-toh)*	print
stile (m)	*(stEEh-leh)*	style
stilista (m)	*(steeh-lEEhs-tah)*	designer, stylist
taffetà (m)	*(tahf-feh-tAh)*	taffeta
taglia (f)	*(tAh-lyah)*	size
tagliare	*(tah-lyAh-reh)*	cut (v)
tessitore (m)	*(tehs-seeh-tOh-reh)*	weaver
tessuto (m)	*(tehs-sOOh-toh)*	fabric
velo (m)	*(vEh-loh)*	veil
vestito (m)	*(vehs-tEEh-toh)*	dress
vita (f)	*(vEEh-tah)*	waist

IRON AND STEEL

English to Italian

alloy steel	la lega d'acciaio	*(lEh-gah dahch-chAh-yoh)*
aluminum	l'alluminio	*(ahl-looh-mEEh-nyoh)*
annealing	la ricottura	*(reeh-koht-tOOh-rah)*
bars	le barre	*(bAhr-reh)*
billets	le billette	*(beehl-lEht-teh)*
blast furnace	l'altoforno	*(ahltoh-fOhr-noh)*
carbon steel	l'acciaio al carbonio	*(ahch-chAh-yoh ahl kahr-bOh-nyoh)*
cast iron	il ferro fuso, la ghisa di seconda fusione	*(fEhr-roh fOOh-zoh), (gEEh-zah deeh seh-kOhn-dah fooh-zyOh-neh)*
chromium	il cromo	*(krOh-moh)*
coal	il carbone	*(kahr-bOh-neh)*
coil	la serpentina, la bobina	*(sehr-pehn-tEEh-nah), (boh-bEEh-nah)*
coke	il coke	*(kohk)*
cold rolling	la laminatura a freddo	*(lah-meeh-nah-tOOh-rah ah frEhd-doh)*
conveyor	il trasportatore	*(trahs-pohr-tah-tOh-reh)*
conveyor belt	il trasportatore a cinghia	*(trahs-pohr-tah-tOh-reh ah chEEhn-gyah)*
copper	il rame	*(rAh-meh)*
crucible	il crogiuolo	*(kroh-jwOh-loh)*
cupola	la cupola	*(kOOh-poh-lah)*
electric arc furnace	l'altoforno ad arco elettrico	*(ahl-toh-fOhr-noh ad Ahr-koh eh-lEht-treeh-koh)*
electrodes	gli elettrodi	*(eh-lEht-troh-deeh)*
electrolytic process	la procedura elettrolitica	*(proh-cheh-dOOh-rah eh-leht-troh-lEEh-teeh-kah)*
ferrite	la ferrite	*(feh-rEEh-teh)*
ferroalloys	le leghe di ferro	*(lEh-geh deeh fEhr-roh)*
ferromanganese	il ferromanganese	*(fehr-roh-mahn-gah-nEh-zeh)*
ferronickel	il ferronichel	*(feh-ro-nEE-kel)*

finished products	i prodotti finiti	*(proh-dOht-teeh feeh-nEEh-teeh)*
finishing mill	il laminatoio finitore	*(lah-meeh-nah-tO-yoh feeh-neeh-tOh-reh)*
flat products	i prodotti piatti	*(proh-dOht-teeh pyAht-teeh)*
foundry	la fonderia	*(fohn-deh-rEEh-ah)*
furnace	la fornace	*(fohr-nAh-cheh)*
galvanizing	la galvanizzazione, la zin-catura	*(gahl-vah-neehds-dsah-tsyOh-neh), (dseehn-kah-tOOh-rah)*
grinding	la molatura	*(moh-lah-tOOh-rah)*
heat	il calore	*(kah-lOh-reh)*
hot rolling	la laminatura a caldo	*(lah-meeh-nah-tOOh-rah ah kAhl-doh)*
induction furnace	il forno ad induzione	*(fOh-rnoh ad eehn-dooh-tsyOh-neh)*
ingot mold	la lingottiera	*(leehn-goht-tyEh-rah)*
ingots	i lingotti	*(leehn-gOht-teeh)*
iron ore	il minerale ferroso	*(meeh-neh-rAh-leh fehr-rOh-zoh)*
limestone	il calce	*(kAhl-cheh)*
malleability	la malleabilità, la duttilità	*(mahl-leh-ah-beeh-leeh-tAh), (dooht-teeh-leeh-tAh)*
manganese ore	il minerale manganese	*(meeh-neh-rAh-leh mahn-gah-nEh-zeh)*
molybdenum	il molibdeno	*(moh-leehb-dEh-noh)*
nickel	il nichelio	*(neeh-kEh-leeh-oh)*
nitrogen	il nitrogeno	*(neeh-trOh-jeh-noh)*
ore	il minerale	*(meeh-neh-rAh-leh)*
pickling	il decapaggio	*(deh-kah-pAhj-joh)*
pig iron	la ghisa, la ghisa di prima fusione	*(gEEh-zah), (gEEh-zah deeh prEEh-mah fooh-zyOh-neh)*
pipes and tubes	le condotte e i tubi	*(kohn-dOht-teh eh eeh tOOh-beeh)*
plate	la lamiera, la piastra	*(lah-myAh-rah), (pyAhs-trah)*

powder	la polvere	*(pOhl-veh-reh)*
pressure	la pressione	*(prehs-syOh-neh)*
process	la procedura	*(proh-cheh-dOOh-rah)*
refractories	i refrattari	*(reh-fraht-tAh-reeh)*
rod	l'asta, il ferro tondo	*(Ahs-tah), (fEhr-roh tOhn-doh)*
rolling mill	il laminatoio	*(lah-meeh-nah-tOh-yoh)*
scale	la scaglia, l'incrostatura	*(skAh-lyah), (eehn-krohs-tah-tOOh-rah)*
scrap	i rottami	*(roht-tAh-meeh)*
sheets	le lastre	*(lAhs-treh)*
slabs	le sbarre	*(zbAhr-reh)*
specialty steels	gli acciai con lavorazione particolare	*(ahch-chAh-eeh kohn lah-voh-rah-tsyOh-neh pahr-teeh-koh-lAh-reh)*
stainless steel	l'acciaio inossidabile	*(ahch-chAh-yoh eehn-ohs-seeh-dAh-beeh-leh)*
steel mill	l'acciaieria	*(ahch-chah-yeh-rEEh-ah)*
super alloys	la superleghe	*(sooh-pehr-lEh-geh)*
temper	il rinvenimento	*(reehn-veh-neeh-mEhn-toh)*
titanium	il titanio	*(teeh-tAh-nyoh)*
toughness	la durezza	*(dooh-rEhts-tsah)*
tungsten	il tungstenio	*(toohng-stEh-neeh-oh)*
vacuum melting furnace	fornace per la colatura sotto vuoto	*(fohr-nAh-cheh pehr lah koht-tOOh-rah sOht-toh vwOh-toh)*
vanadium	il vanadio	*(vah-nAh-dyoh)*
wire	il filo metallico	*(fEEh-loh meh-tAhl-leeh-koh)*

Italian to English

acciai (m) con lavorazione particolare	*(ahch-chAh-eeh kohn lah-voh-rah-tsyOh-neh pahr-teeh-koh-lAh-reh)*	specialty steels
acciaieria (f)	*(ahch-chah-yeh-rEEh-ah)*	steel mill
acciaio (m) al carbonio	*(ahch-chAh-yoh ahl kahr-bOh-nyoh)*	carbon steel

acciaio inossidabile	*(ahch-chAh-yoh eehn-ohs-seeh-dAh-beeh-leh)*	stainless steel
alluminio (m)	*(ahl-looh-mEEh-nyoh)*	aluminum
altoforno (m)	*(ahltoh-fOhr-noh)*	blast furnace
altoforno ad arco elettrico	*(ahl-toh-fOhr-noh ad Ahr-koh eh-lEht-treeh-koh)*	electric arc furnace
asta (f)	*(Ahs-tah)*	rod
barre (f)	*(bAhr-reh)*	bars
billette (f)	*(beehl-lEht-teh)*	billets
bobina (f)	*(boh-bEEh-nah)*	coil
calce (m)	*(kAhl-cheh)*	limestone
calore (m)	*(kah-lOh-reh)*	heat
carbone (m)	*(kahr-bOh-ne)*	coal
coke (m)	*(kohk)*	coke
condotte (f) e tubi (m)	*(kohn-dOht-teh eh tOOh-beeh)*	pipes and tubes
crogiuolo (m)	*(kroh-jwOh-loh)*	crucible
cromo (m)	*(krOh-moh)*	chromium
cupola (f)	*(kOOh-poh-lah)*	cupola
decapaggio (m)	*(deh-kah-pAhj-joh)*	pickling
durezza (f)	*(dooh-rEhts-tsah)*	toughness
duttilità (f)	*(dooht-teeh-leeh-tAh)*	malleability
elettrodi (m)	*(eh-lEht-troh-deeh)*	electrodes
ferrite (f)	*(feh-rEEh-teh)*	ferrite
ferro (m) fuso	*(fEhr-roh fOOh-zoh)*	cast iron
ferro tondo	*(fEhr-roh tOhn-doh)*	rod
ferromanganese (m)	*(fehr-roh-mahn-gah-nEh-zeh)*	ferromanganese
ferronichel	*(feh-ro-nEE-kel)*	ferronickel
filo (m) metallico	*(fEEh-loh meh-tAhl-leeh-koh)*	wire
fonderia (f)	*(fohn-deh-rEEh-ah)*	foundry
fornace (f)	*(fohr-nAh-cheh)*	furnace
fornace per la colatura sotto vuoto	*(fohr-nAh-cheh pehr lah koht-tOOh-rah sOht-toh vwOh-toh)*	vacuum melting furnace

forno (m) ad induzione	*(fOh-rnoh ad eehn-dooh-tsyOh-neh)*	induction furnace
galvanizzazione (f)	*(gahl-vah-neehds-dsah-tsyOh-neh)*	galvanizing
ghisa (f)	*(gEEh-zah)*	pig iron
ghisa di prima fusione	*(gEEh-zah deeh prEEh-mah fooh-zyOh-neh)*	pig iron
ghisa di seconda fusione	*(gEEh-zah deeh seh-kOhn-dah fooh-zyOh-neh)*	cast iron
incrostatura (f)	*(eehn-krohs-tah-tOOh-rah)*	scale
lamiera (f)	*(lah-myEh-rah)*	plate
laminatoio (m)	*(lah-meeh-nah-tOh-yoh)*	rolling mill
laminatoio finitore	*(lah-meeh-nah-tO-yoh feeh-neeh-tOh-reh)*	finishing mill
laminatura a caldo (f)	*(lah-meeh-nah-tOOh-rah ah kAhl-doh)*	hot rolling
laminatura a fred-do	*(lah-meeh-nah-tOOh-rah ah frEhd-doh)*	cold rolling
lastre (f)	*(lAhs-treh)*	sheets
lega d'acciaio (f)	*(lEh-gah dahch-chAh-yoh)*	alloy steel
leghe (f) di ferro	*(lEh-geh deeh fEhr-roh)*	ferroalloys
lingotti (m)	*(leehn-gOht-teeh)*	ingots
lingottiera (f)	*(leehn-goht-tyEh-rah)*	ingot mold
malleabilità (f)	*(mah-leh-ah-beeh-leeh-tAh)*	malleability
minerale (m)	*(meeh-neh-rAh-leh)*	ore
minerale ferroso	*(meeh-neh-rAh-leh fehr-rOh-zoh)*	iron ore
minerale man-ganese	*(meeh-neh-rAh-leh mahn-gah-nEh-zeh)*	manganese ore
molatura (f)	*(moh-lah-tOOh-rah)*	grinding
molibdeno (m)	*(moh-leehb-dEh-noh)*	molybdenum
nichelio (m)	*(neeh-kEh-leeh-oh)*	nickel
nitrogeno (m)	*(neeh-trOh-jeh-noh)*	nitrogen
piastra (f)	*(pyAhs-trah)*	plate
polvere (f)	*(pOhl-veh-reh)*	powder
pressione (f)	*(prehs-syOh-neh)*	pressure
procedura (f)	*(proh-cheh-dOOh-rah)*	process

procedura elettro-litica	*(proh-cheh-dOOh-rah eh-leht-troh-lEEh-teeh-kah)*	electrolytic process
prodotti (m) finiti	*(proh-dOht-teeh feeh-nEEh-teeh)*	finished products
prodotti piatti	*(proh-dOht-teeh pyAht-teeh)*	flat products
rame (m)	*(rAh-meh)*	copper
refrattari (m)	*(reh-fraht-tAh-reeh)*	refractories
ricottura (f)	*(reeh-koht-tOOh-rah)*	annealing
rinvenimento (m)	*(reehn-veh-neeh-mEhn-toh)*	temper
rottami (m)	*(roht-tAh-meeh)*	scrap
sbarre (f)	*(zbAhr-reh)*	slabs
scaglia (f)	*(skAh-lyah)*	scale
serpentina (f)	*(sehr-pehn-tEEh-nah)*	coil
superleghe (f)	*(sooh-pehr-lEh-geh)*	super alloys
titanio (m)	*(teeh-tAh-nyoh)*	titanium
trasportatore (m)	*(trahs-pohr-tah-tOh-reh)*	conveyor
trasportatore a cinghia	*(trahs-pohr-tah-tOh-reh ah chEEhn-gyah)*	conveyor belt
tungstenio (m)	*(toohng-stEh-neeh-oh)*	tungsten
vanadio (m)	*(vah-nAh-dyoh)*	vanadium
zincatura (f)	*(dseehn-kah-tOOh-rah)*	galvanizing

	LEATHER GOODS	

English to Italian

ankle boots	gli stivaletti	*(steeh-vah-lEht-teeh)*
astrakan	l'astrakan	*(ahs-trah-kAhn)*
attaché case	la cartella	*(kahr-tEhl-lah)*
beaver	il castoro	*(kahs-tOh-roh)*
belt	la cintura	*(cheehn-tOOh-rah)*
billfold	il portafogli	*(pohr-tah-fOh-lyeeh)*
blotter	il tampone di carta assor-bente	*(tahm-pOh-neh deeh kAhr-tah ahs-sohr-bEhn-teh)*
boot shop	la stivaleria	*(steeh-vah-leh-rEEh-ah)*
bootmaker	lo stivalaio	*(steeh-vah-lAh-yoh)*
boots	gli stivali	*(steeh-vAh-leeh)*
briefcase	la borsa documenti	*(bOhr-sah doh-kooh-mEhn-teeh)*
calfskin	il vitello	*(veeh-tEhl-loh)*
card case	il portabiglietti	*(pohr-tah-beeh-lyEht-teeh)*
cigarette case	il portasigarette	*(pohr-tah-seeh-gah-rEht-teh)*
cowhide	il cuoio	*(kwOh-yoh)*
coyote	il coyote	*(koh-yOh-teh)*
dye (v)	tingere	*(tEEhn-jeh-reh)*
eyeglass case	il portaocchiali	*(pohr-tah-ohk-kyAh-leeh)*
fitch	la puzzola	*(pOOhts-tsoh-lah)*
fox	la volpe	*(vOhl-peh)*
garment bag	il portabiti	*(pohrt-Ah-beeh-teeh)*
gloves	i guanti	*(gwAhn-teeh)*
handbag	la borsetta	*(bohr-sEht-tah)*
holster	la fondina	*(fohn-dEEh-nah)*
key case	il portachiavi	*(pohr-tah-kyAh-veeh)*
kidskin	il capretto	*(kah-prEht-toh)*
lamb	l'agnello	*(ah-nyEhl-loh)*
leather	la pelle	*(pEhl-leh)*
leather goods	la pelletteria	*(pehl-leht-teh-rEEh-ah)*

leather jacket	giubbotto di pelle	*(joohb-bOht-toh deeh pEhl-leh)*
lizard skin	la pelle di lucertola	*(pEhl-leh deeh looh-chEhr-toh-lah)*
lynx	il lince	*(lEEhn-cheh)*
makeup case	il portatrucco	*(pohr-tah-trOOhk-koh)*
manicuring kit	il completo per la manicure	*(kohm-plEh-toh pehr lah mah-neeh-kOOh-reh)*
marmot	la marmotta	*(mahr-mOht-tah)*
mink	il visone	*(veeh-zOh-neh)*
Moroccan leather	il marocchino	*(mah-rohk-kEEh-noh)*
nutria	il castorino	*(kahs-toh-rEEh-noh)*
opossum	l'opossum	*(ohpahsuhm)*
ostrich skin	la pelle di struzzo	*(pEhl-leh deeh strOOhts-tsoh)*
otter	la lontra	*(lOhn-trah)*
paper holder	il portacarta	*(pohr-tah-kAhr-teh)*
passport case	il porta passaporto	*(pohr-tah-pahs-sah-pOhr-toh)*
pigskin	la pelle di cinghiale	*(pEhl-leh deeh cheehn-gyAh-leh)*
pocketbook	la borsetta	*(bohr-sEht-tah)*
portfolio	la cartella	*(kahr-tEhl-lah)*
purse	la borsa	*(bOhr-sah)*
rabbit	il coniglio	*(koh-nEEh-lyoh)*
raccoon	il procione lavoratore	*(proh-chOh-neh lah-voh-rah-tOh-reh)*
sable	lo zibellino	*(dseeh-behl-lEEh-noh)*
saddle	la sella	*(sEhl-lah)*
saddler	il sellaio	*(sehl-lAh-yoh)*
scissor case	il porta forbici	*(pohr-tah-fOhr-beeh-cheeh)*
sealskin	la pelle di foca	*(pEhl-leh deeh fOh-kah)*
slippers	le pantofole	*(pahn-tOh-foh-leh)*
snakeskin	la pelle di serpente	*(pEhl-leh deeh sehr-pEhn-teh)*
suede	la pelle scamosciata	*(pEhl-leh skah-moh-shAh-tah)*

suede jacket	il giubbotto di renna	*(joohb-bOht-toh deeh rEhn-nah)*
suitcase	la valigia	*(vah-lEEh-jah)*
tan (v)	conciare	*(kohn-chAh-reh)*
tanner	il conciatore	*(kohn-chah-tOh-reh)*
tannery	la concia	*(kOhn-chah)*
tannin	il tannino	*(tahn-nEEh-noh)*
trunk	il baule	*(bah-OOh-leh)*
wallet	il portafogli	*(pohr-tah-fOh-lyeeh)*
watch strap	il cinturino per orologio	*(cheehn-tooh-rEEh-noh pehr oh-roh-lOh-joh)*
whip	la frusta	*(frOOhs-tah)*

Italian to English

agnello (m)	*(ah-nyEhl-loh)*	lamb
astrakan (m)	*(ahs-trah-kAhn)*	astrakan
baule (m)	*(bah-OOh-leh)*	trunk
borsa (f)	*(bOhr-sah)*	purse
borsa documenti	*(bOhr-sah doh-kooh-mEhn-teeh)*	briefcase
borsetta (f)	*(bohr-sEht-tah)*	handbag, pocketbook
capretto (m)	*(kah-prEht-toh)*	kidskin
cartella (f)	*(kahr-tEhl-lah)*	attaché case, portfolio
castorino (m)	*(kahs-toh-rEEh-noh)*	nutria
castoro (m)	*(kahs-tOh-roh)*	beaver
cintura (f)	*(cheehn-tOOh-rah)*	belt
cinturino (m) per orologio	*(cheehn-tooh-rEEh-noh pehr oh-roh-lOh-joh)*	watch strap
completo (m) per la manicure	*(kohm-plEh-toh pehr lah mah-neeh-kOOh-reh)*	manicuring kit
concia (f)	*(kOhn-chah)*	tannery
conciare	*(kohn-chAh-reh)*	tan (v)
conciatore (m)	*(kohn-chah-tOh-reh)*	tanner
coniglio (m)	*(koh-nEEh-lyoh)*	rabbit
coyote (m)	*(koh-yOh-teh)*	coyote
cuoio (m)	*(kwOh-yoh)*	cowhide

fondina (f)	*(fohn-dEEh-nah)*	holster
frusta (f)	*(frOOhs-tah)*	whip
giubbotto (m) di pelle	*(joohb-bOht-toh deeh pEhl-leh)*	leather jacket
giubbotto di renna	*(joohb-bOht-toh deeh rEhn-nah)*	suede jacket
guanti (m)	*(gwAhn-teeh)*	gloves
lince (m)	*(lEEhn-cheh)*	lynx
lontra (f)	*(lOhn-trah)*	otter
marmotta (f)	*(mahr-mOht-tah)*	marmot
marocchino (m)	*(mah-rohk-kEEh-noh)*	Moroccan leather
opossum (m)	*(oh-pah-suhm)*	opossum
pantofole (f)	*(pahn-tOh-foh-leh)*	slippers
pelle (f)	*(pEhl-leh)*	leather
pelle di cinghiale	*(pEhl-leh deeh cheehn-gyAh-leh)*	pigskin
pelle di foca	*(pEhl-leh deeh fOh-kah)*	sealskin
pelle di lucertola	*(pEhl-leh deeh looh-chEhr-toh-lah)*	lizard skin
pelle di serpente	*(pEhl-leh deeh sehr-pEhn-teh)*	snakeskin
pelle di struzzo	*(pEhl-leh deeh strOOhts-tsoh)*	ostrich skin
pelle scamosciata	*(pEhl-leh skah-moh-shAh-tah)*	suede
pelletteria (f)	*(pehl-leht-teh-rEEh-ah)*	leather goods
portabiti (m)	*(pohrt-Ah-beeh-teeh)*	garment bag
portabiglietti (m)	*(pohr-tah-beeh-lyEht-teeh)*	card case
portacarta (m)	*(pohr-tah-kAhr-tah)*	paper holder
portachiavi (m)	*(pohr-tah-kyAh-veeh)*	key case
portafogli (m)	*(pohr-tah-fOh-lyeeh)*	billfold, wallet
portaforbici (m)	*(pohr-tah-fOhr-beeh-cheeh)*	scissor case
portaocchiali (m)	*(pohr-tah-ohk-kyAh-leeh)*	eyeglass case
portapassaporto (m)	*(pohr-tah-pahs-sah-pOhr-toh)*	passport case
portasigarette (m)	*(pohr-tah-seeh-gah-rEht-teh)*	cigarette case

portatrucco (m)	*(pohr-tah-trOOhk-koh)*	makeup case
procione (m) lavo-ratore	*(proh-chOh-neh lah-voh-rah-tOh-reh)*	raccoon
puzzola (f)	*(pOOhts-tsoh-lah)*	fitch
sella (f)	*(sEhl-lah)*	saddle
sellaio (m)	*(sehl-lAh-yoh)*	saddler
stivalaio (m)	*(steeh-vah-kAh-yoh)*	bootmaker
stivaleria (f)	*Steeh-vah-leh-rEEh-ah)*	boot shop
stivaletti (m)	*(steeh-vah-lEht-teeh)*	ankle boots
stivali (m)	*(steeh-vAh-leeh)*	boots
tampone (m) di carta assorbente (m)	*(tahm-pOh-neh deeh kAhr-tah ahs-sohr-bEhn-teh)*	blotter
tannino (m)	*(tahn-nEEh-noh)*	tannin
tingere	*(tEEhn-jeh-reh)*	dye (v)
valigia (f)	*(vah-lEEh-jah)*	suitcase
visone (m)	*(veeh-zOh-neh)*	mink
vitello (m)	*(veeh-tEhl-loh)*	calfskin
volpe (f)	*(vOhl-peh)*	fox
zibellino (m)	*(dseeh-behl-lEEh-noh)*	sable

MOTOR VEHICLES

English to Italian

air filter	il filtro dell'aria	*(fEEhl-troh dehl Ah-reeh-ah)*
alternator	l'alternatore	*(ahl-tehr-nah-tOh-reh)*
assembly line	la linea di montaggio	*(lEEh-neh-ah deeh mohn-tAhj-joh)*
automatic gearshift	il cambio automatico	*(kAhm-byoh ah-ooh-toh-mAh-teeh-koh)*
automobile	l'automobile	*(ah-ooh-toh-mOh-beeh-leh)*
automotive worker	l' operaio	*(oh-peh-rAh-yoh)*
battery	la batteria	*(baht-teh-rEEh-ah)*
belt	la cinghia	*(chEEhn-gyah)*
body	il telaio	*(teh-lAh-yoh)*
brake	il freno	*(frEh-noh)*
bumper	il paraurti	*(pah-rah-OOhr-teeh)*
camshaft	l'albero di distribuzione a camme	*(Ahl-beh-roh deeh deehs-treeh-booh-tsyOh-neh ah kAhm-meh)*
car	la macchina	*(mAhk-keeh-nah)*
carburetor	il carburatore	*(kahr-booh-rah-tOh-reh)*
chassis	la carrozzeria	*(kahr-rohts-tseh-rEEh-ah)*
clutch	la frizione	*(freeh-tsyOh-neh)*
connecting rod	la biella	*(byEhl-lah)*
crankshaft	l'albero a gomito	*(Ahl-beh-roh ah gOh-meeh-toh)*
cylinder	il cilindro	*(cheeh-lEEhn-droh)*
dashboard	il cruscotto	*(kroohs-kOht-toh)*
defroster	lo sbrinatore	*(zbreeh-nah-tOh-reh)*
designer	lo stilista	*(steeh-lEEhs-tah)*
diesel	il diesel	*(deezl)*
disc	il disco	*(dEEhs-koh)*
displacement	la cilindrata	*(cheeh-leehn-drAh-tah)*
distributor	il distributore	*(deehs-treeh-booh-tOh-reh)*
driver	l'autista	*(ah-ooh-tEEhs-tah)*

engine	il motore	*(moh-tOh-reh)*
engineer	l'ingegnere	*(eehn-jeh-nyEh-reh)*
exhaust	lo scarico, lo scappamento	*(skAh-reeh-koh), (skahp-pah-mEhn-toh)*
fender	il parafango	*(pah-rah-fAhn-goh)*
front-wheel drive	la trazione anteriore	*(trah-tsyOh-neh ahn-teh-ryOh-reh)*
gas consumption	il consumo di benzina	*(kohn-sOOh-moh dehl-lah behn-dsEEh-nah)*
gas pedal	l'acceleratore	*(ahch-cheh-leh-rah-tOh-reh)*
gasoline	la benzina	*(behn-dsEEh-nah)*
gasoline tank	il serbatoio della benzina	*(sehr-bah-tOh-yoh dehl-lah behn-dsEEh-nah)*
gearshift	il cambio	*(kAhm-byoh)*
generator	il generatore	*(jeh-neh-rah-tOh-reh)*
grille	la cuffia del radiatore mascherina	*(kOOhf-fyah dehl rah-dyah-tOh-reh mahs-keh-rEEh-nah)*
horsepower	la potenza in cavalli	*(poh-tEhn-dsah eehn kah-vAhl-leeh)*
ignition	l'accensione	*(ahch-chehn-syOh-neh)*
injector	l'iniettore	*(eeh-nyeht-tOh-reh)*
inspection	l'ispezione	*(eehs-peh-tsyOh-neh)*
mechanic	il meccanico	*(mehk-kAh-neeh-koh)*
mileage	il chilometraggio	*(keeh-loh-meh-trAhj-joh)*
model	il modello	*(moh-dEhl-loh)*
odometer	il contachilometri	*(kohn-tah-keeh-lOh-meh-treeh)*
oil filter	il filtro dell'olio	*(fEEhl-troh dehl Oh-leeh-oh)*
oil pump	la pompa dell'olio	*(pOhm-pah dehl Oh-leeh-oh)*
paint	la vernice	*(vehr-nEEh-cheh)*
pinion	il pignone, il rocchetto	*(peeh-nyOh-neh), (rohk-kEht-toh)*
piston	il pistone	*(peehs-tOh-neh)*
power steering	il servosterzo	*(sehr-voh-stEhr-tsoh)*

propulsion	la propulsione	*(proh-poohl-syOh-neh)*
prototype	il prototipo	*(proh-tOh-teeh-poh)*
radial tire	il pneumatico radiale	*(pneh-ooh-mAh-teeh-koh rah-dyAh-leh)*
rear axle	l'asse posteriore	*(Ahs-seh pohs-teh-ryOh-reh)*
ring	l'anello	*(ah-nEhl-loh)*
robot	il robot	*(rohbaht)*
seat	il sedile	*(seh-dEEh-leh)*
seatbelt	la cintura di sicurezza	*(cheehn-tOOh-rah deeh seeh-kooh-rEhts-tsah)*
sedan	la berlina	*(behr-lEEh-nah)*
shock absorber	gli ammortizzanti	*(ahm-mohr-teehds-dsAhn-teeh)*
spare tire	la ruota di scorta	*(rwOh-tah deeh skOhr-tah)*
spark plug	la candela	*(kahn-dEh-lah)*
speedometer	l'indicatore di velocità tachimetro	*(eehn-deeh-kah-tOh-reh deeh veh-loh-cheeh-tAh tah-kEEh-meh-troh)*
spring	la molla	*(mOhl-lah)*
starter	il motorino d'avviamento	*(moh-toh-rEEh-noh dahv-veeh-ah-mEhn-toh)*
steering	la guida	*(gwEEh-dah)*
steering wheel	lo sterzo, il volante	*(stEhr-tsoh), (voh-lAhn-teh)*
suspension	la sospensione	*(sohs-pehn-syOh-neh)*
tire	il pneumatico	*(pneh-ooh-mAh-teeh-koh)*
torque	la forza di torsione	*(fOhr-tsah deeh tohr-syOh-neh)*
valve	la valvola	*(vAhl-voh-lah)*
water pump	la pompa dell'acqua	*(pOhm-pah dehl Ahk-kwah)*
wheel	la ruota	*(rwOh-tah)*
windshield	il parabrezza	*(pah-rah-brEhts-tsah)*

Italian to English

acceleratore (m)	*(ahch-cheh-leh-rah-tOh-reh)*	gas pedal
accensione (f)	*(ahch-chehn-syOh-neh)*	ignition
filtro dell'aria (m)	*(fEEhl-troh dehl Ah-reeh-ah)*	air filter

albero (m) a gomi-to	*(Ahl-beh-roh ah gOh-meeh-toh)*	crankshaft
albero di distribuzione a camme	*(Ahl-beh-roh deeh deehs-treeh-booh-tsyOh-neh ah kAhm-meh)*	camshaft
alternatore (m)	*(ahl-tehr-nah-tOh-reh)*	alternator
ammortizzatore (m)	*(ahm-mohr-teehds-dsAh-tOh-reh)*	shock absorber
anello (m)	*(ah-nEhl-loh)*	ring
asse (m) posteriore	*(Ahs-seh pohs-teh-ryOh-reh)*	rear axle
autista (m)	*(ah-ooh-tEEhs-tah)*	driver
automobile (f)	*(ah-ooh-toh-mOh-beeh-leh)*	automobile
batteria (f)	*(baht-teh-rEEh-ah)*	battery
benzina (f)	*(behn-dsEEh-nah)*	gasoline
berlina (f)	*(behr-lEEh-nah)*	sedan
biella (f)	*(byEhl-lah)*	connecting rod
cambio (m)	*(kAhm-byoh)*	gearshift
cambio automatico	*(kAhm-byoh ah-ooh-toh-mAh-teeh-koh)*	automatic gearshift
candela (f)	*(kahn-dEh-lah)*	spark plug
carburatore (m)	*(kahr-booh-rah-tOh-reh)*	carburetor
carrozzeria (f)	*(kahr-rohts-tseh-rEEh-ah)*	chassis
chilometraggio (m)	*(keeh-loh-meh-trAhj-joh)*	mileage
modello (m)	*(moh-dEhl-loh)*	model
cilindrata	*(cheeh-leehn-drAh-tah)*	displacement
cilindro (m)	*(cheeh-lEEhn-droh)*	cylinder
cinghia (f)	*(chEEhn-gyah)*	belt
cintura (f) di sicurezza	*(cheehn-tOOh-rah deeh seeh-kooh-rEhts-tsah)*	seatbelt
consumo (m) di benzina	*(kohn-sOOh-moh dehl-lah behn-dsEEh-nah)*	gas consumption
contachilometri (m)	*(kohn-tah-keeh-lOh-meh-treeh)*	odometer
cruscotto (m)	*(kroohs-kOht-toh)*	dashboard
cuffia (f) del radiatore mascherina	*(kOOhf-fyah dehl rah-dyah-tOh-reh mahs-keh-rEEh-nah)*	grille
diesel (m)	*(deezl)*	diesel

disco (m)	*(dEEhs-koh)*	disc
distributore (m)	*(deehs-treeh-booh-tOh-reh)*	distributor
filtro (m) dell'olio	*(fEEhl-troh dehl Oh-leeh-oh)*	oil filter
forza (f) di torsione	*(fOhr-tsah deeh tohr-syOh-neh)*	torque
freno (m)	*(frEh-noh)*	brake
frizione (f)	*(freeh-tsyOh-neh)*	clutch
generatore (m)	*(jeh-neh-rah-tOh-reh)*	generator
guida (f)	*(gwEEh-dah)*	steering
indicatore (m) di velocità tachimetro	*(eehn-deeh-kah-tOh-reh deeh veh-loh-cheeh-tAh tah-kEEh-meh-troh)*	speedometer
ingegnere (m)	*(eehn-jeh-nyEh-reh)*	engineer
iniettore (m)	*(eeh-nyeht-tOh-reh)*	injector
ispezione (f)	*(eehs-peh-tsyOh-neh)*	inspection
linea (f) di montaggio	*(lEEh-neh-ah deeh mohn-tAhj-joh)*	assembly line
macchina (f)	*(mAhk-keeh-nah)*	car
meccanico (m)	*(mehk-kAh-neeh-koh)*	mechanic
molla (f)	*(mOhl-lah)*	spring
motore (m)	*(moh-tOh-reh)*	engine
motorino (m) d'avviamento	*(moh-toh-rEEh-noh dahv-veeh-ah-mEhn-toh)*	starter
operaio/a (m/f)	*(oh-peh-rAh-yoh)*	automotive worker
parabrezza (m)	*(pah-rah-brEhts-tsah)*	windshield
parafango (m)	*(pah-rah-fAhn-goh)*	fender
paraurti (m)	*(pah-rah-OOhr-teeh)*	bumper
pignone (m)	*(peeh-nyOh-neh)*	pinion
pistone (m)	*(ppehs-tOh-neh)*	piston
pneumatico (m)	*(pneh-ooh-mAh-teeh-koh)*	tire
pneumatico radiale	*(pneh-ooh-mAh-teeh-koh rah-dyAh-leh)*	radial tire
pompa (f) dell'acqua	*(pOhm-pah dehl Ahk-kwah)*	water pump
pompa dell'olio	*(pOhm-pah dehl Oh-leeh-oh)*	oil pump

potenza (f) in cav-alli	*(poh-tEhn-dsah eehn kah-vAhl-leeh)*	horsepower
propulsione (f)	*(proh-poohl-syOh-neh)*	propulsion
prototipo (m)	*(proh-tOh-teeh-poh)*	prototype
robot (m)	*(roh-baht)*	robot
rocchetto (m)	*(rohk-kEht-toh)*	pinion
ruota (f)	*(rwOh-tah)*	wheel
ruota di scorta	*(rwOh-tah deeh skOhr-tah)*	spare tire
sbrinatore (m)	*(zbreeh-nah-tOh-reh)*	defroster
scappamento (m)	*(skahp-pah-mEhn-toh)*	exhaust
scarico (m)	*(skAh-reeh-koh)*	exhaust
sedile (m)	*(seh-dEEh-leh)*	seat
serbatoio (m) della benzina	*(sehr-bah-tOh-yoh dehl-lah behn-dsEEh-nah)*	gasoline tank
servosterzo (m)	*(sehr-voh-stEhr-tsoh)*	power steering
sospensione (f)	*(sohs-pehn-syOh-neh)*	suspension
sterzo (m)	*(stEhr-tsoh)*	steering wheel
stilista (m)	*(steeh-lEEhs-tah)*	designer
telaio (m)	*(teh-lAh-yoh)*	body
trazione (f) anteri-ore	*(trah-tsyOh-neh ahn-teh-ryOh-reh)*	front-wheel drive
valvola (f)	*(vAhl-voh-lah)*	valve
vernice (f)	*(vehr-nEEh-cheh)*	paint
volante (m)	*(voh-lAhn-teh)*	steering wheel

PHARMACEUTICALS

English to Italian

alcohol	l'alcool	*(Ahl-kohl)*
allergy	l'allergia	*(ahl-lehr-jEEh-ah)*
amphetamine	l'anfetamina	*(ahn-feh-tah-mEEh-nah)*
anaesthetic	l'anestetico	*(ahn-ehs-tEh-teeh-koh)*
analgesic	l'analgesico	*(ahn-ahl-jEEh-zeeh-koh)*
antacid	l'antacido	*(ahn-tAh-cheeh-doh)*
anti-inflammatory	l'antiflogistico	*(ahn-teeh-floh-jEEhs-teeh-koh)*
antibiotic	l'antibiotico	*(ahn-teeh-beeh-Oh-teeh-koh)*
anticoagulant	l'anticoagulante	*(ahn-teeh-koh-ah-gooh-lAhn-teh)*
antidepressant	l'antidepressivo	*(ahn-teeh-deh-prehs-sEEh-voh)*
antiseptic	l'asettico	*(ah-sEht-teeh-koh)*
aspirin	l'aspirina	*(ahs-peeh-rEEh-nah)*
barbiturates	i barbiturici	*(bahr-beeh-tOOh-reh-cheeh)*
bleed (v)	sanguinare	*(sahn-gweeh-nAh-reh)*
blood	il sangue	*(sAhn-gweh)*
botanic	botanico	*(boh-tAh-neeh-koh)*
calcium	il calcio	*(kAhlchoh)*
capsule	la capsula	*(kAhp-sooh-lah)*
compounds	i composti	*(kohm-pOhs-teeh)*
content	il contenuto	*(kohn-teh-nOOh-toh)*
cortisone	il cortisone	*(kohr-teeh-zOh-neh)*
cough (v)	tossire	*(tohs-sEEh-reh)*
cough drop	la pastiglia per la tosse	*(pahs-tEEh-lyah pehr-lah tOhs-seh)*
cough syrup	lo sciroppo per la tosse	*(sheeh-rOhp-poh pehr-lah tOhs-seh)*
crude	grezzo	*(grEhts-tsoh)*
density	la densità	*(dehn-seeh-tAh)*

diabetes	il diabete	*(deeh-ah-bEh-teh)*
digitalis	il digitalis	*(dee-gee-tAh-lees)*
disease	la malattia	*(mah-laht-tEEh-ah)*
diuretic	il diuretico	*(deeh-ooh-rEh-teeh-koh)*
dose	la dose	*(dOh-zeh)*
drop	la goccia	*(gOhch-chah)*
drug	il farmaco, la droga	*(fAhr-mah-koh), (drOh-gah)*
drugstore	la farmacia	*(fahr-mah-chEEh-ah)*
eyedrop	il collirio	*(kohl-lEEh-reeh-oh)*
hexachlorophene	l'esaclorofene	*(eh-zah-kloh-roh-fEh-neh)*
hormone	l'ormone	*(ohr-mOh-neh)*
hypertension	l'ipertensione	*(eeh-pehr-tehn-syOh-neh)*
injection	l'iniezione, la puntura	*(eehn-yeh-tsyOh-neh), (poohn-tOOh-rah)*
insulin	l'insulina	*(eehn-sooh-lEEh-nah)*
iodine	lo iodio	*(yOh-deeh-oh)*
iron	il ferro	*(fEhr-roh)*
laboratory techni-cian	il tecnico del laboratorio	*(tEhk-neeh-koh dehl lah-boh-rah-tOh-reeh-oh)*
laxative	il lassativo, il purgante	*(lahs-sah-tEEh-voh), (poohr-gAhn-teh)*
medicine	la medicina	*(meh-deeh-chEEh-nah)*
morphine	la morfina	*(mohr-fEEh-nah)*
narcotic	il narcotico	*(nahr-kOh-teeh-koh)*
nitrate	il nitrato	*(neeh-trAh-toh)*
nitrite	il nitrite	*(neeh-trEEt-teh)*
ointment	l'unguento	*(oohn-gwEhn-toh)*
opium	l'oppio	*(Ohp-pyoh)*
organic	organico	*(ohr-gAh-neeh-koh)*
pellet	la pallottolina	*(pahl-loht-toh-lEEh-nah)*
penicillin	la penicillina	*(peh-neeh-cheehl-lEEh-nah)*
pharmacist	il farmacista	*(fahr-mah-chEEhs-tah)*
phenol	il fenolo	*(feh-nOh-loh)*
physician	il medico	*(mEh-deeh-koh)*
pill	la pillola	*(pEEhl-loh-lah)*

plants	le piante	*(pyAhn-teh)*
purgative	il purgante	*(poohr-gAhn-teh)*
remedies	i rimedi	*(reeh-mEh-deeh)*
saccharin	la saccarina	*(sahk-kah-rEEh-nah)*
salts	i sali	*(sAh-leeh)*
salve	l'unguento, la pomata	*(oohn-gwEhn-toh), (poh-mAh-tah)*
sedative	il calmante	*(kahl-mAhn-teh)*
serum	il siero	*(syEh-roh)*
sinus	la cavità	*(kah-veeh-tAh)*
sinusitis	la sinusite	*(seeh-nooh-sEEh-teh)*
sleeping pill	il sonnifero	*(sohn-nEEh-feh-roh)*
sneeze (v)	starnutire	*(stahr-nooh-tEEh-reh)*
starch	l'amido	*(Ah-meeh-doh)*
stimulant	lo stimolante	*(steeh-moh-lAhn-teh)*
sulphamide	il sulfamide	*(soohl-fah-mEEh-deh)*
synthesis	la sintesi	*(sEEhn-teh-zeeh)*
syringe	la siringa	*(seeh-rEEhn-gah)*
tablet	la compressa, la pastiglia	*(kohm-prEhs-sah), (pahs-tEEh-lyah)*
thermometer	il termometro	*(tehr-mOh-meh-troh)*
toxicology	la tossicologia	*(tohs-seeh-koh-loh-jEEh-ah)*
toxin	la tossina	*(tohs-sEEh-nah)*
tranquilizer	il tranquillante	*(trahn-kweehl-lAhn-teh)*
vaccine	il vaccino	*(vahch-chEEh-noh)*
vitamin	la vitamina	*(veeh-tah-mEEh-nah)*
zinc	lo zinco	*(dsEEhn-koh)*

Italian to English

alcool (m)	*(Ahl-kohl)*	alcohol
allergia (f)	*(ahl-lehr-jEEh-ah)*	allergy
anfetamina (m)	*Ahn-feh-tah-mEEh-nah)*	amphetamine
amido (m)	*(Ah-meeh-doh)*	starch
analgesico (m)	*(ahn-ahl-jEEh-zeeh-koh)*	analgesic
anestetico (m)	*(ah-nehs-tEh-teeh-koh)*	anaesthetic

antacido (m)	*(ahnt-Ah-cheeh-doh)*	antacid
antibiotico (m)	*(ahn-teeh-beeh-Oh-teeh-koh)*	antibiotic
anticoagulante (m)	*(ahn-teeh-koh-ah-gooh-lAhn-teh)*	anticoagulant
antidepressivo (m)	*(ahn-teeh-deh-prehs-sEEh-voh)*	antidepressant
antiflogistico (m)	*(ahn-teeh-floh-jEEhs-teeh-koh)*	anti-inflammatory
asettico (m)	*(ah-sEht-teeh-koh)*	antiseptic
aspirina (f)	*(ahs-peeh-rEEh-nah)*	aspirin
barbiturici (m)	*(bahr-beeh-tOOh-reh-cheeh)*	barbiturates
botanico	*(boh-tAh-neeh-koh)*	botanic
calcio (m)	*(kAhl-choh)*	calcium
calmante (m)	*(kahl-mAhn-teh)*	sedative
capsula (f)	*(kAhp-sooh-lah)*	capsule
cavità	*(kah-vee-tAh)*	sinus
collirio (m)	*(kohl-lEEh-reeh-oh)*	eyedrop
composti (m)	*(kohm-pOhs-teeh)*	compounds
compressa (f)	*(kohm-prEhs-sah)*	tablet
contenuto (m)	*(kohn-teh-nOOh-toh)*	content
cortisone (m)	*(kohr-teeh-zOh-neh)*	cortisone
cura (f)	*(kOOh-rah)*	medication
densità (f)	*(dehn-seeh-tAh)*	density
diabete (m)	*(deeh-ah-bEh-teh)*	diabetes
digitalis (m)	*(dee-gee-tAh-lees)*	digitalis
diuretico (m)	*(deeh-ooh-rEh-teeh-koh)*	diuretic
dose (f)	*(dOh-zeh)*	dose
droga (m)	*(drOh-gah)*	drug
esaclorofene (m/f)	*(eh-zah-kloh-roh-fEh-neh)*	hexachlorophene
farmacia (f)	*(fahr-mah-chEEh-ah)*	drugstore
farmacista (m/f)	*(fahr-mah-chEEhs-tah)*	pharmacist
farmaco (m)	*(fAhr-mah-koh)*	drug
fenolo (m)	*(feh-nOh-loh)*	phenol
ferro (m)	*(fEhr-roh)*	iron

goccia (f)	*(gOhch-chah)*	drop
grezzo	*(grEhts-tsoh)*	crude
iniezione (f)	*(eeh-nyeh-tsyOh-neh)*	injection
insulina (f)	*(eehn-sooh-lEEh-nah)*	insulin
iodio (m)	*(yOh-deeh-oh)*	iodine
ipertensione (f)	*(eeh-pehr-tehn-syOh-neh)*	hypertension
lassativo (m)	*(lahs-sah-tEEh-voh)*	laxative
malattia (f)	*(mah-laht-tEEh-ah)*	disease
medicina (f)	*(meh-deeh-chEEh-nah)*	medicine
medico (m)	*(mEh-deeh-koh)*	physician
morfina (f)	*(mohr-fEEh-nah)*	morphine
narcotico (m)	*(nahr-kOh-teeh-koh)*	narcotic
nitrato (m)	*(neeh-trAh-toh)*	nitrate
nitrite (m)	*(neeh-trEEh-teh)*	nitrite
oppio (m/f)	*(Ohp-pyoh)*	opium
organico	*(ohr-gAh-neeh-koh)*	organic
ormone (m)	*(ohr-mOh-neh)*	hormone
pallottolina (f)	*(pahl-loht-toh-lEEh-nah)*	pellet
pastiglia (f)	*(pahs-tEEh-lyah)*	tablet
pastiglia per la tosse	*(pahs-tEEh-lyah pehr-lah tOhs-seh)*	cough drop
penicillina	*(peh-neeh-chehl-lEEh-nah)*	penicillin
piante (f)	*(pyAhn-teh)*	plants
pillola (f)	*(pEEhl-loh-lah)*	pill
pomata (f)	*(poh-mAh-tah)*	salve
puntura (f)	*(poohn-tOOh-rah)*	injection
purgante (m)	*(poohr-gAhn-teh)*	laxative, purgative
rimedi (m)	*(reeh-mEh-deeh)*	remedies
saccarina (f)	*(sahk-kah-rEEh-nah)*	saccharin
sali (m)	*(sAh-leeh)*	salts
sangue (m)	*(sAhn-gweh)*	blood
sanguinare	*(sahn-gweeh-nAh-reh)*	bleed (v)
sciroppo (m) per la tosse	*(sheeh-rOhp-poh pehr-lah tOhs-seh)*	cough syrup
siero (m)	*(syEh-roh)*	serum

sintesi (f)	*(sEEhn-teh-zeeh)*	synthesis
sinusite (f)	*(seeh-nooh-zEEh-teh)*	sinusitis
siringa (f)	*(seeh-rEEhn-gah)*	syringe
sonnifero (m)	*(sohn-nEEh-feh-roh)*	sleeping pill
starnutire	*(stahr-nooh-tEEh-reh)*	sneeze (v)
stimolante (m)	*(steeh-moh-lAhn-teh)*	stimulant
sulfamide (m)	*(sohl-fah-mEEh-deh)*	sulphamide
tecnico (m) del lab-oratorio	*(tEhk-neeh-koh dehl lah-boh-rah-tOh-reeh-oh)*	laboratory technician
tossicologia (f)	*(tohs-seeh-koh-loh-jEEh-ah)*	toxicology
tossina (f)	*(tohs-sEEh-nah)*	toxin
tossire	*(tohs-sEEh-reh)*	cough (v)
tranquillante (m)	*(trahn-kweehl-lAhn-teh)*	tranquilizer
unguento (m)	*(oohn-gwEhn-toh)*	salve, ointment
vaccino (m)	*(vahch-chEEh-noh)*	vaccine
vitamina (f)	*(veeh-tah-mEEh-nah)*	vitamin
zinco (m)	*(dsEEhn-koh)*	zinc

PRINTING AND PUBLISHING

English to Italian

black and white	il bianco e nero	*(byAhn-koh eh nEh-roh)*
bleed	la pagina al vivo, smarginato	*(pAh-jeeh-nah ahl vEEh-voh), (zmahr-jeeh-nAh-toh)*
blowup	la gigantografia, l'ingrandi-mento	*(jeeh-gahn-toh-grah-fEEh-ah), (eehn-grahn-deeh-mEhn-toh)*
boldface	il neretto	*(neh-rEht-toh)*
book	il libro	*(lEEh-broh)*
capital	il maiuscolo	*(mah-yOOhs-koh-loh)*
chapter	il capitolo	*(kah-pEEh-toh-loh)*
coated paper	la carta patinata	*(kAhr-tah pah-teeh-nAh-tah)*
color separation	la separazione dei colori	*(seh-pah-rah-tsyOh-neh deh-eeh koh-lOh-reeh)*
copy	il materiale scritto	*(mah-teh-ryAh-leh skrEEht-toh)*
copyright	i diritti d'autore	*(deeh-rEEht-teeh dah-ooh-tOh-reh)*
cover	la copertina	*(koh-pehr-tEEh-nah)*
crop (v)	rifilare	*(reeh-feeh-lAh-reh)*
dummy	il menabò	*(meh-nah-bOh)*
edit (v)	redigere	*(reh-dEEh-jeh-reh)*
edition	il numero	*(nOOh-meh-roh)*
editor	il redattore	*(reh-daht-tOh-reh)*
engrave (v)	incidere	*(eehn-chEEh-deh-reh)*
font	la serie completa di caratteri	*(sEh-ryeh kohm-plEh-tah deeh kah-rAht-teh-reeh)*
form	la forma	*(fOhr-mah)*
format	il formato	*(fohr-mAh-toh)*
four colors	quattro colori	*(kwAht-troh koh-lOh-reeh)*
galley proof	la bozza in colonna	*(bOhts-tsah eehn koh-lOhn-nah)*
glossy	lucido	*(lOOh-cheeh-doh)*
grain	la grana	*(grAh-nah)*

grid	la quadrettatura	*(kwah-dreht-tah-tOOh-rah)*
hardcover	la copertina a tela, la legatura cartonata	*(koh-pehr-tEEh-nah ah tEh-lah), (leh-gah-tOOh-rah kahr-toh-nAh-tah)*
headline	il titolo	*(tEEh-toh-loh)*
illustration	l'illustrazione	*(eehl-loohs-trah-tsyOh-neh)*
inch	il pollice	*(pOhl-leeh-cheh)*
ink	l'inchiostro	*(eehn-kyOhs-troh)*
insert	il volantino	*(voh-lahn-tEEh-noh)*
introduction	la premessa	*(preh-mEhs-sah)*
italic	il corsivo	*(kohr-sEEh-voh)*
jacket	la copertina di libro, la sopraccoperta	*(koh-pehr-tEEh-nah deeh lEEh-broh), (soh-prahk-koh-pEhr-tah)*
justify (v)	giustificare	*(joohs-teeh-feeh-kAh-reh)*
layout	la disposizione di una pagina	*(deehs-poh-zeeh-tsyOh-neh deeh ooh-nah pAh-jeeh-nah)*
letterpress	la parte stampata	*(pAhr-teh stahm-pAh-tah)*
line	la linea	*(lEEh-neh-ah)*
line drawing	il disegno	*(deeh-zEh-nyoh)*
lower case	il minuscolo	*(meeh-nOOhs-koh-loh)*
matrix	la matrice	*(mah-trEEh-cheh)*
matt	non lucido, opaco	*(nohn lOOh-cheeh-doh), (oh-pAh-koh)*
mechanical	il montaggio	*(mohn-tAhj-joh)*
negative	il negativo	*(neh-gah-tEEh-voh)*
newsprint	la carta da giornale	*(kAhr-tah dah johr-nAh-leh)*
on press	in stampa	*(eehn stAhm-pah)*
overrun	superare la giustezza	*(sooh-peh-rAh-reh lah joohs-tEhts-tsah)*
packing	l'imballo	*(eehm-bAhl-loh)*
page	la pagina	*(pAh-jeeh-nah)*
page makeup	la composizione della pagina	*(kohm-poh-zeeh-tsyOh-neh dehl-lah pAh-jeeh-nah)*
pagination	l'impaginazione	*(eehm-pah-jeeh-nah-tsyOh-neh)*
pamphlet	l'opuscolo	*(oh-pOOhs-koh-loh)*

paper	la carta	*(kAhr-tah)*
paperback	in brossura	*(brohs-sOOh-rah)*
pigment	il colore, il pigmento	*(koh-lOh-reh), (peehg-mEhn-toh)*
plate	la lastra	*(lAhs-trah)*
point	il punto tipografico	*(pOOhn-toh teeh-poh-grAh-feeh-koh)*
positive	il positivo	*(poh-zeeh-tEEh-voh)*
preface	la prefazione	*(preh-fah-tsyOh-neh)*
press book	l'ultima bozza	*(OOhl-teeh-mah bohts-tsah)*
printing	la stampatura	*(stahm-pah-tOOh-rah)*
printing shop	la tipografia	*(teeh-poh-grah-fEEh-ah)*
proofreading	la correzione delle bozza	*(kohr-reh-tsyOh-neh dehl-leh bOhts-tseh)*
publisher	l'editore	*(eh-deeh-tOh-reh)*
ream	la risma	*(rEEhz-mah)*
register	il registro	*(reh-jEEhs-troh)*
scanner	l'analizzatore di immagini, lo "scanner"	*(ah-nah-leehds-dsah-tOh-reh deeh eehm-mAh-jeeh-neeh)*
scoring	la raschiatura	*(rahs-kyah-tOOh-rah)*
screen	il retino	*(reh-tEEh-noh)*
sewn	rilegato	*(reeh-leh-gAh-toh)*
sheet	il foglio	*(fOh-lyoh)*
signature	la firma	*(fEEhr-mah)*
size	il formato	*(fohr-mAh-toh)*
soft cover	la copertina flessibile	*(koh-pehr-tEEh-nah flehs-sEEh-beeh-leh)*
spine	il dorso	*(dOhr-soh)*
table of contents	l'indice	*(EEhn-deehOcheh)*
title	il titolo	*(tEEh-toh-loh)*
web offset press	la macchina da stampa offset a bobina	*(mAhk-keeh-nah dah stAhm-pah offset ah boh-bEEh-nah)*

Italian to English

analizzatore (m) di immagini	*(ah-nah-leehds-dsah-tOh-reh deeh eehm-mAh-jeeh-neeh)*	scanner
bianco e nero (m)	*(byAhn-koh eh nEh-roh)*	black and white
bozza (f) in colonna	*(bOhts-tsah eehn koh-lOhn-nah)*	galley proof
capitolo	*(kah-pEEh-toh-loh)*	chapter
carta (f)	*(kAhr-tah)*	paper
carta da giornale	*(kAhr-tah dah johr-nAh-leh)*	newsprint
carta patinata	*(kAhr-tah pah-teeh-nAh-tah)*	coated paper
colore (m)	*(koh-lOh-reh)*	pigment
composizione della pagina	*(kohm-poh-zeeh-tsyOh-neh dehl-lah pAh-jeeh-nah)*	page makeup
copertina (f)	*(koh-pehr-tEEh-nah)*	cover
copertina a tela	*(koh-pehr-tEEh-nah ah tEh-lah)*	hardcover
copertina di libro	*(koh-pehr-tEEh-nah deeh lEEh-broh)*	jacket
copertina flessibile	*(koh-pehr-tEEh-nah flehs-sEEh-beeh-leh)*	soft cover
copiare	*(koh-oyAh-reh)*	copy (v)
correzione (f) delle bozza	*(koh-rehts-tsyOh-neh dehl-leh bOhts-tseh)*	proofreading
corsivo (m)	*(kohr-sEEh-voh)*	italic
diritti (m) d'autore	*(deeh-rEEht-toh dah-ooh-tOh-reh)*	copyright
disegno (m)	*(deeh-zEh-nyoh)*	line drawing
disposizione (f) di una pagina	*(deehs-poh-zeeh-tsyOh-neh deeh ooh-nah pAh-jeeh-nah)*	layout
dorso (m)	*(dOhr-soh)*	spine
editore/trice (m/f)	*(eh-deeh-tOh-reh.trEEh-cheh)*	publisher
foglio (m)	*(fOh-lyoh)*	sheet
forma (f)	*(fOhr-mah)*	form
formato (m)	*(fohr-mAh-toh)*	size, format

gigantografia (f)	*(jeeh-gahn-toh-grah-fEEh-ah),*	blowup
giustificare	*(joohs-teeh-feeh-kAh-reh)*	justify (v)
grana (f)	*(grAh-nah)*	grain
illustrazione (f)	*(eehl-loohs-trah-tsyOh-neh)*	illustration
imballo (m)	*(eehm-bAhl-loh)*	packing
impaginazione (f)	*(eehm-pah-jeeh-nah-tsyOh-neh)*	pagination
in brossura	*(eehn brohs-sOOh-rah)*	paperback
in stampa	*(eehn stAhm-pah)*	on press
inchiostro (m)	*(eehn-kyOhs-troh)*	ink
incidere	*(eehn-chEEh-deh-reh)*	engrave (v)
indice (m)	*(EEhn-deeh-cheh)*	table of contents
ingrandimento (m)	*(eehn-grahn-deeh-mEhn-toh)*	blowup
lastra (f)	*(lAhs-trah)*	plate
legatura cartonata (f)	*(leh-gah-tOOh-rah kahr-toh-nAh-tah)*	hardcover
libro (m)	*(lEEh-broh)*	book
linea (f)	*(lEEh-neh-ah)*	line
lucido	*(lOOh-cheeh-doh)*	glossy
macchina (f) da stampa offset a bobina	*(mAhk-keeh-nah dah stAhm-pah offset ah boh-bEEh-nah)*	web offset press
maiuscolo (m)	*(mah-yOOhs-koh-loh)*	capital
materiale scritto (m)	*(mah-teh-ryAh-leh skrEEht-toh)*	copy
matrice (f)	*(mah-trEEh-cheh)*	matrix
menabò (m)	*(meh-nah-bOh)*	dummy
minuscolo (m)	*(meeh-nOOhs-koh-loh)*	lower case
montaggio (m)	*(mohn-tAhj-joh)*	mechanical
negativo (m)	*(neh-gah-tEEh-voh)*	negative
neretto (m)	*(neh-rEht-toh)*	boldface
non lucido	*(nohn lOOh-cheeh-doh)*	matt
numero (m)	*(nOOh-meh-roh)*	edition
opaco	*(oh-pAh-koh)*	matt

opuscolo (m)	*(oh-pOOhs-koh-loh)*	pamphlet
pagina (f)	*(pAh-jeeh-nah)*	page
pagina al vivo	*(pAh-jeeh-nah ahl vEEh-voh)*	bleed
parte (f) stampata	*(pAhr-teh stahm-pAh-tah)*	letterpress
pigmento (m)	*(peehg-mEhn-toh)*	pigment
pollice (m)	*(pOhl-leeh-cheh)*	inch
positivo (m)	*(poh-zeeh-tEEh-voh)*	positive
prefazione (f)	*(preh-fah-tsyOh-neh)*	preface
premessa (m)	*(preh-mEhs-sah)*	introduction
punto (m) tipografico	*(pOOhn-toh teeh-poh-grAh-feeh-koh)*	point
quadrettatura (f)	*(kwah-dreht-tah-tOOh-rah)*	grid
quattro colori	*(kwAht-troh koh-lOh-reeh)*	four colors
raschiatura (f)	*(rahs-kyah-tOOh-rah)*	scoring
redattore (m)	*(reh-daht-tOh-reh)*	editor
redigere	*(reh-dEEh-jeh-reh)*	edit (v)
registro (m)	*(reh-jEEhs-troh)*	register
retino (m)	*(reh-tEEh-noh)*	screen
rifilare	*(reeh-feeh-lAh-reh)*	crop (v)
rilegato	*(reeh-leh-gAh-toh)*	sewn
risma (f)	*(rEEhz-mah)*	ream
segnatura (f)	*(seh-nyah-tOOh-rah)*	signature
separazione (f) dei colore	*(seh-pah-rah-tsyOh-neh deh-eeh koh-lOh-reeh)*	color separation
serie completa (f) di caratteri	*(sEh-ryeh kohm-plEh-tah deeh kah-rAht-teh-reeh)*	font
smarginato	*(zmahr-jeeh-nAh-toh)*	bleed
sopraccoperta (f)	*(soh-prahk-koh-pEhr-tah)*	jacket
stampatura (f)	*(stahm-pah-tOOh-rah)*	printing
superare (f) giustezza	*(sooh-peh-rAh-reh lah joohs-tEhts-tsah)*	overrun
tipografia (f)	*(teeh-pioh-grah-fEEh-ah)*	printing shop
titolo (m)	*(tEEh-toh-loh)*	headline, title
ultima bozza (f)	*(OOhl-teeh-mah bOhts-tsah)*	press book
volantino (m)	*(voh-lahn-tEEh-noh)*	insert

WINEMAKING

English to Italian

acid content	l'acidita	*(ah-cheeh-deeh-tAh)*
acre	l'acro	*(Ah-kroh)*
aging	l'invecchiamento	*(eehn-vehk-kyah-mEhn-toh)*
alcohol	l'alcol	*(Ahl-kohl)*
alcoholic content	il contenuto alcolico	*(kohn-teh-nOOh-toh ahl-kOh-leeh-koh)*
area of origin guaranteed	la denominazione di origine controllata (D.O.C.)	*(deh-noh-meeh-nah-tsyOh-neh deeh oh-rEEh-jeeh-neh kohn-trohl-lAh-tah)*
blend (v)	tagliare	*(tah-lyAh-reh)*
body	il corpo	*(kOhr-poh)*
bottle (usually 75 centiliters)	la bottiglia	*(boht-tEEh-lyah)*
bouquet	il naso, il bouquet	*(nAh-zoh)*
case	la cassa	*(kAhs-sah)*
cask (225 liters)	il barile	*(bah-rEEh-leh)*
centiliter	centilitro	*(chehn-tEEh-leeh-troh)*
climate	il clima	*(klEEh-mah)*
cooper	il bottaio	*(boht-tAh-yoh)*
cork	il tappo	*(tAhp-poh)*
corkscrew	il cavatappi	*(kah-vah-tAhp-peeh)*
country	il paese	*(pah-Eh-zeh)*
dregs	i rimasugli	*(reeh-mah-sOOh-lyeeh)*
drink	la bevanda	*(beh-vAhn-dah)*
dry wine	il vino secco	*(vEEh-noh sEhk-koh)*
estate (or chateau)	la fattoria	*(faht-toh-rEEh-ah)*
estate bottled	imbottigliato all'origine	*(eehm-boht-teeh-lyAh-toh ahl oh-rEEh-jeeh-neh)*
ferment (v)	fermentare	*(fehr-mehn-tAh-reh)*
fruity	fruttato	*(frooht-tAh-toh)*
grape	l'uva	*(OOh-vah)*
grape bunch	il grappolo d'uva	*(grAhp-poh-loh dOOh-vah)*
grape harvest	la vendemmia	*(vehn-dEhm-myah)*

hectare	l'ettaro	*(Eht-tah-roh)*
juice	il succo	*(sOOhk-koh)*
label	l'etichetta	*(eh-teeh-kEht-tah)*
liqueur	il liquore	*(leeh-kwOh-reh)*
liter	il litro	*(lEEh-troh)*
magnum (2 bottles in one)	il bottiglione da due litri	*(boht-teeh-lyOh-neh dah dOOh-eh lEEh-treeh)*
malolactic fermentation	la fermentazione malolattica	*(fehr-mehn-tah-tsyOh-neh mah-loh-lAht-teeh-kah)*
must	il mosto	*(mOhs-toh)*
neck (of bottle)	il collo	*(kOhl-loh)*
pasteurized	pastorizzato	*(pahs-toh-reehds-dsAh-toh)*
production	la produzione	*(proh-dooh-tsyOh-neh)*
ripe	maturo	*(mah-tOOh-roh)*
skin	la buccia	*(bOOhch-chah)*
sour	agro	*(Ah-groh)*
sparkling wine	il vino spumante	*(vEEh-noh spooh-mAhn-teh)*
sugar content	il contenuto zuccherino	*(kohn-teh-nOOh-toh dsoohk-keh-rEEh-noh)*
table wine	il vino da tavola	*(vEEh-noh dah tAh-voh-lah)*
tannin	il tannino	*(tahn-nEEh-noh)*
tasting (wine tasting)	la degustazione	*(deh-goohs-tah-tsyOh-neh)*
temperature	la temperatura	*(tehm-peh-rah-tOOh-rah)*
type of vine	il vitigno	*(veeh-tEEh-nyoh)*
unfermented grape juice	il succo d'uva non fermentato	*(sOOhk-koh dOOh-vah nohn fehr-mehn-tAh-toh)*
vat	il tino, la tinozza	*(tEEh-noh) (teeh-nOhts-rsah)*
vine	la vigna	*(vEEh-nyah)*
vineyard	il vigneto	*(veeh-nyEh-toh)*
vintage	la vendemmia	*(vehn-dEhm-myah)*
vintage year	l'annata	*(ahn-nAh-tah)*
vintner	il vinaio	*(veeh-nAh-yoh)*
vintry	la cantina	*(kahn-tEEh-nah)*
wine	il vino	*(vEEh-noh)*

wine cellar	la cantina, l'enoteca	*(kahn-tEEh-nah), (eh-noh-tEh-kah)*
wine cooperative	la cooperativa vinicola	*(koh-oh-peh-rah-tEEh-vah)*
winegrower	il viticultore	*(veeh-teeh-koohltOh-reh)*
winepress	il torchio da vino	*(tOhr-kyoh dah vEEh-noh)*
wine steward	l'enologo, il sommelier	*(eh-nOh-loh-goh)*
wine growing areas	le zone di coltivazione delle vigne	*(dsOh-neh deeh kohl-teeh-vah-tsyOh-neh dehl-leh vEEh-nyeh)*
yeast	il lievito	*(lyEh-veeh-toh)*
yield	la resa	*(rEh-zah)*

Italian to English

acidità (f)	*(ah-cheeh-deeh-tAh)*	acid content
acro (m)	*(Ah-kroh)*	acre
agro	*(Ah-groh)*	sour
alcool (m)	*(Ahl-kohl)*	alcohol
annata (f)	*(ahn-nAh-tah)*	vintage year
barile (m)	*(bah-rEEh-leh)*	cask (225 liters)
bevanda	*(beh-vAhn-dah)*	drink
bottaio (m)	*(boht-tAh-yoh)*	cooper
bottiglia (f)	*(boht-tEEh-lyah)*	bottle (usually 75 centiliters)
bottiglione da due litri (m)	*(boht-teeh-lyOh-neh dah dOOh-eh lEEh-treeh)*	magnum (2 bottles in one)
bouquet (m)	*(bou-quet)*	bouquet
buccia (f)	*(bOOhch-chah)*	skin
cantina (f)	*(kahn-tEEh-nah)*	wine cellar
cassa (f)	*(kAhs-sah)*	case
cavatappi (m)	*(kah-vah-tAhp-peeh)*	corkscrew
centilitro (m)	*(chehn-tEEh-leeh-troh)*	centiliter
clima (m)	*(klEEh-mah)*	climate
collo (m)	*(kOhl-loh)*	neck (of bottle)
contenuto (m) alcolico	*(kohn-teh-nOOh-toh ahl-kOh-leeh-koh)*	alcoholic content
contenuto zuccherino	*(kohn-teh-nOOh-toh dsoohk-keh-rEEh-noh)*	sugar content

cooperativa (f) vinicola	*(koh-oh-peh-rah-tEEh-vah)*	wine cooperative
corpo (m)	*(kOhr-poh)*	body
degustazione (f)	*(deh-goohs-tah-tsyOh-neh)*	tasting (wine tasting)
denominazione di origine control- lata (D.O.C.) (f)	*(deh-noh-meeh-nah-tsyOh- neh deeh oh-rEEh-jeeh- neh kohn-trohl-lAh-tah)*	area of origin guaranteed
enologo (m)	*(eh-nOh-loh-goh)*	wine steward
enoteca (f)	*(eh-noh-tEh-kah)*	wine cellar
ettaro (m)	*(Eht-tah-roh)*	hectare
etichetta (f)	*(eh-teeh-kEht-tah)*	label
fattoria (f)	*(faht-toh-rEEh-ah)*	estate (or chateau)
fermentare	*(fehr-mehn-tAh-reh)*	ferment (v)
fermentazione mal- olattica (f)	*(fehr-mehn-tah-tsyOh-neh mah-loh-lAht-teeh-kah)*	malolactic fermentation
fruttato	*(frooht-tAh-toh)*	fruity
grappolo d'uva (m)	*(grAhp-poh-loh dOOh-vah)*	grape bunch
imbottigliato all'o- rigine	*(eehm-boht-teeh-lyAh-toh ahl oh-rEEh-jeeh-neh)*	estate bottled
invecchiamento (m)	*(eehn-vehk-kyah-mEhn-toh)*	aging
lievito (f)	*(lyEh-veeh-toh)*	yeast
liquore (m)	*(leeh-kwOh-reh)*	liqueur
litro (m)	*(lEEh-troh)*	liter
maturo	*(mah-tOOh-roh)*	ripe
mosto (m)	*(mOhs-toh)*	must
naso (m)	*(nAh-zoh)*	bouquet
paese (m)	*(pah-Eh-zeh)*	country
pastorizzato	*(pahs-toh-reehds-dsAh-toh)*	pasteurized
produzione (f)	*(proh-dooh-tsyOh-neh)*	production
resa (f)	*(rEh-zah)*	yield
rimasugli (m)	*(reeh-mah-sOOh-lyeeh)*	dregs
sommelier (m)	*(soh-meh-lee-Eh)*	wine steward
succo (m)	*(sOOhk-koh)*	juice
succo d'uva non fermentato	*(sOOhk-koh dOOh-vah nohn fehr-mehn-tAh-toh)*	unfermented grape juice
tagliare	*tah-lyAh-reh)*	blend (v)

tannino (m)	*(tahn-nEEh-noh)*	tannin
tappo (m)	*(tAhp-poh)*	cork
temperatura (f)	*(tehm-peh-rah-tOOh-rah)*	temperature
tino (m)	*(tEEh-noh)*	vat
tinozza (f)	*(teeh-nOhts-tsah)*	vat
torchio da vino (m)	*(tOhr-kyoh dah vEEh-noh)*	winepress
uva (m)	*(OOh-vah)*	grape
vendemmia (f)	*(vehn-dEhm-myah)*	grape harvest, vintage
vigna (f)	*(vEEh-nyah)*	vine
vigneto (m)	*(veeh-nyEh-toh)*	vineyard
vinaio (m)	*(veeh-nAh-yoh)*	vintner
vino (m)	*(vEEh-noh)*	wine
vino da tavola	*(vEEh-noh dah tAh-voh-lah)*	table wine
vino secco	*(vEEh-noh sEh-koh)*	dry wine
vino spumante	*(vEEh-noh spooh-mAhn-teh)*	sparkling wine
viticultore (m)	*(veeh-teeh-koohl-tOh-reh)*	winegrower
vitigno (m)	*(veeh-tEEh-nyoh)*	type of vine
zone (f) di colti- vazione delle vigne	*(dsOh-neh deeh kohl-teeh- vah-tsyOh-neh dehl-leh vEEh-nyeh)*	wine growing areas

Agriculture, Industry and Resources

The economic map of Italy will give you a good idea of
Italian industrial geography.

MAJOR MINERAL OCCURRENCES

Ab	Asbestos	Mr	Marble
Al	Bauxite	Na	Salt
C	Coal	O	Petroleum
Fe	Iron Ore	Pb	Lead
G	Natural Gas	Py	Pyrites
Hg	Mercury	S	Sulfur
K	Potash	Sb	Antimony
Lg	Lignite	Zn	Zinc
⚡	Water Power	/////	Major Industrial Areas

ABBREVIATIONS

a.a. always afloat
a.a.r. against all risks
a/c account
A/C account current
acct. account
a.c.v. actual cash value
a.d. after date
a.f.b. air freight bill
agcy. agency
agt. agent
a.m.t. air mail transfer
a/o account of
A.P. accounts payable
A/P authority to pay
approx. approximately
A.R. accounts receivable
a/r all risks
A/S, A.S. account sales
a/s at sight
at. wt. atomic weight
av. average
avdp. avoirdupois
a/w actual weight
a.w.b. air waybill

bal. balance
bar. barrel
bbl. barrel
b/d brought down
B/E, b/e bill of exchange
b/f brought forward
B.H. bill of health
bk. bank
bkge. brokerage
B/L bill of lading
b/o brought over
B.P. bills payable
b.p. by procuration
B.R. bills receivable
B/S balance sheet
b.t. berth terms
bu. bushel
B/V book value

ca. circa; centaire
C.A. chartered accountant
c.a. current account
C.A.D. cash against documents
C.B. cash book
C.B.D. cash before delivery
c.c. carbon copy
c/d carried down
c.d. cum dividend
c/f carried forward
cf. compare
c & f cost and freight
C/H clearing house
C.H. custom house
ch. fwd. charges forward
ch. pd. charges paid
ch. ppd. charges prepaid
chq. check, cheque
c.i.f. cost, insurance, freight
c.i.f. & c. cost, insurance, freight,
    and commission
c.i.f. & e. cost, insurance, freight,
    and exchange
c.i.f. & i. cost, insurance, freight, and
    interest
c.l. car load
C/m call of more
C/N credit note
c/o care of
co. company
C.O.D. cash on delivery
comm. commission
corp. corporation
C.O.S. cash on shipment
C.P. carriage paid
C/P charter party
c.p.d. charters pay duties
cpn. corporation
cr. credit; creditor
C/T cable transfer
c.t.l. constructive total loss
c.t.l.o. constructive total loss only
cum. cumulative

cum div. cum dividend
cum. pref. cumulative preference
c/w commercial weight
C.W.O. cash with order
cwt. hundredweight

D/A documents against acceptance;
  deposit account
DAP documents against payment
db. debenture
DCF discounted cash flow
d/d days after date; delivered
deb. debenture
def. deferred
dept. department
d.f. dead freight
dft. draft
dft/a. draft attached
dft/c. clean draft
disc. discount
div. dividend
DL dayletter
DLT daily letter telegram
D/N debit note
D/O delivery order
do. ditto
doz. dozen
D/P documents against payment
dr. debtor
Dr. doctor
d/s, d.s. days after sight
d.w. deadweight
D/W dock warrant
dwt. pennyweight
dz. dozen

ECU European Currency Unit
E.E.T. East European Time
e.g. for example
encl. enclosure
end. endorsement
E. & O.E. errors and omissions
  excepted
e.o.m. end of month
e.o.h.p. except otherwise herein
  provided
esp. especially
Esq. Esquire
est. established
ex out

ex cp. ex coupon
ex div. ex dividend
ex int. ex interest
ex h. ex new (shares)
ex stre. ex store
ex whf. ex wharf

f.a.a. free of all average
f.a.c. fast as can
f.a.k. freight all kinds
f.a.q. fair average quality; free
  alongside quay
f.a.s. free alongside ship
f/c for cash
f.c. & s. free of capture and seizure
f.c.s.r. & c.c. free of capture, seizure,
  riots, and civil commotion
F.D. free delivery to dock
f.d. free discharge
ff. following; folios
f.g.a. free of general average
f.i.b. free in bunker
f.i.o. free in and out
f.i.t. free in truck
f.o.b. free on board
f.o.c. free of charge
f.o.d. free of damage
fol. following; folio
f.o.q. free on quay
f.o.r. free on rail
f.o.s. free on steamer
f.o.t. free on truck(s)
f.o.w. free on wagons; free on wharf
F.P. floating policy
f.p. fully paid
f.p.a. free of particular average
frt. freight
frt. pd. freight paid
frt. ppd. freight prepaid
frt. fwd. freight forward
ft. foot
fwd. forward
f.x. foreign exchange

g.a. general average
g.b.o. goods in bad order
g.m.b. good merchantable brand
g.m.q. good merchantable quality
G.M.T. Greenwich Mean TIme
GNP gross national product

g.o.b. good ordinary brand
gr. gross
GRT gross register ton
gr. wt. gross weight
GT gross tonnage

h.c. home consumption
hgt. height
hhd. hogshead
H.O. head office
H.P. hire purchase
HP horsepower
ht. height

IDP integrated data processing
i.e. that is
I/F insufficient funds
i.h.p. indicated horse-power
imp. import
Inc. incorporated
incl. inclusive
ins. insurance
int. interest
mv. invoice
I.O.U. I owe you

J/A, j.a. joint account
Jr. junior

KV kilovolt
KW kilowatt
KWh kilowatt hour

L/C, l.c. letter of credit
LCD telegram in the language of the
  country of destination
LCO telegram in the language of the
  country of origin
ldg. landing; loading
l.t. long ton
Ltd. limited
1. tn. long ton

m. month
m/a my account
max. maximum
M.D. memorandum of deposit
M/D, m.d. months after date
memo. memorandum
Messrs. plural of Mr.

mfr. manufacturer
min. minimum
MLR minimum lending rate
M.O. money order
m.o. my order
mortg. mortgage
M/P, m.p. months after payment
M/R mate's receipt
M/S, m.s. months' sight
M.T. mail transfer
M/U making-up price

n. name; nominal
n/a no account
N/A no advice
n.c.v. no commercial value
n.d. no date
n.e.s. not elsewhere specified
N/F no funds
NL night letter
N/N no noting
N/O no orders
no. number
n.o.e. not otherwise enumerated
n.o.s. not otherwise stated
nos. numbers
NPV no par value
nr. number
n.r.t. net register ton
N/S not sufficient funds
NSF not sufficient funds
n. wt. net weight

o/a on account
OCP overseas common point
O/D, o/d on demand; overdraft
o.e. omissions excepted
o/h overhead
ono. or nearest offer
O/o order of
O.P. open policy
o.p. out of print; overproof
O/R, o.r. owner's risk
ord. order; ordinary
O.S., o/s out of stock
OT overtime

p. page; per; premium
P.A., p.a. particular average; per
  annum

P/A power of attorney; private account

PAL   phase alternation line

pat. pend. patent pending

PAYE pay as you earn

p/c petty cash

p.c. percent; price current

pcl. parcel

pd. paid

pf. preferred

pfd. preferred

pkg. package

P/L profit and loss

p.l. partial loss

P/N promissory note

P.O. post office; postal order

P.O.B. post office box

P.O.O. post office order

p.o.r. pay on return

pp. pages

p & p postage and packing

p. pro per procuration

ppd. prepaid

ppt. prompt

pref. preference

prox. proximo

P.S. postscript

pt. payment

P.T.O., p.t.o. please turn over

ptly. pd. partly paid

p.v. par value

qlty. quality

qty. quantity

r. & c.c. riot and civil commotions

R/D refer to drawer

R.D.C. running down clause

re in regard to

rec. received; receipt

recd. received

red. redeemable

ref. reference

reg. registered

retd. returned

rev. revenue

R.O.D. refused on delivery

R.P. reply paid

r.p.s. revolutions per second

RSVP please reply

R.S.W.C. right side up with care

Ry railway

s.a.e. stamped addressed envelope

S.A.V. stock at valuation

S/D sea damaged

S/D, s.d. sight draft

s.d. without date

SDR special drawing rights

sgd. signed

s. & h. ex Sundays and holidays excepted

shipt. shipment

sig. signature

S/LC, s. & l.c. sue and labor clause

S/N shipping note

s.o. seller's option

s.o.p. standard operating procedure

spt. spot

Sr. senior

S.S., s.s. steamship

s.t. short ton

ster. sterling

St. Ex. stock exchange

stg. sterling

s.v. sub voce

T.A. telegraphic address

T.B. trial balance

tel. telephone

temp. temporary secretary

T.L., t.l. total loss

T.L.O. total loss only

TM multiple telegram

T.O. turn over

tr. transfer

TR telegram to be called for

TR, T/R trust receipt

TT, T.T. telegraphic transfer (cable)

TX Telex

UGT urgent

u.s.c. under separate cover

U/ws underwriters

v. volt

val. value

v.a.t. value-added tax

v.g. very good

VHF very high frequency

v.h.r. very highly recommended	W/R, wr. warehouse receipt
w. watt	W.W.D. weather working day
WA with average	wt. weight
W.B. way bill	x.c. ex coupon
w.c. without charge	x.d. ex dividend
W.E.T. West European Time	x.i. ex interest
wg. weight guaranteed	x.n. ex new shares
whse. warehouse	
w.o.g. with other goods	y. year
W.P. weather permitting; without prejudice	yd. yard
	yr. year
w.p.a. with particular average	yrly. yearly
W.R. war risk	

WEIGHTS AND MEASURES

U.S. UNIT	METRIC EQUIVALENT
mile	1.609 kilometers
yard	0.914 meters
foot	30.480 centimeters
inch	2.540 centimeters
square mile	2.590 square kilometers
acre	0.405 hectares
square yard	0.836 square meters
square foot	10.093 square meters
square inch	6.451 square centimeters
cubic yard	0.765 cubic meters
cubic foot	0.028 cubic meters
cubic inch	16.387 cubic centimeters
short ton	0.907 metric tons
long ton	1.016 metric tons
short hundredweight	45.359 kilograms
long hundredweight	50.802 kilograms
pound	0.453 kilograms
ounce	28.349 grams
gallon	3.785 liters
quart	0.946 liters
pint	0.473 liters
fluid ounce	29.573 milliliters
bushel	35.238 liters
peck	8.809 liters
quart	1.101 liters
pint	0.550 liters

TEMPERATURE AND CLIMATE

Temperature Conversion Chart

DEGREES CELSIUS	DEGREES FAHRENHEIT
-5	23
0	32
5	41
10	50
15	59
20	68
25	77
30	86
35	95
40	104

Average Temperatures for Major Cities

	JAN	APR	JULY	OCT
Milan	40/32°F (4/0°C)	65/49°F (17/9°C)	84/67F° (26/18°C)	63/52°F (16/11°C)
Rome	52/40°F (11/4°C)	66/50°F (18/10°C)	87/67°F (30/18°C)	63/52°F (17/11°C)
Palermo	60/46°F (15/8°C)	68/52°F (20/11°C)	85/65°F (29/18°C)	77/60°F (25/15°C)

Spring	primavera
Summer	estate
Autumn	autunno
Winter	inverno
Hot, warm	caldo
Sunny	sole
Cool	fresco
Wind	vento
Fog	nebbia
It's snowing	nevica
It's raining	piove

COMMUNICATIONS CODES

Telephone

telephone booth	cabina telefonica
public phone	telefono pubblico
telephone directory	elenco telefonico

long-distance call	telefonata in teleselezione
local call	telefonata urbana
person-to-person call	telefonata diretta con preavviso
tokens	gettoni
operator	telefonista
the line is busy	la linea é occupata
dial a number	formare un numero

For most calls from a public booth, you need to use a special 200-lire token (gettoni).

Area Codes in Italy

Florence	055	Rome	06
Genoa	010	Turin	011
Milan	02	Venice	041
Naples	081		

International Country Codes

Algeria	213	Mexico	52
Argentina	54	Morocco	212
Australia	61	Netherlands	31
Austria	43	New Zealand	64
Belgium	32	Norway	67
Brazil	55	Philippines	63
Canada	1	Poland	48
Chile	56	Portugal	351
Colombia	57	Russia	7
Denmark	45	Saudi Arabia	966
Finland	358	Singapore	65
France	33	South Africa	27
Germany	37	South Korea	82
Gibraltar	350	Spain	34
Greece	30	Sri Lanka	94
Hong Kong	852	Sweden	46
Hungary	36	Switzerland	41
Iceland	354	Taiwan	886
India	91	Thailand	255
Ireland	353	Tunisia	216
Israel	972	Turkey	90
Italy	39	United Kingdom	44
Japan	81	USA	1
Kuwait	965	Venezuela	58
Luxembourg	352	Yugoslavia	38
Malta	356		

POSTAL SERVICES

In Italy

The Italian postal service is not always reliable and mail is often delayed. For business correspondence, you are advised to use telex and special delivery services. All post offices are open from 8 A.M. to 2 P.M., while in the cities the central post offices are usually open 8 A.M. to 4 P.M. Stamps can also be bought at tobacconists. Central post offices also offer tele phone and telegraph services.

In Rome, the main post office (open 24 hours) is at Piazza San Silvestro 00187. In Milan, the main post office (open 8 A.M. to 8 P.M.) is at Piazza Cordusio 20123.

In Switzerland

The postal service is highly efficient and delivery of regular mail ordinarily takes one day. Post offices are open from 7:30A.M. to noon and 1:30 P.M. to 6:30 P.M.,Monday through Friday; 9:30 to 11 A.M. on Saturday. Facilities offer postal, telephone, and telegram service. In Geneva, the office at rue de Lausanne is open from 6:30 A.M. to 11 P.M., every day.

TIME ZONES

Use the following table to know the time difference between where you are and other major cities. Note, however, that during April through September, you will also have to take Daylight Savings Time into account. Since there are four time zones for the United States, eleven zones for the former Soviet Union, and three for Australia, we've listed major cities for these countries.

Note that in most parts of the world, official time is based on the 24-hour clock. Train schedules and other official documents will use 13:00 through 23:00 to express the P.M. hours.

1 PM = 13.00 le tredici (leh trEH-dee-chee)
1.30PM = 13.30 le tredici e trenta (leh trEH-dee-chee ay trEHn-tah)
2PM = 14.00 le quattordici (leh koo-aht-tOHr-dee-chee)
3PM = 15.00 le quindici (leh koo-EEn-dee-chee)
4PM = 16.00 le sedici (leh sAY-dee-chee)
5PM = 17.00 le diciassette (leh dee-chee-ahs-sEHt-teh)
6PM = 18.00 le diciotto (leh dee-chee-OHt-toh)
7PM = 19.00 le diciannove (leh dee-chee-ahn-nOH-veh)
8PM = 20.00 le venti (leh vAYn-tee)
9PM = 21.00 le ventuno (leh vayn-tOO-noh)
10PM = 22.00 le ventidue (leh vayn-tee-dOO-eh)
11PM = 23.00 le ventitrè (leh vayn-tee-trEH)
midnight = mezzanote (meh-tsah-nOHt-teh)

– 8 HOURS	– 6 HOURS	– 5 HOURS	GREENWICH MEAN TIME	+1 HOUR	+2 HOURS	+3 HOURS	ADDITIONAL HOURS
Los Angeles San Francisco	Chicago Dallas Houston	Boston New York Washington, D.C.	Great Britain Iceland Ireland Portugal	Austria Belgium Denmark France Germany Hungary Italy Luxembourg Malta Monaco Netherlands Norway Poland Spain Sweden Switzerland Yugoslavia	Finland Greece Romania South Africa	Turkey Moscow	Sydney (10 hours) New Zealand (12 hours)

MAJOR HOLIDAYS

January 1	New Year's Day	Capodanno
March 31	National Day (Malta)	Festa Nazionale
April 25	Liberation Day	Festa della Resistenza
May 1	Labor Day	Festa del Lavoro
August 1	National Day (in most Swiss cantons)	Festa Nazionale
August 15	Assumption Day	Assunzione
November 1	All Saints Day	Ognissanti
December 8	Immaculate Conception	Immacolata Concezione
December 13	Republic Day (Malta)	Festa della Repubblica
December 25	Christmas	Natale
December 26	St. Stephen's Day	Santo Stefano
March-April	Good Friday (Malta)	Venerdi Santo
	Easter Monday	Lunedì dopo Pasqua
		Lunedì dell Angelo

The following saints' days are celebrated in these cities:

April 25	San Marco (Venice)
June 24	San Giovanni Battista (Florence, Genoa, Turin)
June 29	Santi Pietro e Paolo (Rome)
September 19	San Gennaro (Naples)
December 17	Sant'Ambrogio (Milan)

CURRENCY INFORMATION

Major Currencies of the World

Andorra	French Franc
Argentina	Argentinian Peso
Austria	Schilling
Belgium	Belgian Franc
Colombia	Colombian Peso
Denmark	Danish Krone
Finland	Finmark
France	Franc
Germany	Mark
Greece	Drachma
Hungary	Forint
Iceland	Krone
Ireland	Punt
Italy	Lira
Liechtenstein	Swiss Franc
Luxembourg	Luxembourg Franc
Malta	Maltese Lira
Monaco	French Franc
Mexico	Mexican Peso
Monaco	French Franc
Netherlands	Guilder

Norway	Norwegian Krone
Peru	Sol
Portugal	Escudo
Puerto Rico	U.S. Dollar
Russia	Ruble
Spain	Peseta
Sweden	Swedish Krone
Switzerland	Swiss Franc
Turkey	Lira
United Kingdom	Pound Sterling
Uruguay	Uruguayan Peso
Venezuela	Bolivar
Yugoslavia	Dinar

Major Commercial Banks

In Italy
Banca Nazionale del Lavoro
Via Vittorio Veneto 119
00187 Rome

Banco di Roma
Via del Corso 307
00186 Rome

Credito Italiano
Piazza Cordusio
20123 Milan

Cariplo
Cassa di Risparmio
  delle Provincie Lombarde
Via Monte di Pietà 8
20121 Milan

In Switzerland
Union Bank of Switzerland (UBS)
Bahnhofstrasse 45
Postfach
CH-8021 Zurich

Swiss Bank Corporation
Postfach
CH-4002 Basle

Credit Suisse
Paradeplatz 8
Postfach
CH-8021 Zurich

MAJOR PERIODICALS

The *International Herald Tribune* is the leading English-language newspaper sold in Europe. It is available at most hotels and newsstands. The *Journal of Commerce* is also available at some stands.

In Italy

Newspapers

Avanti!	Il Giorno
Corriere della Sera	Il Mattino
Daily American	Il Messaggero
La Nazione	La Repubblica
La Notte	Il Resto del Carlino
L'Osservatore Romano	Il Sole – 24 Ore

Paese Sera	La Stampa
Il Popolo	L'Unità

Magazines
L'Espressso   Panorama

In Switzerland

Newspapers
Neue Zuercher Zeitung   Finanz und Wirtschaft
Schweiz. Handelszeitung   La Tribune de Genève

(All major business newspapers in Switzerland are in German or French.)

ANNUAL TRADE FAIRS

This is a partial list of annual events. Changes may occur from year to year, as well as during the year, and it is advisable to consult local tourist offices and the Government Tourist offices abroad for up-to-date information.

Rome

January	Presentation: Women's High Fashion Collection
March	International Nuclear Electronics and Aero-space Technology Exhibit
May-June	General Trade Fair
July	Presentation: Women's High Fashion Collection

Bologna

March	International Building and Construction Fair
April	Cosmetics & Perfume Exhibition
	Children's Book Fair
May-June	General Trade Fair
September	Shoe Fair
October	International Building and Construction Fair
November	Farm Machinery Fair

Florence

January	Men's Fashions
	International Footwear, Leathergoods, and Accessories Show
April	International Gift and Handicraft Show
September	International Footwear, Leathergoods, and Accessories Show
November	Leathergoods, Shoes, and Bags Machinery Exhibit

Milan

February	International Housewares Exhibit
	International Tourism Exchange
	International Kitchen Furniture Exhibit*
	Heating, Air Conditioning, and Plumbing International Fair
March	Industrial Automation Exhibit
	Ladies High Fashion Show
	International Shoe Show
April	International Trade Fair
	Gold Italia (jewelry, silverware)
May	International Woodworking Machinery and Tools Exhibit*
June	European Knitwear Fair
September	International Office Furniture Exhibit
	Computers, Telecommunications, and High Technology Electronics Exhibit
	International Hi-Fi, Video, and Consumer Electronics Show
	International Housewares Exhibit
	International Furniture and Lighting Exhibition
October	International Leathergoods Market
	Ladies High Fashion Show
November	International Exhibition of Chemistry, Analysis, Research, and Test Equipment
December	European Knitwear Fair

Turin

February-March	International Vacation, Tourism, and Sports Show
April - May	International Auto Show
October-November	International New Technologies Show

For additional information contact:

Italy-America Chamber of
  Commerce, Inc.
Empire State Building
350 Fifth Avenue
New York, NY 10118
Tel: 212/279-5520

Ente Autonomo Fiera di Roma
Via Savoia, 78
00198 Roma
Tel: 2/851 471

Italian Trade Commission
499 Park Avenue
New York, NY 10022
Tel: 212/980-1500

Relazioni Pubbliche Informazioni
Via Isonzo, 25
00198 Roma
Tel: 06/868 748

*Biennial

Ente Autonomo Per Le
  Fiere di Bologna
Piazza Costituzione, 6
40128 Bologna
Tel: 51/50 30 50

Fiera di Milano
Largo Domodossola, 1
20145 Milano
Tel: 2/34 32 51

Torino Esposizioni
Corso Massino D'Azelio, 5
10126 Torino

TRAVEL TIMES

To Italy

Most international flights go to either Milan or Rome, although there are international flights to other Italian cities less frequently. In Milan, flights arrive at Malpensa, about 40 km from the city. To get into Milan itself, take the airport bus, which leaves the airport every 45 minutes. All domestic flights and flights from other European cities land at Linate Airport, only 7 km from the city and a quick taxi ride into town.

Flights to Rome arrive at Leonardo da Vinci Airport, 35 km from the city. Taxis are very expensive from the airport; better alternative is public transportation.

To Malta

There are some direct flights to Malta from London, but most arrivals are through Rome. The airport is located at Luqa, 5 km from Valletta.

To Switzerland

Flights to Geneva arrive at Cointrin Airport, located about 4 km from the center of the city. Taxis are quick but you can also take the airport bus to the Air Terminal at Gare Cornavin. The airport bus runs every 20 minutes.

Approximate Flying Times to Key Italian Cities

New York–Milan	$7^{1}/_{2}$ hours
New York–Rome	8 hours
Chicago–Milan	9 hours
Los Angeles–Milan	12 hours
London–Milan	2 hours
London–Rome	2 hours, 15 minutes
Sydney–Rome	$12^{1}/_{2}$ hours

Average Flying Times Between Major Italian Cities

Rome-Milan	1 hour
Rome-Genoa	1 hour

Rome–Venice	1 hour
Rome–Turin	1 hour
Milan–Naples	1 hour, 15 minutes
Milan–Bari	1 hour, 25 minutes
Naples–Bologna	1 hour, 15 minutes
Turin–Pisa	50 minutes

Alitalia and Aero Transport Italiani offer domestic flights to most cities. Alisarda also offers domestic flights, including to Sardinia.

Rail Travel

The major Italian train lines are fast and comfortable, although all service slows a bit during the tourist season. Trains have two classes—first and second—with first class being the advisable one to choose. People often disregard the signs distinguishing the classes, thus you are apt to find second-class passengers sitting in first-class seats. Just politely ask the person to move. Passes that are good for unlimited travel within Italy are available to foreigners. They may be purchased for 8, 15, 21, or 30 days. Consult your travel agent or inquire at any railway terminal. The following is a brief description of the varieties of Italian trains.

E.C. Eurocity	High-speed international train making stops only at major cities (supplementary fare necessary; sometimes only first class seats are available)
E.N. Euronotte	Same as E.C., traveling only at night. Often requires reservation of cuccette (berths) or sleeping car
I.C. Intercity	High-speed train whose route is entirely within Italy and makes stops only at major cities (supplementary fare necessary; sometimes only first class seats are available)
Espresso	Express train
Regionale	Regional train (used to be known as the "diretto")
Interregionale	Local, makes all stops
Important symbols:	
WL	Sleeping car
Ac	First class sleeping car
Bc	Second class sleeping car
Ac/Bc	Mixed first and second class sleeping car

In Switzerland, all trains to Geneva arrive at Gare Cornavin, which is conveniently located in the center of the city. There are also link-ups with other major Swiss cities, as well as other European cities.

TRAVEL TIPS

On the Plane

1. Be aware that the engine noise is less noticeable in the front part of the plane. Try to sleep. Some frequent travelers bring along earplugs, eye-shades, and slippers.
2. Wear comfortable, loose-fitting clothing.
3. Walk up and down the aisles, when permitted, at least five minutes every hour to maintain body circulation.
4. Limit alcohol intake—altitude heightens the intoxicating effect.
5. Avoid heavy foods and caffeine, which dehydrates the body.
6. Drink plenty of liquids and eat foods rich in potassium. Pressurized cabins cause dehydration.
7. Take it easy when you arrive. When possible, schedule your first important meeting according to your "at home" peak period.

Jet Lag

Disruption of the body's natural cycles can put a lingering damper on your vacation, so take the following precautions:

1. *Avoid loss of sleep* by taking a flight that will get you to your destination early in the evening, if at all possible. Get a good night's sleep at home the night before your departure.
2. *Rearrange your daily routine* and sleeping schedule to harmonize with a normal body clock at your destination.
3. *Avoid stress and last-minute rush.* You're going to need all your strength.
4. *Rearrange your eating habits.* Start four days early—begin a diet of alternate days of feasting and fasting. "Feast" features high-protein breakfasts and lunches (to increase energy level and wakefulness) and high-carbohydrate dinners (to help induce sleep).

Shopping

Shop hours in Italy change with the season. In the winter shops are generally open 8 A.M. to 7 P.M. with a lunch break between 1 and 3. During the tourist season, shops open and close later in the afternoon (4 to 8). Some remain open on Sundays but most close a half day during the week—often Monday morning or Thursday afternoon. In Switzerland stores are generally open until 6:30 P.M.

Drug Stores

The Italian drugstore doesn't stock the variety of goods available in America. For perfume, cosmetics, etc. you'd go to a *profumeria*. A drugstore has a sign outside—a green or red cross. In the window is a notice telling where the nearest all-night drugstore is.

Clothing Sizes

In Europe, clothing sizes vary from country to country, so be sure to try the garment on. Basically, for men, a suit size is "10" more than the American size; thus, an American 40 is a European or Continental 50. For women, the conversion is the American size plus "28"—thus, an American size 10 is a Continental 38.

Electricity

In most large cities in Italy you'll find voltage for electric lights at 220–230 AC, 50-cycle and voltage for appliances at 220 or 230 AC, 50-cycle. Check the voltage before plugging in your appliance. You may find an adapter plug useful.

Film

Film sizes aren't always indicated the same way in Europe as in America. Check carefully before purchasing.

Telephones

In Italy there are fewer public telephones. Most people use the public phone that can be found in cafes and bars. The cashier supplies tokens *(gettoni)*. Dialing is direct and on an inter-city basis. You'll find area codes in the directory. You must order long-distance calls in advance.

If possible avoid making telephone calls from your hotel as the cost is excessively high.

Driving

You'll need the following when driving: passport; international insurance certificate (green card); registration (log) book; and a valid driving license. An international driving permit may save you trouble. A red warning triangle— for display on the road in case of an accident—is compulsory.

Tipping

Tipping, of course, varies with the individual and the situation. The following amounts are typical: In hotels in Italy 5% is included in the bill; in Switzerland, the porter should receive 1 franc per bag; in Italy, the porter should receive 1000 lire; in Switzerland, the tip for the maid is included in the bill, in Italy the maid should be tipped 10–20,000 lire per week. In restaurants, 5% is usually included in the check; lavatory and hatcheck attendants usually expect a few hundred lire in Italy and a few francs in Switzerland. Taxi drivers, barbers, and hairdressers should receive 5%; ushers and guides are tipped lesser amounts.

MAJOR HOTELS

Rome

Aldrovandi Palace Hotel
Via Aldrovandi, 15
00197
Tel: (06) 3223993
Fax: (06) 3221435
All business amenities available (fax,
    translation service, photocopiers,
    400-capacity meeting room), pool
    and restaurant.

Ambasciatori Palace
Via Vittorio Veneto, 70
00187
Tel: (06) 47493
Fax: (06) 4743601
All business amenities available
    including 200-person meeting
    room. Opposite U.S. Embassy

Bernini Bristol
Piazza Barberini, 23
00187
Tel: (06) 463051
Fax: (06) 4750266

Cavalieri Hilton
Via Cadlolo, 101
00136
Tel: (06) 31511
Fax: (06) 31512241
All amenities both business and per-
    sonal, including pool, sauna, mas-
    sage, Turkish bath, five meeting
    rooms (capaciy 350), and a con-
    vention center (2,000 capacity)

Cicerone
Via Cicerone, 55/C
00193
Tel: (06) 3576
Fax: (06) 6541383
On Vatican side of Tiber, most busi-
    ness facilities including two small
    meeting rooms

D'Inghilterra
Via Bocca del Leone, 14
00187
Tel: (06) 672161
Fax: (06) 6840828
Most business amenities

Eden
Via Ludovisi, 49
00187
Tel: (06) 4743551
Fax: (06) 4742401
Roof restaurant

Excelsior
Via Vittorio Veneto, 125
00187
Tel: (06) 4708
Fax: (06) 4756205
All business amenities. Next to U.S.
    Embassy

Grand Hotel de la Ville
Via Sistina, 69
00187
Tel: (06) 6733
Fax: (06) 620836

Hassler-Villa Medici
Piazza Trinita' dei Monti, 6
00187
Only accepts American Express
Tel: (06) 6782651
Fax: (06) 6799991
All business amenities. Rooftop
    restaurant

Jolly Leonardo da Vinci
Via dei Gracchi, 324
00192
Tel: (06) 39680
Fax: (06) 611182

Jolly Vittorio Veneto
Corso d'Italia, 1
00198
Tel: (06) 8495
Fax: (06) 6122934

Le Grand Hotel
Via Vittorio Emanuele Orlando, 3
00185
Tel: (06) 4709
Fax: (06) 4747307
All business amenities, plus sauna,
    massage, restaurant, afternoon teas

Lord Byron
Via G. De Notaris, 5
00197
Tel: (06) 3220404
Fax: (06) 3220405
Most business amenities, well known
    restaurant: Relais Le Jardin

Mediterraneo
Via Cavour, 15
00184
Tel: (06) 464051

Plaza
Via del Corso, 126
00186
Tel: (06) 672101
Fax: (06) 624669

Regina Carlton
Via Vittorio Veneto ,72
00187
Tel: (06) 476851
Fax: (06) 8445104

Visconti Palace
Via Cesi, 37
00193
Tel: (06) 3684
Fax: (06) 680407

Florence

Baglioni
Piazza Unita' Italiana, 6
50123
Tel: (055) 218441
Fax: (055) 215695
All business amenities. Opposite train
    station

Excelsior
Piazza Ognissanti, 3
50123
Tel: (055) 264201
Fax: (055) 210278
All business amenities, including
    restaurant. Many rooms overlook
    Arno river. Also, roof garden,
    parking, and banquet room

Hotel Park Palace
Piazzale Galileo, 5
50125
Tel: (055) 222 431
Fax: (055) 220517
5 minutes from mid-town Florence.
Pool, park, restaurant

Regency Umbria
Piazza Massimo d'Azeglio, 3
50121
Tel: (055) 245247
Fax: (055) 2342938
Small hotel with all business ameni-
    ties. Well-known restaurant on site

Savoy
Piazza della Repubblica, 7
50123
Tel: (055) 283313
Fax: (055) 284840
All business amenities including
    meeting rooms for 200.

Villa Medici
Via Il Prato, 42
50123
Tel: (055) 261331
Fax: (055) 261336
All business amenities. Pool, sauna,
    beauty salon

Milan

Anderson
Piazza Luigi di Savoia, 20
20124
Tel: (02) 6990141
Fax: (02) 6990331
100 yards from main train station

Carlton Hotel Senato
Via Senato, 5
20121
Tel: (02) 798583
Fax: (02) 798583

Cavour
Via Fatebenefratelli, 21
20121
Tel: (02) 650983
Fax: (02) 651402
Near La Scala

De la Ville
Via Hoepli, 6
20121
Tel: (02) 867651
Fax: (02) 86609

Dei Cavalieri
Piazza Missori, 1
20123
Tel: (02) 8857
Fax: (02) 312040

Executive
Viale Luigi Sturzo, 45
20154
Tel: (02) 6294
Fax: (02) 310191
Congress Center

Excelsior Gallia
Piazza Duca d'Aosta, 9
20124
Tel: (02) 6278
Fax: (02) 311160
Meeting rooms for 25-400, business
    amenities, restaurant, piano bar.
    Near railroad station and air
    terminal

Grand Hotel Fieramilano
Viale Boezio, 20
20145
Tel: (02) 3105
Fax: (02) 331426

Galileo
Corso Europa, 9
20122
Tel: (02) 7743
Fax: (02) 656319

Grand Hotel Brun
Via Caldera, 21
Tel: (02) 45271
Fax: (02) 4526055

Grand Hotel Duomo
Via San Rafaelli, 1
20121
Tel: (02) 8833
Fax: (02) 872752

Grand Hotel et de Milan
Via Manzoni, 29
20121
Tel: (02) 801231
Fax: (02) 872526

Jolly Touring
Via Tarchetti, 2
20121
Tel: (02) 6335
Fax: (02) 320118

Jolly President
Largo Augusto, 10
20122
Tel: (02) 7746
Fax: (02) 76004848

Hotel Madison
Via Gasparotto, 8
20124
Tel: (02) 6085991
Fax: (02) 6073612

Milano Hilton
Via Galvani, 12
20124
Tel: (02) 69831
Fax: (02) 6071904

Palace
Piazza della Repubblica, 20
20124
Tel: (02) 6336
Fax: (02) 654485

Hotel Pierre Milano
Via De Amicis, 32
20123
Tel: (02) 8056221
Fax: (02) 8052157
American bar

Plaza
Piazza Diaz, 3
20123
Tel: (02) 3498205
Fax: (02) 321162

Principe & Savoia
Piazza della Repubblica, 17
20124
Tel: (02) 6230
Fax: (02) 6595838

Quark Hotel
Via Lampedusa, 11/9
20141
Tel: (02) 84431
Fax: (02) 8464190
300 suites, 3 restaurants, 2 bars, pool,
    55,000 square feet exhibition space

Royal Hotel
Via Cardano
20142
Tel: (02) 6709151
Fax: (02) 6703024

Hotel Washington
Via Washington, 23
20
Tel: (02) 4813216
Fax: (02) 4814761
A/C, Cable, business amenities,
    shuttle to Fair grounds

Turin

Jolly Hotel Ligure
Piazza Carlo Felice, 85
10123
Tel: (011) 55641
Fax: (011) 535438

Jolly Principi di Piemonte
Via Gobetti, 15
10123
Tel: (011) 532153
Fax: (011) 221120

Turin Palace Hotel
Via Sacchi, 8
10128
Tel: (011) 515511
Fax: (011) 5612187

If you are traveling to cities other than the ones mentioned here, you may wish to call the central reservation office in Milan for either of the two following chains:
Ciga—02-626622
Jolly—02-7703

MAJOR RESTAURANTS

Rome

Alberto Ciarla—one star
Piazza San Cosimato 40, 00153
Tel: 5818668
Major credit cards accepted

El Toulà—one star
Via della Lupa 29, 00186
Tel: 6781196
Major credit cards accepted

Girarrosto Toscano—one star
Via Campania 29, 00187
Tel: 493759
Major credit cards accepted

Hostaria dell'Orso
Via Monte Brianzo 93, 00186
Tel: 6564250

La Rosetta—one star
Via della Rosetta 9, 00187
Tel: 6561002
American Express, Diner's Club
  accepted

Piperno—one star
Monte de'Cenci 9, 00186
Tel: 6540629

Relais Le Jardin—two stars
Via De Notaris 5, 00197
Tel: 3609541; Telex 611217
Major credit cards accepted

Sans Souci—one star
Via Sicilia 20/24, 00187
Tel: 493504
Major credit cards accepted

Florence

Da Dante-al Lume di Candela
Via delle Terme 23 r, 50123
Tel: 294566
Major credit cards accepted

Enoteca Pinchiorri—two stars
Via Ghibellina 87, 50122
Tel: 242757
American Express accepted

Harry's Bar
Lungarno Vespussi 22 r, 50123
Tel: 296700
American Express accepted

Sabatini
Via de'Panzani 9/a, 50123
Tel: 282802
Major credit cards accepted

Milan

Alfredo-Gran San Bernardo—one
  star
Via Borghese 14, 20154
Tel: 3319000

A Riccione—one star
Via Taramelli 70, 20124
Tel: 6086807
Major credit cards accepted

Biffi Scala
Piazza della Scala, 20121
Tel: 876332
Major credit cards accepted

Casa Fontana—one star
Piazza Carbonari 5, 20125
Tel: 6892684
American Express, Visa accepted

Ratings extracted from the *Red Michelin Guide,* 1993

El Toulà
Piazza Paolo Ferrari 6, 20121
Tel: 870302
Major credit cards accepted

Giannino—one star
Via Amatore Sciesa 8, 20135
Tel: 5452948
Major credit cards accepted

Gualtiero Marchesi—three stars
Via Bonvesin de la Riva 9,
    20129
Tel: 741246
American Express accepted

Turin

St. Andrews
Via Sant'Andrea 23, 20121
Tel: 793132
Major credit cards accepted

Savini—one star
Galleria Vittorio Emanuele II,
    20121
Tel: 8058343
Major credit cards accepted

Al Gatto Nero—one star
Corso Filippo Turati 14, 10128
Tel: 590414
American Express, Diner's Club
    accepted

Del Cambio—one star
Piazza Carignano 2, 10123
Tel: 546690
Major credit cards accepted

Tiffany
Piazza Solferino 16/h, 10121
Tel: 540538
American Express accepted

Vecchia Lanterna—one star
Corso Re Umberto 21, 10128
Tel: 537047
American Express, Visa accepted

Villa Sassi-el Toulà—one star
Strada al Traforo del Pino 47, 10132
Tel: 890556
Major credit cards accepted

USEFUL ADDRESSES

American Chamber of Commerce in
    Italy
12 Via Agnello
20121 Milan

Unione Italiana delle Camere di
    Commercio Industria
Artigianato e Agricoltura
Piazza Sallustio 21
00187 Rome

Associazione Italiana degli
    Industriali dell'Abbigliamento
Foro Bonaparte 70
20121 Milan

Camera Nazionale dell'Alta
    Moda Italiana
Piazza Aracoeli 3
50123 Florence

Unione Industriale Pastai
    Italiani UN.I.P.I.
Via Po 102
00198 Rome

Federceramica
Piazza del Liberty 8
20121 Milan

Associazione Industrie
    Dolciarie Italiane A.I.D.I.
Via 6 Oriani 92
00197 Rome

Associazione Italiana
Industriali Prodotti
 Alimentari
Via Pietro Veri 8
20121 Milan

Federazione Italiana
    Industriali Produttori
    Esportatori ed
    Importatori di Vini,
    Acquaviti, Liquori,
    Sciroppi, Aceti ed Affini
Via Mentana 2-B
00185 Rome

Associazione Italian
    Manufatturieri Pelle
Cuoio e Succedanei—
    A.I.M.P.E.S.
Viale Beatrice d'Este 43
20122 Milan

Associazione Industria
    Marmifera Italiana e delle
    Industrie Affini
Via Nizza 59
00198 Rome

Associazione Italiana
    Editori A.I.E.
Via della Erba 2
20121 Milan

Borsa Valori
Via del Burro 147
00186 Rome

Confederazione Generale
    dell'Industria Italiana
Viale dell'Astronomia 30 Rome

Europe

449

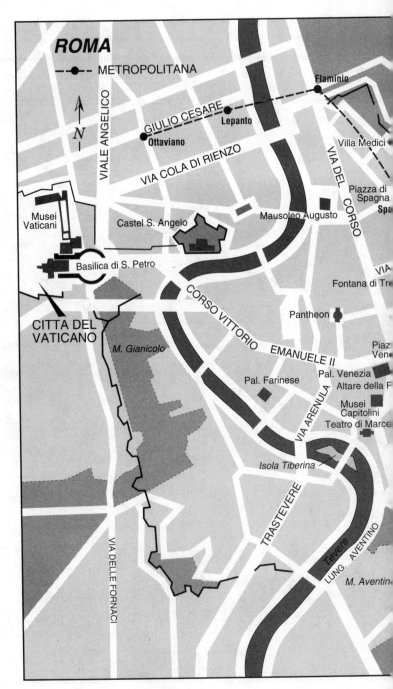

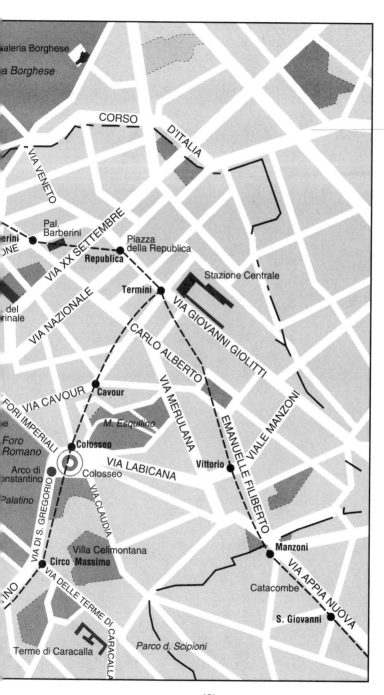

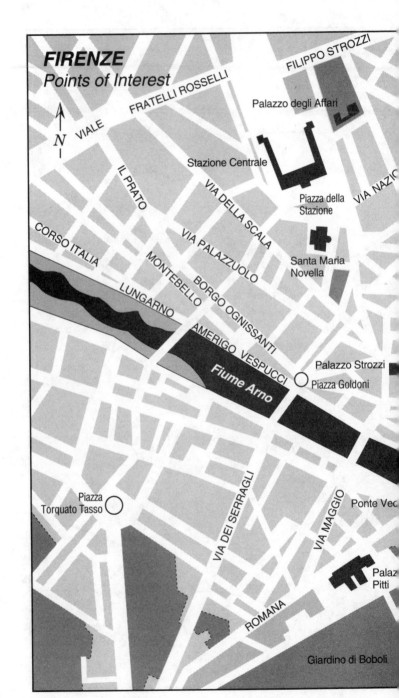

FIRENZE
Points of Interest

N

FILIPPO STROZZI

FRATELLI ROSSELLI

VIALE

Palazzo degli Affari

IL PRATO

Stazione Centrale

VIA DELLA SCALA

VIA NAZIO

Piazza della
Stazione

VIA PALAZZUOLO

CORSO ITALIA

MONTEBELLO

BORGO OGNISSANTI

Santa Maria
Novella

LUNGARNO

AMERIGO VESPUCCI

Palazzo Strozzi

Fiume Arno

Piazza Goldoni

VIA DEI SERRAGLI

Piazza
Torquato Tasso

VIA MAGGIO

Ponte Vec

Palaz
Pitti

ROMANA

Giardino di Boboli

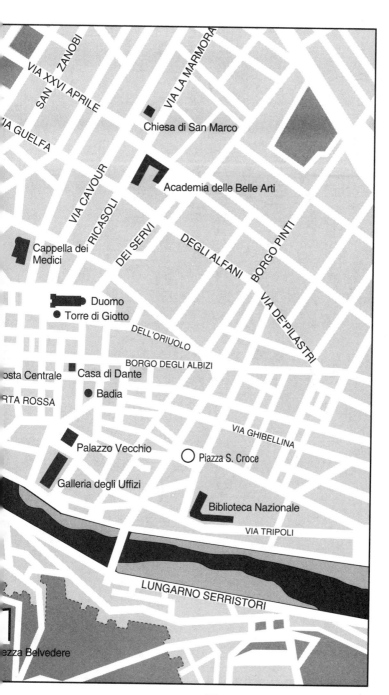

VIA ZANOBI

VIA XXVI APRILE

SAN

VIA GUELFA

VIA LA MARMORA

Chiesa di San Marco

Academia delle Belle Arti

VIA CAVOUR

RICASOLI

DEI SERVI

DEGLI ALFANI

BORGO PINTI

VIA DE'PILASTRI

Cappella dei Medici

Duomo

● Torre di Giotto

DELL'ORIUOLO

BORGO DEGLI ALBIZI

osta Centrale   Casa di Dante

RTA ROSSA   ● Badia

VIA GHIBELLINA

Palazzo Vecchio   ◯ Piazza S. Croce

Galleria degli Uffizi

Biblioteca Nazionale

VIA TRIPOLI

LUNGARNO SERRISTORI

ezza Belvedere

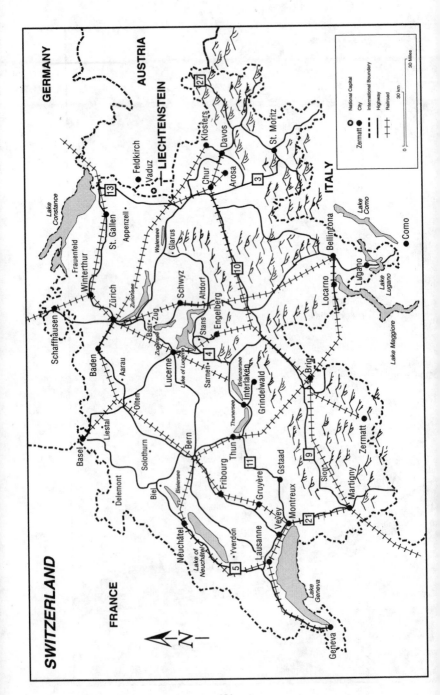

THE COUNTRY
CRAFT SERIES

GARLANDS
&WREATHS

GARLANDS
&WREATHS

Lynn Bryan

Bloomsbury Books
London

Cover photograph: The richness of golden seed pods with pinecones, combined with a vine base, make a wonderful wreath.
Previous page: Single ends of grain seem to flick out of this dried flower wreath decorated in true country style with a dominance of everlasting blooms on a base of heather. It is a very pretty wreath and suits a country kitchen year-round.

Published by Harlaxton Publishing Ltd
2 Avenue Road, Grantham, Lincolnshire, NG31 6TA, United Kingdom.
A member of the Weldon International Group of Companies.

First published in 1994

© Copyright Harlaxton Publishing Ltd
© Copyright design Harlaxton Publishing Ltd

This edition published in 1994 by
Bloomsbury Books
an imprint of
The Godfrey Cave Group
42 Bloomsbury Street, London. WC1B 3QJ
under license from Harlaxton Publishing Ltd.

Publisher: Robin Burgess
Editor: Dulcie Andrews
Illustrator: Sam Denley
Photographer: James Duncan
Typesetting: Sellers, Grantham
Colour separation: G A Graphics, Stamford
Produced in Singapore by Imago

British Library Cataloguing-in-Publication data.
A catalogue record for this book is available from the British Library.
Title: Country Craft Series: Garlands and Wreaths
ISBN: 1-85471-432-5

4

CONTENTS

INTRODUCTION
7
GETTING STARTED
9
TOOLS AND MATERIALS
11
STARTING WORK
17
TECHNIQUES OF THE CRAFT
29
FINISHING TECHNIQUES
35
BEGINNER'S PROJECT
43
INDEX
47

INTRODUCTION

Through this Country Craft series, it is our hope that you will find satisfaction and enjoyment in learning a new skill. In this case, that of making garlands and wreaths using dried and fresh flowers. Throughout past centuries, garlands and wreaths made from natural products have had a positive significance, heralding the beginning of a new cycle of growth and prosperity for the immediate community.

This book provides you with advice on how to make simple country-style wreaths and garlands to hang inside your house for every season and special occasion. Several aspects of the techniques are illustrated, and the wonderful selection of photographs of country-style wreaths and garlands will inspire you to make your garland or wreath in a professional way. The simple Beginner's Project is clearly explained, with step-by-step photographs, and the result is a lovely harvest wreath to display in your home or give as a special gift.

Opposite: This is one of the most unusual wreaths, created from moss and red dried chilli peppers.
Note that they swirl in the same direction, like a whirlpool.
This is a fun wreath to hang in the kitchen.

GETTING STARTED

TO BEGIN A WREATH is to begin a process which has been carried out by people since the earliest days of social ritual. A celebration of mid-winter – in pagan times celebrated on the shortest day – called for a wreath made of everlasting greenery. To celebrate the harvest time, a wreath with sheaths of wheat and corn (grain) was created.

A garland is, to all intents and purposes, similar to a wreath, but is not as rigid. Seen on many an Ancient Greek victor as a symbol of his success, the garland was usually made of laurel leaves. A study of social rituals reveals the use of a garlands as a welcoming gift; a garland of spring flowers around the neck and shoulders of village girls on May Day as they dance around the maypole is a more traditional image of the floral garland that still has social significance. When travellers arrive in Hawaii, a garland (called a *lei*) is hung around their necks as a welcome gift.

To find the origins of the wreath, it is essential to look to pagan societies where evergreens represented survival. While most of the trees in the forest stood tall and bare of leaves, the fir tree remained vibrant and green, so it is easy to understand why branches of the fir were taken from these trees and woven into an unbroken circle. This is why the wreath is so important as a Christmas ritual,

hung on the front door to welcome visitors and travellers from afar; the pagan mid-winter ritual has evolved into a Christmas celebration. We have since taken the lowly fir wreath to our hearts for many special occasions – and to cheer up our everyday lives. We now add bows made from taffeta and satin, from florists' ribbon and craft paper; tiny toys, little gift boxes and candles; real and imitation berries. The wreath is an expression of our creativity and, as such, has become an additional and fashionable decoration in our homes. Its symbolism may have been diluted over the centuries but it is still, for country folk and those city people with an abiding interest in the cycle of life, representative of each seasonal event.

In the pages of this book you will find everything you need to know and the inspiration to help you begin making a wreath or a lavish garland. It is important to read all the advice before beginning, and to think about the final look of your "Beginner's Project". After making a few wreaths, you will find it becomes easier, and there is no doubt that within weeks you could be making beautiful and extravagant wreaths for friends and family. All it takes is confidence. You will also discover the delights of using a new skill that brings such pleasure to others.

Opposite: A natural vine heart-shaped base is delightfully decorated with small terracotta hearts, gorgeous green taffetta ribbons, tiny white rose buds and small tendrils of ivy. Note the top of the heart-shape is the focal point in design.

TOOLS AND MATERIALS

IT IS important to begin making wreaths and garlands with the right tools and materials. The items listed below are not expensive and are readily available from craft and hobby stores or your local florist. Be cautious when thinking about using polystyrene bases. Apart from the fact that these have a tendency to break apart when laden with decorations, their damaging effect on the ozone layer of the atmosphere cannot be denied – therefore I hope you choose not to use them. Natural bases are easier to work with and present a superior finished wreath or garland.

TOOLS
- Florist's wire
- Sharp craft scissors
- Adhesives
- Glue gun
- Wire cutters
- Sticky tape
- Gutta-percha tape

Wire – This comes in two types – one is a light silver and blends well with natural and herbal materials; the other has a green enamel coating which is great for fresh flowers and evergreens. You can buy this on spools (like thread) making it easy to handle as you work. The wire is measured in 'gauges' – 28 provides the flexibility you need when working with finer herbs and drieds. Usually the thicker

wire comes in straight pre-cut lengths. You need this when making up bunches of drieds or fresh flowers to insert into a large garland.

Scissors – Most people have a pair of scissors which they use for craft work or for cutting cardboard. Use these for cutting plant stems and the fine florist's (floral) wire – never use your dress-making scissors for such acts or you will ruin them!

Wire cutters – Use these for cutting lengths of heavier wire.

Adhesives – Experienced makers of wreaths or garlands generally attach decorations and bows to the base with fine wire as this is sturdy and resistant to the bad weather which wreaths hung outdoors always experience. However, adhesives are a useful alternative, especially for indoor wreaths and garlands. They are particularly handy for a wreath which you may want to put together quickly and is only going to be on show for a few days.

There are various types of craft adhesives available and the manufacturers are continually improving their elasticity – an important factor to consider when applying dried plant material. Ideally, a glue should be quick-drying and pliable.

You may like to work with a small glue gun especially designed for craft-workers. The advantage of such a gun is that you can aim the spot of glue accurately, and the glue dries

Opposite: A selection of essential tools – wire cutters, snips, glue gun, florist's foam, a selection of wreath bases, gutta percha-tape, fine florist's wire.

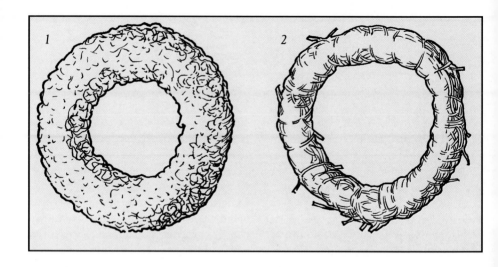

in a moment and the substance is acceptably pliable.

The slight disadvantage of a glue gun is that some people find it awkward to work with, especially when carrying out fiddly movements. Inexperience can leave large unsightly blobs on the item. Also, once the material is in place, it is there forever, giving you no leeway for bad design decisions.

In my experience the best type of glue for dried flower work, and even for attaching brittle pinecones, is any glue sold as a thick white glue and which dries quickly and clearly. Do ask your craft or hobby store owner for advice as they do know their products well.

BASES

The following is an explanation of the different types of wreath bases available at your local craft or hobby supply store or at your local florist.

Cane – These are light and provide a good shape for decorating with masses of dried flowers and ribbons. Made of tubular cane woven into an intricate circle, these look like vine wreaths but do not have the natural elasticity of vines. These look wonderful when painted (using an aerosol paint spray) to match a seasonal setting.

Floral foam – It is best to buy circles of the dry floral foam especially made for use with dried flowers. It is available in beige and can be used more than once if you are careful when creating arrangements with it.

Moss – This is a lovely natural background for herb wreaths and fresh flower wreaths. It also has the advantage of looking attractive from any direction. Stems press in easily and can be hidden away in the mass of moss. Fresh flowers last longer in moss if it is damp. (Fig.1.)

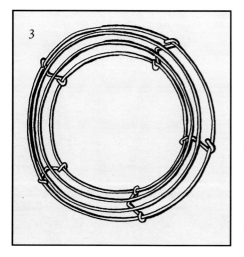

the circle. These are best used when you create a wreath using wired dried flowers. The thickness of the straw base is not really suitable for fresh flower wreaths. (Fig.2.)

Vine – Country craft supply stores and good florists may stock these but you can make them yourself by inter-weaving several strands of a good thick vine into a circle. This type of wreath is great for wrapping ivy and other evergreen plant material around.

Rope – Braided rope forms the basis of these shapes. Strands of hemp rope are woven in an attractive pattern which gives inspiration for the decoration. Dried flowers, dried vegetables (such as green or red chilli peppers) bows and tiny items can easily be glued into place or tied on with thin ribbon. The stems of dried or fresh flowers can be neatly tucked away into the braiding.

Straw – Very good for use with dried flowers, these are made of pressed straw which is kept in shape with a strong thread wrapped around

Wire – These come in a variety of shapes but generally they have two or more circles of strong wire joined in a double layer. (There are single-wire wreath frames available but the less experienced may find these difficult to decorate.) The double-wire frames are best for wreaths which require a sturdy base – such as those made from pinecones only. (Fig.3.)

OTHER DECORATIVE MATERIALS

Plant material can be dried or fresh. Fresh flowers look beautiful in special occasion wreaths for weddings and christenings, or family birthdays. Dried flowers are best for wreaths which are to be part of your decorative scheme for a long time. See 'Starting Work' for more information on both dried and fresh plant material.

Next page: The yellow, blue, red and lavender scheme here was inspired by the lovely ribbon. As you can see, the stems of the dried blooms are gathered in small bunches and wired together as the length is formed, then a full bow is wired before the pattern repeats itself. Yarrow, pinecones, statice, small roses and lavender deserve the credit for the success and beauty of this garland.

STARTING WORK

IN THIS chapter I would like to encourage you to think about the kinds of decisions that have to be made before beginning the creative process. Choosing which style of wreath or garland you want to make is the first question to address. Many readers may wish to make a wreath for a specific occasion like Christmas – this makes your decision easier as the ideal Christmas wreath is likely to be made from an evergreen circle attached to a double-wire frame. A wreath to celebrate harvest time is best made from corn (grain) stalks attached to a double-wire frame, left plain and simple or decorated with natural items.

DRIED FLOWERS

If you wish to make a wreath for everyday, then the ideal materials are dried flowers worked on a moss base, a double-wire base, a vine circle or a straw base. The choice of dried flowers is wide and varied so the next question to answer is – which type of flowers and which colours do you want in the wreath?

A visit to your local craft supply store or florist is essential before you begin to design your wreath. Here you will see all sorts of wonderful shapes of wreath bases and a colourful selection of dried flowers; some are naturally coloured, others have had their colour enhanced to preserve the look. Look for a bunch of dried yarrow (*Achillea millefolium*), a plant which produces a wonderful large, flat head of tiny blossoms. Another favourite of mine is lavender (*Lavendula officinalis*) which not only looks delightful but also has a restful fragrance. Statice (*Limonium latifolium*) comes in a variety of colours and is easy to work with as the stems stand up well to frequent handling. I have included some of the dried flowers you may like to use in a chart. Of course, for a wonderful and different effect you can try using dried red chilli peppers (see photograph opposite the Introduction page.).

For a herbal wreath, lavender, thyme, sage, rosemary, chives, bay leaves and marjoram are the main 'ingredients' to choose from. Herbs, of course, not only look attractive but their permeating fragrances are both pleasant and beneficial. Be sure not to make this type of wreath too large, however, or use too many herbs in the same wreath.

Opposite: Natural vines are entwined and decorated with moss, pinecones and a lovely rich red ribbon which becomes the focal point at the top of the wreath. This is a simple design yet easily achieved by the beginner. Start with the vines, wrapping the ends in and around themselves. Add the pinecones then dot with moss, beginning from the bottom of the circle. Take a long length of ribbon and add it last, working from the top, clockwise, and tie the bow when you reach midnight.

FLOWERS TO DRY YOURSELF

Many types of dried flowers are not easily available in some parts of the country, so to obtain a good selection for your wreaths and garlands, it is useful and rewarding to dry your own. Use this chart as a guide to what to dry and when to pick it for drying.

Suitable plants for drying

In the following chart some of the plants may only be available from specialist suppliers. *Latin names* have been given for easier identification, since common names vary in different areas.

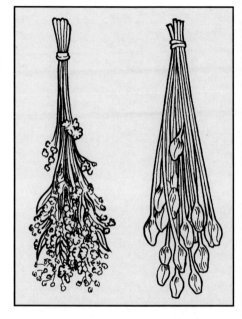

Left: Miniature everlasting in a bunch.
Right: Love-in-the-mist (nigella) blooms.

LATIN NAME	COMMON NAME	TIME TO PICK	PARTS TO USE
Acacia sp.	wattle, (tree-mimosa)	Spring	Flower head, leaf
Acanthus	bear's breeches	Summer	Flower spikes
Achillea sp.	yarrow, sneezewort	Spring	Flower head, leaf
Alchemilla mollis	lady's-mantle	Summer	Flower head, leaf
Althea	hollyhock	Summer	Seed heads
Amaranthus sp.	love-lies-bleeding	Summer	Seed head
Anaphalis	pearl everlasting	Summer	Spray
Angelica archangelica		Summer	Culinary, pot-pourri
Anigozanthos sp.	kangaroo paw	Autumn	Flower head

LATIN NAME	COMMON NAME	TIME TO PICK	PARTS TO USE
Anthemis nobilis	chamomile	Summer	Flower head
Arctotis sp.	African daisy	Summer	Flower head
Aruncus	goat's beard	Spring	Flower head
Banksia sp.		Spring	Leaf
Betula pendula	silver birch	Winter	Spray
Callistemon	bottle brush	Summer	Flower head
Centaurea cyanus sp.	cornflower	Summer	Flower head
Choisya ternata	Mexican orange blossom	Summer	Foliage
Chrysanthemum sp.	chrysanthemum	Autumn	Flower head
Cimicifuga	bugbane	Summer	Seed heads
Clematis sp.		Autumn	Seed head
Clematis vitalba	traveller's joy	Autumn	Spray and seed head
Cortaderia selloana	pampas grass	Evergreen	Silky plumes
Cyperus papyrus	Egyptian paper rush	Summer	Seed head
Cytisus	broom	Summer	Branch flowers
Dahlia sp.	dahlia pompon	Summer	Flower head
Delphinium consolida	larkspur	Summer	Flower head
Dianthus sp.	pinks, carnations	Summer	Seed head
Digitalis	foxglove	Summer	Seed heads

LATIN NAME	COMMON NAME	TIME TO PICK	PARTS TO USE
Dryandra formosa	golden dryandra	Spring	Flower head
Eryngium martimum	sea holly	Summer	Toothed bracts
Eucalyptus cinerea	gum tree	Autumn	Leaf
Eucalyptus globulus	Tasmanian blue gum	Autumn	Leaf, seed head
Fagus cuprea	copper beech	Summer	Spray, leaf
Fagus sylvatica	common beech	Summer	Spray, leaf
Garrya elliptica		Spring	Catkins
Gentiana	gentians	Summer	Sprigs
Grimmia pulvinata	bunmoss	Winter	Leaf
Gypsophila sp.	baby's breath	Summer	Flower head
Helichrysum sp.	everlasting or straw flower	Summer	Flower head
Hordeum jubatum	squirrel-tail grass	Autumn	Grass seed head
Hordeum sp.	black-eared barley	Autumn	Grass seed head
Hydrangea	hydrangea, inc. lacecaps	Autumn	Flower head
Juncus sp.	bog rush	Autumn	Seed head
Larix sp.	larch	Autumn	Seed head
Lavendula spica	old English lavender	Summer	Flower head
Leptospermum	tea-tree	Autumn	Spray
Limonium sp.	statice, sea lavender	Summer	Flower head

LATIN NAME	COMMON NAME	TIME TO PICK	PARTS TO USE
Lunaria rediviva	honesty	Autumn	Seed head
Mahonia aquifolium	Oregon grape	Spring	Racemes
Milium sp.	millet	Autumn	Seed head
Molucella laevis	bells of Ireland	Summer	Spray
Myrtus sp.	myrtle	Summer	Leaf
Myosotis	forget-me-not	summer	Flower spray
Nigella damascena	love-in-a-mist	Summer	Seed head
Olearia sp	daisy bush	Summer	Seed head
Phleum pratense	timothy	Summer	Seed head
Phragmites	reed	Summer	Seed head
Physalis alkekengii	Chinese lanterns	Autumn	Fruit pods
Pinus sp.	pine	Autumn	Seed head, cone
Protea sp.	cape honey flower	Summer	Flower head
Ranculus acris	buttercup	Summer	Flower head
Rosa	rose	Summer	Flower head
Salix myrsinites	willow	Autumn	Leaf, catkins
Solidago canadensis	golden rod	Autumn	Spray
Sphagnum sp.	sphagnum moss	Summer	Leaf
Stachys lantana	lamb's tongue	Summer	Leaf

FRESH FLOWERS

Although fresh flowers look glorious in garlands, the obvious drawback is that they do not last for long periods of time. Therefore, they are best used only for special occasions where they are not needed for more than a few hours; for a wedding, there is nothing more romantic than a small wreath of white and pink roses as a garland around white, pale pink or silver thick, short candles. A combination of fresh and dried flowers is not always successful as each has its own ambience; it is essential to design and plan such a wreath very thoughtfully.

DESIGN CONSIDERATIONS

As with any dried or fresh floral arrangement, the key to its success lies in the combination of colours, textural elements and form. When you see dried blooms in a store, they are always bunched together, presenting a mass of colour and form. When you take just one bunch, both colour and form are less intense so, when you take just a few blooms, there is even less impact.

To plan a wreath or garland needs a great deal of thought. You will see many examples in this book of wreaths completely covered in drieds, and many which are only partly covered, leaving the wreath base on show. Usually, if you use a lovely stripped willow, vine, or straw base, the simplicity of the base is a visual relief from flowers and bows.

COVERING A BASE COMPLETELY

Begin by placing the decorations in groups of the same type and colour.

Move them around the workbench or table top until you are pleased with the colour groupings. Work within the colour spectrum

for harmony – red and pink; cream, yellow, orange and white; blue, purple and lilac. If using just green foliage, try to place different shades of green apart, mixing them through the arrangement.

Once you have made one successful group of drieds – for example, a small collection of yarrow, a bunch of statice and one of lavender – place it at the centre top of the wreath, making sure the centre of the three is in the centre of the wreath base. Then repeat the groupings, working clockwise: yarrow, statice and lavender, yarrow, statice and lavender. Simply place them on the wreath at first, without gluing or attaching with wire. If you are just one group short, then spread the drieds out further around the base, or find one or two stems of something different and place these strategically to fill up the spaces. Once you are happy with the placement, attach your arrangement to the base.

COVERING A BASE PARTLY

Place the base in the position you want it to hang. Place your decorative flowers in colour groups on the workbench. If you are using a bow, place this in the centre of the bottom of the wreath first, then add the bunches in their groupings to either side, working up the wreath base as far as you want to go. Usually, to halfway up each side is fine – you end up with a semi-circle on top of plain wreath base, and a semi circle on the bottom of dried flowers.

If you are not using a bow, but a more special grouping of flowers with a focal point, place this grouping in the bottom central position and work away from this point on either side, ensuring you balance the work. If you use a group of lavender to the left, then

Above: The perfect wreath for a wedding breakfast table consists of blooms of small white clematis flowers, sprigs of jasmine and a central rose in full bloom.
Next page: A vine wreath decorated with miniature pumpkins makes a celebration of harvest-time. The wreath is wrapped around with a natural fibre ribbon but you could also use paper ribbon instead.

use one to the right in the same position.

Again, do not attach your arrangement to begin with; only when you are absolutely sure that the placement is right, use glue or wire to attach your items to the base.

Opposite: Just about every dried flower bloom you can imagine has gone into making this country wreath. It is a wonderful example of how to completely cover a natural moss base with blooms. If you examine it closely you will note the flowers are placed in groups of form and texture around the base so that the various shades of pink, lilac and moss green are found throughout the design.

TECHNIQUES OF THE CRAFT

AS THIS IS A BOOK for beginners, the techniques described here are the easy ways to create stunning effects. There are certain principles of the craft which apply when using dried and fresh flowers; the latter need more patience and care but use the same structural principles.

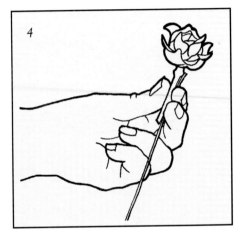

The work begins with the inspiration. There are no mysteries involved with this pastime – just the desire to create something beautiful and well designed. A tube or pot of quick-drying glue is essential, as is sticky tape, be it double-sided, transparent or regular. These two 'tools' make assembling garlands and wreaths easier than you imagine.

A circular shape is the base for any wreath. This can be made of wire, of entwined natural twigs, of interwoven cane, or a floral foam circle bought from a floral craft supplier.

Lay the necessary equipment and tools, flowers and other decorations in groups on the work surface so that they are within easy reach. There is nothing worse than reaching a difficult stage and having to look for the right tool.

Wiring a stem

Many of the flowers you have chosen may need to be wired to make up for the shortness of stem. Stub wire is ideal for this, as it is flexible and strong, and rose wire is excellent to bind. Use gutta-percha tape to disguise the wire. Wiring a flower head is easy if you follow these instructions carefully:

1. Cut off the flower head, leaving about 2.5cm (1 inch) of stem.
2. Hold stub wire so it touches the base of the flower and is next to stem. Wind a length of fine rose wire around the stub wire and stem. Wind down the stub wire for about 7.5cm (3 inches). Cut rose wire and fold in carefully.
3. Hold flower head upside down, place the end of gutta-percha tape behind the stem

Opposite: Hellebores, trimmed natural fir branches, pinecones and a rich flamboyant ribbon herald a glorious welcome to any visitor at Christmas. Note the hellebores are centred, making more of an impact than if they had been dotted around the wreath.

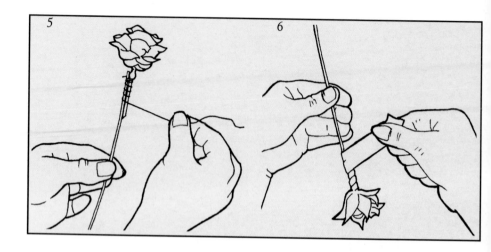

on the diagonal. Keeping the tape taut, wind this down in a spiral to cover the wires. Cut it and neatly fold in the ends. (Figs. 4, 5, 6.)

To create a long-stemmed cluster of flowers or foliage, bind several single stems together with gutta-percha tape and insert them carefully through the openings in the wreath.

INSERTING YOUR MATERIAL

If using a floral foam circle, it is easier just to press the stems firmly into the foam, making sure you cut the ends off should they poke out of the back. The trick is not to be afraid of working with the bloom, dried or fresh. You must begin the process carefully but firmly. Watch a florist put together an arrangement and note the firm manner in which the stems are stripped of excess leaves and boldly placed into the rest of the group. Confidence comes with experience.

When working with cane, vine, wire or twigs, the stems must be manipulated and

woven into the openings in the wreath base. Hiding the stems is a fine art and one which will come with practice.

For small pinecones, slip a piece of florist's (floral) wire through the lowest band of scales, leaving a small length at the beginning, around which to twist the longer stem. (Figs. 7, 8, 9.)

Many modern country-style wreaths feature small 'designer' vegetables and fruits (especially grown for gourmet restaurants and, conveniently, dried flower arrangers!) and the way to prepare these for insertion is simple. Bore two holes in the base of the fruit or vegetable with a metal or wooden skewer. Push a piece of heavy-gauge wire stub through both holes and twist the ends together. (Fig 10.)

SWAG GARLANDS

To make a Christmas garland, using a commercially-manufactured length of green foliage or a length of entwined natural fir tree branches as a base, is really quite simple.

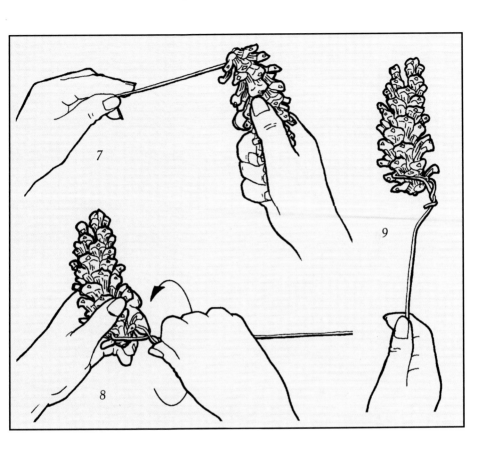

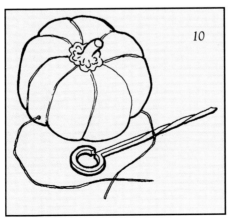

Measure the length you require by running a piece of string along the item which will feature the swag – a mantelpiece or the side of a trestle table covered in a cloth, for example – and cut the greenery to match the length of the string. Imitation fir garland lengths have quite a strong central link around which you can twist the ends of your decorations. If you have made a natural fir length, cut the ends of the branches – this avoids any fear of the garland scratching against a painted surface – and tape them into place. (On a recent Christmas visit to friends in Connecticut, I spent several hours attaching a ready-made imitation fir garland across a newly-painted fireplace – extremely fearful of scratching it. Luckily, the ends of the garland's branches were covered in soft plastic and this, miraculously, prevented any scratching.) Place the garland on a workbench or tabletop and sit at a height that makes it easy to work; this job can take a few hours to do carefully, so it is worth making yourself comfortable. Have everything you need to hand. To decorate, start at one end of the garland, repeating the groupings of dried flowers and other decorations as you work along the central link. Always fold in the ends of bunches and tape them firmly. Sit back and look at the piece as you work along it and, if something does not look right, then take it out and try something else there.

To attach the finished swag to a mantelpiece, I prefer to use a re-usable adhesive stuck at frequent intervals along the garland and pressed firmly to the edge of the mantelpiece. When you take it down, wrap your imitation fir garland in tissue and plastic and store it away carefully – it will look just as beautiful the same time next year.

Opposite: Small branches of evergreen twigs have been bound together to form a length of garland to wind up this staircase for effect at Christmas. Natural red Idesia berries are used in bunches with sprigs of holly and ivy to decorate the evergreen. The ends of the evergreen have been left to hang over the edges of the garland. The ends of the branches are taped to prevent scratching of the painted surface. You can attempt something as demanding as this once you have practised the art of winding evergreen lengths together.

FINISHING TECHNIQUES

WITH THIS CRAFT, a really successful result depends upon those all-important decorative finishing touches. In this chapter you will learn how to tie fabric and paper bows and attach them to a wreath. As we discussed earlier, not all wreaths need a bow; but some bases, particularly stripped willow and cane bases, can be decorated with just a length of ribbon and a bow. You will also learn how to tie a wrapped bow, a small formal bow and how to hang a wreath using a loop of wire.

The bow is an addition about which there are no hard and fast rules. Some wreaths are suited to bows; in others they look out of place. It is a personal judgement but, after making a few wreaths, you will soon be able to judge when a bow will enhance your design. Bows can be made out of a wide variety of natural and synthetic materials, and there is a good choice of ribbons especially manufactured for outdoor wreaths. My preference is for a wider flocked all-weather ribbon, particularly glorious in red for Christmas. This type of ribbon is sturdy and holds its shape well during the winter days. Wrapped bows are absolutely splendid made up in flocked ribbon, but it is a bit too stiff to make into a traditional tied bow. An advantage of the wider ribbon is that you can

split it to the exact width you need; simply place a sharp finger nail into the fabric at the width you want, and it will split all the way down to the length you require (Fig.11).

Less attractive is the type of glossy ribbon which is widely available. I think it always look likes plastic and a shiny look is not ambient to country-style wreaths. This glossy ribbon does not hold its shape well, either. If you require an elegant glossy finish for an interior wreath, use a good-quality satin ribbon, but remember to keep the bow shape small as satin ribbons do not have that much strength. Look for a satin ribbon with a wired

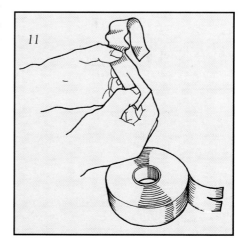

Opposite: Stems of lavender, small rose heads and green leaves sit comfortably amongst a mass of corn (grain) sheaves in this harvest-time wreath. The large calico bow could only be placed at the bottom of this wreath in order for it not to detract from the symmetry of the design.

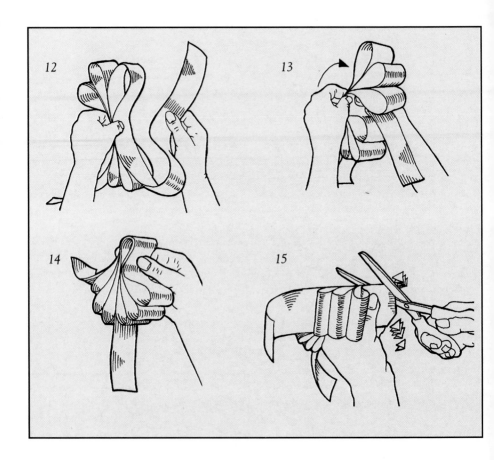

edge if possible, as the wiring does provide strength and the bow will hold its outer shape well.

A WRAPPED BOW

The easiest for the beginner is the wrapped bow. It can be wrapped either with wire or another piece of ribbon. (I was taught how to tie this bow by my dear friend Carol, who loved making bows for clients in our Christmas store. She was patient with me, and especially with my husband when he thought he ought to learn!)

1. Work out how full you want the bow to be. As a rule, it ought to be in proportion to the size of the wreath. After tying a few bows you will be able to judge when it is the right size.

2. Holding the end of the ribbon in your left hand, and leaving a tail the length you think it should be in the finished bow, make a series of loops, one over the other, with your right hand. Leave a tail the same length as the first. Cut the ribbon.

Above: Here is a wreath that looks like a circle but in reality is a bunch of evergreen branches gathered together, caught at the top and hidden with a trimmed bow. A bunch of pinecones and thistle heads completes the effect.

3. Fold the loops of ribbon in half. Neatly snip each corner of the centre fold (to make it easier to wrap the wire or ribbon around). Fold out the loops, holding the snipped centre, keep the loops together.

4. Wind a small length of wire or thin ribbon around the snipped area, twist or tie ends together and cut. Tease the inside of the loops out and up; tease the outside loops down. Pull the trailing ends into place.

The advantage of a wire-wrapped bow is the ease of attaching it to the base. After making a few of these bows, you will get the knack. If you require a fuller bow, make more loops. (Figs. 13-18.)

Paper ribbon is a modern miracle for dried flower enthusiasts. When you first see a roll of it you wonder what the effect will be but, once you rub a small length in your fingers and tease out the full width, its beauty is revealed. It is best to tie the ribbon first then tease out the bow shapes.

A FORMAL SMALL BOW

This attractive bow is more simple to make than it looks.and looks lovely. Take a length of ribbon and wrap it right-hand end over left-hand end. Pinch the centre together and staple firmly. Wrap another smaller length of matching (or contrast, if you want to be different) ribbon around, covering the staple. Tie at the back. If you are tying the bow on to a wreath, leave the ends. If not, glue or stitch the bow to the wreath. Snip the ends on the diagonal with pinking shears for a neat finish. (Figs.18, 19, 20.)

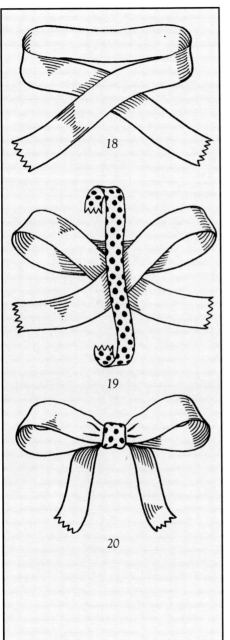

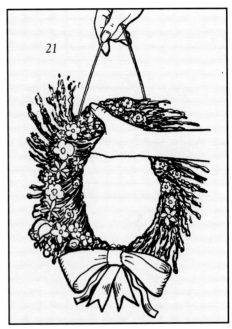

HANGING A WREATH

A popular way of making a loop to hang a wreath is as follows:

Cover a piece of fairly strong stub wire with gutta-percha tape and twist a circle in the middle.

1. Push the ends of the wire in to the wreath base.
2. Pull them back under the frame, which pulls the circle towards the frame.
3. Then push each wire end into the frame on either side to secure it in position. (Fig.21.)

Right: This natural wreath is made from small
branches of an evergreen. To try this yourself,
look for an evergreen with manageable foliage.
Entwine the branches carefully, making sure
that you tuck away the ends into the body of
the wreath. Group the small pinecones together
and glue them to the wreath once you have
decided where you want them to go. This is
hung in an imaginative way – a considerable
number of lengths of white string is pulled
together in a clump, wrapped around the top of
the wreath.

BEGINNER'S PROJECT

THIS IS A LOVELY yet simple country-style wreath, ideal for display at harvest time. It can be hung on the wall over a kitchen bench, or hung from the top of the dresser. Or you may like to rest it on a side table, with a smaller bowl of pot pourri nestling inside its circle.

The great thing about this simple wreath is that you can achieve the look quickly with just a pair of scissors and glue. The pinecone picks are available in a packet; you may have to buy the berry picks separately. The picks referred to here are the type found in a craft supply store. They are a ready-made decoration and are not expensive. Stores which specialize in Christmas decorations are good for picks of berries; you may add mistletoe – place the bunches next to the red berries.

It is a good idea to buy this type of thing after Christmas when stores are selling off this year's stock in time for the new season's decorations. (I always stock up on all sorts of decorations, knowing they will come in handy for a wreath one day!)

The design is a matter of personal choice. I liked the flash of the yellow but you may prefer to use just berries and the small dried rose buds, keeping in the paler tones.

You may feel confident enough to use real pinecones, although they will probably be larger than the ready-made picks. If you do find really small natural pinecones, make sure you wire them through the lower section (page 30). This makes them easier to attach to the wreath base.

You may like to use corn stalks, too. Or add small imitation red apples, tiny, swirling bird's nests, or tiny gift parcels tied with appropriate gingham bows ... the varieties are endless when working on a harvest theme. But do stop adding items when you think it looks crowded enough! Stand back and look at the wreath every now and then to check the design is balanced. Listen to your instinct.

TOOLS AND MATERIALS

- Craft scissors (snips)
- Glue gun or glue tube
- Stripped willow or cane wreath base
- About 25 pinecone picks
- About 12 red berry picks
- One bunch of yellow seed heads
- Small dried rose buds from a pot pourri selection.

Opposite: The richness of golden seed pods with pinecones, combined with a vine base, make a wonderful wreath.

1

METHOD

Step One

Place the wreath on the cleared workbench. Place each of the materials in a separate group. Begin to decorate with bunches of the small yellow seed heads. Cut the stems if they are too long, but leave them long enough to thread in and out of the wreath base. Hide the ends. Begin at the side of the wreath as in the photograph and work with the seed heads facing upwards, and facing the same direction. Insert the next bunch so that it appears to come from the top of the previous one.

Note: The yellow stems are fragile, so be careful when weaving the bunches into the vine wreath base.

Step Two

Begin threading the stems of the pinecone picks through the layers of the base. Place these in the same direction as the yellow bunches.

Step Three

Place the berries between the pinecones and the seed heads, filling the gaps. Apply glue to the base of the bunch of berries. (I cut these off a larger berry pick.) Hold in place on the wreath base until firm.

Step Four

Take tube of glue (or glue gun) and carefully glue into place the small rose buds. Try to create the effect that you have just sprinkled

2

3

4

them over the whole wreath base. If you are going to place the wreath on a flat surface, sprinkle more of the pot pourri mixture, as well as the small rose buds, over the wreath once it is in place. The fragrance is lovely.

To hang your wreath
You will need a medium-sized nail or screw not quite as long as the depth of the wreath base. When you place the wreath over the nail, make sure the nail is hidden.

INDEX

Adhesives 11-12, 29
Apples 43
Bases
  Covering completely 22
  Covering partly 22-7
  Inserting material 30
  Types 11, 12-13, 29
Berries 9, 33
  Picks 43-4
Birds' nests 43
Bows 9, 13, 14-15, 16, 35-9, 43
  Positioning 22
  Small formal bow 39
  Tied 35, 39
  Trimmed 37
  Wired 11
  Wrapped 35, 36-8
Calico bow 34
Candles 9, 22
Cane base 12, 29, 30, 35, 43
Chilli peppers 6, 13, 17
Christenings 13
Christmas 35, 43
  Swag garland 30-1, 33
  Wreaths 9, 17, 28
Clematis 23
Clusters, wiring 30
Colour 17, 22
Corn 2, 9, 17
  Sheaves 34
  Stalks 43
Covering bases 22-7
Design 22
Dried flowers 11, 12, 17-21
  Wreaths 13, 26-7
Drying flowers 18
  Suitable plants 18-21
Evergreens 11, 13
  Garland 33
  Wreaths 9, 17, 37, 40-1
Everlasting 18
Fibre ribbon 24-5
Fir 9, 29, 30
  Imitation 32
Flocked ribbon 35
Florist's foam 11
  Bases 12, 29, 30
Florist's wire 11, 30

Flower head, wiring 29-30
Foliage 22, 30, 32, 34
Form 22
Fresh flowers 11, 12, 13, 22, 29
Fruit, wiring 30
Garlands 9, 14-15, 33
Gift boxes 9, 43
Glossy ribbon 35
Glue see Adhesives
Glue gun 11-12
Gutta-percha tape 11, 29, 30, 39
Hanging wreaths 35, 39, 46
Harvest wreaths 9, 17, 24-5, 34, 43-6
Heart-shaped wreath 8
Heather base 2
Hellebore 28
Herbs 11, 12, 17
Holly 33
Idesia berries 33
Inserting material 30
Ivy 8, 13, 33
Jasmine 23
Kitchen wreath 2, 6
Lavender 14-15, 17, 22, 34
Leaves see Foliage
Laurel 9
Lei 9
Love-in-the-mist 18
Mantelpiece swag 32
Mid-winter 9
Mistletoe 43
Moss 6, 16
  Base 12, 17, 26-7
Pagan rituals 9
Painted base 12
Paper ribbon 23
Picks 43
Pinecones 12, 13, 14-15, 16, 29, 37, 40-1, 42-3
  Picks 43-4
  Wiring 30, 43
Plants for drying 18-21
Polystyrene base 11
Pot pourri 43, 46
Project 43-6
Pumpkins 24-5
Ribbon 8, 12, 13, 14-15, 16, 28, 35

Splitting 35
Rope base 13
Rose buds 8, 43, 46
Rose wire 29
Roses 14-15, 22, 23, 34
Satin ribbon 9, 35
Scissors 11
Seed heads 42-4
Skewer 30
Snips 11
Staircase garland 33
Statice 14-15, 17, 22
Stems, wiring 29-30
Sticky tape 11, 29
Straw base 13, 17, 22
String 40-1
Stub wire 29, 30, 39
Swag garland 30-1
Taffetta ribbon 8, 9
Texture 22
Thistle heads 37
Tied bow 35, 39
Tools 11-12, 29
Toys 9
Twig base 29, 30
Vegetables 13
  Wiring 30
Vine base 8, 13, 17, 18, 22, 24-5, 30, 42
Weddings 13, 22
  table decoration 23
Wheat 9
Willow base 22, 35, 43
Wire 11, 30
Wire base 13, 17, 29, 30
Wire cutters 11
Wire hanging loop 35, 39
Wiring
  Pinecones 30, 31
  Stems 29-30
  Vegetables & fruit 30, 31
Wrapped bow 35, 36-8
Yarrow 14-15, 17, 22